Kocka, Jurgen
White collar workers in
America, 1890-1940

WHITE COLLAR WORKERS IN AMERICA 1890-1940

A Social-Political History in International Perspective

WHITE COLLAR WORKERS IN AMERICA 1890-1940

A Social-Political History in International Perspective

Jürgen Kocka

Translated by Maura Kealey

SAGE Studies in 20th Century History Volume 10

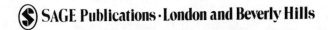

SAGE Publications · London and Beverly Hills

For information address

SAGE Publications Ltd
28 Banner Street
London EC1Y 8QE

SAGE Publications Inc
275 South Beverly Drive
Beverly Hills, California 90212

British Library Cataloguing in Publication Data
Kocka, Jürgen
White collar workers in America, 1890-
1940. — (Sage studies in 20th century history;
vol. 10).
1. White collar workers — United States
I. Title
301.44'45'0973 HD8039.M4U5 80-40572

ISBN 0-8039-9844-9
ISBN 0-8039-9845-7 Pbk

First Printing in English

Translation from the German authorized by
Vandenhoeck & Ruprecht, Publishers, Gottingen

Printed in the United States of America

Contents

Tables

Foreword

This book looks at American social history from a European perspective. It probably shares some of the strengths and weaknesses of the reports of foreign travelers who consciously or unconsciously compare the country they visit with their homeland. For in exploring the United States the foreign observer also seeks to better understand his own society; and if he succeeds, he may present Americans with a new view of their social world. The outsider often sees what the native overlooks, and comparison casts new light on both societies. Of course, the outsider must be careful not to thoughtlessly apply foreign assumptions and categories to the new society so that his portrait is false.

These observations certainly apply to the historian who hopes to explain American social development by comparing it with that of Germany. I can only hope that this book better exploits the opportunities of a comparative perspective than suffers from its dangers.

The book addresses a series of problems which are not usually examined together. It describes and analyzes the development of white collar workers in the US from the late 19th century to the second world war. It places particular emphasis on their fluctuating economic situation, working conditions, and attitudes and conduct, but also looks into to a lesser extent their living conditions, organizations, political behavior, and changing place in US society and politics. A double comparative perspective frames the analysis. First, American white collar workers will be continuously compared with American blue collar workers; the economic, social, psychological, and political significance of the distinction between wage worker and salaried employee — the significance of the 'collar line' in the system of classes and strata — becomes of central concern. The lower and middle levels of the white collar world — sales clerks, office workers, technical draftsmen, and similar occupational groups in the private economy — are the book's chief subjects. In the second place, the analysis draws questions and categories from comparing American white collar workers with their contemporary German counterparts. This cross-cultural comparison opens up a previously thinly researched territory in American social history, i.e., white collar workers, as an interesting problem for historical investigation.

Reciprocally, comparing the history of German and American white collar employees may help to bring the details of German development into clearer focus and, above all, help to explain it. Through the confrontation with the US experience — economically similar, but socially and politically so dissimilar — it is possible to isolate, and interpret the special character of German white collar history from the late 19th century to the triumph of National Socialism. Although this book deals mainly with American developments, and extended archival research was undertaken primarily on the American side, the book's arguments and conclusions are as much a contribution to German as to US history. Comparison with the US places the development of German white collar workers in a new light. Comparison with Germany makes the history of American white collar workers as such a subject worth researching.

Chronologically, the book focuses on the half-century from the first impulses toward 'organized capitalism' in the late 19th century to the second world war (in the US) and the triumph of fascism in Germany; these two countries are at the center of attention. The final section, however, extends the comparison to England and France and also outlines American and German white collar history to the present. Of course, both social groups can be properly understood only within the context of their contemporary societies. Thus in some places, the comparison of white collar workers broadens into a comparison of the basic characteristics of American and German social history since industrialization.

Several interesting theoretical questions fall, implicitly and explicitly, within the scope of the investigation. In Germany and the US, it will be argued, the basic characteristics and chronology of capitalist industrial development were remarkably similar. To what degree did this fundamental socio-economic congruence mean that both countries would also develop similar social-structural, social-psychological, and social-political characteristics? To what extent did similar economic developments in these two bourgeois capitalist systems dictate similar patterns of class formation and social stratification, parallel tensions, protests, and social conflicts? The book concludes by stressing the differences in the two countries' social development despite their great economic similarities. These differences are explained primarily by the impact of diverse pre-industrial, pre-capitalist, and pre-bourgeois traditions, which continued to shape both societies even at a quite advanced stage of industrialization.

The book also contributes to the sociological discussion about white collar workers which has been going on in Europe since the beginning of the century, but which has not yet produced a thorough comparative study. Many authors have analyzed, described, or assumed a distinction between blue and white collar workers as if this distinction appeared in the same way and meant about the same thing in all advanced industrial societies or all industrial capitalist systems. The following investigation demonstrates that the collar line was (and is) much more strongly historically conditioned and culturally varied than sociological studies without a basic historical and comparative perspective can portray.

Finally, this study takes up the still intense and politically relevant debate on the relationship between capitalism and fascism. In both the US and Germany around 1930, bourgeois capitalist systems faced very similar economic challenges from the world depression. In Germany the groups under study, along with other sections of the lower middle class, were overrepresented in the mass base of National Socialism. The extended debate on the connection between capitalist crises, the potential for right-wing protest in the lower middle classes, and the rise of fascism has always and still does draw primarily on Germany's historical experience. (These arguments will be reviewed at the beginning of Chapter 1 and the supporting evidence on the German side presented in Chapter 1, III, 2.) If the line of argument that posits a necessary connection between capitalism, the lower middle class, and fascism is correct, then, under a similar challenge, similar tendencies toward right-wing protest should have appeared in the American lower middle classes (though of course not with the same content and certainly not with the same intensity, in non-fascist North America).

The search for just such a rightist protest potential specific to white collar workers or the lower middle classes has guided this study. The conclusion that emerges is that such a right-wing extremist potential scarcely existed in the US. To explain this difference between Germany and the US one must explain why in one case the capitalist economic and bourgeois social order were perverted to fascism, while in another — despite a similar challenge — they were not. These conclusions should point the way toward working out a future theory of fascism grounded in social history. This investigation can promise only a small, but empirically based, comparatively pursued, and theoretically grounded, contribution to the problem. Comparison can help the historian identify the features of the American social and political system which have contributed to the new world's relative immunity to some of the problems that have burdened the European democracies. And the study may also shed some light on why in recent decades, these European-American divergences seem to have narrowed.

Chapter 1 presents a skeletal explication of the project's design and theoretical foundations. It defines the study's key concepts and places them in the context of several social-theoretical controversies of the last years and decades. It also describes the comparative method selected and justifies the concentration on Germany and the US. A quick sketch of German white collar history to 1933 provides a foil for the detailed analysis of the American case which follows. Chapters 2 through 4 are divided chronologically; they explore American white collar history from the late 19th century to the second world war within the framework of American social history and in comparative perspective. Chapter 5 summarizes the conclusions with reference to the problems raised in Chapter 1. It also extends the comparison to England and France. The study closes with a quick glance toward present-day America and Germany and a brief examination of the implications of the book's conclusions for more general questions of historical sociology.

It is a pleasure to thank a great number of individuals and institutions without whose support and assistance this work would have been impossible or much more difficult. A fellowship from the American Council of Learned Societies allowed me to spend a year and a half as a Fellow of the Charles Warren Center for Studies in American History at Harvard University in 1969/70 and collect the greater part of the materials used in the study. I am very grateful for the stimulating atmosphere at the Center, then under the direction of Oscar Handlin, and for the close working relationship arranged above all by the late Fritz Redlich with the Business History Section of the Harvard Graduate School of Business Administration. The Widener Library of Harvard University, the

Baker Library of the Harvard Business School, the AFL-CIO Library in Washington, DC, the Labor History Archives of Wayne State University in Detroit, the State Historical Society of Wisconsin in Madison, the Ford Archives at the Henry Ford Museum in Dearborn, Michigan, the Archives and Library of the General Electric Company in Schenectady, NY, the New York Public Library and the Firestone Library in Princeton, NJ gave me access to their collections; I wish to thank the archivists and librarians who helped me at these institutions. The early Gallup and Roper Public Opinion Polls used in the study were made available by the Databank of the Public Opinion Research Center in Williamstown, Mass., under the direction of P. K. Hastings, with the financial assistance of Harvard University. Completion of the first version of the study (1972) was facilitated by a useful and pleasant month at the Villa Serbelloni, Bellagio; for it I thank the director, William C. Olson, and the Rockefeller Foundation in New York. Bielefeld University has supported my further research on this project since 1973, particularly into materials on the European side of the comparison. Finally, I owe the time and opportunity to finish the American research and revise the manuscript — and much lively encouragement also — to a seven month stay at the Institute for Advanced Study in Princeton, NJ (1975/76). For reading and criticizing the first manuscript version or individual chapters, thanks are due to Gerhard A. Ritter, Hans-Ulrich Wehler, Heinz Gollwitzer, Hartmut Kaelble, Hans-Jürgen Puhle, Gustav Schmidt and Richard Tilly. Many people on both sides of the Atlantic have assisted me since 1969 with discussions, information, references and criticism. Only a few are mentioned here, with my thanks: Gerald D. Feldman, Frank Freidel, Felix Gilbert, Herbert G. Gutman, George Green, Samuel P. Hays, Albert O. Hirschman, Charles Maier, Arno Mayer, Samuel J. Meyers, Glenn P. Porter, Hans Rosenberg and Fritz Stern. I am grateful also to the participants in discussions at various (mostly American) universities and conferences which have offered me the chance to present theses and conclusions from this study. Heidrun Homburg provided exacting criticism and assistance in the preparation of the manuscript, Claudia Huerkamp prepared the index. For this English edition I have abridged and revised the book which appeared in Germany in 1977 under the title *Angestellte zwischen Faschismus und Demokratie. Zur politischen Sozialgeschichte der Angestellten: USA 1890-1940 im internationalen Vergleich*. Maura Kealey has produced the English manuscript. She has done more than merely translate it, she has written it anew.

Bielefeld, January 1980
J.K.

1. The Framework and the Aims of the Study

I. CAPITALISM, THE LOWER MIDDLE CLASS, AND FASCISM: THE RECEIVED THESIS AS A STARTING POINT

The role of the lower middle class becomes a key question if one wants to explore the social conditions that have nurtured democracy in western industrial societies in the 19th and 20th centuries. Understanding its history is crucial to explaining the creation, destruction, and defense of social and political democracy in the past as well as to assessing present opportunities and obstacles to democracy. Since the rise of fascist movements between the world wars, historians have been critical of the lower middle class. It is commonly regarded as more of a handicap to than a support for democratic society, especially since the end of the 19th century. Many different authors have contributed, explicitly or implicitly, to creating a complex social-historical argumentation about the lower middle class. The present investigation will be basically critical of this argumentation. But I shall use it as a starting point, as a frame of reference, and as a device for structuring a comparative study. So I shall briefly reconstruct it at the outset without even trying to do justice to the individual authors who have contributed to it.

The terms *Kleinbürgertum, Mittelstand, classes moyennes, petite bourgeoisie* and *lower middle classes* (their individual differences will be treated later) describe a social grouping that has appeared demarcated both from manual workers and other lower social strata, on one hand, and from the bourgeoisie and other upper class groups, on the other, since the beginning of industrialization. These boundaries are not sharply marked, but vary from author to author and context to context. Occasionally the term is stretched to include the best situated skilled workers, on one hand, and professionals and academics, on the other. Usually, however, it describes a somewhat narrower grouping with independent craftsmen, shopkeepers and small businessmen (the old middle class) and most lower and middle level white collar workers (the new middle class) at the center. The small town storekeeper, craftsman, insurance agent, and in fact all those who worked for themselves, were part of the old middle class. Only those who made their living by working for others and thus belonged to the broad ranks of dependent labor — even though they performed non-manual work and were paid in salary — will be included in the white collar category and the new middle class as these terms are used in this study.[1]

The old as well as the new middle class, to resume sketching this thesis, were losers in the process of transformation that began with industrialization. The rise of industrial capitalism brought technological innovations and changes in the market which undermined the competitive position of the independent small businessman. Independent producers and small shopkeepers found their economic viability increasingly called into question by big business, on one side, and the workers and the increasingly powerful labor movement, on the other. New life styles and values threatened the cultural and ideological symbols with which the 'old middle class' most closely identified: thrift, hard work, independence, established order and respect for tradition. Relative to other social groups small businessmen's economic opportunity, social status, and often their access to political power declined as well. Although a good part of their sense of identity and self-respect rested on being different from and better than manual workers and the lower classes, in fact they were gradually becoming more like them in income, property, security, education, standard of living, political influence and other objective characteristics. In part this was because the workers, at least those best situated, were advancing more quickly; in part it reflected the actual decline of the 'old middle class'. At least over the long run these small businessmen saw the basis of their independence crumbling and concluded that they were very likely on the way to becoming wage workers themselves. This they viewed as a danger and a threat.[2]

The objective differences between lower and middle level white collar workers (the new middle class component of the lower middle class)[3] and blue collar workers gradually dwindled in much the same fashion. These differences had been quite pronounced in the early stages of industrialization, but they too tended to crumble with changes in technology, the organization of work, personnel policies, the educational system and public values. A large part of the rapidly growing army of white collar workers approached the condition of the better situated manual workers. Both groups' income and job security, skills and career possibilities, opportunity to exercise initiative and authority on the job, share of company social programs, legal position, level of education, and life chances tended to converge. This leveling process was not at all complete; naturally it affected various categories of salaried employees to varying degrees. Nevertheless, the convergence contradicted the sense of identity and self-respect of many white collar employees, who placed great emphasis on the distance between themselves and the workers and who in fact even defined themselves as not belonging to the proletariat.[4]

In other words, both old and new middle class, according to this thesis, felt threatened by some aspects of the modernization that accompanied industrialization. They feared the dismantling of traditional differences between themselves and manual workers and they feared the growing demands of an increasingly organized proletariat. At the same time neither branch of the lower middle class thought they were in the same boat as large entrepreneurs, big landowners, and top administrators, though at times the socially and politically powerful sought to exploit their anti-proletarian anxieties and, by wooing them with minor concessions, to keep them marching behind the banner of an anti-proletarian, anti-socialist politics. Both the old and the new middle class developed defensive-conservative, sometimes even reactionary and backward looking attitudes in the course of distinguishing and defending themselves from those above and below them. They fought to retain their traditional advantages in income, status, and influence. They clung to non-proletarian life styles and ideologies, even though their social-economic basis was becoming questionable. They disapproved of the on-going transformation of their society in which they seemed to be losing ground compared to other groups; they especially resented those groups which they saw as causing or benefiting from these changes. They frequently looked to the state to prop up their special position and to protect them with legislative and administrative measures; they often organized on a socio-economic basis to lobby for such protection.

Under the pressure of an economic crisis like that of the 1930s, the reactionary attitudes and resentments of these groups between bourgeoisie and proletariat became sharper. Most of them shunned left-wing protest movements, since these were egalitarian and identified with the very workers from whom they were emphatically seeking to distinguish themselves. They were much more apt to radicalize to the right; that is, to embrace movements and ideologies which allowed them *at the same time* to vigorously condemn 'those up there', the disappointing system, capitalist and conservative elites; *and* to set themselves off 'from below', to combat the proletarian challenge and the left. Under certain conditions this lower middle class susceptibility to right-wing protest meant that these groups became an important part of the social base for right-radical, proto-fascist or fascist mass movements.

The argument that a gradual leveling process between middle classes and working class was occurring, that lower middle class groups were being squeezed between bourgeoisie and proletariat, and that these groups were suffering from the unfavorable impact of social-economic progress has a long tradition. During the early phases of industrialization it was applied to the old middle class; it was extended to white collar workers by 1890 at the latest.[5] This argumentation emerged as a pendant to the prognosis that society was increasingly divided into two classes — bourgeoisie and proletariat. Yet it also was picked up and generalized from the complaints of the affected groups in the lower middle class. These complaints seemed, on the one hand, to confirm that prognosis; on the other, they served as a basis for demands for measures which would prevent its realization.

Before the interwar years the expectation of a gradual convergence of the lower middle classes and the workers was not usually linked with the anticipation that specific lower middle class resentments and protest would emerge which could serve as a basis for right-wing protest movements. Instead, some hoped (and some feared) that these groups which at present still supported the conservatives or liberals but at any rate the middle class camp would in the long run recognize that their interests lay on the side of the proletariat which they increasingly resembled. Consequently, in the future they might turn to support of leftist reforms or even revolution.[6] There were some dissenting voices.[7] But only with the rise of Italian and German fascism after the first world war was there clearly reason and occasion to tie the leveling and decline thesis to the thesis of a specific lower middle class potential for right-wing extremism.

In the 1920s, authors inquiring into the social basis of fascism from a social-historical rather than an intellectual, constitutional, or purely national historical perspective introduced this thesis about the lower middle class into the debate on fascism. It appealed above all to those with some sort of marxist orientation who, however, did not share the crude and misleading Comintern position developing at that time which held that fascism was nothing more than an instrument of rule for 'the most reactionary, chauvinistic, and imperialistic elements of Finance Capital'. Non-marxist observers seeking to uncover the social base of this new movement also discovered the lower middle class. Their explanations of its behavior paralleled or even overlapped the line of argument sketched above.[8] Up to the present the thesis connecting industrial capitalist development, the situation of the lower middle class, and the development of right-wing protest tendencies has been advanced primarily in the context of the controversy over fascism. Parts of the argument have been contradicted. For the most part it is unclearly formulated, sometimes only vaguely alluded to. It appears with marked shifts of emphasis, in varying contexts, and is qualified with distinctions which this outline has omitted. Yet even when these qualifications are taken into account, this is still the basic thesis that prevails.[9]

This thesis has been based primarily on Italian and German examples. In principle it can take national peculiarities into account, for instance, defeat in the first world war and subsequent inflation as exacerbating factors in Germany. By explicit claim or implication, however, it is also a general social-historical[10] hypothesis which can be transnationally applied: It tries to explain the lower middle classes' *potential* susceptibility to right-wing radicalization as a consequence of transformation processes which typically appear at advanced stages of capitalist industrialization. It builds a connection between certain changes, tensions and contradictions inherent in advanced capitalist societies and the rise of fascist movements. It argues that social-economic, political and cultural changes typical of such societies produce a powerful potential for right-wing protest in the lower middle class, which then, under certain conditions, becomes a social base for fascist movements that contribute to the destruction of liberal-democratic social and political structures.

Thus this thesis not only claims to explain past phenomena; it also implicitly warns of danger spots for democracy in the present and future. It is not limited to accounting for how in the past the lower middle class developed a potential for protest which became a propelling force in the destruction of democracy. It also argues that this potential for protest will in principle continue to exist because and as long as the socio-economic and socio-political processes behind it — industrial capitalism with its tensions, and conflicts — continue.[11] The present study will both use evidence from different countries to check and criticize the received thesis as sketched in the preceding paragraphs, and it will use this thesis to formulate questions and structure the comparison.[12] For these purposes greater clarification of concepts is needed, and the subject of the study has to be further narrowed down.

II. 'LOWER MIDDLE CLASS' AND 'WHITE COLLAR WORKERS': CONCEPTUAL PROBLEMS

A discussion of the history, the meanings and the functions of the concepts of *lower middle class, Mittelstand* and *classes moyennes* will serve this purpose. These concepts are usually used without strict definitions. Their scope varies. Almost always, however, they include the small independent businessmen in trade and commerce, lower and middle level white collar workers in the private and public sectors, as well as less prosperous professionals.[13] These groups vary significantly in class situation,[14] occupation, function, income, status, tradition, education, and other criteria. Why and with what justification are they combined?

This conglomeration of social groups became an object of political interest, scientific discussion and conceptual definition primarily within the framework of a dichotomous class theory and politics. The more that contemporary observers tended to perceive, expect, or fear (and sometimes fight) the polarization of industrial society into two great hostile camps, the more clearly they needed a concept to sum up those groups which did not fit into such a dichotomous model. This need grew as the antagonism between labor and capital, or proletariat and bourgeoisie, was superimposed on the older antagonisms between state and subject, aristocracy and middle class, city and country. At the same time sharper lines of differentiation emerged within the middle class, between the advancing or already established industrial, commercial, and financial bourgeoisie, on the one hand, and the small traders, shopkeepers, and other middle class groups who could only with difficulty be considered part of the bourgeoisie, on the other.

One solution was to adapt older concepts to fit these intermediate groups. Their meaning shifted, though not all at once; the older usage also continued and died out only gradually. The transition that occurred in the concepts *Mittelstand* and *classes moyennes* between the late 18th and the second third of the 19th centuries illustrates this process. At first these concepts tended to encompass the entire middle strata, the propertied and educated classes, who stood between the aristocracy and the common people, between the old ruling elites and the lower orders. Often, these terms were associated with reason and progress, and with general citizenship. However, it gradually became more difficult to include rich and influential capitalists, employers, entrepreneurs, and managers in the *Mittelstand* or *classes moyennes*. These upper strata were increasingly thought of as parts of the bourgeoisie, and no longer as part of the *Mittelstand* or *classes moyennes*. These terms were increasingly reserved for the strata between the bourgeoisie, which was now placed with the older ruling groups, and the growing proletariat. The picture of a simple, modest, but nonetheless middle class way of life became central to both the German and the French concept.[15] The German use of *Stand* kept alive memories of an older social order. The contrary French choice of the anti-corporatist concepts of class even to define these intermediate groups mirrored revolutionary France's clearer rejection of the ancien regime. This linguistic contrast not only indicates divergent German and French paths to industrial society, but probably also corresponds to the differing characteristics of those groups in Germany and France. The tone and connotation of these concepts remained positive in both languages, but the content shifted dramatically from their early associations. More and more distinctly they came to connote the promise of mediation between extremes, the fear of being ground down, the appeal to preserve the so-called 'healthy middle', and the defense of tradition — which was of course painted somewhat differently in Germany than in France. Those who wanted to be able to refer to these groups but also to avoid these conservative implications had to find other concepts. In German this gap was filled with the easily deprecatory sounding term *Kleinbürgertum*. At the latest Marx and Engels gave it a critical edge; it was frequently associated with backwardness and a dim future.[16]

The meaning of the English term *middle class* did not shift as markedly as that of *classes moyennes* and *Mittelstand*. Many authors throughout the 19th and 20th centuries have continued to use the term to include all middle class groups between the aristocracy and manual workers, while on the continent these middle class groups were increasingly divided into *Bourgeoisie* and *Kleinbürgertum, Bürgertum* and *Mittelstand*, or *bourgeoisie* and *classes moyennes*. Apparently English language patterns were not so distinctly stamped by the image of an all-encompassing conflict between capital and labor. Thus there was less need for a concept to segregate the groups which did not form part of that dichotomy. When the need did appear it was satisfied with the fairly colorless term *lower middle class(es)*, which does not resonate nearly as distinctly as *Kleinbürgertum*[17] with the class antagonism between bourgeoisie and proletariat.

The English tendency to blur the line between upper and lower middle classes was even more pronounced in the US. The term *middle class* was relatively little used in 19th century America; compared to Europe, its scope and meaning remained relatively undefined. By the time of the first world war, however, the concept was used to characterize those between big business and big labor, which were now perceived more clearly than before as overly powerful and in conflict with each other. In other contexts, the term *middle class* continued to be used in the comprehensive English sense as well; and *lower middle class* began to appear simultaneously as a label for these intermediate groups.[18]

Thus the necessity for and the practice of placing lower middle class groups in a separate category from those above and below — whether the extremes are labeled 'labor' and 'capital', or 'proletariat' and 'bourgeoisie' — closely correlated with the degree to which the basic model of a dichotomous class society dominated contemporary perceptions of reality. Representatives of very different political and scholarly points of view adopted the idea of a middle class or lower middle class grouping between the two main camps, though with distinct shadings and partly contradictory conclusions. Since the *Communist Manifesto* marxists have predicted that the lower middle class would decline and ultimately be crushed between the bourgeoisie and the proletariat. In making this argument, Marx and Engels were still thinking primarily of the old middle classes. By the revisionism debate of the 1890s at the latest, however, marxists included the new middle class in the concept *Kleinbürgertum* using the same logic. This was true both of Bernstein in doubting the prognosis of lower middle class demise and of Kautsky in continuing to uphold it. Lenin also spoke of a lower middle class that included both small independents and dependent employees, since it was the qualities they shared that interested him. For him, attitudes and behavior distinguished both the old and new middle classes from the bourgeoisie; but they also kept them apart from the proletariat. Furthermore, these groups shared important political characteristics — above all, in Lenin's opinion, a tendency toward vacillating and unpredictable behavior.[19] Marxist and marxist-oriented writers have repeatedly linked small independents and salaried employees exactly because they are reasoning from a dichotomous model, even if they expect these middle groups to eventually merge with the proletariat.[20]

At least since the 1890s conservative authors, partly in reaction, have linked approximately the same groups in order to refute the marxist prognosis of social polarization or to warn that this polarization might begin or progress if the independent and dependent middle ranks were not rescued with appropriate political measures.[21] In one form or another the affected groups and their organizations proclaimed and utilized this last argument. Although small businessmen, white collar employees, and government clerks may have distinguished themselves from one another in most respects, they shared, the sense of belonging neither to the bourgeoisie or the proletariat. This negative self-image shaped their life style, conduct, organizational behavior and political demands; thus it also shaped the responses of other social groups to them and influenced the governments which had to take their perspective, rhetoric, and politics into account. To the degree that not belonging to proletariat or bourgeoisie formed the sense of identity, attitudes, and behavior of the groups in question as well as the way others viewed and treated them, an actual community of interest did appear among those who identified themselves as middle class or lower middle class. At the same time, however, these concepts retained ideological overtones; that is, they exaggerated what these groups had in common for ideological reasons.[22]

Thus the practice of combining artisans, retailers, government clerks, office workers, members of the lesser professions and other such groups under the label of *lower middle class* developed within a theoretical and historical context that was marked by a dichotomous model of class society and corresponding actual social polarization — though this model was never fully congruent with reality and the polarization of society was by no means complete. This linguistic combination was particularly common where, as in Wilhelminian Germany, tendencies toward and theories of class society were particularly prevalent. It surfaced only gradually and at a late date in the US, where the polarization of society into classes was retarded by various counter tendencies and where the contours of the lower middle class remained particularly unclear in the consciousness of contemporary thought.

This may explain why the concepts *Mittelstand* or 'lower middle classes' are rather abstract, and not very useful analytical tools if used outside the type of intellectual or historical context in which they originated. The characteristics which unite the groups considered *lower middle class, Mittelstand* or *classes moyennes* are formal, thin and under some viewpoints less significant than those which divide them. In fact one of the received thesis' weaknesses may well be that it assumes rather than proves the similarities in the situation, attitudes, and conduct of the various lower middle class groups and thus errs in treating evidence about one group as valid for the others as well. In order to investigate the connection between economic situation, interests, status, education, mentality, and organizational and political behavior of social groups within complex industrial societies, it is not possible to combine groups as different in class position, occupation and socio-economic function as the various components of the lower middle class.

The following study does not take the lower middle class as a whole as its subject and does not address itself to the entire thesis sketched above. For practical reasons as well, it restricts itself to only one of the lower middle class groups: lower and middle level white collar workers in the private sector. Its conclusions will apply only to this group, though they will be formulated so that hypotheses to investigate other lower middle class groups, e.g. artisans and small shopkeepers, can be drawn from them. This limitation should reduce the heterogeneity of the social grouping under investigation to a manageable level. Only groups in the same class position will be included: white collar employees. They distinguish themselves from the other great grouping of dependent labor, the blue collar working class, by the fact that they do not perform manual labor (or at any rate not primarily) and that they are traditionally paid in salary not wages. By excluding the managerial and upper ranks of professional employees the investigation excludes those salaried persons who because of their enormous delegated authority, particular qualifications, or influence as specialists differed considerably from most white collar workers in power, status and income, and who it would be impossible, unusual, or at least doubtful to describe as lower middle class.[23] In excluding government employees the investigation eliminates a significant grouping of non-manual salaried employees. In some countries workers in the public sector are so distinguished by legal position and tradition from the private sector that they are called by separate names — e.g. in German, *Beamte* instead of *Angestellte*. Thus occupational groups which either in the US or Germany or in both countries are public employees or officials, such as post office employees, government clerks, teachers, etc., will be dealt with only in passing.[24]

The subject of this study is a social grouping which can be found under different labels and with varying characteristics in all industrializing and industrial societies. The development of this social grouping is so closely connected with the progress of industrialization and its related social changes that the proportion of white collar workers in the labor force as a whole may serve as a rough indicator of the level of economic development.[25] Thus this social grouping can be studied in international comparison, as long as one limits the comparison to societies with somewhat parallel levels of industrialization. Unlike farmers or small artisans, white collar groups do not stagnate at advanced stages of development but instead enjoy above average growth. This expansion is not the least reason why white collar workers deserve so much attention. They have played and will play a major role in the recent past, the present, and the immediate future of developed western industrial societies.

III. THE DIFFERENCE BETWEEN WHITE COLLAR AND BLUE COLLAR AS A RESEARCH PROBLEM

If discussion of the thesis connecting industrial capitalist development, the lower middle class, and fascism is restricted to white collar workers, then the distinction between blue and white collar becomes of crucial importance. For that thesis as applied to white collar groups rests heavily on the hypothesis that salaried employees interpreted their actual situation by comparing it to that of wage workers. It assumes that they took the working class as a reference group and used the multi-dimensional differences between themselves and the workers as support and basis for their sense of self-worth. Any narrowing in this difference was experienced as relative deprivation; that is, as a relative decline and thus as grounds for dissatisfaction, whether it resulted from one's own situation worsening, or the position of the reference group improving, or both.

This conception of white collar workers is compatible with the insights of social psychologists into reference groups and relative deprivation. Research has demonstrated that comparison to other individuals and groups is an important basis for and source of self-esteem and self-criticism for individuals and groups. Furthermore, some groups and individuals are more important foils for comparison than others; it is common to choose a group that is less well off. Diminution in the relevant dimensions of difference between one's own group and the other then becomes a source of growing dissatisfaction; under certain conditions it may become a basis for many kinds of protest.[26] Naturally, these insights from social psychology do not demonstrate that white collar workers are susceptible to right-wing protest at advanced stages of industrialization; they merely make it appear a logical possibility. The primary usefulness of reference group theories here will be to raise a series of questions and issues which this study will try to keep in mind. Why, for instance, did white collar workers choose precisely this reference group and not another, e.g. one better situated in most respects, such as entrepreneurs and managers? Were there other, competing reference groups? Does this entire thesis apply more to some categories of white collar workers than others; if so, how do these categories differ (for instance: social origin, income, status, distance from the reference group)? Does the working class as a whole serve as a reference group, or only particular sections of it? Which ones and why? What dimensions of social stratification were relevant for this distinction; that is, which differences between blue and white collar counted more, which less, which not at all and why?[27] Which dimensions changed more, which less? How intense were the dissatisfactions which arose from this distinction compared to others with other causes? Under what conditions did discontent express itself as protest, and what kind of protest? How did white collar workers explain the blurring of the collar line to themselves?

One can apply such questions to different countries since the difference between manual and non-manual activities, between blue and white collar workers, *ouvriers* and *employés, Arbeiter* and *Angestellten,* can be observed in all industrial societies.[28] White collar workers specialize in performing commercial, administrative, planning, controlling and coordinating functions. Most of them work in commercial establishments, banks and other service institutions, or in the office section of industrial concerns at some physical distance from the factory and the milieu of the worker. Compared to manual workers their tasks are wholely or predominantly non-manual, frequently less routinized, hard to quantify, and more concerned with information than objects. Their working environment is as a rule cleaner, safer, and more comfortable than that of the workers. The mechanization, and automation of work began later in the office than on the shop floor; it is still less advanced today. Furthermore, mechanized and automated procedures have less impact on office workers since they do not dictate the order of work and limit freedom of movement as directly as machine production. The average white collar employee may anticipate more reasonably than the average worker at least some slight advancement in his career. The structure of work and the qualifications required create more continuity between lower and middle and sometimes even top office positions than exists between the skilled worker and the office; furthermore, the office provides more hierarchical rungs to climb than the factory. Many white collar employees, but almost no workers, exercise some delegated authority; they are therefore not at the very bottom of the hierarchical order characteristic of every economic enterprise. White collar workers receive a salary instead of wages, which means that they are paid at longer intervals and they know how much they will earn in advance. Salaries are also less affected by market fluctuations and varying individual abilities; they are more readily tied to a seniority system than wages. On the average white collar workers earn more and are better qualified than blue collar workers.[29] They frequently have somewhat more job security and work somewhat shorter hours. It is due to these objective differences that other things being equal white collar positions confer higher status than blue collar positions. This differential status exists not only at the workplace; it also has consequences for social realms beyond the sphere of work.[30]

The blue collar-white collar line has shifted according to typical patterns in all industrial societies. Everywhere the above average growth of white collar positions had a kind of inflationary effect. The privileges and exclusiveness which had belonged to the very small group of salesmen and early office workers were not completely transferred to most of the rapidly growing lower white collar categories. Most white collar functions had originally been performed by individuals and small groups with little division of labor. These functions were increasingly restructured by that division and by the routinization and mechanization of office work. In consequence most lower and middle level white collar positions became more similar to blue collar positions. General education and declining illiteracy eliminated a factor that had previously distinguished all white collar from most blue collar workers. Everywhere women gained entry to offices and banks; thus another difference between the office and the factory, where women had long been employed, diminished. Furthermore, blue collar workers gained rights, such as paid vacations or limited job security, which had previously been considered white collar privileges. In the first half of the 20th century the difference in earnings between blue and white collar appears to have declined slightly everywhere. The wages of better paid blue collar workers and the salaries of the worst paid white collar employees have increasingly overlapped. In addition, tendencies appeared everywhere to clearly distinguish an upper stratum of white collar workers, who were not losing ground relative to other groups, from the great mass of lower and middle level employees whose situation as a whole approached the workers', though it was not fully identical. It seems likely that these broad social and economic changes would have affected the relative status, sense of identity, and social behavior of white collar workers everywhere.[31]

To recapitulate: the collar line and its transformation may be deduced from the structure and function of production and distribution in industrial capitalist systems. It may be demonstrated that the division of labor, the differentiation of functions, and the separation between giving and carrying out orders creates functionally and occupationally differentiated social groups which differ in indispensability, initiative, the nature of their duties, and their place in the authority structure of the firm even though they share the class position of dependent workers. It would be logical for a firm interested in self-preservation, expansion and profit to treat these groups differently: paying one group by salary, the other in wages; granting one advantages denied the other. It is also possible to show that typical changes in the situation of white collar workers resulted from structural transformations which were visible in all capitalist industrial systems.[32] Thus because the distinction between blue and white collar necessarily emerges in industrial capitalist societies and because it differentiates approximately the same functional and occupational groups everywhere, it may serve as the conceptual basis for a comparative investigation such as the following comparison of Germany and the US.

However, careful analysis of any society reveals that drawing this line of demarcation is a complicated historical process in which the universal features of industrial capitalist systems are not a sufficient determinant of whether specific functional and occupational groups (e.g. foremen) are considered blue or white collar in any given society; nor have the criteria offered above always provided sharp lines of differentiation.[33] Furthermore, as will soon be shown, historical trends have been less distinct than the argument would have it. Large groups of white collar workers were not at all affected by the tendency of salaries to approach wages; furthermore, this tendency was much weaker in some societies than others.[34] Even a superficial knowledge of the situation in different societies suffices to suggest that although the distinction between blue and white collar workers does follow from the structural elements of industrial capitalist systems and is thus common to all, that fact alone says very little about the social, cultural, political, legal and ideological meaning of the collar line.

Which features and advantages raise the white collar workers' position above that of manual workers appears to be dependent on the specific social and cultural histories of individual societies. For example, whether or not the collar line becomes legally significant and legally defined, whether it becomes a basis for separate social legislation for blue and white collar workers, varies directly with the social and political circumstances of particular societies; it is hardly determined by the basic elements of industrial capitalism. The variations in the case of law appear particularly enormous. In part so do the social status distinctions that are linked with the collar line. Although in most instances white collar workers enjoy higher status than blue collar workers, there are wide variations between societies and over time in the size and content of that advantage. Thus it does not appear possible to predict from the basic characteristics of industrial capitalist systems alone how the shifting line between white and blue collar will shape the sense of identity, social contacts, life style, or organizational and political behavior of those concerned. Many economic, social, cultural, and political factors may determine whether or not this distinction becomes so important that other lines of differentiation which are always present, for instance occupational or ethnic ties, appear secondary in comparison. Such factors also determine how important relative to other lines of differentiation the collar line is in the system of class formation and social stratification in a society.[35] To put it another way, and to connect it to the thesis of 'relative deprivation': It does not necessarily follow from the ubiquitous, socio-economically based distinction between blue and white collar as such that white collar status would assume such unequivocally central importance for those who shared it that they would choose a group with similar dimensions — the workers — as a reference group instead of comparing themselves as members of an ethnic group to other ethnic groups or as members of an occupational group to other occupational groups.

If this study uncovers and confirms clear variations in the strength and the meaning of the distinction between blue and white collar workers in different societies, that may mean that the initial thesis connecting capitalism, the lower middle class (including white collar workers), and fascism would apply more directly to some societies than others and would have to be modified as a whole. The following investigation will therefore concentrate on international differences and national peculiarities in the collar line without denying its ubiquity, which is, after all, a methodological prerequisite for the study.

If this comparison finds great variations in the blue collar-white collar distinction, that would also call into question a series of theories about white collar workers which have a particularly rich tradition in Germany. These theories are in fact based on source material from the development of a single society, but they nonetheless present their conclusions as a general 'sociology of white collar workers'; they formulate general characteristics of *the* white collar workers and *the* collar line and then derive them from the basic character of the (capitalist) process of industrialization. Without an adequate historical-comparative perspective, these theories overlook the fact that a good part of the distinction between blue and white collar is socio-culturally and socio-politically shaped by traditions and structures which differ from one society to another. Thus the actual significan e of the collar line cannot be immediately deduced from the divergent functions of blue and white collar workers 'in modern society' or from the logic of the 'reproductive process of capital'.[36] Such a finding would also place a number of investigations of social mobility that use the distinction between manual and non-manual occupations as a yardstick to compare very different societies in danger of assuming more international uniformity and greater continuity over time in the distinction in status between these groupings than is justified.[37]

IV: THE AMERICAN-GERMAN COMPARISON: JUSTIFICATION AND PURPOSE

Thus the set of problems which this study addresses calls for cross-cultural comparative treatment. In order to remain within manageable limits the following study will focus on the comparison of the US and Germany. The choice of these two societies can be justified. It is necessary to compare societies at about the same level of development, with white collar groups that are approximately equal in size, similar in social-economic characteristics, and exposed to similar structural changes, if one wants to find out to what extent such societal similarities led to similar social, cultural, and political characteristics in these groups — or to what extent and for what reasons this was not the case. Concentration on the US and Germany meets this condition. Both countries in the interwar years had bourgeois social orders with liberal-democratic systems of government. Both societies industrialized by private capitalist prescription; both reached parallel stages of development in approximately the same decades. This parallelism may be illustrated by the distribution of the gainfully occupied population or labor force among the economic sectors (see Table 1.1).

It is true that measured by the size of the labor force the immigrant society in the US grew considerably more rapidly than in Germany. In 1850 only about half as many persons were gainfully occupied in the US as in Germany. By 1890, however, the US had attained a slight lead, which continued to widen into the 1920s. Nonetheless, the distribution of the labor force among the economic sectors was remarkably similar. Both societies reached the point at which those engaged in non-agricultural pursuits first outnumbered those in agriculture around 1880, though in the US the relative shrinking of the agricultural population was more pronounced in the following decades than in Germany. In both societies the proportion of the labor force in industry and commerce reached a highpoint in the 1920s; thereafter it increased only modestly. The somewhat greater expansion of German commerce and industry compared to the US was due to the greater importance which transportation and trade had had even in the first decades of industrialization in this large country of dispersed settlements, where mercantile capitalist traditions had developed early.[39] In both Germany and the US, from the end of the 19th century on the

Table 1.1
Labor Force by Economic Sectors: US and Germany, 1850-1940
(as a percentage of gainfully occupied population)[38]

Year	Agriculture, Forestry, Fisheries		Industry, Mining, Manufacturing		Transportation, and Other Public Utilities		Commerce, Banking, Insurance		Domestic Service		Other Services		Total (000s)	
	US	Ger.	US	Ger.	US	Ger.			US	Ger.			US	Ger.
1850a	64	55	18	25	5	4			12	16			7,700	15,028
1860b	59	52	20	27	7	4			12	17			10,530	15,967
1870	53		23		10				13				12,920	
1875		50		29						16				18,643
					US	Ger.	US	Ger.	US	Ger.	US	Ger.		
1880	50	49	25	29	5	2	7	4	6	8	6	5	17,390	19,638
1890	43	43	28	34	6	3	8	5	6	7	7	6	23,740	22,372
1900	38	38	30	37	7	3	9	7	6	6	8	9	29,070	25,548
1910	32	36	32	37	9	4	11	8	6	5	10	10	36,730	29,420
1920	27		34		10		12		5		12		41,610	
1925		32		40		5		10		4		12		31,033
1930	22	31	31	37	10	6	15	12	5	4	14	12	48,830	30,483
1940c	17	27	31	40	8	5	16	10	5	4	16	12	53,300	39,680

a For Germany: 1852
b For Germany: 1861
c For Germany: 1939

proportion of the labor force engaged in trade, banking, insurance and transportation increased significantly faster than that in industry and commerce. Here as there the percentage of domestic servants (which in Germany in the second third of the 19th century had been significantly higher than in the US) declined slowly after 1880. At the same time the numbers engaged in other services (education, the professions, government) increased in a very similar way in both countries until the 1930s. In the US these groups then attained a clear lead over their counterparts in the Third Reich, which more actively promoted industrial development. Since the relative shifts in sectoral shares of the workforce vary in fairly typical patterns during industrialization, they make particularly good general criteria to compare levels of development. These parallel shifts indicate that Germany and the US reached parallel stages of development at about the same time: insofar as this was the case, comparison of these two societies can be based on clearer similarities than a comparison with Great Britain, a south European, or a contemporary developing nation would be.[40]

Structural changes typical of industrial capitalist development also occurred at the same time and in a similar manner in the US and Germany. The factory system became established as a key element in the industrial revolution with a major impact on society here as there in the second third of the 19th century. Insofar as there were measurable discontinuities in the growth of the rate of investment and in industry and commerce's share of value created or the gross national product, there as here they began in these decades. Changes in the relationships among economy, social structure and politics, which can be summed up as the beginnings of 'organized capitalism', appeared in Germany and the US at the end of the 19th century. They included the progressive organization of the market by large firms through combination and concentration, and the simultaneous tendency of these firms to become more systematic and bureaucratic. White collar intensive industries (electrical and chemical, for example) grew at above average rates; so did white collar occupations. A powerful new social group, the salaried entrepreneurs or managers, emerged with the increasing separation of ownership and control at the top of large firms. Formal organizations became more important in the sphere of interest articulation and social conflicts. Government agencies increasingly intervened in the social and economic realm, though less forcefully and at a later date in the US than Germany.[41] The changes in business structure which contributed to the expansion and alteration of white collar positions occurred in a more parallel fashion in the US and Germany than they did, for instance, in Germany and France or in the US and England.[42] Before 1914 the relatively high growth rate of the German economy was more similar to the American case than to the more leisurely pace of France or England; only with the world war and its aftermath did the average growth rate of the German economy fall noticeably behind the American.[43] Finally, the economic crisis around 1930 hit the US and Germany equally hard; it affected the population in these societies more than in either France or England.[44]

Due to these parallels the quantitative development of white collar groups also proceeded along parallel lines in the US and Germany. The figures in Table 1.2 include white collar workers in the private and public sectors, but exclude 'managers, officials and proprietors' as well as independent professionals.

These figures permit only rough comparisons. Here as there the number of white collar workers increased disproportionately after the late 19th century; their share of the labor force doubled in both societies. Although the American figures may be slightly too high

Table 1.2
The Proportion of White Collar Workers in the Economically Active Population, US and Germany, 1895-1940[45]

	In 10,000s		As a % of the Economically Active Population	
	US	Germany	US	Germany
1895		212		11
1900	336		12	
1907		331		13
1910	556		15	
1920	793		19	
1925		544		17
1930	1,092		22	
1933		551		17
1939		773		22
1940	1,254		24	

since they include some self-employed, in reality the proportion of white collar workers was always somewhat higher in the US than in Germany. This lead increased between 1910 and 1930, then shrank in the 1930s. The proportion of women within the white collar group increased in both societies; the temporal lead of the US in this shift was particularly marked.[46] If one looks at the numerical relationship of blue and white collar workers within the industrial sector alone, the same picture emerges: a great similarity between the two countries with a slight lead on the American side (see Table 1.3).

Table 1.3
White Collar Workers in Manufacturing, Mining and Construction, US and Germany, 1925-38[47]
(as a percentage of all employees in these industries)

	US	Germany
1925	12.5	12.9
1929	13.7	13.1
1932	16.3	15.0
1937	12.9	11.7
1938	14.2	11.9

Source: S. Kuznets, *National Income and its Composition 1919-1938,* New York 1941, pp. 557, 600.

These considerations justify the choice of the US and Germany for a comparative investigation which must presuppose similar economic development in order to avoid comparing white collar groups of completely different size, character, and level of development. Comparison with Germany suggests itself for another reason. In recent years interest in the survival of older pre-industrial or pre-capitalist structures and traditions in modern industrial societies has been growing. Alexander Gerschenkron, for instance, has directed attention to the significance which conditions prior to and at the start of industrialization have on the pace and course of economic development.[48] Barrington Moore's comparative study of lords and peasants has renewed awareness of the ways in which social-economic developments reaching back to the early modern era and the late middle ages condition the chances for democracy and dictatorship in modern states.[49] A common thesis is that since the beginning of industrialization, German social history has been particularly influenced by surviving pre-industrial and pre-capitalist traditions and structures. In recent years this thesis has produced provocative questions about and important insights into Imperial Germany (1870-1918), particularly in studies of social groups like the artisans and the agrarians, analyses of cultural processes and the history of consciousness, and investigations of parliament and political parties. The impact of pre-industrial structures and traditions on the development of industry and white collar workers in Germany has also been investigated.[50]

Although in recent years more attention has been devoted to the continuity of pre-industrial factors in American social history as well,[51] there is no doubt that *in comparison with Europe* the role of specific pre-industrial and pre-capitalist traditions was much weaker in American history after industrialization. That feudal, aristocratic, and corporatist traditions were to a great extent absent in America in contrast to Europe is frequently and legitimately emphasized.[52] For this study, it will be particularly important that another type of pre-industrial tradition — that of the bureaucratic authoritarian state — was also to a great extent absent in the US (as in Great Britain) in contrast to most of continental Europe. Thus the comparison of parallel social developments in the US and Germany will make it possible to explore the influence and significance of specific pre-industrial and pre-capitalist structures and traditions surviving in the industrial era. To what extent did the structures and processes, institutions and ideologies, tensions and conflicts which this book hopes to explore result from the effects and characteristics of capitalism itself (so that they should have emerged in all industrial capitalist systems); to what extent were they tied to continuing pre-industrial/pre-capitalist structures and traditions, and thus might be expected to appear in Germany, but not in the US? What effect the continuity of specific pre-industrial/pre-capitalist traditions had in Germany, what the lack of or weakness of such traditions meant in American social history, will be dealt with as concretely as possible in the following chapters. Or, framed in terms of the theme of this study and in relation to the received thesis sketched above: to what extent were the multi-dimensional collar line and the susceptibility of the new middle class to right-wing tendencies a function of the inherent characteristics of industrial capitalism; to what extent were they shaped by the continuity of specific pre-industrial/pre-capitalist structures and traditions?

Perhaps our key concepts need some further clarification. *Capitalism* refers to an economic system based predominantly on private property and private control of capital for the production and exchange of commodities for profit. Key decisions are made by private entrepreneurs interacting mainly through the mechanisms of the market. *Industrial capitalism* is distinguished by some additional characteristics, among them: the factory, that is, a centralized mode of production based on machinery and wage labor; the relative growth of first the industrial and then the service sectors at the expense of agriculture; the uneven but only briefly interrupted increase in the gross national product, even measured per capita; many fundamental social changes like urbanization, and the rise of mass education. Industrial capitalism began (roughly speaking and ignoring many precursors) in England in the last third of the 18th century, in western continental Europe in the first third of the 19th, in Germany and the US in the second third, and in Italy and Russia in the last quarter of the 19th century. In this book *pre-industrial* and *pre-capitalist* structures and traditions will refer to interrelated social, cultural, and political factors which originated before the rise of industrial capitalism and continued in effect in the period of industrial capitalism, though usually in an increasingly weakened and modified form. They were maintained and sometimes even reinforced through different mechanisms which need to be analyzed. They varied from one industrializing country to another. Even when we speak only of 'traditions', we mean not just values, ideologies, and mentalities, but also the peculiarities of class formation and stratification, patterns of behavior, institutions and law. We will be particularly interested in the influence of two specific traditions on emerging industrial society: the corporatist and the bureaucratic.[53] Both were strong in Germany and weak in the US.

These questions are drawn primarily from German historiography. By studying the US in a comparative perspective it is hoped to improve our understanding of the factors underlying Germany's past. This is one of the aims of this study. But equally important is the second aim: By asking this type of 'imported' comparative question it is hoped to explore an area which has up to now been slighted in US history. Of course, there is the outstanding study by the sociologist C. Wright Mills[54] which has, however, remained without followers. There are quite a number of studies on white collar unions.[55] But white collar workers in the private sector were barely organized, and studies of this kind are by necessity very selective as to the questions they ask and as to the time periods and groups they investigate. There are some new departures in American working class history and in women's history which have led to the thematization of important aspects of white collar history.[56] In the last decade social-historical studies of cities have made important discoveries about social mobility and migration which illuminate patterns of entry into white collar occupations and some characteristics of these groups. However, most of these studies have posited the collar line as an underlying assumption rather than actually investigating it. Furthermore, they have not examined white collar workers as a subject in any comprehensive way.[57] White collar workers have been touched upon by a great many recent studies on family history and the history of ethnic groups, on corporate personnel management and the development of educational institutions. American historical literature is extensive and rich, and non-specialists in particular may be sure that they have missed some important article or book. Still, it seems true that white collar employees as a social grouping have remained at the periphery of American historians' interest — quite in contrast to the lively debate underway in Germany since the beginning of the century.[58]

The main reason for the marked neglect of the history of white collar workers in the US is the nature of the subject itself. The characteristics of American white collar employees have inhibited rather than invited conceptualization and study by contemporaries, social scientists, and historians. The following investigation intends to explain these characteristics. A comparison may transform a topic that has been insufficiently interesting in itself into a subject for historical inquiry.

The project was conceived with its investigative questions rather than with the available sources in clear sight. The subsequent search for authoritative sources turned out to be unusually difficult and time consuming. On the one hand, there are hardly any large source collections that bear directly on this theme; on the other, few themes in American social history do not have some possible significance for the history of the employed middle classes. The unfavorable state of the sources also reflects the image of American white collar workers which they themselves and which others hold. It further explains why the following investigation rests on a heterogeneous, widely dispersed collection of materials, and why it has not been possible to treat all questions with equal thoroughness.

Two internally quite heterogeneous groups of white collar workers will be empirically in the foreground: first, sales employees in the retail and parts of the wholesale trade: the great majority of the census category 'sales workers'. In 1900 'sales workers' numbered 1.3 million, in 1930, 3.5 million; in those years they made up 39% and 32% of all salaried employees (private and government).[59] A primary source of information about this group will be its organizations, for example, the retail clerks' union, whose history will be used to provide insight into the social group it represented. For this purpose its failures — the union remained very small — are as interesting as its limited successes. In addition, sources related to their workplace — the history of commercial establishments, professional literature — shed light on this group.

The other chief subject for this study are the commercial, technical, and general office employees of manufacturing firms. In 1920 they numbered 1.4 million or 17%, in 1930, 1.5 million or 13% of all salaried employees.[60] In American occupational statistics these white collar employees in industry were counted as 'sales workers' if they were engaged in sales or related work. If they were general office employees, bookkeepers, secretaries and the like, they belonged to the census category 'clerical and kindred workers'; in 1900 this group numbered 0.9 million or 25%, in 1930, 4.3 million or 40% of the total white collar workforce. To the extent that they were engineers, chemists, industrial economists, technicians, and the like (excluding those who were counted as 'managers' or 'officials') they were placed in the category of 'professional, technical, and kindred workers', which in 1900 accounted for 1.2 million or 27%, and in 1930, for 3.3 million or 30% of all white collar workers. We will include bosses and foremen who were partly placed in the census category 'craftsmen, foremen and kindred workers' and thus counted as blue collar workers.[61] Abundant sources on personnel management, the social policies and social structure of large firms, firm archives, and other sorts of business-oriented materials illuminate this social grouping, which was almost completely unorganized before the 1930s.

Since this study is concerned with the significance of the distinction between blue and white collar, the lower and middle level salaried employees in industry are its chief concern. Upper level white collar employees like corporate officers and division heads, engineers with university degrees and other academically qualified professionals, are treated only incidentally. Frequently, however, neither the personnel structure nor the sources permit the drawing of an unequivocal line between higher and middle/lower level employees.[62] In some cases this problem can be solved by approximation, in others the sources permit the isolation of an upper group which may be defined somewhat differently from case to case. Other materials, for example those on white collar trade unions, refer specifically to these lower level groups. And general sources can often be used to throw light primarily on the dividing line between blue and white collar and the groups closest to the line: lower and middle level white collar employees, on one side, and skilled wage workers, on the other.

Wherever possible the investigation will try to make generalizations that reach beyond the two white collar groups that are at its center: salaried employees in commerce and industry. Occupational and professional literature, sources on labor law and the labor movement, government surveys, statistical reports, urban studies, materials on the history of education and political movements, early public opinion surveys, pamphlets, autobiographies, and information on the history of concepts and terms have been particularly useful. The urban industrial northeast (especially Massachusetts and New York) and midwest (Ohio, Illinois, and Michigan) will dominate, but sparser materials available from other regions have not been ignored.

The decisive time period for this study follows from the problem it seeks to illuminate. Since it is concerned with the connection between economic depression, lower middle class protest, and the rise of right-wing protest movements — in the extreme case, fascism — the economic crisis of the late 1920s and early 1930s and the immediately preceding postwar period must be included. On the German side only the period to 1933 is of interest, since at that date the process under study was terminated by the victory of fascism. In the US there was no parallel point of demarcation; nor was there in France or England. Thus this study will follow American developments through the 1930s and into the second world war, and will briefly sketch the connection between economic development, the employed lower middle classes, and right-wing protest suggested by the received thesis to the present.

There would be no point in trying to establish an arbitrary chronological starting point. Inquiry into the causes of German-American divergence around 1930 quickly forces the researcher's attention back to the years of the first world war and the preceding decades, and partly much further back. Answers to the questions asked are sought wherever it seems fruitful and empirically possible. The period of increasingly 'organized capitalism' in the US, that is, the era of the Progressive reforms in economy, state, and society from the 1890s to about 1920, is particularly important. The 1920s will, of course, be covered, and occasional points will require reaching back to the middle of the 19th century. The entire study is structured by the comparison of American and German development. The latter case, however, will not be presented as completely as the former; instead, its fundamentals will be sketched using the investigative questions developed above so that it can serve as a comparative reference point for the detailed analysis of the US situation which follows. In the course of that more thorough presentation, individual details of the German case will be brought up where appropriate for comparative insight.

V. GERMAN WHITE COLLAR WORKERS BEFORE 1933: BACKGROUND FOR COMPARISON

The distinction between manual workers and salaried employees played an important and much discussed role in German economic, social and political history after the beginning of the industrial revolution, but especially after the late 19th century. In contrast to workers, salaried employees performed very little or no manual labor; on the average they earned more than workers (though earnings overlapped). White collar employees received a salary rather than wages. These characteristics had important consequences for their social situation: salaried employees' earnings were more predictable, less directly dependent on market fluctuations, and less clearly destined to decline after the age of 40 than workers' earnings. White collar workers distinguished themselves from manual workers in their life style, behavior as consumers, and career expectations. As a rule salaried employees enjoyed greater job security and other advantages at work which were denied to wage workers: paid holidays, special status in company insurance plans, bonuses, etc. By granting white collar employees these privileges, top management satisfied their expectations within financially feasible limits and contributed to maintaining and deepening the gulf which stood in the way of any possible solidarity between organized workers and organized salaried employees. The collar line even became fixed in German law. Initiated in response to strong pressure from organized white collar employees, and facilitated by the cooperation of anti-socialist government officials and politicians, after 1911 a series of federal laws favorably distinguished white collar employees from blue collar workers. Separate legal treatment first appeared in social insurance statutes; it permeated the extensive labor legislation passed during the first world war and the early years of the Weimar Republic. Laws requiring employee representation on company committees, for instance, separated manual workers from salaried employees. Thus the legal distinction came to make an independent contribution to widening the conceptual and actual distance between workers and salaried employees. Patterns of organization were also shaped by the collar line. Before the first world war and again after 1932, every third white collar employee was organized, as was every third worker. Yet even the left-wing white collar employees in industry did not join the same trade unions as the workers in their branch of industry.

In the 19th century and the first third of the 20th, the vast majority of white collar employees in Germany did not think of themselves just as members of the labor force and certainly not as workers or proletarians. Instead, they identified with a particular occupation or occupational 'corporation' (*Stand*) such as the 'Mercantile Employees' Corporation' or bank clerks; or they even identified themselves as members of a broad stratum of 'private bureaucrats' analogous to the public bureaucracy. In this way salaried employees saw themselves as members of a middle social stratum that superseded occupational differences; they were divided by position and status from the dependent manual workers, on one side, and everyone who was self-employed, on the other. These two elements — belonging to the class of dependent labor, on the one hand, but, on the other, strictly distinguishing themselves from manual workers — determined the sense of identity, expectations, organizational behavior and other dimensions of white collar employees' existence. They also shaped the way in which white collar employees were viewed and treated by other social groups. The significance of the collar line in German life has been reflected in a lively popular and scholarly literature on white collar workers since the early 20th century.[63]

In the first years of the century it became evident that social change was tending to diminish the differences between blue and white collar workers and thus to call into question essential elements of the salaried employee's sense of identity — which was based in large part on his distance from the workers. The greater their numbers became and the more widely distributed previously restricted educational and technical skills became, the worse the market position of most white collar employees became. Increasingly, salaried employees performed simple, routinized tasks in offices, banks and stores; they became subject to direction and controls that paralleled the workers' situation in the factory. White collar workers also became increasingly interchangeable. In many cases once-frequent contact with the entrepreneur declined. As advanced training or even university education became a prerequisite for entry into upper level positions, the career opportunities of lower and middle level salaried employees clearly declined. Furthermore, during and after the first world war blue collar workers fought for and won advantages which had originally been the preserve of white collar groups, including the right to paid vacations, reduction of the work day, and modest job security.

The social origins of workers and salaried employees also became more similar: whereas previously salaried employees had been drawn from lower middle class and middle class families, they were now often the offspring of working class parents. In the lowest office jobs and in sales work the employment of women was becoming common; this had been the case in some branches of industry in the 19th century, but never in salaried occupations. At the beginning of the first world war, in the 'rationalization' after 1924, and above all in the depression of the late 1920s and early 1930s, masses of white collar employees were thrown out of work. These were new experiences which contradicted their sense of identity and put them objectively in a more similar position to manual workers. Even before the first world war the average gap between wages and salaries appears to have declined slightly; it definitely decreased in the inflationary period 1914-23 and was only partly reestablished by 1933. After the impoverishment of war and inflation the average white collar worker had not regained his 1913 real income by the early 1930s. The average worker, in contrast, appears to have regained his prewar real income by about 1928, before the world economic crisis brought a new retreat for wages and a new widening of the wage-salary differential. In the economic crisis many firms cut expenditures and wiped out another part of what remained of the worker-salaried employee distinction. Now white collar salaries were docked for short time; these reductions contradicted the basic principle of a monthly salary and pushed salaried employees, in the opinion of some of their spokesmen, toward the status of 'hourlies'.[64]

White collar employees met these changes with a variety of ideological and political reactions. Traditionally anti-proletarian and anti-socialist, they were certainly not to be found among the forces favoring change in Imperial Germany and were hardly part of the social base that supported democratic reform. When confronted with a radical egalitarian socialist protest movement and an apparently revolutionary proletariat, only partially integrated into bourgeois society, most white collar workers stressed their membership in the middle class and the anti-socialist camp. The more parallel the working conditions and economic situation of worker and salaried employee became, the more tenaciously and actively most white collar workers defended their traditional privileges. They clung to their increasingly superseded status advantages, and affirmed their now questionable belief that they were different from workers. Only a small minority — though it was growing slightly in the years before 1914 — who were for the most part members of the less important white collar associations (the Bund der technisch-industriellen Beamten and the Zentralverband der Handlungsgehilfen) were ready for limited cooperation with labor unions and the Social Democratic Party (SPD). The world war and its aftermath drove a larger number of white collar workers to a usually very careful and limited leftward reorientation. In these years even the largest, least militant white collar association adopted definite elements of trade union behavior, including strikes and collaboration with manual workers' unions. The tone of their newspapers became more militant; attacks on capitalists, entrepreneurs and conservatives increased. Reform-minded and radical associations grew more quickly than conservative. A noteworthy number of white collar employees took part in the great strikes and revolutionary events of 1918/19.[65]

This very limited white collar swing to the left and the narrowing social and political distance between workers and salaried employees during the war and in the 1918/19 revolution did not continue during the Weimar Republic. In certain respects, it is true, the trend was not reversed: white collar associations continued their trade union policies and were thereby clearly separated from their Wilhelminian past. Polemics against entrepreneurs, capitalists, and conservative elites were not limited to the left wing of white collar organizations but were also found in moderate liberal and right-wing associations. But this persistent radical current, which had flourished in the war and gained renewed strength in the depression, was increasingly paired with right-wing tendencies and linked with new anti-socialist, anti-proletarian protests. The membership figures of the three national white collar federations organized during the war and the revolution demonstrate that white collar employees as a whole leaned more to the right than the left in the years between the revolution and the Nazi seizure of power in 1933 (see Table 1.4).

Table 1.4
Membership in the Three Major Federations of White Collar Associations in Germany, 1920-30[66]
(in 000s)

	1920	1922	1925	1926	1927	1929	1930
Afa	690	658	428	405	396	453	480
Gedag	463	460	411	420	460	558	592
GDA	300	302	313	307	290	375	385
	1453	1420	1152	1132	1146	1386	1457
				(in %)			
Afa	47.5	46.3	37.2	35.8	34.6	32.7	32.9
Gedag	31.8	32.4	35.6	37.1	40.1	40.2	40.6
GDA	20.7	21.3	27.2	27.1	25.3	27.1	26.5
	100.0	100.0	100.0	100.0	100.0	100.0	100.0

The Afa-Bund (General Free Federation of Salaried Employees), which was affiliated with the Federation of Socialist Trade Unions (ADGB) and the SPD, was the largest national white collar federation in 1920 with almost half the organized salaried employees as members; by 1930 this share had dropped to barely one-third. In contrast, the anti-socialist federations gained ground: the Gedag (United Association of German Salaried Employees' Trade Unions), controlled by the nationalistic-antisemitic German National Mercantile Employees' Association (DHV) and affiliated with the Union of Christian Trade Unions in Germany, increased its share of the total in this period from 32 to over 40% to become the largest of the three national federations. The Trade Union Federation of Salaried Employees (GDA), linked to the Hirsch-Duncker unions, followed a liberal, republican, but non- or anti-socialist line; it also made absolute and relative gains. The clearest shift to conservative or right-wing associations occurred between 1922 and 1925 during the inflation and stabilization crisis. Yet the shift in the balance of power was a continuous process, uninterrupted during the decline in the level of organization of white collar employees from 1922-25, the stagnation of membership figures between 1925 and 1927, or their increase after 1927. Elections for representatives to the white collar insurance board in 1927/28 confirm this distribution of power. A united slate entered by the anti-socialist federations Gedag and GDA won a clear majority of 71% over the socialist-oriented Afa-Bund's 29%. Just as they had in 1910, the great majority of salaried employees clearly wished to maintain a special legal status for salaried employees in social insurance programs and to retain the boundary between themselves and the workers. In general in the 1920s, workers' trade unions and salaried employees' associations moved further apart.[67]

After 1929, under the impact of the economic crisis, major disparities in the political outlook of workers and white collar employees became apparent. While the great majority of workers stood to the left of center and voted either communist or socialist, the great majority of salaried employees were politically right of center during the last years of the Weimar Republic. Under the pressure of depression white collar workers were more apt to radicalize to the right than the left. In clear contrast to manual workers, salaried employees were disproportionately strongly represented among the voters, sympathizers, members and functionaries of the rising NSDAP.

Analysis of the election results in July 1932 supports this conclusion. Samuel A. Pratt[68] has used the Pearson formula to correlate the proportion of the vote for the NSDAP and other parties with the proportion of specific social groups in the total population or labor force in 193 cities with 25,000 or more inhabitants. Dividing the population into independents (including top level salaried employees and bureaucrats), salaried employees and bureaucrats (excluding the top levels), and wage workers, he arrived at the following correlation coefficients (see Table 1.5).

Table 1.5
Correlation-Coefficients Between the Proportion of Certain Social Groups and NSDAP/KPD Shares of the Vote in 193 Cities, Reichstag Elections, July 1932

No. of cities	Size	Level of Significance	NSDAP Proportion of Vote Indep.	White Col.	Wkrs.	KPD Proportion of Vote Indep.	White Col.	Wkrs.
93	25-50,000	0.21	0.23	0.25	—0.20	—0.26	—0.37	0.44
48	50-100,000	0.29	0.58	0.57	—0.57	—0.72	—0.74	0.77
52	more than 100,000	0.27	0.33	0.27	—0.27	—0.31	—0.53	0.54

Statistical comparison of ten cities of varying sizes with the highest and lowest proportion of salaried and government employees in the labor force yields a similar result (see Table 1.6).

Table 1.6
Proportion of Salaried Employees and NSDAP/KPD Shares of the Vote in Selected Cities, Reichstag Elections, July 1932

Size of City	Median Proportion of Salaried Employees in Labor Force (in %)	Median Proportion of the Vote (in %) NSDAP	KPD
10 cities with highest proportion of white collar workers			
25-50,000	36.25	43	7
50-100,000	34.7	42	7
More than 100,000	33.65	39.5	14.5
10 cities with lowest proportion of white collar workers			
25-50,000	17.75	32	20
50-100,000	14.5	23.5	26.5
More than 100,000	19.2	27	25

Finally, correlation of the proportion of the labor force in the heavily white collar category of trade and commerce and the NSDAP share of the vote in all three sizes of cities yields significantly positive coefficients (0.21, 0.44 and 0.30); correlation of the proportion engaged in the blue collar category of industry and crafts and the Nazi share of the vote yields significant negative coefficients (-0.23, -0.47, -0.27).

One might be inclined to view these findings with caution since they are frequently only slightly above the line of significance and because of the methodological limits of simple correlation analysis, but the tendency which this evidence suggests is supported by other investigations and by the observations of contemporaries. White collar workers made up about 24% of NSDAP members in 1930 and about 21% in 1932, though they constituted only 12% of the population; only the non-agricultural self-employed were more strongly overrepresented.[69] Analysis of the Nazi leadership also reveals significant white collar overrepresentation.[70] Furthermore, salaried employees — next to public service workers (rail, postal, utilities, etc.) — played a noticeably large role in Nazi cell organizations between 1929 and 1933.[71] A large part of the membership of the right-leaning DHV, particularly the young sales clerks, agitated for close cooperation with the NSDAP after 1929/30, though their more cautious leaders preferred to pursue alliance with the middle of the road bourgeois parties.[72] For keen observers like Theodor Geiger the attraction of white collar workers to National Socialism was beyond doubt in 1930-33.[73] As early as 1929 the social scientist Emil Lederer, who was extremely well informed about white collar workers, wrote that 'Social romanticism is thoroughly at home in these [white collar] capitalist in-between strata, and the fascist idea of building a corporatist world in which activist youth will rule the older social classes in conjunction with certain groups of workers takes root most easily here.'[74] The Nazi mixture of radical polemic against elites and militant defense against socialism and the proletariat corresponded vaguely but effectively to the anxieties and ideologies of white collar workers, which were also expressed in parallel form by demarcating their group both from those above and those below. Under the pressure of the crisis, facing economic misery and the danger of proletarianization, white collar employees developed a radical protest stance which was simultaneously directed against capitalism and socialism. They moved to the right and became a decisive component of the social base of the right-radical protest movement which, with powerful support from ruling groups like large landowners, the military, and the business elite, destroyed the first German republic in 1933.[75]

Of course, this sketch presents only the general trend, which varied greatly in individual circumstances and was partly counteracted by contrary tendencies. There was a strong left wing of white collar workers which remained aloof from National Socialism; although the Afa-Bund had declined, it still represented more than a quarter of organized salaried employees during the economic crisis. The Afa federation frequently took positions to the left of many manual workers' trade unions. It had supported the Independent Socialists and remained on the left side of the ADGB, though it insisted on organizational independence from workers' unions and in order to keep its membership partially supported the separate privileged status of salaried employees in law.[76] And although it is true that workers were underrepresented as members of and voters for the NSDAP, they were by no means completely absent. Studies currently in progress of NSDAP voters in individual cities and precincts seem to find that the line between Nazi voters and opponents was often much less congruent with the collar line than the thesis argued here might suggest.[77] Demands and promises aimed specifically and expressly at salaried employees did not play a large role in the propaganda of the NSDAP, though the two-front stance against elites and socialists was in complete harmony with the politics of many white collar workers. In fact the Nazis refrained from concrete demands aimed at specific interests and groups in their not unsuccessful attempt to become a people's party which could appeal to the most diverse social-economic groups. Furthermore, a variety of other criteria and factors such as age, sex, religion, urban-rural residence, city size and unemployment affected the NSDAP's chances and determined the composition of their social base. In part these factors cut directly across the collar line.[78] One would also have to distinguish between and compare the behavior of individual groups of white collar employees to fully test this thesis.[79]

On the whole, however, the facts of the German case — a sharp distinction between workers and salaried employees, a tendency for the gap between them to narrow, defensive anti-socialist protest stances among salaried employees and their radicalization to the right under the pressure of economic crisis — substantiate the thesis presented at the outset. Small wonder, when one thinks to what extent that argumentation was developed on the basis of German experiences in the 1920s and 1930s. But does the thesis also fit the American case?

2. American White Collar Workers Before the First World War

I. CAPITALISM AND ORGANIZATION: CHANGES IN AMERICAN SOCIETY

1. Growth and Tensions

Although it can be convincingly argued that industrialization was well underway in pre-civil war America, the north's victory over the agricultural, slave economy south in 1865 undoubtedly eased and hastened the subsequent triumphant course of industrial development. In the quarter century after the civil war the nation's railroad network tripled; miles of track increased from 35,000 in 1865 to 167,000 in 1890. The first transcontinental line was completed in 1869, and in 1886 a standard nationwide gauge adopted. Between 1890 and the first world war track mileage doubled again.

Rapid growth of industrial production under the expanding factory system characterized the era after the civil war. If one takes industrial production in 1899 as 100, the figures for 1860 and 1865 were only 16 and 17; for 1890, 71; and for 1914, 192. In 1860 20% of the labor force was engaged in industry; in 1890 it was 28%, and by the time of the first world war the proportion had climbed to about one-third. According to Kuznets' calculations the gross national product grew between 1870 and 1890 from about 9 to about 26 billion dollars; it increased per capita from $223 to $405 even with the rapid population growth. The Department of Commerce reported that between 1890 and 1917 gross national product increased from 27 to 71 billions, or per capita from $424 to $683. These figures, which are expressed in constant prices (1929) and thus take fluctuations in the value of money into account, reveal the enormous growth which occurred. Nowhere in the world did the social product grow more quickly in the four or five decades before the first world war than in the US; even reckoned per capita, the rate of growth in the US led all societies except the industrial newcomer Japan. In the 1870s industry (including mining and construction, but excluding utilities) contributed 20% of the US gross national product. In 1890 industry's share was about 25%, and in the second decade of the 20th century, 27-28%. Industrial products made up 16% of exports in 1860, 21% in 1890 and 49% in 1913. This increase corresponds to the general pattern of industrializing societies, though the US with its extensive arable land and early mechanized, commercial agriculture never experienced the clear shift from a foodstuff exporting to importing country which Germany, for example, underwent in the 1870s and 1880s. Also, since the domestic market absorbed a comparatively large share of industrial production until the 1890s, industrial products were directed into the export trade in great quantities at a relatively late date.

It is beyond the scope of this study to discuss in any detail the pattern of and impetus for this enormously successful economic growth. Such a discussion would have to pay particular attention to the increasingly accessible, rapidly expanding unified home market, the country's great mineral wealth, pro-industrial policies of state and federal governments after the civil war — including protective tariffs, favorable taxation, absence of direct intervention, land grants — as well as the dynamic achievements of entrepreneurs in a social system which had adapted to capitalism through trade and commercial agriculture long before industrialization, and which had few traditions that might have inhibited economic growth. Above all, however, what distinguished this society from Europe was the massive immigration into a land that was continually expanding to the west. In 1840 the US population was seventeen million; in 1860, 36 million; 1890, 63 million; 1920, 106 million; and 1930, 123 million. In that 90 year span the native stock — those born to native born parents — increased from fourteen to 83 million, or not quite six fold; during the same period the foreign stock — immigrants and children with one or both foreign born parents — grew from three to 40 million, or by more than thirteen times. When mass immigration began in 1840 every sixth American was of foreign stock; in 1930 it was every third American. Almost five million immigrants arrived between 1820 and 1860; 13.5 million came from 1860 to 1890, most from northern and western Europe. Between 1890 and 1930 another 23 million immigrated, mostly from southern, eastern, and southwestern Europe. In some years before 1915 more than one million foreigners arrived, or an average of 35,000 every day. Around 1900 40% of the inhabitants of the twelve largest cities were foreign born; their children made up another 20%. In smaller cities and rural areas the proportion was smaller. Both as consumers and workers, the immigrants were a major factor in US economic growth.[1]

The social history of the US between civil war and world war is above all the history of the repercussions of this stormy capitalist industrialization. It shattered the earlier none too stable social relations, already shaken by the civil war, and produced a series of tensions, imbalances and conflicts which, particularly in the 1880s and early 1890s, created a situation approaching crisis.

During the last third of the 19th century US society was increasingly stamped by conflicts between bourgeoisie and the emerging proletariat that were typical of capitalist industrializing societies. Most affected were the rapidly industrializing regions of the east and the midwest. Although average real wages for workers advanced (reverses during recessions notwithstanding) to a higher level in the US than in any European country,[2] American workers nevertheless expressed their discontent through protest. If the US labor movement lacked the organizational and ideological unity of the German, it surpassed that nation in the intensity and violence of some of its struggles. Many factors contributed to this difference. Exploitation by owners and managers in the US was less filtered through patriarchal traditions and state protection than it was on the European continent; class relations seem to have been more nakedly determined by market, efficiency, and profit considerations. In the US there were probably greater inequalities between the mass of ill paid, largely unorganized, unskilled workers who were often new immigrants living under miserable conditions and skilled workers, who in contrast to Germany were not only relatively well paid but also remained closer to their artisan traditions at a later date. This identification helped to generate strong grievances, since these skilled workers continued to measure and condemn their now definitive wage worker status against the ideal type of the small independent craftsman. Religious, radical-democratic, and populist currents also played a role. After 1869 the most important organizational expression of labor discontent and protest was the Knights of Labor, a non-marxist, cooperative, partly utopian organization with some trappings of a secret society. The Knights admitted workers from all occupations, races, and both sexes as well as small businessmen. It agitated against the capitalist wage system, large banks and corporations, railroad companies and large landowners as well as against unrestricted immigration. The organization's membership increased during the depression of 1873-77, then grew more rapidly in the milder recession of 1884-86. After the Knights' victory against Jay Gould's railroads in 1886, membership jumped from 50,000 to 700,000, only to drop precipitously because of defeats, organizational weaknesses, and internal conflict. The number of labor conflicts grew in these years and a few great strikes like bloody Homestead in 1892 and the Pullman strike of 1894 commanded the attention of an increasingly shocked middle class public. On rare occasions there were bloody anarcho-syndicalist attacks and brutal reactions, as at Haymarket Square in Chicago in 1886. Fears of radicals grew among employers and the public at large.[3]

This classic battlefront of industrial capitalist society was overlaid in the US by the lines, differentiation and conflict of ethnic heterogeneity, which sometimes strengthened, sometimes diluted class conflict. Heterogeneity increased with the 'new immigration' after 1890, which transplanted masses of people from the pre-industrial social orders of southern and eastern Europe into the rapidly growing great cities and industrial regions. For a long time they remained clustered together, preserving their traditional family systems and social customs. Most came without special qualifications and with scant knowledge of English. Ignorant of American living standards, they filled the lowest paid, least skilled positions. Only in the second generation did a sizeable number gradually climb the occupational ladder to make room at the bottom for more recent arrivals. In this second generation close cultural and social ties to their own ethnic group remained strong. These new immigrants provided a mass base for the urban bosses, the ward or citywide political leaders who proliferated after the 1880s. They ruled with the help of patronage, corruption, and the public officials who depended on them. If the political power structure they created bore little resemblance to the principles of American constitutionalism, the boss nonetheless became an important source of relief and aid to these immigrant groups. Older settlers of Anglo-Saxon, Protestant descent, already shaken in cities like Boston and Milwaukee by power struggles with earlier Irish and German arrivals, began to flee to the suburbs as these new immigrant masses further threatened their way of life, their values, and their power. In reaction WASPS joined the temperance movement, supported campaigns for clean government against the bosses and political machines, and proposed initiatives for public schools in the cities to counteract the largely ethnic Catholic schools. They flocked into organizations that proclaimed the pride and strength of the older heritage — the Sons of the American Revolution was founded in 1889, the Daughters of the American Revolution at about the same time — or they contributed to the growing strength of nativist, xenophobic, anti-Catholic and anti-semitic currents — the American Protective Association, centered in Michigan, Iowa and Minnesota, grew between 1893 and 1894 from 70,000 to half a million members. These tensions, anxieties, and reactions multiplied during the depression years 1893-96.[4]

The third great battle line ran between the city and the country. Fused with the conflict between small independents and great corporations, urban-rural antagonism found powerful if confused expression in the populist movements of the early 1890s. Populism combined many heterogeneous elements. Its nucleus was small and medium sized farmers protesting the price system, the mechanisms of an impersonal market, middlemen and transportation costs, the interests and the capitalists of the big cities who were held responsible for the changes in and increasing difficulties of the lives of small men on the land. At an early date this basically economic conflict became closely linked with symbolic cultural conflicts. Country people were deeply suspicious of new city life styles which deviated from inherited American values. They decried the great anonymity, new dependency, provocative forms of life, spectacular riches, and highly visible poverty of the great cities. The grievances of producers and traders in towns and smaller cities against the railroads meshed with this rural protest. The utter dependence of small shippers' well being and very existence on railroad magnates, bankers and managers, in sharp competition with each other and whose rate and scheduling decisions were often erratic, stirred up anxiety and resentment against big business, finance capital, and the powerful urban rich. In the cities, anxieties and protests developed among small independent businessmen which paralleled the reactions of the old middle class in Germany in that they were above all reactions to the challenge of competition from new large enterprises aimed at preserving or reviving older circumstances.

In contrast to the old middle class in Germany, however, American small business did not reason from pre-capitalist guild assumptions (which had never been strong in the US, and which had completely decayed by the late 19th century); nor did they look to the state for special privileges and protection as much as did their German counterparts. Instead, they clung to a belief in an older competitive capitalism of small and equal enterprises against the trusts and holding companies, giant corporations, and concentrations of economic power which undermined their independence and threatened the old decentralized system of competition. At the same time these American small businessmen — in contrast to their German counterparts, but not so different from corresponding groups in France — supported radical-democratic reforms in the American political tradition. For that reason alone their separation from the emerging proletariat was not as distinct as that of the German craftsman and small shopkeeper. Finally, regional antagonism overlapped these social conflicts. The western states, primarily the Dakotas, Nebraska and Kansas, and the agricultural south (North and South Carolina, Mississippi and Texas), which were home to a good part of the populist movement, expressed a multi-faceted antipathy to the industrial, urban north-east.

Populism combined an extraordinarily diverse bundle of elements. In some southern states it amalgamated with nativist, anti-semitic, racist components, which found the anti-urban, anti-intellectual strains in the movement quite compatible. Elsewhere — in Kansas and other midwestern states — populism had a more social-democratic profile. These populists advocated increased government controls to end private industry's power abuses. They favored female suffrage and social welfare legislation; they had little use for the regressive, anti-modern currents in the movement. Demands for state-owned storage and distribution facilities paralleled some demands of the big German landowners in the 1890s. The ever more central demands for the silver standard and easy money also paralleled the European situation. With the electoral defeat of the People's Party in 1896 and the return of prosperity after 1897 the movement disintegrated. On the whole it is not an unjust assessment to say that populism was a relatively poorly organized, extremely heterogeneous, ideologically confused protest of the 'little man' against the progress of an industrial capitalist, urban, impersonal society. It was the last concerted stand of these older social groups against 'modernization', even though the populists had their 'modern' side: they correctly diagnosed some unacceptable weaknesses of and suggested ways to humanize the new order which were incorporated into later reforms.[5]

These interlocking, overlapping lines of conflict were part of a cluster of inequities and antagonisms which developed from the contradiction between an extremely fluid, decentralized, rural-small town, small business social structure, on the one hand, and the impact of industrial capitalist growth, on the other. The unfettered aggressiveness of the American self-made man, the business practices of a speculator willing to risk all or a hectic promoter looking for a quick profit, became qualitatively different phenomena when transferred from a mill owner in a small city or a medium sized robber baron to the rulers of empires the size of Standard Oil or US Steel. These qualities could become sources of inefficiency and irrationality in concerns which demanded rational planning, continuity, and systematic management. Furthermore, they could become public evils when the welfare of an entire branch of industry and whole communities might depend on the unpredictable decisions of one powerful man. Systematic, coordinated management methods and government regulation were possible paths toward a solution, yet it was just this sort of help that the traditional decentralized, unbureaucratic political system was not in a very good position to provide. The more all encompassing and impersonal the economic system became, the less its crises — 1873-77, 1884-86, 1893-96, 1907 — could be solved by private improvization alone. Linkages between towns, economic regions, and producers increased in the US, but neither the inherited modes of thought nor the rather insular political institutions were prepared to accept and cope with these new interconnections. The more significant administrative and legislative decisions became for the daily life of ordinary people, in the administration of city services, for instance, the more unbearable the archaic features — inefficiency, corruption, and a spoils system mentality — of the political system became.

The official declaration of the 1890 census that the western frontier, which had long been regarded as a last escape valve for the tensions and conflicts produced in the urban industrial east, was now closed contributed to the widespread sense that society's automatic relief mechanisms were no longer functioning and that America was becoming more like Europe. The popular values preached from the pulpit and in the schoolroom — thrift, individual self-help, hard work, honesty, competition and the free play of talents — might inspire anti-urban, anti-corporate, anti-modern protest movements; they were hardly a suitable foundation for dealing successfully with the emerging world of interdependent large organizations. Social Darwinist ideologies might be sufficient to legitimate the successes of small, middling, and great competitors in a society without great structural inequalities; they became less convincing, however, when men were faced with conditions in the inner cities and their own ever more clearly perceived dependence on impersonal powers beyond their reach. They offered no help at all for social efforts to redress the wounds which the capitalist industrial system at this stage of development was inflicting on broad sections of the public.[6]

2. The Beginning of Organized Capitalism

At the end of the 19th century new structures and patterns of order capable of stabilizing this social and economic disequilibrium to some extent and reducing tensions were slowly developing. At the same time, however, they were becoming the source of new frictions and protests. In American history these changes have been summed up as the 'Progressive Era', as an organizational revolution, or as the rise of corporation capitalism or political capitalism.[7] These terms cover only part of what will be included in the following sketch of the beginnings of 'organized capitalism' in the US. By using this concept[8] one can try to understand central American developments in the 'Progressive Era' as a particular case of a general process which took place in all advanced western industrial societies in the late 19th and early 20th centuries. The concept refers to a cluster of interlocking shifts in economy, society and state which appeared at an advanced stage of capitalist industrialization in reaction to the disequilibrium, tensions and problems that accompanied the preceding industrial progress. These alterations were also apparent in European industrializing societies, above all in Germany, at the end of the 19th century. In the US they were shaped by this nation's unique traditions and characteristics. They pushed the factor of 'formal organization' to the front in the most diverse areas of life as change upset traditional structuring principles; in very disparate fields of action they emphasized collective over individual components. They tended to produce greater specification, formalization and institutionalization of social roles. They initiated and accelerated tendencies toward centralization of social functions and the exercise of power. Yet as must also be emphasized, these tendencies toward more systematic organization describe a process which was only partially realized, and which was in its early stages before the first world war. The slow emergence of 'organized capitalism' in the US before the first world war can be summarized under the following six points.

1. Trends toward concentration and combination appeared in some industries, transportation and banking, and to a lesser extent in commerce and insurance. These developments were primarily a reaction to uneven growth and economic crisis, but (for instance in the railroads) they were also consciously designed to coordinate the actual economic interdependence which already existed. Changes in technology and marketing also furthered this development, since they promised economic advantages to management which could only be exploited by large concerns or combinations of firms. The drive for power of ambitious entrepreneurs was often a propelling force. Giant firms, industrial agreements, trusts and holding com-

panies increased rapidly, primarily in capital-, energy-, and management-intensive branches of industry (railroads, mining, banking, metal fabrication, foodstuffs, petroleum, machinery); in the mushrooming electrical and chemical industries; and eventually also among vehicle manufacturers. These concentrations and combinations triumphed despite hostile public opinion, anti-trust laws, and adverse court decisions. The years from 1893 to 1900 could be called the golden age of railroad mergers. Standard Oil pioneered the holding company in 1899, an organizational form less vulnerable to legal attack than the trust. Between 1898 and 1902 a wave of mergers took place, the intensity of which was only reached again in the 1920s. The first corporation capitalized at one billion dollars was US Steel in 1901. Great banking houses such as J. P. Morgan, Kuhn & Loeb, and the National City Bank of New York often played a directing and coordinating role in these combinations; they thus attained great and lasting influence on these industrial concerns. Production and commerce, which had previously been subject to the principles of a competitive market and free competition, were now increasingly controlled by agreements and conscious organizational efforts of the major firms. Of course, these controls remained partial; they transformed and supplemented rather than eliminated competition.[9]

2. Rapid changes also occurred within the corporations after the 1890s; they were designed to reorganize and systematize traditional personal, casual, or supply and demand structured work and authority relationships. The separation of ownership and control and the consequent rise of the managers, especially in firms with widely held stock ownership, hardly altered the basic goals of the firm. But these employed managers were more open to the techniques of systematic, scientific management; they showed greater readiness to introduce specialization and to divide functions. Authority relationships became clearer; there was a definite concentration on efficient organization and planning. Relationships within the firm became more formalized; specific educational qualifications became more important prerequisites for performing certain tasks. Parallel changes in the educational system simultaneously caused and resulted from this process. Specialists appeared in technical fields, in sales, company and personnel management, who had prepared for their jobs in specific courses of study at trade schools or colleges. Written communication increased within the firm; the number of office departments increased and with them, the number of white collar workers. Manual and non-manual jobs, and thus blue and white collar functions, became more rigidly separated. Scientific management methods were introduced by engineers like Frederick W. Taylor to organize the

work process on a more rational basis. They were propagated as harbingers of a new efficient social order; their technocratic elements fit well into the theories and programs of progressive reformers like Herbert Croly or Frederick C. Howe. Great firms internalized many functions which had previously been performed by independent market-related institutions, for example, in sales, law, and research. The consequence was the transformation of some independent professionals like lawyers into employees of large firms and the creation of functionally diversified, functionally integrated, big business. Thus the expansion of business firms and their internal reorganization partly replaced the market. The management problems created by these developments were at least partly solved by the new systematically ordered, vertically integrated, departmentalized, yet highly centralized corporate structures.[10]

3. These tendencies toward specialization, systematization and professionalization within large firms paralleled and influenced the division of labor in the entire economy and society. One consequence was an above average increase in all categories of lower and middle level clerical workers (i.e., without academic or with quasi-academic training). The history of this social grouping will be the subject of the next chapter.

Table 2.1
Clerical and Kindred Workers, US, 1870-1930[11]

	1930	1920	1910	1900	1890	1880	1870
In 000s	4025	3112	1718	737	469	160	82
As a % of the Labour Force	8.2	7.3	4.6	2.5	20	0.9	0.6

A related development was the emergence somewhat above the clerical stratum of an occupational group with academic or advanced training (the professions),[12] which included a growing number of salaried employees. The growth, shaping, and increasing significance of the professions was one of the most important social changes occurring in the US around the turn of the century. In extreme contrast to Germany, the professions — doctors, lawyers, engineers and teachers — lacked an old, secure, distinctive tradition in the US. They were not encouraged and molded by the requirements of an absolutist-bureaucratic state; when they did emerge, they were immersed in US democratic traditions that were inimical to privileges, titles, and monopolies. Whatever remnants of older, imported traditions of professional exclusiveness there had been had largely dissolved in the 1830s and 1840s. Toward the end of the 19th century the country showed only scant traces of clearly demarcated professions, i.e., that were defined by formal qualifications, endowed with exclusive functions and privileges, and able to restrict and regulate admission to their group.

This picture changed decisively in the 1890s and the first years of the new century, in response to the requirements of an increasingly industrial and urban way of life. Legal education and training, for example, began to shift from the lawyer's office to the new or expanding university law schools. After 1894 individual states introduced a publicly administered standardized examination, bar associations were founded, and a 'craft' became a 'profession'. At about the same time the medical profession experienced a similar transformation. New medical science imported from Europe began to turn the 'people's doctor' into a medical-scientific expert, with income, status, and power claims which the American Medical Association, reorganized in 1901, began to pursue. Teachers followed doctors and lawyers, though at a somewhat later date and with far less success. Still, the teaching profession was gradually raised from an unprestigious, poorly paid, transitional career stop for those on their way to better things or for women before getting married. With the creation of teachers' colleges and the standardization and regulation of qualifications, teachers began to approach civil servant status. After 1905 they organized by joining the NEA (which up to that point had only accepted school administrators). This professionalization of teaching went hand in hand with compulsory school atendance — required in only six states in 1870, introduced in all by 1900 — with the extension of public secondary school systems — they quadrupled between 1890 and 1910 — and with the expansion of trade schools and the increase of practical education courses within the general secondary school curriculum. The same trend occurred in other professions, including the various branches of engineering, and — to some extent — social workers and accountants. Businessmen and managers, particularly those from large corporations, also showed limited professional tendencies. Around 1900 they joined trade associations which in rhetoric and increased emphasis on special qualifications imitated professional models.

These new or better defined professions, that is, groups which were becoming internally more cohesive and more clearly demarcated from outsiders, also enjoyed above average growth, though it was not at first as rapid as that of clerical workers.

Table 2.2
Members of the Professions, US, 1870-1930[13]

	1930	1920	1910	1900	1890	1880	1870
In 1000s	3254	2171	1711	1181	876	550	342
As a % of the Labour Force	6.7	5.1	4.6	4.1	3.8	3.2	2.6

Doctors, lawyers, academically trained managers, engineers, teachers, and similar groups varied tremendously, yet they all also exhibited a set of common characteristics. This included an emphasis on specific competence and specialized functions as a basis for their sense of identity: numerical increases in and sharper delineation of the group; advanced education, increasingly with formalized degrees at the university level, as a standard prerequisite for membership; attempts to control entry and occupational behavior primarily by the profession itself (through associations, titles and licenses); rising claims to status and income, in some cases stress on public 'service' and responsibilities. They introduced an alternative basis for status and self-esteem into a society whose dominant model had traditionally been the independent small businessman in town or on the land: that of the expert. In contrast to the jack of all trades image of the self-made man, the professional's success and achievements were the rewards of a long course of specialized training. The professions were primarily an urban phenomenon. Although professionals usually practiced as individuals, they showed a great willingness to engage in collective behavior, particularly by forming and joining professional organizations. The contacts which made these groups feasible only developed in the US with the extension of the transportation network and the emergence of dense centers of population. Professionals viewed and organized themselves at least partly on the basis of loyalties which ran counter to traditional ethnic or local/regional associations.[14]

4. In other parts of the labor market and with respect to conflicts of interest in general, the principle of conscious collective organization increasingly supplemented and tended to displace the principle of individual exchange and contract. Organizations devoted to one specific purpose replaced more diffuse movements

which had combined instrumental and symbolic goals. The American labor movement exemplified this trend. In the recession of 1884-86 the Knights of Labor had reached their peak. In 1886 the American Federation of Labor (AFL) was founded, which united the older trade unions of skilled workers — printers, masons, machinists, for instance — at the national level. In contrast to the rapidly declining Knights, the AFL accepted the industrial capitalist system. It accepted wage worker status, large firms, and management control of the enterprise. Within this system the AFL fought to improve the economic and social position of organized labor by negotiating wage contracts with private industry and to a lesser extent by influencing legislation; naturally also by providing services to its members. In contrast to older workers' associations, the Federation organized narrowly defined groups — wage workers in specific occupations. It excluded the self-employed, farmers, and most unskilled workers. The Federation's aims were limited and clearly defined. Also in contrast with the Knights and the older National Labor Union (1866-72), the AFL achieved stability and grew: in 1897 it had 447,000 members, in 1907 about two million, and in 1917 about three million members. Within the framework of this fairly conservative business unionism (measured by earlier American and by continental European criteria), the AFL won major victories for its members — often against the bitter resistance of the employers.

A parallel process of integration and specialization can be observed in the transformation of farmers' organizations from the Grange and populist movements to the various self-help and interest groups which affiliated in the American Farm Bureau Federation in 1919. Businessmen also organized, partly in opposition to the organized workers. In 1895 organizations of local businessmen founded the National Association of Manufacturers (NAM), in which for the most part small and medium sized concerns pursued conservative programs. Some big businessmen experimented at the turn of the century with looser organizations such as the National Civic Federation, in which they met with labor leaders and representatives of the public for discussion and limited joint initiatives. In 1912 local and regional chambers of commerce united in the US Chamber of Commerce; not the least of their motives was to lobby for the interests of the growing export trade with the government in Washington and abroad.[15]

5. Organization was also the medium in which the reform impulses of the 'Progressive Era' found expression. From 1900 to 1917 reform currents achieved great influence on public opinion, in both major parties, and with three presidents: Theodore Roosevelt, William Taft and Woodrow Wilson. Reform clubs and associations

were organized locally, in various states, and finally on the national level. Their leading members came from very diverse backgrounds, though the same circles that produced other political leaders predominated: journalists, lawyers, teachers, frequently also businessmen, active church members, and sometimes reform-oriented trade union leaders as well. They belonged to a great extent to the rising professional strata. Younger, well educated, indigenous Protestants were in the majority. In contrast to earlier reform movements the progressive programs accepted the fundamental principles of the increasingly organized industrial capitalism; they were at home in the new urban-industrial environment. They knew how to make good use of the national press; they organized for definite purposes and understood how to influence the political process to achieve specific goals. Many of their efforts were concentrated in the great cities of the east and midwest.

These reformers campaigned for very diverse goals, which varied from group to group and region to region. Many directed their critique of society against the extravagance of the rich, the uncontrolled power of the trusts, the exploitative practices of big business; they campaigned against social injustice, the decline of the inner city, the corruption of local government. They decried the spreading slums and the poverty and vice in the living arrangements of the new immigrants that they hoped to make into good Americans. They favored the extension of public control over necessary services (gas, water, electricity), public control of the railroads and some state enterprises (e.g., insurance); they advocated taming the political and economic power of big business through legislation and good administration. They fought for social welfare programs, against child labor, for public health, for laws to regulate female labor. Many of these progressives put their faith in systematic administration and the application of science to public affairs. They thought that social problems could be solved not through conflict and not primarily through redistributing wealth, but instead by efficiency, by eliminating waste, by expertise and reorganization. These reformers urged better education for all citizens and systematic training for civil servants; sometimes with reference to the model of the German bureaucratic state, they advocated upgrading or developing a career civil service. Conservation measures to protect the land and nature from the incursion of private interests were among their goals. And many reformers also campaigned for more democracy and citizen participation: governments should not only be made more effective, but also more responsible and more responsive to the electorate. They supported the referendum, initiative, recall, popular primaries, and women's suffrage.

Progressive reform currents remained a very mixed stream. Often older campaigns, such as the anti-trust efforts aimed at dismembering the large corporations, continued to exist; they were joined and then displaced by the new — in this case, efforts to impose public control on big business without destroying it. With minor exceptions progressivism was not a socialist movement; most adherents respected private property and felt committed to middle class American ideals in the tradition of Jefferson *and* Hamilton. Sometimes they revealed clear nativist elements or strong distrust of the new immigrants, which they combined with special pleading for their 'Americanization'; that is, for their simultaneous social uplift and adaptation to older middle class American values. These progressives were no strangers to anxiety about the waves of foreigners and fears about the radicalization of the masses. Their nativist sentiments were often combined in somewhat contradictory fashion with radical-democratic reform demands and often with radical, though still middle class, social criticism. Social Christianity entered the picture. The effort to rationalize the system of government, to remove old irritations. to achieve efficiency and organization, was a common thread. This was precisely the point where the progressive movement received support from many businessmen, particularly big businessmen, who recognized that public controls would be useful in ending outmoded, unprofitable competitive practices. These businessmen welcomed the modernization of the political system, even if reform might mean some slight loss of independence or paying slightly higher taxes. Thus the reformers — in the optimistic hope of advancing social justice, social peace, freedom and democracy — demanded much that fitted well with or furthered the structural changes that marked the US path toward organized capitalism. In this respect the progressivism of the first two decades of this century functioned as an ideology that justified those changes which were slowly, with difficulty, displacing the structures of an earlier stage of capitalist development. The uniquely liberal-democratic, traditionally American character of the progressive movement was its simultaneous promise of efficiency and uplift: it saw no contradiction between the organization of capitalism, social justice, and democracy. And furthermore, its campaign for organization and order in the political system was not primarily designed (as was the case in Germany) to prop up the position of traditional rulers and preserve traditional privileges.[16]

6. A good part of progressive reform demands addressed themselves to the relationship between society and state. They aimed at increasing state controls and intervention to produce greater social stability and justice; they aimed to reform the political struc-

ture to accomplish these goals and at the same time to make it more democratic. Some of these demands were won. Reorganization of local government made corruption more difficult and weakened the power of political bosses and machine politics. The archaic patronage system was supplemented and partly replaced by the beginnings of a career civil service system. Progressive reforms supplied governments with new means to regulate necessary public services, to supervise building and construction, and to perform other tasks of great public significance. Individual states enacted protective legislation for children, limitations on female labor, workmen's compensation and similar laws: state governments grew larger and more effective. Between 1911 and 1913, 21 states adopted some form of protective labor legislation. In 1906 the federal government took on responsibility for regulating the production of food and drugs. In the same year the strengthening of the Interstate Commerce Commission (established in 1887) increased federal influence over companies doing business in more than one state, particularly over the business, rate-making, and labor policies of the railroads. A Bureau of Corporations (1903) was established within the new Department of Commerce and Labor to collect and make public the facts about these large firms. The Federal Trade Commission Act of 1914 established a five-man commission which would have authority to prohibit unfair competitive practices. Many other examples could be given. Government agencies began to play a greater role in arranging and securing the economic affairs of American companies in other countries. To an increasing extent after the 1890s, these efforts developed into imperialistic, expansionist policies serving primarily economic purposes.

Areas under the jurisdiction of civil servants increased; their status very haltingly, but nonetheless, became more secure after 1883. Thus at a much later date and more slowly than in Europe, the US began to create a career civil service or professional bureaucracy which in the long run would increase the efficiency, honesty, and continuity of public administration. The situation and standing of public officials, who had been poorly paid and little regarded, slowly began to improve. Under Roosevelt and Wilson the White House, with its expanding staff, gained initiative and influence vis-à-vis Congress; at the same time congressional procedures were also reformed to better handle the increased workload of government. Lobbying became more systematic; it became standard practice, for instance, to consult affected interest groups as part of the law-making process. All in all, decision-making processes and administration gained continuity and force.[17]

With these changes the American political system began to reveal traces of the sort of government intervention in economy and society that were typical of organized capitalism. These reforms were often achieved against the resistance of business interests which feared for their independence and profits; the reformers often viewed the established economic, social and political ruling groups with distrust and criticism. Nonetheless, reform was usually realized by compromises which not only respected the veto power of big business but which also guaranteed such interests a major say in the new system. Thus the railroads had a strong voice in railroad regulation, as did bankers in the Federal Reserve System. Such reforms were also frequently openly supported by farsighted businessmen who reasoned that these measures were more apt to stabilize than destroy private enterprise.[18]

And in fact, many of the progressive reforms did tend to stabilize the system against more radical challenges; many progressives were thoroughly aware of this connection. The formation in 1905 of the radical Industrial Workers of the World (IWW), the 'Wobblies', with their anarcho-syndicalist ideology and militant practice, alarmed not only the rich upper classes but also many reformers. The IWW primarily organized groups ignored by the AFL: migrant farm workers, lumbermen, railroad construction workers in the west, unorganized textile and sawmill workers in the exploitative south, where labor conditions were in many ways still pre-industrial. New immigrants performing unskilled labor in the textile factories and mines of the east, also largely neglected by the AFL, were receptive to Wobbly organizers and leaders. The IWW led at least 150 strikes between 1908 and 1916, mostly militant and not at all 'business-like'. Some were violently put down by employers and citizens, who either took the law into their own hands or, with government support, used the courts, police, state militia and the military. Despite persecution the Wobblies grew to about 60,000 members in 1916.

One would not be entirely mistaken in interpreting the Wobblies as a protest against an older type of social relations and authority which was now anyway gradually changing and becoming more organized in large areas of the economy. In long range perspective though perhaps not to contemporaries, the Socialist Party of America led by Eugene V. Debs would have to be considered a more important challenge to the American system, even though it was never as militant as the Wobblies but sought to work within the AFL, and was ideologically no more radical than many of the most decisive progressives. Formally established in 1901, the Socialist Party attracted one million voters in the 1912 presidential election. When the first world war began, socialists had elected two representatives to Congress, 28 representatives and five senators to thirteen state legislatures, and 22 mayors. Within the AFL they were unable to reattain the power they had had in the 1890s, when Gompers had almost been defeated by a socialist opponent. In 1910, however, the socialists controlled individual AFL unions in the garment industry, brewing and baking; they were influential in the machinists', mineworkers', and cigarmaker unions as well as in the printers'. Yet already in the last years before the war the Socialist Party appears to have lost influence; its decline was usually explained by the success of progressive reforms at the local, state, and national level in taking the wind out of the sails of this more radical alternative.[19]

If one takes these radical challenges to the American system of government seriously, and adds to them the monumental problems which massive immigration was creating in the large cities, the stabilizing function of the progressive reform movement can hardly be overestimated — a function it shared with the differing paths toward organized capitalism taken by other industrializing societies.

Concentration and centralization in the economy; more systematic, specific work and authority relationships in large concerns; the emergence of professional groups and the growing number of white collar workers; the organization of the labor market, of class conflict and of interest representation; increasing crossovers between the social-economic and political-governmental spheres; increased capability of the state apparatus; and the development of new ideologies and patterns of thought which placed greater emphasis on collective action and organization — these were the elements which characterized emerging organized capitalism in the US and Germany after the 1890s. Here as there these tendencies did not go beyond the early stages before the first world war; here as there the war speeded up this development.[20]

American and German developments diverged, however, in important respects, primarily because of the constellations from which they began. One crucial variable was the continuing impact of corporatist traditions on parts of German society; the organizational impulses of the late 19th century could, on the German side, reach back and build on or modify these traditions. The way that the chambers of commerce and industry expanded and multiplied their functions was but one example of this mixture of old and new. Such traditions were almost completely absent in the US at the end of the 19th century. The consequences of this divergence will be a recurring theme in the comparison of American and German white collar workers in the era of emerging organized capitalism. Secondly, organizational tendencies in Germany were able to latch onto hardy bureaucratic structures and traditions of absolutist origins, which had never been radically challenged by a successful revolution, but which had succeeded in surviving by adapting to changing conditions. These traditions were also absent from the US. The more modest extent of and a certain time lag in the trend toward organized capitalism in the US compared to Germany may be partly explained by this combination of circumstances.

These contrasting starting constellations also meant that the individual factors which shaped emerging organized capitalism in the US and Germany would vary in significance. In both societies the organization of the economy by large firms created tensions with the government's increasing intervention in economy and society. Compared to Germany the collective efforts of private economic interests were much more important and successful in the US, since here the state had first to create an effective instrument, a relatively independent bureaucracy, before it could effectively intervene. Furthermore, the basic differences in points of departure also meant that professionalization and certain professions (engineers, managers, lawyers, and teachers) would play a much greater role in the US than in Germany. There an old bureaucratic tradition and new bureaucratic tendencies took on the new tasks, or had even been performing them for some time. German bureaucrats had long occupied the place that the professions now began to assume in US society.[21]

This at least tendential distinction: bureaucratization and state organization of society in Germany, professionalization and stronger voluntary organization by relatively autonomous social groups in the US, correlates with a fundamental social-political and cultural difference between the German and American paths to organized capitalism. In contrast to the US, progressive reforms and ideologies found little resonance and did not play an important role in Germany. German ruling elites identified far too thoroughly with traditional, pre-democratic and partly with pre-industrial stances which could hardly be defended in the long run: the undemocratic three-class suffrage, blocked parliamentary development, hierarchical social structures and a rigid class society, defensive barricades against the working class. These commitments made them incapable of implementing moderate or conservative reforms, which in any case would have been more difficult in Germany than in the US because of the radical opposition of the militant proletariat. Even without a national emergency US labor leaders joined integrative associations devoted to compromise with big business and banking interests; there was no parallel in Germany before the domestic 'truce' of the first world war. American social planners could conceive of putting rather radical ideas into practice in experimental open factories.[22] Germany lacked the equivalent of the broad, multi-faceted, progressive consensus, which was partly liberal (as historians were prone to emphasize some years ago) and partly conservative-stabilizing, as the revisionist historiography of the late 1960s has argued. To a German historian looking at North America, in spite of sporadic violence, social inequalities, repression, and crisis, that consensus continues to be striking. In particular the progressive confidence in simultaneous efficiency and uplift, in solving conflicts through better understanding, organization, and material progress, was much weaker among German liberals, democrats or social democrats. There such beliefs took second place to social imagery penetrated by notions of classes and ranks and structural conflicts so distasteful to the American 'Progressives'. The model of a 'zero-sum game' often characterized public opinion in Imperial Germany: conventional wisdom held that the advantage of one necessarily meant the disadvantage of the other. The conviction that this was not so, that social, political, and economic improvements were possible without decisive losses and sacrifice by individual parts of the whole, was by contrast typical of the thought and rhetoric of 'progressive' reformers in the US at the beginning of this century.

The history of white collar workers in the period of emerging organized capitalism will be approached within the framework of these similarities and differences.

II. SALES CLERKS AND CLERKS' UNIONS

1. Formation, Goals, and Activities of the Retail Clerks' International Protective Association (RCIPA)

Of the few older American white collar associations[23] whose development can be traced through this entire period, the RCIPA invites investigation not only because of the relatively good source material available. This particular white collar group must be of special interest to a work which has formulated its basic questions with the German case in mind, since at an early date the German mercantile employees' organizations (particularly the largest, the Deutschnationale Handlungsgehilfen-Verband [DHV]), showed marked tendencies toward the sort of lower middle class self-concepts and demands, ideology and alliance policy, which became right-radical protest in the last years of the Weimar Republic.[24] The basic structure and character of the RCIPA developed in the two and a half decades before the first world war.

Before the foundation of this first American sales clerks' trade union in 1890, only isolated local associations of clerks existed. In 1820, for example, sales clerks founded the New York Mercantile Library Association. The Association aimed at the professional and general improvement of clerks in counting houses and stores and tried with some success to obtain the good will and financial support of the store owners. After the 1830s it actively sought to find jobs for its members. Among other things the Association promised the store owners to guarantee the honesty and competence of clerks hired through its offices — a promise that, in view of the widely deplored but then frequent embezzlements, may have been favorably but skeptically greeted by business and store owners. In 1845 the Association claimed as members[25] about 20% of the 10,000 clerks in New York in the wholesale and retail trade, counting houses, and offices.

In 1869, also in New York, there was a 'Society of Commercial Travellers' which worked to convince the public and the state legislatures to repeal the Drummer Laws which discriminated against travelling salesmen in favor of local trade.[26] Many local organizations of clerks certainly existed as well. In distinct contrast to Germany, however, the need for sociability does not seem to have been a prominent motive for founding clerks' associations. Social needs appear to have been satisfied in the US by the widespread social clubs, lodges, and brotherhoods which, despite undoubted social gradation, did not separate individual occupations. Ethnic and religious organizations and women's leagues also helped to satisfy needs for sociability.[27]

By the mid-1830s at the latest, retail clerks joined together on a local and temporary basis to persuade their employers to adopt a common early closing time.[28] In 1864 New York dry goods workers struck successfully to prevent the imposition of a longer work day. From the 1880s into the 20th century local clerks' assemblies affiliated with the Knights of Labor, which in addition to workers accepted self-employed businessmen, farmers, artisans and middlemen.[29] In 1888 the first sales clerks' local joined the fledgling AFL. The 'Retail Clerks' National Protective Association' was organized as a national trade union within the AFL. In 1899 Canadian locals were admitted, and the association changed its name to RCIPA (since 1947, 'Retail Clerks' International Association'). This organization, with its chief strength in the midwest, reached 4,200 members (in 41 locals) in the good years 1890-93, a figure the following years of depression wiped out and which was reattained only in 1897. During 1903-08 the union reported 50,000 members; 1909-18, 15,000; 1919-21, 21,000.[30]

The organization, which to be sure not in its name but otherwise always referred to itself as a union, worked to limit sales clerks' work day to no more than ten hours instead of the then not unusual fourteen-sixteen hours a day. Other goals included Sundays off, a fair wage, and equal pay for equal work for men and women. The clerks' union also sought to influence the public and political authorities — in combination with other organizations, in particular the blue collar unions — to support a general improvement in the situation of store clerks and workers. In its first years the union advocated legal regulation of apprenticeship, though by 1901 at the latest it had dropped this demand. It arranged insurance and employment programs for its members.[31]

In fact, however, until about 1905 the early closing campaign and the recruitment of new members took priority in the organization's activities. Store hours from 6 a.m. to 10 or even 11 p.m. (Sundays from 6 a.m. to noon) became the clerks' chief complaint and drove them to collective self-help.[32] Especially in small stores and small cities, when the boss closed the store often depended on when the last customer left. Some locals of the RCIPA called themselves just that: Early Closing Associations.[33] The organized sales clerks tried to negotiate individual or collective contracts with their employers, which most importantly provided for evenings, Sundays, and holidays off.

The clerks pursued this goal with a variety of means. They tried to persuade the employers that early closing, if adopted at the same time by all competitors, would not harm their business interests; just the reverse, it would lead to better performance on the job by their then less overtired employees. In fact the union found many businessmen who agreed — particularly the owners of large firms, for whom it was unprofitable to keep the establishment open for a few late customers.[34] Since there was no regulatory legislation and since up to the first world war the primarily small business retail trade was unable to combine in order to control competition, the early retail clerks' union was one of the few means available to even slightly curtail cut-throat competition — although of course the membership's free time was also at stake.

The clerks' main weapon against employer resistance was the consumer boycott, often undertaken in cooperation with the local trade unions. The eight hour day was a dominant demand of labor organizations in the 1880s, which contributed to reinforcing and organizing the clerks' claims.[35] The sales clerks' union worked through the local Labor and Trades Council, to which all AFL locals including the RCIPA usually belonged, to convince working people not to buy in certain stores until they complied with the clerks' demands. They relied on techniques such as the store card and the union label. The public would be called upon to patronize stores that displayed the RCIPA store card. Store owners could obtain this card by signing a contract with the RCIPA and agreeing to hire union members. Conversely, the organized sales clerks promised the trade unions that they would promote the sale of goods with the union label. The success of these techniques depended on the size and solidarity of the local trade union movement (including the solidarity of the working class women who did the shopping). From place to place and time to time the store card was in great demand among shopkeepers. In at least a few cases, merchants were prepared to pay the union's initiation fee and dues for some of their employees in order to be able to display the RCIPA's store card in the window. But these techniques failed to achieve general or lasting success.[36]

In addition, the RCIPA appealed to the general public in every possible way — meetings, circulars, demonstrations in front of stores, advertisements, boycott lists — to reduce late shopping and to put pressure on stores that stayed open late. The union often found support in the press, from church groups who agitated for Sunday closing, and above all from numerous middle class reform and women's associations. Long hours,[37] but above all the exploitation of the sales girls, who were usually under-age and incapable of organizing themselves, mobilized citizens' campaigns beginning in the early 1890s. The fight for better working conditions for clerks (shorter hours, a minimum wage, overtime, and improved safety and hygiene) was the main impetus behind the founding of the soon nationally federated Consumers' Leagues after 1890, which sometimes made even broader demands than the RCIPA.[38]

Finally, at the latest by 1900, the RCIPA organized isolated walkouts and strikes to achieve their demands. In view of the modest membership dues and the absence of a strike fund, however, for financial reasons alone these actions had to be undertaken cautiously.[39]

The prominence of early closing among the RCIPA's goals was linked to the instability of its membership. Many clerks lost interest in their organization once they had won the early closing battle. In that event the local might easily fall apart, and often the result was the renewed curtailment of the clerks' leisure time.[40] Pressure from reform groups and unions, the interests of large businesses and department stores, the impact of the gradual shortening of the work day in the industrial sector, finally also the growing tendency to pass legislation limiting women's, children's, and Sunday work (at first for factories, after 1896, however, extended to the mercantile sector)[41] gradually improved the sales clerks' situation, at least as far as their work day was concerned. On the occasion of the union's twentieth anniversary the RCIPA leadership asserted, though not entirely without exaggeration, that 6 p.m. closing (except on Saturdays) and Sunday closing were now in effect almost everywhere.[42]

After 1905, at the urging of the RCIPA leadership, the locals also began to agitate for a minimum wage, compensation for overtime, paid vacations,[43] and for fixing the maximum work day (as opposed to agreements about closing time).[44] The minimum wage was to be $9 a week, a much greater sum than female clerks in particular received in these years. The locals retained great freedom in determining what minimum wage they would actually demand, however. Contrary to the national platform the minimum wage asked for women remained without exception under $9 before the first world war.[45]

Along with broadening their objectives, the RCIPA stepped up their efforts to recruit members. More clearly than in its first years the union urged its locals to insist on the closed shop in their contracts with employers. The RCIPA hoped to establish that within two weeks newly hired clerks would be required to join the union.[46] These new demands, which made the RCIPA more like other unions, seem to have stiffened the resistance of the employers. The limited support or toleration of the large concerns evaporated; store owners instead organized local employers' associations.[47] Sympathetic treatment of the common interests of employers and employees had prevailed for a long time in leading articles of *The Advocate*, the RCIPA's newspaper.[48] This sentiment did not entirely disappear,[49] but the level of anti-business polemic in the columns of the paper gradually increased. It reached a temporary highpoint in the years 1914-17. The poor paying, proliferating chain stores and branch outlets were at the center of the clerks' critique.[50] Yet reading the unsystematic, not statistically compilable reports of success from the locals creates the impression that the union was as a rule unable to get a foothold in large concerns, particularly not in the branch and department stores. Department store closing hours provided less ground for attack; and already before 1914, large stores had begun to offer their employees insurance, bonuses, and company benefit programs with which the union could not compete. It was also more difficult to bring a big store to terms with a consumer boycott than a medium sized merchant in a small or medium sized city, who was often dependent on discrete sections of a public that could be surveyed and mobilized with relative ease.

The Association's scant success can be read in its membership figures. Even according to the union's own, probably exaggerated data, the RCIPA never organized more than 5-10% of its potential membership, in 1918-19 in fact only about 2%.[51] It is not possible to determine how many union shops,[52] salary increases, and maximum work day agreements the clerks' union won. In 1916, one of its best years, the RCIPA reported that it had led five strikes and founded 80 local organizations.[53]

The pro-labor and pro-union policies (compared to earlier years) of the Wilson administration and the generally favorable organizing conditions of the war years helped the RCIPA achieve a certain boom — even though sales clerks were not crucial to the war effort and their organization received no direct government assistance. The decline of the dollar led to an absolute and (compared to wage workers) relative decline in the purchasing power of the poorly organized white collar employees. The pressure of inflation on the unorganized 'White Collar Slaves' became one of the sales clerks most frequently discussed grievances.[54] The union's conflicts with employers, which included lockouts, arrests, and sporadic violence, increased. They were now sparked primarily by salary questions and demands for a minimum wage, particularly for women. If one considers their financial circumstances, radicalism, and breadth of demands, the sales clerks' union reached a temporary peak in 1918-19.

Three sets of features typical of the early RCIPA will be briefly examined: its organizational basis, its relationship to manual workers, and its sense of identity. We will look into this union in order to understand more of the occupational group it tried to organize. Comparison with the German side will help to clarify peculiarities of the RCIPA and to put them into the context of the present study.

2. The Organizational Basis of the RCIPA

(a) Recruitment and Scope

German retail clerks[55] of the 19th and 20th centuries did not form retail clerks' or shop assistants' associations like those in the US and in Britain, they rather belonged in large numbers to the associations of *Handlungsgehilfen*, i.e. mercantile assistants or mercantile employees. According to the German Commerce Code of 1897 and several earlier legal definitions, the term referred to anyone who was employed in a 'mercantile business' (and that included large merchant houses and small stores as well as manufacturing firms and other private enterprises) and who performed mercantile services for compensation. In other words, *Handlungshilfe* included several related occupations like retail clerk or shop assistant, wholesale clerk, traveling salesman (if not self-employed) and salesmen in manufacturing enterprises. The term still predominated in the early 20th century. It carried strong corporatist overtones, and was meant to do so. For centuries it had referred to a specific stratum within the mercantile corporation (*Handelsstand*), to the assistants in contrast to the principals (masters), and the apprentices.

For a long time the mercantile assistants, including the retail clerks, adhered to such a preconception of a mercantile or merchant corporatist group including employers and employees. For a long time they drew the organizational conclusion that independents should be eligible for membership; as late as 1890, every fourth member of the mercantile assistants' organizations was self-employed. During the depression of the 1870s, when interest conflicts typical of a class society came to the fore in many of the larger mercantile establishments as well, and the relationship between employer and employee was clearly emerging from its corporatist-harmonious shell, sales clerks' own interests partly dispelled their lingering corporatist preoccupations. Gradually the self-employed merchants were deprived of power, pushed aside and attacked in the associations, and by 1918-19, expelled.

This drawn out process of expelling the self-employed, carried out differently from organization to organization, charted the inroad of class viewpoints and trade union principles in a crumbling occupational-corporatist organization. In two respects, however, the corporatist principle was clearly maintained. Mercantile assistants' associations never tried to organize all those employed in a trade along the lines of an industrial union. Packers, transportation workers, and other manual workers in the mercantile sector remained — as a sub-corporatist stratum, so to speak — barred from the mercantile assistants' associations. This demarcation hardened to the extent that a radical, anti-bourgeois proletariat emerged as a fundamental challenge to society and state and impelled many mercantile employees to assert their membership in the middle class and their distance from the workers. In fact, this distancing from the workers corresponded to the pattern in which the rest of their corporatist identity began to fall into place with the lines of cleavage and conflict of a class society.

The other way in which the German mercantile assistants' associations perpetuated their corporatist tradition was in continuing to organize mercantile employees in wholesale, retail, and manufacturing industries together. The old concept of *Handlungsgehilfe* — mercantile assistant — ignored the basic difference between specific occupations and different industrial sectors in favor of what all those who pursued 'mercantile services' for compensation supposedly had in common. In that it mirrored a much less differentiated or at least different occupational world of pre-industrial times. By the same logic the mercantile assistants' associations ignored the great disparities in activities, function, and workplace between store clerks, counting house clerks, commercial agents and the salesmen — not the technicians! — in the export division of a large industrial concern. They recruited these occupational groups together because of their common membership in the traditional mercantile corporatist group; appropriately, they emphasized not the increasingly divergent *specific occupational* characteristics of their members, which originated in an increasingly differentiated economic structure, but rather their common membership in a *broad occupational* group (*Berufsstand*). They did not choose to recruit members on the basis of specific occupations —for instance, retail clerks, accountants, industrial salesmen or commercial travelers — but they tried to unite them under a traditional semi-corporatist banner. In consequence the criteria which shaped their sense of identity, organizational behavior, social expectations and political demands came from their common mercantile education and training, beliefs, life style, and social prestige. This development was at the cost of a general workers' let alone class consciousness, but also at the cost of a sense of identity adapted to their specific occupational function and workplace. Their organization was not oriented to their specific problems on the job. This organizational and ideological basis forced the associations to cloak their economic, job-related demands in corporatist ideology and emphasize status over class, education and belief over function and interest.

As a trade union affiliate of the AFL, the RCIPA excluded employers from membership; it stood on the principle of a limited conflict of interest between employers and workers in the same concern, trade, or branch of industry. The RCIPA staunchly maintained this principle, in contrast to the majority of contemporary German mercantile employee associations before 1900. Clerks who became self-employed were given an honorable discharge. Individual decisions about admitting salaried employees in higher and managerial positions were left to the locals. After 1907 the national tightened this rule, however, by excluding all managers not directly engaged in the sale of goods and all salaried employees who accepted stock worth more than $500 in their own company.[56] Despite its predominantly conciliatory stance toward the employers, the RCIPA considered itself a labor union. Preconceptions about occupational-corporatist harmony never influenced its membership criteria. There were no corporatist organizations like the German mercantile assistants' associations on the contemporary American scene.

It is true that in the US, as well as in Germany, there had originally been a close relationship between wholesale and retail clerks, since in fact a division between these mercantile branches had hardly emerged in the early 19th century. Changing jobs from counting house to shop and back — interrupted perhaps by periods of self-employment — may have been more the rule than the exception.[57] But a number of factors contributed to breaking up this relationship: functional and institutional differentiation of wholesale and retail, differentiation in the branches of trade, the growth of industrial firms uniting production and wholesale functions, the expansion of commerce, the increasing division of labor in businesses, offices and counting houses, the separation of transporting from merchandising goods, the general increase in the ability to write and figure and the consequent erosion of a special mercantile education which everyone employed in trade had shared. And in actual fact mercantile employees in different occupations, for instance sales clerk or counting house clerk, came to differ considerably in their duties, hours of work, earnings, prospects for advancement, education, and social prestige.[58]

When the RCIPA was formed there appears to have been no debate over whether the union should admit mercantile employees other than clerks. In view of the organization's main goals — early closing scarcely concerned wholesale employees — these American employees seem to have fairly automatically combined just as retail clerks. They followed a narrow craft union principle, although, as will be shown, principle and practice never fully coincided. There were no discernible impulses toward creating a more inclusive occupational-corporatist association. When in 1905 the question arose whether wholesale clerks should be admitted to the organization, the executive committee decided that they should either join the AFL or the local Labor and Trades Council as individuals, or with the RCIPA's support organize their own union within the AFL — but under no circumstances become affiliates of the RCIPA.[59] The union never considered admitting or organizing sales personnel in industry. By contrast, in 1910 the largest German mercantile employee association demanded the right to combat functional differentiation within the mercantile sector and to keep a corporatist community alive among all employees with mercantile ties by cultivating corporatist ways of thinking and education.[60] Such a demand would probably not even have been properly understood by American sales clerks. They would even have lacked a current equivalent term for the German *Handlungsgehilfen* (mercantile assistants). The decidedly functional, matter of fact terms 'clerk', 'sales clerk', 'salesman', 'sales woman', referred to only part of what *Handlungsgehilfen* denoted. 'Sales workers' and 'commercial employees' lacked the German term's demarcation from manual workers. None of these American terms caught the sweep, much less the pathos, with which its traditional corporatist past continued to stamp the term *Handlungsgehilfen*. The English characterization 'shop assistant' came closer; significantly enough, this term appeared infrequently in America.[61] Still, 'shop assistant' had a much more specialized meaning than the broad term *Handlungsgehilfe*.

Insofar as the RCIPA departed from the narrow craft or trade union principle, the American clerks did not tend to move in an occupational-corporatist direction, as did the German commercial employees, but rather toward industrial unionism, that is, toward organizing all employees in retail trade, including manual workers, without regard to occupation. After salary demands became the key issue and early closing declined, and as the union went through its most radical phase, a majority at the RCIPA's 1915 convention voted for just such an extension of the membership domain and a corresponding name change to 'Mercantile Employees' Association'. This was denied by the executive committee of the predominantly craft based AFL.[62]

The RCIPA was more apt to include manual workers employed in mercantile concerns — for instance, messengers, drivers, warehousemen and other unskilled workers, in its organizing drives than other mercantile let alone non-mercantile clerks. Compared to the German shop assistants' associations the American sales clerks paid little attention to the distinction between blue and white collar. Their constitution first permitted them to organize all persons actively employed in a retail store (1901); then (1905) those working in any branch of retail, mail order, or exhibition merchandising; and finally (1918-35) all persons employed by a mercantile or mail order firm actively engaged in handling or selling goods.[63] These formulations permitted the organization of manual workers who were also employed in the sale of goods. The clerks' union frequently got into jurisdictional disputes with the Teamsters, Butchers, and Tailors which had to be arbitrated by the AFL leadership.[64] The organizational behavior of the RCIPA seems to indicate that the union attached more significance to the characteristics that separated sales clerks from other commercial white collar employees than to those separating white collar clerks and manual workers in the same store or branch of commerce.

(b) Apprenticeship

The continuing impact of corporatist traditions on German mercantile employees and the absence of such traditions in the US account for a further difference between German mercantile assistants' associations and the RCIPA: their treatment of apprentices as potential members. Next to long, irregular hours of work the German mercantile employee associations' main complaint before 1915 was the so-called practice of 'breeding apprentices'. Employers tended to meet what seemed to the clerks an unreasonable proportion of their staff needs with low-paid young 'apprentices' and thus to limit job opportunities for assistants and to put their earnings under competitive pressure. At bottom these complaints reflected the conflict between the economic and social pretensions of the mercantile assistants, which had become intertwined with tradtional corporatist recruitment methods and modern business reality around 1900. The patterns of recruitment and training practices they had inherited from their corporatist past were rendered increasingly obsolete by changes in merchandising, the progressive division of labor, and lowered educational and training requirements for a large number of employees. The German mercantile assistants' associations tried with great resentment but scant success to maintain or even increase the distance between apprentice and assistant. They sought to reduce the proportion of apprentices among sales personnel, and to require mercantile education and training for apprentices. As a rule the association required a nearly completed apprenticeship as a condition for membership. Their motives for demanding legislation to regulate apprenticeship were not only economic but also social and political.[65]

In the US the apprenticeship system played a more important role in the skilled trades around the turn of the century than in white collar occupations. Even in pre-industrial America apprenticeship was less important than in Europe.[66] In part this reflected the almost complete absence of a medieval and early modern guild tradition, but also, compared to Europe, opportunities were plentiful and alternatives available in this unsettled country. The consequent mobility, shortage of labor (relative to available land), flexible occupational structure and relatively weak government regulation (trade laws, for example) were also factors. In the last third of the 19th century, industrialization and swelling immigration sharply undermined the few rudimentary apprenticeship programs existing in the US. Naturally, some crafts like printing were less affected than others like mining. In the last decades of the 19th century, however, craft unions succeeded in reintroducing more stringent controls over training and apprenticeship into their collective bargaining agreements. Contractual agreements governing the period of training (three-five years), apprentices' wages and the proportion of skilled workers to apprentices (between 15:1 and 5:1) served the craft unions as a means to control entry into their trade and thus to improve their bargaining position and working conditions. Like the English trade unions they carried occupationally restrictive policies much further than most German trade unions. The craft unions' apprenticeship policies were aided by the more consciously felt need of many industrial concerns for qualified skilled workers, a need which was no longer being met as the origins and skills of the new immigrants changed. Large firms especially began to introduce their own training programs (which were often called an 'apprenticeship system'), while smaller companies relied on the nascent trade schools and technical courses in the secondary school curriculum.[67]

Although the name 'apprentice' was commonly used to describe the poorly paid young beginners in shops and counting houses, in early 19th century America access to and training for jobs in commerce were much less apt to be regulated by a formal apprenticeship system than in early 19th century Germany.[68] Contracts of apprenticeship could still be found mainly in the commercial cities of the south and north-east — though by continental standards, even there only in abbreviated form.[69] The standard contract included a fixed number of years of extremely poorly paid (or initially unpaid) service. It obligated the master to provide systematic, thorough, and practical education and training in his craft as well as general care and schooling; the apprentice (who lived in the master's house) promised unqualified loyalty and obedience. As far as actual practice can be pieced together from diverse sources, it was true that the beginner had to master all required tasks for very little pay; in the process he generally learned what there was to learn. As a rule, however, he did not have a contract of apprenticeship and changed bosses within a year or less. He very seldom lived in his employer's house and was hardly subjected to his patriarchal care and discipline. He experienced the transition from apprentice to clerk not as a sudden leap, but as a gradual transition in earnings, function, and status.[70] With the expansion of trade in the 1840s, moreover, whatever orderly master-apprenticeship relationships had existed for the most part collapsed.[71] Around mid-century a common view was that if a young man had a good character and good handwriting he was well prepared to become a clerk.[72] In 1887 Philadelphia department store magnate John Wanamaker supported business colleges with the argument that in the US unlike Germany or England there was no apprenticeship system. After 1890 he became one of the first entrepreneurs of commerce to introduce in-house training programs and continuing education courses for his employees.[73]

Insofar as apprenticeship was a central institution of the corporatist occupational order, as it was at least in the minds and hopes of contemporary German mercantile assistants, it could hardly have been among the RCIPA's demands. There was almost no tradition in American commerce that paralleled the German system of apprenticeship. In Germany it had served as a means to recruit a socially acceptable next generation, who were then educated and socialized in corporatist attitudes and life style as well as taught occupational skills. Insofar as apprenticeship programs provided an outstanding means to improve the clerks' bargaining position and general circumstances, they were eagerly sought by the RCIPA from time to time. Unlike some of the skilled craft unions, however, the clerks were usually too weak to win these campaigns. Moreover, their chances of success were eroding, since even the limited skills still required by clerks' jobs in 1900 were tending to decline rather than increase. In 1891 the union convention supported legislation on apprenticeship. This was not a realistic demand, and was in fact dropped from the next platform. As late as 1901 the union required a one year 'apprenticeship' as a prerequisite for membership.[74] In practice (which did not always strictly follow the rule) it seems that minors under the age of eighteen or even sixteen were considered apprentices. In 1907 when the RCIPA stressed the demand for a minimum wage, it struck all references to 'apprenticeship' and 'apprentice' from its constitution, declaring that the union should insist that everyone engaged in sales work be considered a salesperson, and treated and paid accordingly.[75] Before and after this decision, the apprenticeship issue in any event played only a modest role in the demands and agitation of the RCIPA.

(c) The Employment of Women

Corporatist traditions of organization, group identity, and social behavior also put the problem of working women in a different perspective for German mercantile assistants than for American sales clerks. In the US as in Germany, women began to seek and find jobs as sales clerks long before the first world war. Most female clerks were young and unmarried; they usually came from native stock. They were most apt to be hired in big cities, especially in department stores; in fact female clerks or 'saleswomen' began to push men out of certain occupational categories and departments (e.g. underwear) altogether.

Table 2.3
Sales Clerks by Sex, US, 1870-1930[76]

	All Clerks (000s)	Female Clerks in 000s	in %
1870	241	9	4
1880	386	31	8
1890	615	98	16
1900	970	216	22
1910	1,264	362	29
1920	1,540	527	34
1930	2,390	706	30

The feminization of the sales profession had proceeded even further in Germany. In 1882 19% of the 166,000 German retail clerks were women; in 1895 30% of 269,000 and in 1907 42% of 406,000 clerks were female. [77] This German lead, which may be somewhat exaggerated by differing census categories, nonetheless corresponds to the varying composition of the entire labor force in the two societies; the proportion of women in the gainfully occupied population was always considerably higher in Germany than the US.[78]

Most male mercantile assistants in Germany seem to have perceived the employment of women in stores and offices not only as detrimental to their economic interests (they were being underbid by a traditionally cheaper labor supply), but also as a threat to their status and beneath the dignity of their occupation. Before 1914 most associations refused to accept women as equal members, so female mercantile employees organized separate associations. The most powerful mercantile employee association agitated actively — though without success — against the employment of women in commercial establishments.[79]

In the RCIPA as well there was some open resistance to the admission of women.[80] For a time various in-between organizational compromises were tried, mainly women's auxiliaries that affiliated with the RCIPA locals.[81] Now and then *The Advocate* marshalled economic arguments against the employment of married and well-to-do women.[82] In general, however, it became union policy to organize women as equals and to demand equal pay for men and women, even though this demand was unrealistic. Women participated in trade union activities, including strikes.[83] In the years after the turn of the century women became a favorite topic for the union newspaper. The exploitation of the growing number of saleswomen aroused the RCIPA's anger as well as that of reform groups.[84] *The Advocate* condemned their long hours spent constantly on their feet, their low pay, and the complete lack of insurance for women. However much male members of the RCIPA might see their economic position endangered by the employment of women,[85] their union newspaper strongly upheld the right of women to be sales clerks. When working conditions were more reasonable, the paper even described their employment as a means toward the general emancipation of women. Several articles characterized the sales girl as the 'New Woman', the 'woman who is leading the new industrial life', and who was thus more modern and could look forward to a brighter future than the simple housewife or wealthy club woman. These articles were clearly intended to appeal to the paper's female readers.[86]

The RCIPA had only limited success with female clerks for a variety of reasons. To begin with the union was too weak to eliminate the male-female salary differential. Many girls and young women may have viewed working in a store as a way to pass the time between school and marriage. More importantly in view of the meager alternatives open to women — domestic service, farming, factory work — their duties as sales clerks may not have seemed all that bad. At any rate, female clerks appeared to have had only slight interest in committed trade unionism. Their failure to actively participate may explain part of the instability and weakness of the RCIPA. For all that, in some locals women made up a third to a half of the membership.[87]

3. Sales Clerks and Wage Workers

(a) The RCIPA as Part of the Labor Movement

The German mercantile employees' effort to distinguish themselves from manual workers deeply affected their sense of identity and their expectations in the modern world. The effort to distinguish white collar clerks from the proletariat to the former's advantage determined the programs of almost all their associations as well as their social-political demands and behavior. The partly real but increasingly ideological distinction between salaried employees and wage workers played a central role in the revival of clerks' associations and their politicization in the 1880s. The collar line underlay the emergence of white collar workers as a separate social group in the two decades before the first world war, the creation of a special body of law to cover them, and in fact the very definition of the term. There was almost no cooperation between labor unions and white collar associations before the first world war. Even during the Weimar Republic blue and white collar workers still did not organize together.

The RCIPA never drew this kind of boundary line between white collar clerks and blue collar workers. Their constitution and membership criteria, in fact their own membership in the AFL, suggest just the opposite: the RCIPA considered itself part of the American labor movement. Progress reports in *The Advocate* reveal how fully the RCIPA's victories — whether achieved by consumer boycott or strike — depended on the support of the local Labor and Trades Council, the leaders of the AFL, and individual trade unions. The AFL helped finance the union organizers who traveled across the country recruiting members, starting new locals, and helping old ones get through crises.[88] The sales clerks' initial organizing meeting often took place in the local union hall.[89] The Labor and Trades Council paid for advertisements and leaflets to urge shoppers to boycott stores in support of the clerks. During consumer boycotts labor's delegations comingled workers and clerks. If working class women had not participated in these boycotts and taken their business to stores with the RCIPA card in the window, the clerks would not have had a chance.[90] When the sales clerks did go on strike the labor movement supported their struggle with money and publicity. The Labor and Trades Council supplied pickets; members of other unions, the Teamsters, for instance, honored their picket lines.[91]

The RCIPA acknowledged the clerks' dependence on the labor movement in many ways. Time and again they reiterated the solidarity of all workers and the unity of the toiling masses, using just such phrases.[92] They exchanged telegrams of greeting and solidarity with other AFL unions. RCIPA officers also held important positions in local trade union councils and the national Federation.[93] The RCIPA had more than a paper commitment to the AFL. The Federation was a comfortable as well as a useful home for the clerks' union. Its loose, decentralized structure allowed ample room for union constitutions that suited the particular needs of each occupation. The AFL usually avoided explicit statements about politics and philosophy. Nevertheless, the Federation clearly followed a gradualistic, pragmatic line aimed at the concrete improvement of working conditions within the capitalist system rather than fundamental social reform. The national Federation united many extremely diverse groups of workers, requiring from them a bare minimum of common beliefs and politics.[94] This restraint in organizational and ideological matters may explain why the RCIPA's extremely infrequent, explicit ideological statements did not deviate to the right or the left of the AFL line. It was thoroughly compatible with membership in the AFL for the RCIPA to vacillate between a moderately progressive workers' consciousness and a specific sales clerks' occupational consciousness.

In complete agreement with the leaders of the AFL the sales clerks' union steadfastly rejected the idea of 'one big union'.[95] In doing so the RCIPA always dwelt on the unique qualifications required of sales clerks and the peculiar characteristics of the sales 'profession'. *The Advocate* never tired of articles which discussed the advantages and disadvantages of the clerks' profession, as in a series entitled 'Clerkology'. Their occupational pride was not necessarily in conflict with trade union consciousness as it was understood in the American Federation of Labor. The RCIPA's appeal to sales clerks to become active trade union members rested squarely on their job consciousness. Sales clerks should be protected by trade union organization just as the 'other crafts of skilled labor' were, since 'we in our craft are just as skilled in our labors as are the carpenters, the painters, the plumbers, or such other trades...' These, however, had better luck than the sales clerks at improving their situation through trade union action.[96]

The clerks expressed their workers' consciousness by using terms such as 'employee', 'worker', 'wage earner', 'toiler', and 'working class' to describe themselves. They were soldiers 'in the great battle for bread and butter', but also allies 'in the great war for the freedom of the worker', in 'the coming battle for the emancipation of the workers', for the 'regeneration of society and the uplifting of humanity'.[97]

This rhetoric of general emancipation was more completely expressed in the RCIPA's support of the basic political stands of the AFL. In 1919 *The Advocate* approved 'in principle' (with the Federation) the League of Nations, disarmament, the protection of free speech and the right of assembly, and the repeal of restrictive wartime laws which infringed on these basic rights. The clerks added their assent to women's suffrage, public ownership of the railroads, and to strengthening direct democracy in the states through constitutional amendments and the introduction of the referendum and recall.[98] After war broke out in Europe, *The Advocate*'s leading articles adopted a vehemently anti-war, anti-preparedness stance that focused on the social conflicts at home. The paper gave Gompers less space than UMW president John P.

White, who stood considerably to his left.[99] As late as May 1919 *The Advocate* poked fun at the spreading fear of Bolshevism and attempted to unmask the postwar wave of anti-communism as a cover up for a general attack on social reform.[100] Yet shortly thereafter, the RCIPA capitulated to the Red Scare and followed the AFL in condemning leftist radicals.[101]

The RCIPA's positions on ethnic and race questions were also well within the AFL framework. To properly understand their stance it is important to keep in mind the ethnic composition of the occupational group which the clerks' union was trying to organize. In 1870 and 1880 about 20% of the male and 15% of the female clerks were foreign born; between 1890 and 1920 only about 15% of men and 12% of women clerks were immigrants. Thus the sales clerks' occupation became less accessible to immigrants as the new arrivals began to come in increasing numbers from southern and eastern Europe. The proportion of clerks with one or both foreign born parents was higher, however: between 25 and 30% from 1890-1920, with the men showing a slight increase before 1910, the women a slight decrease after 1900.[102] The following table (2.4) shows the degree of under or overrepresentation of immigrants and second generation immigrants among sales clerks and some non-agricultural occupational groups selected for comparative purposes. The numbers refer to the relationship between the proportion of immigrants or their children in each group and the proportion of immigrants or their children in the total white gainfully occupied population. One hundred would be the normal distribution; thus the lower the figure, the more clearly foreigners or their children were underrepresented in each occupational group, and vice versa.

The occupational groups in Table 2.4 are listed in order of the degree of under, then of overrepresentation of immigrants. Underrepresentation was most prevalent in the prestigious professions, overrepresentation greatest in manual occupations, particularly semi-skilled and unskilled jobs such as cotton textile operative and cutter. Sales clerks fell in the middle, with a slightly higher share of immigrants than other white collar occupations, but fewer than the self-employed in industry and trade. Sales clerks were distinctly more indigenous than manual workers or servants. Clearly, the occupation of sales clerk was one which the immigrant had difficulty entering, whether because of his or her insufficient knowledge of the language and customs or because of prejudice and discrimination.[104] 'Many customers attach importance to being served by Americans', a thorough study of six large department stores in Philadelphia in 1909 concluded. The study found that the great majority of female clerks were born in the US and had Anglo-Saxon,

Table 2.4
Under or Overrepresentation of Immigrants and Children of Immigrants in Selected Occupations, 1890-1950[103]

	1890				1900				1910				1920				1950			
	Male		Female		Male		Female		Male		Female		Male		Female		Male		Female	
	I	C	I	C	I	C	I	C	I	C	I	C	I	C	I	C	I	C	I	C
Lawyers and Judges	26	75	—	—	27	89	—	—	25	102	—	—	28	106	—	—	54	133	76	111
Teachers and Professors	34	74	22	89	39	74	25	95	39	75	27	95	39	78	27	83	56	87	37	80
Stenographers, Secretaries, etc.	47	152	24	120	37	153	32	134	27	167	28	147	29	174	36	133	51	126	41	115
Clerks	56	178	39	146	55	164	43	136		included in				'Bookkeeper'						
Officials (Government)	60	105	26	56	55	96	23	64		?				?				?	?	
Bookkeepers	62	153	30	140	63	150	39	143	44	157	35	138	45	147	40	121	56	119	45	109
Salesmen/Women	64	157	45	183	66	146	55	155	65	141	54	139	67	130	64	111	72	107	81	96
Engineers	69	105	—	—	63	96	—	—	47	104	—	—	52	108	—	—	68	87	103	110
Manufacturers, Managers	100	102	—	—	108	110	104	100	[91	114	99	88	85	113	97	87]		?	?	
Merchants, Designers, etc.	103	103	184	78	119	104	196	85	[132	109	108	109	152	99	157	99]		?	?	
Carpenters	103	81	—	—	113	85	—	—	109	87	—	—	116	86	—	—	108	78	149	78
Draftsmen, Designers, etc.	106	122	—	—	98	128	—	—	[90	137	100	122	83	141	127	114]		?	?	
Foremen and Overseers	144	105	—	—	122	106	—	—	107	120	88	142	97	118	78	159	99	111	124	138
Servants and Waiters	178	109	155	83	182	106	161	91	173	87	169	80	193	81	183	79	205	85	197	79
Cotton-Mill Operatives	192	124	171	98	166	75	174	66	177	111	150	114	172	108	163	113	102	78	110	91
Tailors	280	90	122	158	331	73	174	133	330	50	200	130	374	39	250	114		?	?	

I = Immigrants C = Children of Foreign Born or Mixed Parentage (Second Generation)

German, and northern European backgrounds. Local prejudices were particularly important, since the job involved so much contact with customers.[105] The largest contingent among the foreign born clerks in 1900 was the Germans; natives of England (including Wales) followed. These two groups had furnished the greatest part of the immigrant sales clerks in the preceding decades as well. Scots and Canadians were also less underrepresented than most foreign born, but this was less significant because the total migration from these countries wass so much smaller than the German and English totals. The same was true of the large proportion of Russian (probably Jewish) immigrants who went into sales work at this time — their total number in 1900 did not add up to 1% of the total sales force. Distinctly underrepresented in contrast were the Swiss, Poles, Hungarians, Swedes, Norwegians, and Irish.

Sales work, along with other lower and middle level white collar positions, provided a first rung up the ladder for immigrant sons and daughters before the first world war. In 1890 the proportion of immigrant children among salesmen and saleswomen was higher than in most other occupations. The 'second generation' was particularly common among female clerks in the late 19th century. German and English descendants were also the most numerous in this second generation. Not that they were particularly attracted to sales work (in fact, just the reverse seems to have been true where there were more lucrative alternatives), but they continued to have a numerical superiority in the second generation. This also explains the presence of a great number of second generation Irish in sales work, even though compared to their proportion of the labor force they were still underrepresented. Also still underrepresented were the children of French Canadians, Norwegians, Swiss, Bohemians, Danes and Scots. In contrast, smaller and in part newer groups of immigrant children attained a particularly high degree of overrepresentation: the descendants of Austrian, Hungarian, and once again, Russian families.[106]

The names and biographies of RCIPA leaders, but also the names of ordinary members which appear in the sources, convey a distinct picture of a trade union run overwhelmingly by indigenous Americans or British, German, and Scandinavian immigrants, and probably also composed of these groups.[107] There were apparently no special campaigns to organize new immigrants and their children. On the other hand, there is no indication of open discrimination against minorities. To be sure, racist overtones occasionally appeared in the union's economically motivated demands to restrict immigration: in a discussion of the Japanese on the west coast, for instance. The leaders reiterated their opposition to unrestricted immigration before the war, but this question was not a central concern in the locals and the lives of the membership. And even in the heyday of imperialistic propaganda just after the Spanish-American war, rejection of wage-depressing competition from immigrants was coupled with a firm rejection of imperialistic expansion and territorial conquest.[108]

In contrast to some AFL unions that formally barred non-white Americans from membership (in violation of AFL principles), the RCIPA constitution contained no explicitly racist clauses.[109] The RCIPA leadership defeated a proposed racial exclusion clause in 1901 by citing AFL standards, which forbade discrimination on the basis of race, nationality, religion or sex.[110] After 1913 there was at least one sales clerks' local in Puerto Rico, which the union newspaper occasionally addressed in Spanish.[111] It is very likely, however, that RCIPA locals, like most other trade unions, informally but effectively excluded non-whites. Union conventions and the union newspaper avoided the problem, which was also less pressing for sales clerks than for many factory workers. If one disregards stores run by blacks for blacks (which before 1914 were almost exclusively found in the south, and which were definitely not organized by the RCIPA), blacks were rarely hired by retail stores in any case.

Finally, the RCIPA's stance on political action was generally in agreement with official AFL policy. In complete contrast to the German mercantile employees' associations, American sales clerks had little faith in protective legislation except for immigration restriction, compulsory education, restrictions on prison labor, Sunday closing, and from time to time also campaigns for the eight hour day and apprenticeship regulation. As a rule the RCIPA concentrated on collective bargaining agreements with the typical AFL argument that because of shifting parliamentary majorities and the power of conservative courts, progress through legislation was unlikely. Yet even though the weak clerks' union could hope to achieve far less through direct pressure on employers than a strong craft union, they were still only slightly less skeptical about political action than the Federation's leaders. The RCIPA did support the demand for a legal minimum wage for women in 1914. And sales clerks emphatically favored the stronger legislative program of the AFL in 1905/6. In 1905, for instance, the RCIPA president advocated in fairly unambiguous language a separate, united political representation for the working class. This demand was not in complete accordance with AFL policy and, as is well known, was never realized in the US.[112]

(b) The Skilled Workers as Reference Group

This chapter has already shown how in contrast to German mercantile employees' associations, the American sales clerks' union allied with organized labor and shared the fundamental ideological positions of the labor movement. A second aspect of the relationship between American white collar workers and manual workers comes into focus through comparison with Germany. An important root of German mercantile employee protests in this era and later was their fear of 'proletarianization': that is, they feared that in earnings, life style, education, work, contact with employers, chances for mobility, and legal situation their status would become more like that of wage workers. In other words, the mercantile employees' associations were not only concerned with the actual difficulties in their members' economic and social situation. Since they viewed these problems in a particular historical perspective, they saw them as a stage in a process, as indices of a progressive loss and decline. Thus they protested not primarily against their *bad*, but above all against their *worsening* circumstances, using wage workers as a measuring stick and negative reference group.

These protests against leveling and decline were more or less consciously fueled by feelings of superiority; they were nurtured by the group's corporatist roots. As the social and economic changes that accompanied industrialization increasingly called their actual superiority into question, this feeling became transformed into claims to the right to superior status and, finally, when it was not forthcoming, into demands for privileged treatment and protest. These anti-egalitarian sentiments became politicized only in the 1880s. Mercantile employees responded to the sharply emerging class antagonisms of their industrializing society by identifying with various anti-proletarian, anti-socialist points of view. Reformulation under the impact of class conflict fixed and sharpened these traditional corporatist claims and gave them a new quality. The protests by mercantile employees were increasingly addressed to the political-bureaucratic authorities in the new interventionist state which was emerging at the same time.[113]

American sources contain almost no trace of this kind of view. Sales clerks in or out of the RCIPA did not refer to the danger of 'proletarianization'. The concept did not belong to the political rhetoric of the time, nor to the groups under study. Sales clerks did not seem to feel that they were engaged in a defensive struggle, that they were defending a crumbling position or demanding a return to former circumstances. They were not resisting the 'leveling tide' of the proletariat, which was also a much less closed and threatening group (as well as less repressed, excluded, and discriminated against) in the US than in Germany. Quite the contrary: German relationships appear to have been turned upside down when spokesmen for the RCIPA held up the pay, status, and organizations of skilled workers as a model for the sales clerks to emulate. While German mercantile employees were trying to defend their advantages against the mass of workers, the RCIPA fought to catch up with the mainstream of organized labor. 'For many a long day the poor clerk has been told again and again that he is a nobody. He has no trade, he has no skill, and, the greatest lack of all, he has no tools. He works not in iron, nor in wood, nor in cloth. He is in the class designated in the Good Book as "those who toil not, neither do they spin".' Some feeling that they were inferior to skilled craftsmen was also expressed in the complaints of sales clerks that they could easily be replaced, had few qualifications, and were incapable of controlling entry into their occupation as did printers, plumbers, and ironworkers. The craft union of the skilled worker was a model which these sales clerks would have liked to imitate.[114]

Employees involved in jurisdictional disputes between the sales clerks and the Teamsters' or Butchers' Union almost never chose to be organized as white collar clerks by the RCIPA; the greater clout of the skilled craft unions proved far more attractive. When, during the war, sales clerks were transferred into war-related production, their former union commented on their advancement. They would probably not be back. The RCIPA justified its demands for a minimum wage with the argument that one would have to be serious about this fundamental trade union principle to be fully accepted by other AFL affiliates.[115] The clerks' union defended raising the relatively low membership dues and a program of modest death and sickness benefits with the same arguments.[116] While German mercantile employees enjoyed legal advantages over blue collar workers,[117] the slowly developing labor law in the US accorded no special advantages to white collar workers. On the contrary: protective legislation was at first restricted to factory workers, and the sales clerks had to fight to be treated as the workers' equals.[118]

The primary inequality between sales clerks and (especially skilled) manual workers appeared on pay day. Most clerks received a weekly salary with no overtime; if they missed a day, however, they were docked.[119] Their incomes varied greatly depending on the kind of store and the clerk's position. Men's clothing, shoe stores, and some food and drug stores paid best; cigarette, floral, and dry goods shops paid worst.[120] Department stores fell somewhere in the middle. On the average sales clerks earned more than unskilled laborers, but less than skilled workers (see Table 2.5).

Table 2.5
Weekly Wages and Salaries in Selected Occupations (Men) in Mercantile Establishments in the Boston Central Business District, 1902 (in dollars)[121]

Occupation	No. of Persons	Weekly Average	High	Low
Clerks	106	9.76	28.00	4.00
Drug Clerks	9	12.22	16.00	9.00
Salesmen	2,146	14.99	60.00	3.00
Packers	136	10.99	15.00	5.00
Drivers	164	11.27	15.00	8.00
Porters	274	10.18	18.00	4.00
Bookkeepers	172	19.73	38.50	9.00
Cashiers	8	13.20	23.00	5.00
Managers (Excluding Floor Managers)	43	30.15	125.00	18.00
Stenographers	10	12.03	16.00	8.00
Salesmen, Traveling	56	28.22	100.00	10.00
Cooks	23	16.49	34.62	10.00
Workmen (Carpets and Rugs)	12	18.00	25.00	9.00
Carpenters	6	16.33	25.00	13.00

Weekly Earnings of Skilled Workers in Massachusetts, 1904

Bricklayers	15.96
Carpenters	15.37
Smiths	13.48
Masons	17.12
Modelmakers	19.72
Painters	13.78

The earnings of saleswomen also fell between the wages of unskilled and skilled workers. More clearly than for male clerks, their earnings were well beneath what could be earned in an office with stenographic, typing, or bookkeeping skills (see Table 2.6).

The earnings of female clerks were thus distinctly lower than those of male clerks. Furthermore, they were frequently beneath the minimum level considered necessary for a single woman to live on in their locality. An investigation of 4,048 women in 60 stores in Baltimore (1909) found that 54% earned less than $5, 81% less than $6 a week. Only 658 women earned between $7 and $11, only

Table 2.6
Weekly Earnings in Selected Occupations (Women)

a. Massachusetts 1872[122]

Occupation	Total No. Employed	General Average Wages per Week
Saleswomen	680	$6.28
Barmaids (with Board)	174	4.33
Seamstresses (Dresses & Cloaks, Wholesale)	1,945	7.77
Shirtcutters	28	10.28

b. Mercantile Wages and Salaries in Boston, 1902[123]

Occupation	No. of Persons Considered	Average Weekly Wages & Salaries
Clerks	75	$7.31
Saleswomen	2,404	8.04
Waitresses	258	4.83
Kitchen Girls	70	4.49
Dishwashers	21	4.17
Bookkeepers	215	11.06
Stenographers	44	10.86

124 from $11 to $15 a week. The investigators concluded that in only 19% of the cases were earnings above the local subsistence level for single women.[124] This minimum was reckoned at $8.25 for Boston by the Massachusetts Minimum Wage Commission in 1916. The actual average earnings of 1,152 female retail employees in Boston at this time amounted to only $6.09 per week; even if one considers only the actual time worked by excluding lay offs in recessions, part-time work, etc., their average weekly earnings rose only to $7.54.[125] One may assume that the subsistence minimum was overstated and that many female clerks, who were usually under 25 and often under eighteen, received support from their parents or friends (it was apparently very rare for married women to work as clerks);[126] even so, such figures have to be taken as an index of dependence, need, and exploitation. To make matters worse, during the slack seasons after Christmas and in the summer large stores frequently laid off part of their sales force from one day to the next. Most stores did not continue to pay wages in cases of illness. These modest earnings reflect the low social esteem accorded working women, as well as the increasingly fictitious convention that

women were basically cared for by their husbands or families and that their own earnings were only pin money.[127] Without the support of friends or family, without additional income — whether earned by prostitution or similar connections — it was hardly possible to live on a saleswoman's salary.[128] The view that these women were only passing the time before marriage, ignorance and popular misconceptions, made this kind of exploitation possible before the first world war. Futhermore, the wages paid to unskilled women in factories were scarcely better. And there were few higher positions available for the many women with a secondary school education, except for poorly paid teaching jobs.[129]

As these figures indicate, it was primarily male sales clerks who could reasonably hope to raise their salary to the level of skilled workers' wages. Their demands for higher salaries were often phrased with just that goal in view.[130] The relationship between industrial wages and male clerks' salaries remained fairly constant, however, from the turn of the century to 1916. In the recessions of 1908, 1913, and 1915 industrial earnings were more susceptible to decline than the relatively resistant salaries of clerks. In the wartime inflation from 1917-20, however, the gap between wages and clerks' salaries increased noticeably (see Table 2.10 below).

(c) The Absence of Corporatist Traditions and Claims

The fact that fear of proletarianization, awareness of declining status, and consequent claims for special privileges from employers or government had practically no impact on American sales clerks did not mean that their objective situation was better than that of their German counterparts. American and German clerks were probably affected in very similar ways by relatively low earnings and long hours. Sales clerks were easily replaced in both societies, and increasingly so because of innovations in merchandising and the expansion of basic education. In both countries clerks were subject to the harsh conditions of the capitalist labor market. Their competitive position worsened with the recruitment of women and those with only average schooling into the occupation.[131] Any real hope of becoming independent was also decreasing (even if somewhat later and more slowly in the US than in Germany).[132] In fact, American sales employees lacked some of the legal protections their German counterparts enjoyed. For instance, they had no guarantee against sudden dismissal. Unemployment among sales clerks was at least as well known in the US as in Germany, though it apparently occasioned no specific protests. In Massachusetts in

1887, for instance, 7% of male and 12% of female clerks were without positions.[133]

Several factors explain why German and American clerks reacted so differently to similar challenges, among them the different characteristics of the German and American working class movements. We will come back to this. First we should like to stress some socio-psychological differences between American and German clerks, which themselves resulted from different backgrounds and collective experiences.

American sales clerks' reactions were less focused and militant because they did not measure their economic and social development within a framework of corporatist or semi-corporatist expectations, and thus — lacking an elevated point of departure and traditional standards — they did not register what was happening to them as a radical threat or an oppressive decline. In Germany the traditional occupational-corporatist status expectations of mercantile employees (which at least for some time partly corresponded to social reality)[134] collided abruptly with industrial progress. Because these expectations were largely lacking in the US, they could not be disappointed with parallel consequences. Thus the increasingly impersonal relationship between employer and clerk in large concerns did not intrude in the US on the employee's belief that relations between 'principal' and 'assistant' should in some ways be patriarchal and corporatist. Just as apprenticeship was relatively undeveloped in the US, it was a great exception for the American clerk to live with the family of his or her 'principal'. Most clerks lived in boarding houses or with families who rented rooms.[135] The employer had little say over the private life of the clerk — that is, if the long work day did not make the very idea of a private life illusory, and if the clerk had not so internalized business principles that he 'voluntarily' modeled his life on them.[136] Advice books by authors who had worked in mercantile establishments in the late 19th century suggested that employees should be judged almost exclusively by their 'business performance', not by how they measured up as a whole person. There are two exceptions: since clerks were trusted with the businessman's own money, their honesty should be tested continually; also in the interests of the business, the clerk should have the impression that he was fairly treated.[137]

If their working hours permitted, American sales clerks were apt to look for part-time outside jobs, for instance as bookkeeper for a small business, to supplement their earnings.[138] In distinct contrast, the German Commerce Code prohibited most mercantile employees from holding such outside jobs.[139] This prohibition rested on the image — increasingly fictional — of a relationship between assistant and boss which went far beyond a mere work contract/exchange relationship. The Commerce Code foresaw a 'relationship of service' (*Dienstverhältnis*) which obligated the clerk to 'trustworthiness', 'faithfulness', and 'good morals' in private life and at work; the master was obligated to educate his assistants.[140] Although in fact a narrow economic relationship between employer and employee was well developed in German commercial establishments, the law and many of those involved still proceeded as if the exchange of work for wages was not the essence of the bargain between principal and assistant. Instead, they viewed the relationship as a multi-dimensional obligation which involved the whole person on both sides. The proof was payment in salary, sick benefits, protection against dismissal, and other provisions which exceeded a mere labor contract. In 1892 just under half of all German retail employees still lived and boarded with their employer.[141] For many the sort of patriarchally molded social relations portrayed in a stylized way in Gustave Freytag's famous novel *Soll und Haben* (1855) were still norm and reality. Spokesmen for German mercantile employees criticized the breakdown of this tradition, the transformation of the assistant into a mere employee, and the triumph of a narrow profit mentality in the larger stores. They bemoaned the crumbling of traditional standards of obligation and trust which, if outmoded and often idealized, had nonetheless not been manufactured out of thin air. In 1890 the chairman of a mercantile assistants' association passed judgement on this situation:

> The boss no longer accepts the assistant's company. The affectionate tone which used to be the rule between principal and assistants is hardly used; instead, unfortunately, every possible barrier is raised between them. The assistant is no longer regarded by the principal as flesh of his flesh, he is no longer treated as his co-worker but now only as his worker. Naturally then the bonds within the mercantile corporation must also be loosened, and a certain degree of resentment between assistants and employers enters the picture.[142]

No such complaints were heard from American assistants; they would probably not even have understood them.

Changing positions frequently was considered unseemly by many German shop assistants, who viewed the artisans' 'wandering years' as beneath their status.[143] Although no formal institution of 'wandering' existed in the US, frequent and rapid job turnover was accepted as normal by employees and employers. Geographic mobility was in general socially more acceptable in the US than in Europe; it seems also to have been more common, though this assumption has not yet been proved. Newspaper announcements, information from friends, or direct application at a number of businesses were the means used by American sales clerks to change jobs.[144] Store owners were even advised not to keep their clerks too long, since they were apt to become restless or lazy.[145] Seniority probably conferred fewer advantages in the US than in Germany. A certain element of risk in their position — more frequent dismissals, changes in their jobs corresponding to market and business cycle patterns, as well as being judged by dollars and cents results — probably seemed inevitable and relatively acceptable to most American clerks.[146] These features of a private enterprise economy had also become the norm in Germany with the industrial and commercial development of the last third of the 19th century. But there they often seriously contradicted the mercantile assistant's fundamental sense of identity.

Compared to Germany the relationship between employer and clerk in the US was a relatively impersonal labor contract in which services were exchanged for money. One reflection of this difference was that American clerks were usually paid weekly or bimonthly, not by the month. The agent of the New York branch of a large German mercantile assistants' association reported this back to the readers of the association's journal in Germany. He added: 'This may be explained by the fact that in American business life the requirement to give notice before dismissal is unknown. One is hired by the week and can be let go any Saturday.' He warned his colleagues in Germany against coming to New York to find a better position; even if they were looking for a better standard of living, with more entertainment and artistic enjoyment, they would be better off remaining in the old country. And in fact many shop assistants who did emigrate returned in disillusionment to Germany.[147]

One should not underestimate the fact that most sales clerks were paid weekly wages instead of a monthly salary — in contrast to the German situation. A monthly salary meant more security and reliability; it was less dependent on quick market changes and unforeseen circumstances; it carried more status and prestige; and, on the German side at least, it was one of the major features distinguishing a (salaried) white collar employee from a blue collar (wage) worker. While the semantic distinction between 'salary' and 'wage' has never been quite as clear-cut as the distinction between *Gehalt* and *Lohn* in German, the difference of meaning pointed in the same direction in both languages. In 1902, the Massachusetts Report of the Statistics of Labor, noting that for the first time it was dealing with 'persons employed in what is generally designated "Trade"', also found it necessary to distinguish between wages and salaries.

> By 'salary' is understood the sum paid for specific service in employments mainly mental, or in those requiring a higher grade of ability than the occupations where the labor performed is manual or mechanical. Where salaries are paid, deductions for lost time, vacations, etc., are seldom made, especially in the case of trusted employees, or those whose ability and knowledge are such that the omission of deductions for vacations, etc., is taken as an indication of appreciation on the part of the employer.[148]

Sales clerks who were paid by the week, docked for time lost, and were not usually entitled to a vacation (certainly not paid),[149] and whose earnings were usually characterized as wages, had little better claim to belong to this upper stratum of the labor force than manual workers. Referring to sales clerks' earnings as salaries around 1900 was flattering, and it easily shaded into propaganda and ideology.[150]

Thus, around 1900 there were many indications that the social position of an American clerk was less clearly demarcated from that of a (skilled) manual worker than it was on the German side. But even in the early 19th century, American sales clerks were not distinctly elevated above journeymen artisans and manual workers in their own self-image or in the general public's assessment of their status and prestige, while their German counterparts were.[151] Most of the evidence for this conclusion is implicit rather than direct. Advice books from the middle of the century addressed 'apprentices, clerks, and laborers' in one breath, recommending the same virtues and techniques for getting ahead to all.[152] Lectures about correct employer-employee relations addressed manufacturing and commercial entrepreneurs in identical fashion.[153] Without corporatist traditions no separate commercial and mercantile labor law developed (equivalent to the German Commerce Code). Labor law regulated the situation of employees pure and simple; it might distinguish between them by standards of need, but not by criteria of corporatist status.

Life style, education, and social esteem were significant elements of corporatist self-image in Germany. Appropriately, social life, educational programs, and upholding the group's honor — which went as far as providing a decent burial for an impoverished colleague — were central activities for German mercantile assistants' associations.[154] Interest in sociability and education was not completely absent in American clerks' organizations either. But it was telling that the educational, social, Protestant-philanthropic YMCAs which young clerks founded on the English model accepted members from all occupations, including manual workers.[155] Calls for education and moral uplift seem to have been much less frequently based on occupational or corporatist feelings of togetherness in the US than in Germany. Such issues were insignificant in the RCIPA at the turn of the century.

German mercantile employees applied corporatist categories to the work that they did. They were extremely unwilling to perform tasks they considered appropriate for manual helpers, maids or drivers, because to do so would offend their 'sense of honor'. Even though their actual daily activities became increasingly limited to tasks that did not require special abilities, many mercantile employees continued to see their work in a larger frame of reference. 'The mercantile spirit goes beyond the ordinary dexterity required to pack a pound of coffee or cut a meter of cloth'.[156] Such attitudes were uncommon among American clerks. Whoever was unwilling to perform tasks which would be considered beneath his standing in the old country should not come to New York, the same agent warned his German colleagues.[157] The absence of corporatist ballast allowed the RCIPA to concentrate in a fairly one-dimensional fashion on economic problems and for the most part to ignore the bundle of overarching social, ideological, and political issues which dominated the activities of German associations. The clerks' union left all such matters to the individual members. They were expected to satisfy these needs largely outside their occupational association — perhaps in their family, ethnic group, lodge, church, or local political party organization. American labor unions tended to differ from the multi-functional German trade unions in a parallel way. To this extent differentiation of roles, and the expectation that different needs would be fulfilled by overlapping rather than multi-purpose institutions, was more advanced in the US at the turn of the century than in Germany.

4. The Sales Clerks' Sense of Identity

(a) Superior Status

The arguments advanced up to now have perhaps gone too far in minimizing the differences in status and prestige between manual workers and retail employees in order to distinguish the German and American situations. Some modifications are in order.

The relatively small proportion of immigrants, particularly 'new immigrants' from southern and eastern Europe, in sales work reflected a certain status advantage over skilled and even more distinctly over unskilled manual occupations. This conclusion follows from the markedly lower status of these immigrant groups compared to the native born. For second generation immigrants, however, entry into the occupation of sales clerks was an attainable step up the social ladder from manual work — as revealed by the significant overrepresentation of the children of immigrants. Thus the greater accessibility of sales work to these second generation immigrants compared to their representation in the professions and (though with less contrast) among office employees defines the limit of the clerks' superior status. It also highlights the modest qualifications required to become a clerk and the inability of these white collar employees to control entry into their own occupation.

In the US as well as Germany, varying degrees of esteem and value attached to manual and non-manual work. This was particularly true of women. In spite of the modest earnings (which must, however, be judged against the alternative of factory jobs which paid even less), sales clerks' positions were much sought after by women. Positions in department stores and fine specialty shops seemed particularly desirable. Before the first world war, in large cities like Pittsburgh, Portland, and Washington, DC, department stores kept waiting lists of the girls and young women who had applied for jobs and been turned away. Native-born women where possible avoided factories and sought 'white-handed' occupations — offices, if they had time for some training, stores if they had not. In stores, untrained women could earn 'pin money' without total loss of social position.[158] Clean working conditions and good clothes, greater opportunities to meet eligible batchelors, avoiding contact with the new immigrants who worked in the factories, the chance to acquire skills which would be useful in running a household, proximity to luxury goods and rich customers, sometimes the prestige of a good store, certainly the assumption that their work was appropriate for women—all contributed to the popularity of sales work (and explain the oversupply of female clerks despite the poor pay).[159] It was also true that for female clerks, in contrast to males, the job was usually considered a temporary step before marriage. Since most clerks lacked training for other jobs, their only alternative was unskilled factory work or employment as a domestic. It is also true, however, that many more young women than men had high school diplomas at the turn of the century; they were thus better qualified for the expanding number of white collar jobs.[160]

Male clerks also felt a certain sense of superiority toward manual workers which often extended to a disdain for trade unions as well. An article in *The Advocate* reproved clerks who wore a high collar and went around as 'gentlemen', thinking themselves too good to associate with those who labored in overalls. The RCIPA strongly recommended good, well-kept clothing, however; particularly when applying for a position, the clerk should exude 'an air of prosperity and gentility'. Collar, tie, and starched shirt were important; the clerk should choose a good, simple business suit and avoid looking like 'a college chap who delights in startling contrasts'.[161] The collar and white shirt became symbols of the sense of superiority and claims to higher status than manual workers of the 'white collar man' in the US. In Germany, on the other hand, this status rested on performing mental, non-manual labor which required some education, on non-proletarian status, job security, and a special relationship to one's superiors rather than differences in appearance — as the different etymology of *Angestellter* and white collar worker indicates. Repeated warnings against snobbery from the RCIPA leadership, but even more resentment and criticism from the workers' side, trace the tendencies of sales clerks to claim superior status. 'What do you expect to do with these white collar stiffs?...a $15 a week collar and cuff clerk thinks he's far superior to a $25 a week blouse and overall mechanic', a member of the Plumbers' Union complained in 1888 in a discussion about cooperating with the local RCIPA. In 1902 *The Advocate* complained in return that some coal miners held unreasonable prejudices against those who worked with clean clothes and clean hands. The RCIPA repeatedly condemned the indifference of sales clerks to trade union organization and their preference for joining clubs.[162]

Such quotations suggest some reasons for the limits to the cooperation which the labor movement was prepared to offer white collar workers. The resentments of workers against these 'white collar stiffs' seem to have been as prevalent as the reverse prejudice. Labor leaders did not take the clerks entirely seriously as trade unionists, partly because they showed so little readiness to organize.[163]

(b) The Businessman as a Model

These quotations also highlight an element in sales clerks' sense of identity which was not fully compatible with the RCIPA's strong identification with the labor movement, and which in fact made the task of organizing this occupation more difficult. Two types of special group consciousness and related aspirations may be ideal-typically distinguished, according to which was the major reference group: businessmen or professionals.

On the one hand, clerks saw themselves as potential future store owners. In their sense of identity and self-image they thus shared the positive image and relatively high prestige of the entrepreneur or businessman. And the sources seem to indicate that the esteem accorded the average clerk by the public attached less to his status, education, non-manual work and white collar[164] than to his greater chance than most workers at the turn of the century of someday running his own business. 'For most raw country boys the hope of becoming an apprentice, chore boy, or clerk, and eventually the proprietor of his own store, far outdistanced any other prospect they could reasonably compare with it.'[165] The image and virtues of the small businessman had always been particularly important in a society where a peasantry had never existed and which even in pre-industrial times was dominated by agricultural small businessmen; where the absence of an autocratic-bureaucratic tradition meant that the model of a dependent but powerful and prestigious high official did not exist.[166] Permanent employment in a dependent position (even non-manual) was looked on as a greater disgrace for a longer time in the US than in Germany.[167] Thus if the clerk appeared better off than the mechanic, if his status seemed higher than the manual worker's, this was primarily so because he seemed to be that much closer to becoming an independent businessman.[168]

The assumption that clerks might become future store owners was widespread. In 1905 the RCIPA estimated that about 50% of sales clerks viewed their position as transitional. The union sought to convince these clerks that the saying 'the clerk of today is the merchant of tomorrow' no longer held true. They fought identification with the businessman as false consciousness and the chief obstacle to their organizing efforts.[169] It must be kept in mind, however, that the American clerk's chances of owning his own store were by no means insignificant at the turn of the century; in any case they were greater than those of his German counterpart. Already by 1895 employees outnumbered the self-employed in the German commercial sector. In contrast, in the US in 1900 independents still made up 53% of those engaged in trade and commerce (see Table 2.7). If American clerks were more apt than German shop assistants to see themselves as future businessmen, they also had in objective terms more reason to do so, though for many this idea became more and more clearly a mere hope, illusion, and ideology.

The identification of sales clerks with businessmen explains a series of ideological characteristics frequently mentioned in self-help and advice books as well as in biographical sources and articles in *The Advocate* as the mark of a good clerk. The ideal clerk they portrayed accepted competition 100%.[171] He was responsible for his own happiness and could be sure that steady effort, firm pur-

Table 2.7
Independents and Employees in American and German Commerce, 1895-1939[170]

	Independents (in 000s)	Employees (in 000s)	Independents as % of all those Engaged in Commerce
		US	
1900	1,337	2,502	53%
1909	1,630	3,585	45%
1919	1,759	4,213	42%
1929	2,115	6,123	35%
1939	2,328	6,426	37%
		Germany	
1895	578	627	48%
1907	667	1,073	38%
1925	936	2,035	32%
1933	987	1,739	36%
1939	958	2,116	31%

pose, self-control and achievement would lead to success.[172] Individuality was his highest value. Intelligence, imagination, and daring were demanded of a good clerk, who the self-help literature frequently described in Social Darwinist metaphors as an aggressive 'fighter', 'as nervous as a thoroughbred horse', a successful 'business-getter'.[173] Complete identification with his firm, enthusiasm, self-confidence and optimism were recommended. 'The reason you are not selling more goods. . . is that you haven't sold yourself yet'. 'Electric sparks of enthusiasm' over the article should flow from the clerk to the customer.[174] This ideal clerk was convinced of the identity of interests between himself and his firm. 'Remember that the success of your firm is your success' appeared even in the trade union newspaper, which especially in its early years appealed to potential members by stressing the harmony of interest between employers and employees and the union's conservative business practices.[175]

In 1914 *The Advocate* portrayed a trade unionist addressing the sales clerks:

> Mr Store Clerk, you are making a serious mistake. You should not look upon yourself as a superior being, for you aren't. You're just a workingman, even though you don't care to admit it. You may draw a salary instead of wages, and

> you may have a position instead of a job, but you are a plain wage slave, exploited like the rest of the workers — yes, even more so. You, Mr Store Clerk, get an average wage of $12 a week. You know that isn't enough to live on decently. Isn't that a fact? You know that you can never hope to marry and keep a family on that miserable wage. A union workman would fight his head off rather than accept what you take as a matter of course. We realize that you clerks are the hardest people to reach. Why is that so? The answer isn't hard to find... Your minds reflect the ideas of your employers... You have the idea that you are 'above' the working class; your mind is thoroughly capitalistic.[176]

It is clear that this ideological identification with the independent businessman, which was not unique to sales clerks but tended to stamp many groups in American society in the late 19th and early 20th centuries,[177] inhibited the growth of white collar trade unions like the RCIPA. This ideology not only hindered trade union activity, but also impeded steps toward forming collective interest groups or protest organizations outside the labor movement. Individual interpretation of success and failure, of rise and decline, was as central to this ideology as the conviction that an individual shaped his own destiny.[178] This way of thinking blocked the clerks' ability to comprehend the collective, socially conditioned character of their individual situations.

This is not to suggest that American clerks always saw themselves as future entrepreneurs and capitalists. But to the extent that they did develop a sense of identity that raised them above the workers and the labor movement, this self-image was such that it did not become a basis for collective representation of their interests and for collective protests, in contrast to the German mercantile employees. The hope of independence was less important for German sales clerks than their occupational-corporatist new middle class ideology.[179] To put it briefly and roughly: American clerks had only the choice between organizing as workers and not organizing at all, relying on individual, entrepreneurial mastery of their own situation. The third course which their German counterparts adopted, that is, collective organization independent of both workers and businessmen, was not available.

(c) Would-be Professionals

The ideal of individualism and the independent businessman was not of course the whole picture. The RCIPA, as mentioned, attempted to nurture and promote the occupational consciousness of sales clerks. As members of a craft clerks could claim specific skills, such as understanding human nature, politeness, knowledge of the wares, and practical, all-round experience in all aspects of merchandising. Since such occupational pride was borrowed from crafts with strong unions like the masons, carpenters, and toolmakers, it was not an obstacle to belonging to a labor movement which recognized occupation as the most important basis for organization.

Between the turn of the century and the outbreak of war this occupational consciousness took on overtones which divided the clerks from the manual workers, including the skilled crafts, and their organizations. '...[S]alesmanship is really a science and a profession, and is fast becoming recognized as such...', *The Advocate* proclaimed in 1909. 'Salesmanship is the greatest of all professions. We are salesmen, in that we have something to sell — either merchandise, our own services, or the services of others'. Previously, *The Advocate* had characterized sales work as a craft, trade, vocation, or occupation, sometimes even as a calling. Now the paper began to refer more and more frequently to their profession to emphasize the rising importance of the sales clerk. 'The salesman — meaning also the saleswoman — is more and more the deciding factor in the success or failure of a retail store...this calling is being hailed as the fourth profession...the conditions of their calling are steadily improving'.[180] These early efforts to portray sales work as a profession were particularly pronounced in the mushrooming handbooks and textbooks on 'salesmanship'.[181] They fit in perfectly with the emphasis on functionalism, specialization and professionalization in the popular enthusiasm for rationalization and scientific management characteristic of the Progressive Era.[182]

The individual elements of this emerging professional consciousness were not very well developed. Expert qualification, demonstrated by extreme competence at one's job, became the central characteristic of the good salesman. The specialized knowledge and ability of the 'expert salesman' — formulated in ever new guises in the handbooks — increasingly functioned as a basis for the clerks' claim to social recognition. Knowledge about branch stores, basic business organization, advertising and bookkeeping were part of this image along with understanding the techniques, strategy, and psychology of selling. One's own personality — attractiveness, politeness, dynamism, enthusiasm, adaptability, tact and the ability to be convincing — was to be developed and trained according to a definite plan and principles to be an instrument of more efficient 'salesmanship'.[183] The interpersonal relationship between customer and clerk became a subject for conscious reflection and recommended study in order to maximize success in selling. The details of this system of rules, which were no longer to be learned by imitation but instead by teaching and study, and which were often called a science, do not need to be presented here.

Interest in educational programs, which had formerly been missing in the RCIPA, began to appear with the emergence of this quasi-professional consciousness. *The Advocate* applauded the establishment of courses in 'salesmanship' at some colleges and encouraged others to follow suit.[184]

Commercial schools in the US, in contrast to Germany, were usually private undertakings without formal admission requirements or accreditation. There were about twenty such schools in 1850, 373 in 1900 and 902 in 1920. After the 1880s they featured bookkeeping, typing and shorthand to prepare students for jobs in banks and offices rather than in mercantile establishments. The increase of commercial courses in public high schools after 1900 was likewise intended mainly to prepare students for office work; even the new high schools of commerce created after the turn of the century paid almost no attention to salesmanship.[185] The business colleges which also began to appear after the turn of the century (except for the Wharton School in Philadelphia, founded in 1886) also reflected this trend toward professionalization in trade and commerce. Their purpose, however, was educating top management and leadership, not sales clerks.[186] Before 1914 the special education courses for clerks[187] which the handbook literature so enthusiastically recommended were instituted for the most part by large department stores interested in improving the efficiency and loyalty of their sales force. Training courses, advanced studies, and inspirational meetings of all employees became key management techniques in these large establishments. They had little impact, however, on small and medium sized shops.[188]

The first traces of a 'service' ideology, which would later become extremely popular, developed hand in hand with this attention to competence and systematic training in sales work. Ideologically, emphasis shifted from maximizing profits to rendering good service to the customer. As 'the most important and binding contact between producer and consumer' the sales clerk had a heavy social responsibility. Though it was usually not reflected in his salary, it might nonetheless bring him inner satisfaction of a non-material kind.[189]

Emphasis on functional competence based on generalized, systematic knowledge; corresponding claims to functional authority and social recognition; and the aspiration to serve the public rather than pursue individual profits are central features of professional thought and behavior as traditionally formulated, practiced, or at any rate pretended by lawyers, doctors, and engineers.[190] There were limits, however, to the sales clerks' attempted professionalism. They did not claim other characteristics of professional groups such as accreditation and titles, public examinations, codes of honor with specific occupational ethics, or group self-policing mechanisms.

These professional aspirations undoubtedly remained far removed from the reality of the average sales clerk's day. Generally, his job demanded only modest qualifications; there were few training programs available. Devotion to serving the public did not replace interest in commercial profits. But these traces of professional consciousness did represent a new, even if at first very limited, factor in the ideology of white collar sales clerks. Furthermore, professional aspirations were not entirely compatible with the clerk's primary identification with the independent businessman. Clerks still shared the small businessman's distrust of theory and schooling, his reliance on learning through practice, and his respect for profits and belief in competition. Yet this partial ideological reorientation did fit well with the changing atmosphere and reality of American society on the way to organized capitalism.[191] Professionalism, with its emphasis on theoretical-scientific qualifications, functional basis for authority and devaluation of financial gain compared to the inherent immaterial rewards of the work itself, gradually distinguished the occupational consciousness of even the organized clerks from that of the rest of the labor movement. After the turn of the century[192] professionalism became a new obstacle to trade union organization among sales clerks. Unlike their entrepreneurial identification, this barrier became more effective as the hope of future independence vanished. Especially after the first world war, appeals to the 'professional pride' and 'professional superiority' of the clerks were strong anti-union arguments.[193]

III. WHITE COLLAR WORKERS IN INDUSTRY

1. The Collar Line in Manufacturing Firms

(a) Criteria and Status

In every process of industrial development functional requirements divide the industrial labor force into white and blue collar categories. The strength, mode of expression, and significance of the collar line differs at different stages of industrialization; it is even more decisively shaped by varying historical, economic, social and political conditions.[194] A distinction between employees receiving a salary and workers paid in wages was clearly present in the US in the last decades of the 19th century. In 1876, for example, the

Bureau of Labor Statistics in Massachusetts published a representative social sample of citizens of the state in which the main criterion used to divide the sample was the line between 'salary receivers' and 'wage receivers'. In fact, the investigators relied on other information than the never fully clarified distinction between salaries and wages. All occupations of primarily non-manual character were placed in the class of 'salaried persons' — as were those who were particularly well paid. Those who worked with their hands and with tools were counted as 'wage earners'. Good pay, high qualifications, and special perquisites (such as regular vacations) were considered marks of the 'salaried class'. This group was implicitly accorded higher status than the 'wage earners' for reasons that went beyond superior earnings.[195]

The Federal Census also distinguished between 'wage earners' and 'salaried employees' (sometimes 'salaried officers and employees') in industry after the 1890s. Type of work, however, rather than the length of the pay period was the Bureau's chief standard.[196] Such formulations obviously allowed firms a certain leeway in deciding who to report as 'wage earners', who as 'salaried employees'. Consequently, there is an element of uncertainty which cannot be eliminated from the occupational statistics available to historians. The census definition is substantially in accord with the German concept of salaried employees (*Angestellten*) which developed in the decade and a half before the first world war. In the US in contrast to Germany it appears that some foremen and lower level white collar workers who actually were employed in factory buildings were counted as wage earners. In Germany, on the other hand, managers appear to have been excluded from the salaried employees and counted instead as independent proprietors more often than in the US.[197]

Just as the division between blue and white collar workers seems to be common to all patterns of industrialization, an increase in the proportion of white collar employees in the labor force appears to characterize all societies during advanced industrialization. Historical and cultural factors, varying firm size, or differing centers of gravity in the distribution of the labor force among the branches of industry may, however, lead to slight variations in the proportion of blue to white collar workers in societies which are at roughly parallel stages of development.[198] The following figures indicate that the number of salaried employees in industry in the US increased almost twice as fast as the number of industrial wage earners from the end of the 1890s to the first world war (see Table 2.8).

A parallel shift in the relationship of white to blue collar workers occurred at about the same time in Germany, though apparently at

Table 2.8
Blue and White Collar Workers in American Manufacturing, 1899-1938[199]
(in 000s)

	Blue Collar	White Collar	Blue: White Collar
1899	4,496	349	11.4
1904	5,173	546	9.5
1909	6,256	750	8.3
1914	6,592	911	7.2
1919	8.482	1,384	6.1
1921	6,487	1,087	5.8
1925	7,873	1,270	6.2
1933	5,787	1,003	5.8
1938	7,086	1,246	5.7

a somewhat later date and then more decisively. At the end of the 1890s the proportion of salaried employees in the industrial labor force was still smaller in Germany than in the US;[200] by 1925, about the same relationship — one white collar to six blue collar workers — had been reached in both societies (see Table 2.9).

Table 2.9
Blue and White Collar Workers in German Manufacturing, 1895-1939[201]
(in 000s)

	Blue Collar	White Collar	Blue: White Collar
1895	4,216	186	22.6
1907	6,119	510	12.0
1925	7,660	1,257	6.1
1933	8,951	1,205	7.4
1939	9,705	1,628	6.1

This absolute and relative increase of white collar workers in industry was related to a number of developments: increasing commercialization and bureaucratization of industrial firms; the consequent separation of head from hand work; isolation of the functions of planning, preparation, and administration/control from the once more unitary work process; increasing division of labor within the entrepreneurial and managerial functions; an increase in administrative and supervisory tasks in larger firms; paperwork required by more extensive contact between state and economy; and the mechanization of and the application of science to production. Though all these factors played a part in the increase of white collar workers in the US, Germany, and other societies at parallel stages of development, their exact impact and interrelations are by no means fully explained.[202]

In large German firms during the two decades before the first world war, the distinction between salaried employees and workers, between office and factory, had become a significant part of social and economic reality for those involved and for observant contemporaries. These two social groupings were distinguished by their duties, the kind and amount of payment they received, their educational level, career opportunities and expectations, and by their share of authority and privileges within the company. In spite of remarkable heterogeneity within both groupings, each had a separate sense of identity and status, and a different social world at work. Though many of these distinctions were blurred, and some tended to diminish rather than increase over time, they were nonetheless respected or even encouraged and exploited by management. The result was often increased mutual distrust and distance between white and blue collar groups.[203]

The objective situation in large US firms was basically similar. In mid-1892 the Thomson-Houston Electric Company in Lynn, Massachusetts (founded 1880-83, merged with the newly formed General Electric Co. in 1892) had a total workforce of 4,000. The physical plant included eight factory buildings and a brand new office building (completed 1890). It stood three stories tall, had a foundation of 130 by 53 feet and housed twelve office, drafting, and library rooms as well as a laboratory in the basement. Already 97 draftsmen and technicians were at work in the drafting room. The copy room was always busy, every room had a telephone, and only the director and superintendent of works occupied private offices with personal secretaries. The firm's general office and sales division were in Boston.[204] In 1904 the General Electric branch in Schenectady, New York, employed about 10,000 people. A five-story office building with elevators, pneumatic tubes, telephones and telegraphic connection housed the administration, technical and sales divisions, and the bookkeeping, supplies, production, law and patent departments. Three hundred draftsmen and technicians produced 25,000 new models a year. Two hundred thousand drawings were indexed on a system of 900,000 cards and fireproofed. Another group of technical white collar employees worked in small offices near the factory floor.[205] Such examples could be multiplied. Relatively separate office divisions or 'white collar factories' emerged in US industry at probably about the same rate as in Germany before 1914.

There are some traces in American sources of office employees expressing contempt for the wage worker in overalls that reflect the distance between white and blue collar.[206] Of 223 firms with company cafeterias surveyed at the end of the war, eighteen served only their white collar workers, while the majority of the others had separate rooms for factory hands and office employees. Minor distinctions could be noted: white collar employees ate à-la-carte more often than blue collar; they paid slightly more for each meal. The separate treatment of ethnic and racial minorities was frequently more pronounced, however, than distinctions between blue and white collar. At one firm office employees and factory workers were 'served' meals for 23 and 21 cents respectively in separate cafeterias, while the 'colored workers are fed in a separate canteen, standing at long high tables'. Only a small minority of American firms built separate club rooms for blue and white collar workers, as German firms often did. Again, it was more common to segregate ethnic groups and races. An unnamed firm operated three clubs for their workforce: 'one for Americans, one for foreigners, and one for Negroes'.[207] Since foreigners made up a relatively small proportion of white collar workers, this ethnic consciousness indirectly underlined the status distinction that separated them from the more heavily immigrant blue collar workers.[208]

There are also scattered hints in the sources that indicate that factory workers considered the white collar office staff as belonging to the other side. Some firms reported that they provided separate dining facilities not to respect white collar feelings of superiority, but because factory workers preferred to eat among themselves — because office employees were better dressed, or because they felt more at ease without their superiors present.[209]

The foreman, who often wore a suit and tie, liked to be called 'sir', while he addressed the workers by their first names.[210] Before the 1920s the foreman's power over individual workers was almost unrestrained. In most factories he hired and fired, ordered overtime work and set overtime pay. He dictated fines and, in fact, the actual terms of the work contract. Only a few large companies had already divested him of these functions by creating labor and personnel departments before the first world war, in spite of the high interest in 'scientific factory management' and 'scientific personnel administration' at the time. An observer could still comment as late as 1920, 'the foreman is everything to the worker'.[211] His immense authority seems to have continued much longer in the US than in Germany.[212]

The management hierarchy above the foreman appeared impenetrable to most factory workers. This was partly because before 1914 linguistic and ethnic barriers separated many workers from higher supervisory and office personnel, while the foremen and bosses frequently belonged to immigrant ethnic minorities.[213] The lowly but well dressed American clerk in the payroll department was also able to communicate to the worker in overalls a sense of the distance and power he claimed as a 'member of management'. The office was elevated above the factory floor here as well as in Germany, as one foreman's ironic remark to a worker indicates: 'Say, young fellow, you're in the corony pew here. They want bright boys like you over to the head office; you are too good for this. . . But as long as you're here, just grab that barrel and rustle it over the gravel. . .'[214]

White collar advantages included a significantly shorter work day[215] as well as the one or two week paid vacation granted most office employees but hardly any workers before 1914.[216] White collar employees were less apt to be docked for hours lost (for holidays, temporary work shortages, short illnesses) than manual workers.[217] Office workers were seldom paid in piece rates. Longer pay periods and greater security distinguished the average white collar employee in industry from the average blue collar worker, even though job security was not nearly as well developed for white collar positions as it was in Germany.[218]

(b) Earnings and Sex

American-German parallels also appear in the patterns of white collar earnings before the first world war. In both of these societies (though probably not in England), real wages increased from 1890-1913/14: the increase was more rapid in the US and it continued during the last years before the war; it was slower in Germany, especially between 1907 and 1913.[219] In both countries white collar industrial employees as a group earned more than industrial workers. In 1903 the average German salaried employee at Siemens earned about 2.3 times as much as the average Siemens worker. In the same year the average white collar salary in American manufacturing industry was 2.5 times higher than the average industrial wage.[220] In the US, however, and perhaps also in Germany,[221] the average wage-salary differential declined slightly from the end of the 1890s to 1914, whereas before 1890 it had been on the increase (see Table 2.10). During the depression years 1893-96 the differential had risen temporarily, but thereafter the trend was in the other direction.

The shrinking wage-salary differential can be partly explained by the differing effect of economic booms and stagnation on wages and salaries. Salaries were not depressed in short term recessions as wages were, but they also did not climb as high during upswings. Real wages were even more strongly affected, since as a rule the cost of living rose and fell with the business cycle.[222] Thus it was logical for the distance between wages and salaries to decline in the US as well as in Germany in the predominantly good years between 1897 and 1913.

At least as important conditions for this apparently universal leveling process between wages and salaries at advanced stages of industrialization were the increasing division of labor in the office and the mechanization[224] and increase of office work. These changes made it possible to use employees who were less qualified and more easily controlled. In both the US and Germany, a rapidly growing number of poorly paid employees, increasingly women, entered the offices of industrial firms.

As late as the early 1880s, there were almost no women employees in the (usually small) offices of industrial firms. Only when the typewriter conquered the office at the beginning of the decade — with, among other promotional gimmicks, advertisements and demonstrations in which the 'Remington girl', the young receptionist and stenotypist, was used as an allurement — did young women follow the machine. (They were known, in fact, in deprecating fashion as 'typewriters' for a few decades.) Next to the teaching profession, which had been 'feminized' between 1840 and 1860, and sales work, which had very gradually been opened to women after the civil war (see Table 2.3 above), a new occupation above the level of manual work and domestic service emerged which from the beginning was performed by women. At the same time the field of activities in the office expanded and changed from when a few, almost entirely male, stenographers and secretaries (who were now also increasingly being replaced by women) had performed the work. Table 2.11 traces this transformation (though the figures represent office workers in all sectors, not only those in industry).

Table 2.10
Earnings of Blue and White Collar Workers (Yearly Averages) in American Manufacturing, 1890-1926[223]

Year	Nominal Wages (in Current Dollars Per Capita and Year) Blue Collar	White Collar	Quotient 2:1	Cost of Living Index (1914=100)	Real Wages Per Capita & Year Blue Collar in 1914 Dollars	(1929 = 100)	White Collar in 1914 Dollars	(1929 = 100)
	1	2	3	4	5	6	7	8
1890	439	872	1.99	91	481	83	959	72
1891	442	889	2.01	91	486	84	975	74
1892	446	914	2.04	91	490	85	1,005	76
1893	420	954	2.03	90	467	80	1,060	80
1894	386	961	2.49	86	449	77	1,120	84
1895	416	973	2.33	84	495	85	1,160	87
1896	406	987	2.43	84	483	83	1,175	88
1897	408	1,006	2.46	83	492	84	1,210	91
1898	412	1,052	2.55	83	496	85	1,270	95
1899	426	1,046	2.45	83	513	88	1,260	95
1900	435	1,052	2.41	84	518	89	1.250	94
1901	456	1,048	2.29	85	536	92	1,232	93
1902	473	1,061	2.24	86	550	94	1,232	93
1903	486	1,087	2.23	88	552	95	1,232	93
1904	477	1,106	2.32	89	536	92	1,241	93
1905	494	1,121	2.27	88	561	96	1,320	99
1906	506	1,129	2.23	90	562	96	1,251	94
1907	522	1,144	2.19	94	560	96	1,219	92
1908	475	1,162	2.48	92	516	88	1,262	95
1909	518	1,188	2.29	91	569	98	1,305	98
1910	558	1,218	2.18	95	587	101	1,281	96
1911	537	1,277	2.38	95	575	99	1,340	101
1912	550	1,268	2.30	97	567	97	1,306	98
1913	578	1,294	2.23	99	584	100	1,307	98
1914	580	1,323	2.28	100	580	100	1,323	100
1915	568	1,327	2.33	101	562	97	1,312	99
1916	651	1,427	2.19	109	597	103	1,308	99
1917	774	1,552	2.00	128	606	104	1,211	92
1918	980	1,765	1.80	150	653	113	1,173	88
1919	1,158	1,999	1.73	173	669	115	1,152	87
1920	1,358	2,243	1.65	200	680	117	1,120	85
1921	1,180	2,236	1.89	178	662	114	1,255	95
1922	1,149	2,164	1.88	167	687	118	1,299	98
1923	1,254	2,223	1.77	170	737	127	1,310	99
1924	1,240	2,299	1.85	170	730	126	1,350	102
1925	1,280	2,348	1.83	175	731	126	1,341	101
1926	1,309	2,428	1.85	176	743	128	1,380	104

Table 2.11
Number and Sex of Selected Categories of Office Employees, US, 1870-1930[225]

Year	Stenographers and Typists Number	Stenographers and Typists % Female	Bookkeepers, Cashiers, Accountants Number	Bookkeepers, Cashiers, Accountants % Female	Clerks (Except in Stores) Number	Clerks (Except in Stores) % Female
1870	154	4.5	38,776	2.3	29,801	3.1
1880	5,000	40.0	74,919	5.7	59,799	0.5
1890	33,418	63.6	159,374	17.4	187,969	12.9
1900	112,364	76.6	254,880	29.1	248,323	7.4
1910	316,693	83.1	486,700	38.5	720,498	17.0
1920	615,154	91.8	734,688	48.9	1,487,905	31.7
1930	811,190	95.6	930,648	51.9	1,997,000	35.4

Already in 1900 three out of four stenographers and stenotypists were women; by 1920-29 the proportion was nine out of ten. Other office functions such as bookkeeping were much more slowly feminized. Women accounted for only a small minority of low level technical employees: 2% in 1880, 5% in 1900, and 9% in 1930.[226] Their proportion among engineers, superintendents, and managers was even smaller. 90% of female office employees were unmarried around 1910; the great majority were under 25 years old. They included very few immigrant women, but many daughters of immigrants. The great majority had a high school diploma: that was especially true for secretaries, somewhat less often the case among stenotypists and bookkeepers. Perhaps every second or third general office employee or clerk had a diploma. The proportion of female sales clerks who were high school graduates was much smaller. Many women working in offices (perhaps a third or half) had also taken special courses in stenography or typewriting in public school or at one of the private business schools which multiplied after 1881. In 1880 only 10% of business school students had been female; by 1910 women were already 46% of the total. Most office employees had also completed more special training courses than had sales clerks.[227]

Young women also earned more in offices than in stores. In 1902 the average wage of Boston saleswomen was $8, of female bookkeepers and stenographers, $11 a week. In a random sample of 509 Boston female office employees in 1913, 23% earned under $8, 49% between $8 and $12, 19% between $12 and $15, and 9% over $15 a week. Secretaries earned more than bookkeepers or stenotypists; they in turn earned more than simple clerks. Although there were great variations from branch to branch and position to position, office workers in industry appear to have been somewhat better paid than those in commerce, but somewhat worse than those in banks.[228]

It is easy to understand why young women with the necessary qualifications flocked to these positions, which in 1890 — though hardly in 1910 — had a slight tinge of adventure and emancipation. Office work presented one of the few paths for women into a business world which had previously been reserved entirely for men. And office positions offered better working conditions, shorter hours, fewer deductions, more frequent vacations, better sanitary conditions and more status than sales work, let alone jobs in factories or as domestics.[229]

The opportunities for advancement proved quite limited, however. The areas of the office world that had been quickly and thoroughly feminized offered the possibility for small careers: one could advance from clerk to bookkeeper (whose functions had become divisible and routinized) to personal secretary with the right qualifications. Positions with authority and professional prerequisites, however, were restricted to men — who, partly because of the flood of women employees, were spared the tedium of multiplying routine paper work. Thus in spite of the entry of women into previously male positions, segregation by sex at the workplace remained. Typical female and typical male worlds of work emerged; as a rule, they were distinguished by clear gradations of authority, prestige, and earnings. The pay earned by female employees was often insufficient to guarantee an independent existence. In 1912, a government commission established $8 a week as the subsistence level for single women in Boston. One year later, of the 509 female office employees mentioned above, 59% of the clerks, 43% of the stenographers, and 13% of the bookkeepers earned less than $8 a week. In another random sample of 1,200 Boston women in office work, 5% of the stenographers and 26% of the clerks fell below subsistence earnings. Men doing similar work at about this time probably earned about 50% more.[230] Thus one contribution to the reduction of the wage-salary differential was the feminization of large areas of office work.

2. Schools and Jobs

(a) Changes in Industrial and Technical Education: Some American-German Comparisons

The increasing supply of literate applicants for white collar positions which the extension of the educational system, particularly at the secondary level, brought also had a depressing effect on average white collar earnings. In 1870 and 1890 the number of high school graduates made up only 2% and 3.5% respectively of all boys and girls seventeen or younger. By 1910 it was 9%, and by 1920, 17%. In 1930 this percentage was 29, in 1940, 51%. Illiteracy in the general population fell from 20% (1870) to 6% (1920), and among whites from 11.5% to 4% in these years.[231]

After the mid-1890s commercial branches and courses which prepared students for all types of office work appeared in the high school curriculum. These 'practical education' courses had less prestige, sent the fewest graduates to college, and tended to attract students of moderate or lowly origins. In 1913 in Boston, two-thirds of all female high school pupils were enrolled in such institutions.[232] Thus public schools began to compete with private institutions, which had been offering a variety of preparatory courses for office work since the beginning of the second third of the century. At first they had specialized in teaching penmanship, arithmetic, and bookkeeping. Later they expanded their curriculum to include shorthand, typing, the basic principles of commercial law and the practical skills required in office work. A total of 150,000 students were enrolled in some sort of commercial education course in 1893/94: only 10% in public high school and 77% in private commercial schools. In 1909/10 35% of 234,000 commercial students attended public school, 58% private institutions. The relationship between public and private was reversed only after the first world war.[233]

Technical education developed at a later date and more haltingly in the US than commercial education; it developed much later and less systematically than in Germany.[234] In 1869 a petition from New England manufacturers complained that their European competitors enjoyed the advantage of publicly financed trade and technical schools which they did not. 'At this time almost all of our really good draftsmen are men who were trained abroad.'[235] In the following years public elementary and middle level schools began to introduce mechanical drawing into their course of studies. It became part of general manual training courses which were very popular in the US in the 1870s, 1880s, and 1890s.[236]

Outside the public school system there were trade and technical schools, either profit-making or privately subsidized, which often trained both skilled workers and technicians. A few dated back to the early years of the 19th century, but most had originated in the last third. They had no general admission standards, nor did they supply their graduates with academic credits or prerequisites for other institutions.[237] A clear separation of trade or industrial education from technical schooling emerged only gradually, without organization or planning.[238]

For a long time only two American institutions offered theoretical, advanced engineering courses: West Point, for Army officers, after 1812; and the privately founded Rensselaer Polytechnic Institute in Troy, New York, after 1823/24, which sent about 1,000 engineers and architects into the economy between 1826 and 1899.[239] Other technical universities were founded in Cambridge and Worcester, Massachusetts, and in Princeton, New Jersey, only after the middle of the century. Most of those who then called themselves engineers had learned their craft through practice and had no academic training. With the help of legislation such as the Morill Act (1862) and growing demand, engineering schools which required a high school diploma for admission grew rapidly after the 1870s. Most were part of established liberal arts colleges, but there were also separate technical schools like the Stevens Institute of Technology in Hoboken, New York, and the Case School of Applied Science in Cleveland, Ohio. In 1870 seventeen, in 1880 85, in 1896 110, and in 1915 126 institutions at the college level conferred a bachelor's degree or its equivalent in engineering. According to an older computation, fewer than 900 engineers graduated from American schools before 1870, 2,300 in 1871-80, 3,900 in 1881-90, 10,400 in 1891-1900, and 21,000 in 1901-10.[240]

Two differences between the American and the German system of technical education should be stressed. Technical schools developed earlier in Germany than in the US, and at least quantitatively they maintained a lead in the early 20th century, although by then the American side was quickly catching up. A system of government-run industrial and technical schools had started to develop in the German states in the 1820s. In the following decades a minority of these schools underwent a process of 'academization'. They raised the formal entrance requirements and age; they stressed scientific principles, theory and research; they restructured their courses and internal organization in imitation of the universities, which traditionally did not offer engineering training at all. Finally, they became less accessible for the offsprings of lower middle class and working class families who had been the majority among the students of the technical and industrial schools at the start. Some of these upgraded 'technical academies' or 'polytechnical schools' merged with public institutions of higher learning which had trained architects and engineers for the civil service since the late 17th or 18th century. By the 1870s they had acquired the name 'technical universities' (*Technische Hochschulen*). There were eleven of them, and around 1870 they enrolled about 4,000 students (a minority of whom studied architecture). In contrast there were, in 1870, only about 1,400 engineering students in the US, and this figure includes students at institutions which, due to lower entrance requirements, lower entrance age, and less orientation to strictly scientific studies, would probably, on the German side, not have belonged to the technical universities, but to the professional technical schools existing below the university level (whose students are not included in the 1870 figure of 4,000).[241]

German technical universities did not expand further and even shrunk a little in the depression of the 1870s and early 1880s; they then grew again (1902: 13,000 enrolled students), but more slowly than similar institutions in America. In the last decade before the first world war the number of students in German technical universities remained steady, in contrast to growing enrollment in American technical colleges and engineering courses. In early 20th century Germany, students were warned against taking up courses in engineering because of overcrowding. Around 1910 a German association of white collar technicians protested a proposal to extend technical education, arguing that the 'proletariat of technicians' should not be further enlarged.[242]

Exact quantitative comparison is impossible because of institutional non-comparability. According to Wolfle's figures 12,400 engineering degrees (bachelors and first professional degrees) were received in the US between 1901 and 1910. It can be estimated that, in the same period, German technical universities granted an equal number of final engineering degrees (*Diplom*) or even more, even though the US had 76 million, and Germany just 56 million people in 1900. In addition, there were, below the technical universities, about twenty high caliber professional technical schools (*Höhere Maschinenbauschulen, Technische Mittelschulen* — the names varied), some of which resembled American colleges in entrance requirements, age of students, and structure of courses. There seems still to have been a German lead, though it was quickly being reduced.[243]

Secondly, the hierarchical structure of the technical school system was much more clearly developed in Germany than in the US, and there was, in Germany, more of a correspondence between specific levels of schools and specific types of jobs. The industrial and technical schools had been founded in the 1820s to provide practical training for artisans, small businessmen, foremen and technicians. By the 1870s they had changed. Either they had been 'academized', as mentioned before, or they had succumbed to the powerful movement toward general education which carried so much status and prestige in 19th century Germany. They had raised their standards and broadened their curriculum; they tried to prepare their students so that they could later enter institutions of higher learning; they were transformed — or rather they transformed themselves — into a special type of general secondary school. The quest for social prestige and acceptance explains more of these changes than the emerging needs of the industrializing economy. The resulting vacuum on the lower and middle levels of trade and technical education was, in the 1880s and 1890s, filled by two new types of school: First, there emerged the lower trade and industrial schools which accepted students with just elementary schooling and some practical business background; they trained them, within one or two years, for lower salaried positions such as foremen, technicians and the like, or for a career as small self-employed businessmen (*Maschinenbau-* and *Werkmeisterschulen*). Second, middle professional schools (*Höhere Maschinenbauschulen* and *Technische Mittelschulen*) were founded, as mentioned before. As a rule, they accepted only high school graduates with at least ten years previous general education and some practical experience; their courses were advanced, but related to practical problems. In two to three years they were expected to produce the 'connecting link between the university trained engineer, on the one hand, and the foreman on the other', as the Cologne chapter of the Association of German Engineers put it. The uppermost level was provided by the technical universities which usually required the *Abitur* before registration, i.e., twelve or thirteen years of elementary and advanced secondary general education leading to a specific certificate. The large majority of blue collar workers would not be trained in any of these three types of technical school. After eight years elementary school education they would either commence employment or an apprenticeship accompanied by courses in public extension or vocational schools, usually in the evenings or on a special day of the week. This was generally the emerging pattern, but there were many exceptions, regional variations and changes over time.[244]

This system was structured according to bureaucratic models. Different types of courses and schools leading to specific examinations and degrees opening up specific careers — this was the central principle of bureaucratic recruitment as it had developed in Europe since the late 18th century, and as it has been classically analyzed by Max Weber.[245] Civil servants played a major role in developing this stratified system of technical education. Status claims of teachers and students, alumni and engineering associations contributed to its emergence. Demands by employers had an impact, too, but it is very doubtful whether the needs of industry alone would have led to the emergence of such a formalized and stratified system of technical education. At any rate, this system of technical and industrial education corresponded well with the strict bifurcation so typical of European general education until recently, in contrast to the American tradition of comprehensive schools. In this pioneering system of bifurcation an early separation took place between the large majority of children (in late 19th century Germany about 90%) attending elementary school for eight years and then taking up an apprenticeship or just a job, and the minority (10% or so) moving into some type of secondary education which could lead further to rather elitist institutions of higher learning. This separation took place at the age of ten or even earlier, since institutions of secondary education (especially the *Gymnasium*) frequently offered their own preparatory classes even for pupils younger than ten. This decision later proved hard to revise and tended to reflect and reinforce given social inequalities.[245a]

Lacking a comparable bureaucratic structure in the 18th and early 19th century, the US did not develop such a formalized and stratified system of education. Despite all the admiration that American administrators at the end of the 19th century had for the German system of technical and industrial education, they did not usually like its strict stratification and its close fit to the stratified system of jobs and careers. It was argued that democratic values, the postulate of equal opportunity for all, combined with the hope that school would serve as a means of social and political integration for new immigrants, made the European alternative seem not quite appropriate for the US. The idea was that the educational system should provide an avenue of social mobility, not just prepare students to be efficient workers.[246] These ideas had some effect although, of course, unequal distribution of education corresponding to socio-economic class was by no means absent in the US. Private schools for the rich, great local differences in the quality of public schools, and the greater tendency for lower class children to drop out or repeat grades worked in this direction.[246a] On the other hand, German (and English) observers who visited the US just before the first world war, were amazed that hand and head workers (manual and non-manual) were educated together in the US. They expressed their surprise primarily that there were no purely workers' schools, but they also noted the lack of specialized instruction for those who would enter low and middle level technical occupations.[247] Compared to Germany, American industrial and technical schooling was unsystematic, did not clearly demarcate categories of workers, was extensively private not public, and was not integrated into a system of formal qualifications and certification.

It therefore seems likely that the distinction between blue and white collar and between individual categories of white collar employees was less clearly connected in the US than in Germany to differences in education and training. It would follow that schooling did not determine occupation to the same extent in the US as in Germany, and thus that the choice of occupation would frequently be made at a later age. This variation in the function of education may partly explain the higher degree of inter-generational upward mobility from the lower classes into the lower middle and middle classes — e.g., the greater accessibility of white collar positions to the sons of manual laborers — which seems still to have existed in the first decades of the 20th century in the US compared to Germany.[248] It would seem that workers' children could advance to white collar positions more frequently where entry into these occupations was not that clearly predetermined by the need to attend schools which were less accessible to lower class children than to middle and upper class offspring. At the present state of research this is a very plausible and likely hypothesis. Detailed information about the education and careers of comparable samples of American and German white collar workers would be necessary to test it. Unfortunately, these data are not available. In general, we know much more about the 'supply side' of education than about the actual behavior of those responsible for recruitment, dismissals, and promotions.

(b) The Officers of the National Cash Register Company in Dayton, Ohio (1904)

One source that is available is a report on the age, schooling, and career patterns of the 49 top white collar employees of the National Cash Register Company (NCR) in 1904. In comparison to one or two German cases it seems to support the hypothesis, and offers some revealing insights into the connection between education and occupation. The NCR took pride in its progressive personnel policies, sales methods, and management in general. It was one of the few companies which sought to use this progressiveness for public relations profit; the company therefore made public details about its internal structure to an unusual degree.[249]

At the beginning of April 1904, the NCR had 3,357 employees (not counting the personnel of the large foreign sales division). Five hundred and eighty-eight or 17.5% worked in the office; another 93 (3%) were in technical and supervisory positions in the factory. About 160 or 27% of the office employees were women; they worked almost exclusively (157) in the typing division. Thus the other office divisions of this large corporation were staffed almost entirely by men in 1904.[250]

Table 2.12
School Attendance and First Job of the 49 Top Employees of National Cash Register, Dayton, Ohio, 1904[252]

School Attendance	All Top Employees (N = 49)[256]	Top Employees Under 36 Years Old (N = 26)	Top Employees 36 and Older (N = 23)
1. College or University	6	5	1
2. High School Plus Commercial or Other Special School[253]	11	9	2
3. High School	13	3	10
4. Grade School Plus Industrial or Commercial School[254]	8	5	3
5. Grade School[255]	10	3	7
6. Unknown	1	1	
Total	49	26	23
First Job			
Manual Occupation	14[258]	1	13
Non-manual Occupation[257]	35	25	10

Not least to demonstrate the opportunities for advancement at NCR, the company published brief biographies of its 49 top employees, including the executives, heads of divisions, and some foremen and assistant division chiefs. All were men.[251]

In 1904 61% of these top white collar employees had at least attended high school.[259] On the other hand, a good fifth had only an elementary school education. Furthermore, a majority of the top seven — president, vice-president, director of European affairs, general auditor, treasurer, US sales director, director of production — had not gone as far as high school. 39% of the total group had supplemented their public schooling at private commercial (or very rarely at industrial technical) schools. University or college attendance was still the great exception.[260]

The average age of the group was 36.1 years. (The top seven were still younger: 34 years on the average.) 63% of those under 36 years old had attended high school, but so had 56% of the older group. The younger men had a clear lead in attendance at special commercial or evening schools: 53% compared to 22% in the older group. Five of the six with some university education were in the younger group.

Fourteen of the 49 employees surveyed (29%) had begun their

careers as manual workers. They included the seven foremen, who all came from the skilled crafts. They also included the five members of the factory committee (including the chairman), who had risen from skilled worker to foreman to superintendent. One factory committee member, also the head of the drafting department, had made his way up through a detour as draftsman and head of the patent department. The 51 year-old chief of the inventions department had begun as a manual worker. After high school he had been trained as a machinist, had worked as a foreman, and was then self-employed for five years; he held five more jobs as a skilled worker and foreman before starting at NCR as a head foreman and working his way up. The 42 year-old assistant sales director for the US had begun his career as a skilled molder and had been promoted to factory director. He then transferred to become a sales representative for NCR (supplying his own team and wagon) and worked his way up in the sales department. Only one of these upwardly mobile men was younger than the average: a foreman who was 35. The majority (eight) of the fourteen whose first job had been as a manual worker had only a grade school education (some had supplemented it at a special evening or business school). Still, six of the fourteen had also attended high school, at least for a while.

The first jobs of those who had not been workers were frequently cited as office boy, clerk, messenger, bookkeeper, stenographer, draftsman, retail sales, railroad clerk, teacher. Apparently this last group was especially apt to find the time to attend special schools and learn the office skills which would enable them to transfer to a corporate office offering better pay and greater hope of advancement. High school or grade school education did not correlate significantly with first jobs.

Eighteen of the 49 belonged to the technical or production side of the firm: seven foremen, seven members of the collective 'factory committee' which directed production, the director of the mechanical improvements department, assistant patent attorney, director of testing and inspection, as well as the director of the inventions department. Thirteen, or almost three quarters of these eighteen, had risen from manual positions (all of the foremen, five production directors and the director of inventions). Three others had started as non-technical, non-manufacturing employees: the mechanical improvements director as a grocery store clerk, the director of testing and inspection as a low level clerk in the wholesale grocery business, and one of the production directors as an office boy (who then went on to train in a skilled craft). The eighteen technical/production employees differed only slightly in educational background from the others: 50% had only elementary, 50% some high school education. Some had also attended commercial college. None had studied at industrial or technical institutions, with the exception of the two academics: the factory engineer and the patent attorney.

Eight of the 49 managing and top employees had begun their career with NCR, which was 22 years old in 1904. Four of these eight stalwarts belonged to the leadership group of the top seven. The others, especially the older men, had changed jobs four, five, or six times, though only in exceptional cases had they spent any length of time as workers or self-employed. For these higher and managing white collar employees, the status of salaried employee was already a relatively permanent condition.

The following conclusions may be drawn:

First: High school education was already one of the ingredients in an industrial white collar employee's career in a majority of cases, but it was neither a prerequisite nor a general rule. A tendency for high school education to become the norm was not reflected in 1904 in the top 49 or the top seven employees at NCR. Yet by 1904 it had become company policy to hire as office workers only those people who had completed at least two years of high school — this condition expressly did not apply to new factory workers.[261] It seems likely that the percentage of the office staff (including lower and middle levels, and thus many newly hired employees) with some high school education was at least as high as the proportion of the top 49 who had attended high school, if not even higher.[262] One might infer that high school education only became a necessary qualification for white collar careers in industry around the turn of the century. Thus the top employees, who had all worked for NCR for at least five years, were not affected; they had been selected by other criteria. On the other hand, a large minority of the former manual workers among them had attended high school, indicating that in the second half of the 19th century it was by no means a privilege of non-manual workers.

Other sources show that attendance at high school had become a normal prerequisite for the average technical draftsman before 1914, just as college was for the architect.[263] In 1913 a random sample of 1,114 female office employees (primarily stenographers, typists, and general clerks) in various types of office (not only industrial) in Boston found that 36.7% were high school graduates and another 42.4% had attended high school without graduating. (This investigation had partially excluded the upper level of women office workers, the secretaries.) 21.4% of those surveyed had gone only to grade school (or could not be assigned to either group). At the same time another Boston survey revealed that a positive relationship existed between level of education and type of office job.

95.2% of the secretaries, but only 48.9% of the simple clerks surveyed had high school diplomas. Typists and bookkeepers fell in between. Some former college students also appeared among the secretaries. Within the same specialization more education meant a higher starting salary, and more punctual, frequent raises. In this respect — though not in a higher final salary which would be reached after some years — education clearly paid.[264] Contemporary investigations of the career choices of high school pupils found that hardly any of them were working toward a manual occupation. For boys, engineering was the top choice; in New York businessman, lawyer, and teacher followed. In Ohio the list of most favored professions read: engineer, farmer, businessman, lawyer, doctor, salesman, and bookkeeper/stenographer. The great majority of girls wanted to be teachers. Bookkeeper/stenographer was in second place, followed by careers in nursing or some field of music.[265] At the same time that high school — even if only commercial or practical courses — was becoming a prerequisite for non-manual occupations, high school students themselves were ruling out manual occupations. In 1914, more so than in 1890, high school education and a non-manual career tended to belong together.

Second: As the analysis of the 49 NCR employees illustrates, the impact of the spread of commercial schools on industrial white collar workers preceded the tendency to pay more attention to high school education. The trend was clear in the divergent schooling of the older and younger groups in the 1904 survey. Often the employee had attended the special commercial or evening school after working some years as a manual worker, low level office employee or teacher. The expansion of this unaccredited vocational/professional school system thus permitted continuing flexibility in career patterns. A study of female office workers in Boston in 1914 concluded that one or two years at a business or commercial college (after elementary or high school) paid off with better starting salaries and positions.[266]

Third: The officers of NCR had had practically no special technical education in 1904. This fact is particularly striking in a company which to be sure was not involved with as complex technologies as electrical or technical firms, but which did mass produce complicated machinery. College or university education was also the exception. Particularly in technical fields and production, career patterns in American industry seem to have been determined less by preparatory schooling, training, and degrees than in Germany.[267]

Fourth: Despite this less significant correlation between education and career in the US, transfers from manual occupations to higher white collar positions occurred in only a minority of cases even by 1900. The transfers that did occur were in technical fields and production, where in large part the absence of a hierarchically structured, well developed industrial/technical educational system meant that even top managers were still usually recruited from the skilled workforce.

In 1907 a Massachusetts commission concluded that all industries were in need of more competent foremen, factory directors and managers than were then available. Industry needed men who had broad perspective and interests as well as the qualifications necessary to organize and direct a department or a factory division. Those currently in such positions, whether workers, foremen, or directors, had arrived there by chance — they were of necessity 'self-made men'. This situation — which the NCR data corroborate — stood in contrast to the scene in contemporary Germany, where theoretically trained university and technical school engineers had long since begun to replace foremen who had risen from the ranks in management. This generation refers only to the technically advanced and larger firms in Germany — but that category certainly included the NCR in the US.

(c) Increasing Correspondence of Schooling and Careers

On the preceding pages I have argued that in the late 19th century there was less correspondence between schooling and career in the US compared to Germany. There were also some indications that this correspondence became rather closer, in the US too, in the early 20th century. To the extent that such a tendency existed it would seem to fit well into some of the major themes in the early 20th century debate about educational reform.[268]

On the one hand, public attention was increasingly focussed on the functional differentiations within large firms and in the economy in general, and on the educational requirements following from such differentiation. The Massachusetts Commission on Industrial Education of 1911 noted that between the man who works with his hands or runs the machine and the engineer who conceived the task, there were a great many supervisors of varying rank, knowledge, and authority, whose exact number depended on the type of work and the size of the firm.[269] A consensus developed that the existing public school system was not adequately meeting the needs of modern industry. Either it provided a general education of use primarily to the 10-20% of the pupils who aspired to and would be able to enter one of the professions or an independent business career, or — since the extension of public commercial schools — it prepared students for careers in commerce. In both cases, in the name of educational and equal opportunity for all, it had produced too many theoreticians, professionals and clerks, and had in fact ignored the needs of the great majority.[270] The necessary foremen, technicians, superintendents, or draftsmen were not being trained, nor were a sufficient quantity of skilled workers produced. The discussion was particularly heated at this time because immigration — now primarily from industrially less developed areas — no longer supplied the majority of skilled workers. The desire for a more competent labor force and more efficiency lay behind this argument. It was supported particularly by business groups.

On the other hand, there was the social reformers' critique of the general education system, which seemed to offer little to just those poorer, less motivated, immigrant groups who went into the workforce with few qualifications at fourteen or sixteen. Confused, disoriented, in need of immediate earnings, they frequently fell into jobs with little future and became part of a steadily growing proletariat. In this view general education had produced masses of occupationally helpless, unhappy youths, who would have been better off had they been prepared for a narrowly circumscribed, specific occupation.

The desire for more efficiency and the attempt to solve social problems by educational reforms merged, and initiated discussions about the educational system and the world of work.[271] Greater weight was attached to the suggestion that preparation for particular functions and jobs should be as important a task of the educational system as opening up chances for upward mobility and transmitting democratic and general cultural values — in the interest of a well functioning society *and* the greater happiness of many individuals. A system of differentiated schools was advocated which would prepare for differentiated occupational paths and careers. The advocates of the 'life career' principle seemed to win ground. Their views implied a break with more traditional concepts of success, which had attached less value to permanent membership in one or another manual or white collar occupation or to mobility within the same occupation than to a restless climb through many non-permanent career stations until one became an independent businessman, lawyer, or farmer.[272]

On the opposing side, which was growing weaker, stood the defenders of non-instrumental general education and equal education for all, who continued to emphasize the need to assure mobility through education, to hinder the formation of permanent social classes, and to guarantee everyone a free choice of education.

In order to advocate a state supported school system for lower and middle level white collar employees, it was necessary to clearly distinguish between technical education for white collar positions and industrial education for blue collar occupations.[273] Various public committees and the NAM referred to the German system as a model in making these distinctions.[274] It was also necessary to reflect on what criteria would be used to steer pupils into these diverse schools or curricula. If I am correct, this was the first occasion for serious public discussion in the US about the distinction between manual workers and white collar employees, between the 'abstract-minded class' and 'hand-minded class', or between 'mechanical pursuits' and 'white collar jobs'.[275] The concept 'white collars' first appeared at this time (1903) as a new, somewhat disrespectful collective term for various occupations which had only previously, if at all, been combined in the abstract categories of statisticians (such as 'salaried employees'). The term 'white collar' was probably first applied to technical draftsmen, that is, to employees who in background and workplace stood close to factory workers but were at the same time beginning to separate themselves from them.[276] At the same time the voices multiplied that argued that certain categories of people were more suited to certain categories of jobs, and that it was the task of education to channel pupils into their proper category. Schools should provide counseling and guidance, then prepare students for their future place in life.[277] Even before the world war, in isolated cases psychological tests were given students to distinguish the 'mind-workers' from the 'handworkers'.[278] Beginning in 1907 some Boston elementary schools introduced special industrial arts classes for 7th and 8th grade boys and girls who were thought to be inclined toward handwork. Few were surprised that it was primarily the worst students, often children from poorer immigrant families, who were placed in these classes.[279] Thus a new tendency appeared (at first in hazy outline only) to extend differences between social-economic classes, strata, and opportunities back into the realm of education. This use of the educational system — which had long stamped German society — threatened in the long run to sharpen and reinforce the social-economic differences which it at first reflected.

The increasing adaptation of the public school system to the differentiated needs of the private economy was most visible in the multiplication of industrial, technical, and extension schools. In particular the National Society for the Promotion of Industrial Education, founded in 1906 with close ties to industrial interests, and other reform organizations worked to increase their number and achieve state financing for these schools. Pointing to German competition, the representatives of small and medium sized firms that could not afford their own training programs were most vocal in recommending that the US borrow key elements of the German system, including a purely industrial education for future workers and public financing. They did not wish, however, to borrow the strict state controls which were also the norm in Germany.[280]

Increasing coordination and synchronization of the public school system and the economy was also evident in the further expansion of commercial high schools and, after the turn of the century, commercial colleges.[281] Industrial and technical subjects, with a characteristic lag vis-à-vis commercial, also gradually entered the general education curriculum between the turn of the century and the first world war. Four-year technical high schools were created which taught industrial and technical skills. In fact, they primarily prepared students for engineering colleges and universities or for technical and middle management positions in industrial firms. Thus shortly before the first world war, institutions began to emerge in the US (at least in industrial areas) to train middle level technical and supervisory white collar employees who had previously come almost exclusively from the workshop.[282]

There was a further expansion of industrial education with the creation of vocational junior high schools. They segregated part of the pupils in the last classes of grade school and thus strengthened the tendency to differentiate students at an earlier age according to their future occupation.[283] In Boston a rapidly growing vocational guidance movement sprang up in 1908/09 and contributed to bringing the question of the relationship between education and occupation before an interested public.[284] The debate over education sharpened the awareness of the distinction between blue and white collar on both sides of the collar line and in the general public.

But these were only halting tendencies. Certainly, high school became more important as a prerequisite for non-manual occupations; the decision over entry into non-manual or manual work was tending to shift from the stage of application and hiring back to the stage of schooling and testing. With this shift the child's social and economic milieu undoubtedly became a more important determinant of the future adult's; the sons of working class families were less likely to enter high school than those with a middle class background.[285] But the quickly expanding high school system was not inaccessible for the offspring of manual workers' families, especially not for daughters of skilled workers.[286] In addition, it was not completely impossible to make good after missing a high school education because of a lower class early family background. Private special and extension schools (including a well developed correspondence school system) continued to educate blue and white collar workers together.[287] Night school education continued to develop, though its quality and achievements were sometimes disputed.[288]

In reaction to the inadequate public schools, companies had begun to found their own education and training programs as early as the 1870s. These private programs grew quickly after 1905; between 1910 and 1920 many large corporations supported some sort of company extension school. Although previous education did influence chances to enter and succeed in these private programs, they nonetheless created further channels for advancement which an ambitious, hardworking manual worker could use to enter white collar positions even if he had not begun work with the necessary schooling. A corollary of these company programs' greater degree of unbureaucratic flexibility, however, was a greater degree of managerial discretion: loyal, adaptable workers were usually admitted to these programs, and they were taught not only functional skills and knowledge but also company loyalty.[289]

Finally, many firms did not yet care much about formal educational background when they hired, promoted and paid their employees. While corporations like NCR and GE were increasingly apt to require high school education of their white collar workers, smaller firms in less highly rationalized industrial branches did not begin this practice till much later. Garment factories and mercantile firms in New York in 1914, for instance, paid no attention to high school qualifications at all when determining the pay of their employees.[290] And even in large firms educational background was only one among several factors determining success.

As a general rule, industrial firms rely less on formal, scholastic qualifications in hiring and promotion than state bureaucracies. If this was true for a highly bureaucratic firm like Siemens, it was even more true of American corporations. It is difficult to form a definitive conclusion from the materials available on the business history of this era, but they seem to indicate that at least before 1914, bureaucratic, scholastic promotion procedures were fairly undeveloped in American firms. Getting ahead in large corporations was a more 'political' process than in Germany (at least, more openly so): pull, personal power and rewards, friendship, personality, achievements and favors often played a much greater role than seniority and education.[291]

To sum up: in the decades before the first world war, the acceptance of lifetime careers undoubtedly increased in the US. Orderly promotion according to seniority and education became more of a norm; distinct career paths, principles of efficiency and functional justification in personnel management, and rational training and selection instead of the traditional individualistic methods became more common.[292] Such changes marked a tendency toward rigidity and consolidation in education and economic life. The distinction between blue and white collar became more pronounced. Entry paths to some white collar groups altered: the ways and means of advancing from manual worker to salaried employee were gradually transformed. Barriers erected before the youth entered the world of work became more important. It appears highly probable that within industry transfers from blue to white collar status, from the factory to the office, declined — at least in proportion to the number of white collar positions. It also seems likely that career mobility diminished at this crucial place in the social pyramid.[293]

These developments were all part of the transition from the decentralized, market-oriented capitalism of the 25 years which followed the civil war to a more organized phase of industrial capitalism. One aspect of this shift was that traditional self-regulating mechanisms in economy and society which had allowed greater leeway for individual competition were *partly* being replaced by newer, more organized and planned, collective mechanisms. These changes coalesced in that era of American history which has fittingly been called a 'search for order'.[294] But the limits of that search, and the particular difficulties it encountered in this new land without strong bureaucratic and corporatist traditions of order, must be kept in mind. So also must its late start in comparison, for instance, with Germany. A trend toward fixed careers, the synchronization and categorization of education and work, and a clearer crystallization of stratification patterns characterized the US before the first world war, but it remained rather limited.

3. The Indistinctness and Relative Insignificance of the Collar Line in Industry

(a) Technicians, Engineers, and Mechanics

The less significant role of the US educational system in channeling and stratifying the labor force was one factor that diminished the distinction between blue and white collar workers in American industry in the late 19th and early 20th centuries compared to Germany. Draftsmen and technicians are a case in point. In technically advanced German firms they belonged to the salaried personnel. They enjoyed privileges which elevated them above the workers; they worked in drafting rooms that were separated from the workshop. Although for a long time they were recruited from the skilled workforce and then given supplementary training, by the end of the 19th century they came increasingly from special technical schools. Already in the 1880s they had organized as technicians and thus demarcated themselves from the workers.[295] The situation in America was different. At least until the turn of the century, census takers vacillated on whether draftsmen and foremen should be counted as 'salaried persons' or 'wage earners'.[296]

The Draftsman, a newspaper founded in 1902 in Cleveland, stressed the transitional character of this position and the frequently unclear line of division between draftsmen and workshop mechanics. The paper complained that whereas in other countries mechanical drawing was considered an occupation in its own right and draftsmen practiced a respected profession through their entire lives, in the US the situation was different. Businessmen were only beginning to pay more attention to construction and drafting. To many business owners the draftsman remained an expensive luxury. Particularly in small and medium sized firms, most mechanical drawing was done by workshop practitioners, toolmakers or mechanics who had taught themselves the fundamentals of drafting from a handbook in their free time. Aside from practical experience in the workshop, entrance prerequisites were extremely modest. It was almost enough to be able to draw a straight line. The paper complained that the technical draftsman was still an unknown man to public opinion.[297] The typical representative of this occupation was a very young man, usually paid by the week, who was frequently laid off if work or contract conditions changed. He traveled often, never spending many years in one place, and was sometimes compared to a vagabond. 'A sort of free masonry brotherhood exists between them'. 'It is a puzzle what happens to draftsmen when they get old. Perhaps they don't live long. At any rate, draftsmen that are past middle age [and that meant 30] are rare'.[298] If young mechanics nonetheless worked to become draftsmen, that was primarily because they hoped that the drawing board would be a springboard to a better position as a factory superintendent, engineer, manager or independent businessman.[299]

This portrait of the technical draftsman at the turn of the century is undoubtedly exaggerated and incomplete. In American industry in the 1890s there were also well developed drafting and construction offices, which could not be shut down in slow times. Railroads and electrical firms led the way in this development.[300] Not all employees in drafting and construction were former skilled workers from the factory. Most graduates of engineering school spent some time at the beginning of their career in industry in the drawing room.[301] A minority also remained in such jobs. It is not possible to prove or disprove *The Draftsman*'s portrait's representativeness. But since the paper was trying to find an audience among mechanical draftsmen, it could not have presented too distorted a picture.

The autobiography of a draftsman born in Hungary in about 1870, and who had come to the US in the 1890s, appears to support *The Draftsman*'s views. Anton Bem traveled on foot from city to city in the midwest and south seeking out local architects to ask for work. Sometimes he was lucky (if a church or many houses were about to be built); usually he was paid by the day and he was seldom able to stay longer than one year (frequently only a few weeks) in one place, even though he was very eager to find a permanent job. This Hungarian-American did not earn enough to send for his wife and child, spent most of his time traveling and living in cheap hotels searching for work, and had no property. Occasionally he was reduced to washing clothes and other menial jobs to survive. 'In my humble opinion, lucky are those who can have work'. Nonetheless, he regarded his unsteady, proletarianized existence as better than he might have expected in his homeland![302]

Again, we cannot tell how typical this case was. There were, at any rate, many immigrants among the technical draftsmen and technicians in 1890; they were overrepresented in these categories compared to the proportion of immigrants in the entire labor force (see Table 2.4 above). Both sources emphasize the instability of this career, its transitional character and lack of security, the indistinct contours of the occupational group, its proximity to factory and workplace. All these characteristics would markedly distinguish the American from the typical turn of the century German 'technical-industrial bureaucrat'.[303]

A similar point can be made with respect to the engineers. The process of differentiating mechanics and manual workers, on the one hand, from engineers, on the other, had occurred in Germany in the second third of the 19th century. Decisively aided by the development of technical schools and universities, German engineers organized as an occupational group distinctly separate from skilled workers and simple technicians. There were strong influences from the civil service and the military where engineers had long played an important role. The engineers' common theoretical, technical-scientific education served both to demarcate them from other groups and to create a basis for internal unity that transcended increasing internal specialization. Their most powerful professional association, the Verein deutscher Ingenieure (VDI), was founded in 1856 by graduates of the Berlin Technical Institute: here the connection between advanced technical education and the emergence of engineers as an occupational group was indeed a straight line.[304]

A common technical-scientific education seems to have played a lesser role in the emergence of the American engineering profession which, correspondingly, was more fragmented than its German counterpart. Although the American Society of Civil Engineers, founded in 1852 (active after 1867), claimed for a long time to represent all specializations, mechanical engineers, mining engineers, and electrical engineers all organized their own associations, stressing their functional specialization. None of these organizations — not the elitist American Society of Civil Engineers, nor the practical American Institute of Mining Engineers (1871) nor the American Society of Mechanical Engineers (1880), not even the most professional and scientifically-oriented American Institute of Electrical Engineers (1884) — made definite educational prerequisites a criterion for membership as did the German VDI. Their vague membership requirements focussed instead on the applicant's having performed the tasks of an engineer (without defining these more specifically) within that particular field for a given number of years — and in the case of civil and electrical engineers, on mastering certain definite skills. Even after the turn of the century, many mechanical and mining engineers in particular considered their practical training at the workplace more important than technical-theoretical education.[305] Just as the American sales clerks lacked a common mercantile corporatist education and consequent sense of community comparable to their German counterparts, a common scientific-technical educational background played little role in shaping the engineers' sense of group identity. Attempts to found an overarching organization that would join all specializations failed in the US.[306]

Another consequence of the delayed development of a clearly differentiated technical and technical-scientific school system, as well as of the lesser role education played in the emergence of engineering as a profession in the US, was the lack of a sharp line of division between engineers and mechanics or machinists in the 19th and early 20th centuries. In 1895, according to the president of the Society of Civil Engineers, anyone who was able to understand and take care of a machine could be called a mechanical engineer.[307] Into the 20th century, at work and in their organizations, the lines between mechanics, machinists, technicians, draftsmen, and the various categories of engineers remained relatively indistinct. The emergence of stronger professional aspirations among engineers in the last decades of the 19th century led to repeated complaints about the lack of protection of the title of engineer in the US compared to Europe.[308] A sharp distinction between the skilled worker, whose technical qualifications were acquired through practice, and the theoretically educated professional, between the mechanic and the engineer, emerged only gradually in the US. Even today the

English term 'engineer' is broader than the German *Ingenieur*, and less likely to exclude machinists and mechanics.

In other respects also the boundary line between white and blue collar appeared less clear in American industry than in German. At Siemens & Halske in Berlin, the difference between wages and salaries, between workers and 'private bureaucrats' (*Privatbeamte*) was recorded with the introduction of systematic cost accounting which kept separate lists of wage workers and salaried employees. This distinction was strictly maintained within the firm.[309] In contrast, the Waltham Watch Company mixed factory workers and office employees on the same payroll lists in the 1870s and 1880s; furthermore, it calculated the pay of many office employees in daily wages. Only office supervisors and managers were recorded on separate lists. In 1906/07 the payroll listed between 150 and 200 employees under the heading 'office': it seems that only seventeen of them received a real monthly salary. The others were paid weekly on the basis of daily or hourly earnings.[310] At about the same time an agricultural machinery firm in Chicago listed at least some of their technical draftsmen with factory hands on their wages payroll instead of on their salary list.[311]

Thus, as the absence of a clear definition of salary and wages has already suggested,[312] distinctions between those who received salaries and those who received wages were not firmly fixed; they were certainly less exact categories than was the case in Germany. Furthermore, legislation was more apt to confuse than clarify the issue.[313] In view of the close, consequential connection in German economic and social history between the distinction between wages and salaries, on one side, and between manual workers and salaried employees, on the other, this contrast supports the argument that both objectively and subjectively the distinction between blue and white collar was less distinct in American industry.

(b) Personnel Policies and Managerial Ideologies

What role did the differentiation of white and blue collar workers play in company welfare policies and in the personnel administration of large firms? American industry had begun in the 1890s to follow the lead of several pioneering corporations in developing new techniques of personnel management to integrate their employees into the company. On the one hand, they were responding to social tensions and conflicts. Industry found itself contending with the rapid growth of an organized labor movement (albeit predominantly non-radical). The problems of industrial cities aroused intense public scrutiny and concern, as masses of poor, strange immigrants pushed into the inner cities. There was a growing sense of disorientation and change in all areas of life. All these conditions provoked not only the traditional repressive defenses — bloody defeat of strikes, persecution of moderate trade union activities through the courts, terror hunts for alleged anarchists, militant campaigns by employers' associations like the NAM to defend the open shop — but also the beginnings of a conservative, stabilizing, reform effort. A loose coalition of flexible, 'enlightened' managers and bankers, reform-minded social workers, and trade union leaders committed to compromise with capital worked to initiate reforms within the great corporations that paralleled some of the aims of the Progressive movement in society at large.[314]

The chief focus of this corporate reform movement was on company welfare policies, which were rare before 1890. Companies introduced medical, hygienic, and physical improvements; restaurants and canteens; social clubs, sports facilities, company newspapers, sometimes even vacations; libraries; bonuses; classes and educational programs; accident, health and life insurance as well as pension plans; and in rare cases even workers' committees in order to combat trade unionism and increase the workers' loyalty to and dependence on the company. These efforts were also intended to contribute to the solution of the general social crisis and to uplift the lower classes; in short, they were intended to create happier and more efficient workers.[315]

On the other hand, this so-called welfare capitalism represented an attempt to find answers to a second set of challenges that faced big business after the 1890s, which had also motivated business support for industrial and technical education. The demand of more stable and complex enterprises for a well integrated and well qualified workforce was not being met by the changing character of the labor supply which the waves of new immigrants provided. After the turn of the century increasingly cost and efficiency conscious industrial managers began to discover and quantify the 'waste' that was implicit in the traditional view of labor as a supply and demand commodity under the conditions of more complex organizations and technologies. About a decade after the welfare capitalism movement began, a highly publicized personnel management movement began to discuss (and some advanced corporations began introducing) programs to reduce high labor turnover, and for training and education, systematic, scientific, and sophisticated employment techniques, the emergence of personnel administration and the new 'profession' of the personnel manager, orderly promotion schemes, and similar concerns. The discovery of the 'human factor' in industrial and business success required that traditional instruments of motivation and discipline (threatening to fire workers, fines and rewards) be supplemented with new, indirect means which were aimed at integrating the whole person into the organization.[316]

This alliance of the welfare capitalism and systematic personnel management movements merged efforts to achieve social reform and to maximize the productivity of industrial firms; it linked the desire for greater social justice with the search for more efficient organization. In the minds of these progressive-conservative reformers, whose ultimate conviction was that social conflict could be resolved through incremental change and compromise and who had little use for a class-conflict model of society, there was no contradiction in these paired objectives — quite the contrary.[317] Furthermore, the costs of welfare capitalism and new personnel policies could be more easily absorbed in this prosperous economic era than in the early 1890s or later in the 1930s.

Big business welfare policies experienced a great renaissance in the late 1890s in Germany also — by no means only under the antiquated, conservative, partriarchal banner of a Krupp or Stumm, but also, at Siemens and Bosch, for instance, with liberal elements such as workers' committees. Large scale German employers also created personnel departments and company schools; they had curtailed the arbitrary power of the foreman even before their American counterparts. They too sought to stabilize their workforce. But these modern methods of integration and rationalization were strongly stamped by the habit of thinking of classes, strata, hierarchies and privileges. Thus distinctions between salaried employees and manual workers, and the consciously privileged treatment of the former over the latter in these new company welfare programs and personnel policies, became important ingredients in the labor integration efforts of German management.[318]

By contrast, except for differential treatment in matters like vacations and cafeterias,[319] the distinction between blue and white collar workers as such hardly played a role in distributing the benefits of welfare capitalism and applying these new policies in American firms before the first world war. Almost all pension plans, for instance, covered both categories of employees. Contributions and payments were usually graded by earnings, age, and length of employment of the employee, without distinguishing between manual and non-manual workers. Only top management was treated separately and usually excluded from such plans.[320] Company accident, health and life insurance plans often did not differentiate the rights and duties of members; if they did, it was by criteria such as earnings and length of employment. Sometimes, particularly for accident insurance, they used the degree of risk of each occupation. Blue and white collar workers were almost never distinguished as such.[321] The perusal of a great number of welfare plans and descriptions, of discussions about correct personnel administration practices and the policies actually implemented, conveys a clear picture that the collar line was extremely peripheral and insignificant in American personnel policies.[322]

Of course, many individual personnel policies affected office employees and factory hands differently. The tennis courts and golf course of one firm were primarily used by better off white collar workers, apparently because the expense of outfitting themselves tended to exclude most workers, but perhaps also because of unspoken status distinctions. The social evenings and excursions of another firm were open to all employees,[323] but that certainly did not mean that all groups made equal use of them. If anti-union motives were uppermost in the firm's intentions, for instance in the creation of workers' committees or company unions, it was logical that factory workers would be the chief target. White collar workers, whose loyalty seemed fairly secure, were ignored in such cases, though coincidentally rather than deliberately. There was no effort to formulate a special policy for white collar employees, let alone to treat them preferentially. Before the 1930s American industry did not establish parallel committees to represent white and blue collar workers, as many German firms did even before the first world war, and all were required by law to in 1916. Office employees were included in the committees set up for the general workforce or they were ignored.[324]

Profit sharing and stock options were usually granted only to particular categories of personnel, with the top level white collar employees usually though not always receiving preference.[325] As has already been mentioned, many office employees enjoyed somewhat greater protection against arbitrary dismissal than most workers. Neither law nor company regulations, however, mandated different periods of notice for blue and white collar workers in the US (as they did in Germany). Indeed, in order to avoid misunderstanding, the management of the Ford Motor Company informed all office workers in the recession at the end of the war that regardless whether they were paid in salary or daily wage, they were employed for an indeterminate period of time and their employment could be terminated by the company without prior notice. Ford's erratic personnel policies may be considered atypical. But at another firm in 1908, a twenty-year employee could be dismissed on the spot without cause. The half-month's salary allowed the man was actually viewed as a token of the company's gratitude and generosity.[326] Thus on the issue of job security, American industry also failed to recognize a distinction based on the collar line comparable to Germany.

As a general rule, American firms did not elevate the mass of white collar employees above blue collar workers. Special treatment (profit sharing, exclusion from ordinary company welfare programs, etc.) was only accorded an imprecisely defined group of top managers, executives or officers. Merely holding a non-manual, 'mental' position, office work in and of itself, did not justify special privileges. Instead, it was the greater authority, decision-making responsibility, and achievements (perhaps also qualifications) of top management which legitimated their privileges. This distinction was mirrored in internal company communications. While the German company director addressed himself around 1910 to his *Arbeiter und Angestellten* (workers and salaried employees), or the synonymous *Arbeiter und Beamte* (workers and bureaucrats), his American counterpart spoke to his 'employees', or to the 'officers and employees', or 'management and employees'. The boundary line in the US cut through the white collar group, elevating a small minority and casting the great mass in with the general workforce. We will again encounter this principle of classification, so different from the rule in Germany, in other areas of life.

Other lines of division ran vertically, separating categories of employees by functional criteria. The NCR, for example, did not publish separate company newspapers for white and blue collar workers, but rather for the 'sales pyramid', the 'office pyramid', and the 'making pyramid'. Significantly, the last jointly addressed factory workers, white collar employees in technical fields, and production management. After about 1900 many companies encouraged organizations of employees for health, social, artistic and educational purposes. Such groups very rarely organized along the collar line. Next to clubs for top management (the 'Officers' Club'), function was the basis for group formation: foremen's or salesmen's clubs, the 'Janitors Glee Club', the graduates of a company training program, technical graduates, or the particularly successful skilled workers, foremen, and white collar staff who might be coopted into the 'Advance Club'.[327] Thus in these relatively informal but nonetheless company-run clubs, the dividing line between blue and white collar was quite blurred.

The model of the government bureaucrat played a major role in shaping the sense of identity of salaried employees in German industry; it was a source of expectations and claims, and then of protest when these were disappointed. These salaried employees often thought of themselves as private bureaucrats, that is, as members of a class or layer which cut across and united diverse occupations (technicians, salespeople, bookkeepers, etc.) on the basis of a common status. It demarcated them from the workers 'below' and company management 'above'. In their search for additional means to integrate their employees and for anti-union, anti-socialist measures, German employers found it profitable to accede at least in part to these white collar expectations. Management continued to respect some of their claims to separate treatment for social and political, if not for strictly economic reasons.

Materials from American firms before the first world war contain no hint of a corresponding sense of identity among industrial white collar employees or of comparable personnel policies. Without parallel bureaucratic traditions and models, white collar workers in American industry were apparently much less inclined to see themselves as members of an intermediate layer or class cutting across occupational and functional differences with claims to special treatment and privileges over the mass of manual workers. Even the terminology of German private bureaucrats and employers posited a three-step hierarchical model that accorded salaried employees (like state officials) a special intermediate status; this model also shaped part of the reality of the German firms. In the US, white collar groups conceived of themselves primarily as electrical engineers, salesmen, foremen, etc.; they did not identify themselves as white collar workers per se on the basis of their common quasi-bureaucratic status. Management seldom clothed propaganda in this kind of hierarchical image. More typical was John D Rockefeller, Jr.'s speech to representatives of the workforce and the officers of the Colorado Fuel and Iron Company in 1915 when, after a period of bloody labor conflict, he had decided to create a company union. Every concern, he said, consisted of (1) the stockholders, (2) the directors, (3) the officers, and (4) the employees. These four parties had identical interests. He used a small square table to illustrate his concept of the firm: it would not be complete without all four sides. Each side was necessary and distinct, each had its own role to play. Yet all four were in perfect harmony, each supported by the leg on its side to make an even, level table. In just this way the four parties united in a business concern carried equal responsibility.[328]

Two points about this analogy deserve comment. First, such rhetoric utilized strictly functional, quasi-technocratic categories. By contrast, a hierarchical three-step construct postulated a mediating function for the middle level which also participated in exercising authority: the model thus assumed the existence of authority and conflict. Rockefeller's functional, technocratic analogy, however, negated all authority and conflict. Second, in the absence of a hierarchical model with its implications of authority and bureaucracy, the preconception of an industrial middle class becomes difficult. Thus Rockefeller's analogy did not distinguish between white collar employees and blue collar workers, but instead elevated management above the entire workforce on the basis of function. We will return to the divergent images of society underlying these varying stratification models.

IV. THE RETARDED FORMATION OF A CLASS: WHITE COLLAR WORKERS IN THE AMERICAN SOCIAL STRUCTURE

It has been argued in the preceding chapter that the distinction between blue and white collar workers, which is anchored in the work process and appears in all developed industrial societies, receives its varying sharpness, form, and significance in different societies primarily from social factors that are outside the firm. The question can also be turned around to inquire whether and in what way the difference between blue and white collar which stems primarily from their situation at work stamps their lives away from work: to what extent does this differentiation in the economic sphere spill over into other social realms? Even on the level of the firm it has proved difficult to investigate white collar workers because they were more apt to group themselves and be grouped as foremen, salesmen, or mechanical engineers than as white collar workers per se.The traces they have left reflect above all the fragmentation and indistinctness of the white collar category in the US. It is even more difficult to find sources that portray white collar workers as such outside the firm.

1. The Social Meaning of the Collar Line

(a) A White Collar Worker in Boston

In 1911 a Massachusetts construction contractor, who had been a middle level white collar employee in a Boston industrial firm until his late 30s, published his autobiography. The book was also intended to give advice to the many urban, dependent middle class Americans confronting the economic difficulties and social pressures he had faced. In *One Way Out: A Middle Class New Englander Emigrates to America*, the author (writing under the pseudonym Carleton) tried to portray the typical features of white collar middle class life in New England. His values — probably unrepresentative — were clearly shaped by his own return to manual labor, which he strongly advised, and his subsequent success in independent business.[329]

Carleton's father lost his lumber business in the civil war. Like many Americans even after the turn of the century, he considered charity degrading, so he refused to accept a government pension.[330]

Instead, he became an office worker — the 'head clerk' of an old established lumber company. After his mother died, Carleton's father sold the house they had owned — as was typical for their circle — and 'we boarded'. Frugality enabled the boy to get a high school education. In the mid-1880s eighteen-year-old William, through a friend already working there, got a job in the office division of the 'United Woollen Company' in Boston. His duties consisted of general office work (never precisely described) which required no special preparation or training. His work did not mean too much to him. He was apparently unaware of or uninterested in the situation and structure of the company as a whole, or the connection between his own work and that of other divisions. At any rate he did not mention them. He did report that the work was not hard, the hours were short, and his associates pleasant. After a while he felt a certain pride at being part of this great concern. Like other old Boston firms, his company did not hire immigrants. In six years he received four raises, from $5 to $20 a week, without a corresponding change in his responsibilities — 'apparently automatically'.

All office workers hired together advanced together. They also spent much of their free time together, and raised their standard of living at the same time. Unconsciously, every raise meant that they wore better clothes, lived in better houses, ate in better restaurants, smoked better tobacco and went out more often. It seemed unlikely to Carleton that he would be able to rise above the level of $2,000 a year. Level of earnings was apparently the decisive criterion for which employees socialized together, and where.

When their salaries reached $25 a week, the group joined a small country club. There Carleton met his future wife, a farmer's daughter. When he married at 26, in the late 1890s, he successfully petitioned the company for another raise. He rented a house, since it would not be like being married to continue boarding — as far as he knew, no one in his family had boarded once they married. His one-story house in the suburbs — eight rooms, a small porch and yard — cost $40 a month, or about one-third of the family's income. They furnished the house for about $1,000 on the installment plan.[331]

Now Carleton belonged to the suburban half — that is, the better off half of the population of Greater Boston which had begun to move out of the inner city long before 1900. Factories and workshops, stores and banks, administrative offices and the large businesses remained and continued to draw suburban patrons. The city's residential areas, however, declined in conveniences, comforts, appearance, security and prestige. Only the less well off lower and lower middle classes, including many immigrants, continued to live in them — and it was usually their goal also to move out to the suburbs as soon as possible. The boundary between these two clearly marked halves was permeable. There were subtle ethnic barriers, but they did not prevent the move to the suburbs if — and that was decisive — one could afford it. This focus on moving out and up had definite consequences for individuals and for society as a whole. The individual's efforts to reach the suburbs — which many were doing every day — and thus as a practical matter to rise into middle class America, meant that there was little impetus for collective action to halt the decline of the inner city. In similar fashion the backwardness of the US in social legislation went hand in hand with emphasis on the individual's ability to raise himself out of the lower class; there was little effort to ameliorate the conditions of the poor through collective, legislative action. So much the worse for individuals and groups which, for whatever reason, could not avail themselves of the opportunities to advance the country offered, but which nonetheless felt the full force of the costs which were indivisibly linked with opportunity.[332]

As residents of West Roxbury or Dorchester,[333] The Carletons ranked as middle class. They lived exclusively on the husband's earnings in a relatively crime free, healthy neighborhood. His position and source of income appeared secure; the later construction or purchase of a house probable, and hopes for advancement not unreasonable. Carleton left the house at 6.30 a.m. and probably took the streetcar into the city. He took his lunch to work. He left the office for home at 5 p.m., unless his work required him to stay later. Almost all of his neighbors were middle level white collar employees at banks, industrial firms, or the telegraph company. All had about the same income and lived in the same sort of house. It was usually the behavior or clothes of the wives rather than the husbands that revealed who made more than $2,000 a year. The families enjoyed a lively social life. There were neighborhood clubs, sewing circles, and whist parties. They took turns hosting dinners and dancing parties; these had to come up to neighborhood standards and were expensive. Most of his neighbors followed the market and talked about how they might make a quick fortune if they could only get their hands on a few thousand dollars capital. All expected promotions, and looked towards the 'job ahead'.

When the Carleton's son was born, they hired a maid for $4 a week. Prices were rising quickly (it was around 1900), and they began to budget. They gave up going to the theater and concerts. His wife began to make her own clothes, but then had to suffer her neighbor's raised eyebrows. The pressure to maintain their conspicuous consumption and to participate in the 'social business' was enormous in this neighborhood of middle level white collar workers. For the Carletons, it conflicted increasingly with what was financially possible, and with the birth of their second child they had to stop. Then their school-age boy had to be sent to an expensive prep school. Soon he wanted to join the tennis club and go to dancing school with his friends. It was scant comfort to discover, as the Carletons did the more they knew about their neighborhood, that all were engaged in the same bitter struggle. Carleton quit smoking and wore his clothes longer. The servant girl had to be given up.

Then office methods and procedures began to change. Carleton felt lucky to be able to hold onto his job. Mechanical adding machines had replaced a dozen men; a dozen more were rendered superfluous by a new bookkeeping system. In a bad year for woollens two or three more departed, including the friend who had helped Carleton get his job. Since the man was unmarried, he left Boston for 'somewhere in the west'. When business picked up again, he was replaced by a younger man, who could do the same work for a few hundred dollars less pay.

One day Carleton was called in by his supervisor. He was informed that his salary would be cut by $500, since his former assistant was ready and willing to take over more of Carleton's work for less money. Carleton's protest was interpreted as giving notice, and an hour later he stood out on the sidewalk, with a draft for a half-month's salary in advance. He was 38 and had worked for the company for twenty years. He had no special skills: he was not a bookkeeper, stenographer, or otherwise specialized office worker. In the telephone book he was listed as a clerk. His neighbors and friends knew him as a 'United Woollen man'.

After Carleton had looked for work for two months without success — without a usable specialization he was an old man at 38! — the family was in desperate circumstances, which they could not show without endangering their social position. For the same reason he could not take a job doing unskilled labor.[334]

Finally, he decided to 'emigrate'. He sold their furniture, said goodbye to the neighbors without saying where they were going, and moved his family to 'Little Italy' — a crowded immigrant district of Boston near the harbor — and became a construction worker. Although his former office was within walking distance, this part of Boston was as foreign to Carleton as Europe. The family's life style changed: they lived in a large tenement and shopped in the cheapest stores; before they had had their groceries delivered. Carleton went to night school and learned the basics of the construction business. His son attended public school and sold newspapers in his free time. The Carletons' story then becomes an epic of American success — the family is full of pioneer spirit, and the author romanticizes manual labor, the rough self-made man, and the opportunities for immigrants. He became a supervisor, and after three years an independent construction contractor. Carleton declined to return to the suburbs, however, so the family moved into a deserted farm house outside the city. The oldest son went to college and they were able to afford another child.[335]

It is not necessary to give too much credence to the message of this unusual adviser on upward mobility[336] to accept his story as evidence for the great distance between an orderly white collar office worker's life and the existence of most manual workers, especially the new immigrants. Carleton's account painted the rigid divisions in Greater Boston, with about one million inhabitants around 1900; it confirms that it was at any rate not unusual for industrial white collar workers to belong to the increasingly suburban, heterogeneous middle class. The role that status — determined by earnings, neighborhood and life style, visible consumption, the reputation of the firm, ethnicity and many other factors — played in the life of white collar workers becomes clear in his account; so also does the vulnerability of this status and the white collar clerk's lack of security in this unidentified recession.[337]

(b) Aspects and Limits of the Status Difference Between Blue and White Collar

Other, scattered sources confirm that the distinctions in earnings, function, and status between blue and white collar that originated in the work process extended into areas outside the world of work. In the cities of the anthracite region of eastern Pennsylvania in 1904, for instance, sales clerks, technicians, and office employees belonged to the same educational societies, but not mineworkers. Middle class clubs in these areas excluded miners from their functions, e.g., dances and picnics. Manual workers had their own clubs and festivities, which cost less and observed different customs. (For example, men kept their hats on indoors.)[338] While workers frequented the saloons of the great industrial cities, such behavior was unheard of for industrial and office white collar employees in 1913.[339]

The status distinction between the predominantly native born white collar employees and the strongly immigrant unskilled workers must often have been concealed behind or congruent with ethnic prejudice and status distinctions. In 1920, 75% of the American population was white and native born; 90% of white collar workers (excluding executives and professionals) belonged to this ethnically privileged majority. White immigrants made up

12.8% of the population, but only 8.5% of this white collar group. Blacks, with 9.8% of the total population, amounted to only 1.2% of white collar workers. This underrepresentation existed even though the proportion of immigrants among stenographers, secretaries, bookkeepers, sales clerks, technicians and most other white collar categories had increased between 1890 and 1920. These figures reflect white collar 'encapsulation' vis-à-vis the new immigrants. The marked difference in the composition of white collar and blue collar occupations also indicates one way that ethnic heterogeneity tended to reinforce the collar line. Ethnic composition was thus one visible mark of the higher status of white collar occupations. On the other hand, the much greater proportion of immigrant children in these occupations indicates that the barriers surrounding them and thus the condition of their relative exclusiveness were not all that fixed. Professions like medicine, law, and teaching were much less hospitable to second generation American than lower and middle level white collar careers. And above all, the new immigrants found it difficult to enter not only these white collar occupations, but many of the skilled crafts as well. This fact threw white collar employees and skilled workers together in a way that formed a common boundary between them and unskilled workers.[340]

Contradictory information suggests that the status difference between blue and white collar may have varied from region to region as well.[341] If any clear trend on this question can be discerned between 1890 and 1914, it would be that the broad public was increasingly able and apt to identify a social grouping between the self-employed on one side, and manual workers on the other, of 'salaried men' or 'white collars', disregarding variations in their occupation and branch of the economy. The higher rank, status advantages, and greater desirability of white collar positions per se also seemed more evident in 1914 than in 1890. Different categories of employees — 'clerk, salesman, bookkeeper, drummer, buyer' — were referred to as a 'class' with a higher rank in the social order than the working class.[342]

The career choices of high school students in 1913/14 showed that white collar occupations — and the sources listed not only individual occupations like engineer, bookkeeper, or teacher but also used the collective term — were clearly preferred; the long discussion over education and career choice had sharpened the awareness of such categories. Not only the concrete advantages of white collar working conditions (e.g., relatively short hours, vacations) and the hope (primarily for men) of moving more easily from white collar positions to independence or management[343] determined these preferences. They also rested on the conviction that success in the office, in contrast to the factory, depended on personality, appearance, style and etiquette, cleanliness, the right clothes, and good character.[344]

This awareness of etiquette and appearance had also increased in the decades before 1914 in the US. In the first two thirds of the 19th century it had certainly been less marked than in European societies with their feudal, bureaucratic, and corporatist traditions. This new interest necessarily directed attention to the white collar and clean hands which white collar employees had in common, in contrast to the workers in overalls. The long term changes which made it easier to conceive of white collar workers not just as an abstract statistical category, but as a group with concrete common features (despite many differences), and to demarcate them both from workers and the self-employed were linked to the broad transformation American society was undergoing. They were aspects of a multi-dimensional tendency toward stronger status consciousness, clearer stratification and group segmentation in many areas of life, which were in turn linked to reactions to the masses of new immigrants, to the decline in social-occupational mobility (and even more to the awareness of this decline), and ultimately to the transition from an expanding agricultural society to an industrial nation without an open frontier.

The limits to these tendencies toward social differentiation are equally important, however. The collar line in America remained less distinct and socially and politically less significant than it was in Germany.

Shortly after the turn of the century a German immigrant, a worker in a Chicago bicycle factory, answered the question why he did not want to return to his homeland:

> [America is] even better. Forget about high wages and good living. Just think how differently we stand before the boss here. Do we so much as take our hats off to him? It wouldn't occur to us. We are just as good as he is, on the street and in the tavern, everywhere. No one looks down on manual workers; the pen pusher gets no extra sausage. And that's the way it should be too![345]

There are other comparative accounts which make similar points.[346] They seem to show that manual labor, especially if combined with some skills,[346a] was at that time less despised in the US than in European societies. The absence of feudal and bureaucratic traditions which associated non-manual activity with power,[347] strongly egalitarian elements in the political culture, the influence of the frontier, but also the agrarian tradition of North America where with a few exceptions cities first appeared with industrialization, were all important differences, though the exact impact of each of these interlocking causes is difficult to determine.

The expressions of low esteem for working with one's hands found in this period, which were often linked to prejudice against immigrants, qualify this thesis but do not contradict it.[348] For one thing, contrasts between the US and Germany or Europe cannot rest on comments on the American scene in isolation. For another, reports of contempt for manual labor in the US were usually contained in arguments intended to combat this prejudice. These critiques paralleled the industrial education movement and tendencies to label handwork 'democratic' and 'really American'; they were sometimes fueled by anti-intellectualism, social romanticism and anti-urban feelings. They do demonstrate, however, availability of rhetoric and stereotypes that held working with one's hands in some esteem. There was hardly a parallel in 18th or 19th century Germany.[349]

The less marked disdain for physical labor in the US compared to Germany was part of a larger contrast between the US and western Europe that frequently struck foreign observers. Visitors who were used to German circumstances were particularly impressed by the relatively good street clothes of young factory girls, who were proud of their independence and turned up their noses at domestic servants. Many could not be distinguished from their office counterparts on the way to work.[350] In 1906 Werner Sombart described the relatively 'luxurious clothing' of native born American workers — in contrast to that of the new immigrants — and reckoned that the American worker spent in absolute terms three times, or relatively one and a half times as much as the German on clothes. German and English visitors noted shortly after the turn of the century that most American factories provided washrooms and lockers. At the end of the shift work clothes — in Germany at the time separate smocks or overalls for work were not at all common — could be exchanged for street apparel. Many men put on a collar and tie, and left the factory indistinguishable from an office worker. 'When. . .they discard their overalls, one hardly sees them as workers anymore'. An American visitor to England and Germany at the end of the first world war was struck by the reverse contrast. He saw a great physical and psychological contrast between leaders and followers, and noted that the lower classes knew their place. He was surprised that even clothing revealed the difference in social class. An Englishman had complained to him that on a visit to America he had not been able to tell what class or occupation a man belonged to by his clothes.[351] Thus even in the sphere of consumption,[352] the extension of the work-related distinction between white and blue collar into the world outside the workplace was less marked in the US than in Germany.

A big difference between Europe and the US was in housing. In 1876 the Massachusetts Bureau of the Statistics of Labor compared the earnings, consumption, savings and libraries of salaried employees and wage workers. Although the average salaried employee was way ahead of the average wage worker in most categories (the difference was surely greater than that which existed by the time of the outbreak of the first world war), housing was an exception. 23% of the 55,515 male workers responding owned a house, compared to only 20% of the 7,748 salaried men.[353] The economic-financial superiority of white collar workers (this survey included everyone from sales clerks to the Chief Justice in the salaried category) was not reflected in the distribution of home ownership. It is unfortunately impossible to tell if this was due to the relative youth, single status, or greater mobility of the white collar group, or to the ease of home ownership in Massachusetts at that time. The existence of fewer tenements, and the tendency of workers even in the big cities to live in one or two-family houses, seemed to German observers an especially important contrast to the situation at home.[354] Higher real wages, open and relatively cheap land, cheaper construction methods (wooden houses were and are extremely rare in most parts of Germany), the importance attached to owning one's own home in this agrarian-individualistic value system, and the early development of transportation networks may explain the frequency of home ownership in the working class. Boarding, whether with a family or in a boarding house, was considered either a transitional stage or a sign of failure by many workers as well as white collar employees like Carleton.

In this connection, it is particularly interesting that most residential areas were not segregated along the collar line. Apart from ethnic or racial discrimination and the existence of exclusive preserves for the upper class in the northeast and the south, what counted primarily was income, and not so much the color of one's collar or one's occupation in and of itself (but only as a prerequisite for income). An 1898 investigation of Boston's South End — a poor inner city district, but not a slum — found a great variety of social gradations in lower and lower middle class living arrangements. Poor young sales clerks and low level office clerks not only lived in close proximity to the better off workers, they also socialized together. Further up the income ladder, skilled workers who earned enough lived in the same suburbs as middle level salesmen, professionals, and the better paid office and sales employees.[355]

The popular press and contemporary public opinion, in fact, hardly seemed aware of a status distinction between skilled workers and lower and middle level white collar workers. They were usually mentioned in one breath, and jointly distinguished from the new immigrants who made up the mass of unskilled workers. Their living quarters were contrasted with the slums, where skilled as well as white collar workers hardly ever lived.[356] An investigation of Pittsburgh brothels in 1914 reported a fairly uniform price and quality gradation between houses that corresponded to the social status of their customers: 'clerks, salesmen, mechanics and railroad men' went to the same category of relatively cheap establishments ($1-$2). These were distinguished from the expensive palaces catering to the upper middle classes, but also from the 50 cent houses, frequented by new immigrants and less skilled workers, and from the even cheaper establishments run by Negroes for Negroes.[357] In many respects the dividing line between unskilled and skilled workers was much more important than the distinction between manual and white collar workers[358] — quite in contrast to Germany.

(c) Underlying Structures: Germany and the US Compared

The significance of this stratification pattern must be interpreted in three larger contexts which can be mentioned only briefly. In the first place, the relatively indistinct collar line underlines the overriding importance of economic-financial lines of social differentiation in post-civil war America. Visible earnings and property counted for much more in this expanding nation without corporatist traditions than non-economic status distinctions did.[359] Certainly, this plutocratic capitalistic principle was modified by such factors as ethnic and racial discrimination, the elitism of those who could trace their ancestors back to the Mayflower, the exclusivity of old families against the new rich, etc. But *compared to Germany* the dominant role of strictly economic criteria of distinction in the US around 1900 is striking.

Secondly, the indistinctness of the collar line was tied to the force and visibility of other lines of stratification and conflict. Among them, ethnic divisions were the most important. They were weak in Germany, except in some regions like the Ruhr and Silesia. In an ethnically heterogeneous society membership in a particular ethnic group could be much more important than membership in a particular socio-economic category. Ethnic group consciousness made it difficult — objectively, for others, and for the group itself — to draw a clear profile of a white collar group (or for that matter, of a working class or of individual occupations either). The division of society that was uppermost in public opinion around 1900 was the line between new immigrants and older residents; it was less congruent with the blue collar-white collar distinction than the line between unskilled and semi-skilled laborers and other lower class groups, on one side, and skilled labor and white collar workers, on the other. Thus in pre-first world war America ethnicity worked directly against a clear recognition of the manual worker-white collar distinction. Furthermore, insofar as ethnic variety characterized white collar occupations, it counteracted the formation of occupational groups and organizations. This effect was particularly pronounced if such organizations attempted to pursue other than purely economic goals, for instance if they also took on social, cultural and political functions (as German occupational and white collar associations did as a matter of course). In 1905, for instance, the attempt to found an occupational association for technical draftsmen (a group which included a relatively large number of immigrants) collapsed in a fight over whether only white American born draftsmen should be admitted.[360]

Finally — and closely connected to the preceding arguments — the indistinctness of the collar line in the US was a function of the character of the American working class and the labor movement. Again, a short comparison with Germany may help to illustrate this American peculiarity. In Germany the class conflicts typical of every capitalist industrial system were superseded, influenced and often sharpened by surviving pre-industrial traditions of corporatist-feudal and of bureaucratic origins. The power structure and the predominant patterns of authority and rulership were not those of a fully developed bourgeois class society. Rather, the tenacious hold of a privileged class of large landowners on social esteem and political power, and the relative autonomy of a public bureaucracy with strong power, high prestige and pronounced esprit de corps characterized the German system at least until the first world war — quite in contrast to the US. The strong position of these two pre-industrial elites hindered the development of a parliamentary system which in Germany emerged much later than in the US — not before 1918. Democratization of state and society was particularly late and slow, in contrast to the US where, in principle, democratization of the suffrage and political institutions preceded industrialization. The German working class movement had not only to fight capitalist employers; it did not only criticize certain principles of the capitalist economy and the bourgeois system. It had also to oppose what was left of the old order which had never been successfully challenged by the bourgeoisie. The retardation of liberal-democratic developments in Germany doubled the opponents confronting the emerging labor movement, which in turn became more comprehensive and political, less divided along skill and craft lines, more excluded from state and society, more inclined to accept a position of fundamental — and sometimes fundamentalist — opposition.

Clashes of interest between employers and workers were as bitter in Germany as in the US. There was harsh exploitation, social inequality, hardship and protest of the type one finds in most industrial capitalist systems. But in Germany, in addition, because of surviving older patterns of social perception and behavior, many middle class people defined the emerging industrial working class as inferiors subject to discrimination and rule. It was not just a matter of conflicting interests, but of life style and culture, of social existence and ideological principle as well. Consequently, a high degree of multi-dimensionality and comprehensiveness characterized the relationship between the classes in Germany. The educational system reflected and reinforced this pattern — in some contrast to the US, as mentioned above. Patterns of paternalism or hierarchical rigidity were more characteristic of German firms than American. They had grown out of corporatist traditions or had been implemented according to bureaucratic models. They probably softened some of the brutality of early industrial labor conditions. But they also produced illiberal patterns of authority relations and comprehensive styles of dependence which involved the whole person of the employee and which, once called into question, led to a correspondingly comprehensive and principled type of protest. Being a worker defined a man's and his family's social existence in a definite way, outside the workplace as well as within it. As a response to comprehensive exclusion and everyday discrimination a much discussed workers' subculture developed, including different crafts and skill groups, not fragmented by ethnical division.

In all these respects the American situation was different, at least by degree. Due to the absence of these aggravating traditions the inequality of the American working class (despite income differences, which tended to be greater in the US than in Germany) was less rigid and less strongly perceived. The outsider status of the working class did not seem so obvious and was less clear and less irrevocable, the discrimination that workers did encounter was less comprehensive, though not necessarily less harsh. To be a worker in American society was a less inclusive identity than in Germany; it did not completely dominate as many aspects of a man's life. It did not mean in America to the extent that it did in Germany a ghetto and subculture existence — partly because it was crisscrossed by other ghettoes and subcultures of an ethnic kind. In the US it was more possible for the individual to separate his role at work from his role at home or in 'public life' — as part of an ethnic neighborhood, for instance, or as a member of a club. For all these and some other reasons the basis for the emergence of a proletariat and radical, emancipatory proletarian protest was so much weaker in the most capitalistic western society than in Germany with its strong pre-industrial and pre-capitalist traditions.[361]

In many respects, German white collar employees' very existence as a social group superseding occupational boundaries and distinctions of rank and earnings depended on their reaction to the formation of a relatively united, radical proletariat that embraced all categories of skilled and unskilled manual workers. One can demonstrate that the mobilization and organization of mercantile assistants advanced quickly as a reaction to and safeguard against the growing challenge of organized labor. The largest and most important association of clerks was founded in 1893 with an anti-socialist program, and with the intention of stopping the expanding blue collar unions from either recruiting white collar workers or challenging their relative superiority. Employers' readiness to grant white collar employees a slightly privileged position within the firms was partly an attempt to keep them separate from the challenging labor movement. When, in 1911, the Imperial government conceded white collar demands and enacted a law giving a special social security status to non-manual employees, this move was partly motivated by anti-socialist concerns: the white collars should not be driven into the growing leftist camp. And on the level of self-perception and mentality, the wish not to be a worker was a central part of many white collar employees' self-image — something they shared in spite of many differences in other respects.[362]

This kind of class polarization was much less pronounced in the US. Without a relatively united proletariat, the line of division between blue collar worker and white collar employee remained relatively diffuse in most areas of life: in the educational system and at work, in daily life, and even in social concepts and terms. The machinist remained a machinist in his own thinking and to others; he was separated from carpenters, even more distant from unskilled laborers, and less closely amalgamated with these groups than with workers per se. In the same way the draftsman remained a draftsman and did not become a white collar worker. Vertical, functional, and ethnic-racial cleavages fragmented and blurred horizontal class formation in the US much more strongly than they did in Germany.

It was not only the emergence of a relatively united proletariat but also the impact of early state intervention in society that contributed to the consolidation of a white collar class as such in Germany. Already in the 1880s, social insurance legislation provided a motive and an occasion for various white collar occupations to unite on the basis of common status in order to demand privileged treatment vis-à-vis manual workers. After 1900 white collar associations redoubled their efforts to get a special white collar insurance law passed, and they succeeded in 1911.[363] Government's early attempts to intervene in economic and social processes with the aim of stabilization, redistribution and sometimes reform worked as a powerful incentive for social groups to organize and try to influence the governmental process collectively. These two trends within 'organized capitalism' — systematic state intervention in society and collective organization of groups and interests — reinforced each other. The formation of a distinct white collar class was facilitated by this mechanism.

In the US, white collar workers lacked such practical political motives for constituting themselves as a group. Government intervention to stabilize the social system appeared later than in Germany. Efforts to establish and maintain a precarious, shifting social equilibrium were left to non-governmental initiatives and organizations for a much longer time, partly because they disposed of stronger self-regulating capabilities, partly because a parallel German tradition of modernization and reform 'from above' was simply not available as a supplementary or alternative strategy. Labor and social insurance laws remained modest in the US. Only in the 1930s did they reach approximately the same level as the German labor and social legislation of the 1880s — a 'lag' of almost 50 years![364]

American 'backwardness' in developing a social interventionist state meant that the governmental levers that shaped the social structure in Germany, which were particularly important in forming the white collar class, were absent. But even if there had been an earlier evolution of an interventionist state in the US, it would hardly have created a parallel to the German situation, where the law not only adopted and reflected the distinction between manual workers and salaried employees, but then clarified and strengthened it. For insofar as federal or state governments in the US passed laws regulating hours, workmen's compensation, minimum wages and related questions before the first world war, the distinction between blue and white collar workers played no role in distributing duties or rights. Labor law covered 'employees' in general, and what differentiations existed were based on sex or branch of industry, not the collar line. New Deal social legislation followed the same path, tending to isolate only top managers and officers.[365] The strongly egalitarian and individualistic ideological landscape of the US inhibited the formulation of demands for special collective privileges from the state that paralleled German white collar employees' claims for official support and protection of their traditional status advantages over ordinary workers. This they succeeded in realizing in the White Collar Insurance Law of 1911 and subsequent special legislation (continuing in diluted form up to the present). Furthermore, the ruling groups in the US — in contrast to Germany — seem to have had neither the inclination nor the opportunity to use the collar line as a cornerstone of stabilizing divide-and-conquer policies which might have strengthened the distinction between blue and white collar workers. Anyway, there was no comparable proletarian/socialist challenge to counteract in the US with a policy that favored the white collar salaried middle class. And finally, other conflicts, such as race or ethnicity, probably offered better grounds for playing off one group against another. Thus the role which agitation for special privileges played in shaping German white collar employees into a class could not be matched in the social-economic conditions and political culture of the US. Neither within the world of work nor in society as a whole did the blue collar-white collar distinction become a vehicle for a social integration policy.

2. Professional Tendencies in Place of Bureaucratic Traditions

The preceding section argued that the state in Germany, but not in the US, promoted the formation of a white collar class through social legislation and policies aimed at social integration. The tradition of a strong state and state bureaucracy helped shape the white collar class in Germany in another less direct way also. The ideal type of bureaucrat served as a model for German industrial white collar employees' (and white collar workers in general) sense of identity.[366] One of the characteristics of the German bureaucracy was that it encompassed members of different professions. Thus jurists and technicians in state service identified themselves by their common position vis-à-vis first the ruler, then public power, instead of distinguishing themselves from each other because of their separate occupation or profession. The *Beamtenstand*'s or bureaucratic estate's constituting principle cut across the dominant occupational/vertical lines of division between groups.[367] By definition the bureaucracy occupied an intermediate position. It stood between two elements external to it: on one side it took orders from a ruler, to which it was in principle subordinate; on the other it governed and cared for the masses of subjects, later citizens.[368] Just these characteristics became bound up in the conception, sense of identity, image, and partly also in the objective situation of German industrial white collar employees after the mid-19th century. As *Privatbeamte* — private bureaucrats — they loved to compare themselves and identify with prestigious, powerful, secure, well educated public officials. The state bureaucracy became their normative reference group, whose social situation served as a guideline for their own social demands. Industrial white collar workers with various occupational qualifications (technicians, salesmen, foremen, etc.) thought of themselves as private bureaucrats. They were clearly divided from and at the same time related to a supra-bureaucratic authority, the entrepreneur (the US concept of 'management' ignored or negated just this division between entrepreneur and administration), and they were completely separated from the workers, a group subject to their authority. When white collar employees from different occupations and industries began to unite on the basis of their common position and to found collective organizations outside the workplace, the public bureaucracy provided the image of group unity and a social-political model. Not that a desire to emulate public officials was the motive for these supra-occupational combinations. But identification with this highly esteemed ideal type eased and promoted the formation of a group that united some occupations but definitely excluded others — those 'above' and 'below'.[369]

The US situation was fundamentally different. Industrialization preceded bureaucratization, and the absence of an absolutist past meant that modern society had not inherited a strong central government and administration. The revolution and Jacksonian reforms further reduced whatever bureaucratic tendencies had developed. Without a feudal tradition to counteract, the basic rights of a bureaucracy (appointment on merit, protection against dismissal, the right to a pension) could not be formulated and instituted as progressive-liberal demands against princely despotism, as they were in late 18th century and early 19th century Germany. It was only in the 1883 Pendleton Act which was modeled on English examples, through some of the administrative reforms of the Progressive Era which were strongly influenced by German precedents, and more seriously with the New Deal reforms, that the US granted bureaucratic status to a gradually increasing group of civil servants.[370]

The Prussian-German bureaucracy played a central role in the most diverse modernization processes of the 18th and 19th centuries — sometimes advancing, sometimes retarding, but always shaping social change. In contrast, the role of state administration in America remained peripheral and rudimentary until the 1930s. Effective bureaucracies emerged in the private sector in the US before they did in the public. Whereas state bureaucratic techniques were adopted by private firms in Germany, the relationship was reversed in the US: urban and regional administrative reforms after 1900 borrowed forms of organization, techniques of administration, and personnel from the private sector which was admired for its efficiency.[371]

The extremely low prestige of government employees in the US reflected this real distribution of power. It also suggested the influence of dominant social values: individual achievement measured primarily by economic criteria of success; idealization of the businessman, the pioneering spirit, the self-made man without formal qualifications; the pursuit of property and independence; the acceptance of the market, competition, and risk. These values were all diametrically opposed to the values of bureaucracy, which emphasized security, fairness, respect for rules, education, formal qualifications, and non-economic criteria of success.[372]

> Since the early 19th century in Prussia the civil servant has been regarded as a social ideal, because his service to the state has raised him from the realm of social necessity into the realm of 'freedom'; since the frontier era in America the civil servant has been considered a social cripple, because. . . he has withdrawn from the free play of social forces.[373]

Around 1910 it was not easy for government agencies in the US to attract qualified personnel. If government service was presented as desirable, it was often with the argument that it would later be a useful springboard to a more valuable job in the private sphere. Administrators told employees that their salary bought only their time during office hours. Whatever part-time positions a public servant held in his free time was none of their business! Government recruiters were the first to emphasize that the position was not guaranteed for life — apparently to avoid the charge that they harbored drones and slackers. They also had to admit that government service was not the way to get ahead, since the answer to the common question 'does it pay?' was unfortunately, 'no'. Almost the entire literature about civil servants and government departments consisted of attempts to describe and criticize their mistakes, weaknesses, corruption and sinecures. No attempt was made to propagandize government service and civil service jobs by connecting them to such values as being close to authority, requiring an education, or conferring security. It seems that the public would have looked on these arguments as poor excuses. Instead, government recruiters used democratic propaganda: many citizens should spend some time in public service and do their part to prevent the government from falling into the hands of a small privileged class.[374] In the US, the German situation appears to have actually been turned upside down.[375]

Under these circumstances it is not hard to understand why the sources contain no trace of a bureaucratic sense of identity among white collar workers in American industry. The example of an influential, prestigious, secure, strong bureaucracy was not available to channel white collar workers' social demands and expectations. Nor could it serve as a reference group and model for a specifically white collar consciousness that spanned occupations and divided the group from above and below. A three-step hierarchical schema in which their role was a functional equivalent of the state bureaucracy's was no more noticeable in the thought of these industrial white collar employees than in the structure of company personnel policies.

If the bureaucratic model which inspired German salaried employees' group identity was not available, was there any sort of functional equivalent that could serve as a model for a special white collar consciousness in the US? In other words, if as has been shown the growing class of white collar employees in American industry did not see themselves simply as workers, and if they no longer could or would believe in a future as independent businessmen, what categories and models did they turn to, which characteristics, expectations, and claims did they emphasize, in order to conceptualize themselves as a group? The closest equivalent for some was to emphasize their particular specialization, competence, expertise and qualifications in order to construct a sense of identity modeled on the professions.[376] This professional or semi-professional consciousness was weakly developed before 1914. Nevertheless, it fulfilled some of the functions which a private bureaucratic consciousness met for some categories of white collar employees in Germany. It justified a certain vague elevation of one's group above the masses of workers; it served as the basis for special occupational and social expectations; and it legitimated group claims to recognition and prestige. But in contrast to Germany, for a long time professional identification was too weak a platform for effective organization.

The technical draftsmen, a group whose indeterminate position between blue and white collar, lack of contours as an occupation, and transitional character, scant cohesiveness, and low prestige have already been discussed, may serve as a case in point to exemplify this professional tendency.[377] When *The Draftsman* (1902-1906) began to address this occupational group and to seek a readership among them, it attempted to formulate a basis for and to strengthen a sense of group identity among draftsmen. The paper emphasized that technical education was increasingly necessary to raise the 'profession of draftsmen', which was already recognized abroad, above the level of mere workshop practitioners. The paper recommended technical books and called attention to new schools. The editors hoped that the lamentably low requirements for entering the profession would rise with the spread of technical schools, and attempted to prove (what was apparently not self-evident) that special technical education paid off even then (1904) in salaries and opportunities for advancement. *The Draftsman* stressed and exaggerated the similarity between technical drawing and professions like architecture and engineering. The paper's primary function would be to provide professional information and education; in the second place it would promote the discussion of occupational problems while avoiding controversial political questions.

In 1905 and 1906 the editors of *The Draftsman* tried to found an organization for technical draftsmen; they were at least partially motivated by the search for a wider and more stable circle of readers. The 'American Society of Draftsmen' was open to draftsmen with at least two years practical experience; drawing assistants would be accepted as associates. The organization's primary aims were to provide special education and a social meeting place; representing the group's economic interests was only a secondary goal. Group insurance plans were also considered. 'We are protected neither by law as a profession nor by organization as a trade', the editors told their readers. An association of technical draftsmen would have to work to improve standards within the occupation in order to assure the quality of 'first class workmen'. Then earnings would go up automatically. A reader's letter proposing the formation of a trade union was rejected by other letters referring to the (potential) professional character of the group. 'A labor union does not provide its members with technical education, without which the drafting world cannot expect to attain the rank of profession'. The 'standard of the drafting profession' would be raised through independent self-organization. The American Institute of Architects was expressly taken as a model for their own organizing efforts, and a corresponding membership definition proposed.

This attempt to found a technical association failed. Apparently without the impetus of a campaign to influence public opinion or the political process (for instance in connection with agitation for social insurance), the common interests addressed were insufficient to overcome the draftsmen's lack of cohesion, ethnic antagonisms and unwillingness to pay dues. What is important for our thesis is that *insofar* as a group of white collar workers undertook to define their collective identity through organizing, they adhered to a strictly occupational, semi-professional model. It differed from the model of the private bureaucrat adopted by salaried employees in Germany in that it did not provide a bridge to link diverse occupations on the grounds of common status. German technicians developed a parallel occupational consciousness, but as their organizational behavior reveals, occupation tended to take second place to identification with the broader class of salaried employees.

Other categories of white collar workers in the US revealed comparable professional tendencies in their sense of identity and in their real situation as well, for instance in the development of technical education, the increasing specialization and creation of regular promotion in the most systematic firms, and also in establishing occupational associations with professional touches. Groups with the highest qualifications had the greatest success. The best example is the engineers, whose attachment to professional expertise and specialized competence was so extreme that their associations reflected the increasing fragmentation of an occupation which remained united in Germany — in the US they divided into associations of civil, mechanical, mining, and electrical engineers.[378]

A parallel case was the top strata of bookkeepers and accountants. They organized on a professional basis in the 1880s, taking lawyers' and doctors' associations as a model, in order to work toward raising the academic and scientific qualifications of their occupation. They concerned themselves with questions of examinations and titles, edited the *Journal of Accountancy* (after 1905), and held conventions. As with doctors and lawyers, this professional identity partly counteracted the emergence of white collar consciousness, since accountants employed by corporations as well as independents and partners in accounting firms belonged to this association.[379]

Managers of large firms were also caught up in the movement toward professionalization. But instead of simply organizing as managers without reference to occupational differences (as they did in Germany after the first world war),[380] these groups combined (if at all) along the lines of particular specializations. Thus local organizations of personnel managers were established after 1913 (which in 1918 joined together in the National Association of Employment Managers); there were also professional associations for sales managers and office managers.[381]

Even intermediate and low level employees in and out of industry imitated the professional model to a certain degree. In the 1880s a General Passenger and Ticket Agents' Association met every two years; in addition to exchanging experiences and socializing, the organization helped standardize the treatment of the public on America's decentralized railroads.[382] In 1900 bank employees, with the support of the banks, formed the American Institute of Bank Clerks, which was primarily intended to fulfill professional educational and social functions.[383] Teachers were also increasingly successful in their struggle for professional status. In contrast to Germany, throughout the 19th century in the US a teaching career was rewarded by very low pay and prestige. Teachers lacked job security, and were hardly regarded as professionals. The 1890s brought a gradual change in their situation, and eventually teachers' social standing approximated that of the German elementary or middle school teachers.[384] Office work was also occasionally referred to as a profession, and thereby elevated above the trades of skilled workers.[385] And even sales clerks had begun to speak of their work as a profession before the first world war.[386]

In spite of the objective tendencies which advanced the actual professionalization of white collar occupations and thus justified this white collar self-image — the expansion of technical and commercial education, increasing specialization, rationalization and a larger role for science and system in big business, the creation of lifelong careers — to refer to most middle and low level white collar workers as professionals undoubtedly elevated their real situation in a flattering manner. They lacked occupational associations with professional characteristics (meetings, distribution of professional literature, codes of honor, setting standards for members). They were unable to control entry into their occupation. Their work was for the most part not in and of itself rewarding, nor did it require academic training or high qualifications.

Thus the application of the term 'professional' to these lower or middle level white collar groups had an ideological function which was somewhat comparable to the function of the term 'private bureaucrat' for industrial white collar employees in Germany. The old professions, doctors or lawyers, for instance, were among the most respected members of the community, even if their status was somewhat threatened by the new plutocracy; some of this social prestige rubbed off on those who could claim to belong to even the outskirts of the professions. The professional claim was enormously important at the turn of the century as the new requirements of an increasingly urban industrial society stimulated the growth of new professions as well as contoured the old and placed them on a firmer scientific basis. Thus a process of professionalization was set in motion in the US which had been under way in Germany, under the influence of the state administration and a state school system, since the beginning of the 19th century. In America the professions rather than the bureaucracy became a partly illusory model and object of identification for white collar groups for whom the chance for independence and thus also the ideal of the independent businessman had been strongly reduced by the turn of the century.[387] The professional sense of identity which first emerged among American white collar workers at this time paralleled the

German salaried employees' bureaucratic sense of identity by supplying a basis for claims to social prestige and authority.[388] Yet this justification of status and authority differed from a bureaucratic orientation: it was based on function, education, and competence, and was thus more specific than the self-image of the quasi-bureaucrat.[389] To be sure, members of the modern bureaucracies of the firm, the state, and other organizations in Germany also had this kind of specialized education and competence. But additionally (or rather primarily), their status rested on holding a position as the representative of delegated authority, on being an instrument of authority legitimated not by function but by property, election, dynastic law, etc.[390]

American white collar workers who based their claims to social prestige on a professional model were not forced to define the working class as a subordinate group subject to their authority, at any rate not to the extent which a hierarchical three-step schema required of German private bureaucrats. The gulf between white collar employees and skilled workers was correspondingly less rigid in the consciousness of US employees; it was also not defined as a difference in authority but rather in competence. Furthermore, the working class was significantly less important as a negative reference group for American white collar employees with professional aspirations than it was for their German counterparts.[391] Thus changes in earnings, vacation rights, hours, and self-determination which narrowed the gap between white and blue collar posed less of a threat and were less apt to be experienced as relative deprivation in the US than in Germany, where the private bureaucrat defined himself precisely by his distance from the workers.

Furthermore, German white collar workers' attachment to their quasi-bureaucratic status introduced a distinct anti-capitalist strain into their sense of identity and expectations which was apparent in their propaganda. Their struggle for security, suitable earnings, their bureaucratic concept of success, belief in seniority and formal qualifications, as well as their claim to protection (by employer or state) against economic need or declining status almost necessarily collided with some fundamental principles of private enterprise: the chances and risks of the market, pressure toward measurable achievements expressed in the last analysis in profits, and the principle of individual competition.[392] The semi-professional, non-bureaucratic sense of identity of American white collar workers considerably lessened this danger. In modeling themselves on doctors, lawyers, architects and civil engineers, these white collar groups chose occupations which were far more directly subject to the laws of supply, demand, and competition than German bureaucrats ever were.[393] For that reason alone professionalism was much less suited to become a basis for anti-capitalist protest in times of crisis than the bureaucratic expectations of German salaried employees, which almost necessarily clashed with changing economic and social reality.

The traditional bureaucratic sense of identity adopted by German salaried employees was becoming increasingly untenable even in normal times. A growing number had to recognize that they were dependent workers, whose tasks were controlled and directed by others; they themselves exercised little or no authority. If our analysis holds true, in the German case the split between the 'private bureaucracy' ideology and the real circumstances of salaried employees was widening. Mercantile assistants, whose expectations were still partly based on corporatist models and an idealized group past, experienced a parallel gap between ideology and reality.[394] In contrast, the distance between the emerging professional sense of identity of American white collar workers and their real situation at work and in society was not increasing, but may even have narrowed.

Of course, many of the advantages which lower and middle level white collar workers had enjoyed over blue collar also leveled off in this country, including their higher average wages, shorter hours of work, vacations, and relative freedom at work. Routinization and mechanization of office work increased dramatically in the US; the growth of huge offices, impersonal work relationships, and the increase of bureaucratic controls over individual employees were hardly unique German problems. These trends also contradicted the professional's claim to personal control over his own work.[395] But two important distinctions between the situations of German and American white collar workers must be reiterated:

1. Leveling tendencies were much less threatening to white collar workers who thought in professional-ideological categories and values than to salaried employees with a bureaucratic ideology which was more directly dependent on their distance from manual workers. What appeared as degradation and an occasion for protest within the framework of an outmoded private bureaucracy ideology in Germany was less objectionable within the context of an emerging professional sense of identity in the US. Furthermore, strongly egalitarian traditions in American political rhetoric and culture made it very difficult to mount a direct attack on relative loss of status and social leveling — these elements were inseparable from the political agitation of white collar workers in Germany after 1900.

2. Not only in ideological respects, however, but also in objective terms the starting positions of American and German white

collar workers in the early 1890s appear to have been so different that the experiences of the next two decades affected them differently. In the US such new trends as the acknowledgement that a lifelong career as a dependent employee was one way to be successful in life, tendencies within the corporations to guarantee greater job security,[396] the extension and growing recognition of special and technical education, the Progressive Era's emphasis on science, rationality, expertise, efficiency, and the increasing importance of scientific and professional tendencies in almost all areas of life all contributed indirectly to raising the status of white collar workers. In the absence of a bureaucratic tradition they had previously been regarded as 'hired men' or 'hirelings', and as such accorded little prestige or security; they had had very indistinct contours as a social category or group. These beneficial effects of broad social changes at the turn of the century differentiated the experience of US white collar workers from that of their German counterparts. Parallel tendencies to order and organization in business and society certainly appeared in Germany, but since they replaced a less disorganized capitalist/agrarian world they were a less radical departure. Most crucially, German salaried employees could not gain the same objective and subjective advantages (job security, prestige despite permanent dependence, honor accorded education and training, respect for their competence, contouring as a group) since they had long had them.

Thus similar social-economic changes on the way to organized capitalism did not have the same impact on the new urban-industrial middle classes in Germany and the US. Change in corporatist and bureaucratically molded German society upset relatively fixed images of social order and stratification. Social change called into question and partly destroyed ideologies specific to particular groups which were based on traditional models and the high expectations they produced. One consequence was the emergence of tensions, resentments and protests among groups that saw themselves as relative losers in modernization. In the US, industrialization and urbanization by no means lacked such destructive potential: the protests of rural and urban small businessmen, the populist movements from the 1870s through the mid-1890s bear adequate witness to that. But protest against change was not the dominant trend in this era. Stronger than the resistance of the old was the emergence of what had previously been absent or weak in the US: ever more fixed lines of stratification, contoured occupational groups, career patterns and classes, and specialization, system and order in business and in society as a whole. Protests against modernization arising from the collision of outmoded structures and ideologies with emerging social transformations strongly stamped

German society until after the second world war; they were much weaker in the US. In America, such protests were much more strongly focused on other fronts — ethnic, religious, region and race — which are not under discussion here.

Lower middle class protest directed simultaneously against those above and below had emerged among German salaried employees before 1914, even though it became really virulent only in the 1920s and 1930s. With these reflections in mind, it seems hardly surprising that a parallel to the pre-1914 German salaried employees' protests, or to the relatively successful and influential mobilization of the new middle class in Imperial Germany, did not exist in the US. The transformation of white collar workers from an academic social category to a social group, which could be conceived of and experienced as such by its members and by outsiders on the basis of notably similar characteristics, attitudes and behavior, had not sufficiently progressed. Tradition and ideology did not predispose American white collar workers to resentment and protest against the ongoing changes in economy and society as they did their German counterparts.

To be sure, there were some traces of complaint and critique about the particular fate of the employed middle classes before 1914. The office worker Carleton's complaints about the degrading changes at the workplace and the contradictions between the financial means and social expectations of white collar suburban dwellers were certainly less atypical than the pioneer/immigrant-inspired 'way out' which he proposed.[397] Now and then newspaper articles recognized that 'salaried men' were not always so well off in view of rising prices and declining chances for independence, particularly when they were compared with big business and organized labor. The white collar employee — whether office worker, sales clerk, bookkeeper or buyer — did have some special claims, which he might justify because of his greater education, ability, diligence, intelligence or loyalty to the company: he expected regular promotions, for instance, and anticipated maintaining or improving his and his family's standard of living in the suburbs. Frequently, however, his salary stagnated after he reached 30, just when his children were ready for school (private school, if possible) and his needs and expectations were greater than those of a twenty year-old beginner. Hopes for advancement often proved illusory. After 40 his age became a disadvantage; competition from more enthusiastic, younger men willing to work harder for less pay became more threatening. The white collar worker felt his powerlessness, he feared the merger or liquidation of his firm or a change of bosses, because such circumstances could easily cost him his job. He usually had scant savings, and his financial needs frequently exceeded his means.

> . . . the greatest discontent now existing is not among the working class, but is to be found in a class higher in the social scale, which for the sake of convenience may be called the middle class, that great human stratum which lies between the working man and the prosperous rich and very rich, the great body of salaried men.[398]

Opinions like this last author's remained rare, however. The discontent which they revealed did not appear too highly pitched or pervasive. And even if resentment was felt and formulated, it was not usually translated into demands to protect and guarantee the privileges of the middle class as such — that would not have fitted very well into the ideological landscape of the US. In fact white collar complaints were probably not usually expressed as the discontent, resentment, complaint or protest of a particular occupation or class, since they could hardly have hoped for a sympathetic reception from a public opposed in principle to special privileges. More democratic and egalitarian symbols took the place of class or occupation. The consumer, the taxpayer, the ordinary man, the public, and the forgotten man were common slogans in newspaper articles attacking 'private interests', 'special interests', rising prices, corruption, trusts and big business, or exploitation by capitalists and the claims of organized labor.[399] This rhetorical tradition had no room for specific white collar demands, and it undoubtedly made it more difficult for white collar groups — or other individual occupations and interest groups — to conceptualize themselves as distinct groups with group-specific characteristics and claims.

In fact, insofar as discontent and protest came from the white collar employee's corner, they were most apt to intermingle with the broad, multi-faceted, classless reform sentiment so typical of the Progressive Era. Even the passage quoted above, unusual in that it referred to specific complaints of white collar workers, concluded by regretting that at night in their suburban houses these frustrated salaried men read muckraking journals' polemics against trusts, the extravagance of the rich, social injustice, the decline of the inner city and corruption.[400] White collar workers thus would appear to have supported moderate-progressive, democratic reform politics which incorporated a great variety of interests and listened to spokesmen from the educated elite, businessmen, trade union leaders and committed social reformers. They joined a movement which was also supported by members of the working class and other lower class groups.

But this picture of white collar politics is more a matter of supposition than a firmly documented conclusion. Other studies have found that in other situations lower and middle level white collar workers tended to view progressive reform politics skeptically and ally themselves with conservative, anti-progressive forces.[401] Furthermore, the white collar group was still relatively small, and its political views hard to determine. There are many indications that the political views and behavior of white collar workers were strongly shaped by religious and ethnic determinants, which was quite typical for American politics in those decades. It may also be supposed that the many children of immigrants who filled the ranks of these lower and intermediate white collar categories were unlikely to see themselves as threatened with decline or as victims of relative deprivation. Their reference group was probably much more their parents' generation or other ethnic groups than the working class in general; their experience of upward mobility in American society was still fresh, and a small decline in their relative position within the newly attained occupation secondary. Whatever else these perceptions may have meant for their political orientation, a fear of social leveling and proletarianization was probably not a central problem.

In any case, in contrast to Germany, in the US before the first world war there was hardly a trace of anti-proletarian white collar protest which simultaneously differentiated white collar workers from other middle class groups in order to maintain and strengthen outmoded, threatened privileges. This kind of protest was lacking not only because the general political and ideological landscapes in the US were unfavorable. Even if the corresponding resentment and tendencies had been present, American white collar workers would have had a hard time organizing to express them politically. But even more to the point, in the US in contrast to Germany, a viable basis for such protests did not exist within the groups themselves. Before we can ask whether this German-American difference would also hold true in the economic crisis around 1930, we must first examine the experience of the world war and the 1920s.

3. American White Collar Workers in the World War and the 1920s

I. WHITE COLLAR WORKERS AS LOSERS IN THE WAR

1. Lost Ground and Traces of Protest

Rapid social and economic change during the first world war further advanced the trend that was already visible before 1914 for both insiders and outsiders to perceive the white collar social grouping as more than just an abstract statistical category. The social group's shifting image and identity partly reflected its greater willingness to engage in collective action and protests (which had been almost non-existent before the war); in certain respects its attitudes and behavior now faintly echoed the types of specifically lower middle class reaction that characterized its counterparts in Germany. The more distinct contouring of white collar workers as a social group was among the social consequences of a war in which American white collar workers received as scant a share of the relative winnings as German salaried employees.

The adverse impact of the war on white collar workers was especially clear when their situation was contrasted with the wartime gains of manual workers. Prosperity from producing armaments and other war materials (which had begun before the US entered the war) and the postwar boom that continued into the spring of 1920 drove wages up more rapidly than salaries. The abrupt halt in immigration, the departure of four million men to the military, and the sudden demand for all kinds of war-related goods put manual workers in an unusually good bargaining position. Wartime wage increases were sufficient not only to compensate workers for the decline in the value of the dollar, but even to allow them to advance. In the US as well as Europe, the strategic importance of the working class in a war which economic strength would decide became ever more apparent. Government authorities were now prepared as never before to intervene in economy and society in order to maximize production or pacify internal conflicts which might weaken the country's war effort. In consequence the US took a large step forward on the path toward organized capitalism. The Administration and Congress were now ready to go much further to accommodate organized labor than the moderately favorable legislation of the immediate prewar years. Trade unions were granted practical recognition as bargaining agents for industrial workers; collective bargaining and the eight hour day (which did not reduce the actual hours worked, but guaranteed pay for overtime) received government support and sanction; legislation and administrative rulings mandated better working conditions and established pro-labor arbitration and conciliation boards. These developments improved the social-economic position of most industrial workers and strengthened their rapidly growing trade unions. The recently legitimated American labor movement would play an important role in this interventionist interlude in American history.[1]

Like most unorganized groups, white collar workers were largely ignored in this restructuring of government-interest group relations. Since they hardly ever threatened to strike, they were seldom in a position to profit from the intervention of the War Labor Board or other government agencies. As in Germany, white collar workers saw themselves passed over in favor of the great organized interests;[2] here as there, they were also not the beneficiaries of the tight labor market during the war years to the same extent as manual workers.

Before the war the average wage-salary differential had remained fairly constant, but during the war years wages far outpaced salaries. White collar workers' real earnings were rising slightly or at least holding their own before the war, but now even their nominal earnings fell behind the rising cost of living. Between 1915 and 1920 the cost of living index almost doubled (from 101 to 200). Wage increases in these years were frequent and substantial enough to add up to a 20% increase in real earnings for the average industrial worker. In the same period, however, the real earnings of the average white collar employee in industry sank by about 14%.

In 1915 the average white collar employee in industry earned 2.33 times, but in 1920 only 1.65 times as much as the average production worker. Wage-salary differentials outside industry were also decreasing. The experience of white collar workers in the US was not unique; this leveling process occurred in all advanced industrial societies during the first world war. And compared to their German counterparts, whose country's participation in the war was much more protracted and devastating, the difficulties American white collar workers experienced could even be called mild; at any rate their salaries remained much further above the minimum necessary for existence. The gap between wages and salaries had also narrowed more dramatically in Germany than in the US during the war.[3]

Thus wartime inflation, which hit white collar workers especially hard and clearly separated them from both wage workers and the self-employed, intensified their previously weak tendency to see themselves as a distinct social group. So did the increasing trade union organization of industrial workers and the wartime cooperation between organized interest groups and the government. Other wartime changes, such as the rapid increase in the proportion of women in some white collar occupations, also changed the character of the group in ways that could not be reversed after the war. Ohio's unusually good occupational statistics chart this feminization of office work (see Table 3.1).

Table 3.1
Female Bookkeepers, Stenographers, and Office Clerks in Ohio, 1914-29[4]

	All Economic Sectors		Industry	
Year	Number	% of total	Number	% of total
1914	23,838	40.5	13,352	37.5
1915	27,523	41.3	15,368	37.0
1916	33,008	41.6	18,120	36.9
1917	39,688	43.5	21,436	38.5
1918	50,269	48.2	26,839	43.2
1919	57,337	49.3	29,760	43.6
1920	64,312	49.1	31,172	42.7
1921	54,678	49.5	25,252	43.6
1923	62,472	49.4	28,159	43.0
1924	65,779	49.4	28,220	42.8
1925	68,945	49.7	29,536	43.2
1926	73,008	49.9	30,973	43.5
1927	75,842	50.3	31,346	43.7
1928	76,946	49.9	30,951	43.0
1929	84,870	50.5	34,769	43.9

Furthermore, in the sharp recession of 1921 white collar workers suffered high unemployment; it was an especially hard blow after their losses to inflation during the war.[5] The term 'white collar' came into more common usage, sometimes in dramatic references to 'white collar slaves'.[6] To discuss their common plight authors began to lump various white collar groups together which, except in census tables and the debate about education and career patterns, there had previously been little occasion to link.[7]

White collar discontent and protests that sounded a similar note to lower middle class agitation in Germany became more audible. The hazy concept of the public took on more distinct socio-economic contours: next to the small businessman, minor professionals, and other traditional social types the salaried 'head worker', the 'white collar man' now began to appear behind 'Mr Public' and to fill in the picture of the sketchily defined 'forgotten man' in America. Salaried men were portrayed as having been shortchanged during the war; squeezed by high taxes, they appeared to be in danger of being crushed between capital and labor.[9] The actual level of misery of this social group was not the main theme in these complaints. Instead, they focused on the group's economic and social losses relative to other social groups (particularly manual workers) which the war had made so clear.[10] In these protests against their relative deprivation and in their bitterness over economic and social displacement,[11] white collar workers began to reveal a reactionary side. One middle level salaried employee donned overalls to break a strike in a vital industry because he believed that the 'health of his wife and the lives of his children were threatened, together with his tradition of national order and efficiency, solidarity and service'. Protests against high taxes by white collar workers asserted that far too much money went to free education for 'aliens', i.e., the children of immigrants, and for social welfare programs. Some white collar authors also attacked communist influence in the labor movement, rejected the illusion of equality (which now worked against the middle classes), and expressed the fear of being 'overrun' by other races.[12]

In 1919 a caricature of an ugly, paltry, frustrated little white collar man who leaned toward reactionary attitudes and behavior appeared on the stage. Elmer L. Rice's social-critical play *The Adding Machine* sought to capture the mood of the immediate postwar years polemically. At the center of the drama is Mr. Zero, a petty bookkeeper. He is a 'white collar slave', equally frustrated in his career ambitions at work and his sex life at home. All day long he and an assistant sit in one room on high stools adding columns of figures; Mr. Zero daydreams about praise from his superiors or his own courage in standing up to the boss. In reality, however, as his unhappy wife reminds him daily, he has plodded along for 25 years

Table 3.2
Blue Collar and White Collar Earnings in American Manufacturing 1919-38[8]

Year	Gainfully Occupied (in 000s)		Nominal Earnings Per Capita Per Year (in Current $)		Quotient 4:3	Cost of Living Index (1914 = 100)	Real Earnings Per Capita Per Year (in 1914 $)			
	Blue Collar	White Collar	Blue Collar	White Collar			Blue Collar in 1914 $	Blue Collar 1929 = 100	White Collar in 1914 $	White Collar 1929 = 100
	1	2	3	4	5	6	7	8	9	10
1919	8,482	1,384	1,141	2,012	1.76	173	662	87	1,172	75
1920	8,413	1,343	1,376	2,257	1.64	200	690	91	1,130	72
1921	6,487	1,087	1,149	2,236	1.94	178	655	86	1,251	80
1922	7,198	1,152	1,111	2,155	1.94	167	666	88	1,290	83
1923	8,206	1,286	1,238	2,224	1.79	170	729	96	1,311	84
1924	7,618	1,272	1,246	2,282	1.83	170	730	96	1,340	86
1925	7,873	1,270	1,267	2,344	1.84	175	725	95	1,342	86
1926	8,048	1,316	1,281	2,421	1.89	176	727	96	1,371	88
1927	7,866	1,362	1,285	2,513	1.95	173	745	98	1,461	94
1928	7,863	1,381	1,296	2,653	2.04	171	759	100	1,550	99
1929	8,386	1,503	1,299	2,669	2.05	171	760	100	1,561	100
1930	7,330	1,468	1,208	2,679	2.21	166	725	95	1,609	103
1931	6,179	1,273	1,084	2,527	2.33	152	715	94	1,668	107
1932	5,246	1,085	879	2,219	2.52	136	645	85	1,628	104
1933	5,787	1,003	853	2,102	2.46	129	663	87	1,630	104
1934	6,751	1,138	942	2,141	2.27	133	706	93	1,603	103
1935	7,203	1,187	1,014	2,177	2.15	137	742	98	1,591	102
1936	7,822	1,241	1,081	2,221	2.13	138	782	106	1,609	103
1937	8,569	1,348	1,180	2,294	1.94	143	823	108	1,598	103
1938	7,086	1,246	1,089	2,247	2.06	141	775	102	1,600	103

in the same position without a single promotion. Finally he is pushed aside (without notice) when a new adding machine arrives that can do his work more cheaply. When friends gather at his modest rented apartment, the conversation quickly turns to diatribes against strikes, foreigners, Catholics, and other races: 'America for the Americans'.[13]

It is hardly surprising that such views appeared by and about American white collar workers in the wake of inflation and declining salaries (absolute in purchasing power, relative to wages). Their protests were swelled by a sense of confrontation with a large and powerful labor movement and their conviction that government intervention had contributed to the economic and social displacement of the unorganized middle classes. Yet these were still new and transient experiences for American white collar workers compared to the harsher situation of their German counterparts.

It is highly doubtful that such voices really represented the emergence of a specifically lower middle class type of white collar protest movement in the US comparable to that in Germany. There are some indications that white collar workers along with blue collar workers were strongly represented in the urban branches of the revived Klu Klux Klan in the early 1920s; they thereby supported its anti-modern, anti-Catholic, anti-black, anti-semitic, anti-communist, anti-urban and anti-intellectual stance.[14] But the Klan made little effort to appeal to social-economic groups or strata as such; there were no arguments or recruitment programs aimed specifically at white collar workers.

The salaried middle classes probably did participate in significant numbers in the anti-leftist, xenophobic, and partly anti-trade union mass hysteria of the 1919-21 Red Scare. Sources report white collar workers acting as strike breakers and joining anti-union special militias.[15] Many of them voted for Harding, and thus approved the conservative turn away from progressive reform politics which he represented. One might infer that they supported his administration's steps to reverse the wartime strides toward the interventionist state. Available sources do not reveal the extent to which the salaried middle classes were over or underrepresented on the conservative side of the political spectrum after the war, however.

2. White Collar Organizations and the Labor Movement During the War

For whatever reasons, a relatively well defined white collar protest movement did *not* develop during the war or the 1920s in the US. The specifically white collar groups that were formed were not anti-labor or reactionary. In fact, the economic and social demands of white collar workers were more apt to be submerged in diffuse crusades like prohibition than channeled into white collar interest groups. Of course, they were then invisible as *white collar* protests. (Supporters of prohibition can to a certain degree be linked with urban/rural and regional variables but only tenuously with social classes or strata.)[16] White collar organizations, whether long standing or recently formed, did not consciously separate themselves from the general labor movement and demand special treatment as white collar workers or as members of a 'healthy lower middle class'. White collar workers' organizational alternatives remained limited: they could either join social-economically vague causes like prohibition, cling to their small, isolated, non-political professional associations (like the mechanical engineers, for instance), or follow the RCIPA's example and try to find a home for themselves within the labor movement.

Technical draftsmen are a case in point. Even before the war local draftsmen's and technicians' clubs had fulfilled social and professional purposes but refrained from trade union activities.[17] Public and private shipyard technicians and draftsmen had organized many such clubs on the east, west and Gulf coasts as well as the Great Lakes. In 1913/14 they copied professional associations and founded the 'National Society of Marine Draftsmen'. Questions relating to salaries were not among the association's concerns. As their unhappiness with their economic situation increased during the war, however, disaffected draftsmen got in touch with local trade unions. With labor's help draftsmens' locals were formed within the AFL beginning in September 1916. They were recognized as a national union in September 1917; in May 1918 they became the 'International Federation of Draftsmen's Unions'. The union reported 700 members in July 1918 and 2,300 members in 25 locals in January 1919. Membership peaked in 1920 with 3,500 organized draftsmen reported.[18]

The draftsmen's union pursued the same basic goals as its brother unions in the Metal Trades Department of the AFL and wherever possible they worked closely together. The draftsmen modeled their demands on these unions; they too asked for a shorter work day, minimum wage, overtime payment and improvements in working conditions. The draftsmen also tried to institute an apprenticeship program modeled on that of the metal craft unions to enable them to control access to their occupation and thus to improve their bargaining position. When government officials at first excluded draftsmen at war shipyards from the classifications 'laborers' and 'mechanics', and thus denied them the eight hour day/overtime contract the AFL had gained for manual workers, they protested. Their petitions and delegations to the Navy and the appropriate congressional committees succeeded in remedying this 'discrimination' — not to be counted as a manual worker!

As the regulation of wages and working conditions during the war fell increasingly to government agencies and compulsory arbitration boards, organization became a necessary precondition for a group to be able to represent its collective interests. Technical draftsmen had already begun to contrast their own lack of cohesion with the organized labor movement as manual workers made gains early in the war; this further shift of authority to what was in the last analysis a decision-making process based on a political/bureaucratic effort to bring competing interest groups into some sort of equilibrium was a decisive push toward organization.[19] Under different circumstances and at a much earlier date, German technicians had found the activities of an interventionist state a sufficient prod toward organization to represent their collective interests.[20] But while German circumstances had produced interest groups that encompassed the entire 'corporation of technicians' to underline their distance from the working class, in America technical workers organized along craft lines — e.g., draftsmen — and sought affiliation with the AFL.[21] Their tactics and alliances were standard labor practice.[22]

Restricting the membership to technical draftsmen soon appeared too narrow to the union's leadership, however. In the real world it was difficult to draw distinct boundary lines around the various technical occupations. Although the traditional confusion between engineers, draftsmen and mechanics had gradually declined, delegates to the union's 1919 convention still found it difficult to exactly define its membership criteria. Many technicians spent only part of their time at the drawing board, the rest on projects in the shop. The union also recognized that technicians who did not join were a constant source of competition for those in the union and an obstacle to union control of the workplace. These pragmatic considerations — not a common technical education, let alone feelings of technical-corporatist unity — were behind the union's decision (after lengthy debate) to abandon the craft principle and henceforth to recruit 'all technical men'. The 1919 convention approved the prior decisions of several locals and formally adopted this expansion of the union's jurisdiction. It changed the name to the 'International Federation of Technical Engineers, Architects, and Draftsmen's Unions' and voted to admit (unable to agree on a more specific definition) 'all technical, engineering, architectural and drafting employees'.[23]

The limited successes of the draftsmen's union also point up the great difficulties white collar organizations faced. The union had begun as a professional association; the step to forming a trade union had been taken with great difficulty under the unusual strain of wartime. And even in these unfavorable economic times, the majority of draftsmen continued to consider trade union organization beneath their professional dignity. Those who did join saw their membership in purely instrumental terms: as a means to achieve limited economic aims which otherwise appeared impossible.[24]

With the government's withdrawal from economic life at the end of the war, in the recession and unemployment that followed the brief postwar boom and the increase in anti-trade union agitation as public opinion turned conservative, finally also with the restabilization of salaries, many technicians who had organized under wartime conditions began to lose interest in the International Federation. By 1923 it had shrunk to 600 members in twelve locals and could no longer raise the money to send its president to the AFL convention, which was held in the northwest that year. An honorary member attempted to explain this decline to the other delegates:

> So many of our members are obsessed with the idea that they are members of a learned profession; that they are able to go along and do for themselves, make their mark in the engineering world. . . Our members have fallen away.[25]

In the 1920s the membership became limited to technical employees of city, state and federal governments; a strong contingent worked for the Navy.[26] Technicians in private industry, however, had dropped out. The union devoted most of its efforts to negotiating personnel classifications, salary and seniority questions, pensions and hours with political authorities. The Federation continued to stress its labor union status and AFL affiliation, however. Its ideological positions echoed those of other AFL unions; some public employee unions even went on strike.[27]

What other white collar organizations there were (mostly outside industry) followed the draftsmen's pattern. The RCIPA's membership grew from 15,000 before the war to 21,000 in 1919/20; *The Advocate* used increasingly radical rhetoric during the war. With the active participation of female clerks, the union won several major strikes and reached its strongest point in 1919; in this and most other respects, the RCIPA paralleled the development of skilled craft unions.[28]

After 1904, regularly after 1909, delegates from local bookkeepers' and stenographers' unions attended AFL conventions and sought unsuccessfully to affiliate. Before the war (1913) eight cities had local bookkeepers', stenographers' and accountants' unions;

after the war there were locals in 40 cities with 2,000 members. These white collar unions tried to organize banks and, after 1927, insurance companies. The AFL continued to refuse to grant them a national charter; after 1922 the Federation even recalled some local charters because of suspected communist influence.[29]

The attempts in 1916 and 1918 to organize insurance agents hardly survived the war. An Insurance Mutual Protective Association which reported 6,000 members in Boston, Chicago, Philadelphia, Providence and New York struck the Prudential Insurance Company in 1916; the company accused it of belonging to the IWW. The AFL had refused to grant the petitions from local insurance agent organizations for affiliation since 1895.[30]

During the war the AFL National Federation of Post Office Clerks, which had organized locals after 1900 and become a national union in 1906, drew even with the conservative United National Association of Post Office Clerks which high Post Office officials dominated: the AFL union grew from 10,000 members in 1914 to 25,000 in 1920. The impulse toward unionization was so strong even in the older organization that it initiated discussions with the AFL about fusion with the National Federation. These came to nothing, however. In 1915, for the first time, there was something like a strike of postal employees. The previously conservative, independent Railway Mail Association (1920: 14,000 members) and the National Association of Letter Carriers (1920: 22,400 members) suddenly joined the AFL in 1917. Thus the dissatisfaction of government employees who were losing out in the war did not propel them into specifically lower middle class protest movements in the US. Instead, they joined in the temporary triumph of trade unionism, by thoroughly integrating themselves into the general labor movement. Public employees, whose organization had been condemned as a 'radical and dangerously revolutionary step' in 1905, showed the private sector the way.[31]

The Brotherhood of Railway Clerks was organized in 1899 from local social and benevolent societies. In 1908 the Brotherhood affiliated with the AFL; its ideology, goals, and tactics were indistinguishable from those of other AFL unions. The railway clerks' union grew with considerable government assistance from 5,000 to 186,000 members between 1915 and 1920 (though by 1924 its membership had declined to 88,000). The railway clerks were not only not concerned about white collar separatism, they went as far as extending their jurisdiction along industrial union lines to take in some categories of manual workers. The AFL-affiliated Order of Railroad Telegraphers, which also organized white and blue collar workers together, grew from 25,000 members in 1914 to 78,000 in 1920. These white collar employees of public utilities thus followed in the footsteps of government employees: they channeled wartime discontent into commitment to trade union action and the labor movement.[32]

The International Brotherhood of Electrical Workers had organized white collar employees of the great telephone companies (who were mostly young women) before 1920. Despite their militancy during the war, however, their union remained ineffective because of the lack of government support (the government had assumed formal control over telephone and telegraph services in mid-1918) and the bitter opposition of the private telephone companies. The companies were strong enough after 1919 to impose company unions on their employees which blocked further union organizing efforts.[33] Employees of private telegraph companies had the same experience.[34]

Other white collar government employees also turned to trade unionism in response to their wartime grievances. After 1917 the National Federation of Federal Employees organized blue and white collar workers employed by the federal government together.[35] The American Federation of Teachers (AFT), building on scattered forerunners dating back to the late 1890s (particularly in Chicago) that had been part of the progressive movement, affiliated with the AFL in 1916. In contrast to the purely professional National Education Association (1857) which school administrators dominated, the AFT combined reform politics with concrete trade union demands. Its membership increased from 2,700 in 1916 to 9,300 in 1920.[36]

One conclusion seems evident:[37] to the extent that American white collar workers translated wartime discontent into collective organization, they followed the craft or occupational principle and joined the general labor movement. Their alternative was not to join specifically white collar or lower middle class organizations that excluded the working class, but rather, not to organize at all.

II. WHITE COLLAR WORKERS IN THE 1920s

Almost all of these war-related causes of white collar discontent evaporated at the beginning of the 1920s with the 'return to normalcy'. The cost of living index (1914 = 100) fell from 172.5 (1919) to 166.9 (1922) and remained fairly constant during the 1920s (1928/29: 170.9). Inflation came to an end.[38] The rapid reprivatization of enterprises that had been under government control in the war — the railroads, telephone and telegraph companies for instance — signaled the return to greater government restraint in directing economic and social policy. Not that a model free enterprise economy regulated only by market mechanisms was established; but after the early 1920s corporate combinations (trusts and mergers and industry-wide cooperation) were a greater obstacle to free competition than state intervention.[39] Government support for the labor movement eroded; legal decisions in particular went against the unions. Employers' open shop drives, aided by a sharp pro-business turn in public opinion, got the upper hand and labor unions lost members, respect, and influence. Though labor's fortunes had begun to shift in the sharp recession of 1921, the slide continued during the following years of relative prosperity.[40]

The prosperity of the 1920s has undoubtedly been exaggerated by contemporaries and historians looking back from the vantage point of the severe depression that followed. The distance between incomes increased rather than decreased in the decade following the first world war; broad sections of the population lived on less than contemporaries defined as the minimum necessary for existence, the poverty line, or an 'American standard'.[41] The exploitation and poverty of some groups of workers, particularly the unskilled recent immigrants and blacks but also poor whites in the economically backward southern states, approximated conditions in early industrial England.[42] The already meager earnings of agricultural workers and many farmers stagnated.[43] Unemployment was high. In Columbus, Ohio, an industrial city and a state capital, 11.6% of the labor force was out of work in 1921. National unemployment stood at 5.2% in 1922, 5.7% in 1923, 3.8% in 1924, and 7.6% in 1925. The percentage of white collar workers without jobs in these years (1921-25) was 6.2%, 2.8%, 3.1%, 3.6%, and 6.1%.[44] In April 1929, that is before the depression had begun, 10% of Philadelphia's manual workers were looking for work.[45] Prosperity bypassed enough groups to make one wonder at the absence of visible and audible protest.

Yet on the other side of the picture, national income increased by more than 35% between 1919 and 1929; real income that came into blue and white collar workers' hands in the form of wages and salaries did increase slightly (though much less than the increase in profits, dividends and interest). If one hazards a cross-cultural comparison on the basis of uncertain estimates, between 1913 and 1929 real national income (per capita) increased by 44% in the US, 1% in Germany, and 12% in Great Britain.[46] With the exception of 1925, the real wages of the average American worker increased continuously from 1920 to 1929 — in contrast to German workers who suffered from the after effects of the war and the inflation. In 1920 the average fully employed non-agricultural American worker earned $1,426 a year; in 1929, $1,534. Expressed in 1914 dollars, he earned $714 in 1920 and $898 in 1929. That was a real increase in earnings of 25%. Even if agricultural workers are included, the increase in real income for the average worker still came to just under 20%.[47] Furthermore, the quantities and variety of consumer goods available in the 1920s, including cheap automobiles, allowed large parts of the population to visibly improve their status as consumers. They were better off than citizens of other countries, and as immigrants or the children of immigrants, many were in a position to make such rough international comparisons.[48]

1. Sales Clerks and the RCIPA

The impact of these general changes in the social, economic and political situation on white collar workers will be analyzed first as they affected retail clerks and the RCIPA. The history of the RCIPA in the interwar period may be divided into a period of steady decline (1917/18 to 1933) and a subsequent phase of expansion, revival, and limited radicalization. Official membership was reported as 21,200 in 1921, 10,000 in 1929 and only 5,000 in 1933; actual membership was certainly much lower.[49]

During the 1920s the trend toward larger firms and an increasing proportion of dependent workers in the commercial sector continued, even though new economic activities dominated by small business — service stations were a prime example — were also coming into existence. The self-employed in commerce declined from 53% in 1900 to 35% in 1929. The US figure remained several percentage points higher than Germany's, however, which meant that the average American clerk still had a slightly better chance to become his own boss than the average German. The total labor force in commerce grew more quickly than the labor force as a whole.[50] Thus the embarrassing decline in the RCIPA's actual membership stood in marked contrast to the increase in its potential membership.

In 1921 the RCIPA had to cancel its already scheduled convention for financial reasons. The 60 delegates who finally assembled in 1924 represented only 10% of the locals. They voted to eliminate hospital benefits which the union could no longer afford. Conventions would be held only every five years. As the next scheduled date (1929) approached, however, a referendum of the membership favored an indefinite postponement. Only 1,400 members in 54 locals took part in the voting.[51] (In fact, the next RCIPA convention was not called until 1939.) Articles in *The Advocate* became increasingly defensive.[52] Overall the RCIPA's losses were much more serious than the general decline of the American labor movement between 1920 and 1933.[53]

The RCIPA's fate must also, however, be viewed in the perspective of the increasing prosperity of the 1920s which by and large had benefited sales clerks. After falling well behind industrial workers' wage gains from 1915 to 1920, white collar workers in commerce had made up this relative loss. At the end of the 1920s the average earnings of commerce employees again ranked (as they had before the war) just above the average earnings in manufacturing.[54]

Ohio statistics permit a more exact comparison of blue collar and white collar workers in industry and commerce. Between 1920 and 1929 the earnings of salaried employees in commerce (mostly sales clerks) increased by a greater percentage than the earnings of wage workers in commerce. Yet salaries in commerce still lagged behind the average wages of skilled and unskilled workers in both industry and commerce.

Table 3.3
Average Yearly Wages and Salaries in Industry and Commerce in Ohio, 1918-29 (in Dollars)[55]

Year	All Economic Sectors			Industry			Commerce		
	All Empl.	Wage Earners in Commerce	Sal. Empl.	All Empl.	Wage Earners in Commerce	Sal. Empl.	All Empl.	Wage Earners in Commerce	Sal. Empl.
1918	1,098	1,109	894	1,162	1,159	1,496	854	870	770
1919	1,245	1,246	1,039	1,304	1,285	1,688	1,000	1,015	914
1920	1,524	1,543	1,250	1,602	1,598	1,981	1,212	1,230	1,092
1921	1,284	1,252	1,271	1,293	1,252	1,971	1,243	1,264	1,135
1922	1,304	1,250	1,216	1,350	1,270	1,796	1,167	1,152	1,097
1923	1,425	1,422	1,332	1,449	1,428	2,037	1,248	1,248	1,171
1924	1,419	1,406	1,316	1,456	1,429	1,980	1,280	1,296	1,165
1925	1,445	1,435	1,367	1,497	1,467	2,226	1,224	1,261	1,151
1926	1,426	1,418	1,395	1,479	1,448	1,092	1,258	1,280	1,194
1927	1,455	1,431	1,417	1,502	1,464	2,129	1,273	1,276	1,238
1928	1,469	1,448	1,407	1,528	1,496	2,163	1,268	1,293	1,220
1929	1,480	1,457	1,374	1,535	1,499	2,171	1,237	1,281	1,164

In Boston in 1911, 12% of 3,328 women and girls employed in retail sales had earned less than $4 a week, 39% less than $6, and 66% under $8. In one week during the fall of 1926, Filene's (which may have been among the better paying stores) paid its employees:[56]

Earnings in Dollars	Men Number	%	Women Number	%	Total Number	%
0	22	2	105	5	127	4
Less than 10	14	2	47	2	61	2
10-15	49	5	322	16	371	13
15-20	118	13	645	31	763	26
20-25	108	12	498	24	606	21
25-30	112	13	196	9	308	10
30-40	179	20	115	6	294	10
40-50	102	11	59	3	161	5
50-75	113	13	43	2	156	5
75-100	36	4	17	1	53	2
100 or more	44	5	12	1	56	2
Total	897	100	2,059	100	2,956	100

Thus by the 1920s most employees of Filene's earned between $15 and $20 a week. Branch and chain stores, particularly the 'five and dimes', relied on a cheap, rapidly changing labor force made up almost entirely of young girls. These stores paid much less: the median earnings of these girls in 1928 (according to a study of 6,000 clerks in eighteen states) was $12 a week.[57] *The Advocate* directed most of its attacks in the 1920s against the practices of chains like Kresge and Woolworth.[58] It was a losing battle, however; the census reported a rapid increase in the number of chain stores:[59]

1878:	3	1898:	38	1918:	645
1888:	8	1908:	212	1928:	1718

In 1928 21% of all retail goods — 39% of groceries — were sold in stores owned by a company with at least four outlets.[60] By the 1920s many grocery and department store chains had already moved out of the city center; stores followed people to the suburbs, then gradually adapted locations to suit the convenience of shoppers with automobiles.[61] Supermarkets had already assumed the basic characteristics they still exhibit today.[62]

Other factors diminished retail clerks' already meager interest in organizing. The era of moderate progressive reform came to a standstill with the end of the first world war and the defeat of Woodrow Wilson. While not wholeheartedly in favor of trade unions, progressive politics during wartime had been tolerant of and sometimes helpful to the labor movement. After the war public opinion turned against labor, and employers were quick to seize their chance to attack the wartime gains of unions. The National Association of Manufacturers (composed mainly of small and medium sized firms) led a vigorous campaign against the closed shop under the banner of the American Plan. High postwar unemployment rates were their invaluable ally. The RCIPA was too weak to resist a united assault by local merchant associations; many locals were broken by lockouts and mass dismissals. Even while *The Advocate* condemned these massive open shop drives it joined employers in also condemning the 'unprincipled red agitators' in the labor movement, perhaps in order to avoid providing another target for an aroused public. Other articles emphasized the RCIPA's 'businesslike' character and its reliance on moderate, constructive methods.[63]

Shifts in public opinion had a much more immediate impact on the organization and behavior of retail trade employees than on industry. Both sides — store owners and clerks — were in direct contact with and directly dependent on the public. Merchants who offended a pro-union public would be apt to see their sales drop directly, while manufacturers were several steps removed from public pressure. After 1920, of course, American store owners had little to fear from such pro-labor sentiment. A factory worker, on the other hand, could continue to perform his work relatively untouched by anti-union sentiment in the general public (if he was not fired), while sales clerks who wore a trade union pin would risk the displeasure of customers and lose their effectiveness. These considerations were particularly important in an occupation with professional literature emphasizing that the clerk's compliance with and subordination to the customer was a primary virtue. Thus the anti-union atmosphere of the 1920s had a much more direct impact on sales clerks than on many workers in industry.[64]

Against this background the particularly steep and rapid decline of the RCIPA in the 1920s becomes understandable. Their peculiar sensitivity to public opinion exacerbated the traditional factors that had always hindered their ability to organize: that for many it was a temporary, transitional occupation, the heterogeneity of tasks and branches, the increasing employment of women and minors, the problem of easily hired 'extras' for peak periods, the ease with which clerks could be replaced, their weak financial position.

Changes in company personnel policies also hindered trade union organization. Since about the turn of the century large corporations had led the way in developing new techniques to manage their employees. Without direct reference to the patriarchal traditions of the 19th century, several corporations introduced personnel policies in which paternalism was packaged as partnership and adapted to the needs of big business and exact, impersonal management. Sometimes with advice from social workers in the early years, later under the supervision of specially trained personnel managers, these corporations amalgamated paternalism, scientific management and industrial psychology. This new style of management was a response to social conflicts inside and outside the firm and also a reaction to the reform spirit of the Progressive Era; scientific managers particularly liked to clothe their innovations in an ideology of public service. The personnel management movement was also an answer to big business' growing demand for qualified personnel, which was especially acute as immigration came to an end. Their new techniques aimed to tie employees to the company, to regulate their training and motivation, and thus increase productivity. They stressed the importance of 'human relations' in business and preached the harmony of interests between employer and employees; the social responsibility of big business also belonged to this new movement's ideological baggage. It was called either 'welfare capitalism', with the emphasis on company social policies, or 'personnel management', accenting planned, scientific direction and organization of all employee relationships. Wartime labor shortages and the increase in planning promoted these new approaches. They were the carrot opposed to the stick of dismissals and lockouts in the successful repression of the trade unions after 1918; in the 1920s they buttressed big business' campaign to find public legitimacy in American society.[65]

The largest retail establishments jumped on the welfare capitalism bandwagon. In 1916/17 the Office of Labor Statistics surveyed company welfare measures at 431 firms,[66] including 47 large department stores employing 124,773 persons. The selection of firms was not representative, and the results undoubtedly present too favorable a picture for most employees in retail. The contrast between retail stores and other businesses is nonetheless interesting.[67]

	Department and Other Retail Stores (47)	All Businesses (431)
Company Doctor	32	171
Work Breaks	22	106
Washroom or Showers	47	409
Employee Lockers	47	351
Restaurant or Cafeteria	41	224
Quiet Rooms	21	105
Clubrooms, Recreation Rooms	13	152
Social Programs, Lectures	28	239
Leisure Time Facilities	18	219
Benefit Societies	0	80
Pension Programs	0	75

Thus with the exception of benefit societies and pension programs — lacking perhaps because of the relative youth of sales clerks — the retail stores surveyed were more apt to have welfare and social facilities than the average business. Up to 1926 stores continued to stay slightly ahead of other businesses in increasing benefits,[68] again except for old age and insurance funds.[69] Paid vacations became increasingly common; thus along with office, bank, and insurance employees most sales clerks enjoyed an advantage most factory workers lacked at the end of the 1920s.[70] Since as a practical matter there was no trade union threat, retail stores did not participate in the company union movement of the 1920s. (In 1928 1.5 million American workers belonged to company unions; this was almost half the number organized in all non-company unions in or out of the AFL.)[71]

Retail personnel managers relied instead on instilling loyalty and competence through company training programs (half of 50 large department stores surveyed in 1934 had an independent personnel department).[72] Macy's became the model for professional writers; their dictum that 'the salesperson is a human being, a social unit, a bundle of aspirations. . . a human entity with unlimited possibilities for development' was often quoted.[73] Systematic training for sales clerks was intended to serve two sets of purposes: (1) to transmit concrete information about general merchandising practices, arithmetic, labeling and display, sales tactics and store management. The firm could also build in channels to select and train future managers; internal promotion had become one of the norms of good personnel management in the 1920s.[74] (2) Another purpose of the personnel management approach was to indoctrinate employees with loyalty to their firm and their work. In addition to house newspapers, social meetings, banquets, etc., some stores held daily 'inspirational assemblies' with three minute pep talks from managers trained in public speaking and a few happy songs.[75]

Scientific management spread rapidly in retail during the 1920s. Employment examinations, physical and psychological testing, careful personnel record keeping, regular review of performance and earnings, experimentation with the most efficient methods of payment (e.g., bonus and commission systems) and a major effort to lower employee turnover were part of this expanding movement, especially in large stores.[76]

Although education was becoming more important (in the glutted labor market after 1929 some department stores began to recruit college graduates),[77] the average education of retail clerks remained modest. Information about education was available for 2,745 of Filene's nearly 3,000 employees in the mid-1920s. 37% had attended only grade school (25% of these without graduating); 57% had been to high school, but only 13% of this group had received a diploma. 6% had some higher education, but again only 13% of the group a higher degree. Of the 89 executives, 26 had only a grade school education. Forty-one had been to high school, and 22 (most without graduating) had been to college. The great majority had started out as retail clerks.[78] It seems that in the 1920s, higher education was still not a prerequisite for advancement in retail.

A flood of books appeared to spread the rules and techniques of modern personnel management in the retail trade. Retailing was now a subject for university teaching and research; colleges had been turning out professional personnel managers since the world war. Business groups held conferences and sponsored papers on personnel management; in 1924 the largest retail association in the nation established a 'Store Manager's Division' that met regularly to exchange information.[79]

Actual practice, however, particularly in small shops and chain stores, probably ignored most of these teachings. Handbooks on selling, for instance, advised managers to reduce employee turnover. In reality, a fantastic level of insecurity and fluctuation continued. Stores were known to fire their entire staff except for a few top people at the end of the year in order to start over with a fresh crew. Chain stores made a practice of replacing local branch managers at frequent intervals; new managers were apt to fire the old staff to bring in their own people.[80] A random sample of 500 businesses in Wisconsin found that a separation rate (the number of terminations and dismissals as a percentage of the number employed in that year) of 65.5% to 73.9% was average for industrial firms; in the 23 retail stores surveyed, the separation rate was between 88.5% to 150.5%.[81] Although the large department stores that were the real home of scientific management in retailing were an important segment of the retail trade — the 42,500 such stores in 1929 amounted to only 3% of the 1.5 million retail stores; however, they employed 700,000 persons, or 12% of all retail employees[82] — they did not shape the average clerk's working environment.

In the 1920s the rhetorical commitment to working class consciousness of earlier years faded in the RCIPA. There were no more proclamations of solidarity 'with the toiling masses' in *The Advocate*; criticism of the propertied classes (particularly the clerks' employers) also dried up. The tendency among clerks to see themselves as a distinctly white collar class set apart from manual workers caused the sales clerks' union more trouble in the 1920s than it had before. The clerks, it seems, no longer identified only with their occupation or 'craft', they were beginning to identify with a white collar class encompassing many occupations.[83] The popular press also showed a somewhat greater interest in white collar employees as such in the 1920s than it had at the beginning of the century. Though difficult to verify, awareness of and sensitivity to fine status distinctions between blue collar and white collar workers that could not be reduced to income or occupation seems to have been increasing. The rank orders used in contemporary sociological works point in this direction.[84]

Occupational identity rather than generalized identification with a white collar class continued to be dominant among sales clerks, however. The RCIPA usually referred to sales clerks; high school graduates drew a sharp distinction between the status of the stenotypist and that of the retail clerk, even though both were white collar positions.[85] When clerks were assured that their social position was improving, it was not because they had white collar status; nor was it primarily — though this refrain persisted — because of their hope of future independence. Instead, the evidence brought forward pointed to their professional qualifications and qualities. A corollary of the increased emphasis in sales textbooks on training, education, scientific personnel management and the establishment of regular ranks and career paths was the effort to instill clerks with a sense of professionalism. Sales clerks and those writing for and about them did not focus on any social stratum that superseded occupation (not the working class, but also not a white collar class); they drew attention to specific occupational skills, knowledge, and scientific training. The good salesman and the ideal saleslady were presented as experts in selling, to be sure, but they were at least equally motivated by the ideal of service to the public as by profits. This literature also copied the professions in advocating a code of honor for sales clerks and the establishment of practices (conventions, newsletters) typical of the professions. In this view, the top of the retail profession was not the bold entrepreneur who relied on instinct but the upwardly mobile (and 'scientifically' trained) department manager or executive of a large store.[86]

It is difficult to determine what impact this stress on professionalism and scientific selling had on the masses of sales clerks. The few autobiographical materials available say little about the clerks' work. They suggest that sales clerks were involved with the actual work they performed and to a certain extent identified with their company. There is no evidence that a general white collar consciousness was a source of self-esteem, but definite evidence of clerks' professional identification is also lacking.[87] *The Advocate* used the terms 'salesman' and 'saleslady' more frequently than before the war; the word 'clerk' was pushed into the background (its connotations were somewhat slighting) but never entirely disappeared. This linguistic shift also indicates that the special activity of clerks — selling — was becoming more prominent than when the unspecified term 'clerk' was used to connote the general, transitional character of the occupation.[88] Hints of professional consciousness also appeared in *The Advocate*'s stories about the special demands of and training for particular types of sales work.[89] In 1924 a local store manager addressed the RCIPA convention; in a well received speech, he painted the usual ideological picture of the 'science of merchandising' and 'public service', which he stressed rested on cooperation between store owners and their 'assistants' — a term not commonly used by the RCIPA.[90]

On the whole, however, the RCIPA was skeptical about the professional aspirations of sales clerks. The leadership rightly viewed professionalism as one of the ideological factors inhibiting clerks' readiness to organize. Appeals to the semi-professional character of sales clerks were particularly prominent in the anti-union propaganda of drug store and pharmacy owners, since as a rule their clerks had to meet certain educational prerequisites. Thus the *American Druggist* condemned the RCIPA's campaign to organize pharmacy clerks because it was unseemly for members of a profession responsible for the health of the public to belong to a labor union.[91] Employers only began to marshall such arguments in any number during the depression, however, when sales clerks along with most workers became more accessible to trade union organization.

2. Salaries, Education, and Mobility

White collar workers in industry's real earnings, both in absolute terms and relative to production workers in industry, improved in the 1920s because of industrial workers' weak bargaining position and the end of government aid for trade union organization. Economic growth and the (however incomplete) prosperity of the era were also important. The gap between wages and salaries widened, though the prewar span was never reestablished: In 1898 the average white collar employee in American manufacturing had earned about 2.5 times as much as the average blue collar worker; in 1913 the figure was 2.2, in 1920 1.6 times as much. By 1928 the white collar advantage had again risen to 2.0.[92]

Comparable shifts in the wage-salary differential also took place in the individual industries investigated and in transportation between 1920 and 1928.[93]

Ohio's unusually precise statistics confirm this trend and permit generalization about white collar workers outside industry. Ohio statistics also make it possible to exclude higher and managerial white collar workers as well as most technicians and engineers (who were included in Kuznets' figures, which were the basis for the national wage-salary differentials cited above). Table 3.4 compares blue collar wages with the salaries of sales clerks, bookkeepers, stenographers and other lower and middle level office employees. As the table reveals, lower and middle level white collar salaries in manufacturing and construction but also in service and transportation increased more steadily and at a higher rate in the 1920s than the wages of manual workers. White collar workers in industry and other economic sectors[94] clearly benefited from prosperity; they probably belonged to the class able to buy the wide variety of consumer goods becoming available.[95]

These statistics also demonstrate that the course of American white collar earnings was quite different from German salaried employees' in the same years. In Germany the greater devastation of the war, postwar inflation and slower economic growth were responsible for the fact that average real wages only reached their prewar level in 1928 (even though a greater share of national income went to wages and salaries in Germany than in the US). And that gain was only true for manual workers; the real earnings of salaried employees were still beneath their prewar level in 1929 when the depression began.[97] In the US, real wages for industrial workers sank below their 1913 level only once (in 1915); white collar salaries (after a definite decline during the war) reached their prewar level again in 1924 and continued to climb. The divergent reactions of German and American white collar workers to depres-

Table 3.4
Yearly Income of Blue and White Collar Workers in Ohio, 1918-34[96]
(1929 = 100)

Year	All Economic Sectors		Industry		Construction		Services (Nongovt.)		Public and Private Services	
	Blue	White	Blue	White	Blue	White	Blue	White	Blue	White
	1	2	3	4	5	6	7	8	9	10
1918	76	66	77	60	66	64	61	63	69	58
1919	86	78	86	81	85	80	69	68	81	65
1920	106	91	107	90	102	94	87	80	100	83
1921	86	90	84	87	83	94	89	86	94	86
1922	86	99	85	111	82	89	87	77	89	96
1923	98	92	95	90	117	95	89	84	94	86
1924	97	94	95	91	98	98	94	80	96	119
1925	98	95	98	96	99	100	99	84	95	95
1926	97	96	97	95	97	102	97	89	99	96
1927	98	99	98	99	97	103	103	91	98	96
1928	99	99	99	98	97	104	95	94	101	102
1929	100	100	100	100	100	100	100	100	100	100
1930	92	99	91	100	93	100	95	92	100	98
1931	81	91	79	92	80	92	90	87	96	98
1932	67	81	64	84	59	84	80	75	85	91
1933	64	76	63	78	49	78	68	76	82	88
1934	72	79	72	81	57	81	70	76	88	90

sion and crisis cannot ignore these divergent patterns in the course of wages and salaries.[98]

Compared to the broad German literature on white collar workers in the 1920s, publications in the US were extremely meager. Specific white collar sources of discontent and/or susceptibility to protest were hardly mentioned.[99] Writers on social problems, labor questions and industrial organization, who in Germany at least mentioned the difference between blue and white collar workers and often discussed it at length, continued in the US to refer to employees in general and ignore white collar workers as a special topic.[100] Except for the large Brotherhood of Railway Clerks and the tiny RCIPA, at the end of the 1920s there were no white collar unions in the private sector.[101] In 1930 no American organizations belonged to the International Association of Sales, Office, and Technical Employees, which had been established in Amsterdam by socialist and liberal unions from many industrial countries in 1920.[102]

When the dark side of the white collar workers' situation did come up in public discussion, the attitudes expressed remained hazy and moderate. In 1925 *Harper's Monthly* published an anonymous article by a New York lawyer's wife (in her mid-30s, the mother of two). In sober, non-ideological language she described how the income of her moderately successful spouse, occasionally supplemented by her part-time earnings, did not quite meet the demands of their way of life (which undoubtedly exceeded those of a sales clerk's or bookkeeper's family). Their standard of living included a house (bought for them) in New York City, a modest beach cottage on Long Island where they spent every vacation, a cook, maid, and nursemaid, shopping by telephone, a life insurance policy as the only form of savings, high doctor's bills, two or three evenings out a week (dinner, concerts, films, visiting), two or three dinner parties a month, no travel. Without any hint of resentment against another group, without mentioning general social, let alone political questions — although this woman frequently spent evenings at lectures and discussion groups — but concentrating solely on consumption, life style, and finances, the author concluded: 'We are at an impasse'. Although they could anticipate a gradually rising income, they also had to count on their expenses increasing at a faster pace — particularly educational and medical costs for their children. Her husband felt slightly bitter and ashamed that he had had to take money from his mother for the house and that he 'allowed' his wife to work. They were unable to afford presents for themselves or others; they had to borrow books from the library rather than buy them; they were not always sure they would be able to pay all their bills each month. 'The lack of a bank balance is the essence of negation.' The editors noted only that the article described a situation confronting countless families.[103]

Other articles also lamented white collar workers' low salaries, which seemed even less adequate compared to the high wages of skilled workers. A bookkeeper wrote: 'Sometimes I am almost sorry that I did not learn a good trade. It's the people in my profession that are having the hardest time'.[104] Such complaints did not lack a basis in fact: despite the overall widening of wage-salary differentials in the 1920s, a large group of lower level white collar employees continued to earn much less than most skilled workers.[105]

Even in the good years after 1921/22, white collar unemployment was not unusual. Lower and even middle level white collar workers seemed as vulnerable as blue collar workers. Although unemployment was talked about as a source of white collar workers' discontent, it was viewed as the same sort of phenomenon with the same significance as blue collar unemployment.[106]

Ten to fifteen years later than in Germany, US observers began to comment on the social and ideological consequences of the 'industrial revolution' in the office. Mechanization, specialization and the division of labor, routinizing and simplification of office tasks, huge white collar 'factories', occasional attempts to pay draftsmen and other office employees by piece rate — these developments had begun at the same time in the US as in Germany, but before the 1920s they had been discussed primarily from the perspective of efficiency and organization. The insight that this revolution also meant a loss of status for office workers first appeared in the mid-1920s, and then mainly in writings by pro-labor authors who saw in this trend reason to hope that in the long run large numbers of white collar workers would be drawn to the labor movement.[107]

Contemporary observers were most impressed by white collar workers' declining chances for promotion and advancement. They thus reflected the traditional view that greater mobility was the chief advantage of a white collar over a manual occupation.[108] It is difficult to assess the validity of the declining mobility thesis. We are fairly certain of a few facts about inter-generational mobility. In 20th century America workers' children's chances to move into white collar positions, as well as the opportunity for the children of lower and middle level white collar workers to reach professional or managerial positions, did not decline; they may have increased, but probably remained about the same until the second world war. About one-third of the non-technical lower and middle level white collar workers in the US (male) at the beginning of the century were children of manual workers; the same ratio existed at the beginning of the 1930s, though there were enormous variations from place to place. At the turn of the century in Germany this figure was certainly much lower, but by 1930 the percentage of manual workers' children holding salaried positions probably matched the American ratio.[109] Opportunities for the sons of lower and middle level white collar workers to advance to semi-professional, professional, or executive positions apparently did not decrease in the US in the 20th century; the danger of falling into the working class (which was slight anyway) did not increase. Lower and middle level white collar occupations were like skilled and semi-skilled crafts: their members (in contrast to professional and semi-professional occupations) showed little tendency to hand over their positions to their sons. The other side of the coin was that these positions allowed the sons (and daughters) of other occupational groups relatively easy access.[110]

Those who expressed the fear that white collar workers' opportunities to advance were declining were thinking primarily of individual lifetime careers rather than the fate of the next generation, of course. The scattered evidence about intra-generational mobility that is available suggests that individual upward mobility did not decline in the US from the late 19th century on; if anything, it improved. Systematic comparisons over long time periods are rare, however, and as a rule they employ categories that are too broad to permit the isolation of lower and middle level white collar workers' chances.[111] Only a few examples and problems can be mentioned.

The number of white collar positions in industry and in all economic sectors did increase more slowly in the 1920s than in the first decade of this century. This slowdown was primarily caused by the slower growth of lower and middle level office and sales jobs; the number of professional, technical, and managerial positions increased more rapidly between 1920 and 1930 than in the decades 1910-20 or 1900-10:

Table 3.5
Growth of Selected Occupational Categories, US, 1900-40 (in %)[112]

	1900-10	1910-20	1920-30	1930-40
1. Managers, Executives, and Proprietors, Except Farm	45	14	28	4
2. Professional, Technical and Kindred Workers	42	33	45	17
3. Sales, Clerical and Kindred Workers	71	45	36	14
4. White Collar Workers (1+2+3)	61	41	35	15
5. Blue Collar Workers	37	14	19	11

These shifts in the occupational pyramid do not indicate that the number of positions into which to rise decreased, and thus that opportunities for lower and middle level white collar workers to move up to a higher category declined — on the contrary. Some target groups, such as buyers and department managers in industry and commerce (included in Category 1) increased dramatically: 68% between 1920 and 1930. (The 1930s will be discussed separately below.) Another avenue of approach is to ask what influence changes in education and training had on career opportunities for lower and middle level white collar workers.

A 1926 representative sample of 6,050 lower and middle level office employees found that 86% had spent some time in high school, but only 9.5% had attended college; in addition, 64% of the group had some special commercial education or training.[113] Thus to a greater degree than before the war, high school had become a prerequisite for office work even though in purely practical terms it overqualified applicants for many modern office jobs. Office managers nonetheless continued to give preference to the plentiful supply of applicants with high school education or degrees.[114] They may have sought employees who could more easily adapt to a number of detailed tasks; status may have been a consideration; or perhaps they expected that social skills which were more important in the office than the factory would be more highly developed among high school than grade school applicants. As a rule lower and middle level white collar workers in technical fields such as draftsmen had also attended high school by the end of the 1920s. Special technical courses, whether in high school or at a private institution, were even more important for these positions than commercial courses were for general office work. Promotion from the factory floor continued to be possible, however, especially since a growing minority of blue collar workers had also attended high school by this time.[115]

As high school education became a matter of course for commercial, technical, and clerical white collar workers, however, it became less sufficient as a qualification for advancement to higher white collar positions. This shift was not only a function of the quasi-inflationary devaluation of high school education, but also reflected the expansion of commercial and technical higher education. As the NCR survey illustrated, academically trained employees had not been numerous in top white collar positions around 1900.[116] By the end of the 1920s the situation was quite different. The slower increase in the number of engineering colleges between 1925 and 1930 may have reflected a temporary saturation of the market for college trained engineers;[117] after the rapid increase in the supply of engineering graduates between 1900 and

1925 that would not have been surprising. Commercial colleges (which had almost without exception been founded after 1900) expanded even more rapidly, and supplied a rapidly growing number of graduates for non-technical positions.[118]

Table 3.6
College Degrees (BA or Equivalent), 1901-40[119]

Years	All Fields	Engineering	Business/Commerce
1901-05	149,500	4,900	300
1906-10	173,300	7,500	700
1911-15	206,000	12,500	1,400
1916-20	216,700	20,100	4,900
1921-25	360,200	37,100	20,900
1926-30	550,700	38,800	30,800
1931-35	684,800	54,800	47,600
1936-40	824,700	62,600	72,700

Leaving aside engineers who graduated before 1900 as well as those who were counted as engineers between 1900 and 1910 but had left the profession by 1920, one can calculate that despite some slowdown after 1925, the number of engineering graduates still grew more quickly during the 1920s (+96%) than the number of employed engineers (+67%). Under these circumstances the chances of becoming an engineer without a college degree must have declined.

The number of college degrees awarded also increased faster than the growth of population. For every 1,000 persons who were 22 years old in the first decade of the 20th century there were twenty college graduates (BA or equivalent). In the second decade there were 22 per 1,000; in the 1920s, 45; and in the 1930s, 68. The number of engineering graduates per 1,000 22 year olds was 1, 2, 4 and 5 in these decades; there were about the same number in business and commerce.[120] The census reported a total of 43,240 engineers in 1900; 88,760 in 1910; 136,120 in 1920; 227,590 in 1930 and 277,870 in 1940.[121] The increase in the second decade (54%) and the fourth (22%) thus fell distinctly below the increase in the first (105%) and the third (67%) decades of the 20th century.

The National Industrial Conference Board (NICB), a business association, circulated a questionnaire in 1926 or 1927 which revealed the extent to which an academic background had already become the norm for managerial and executive positions. The survey covered 54,000 'technical and supervisory men': supervisors from foreman and department manager up and all technically qualified white collar workers. It thus included the great majority of positions which could be considered targets for upwardly mobile lower and middle level white collar workers; these were also positions it made sense to fill with candidates who had higher education. The results: employees who had been to college held 47% of the office positions, 49% of engineering and technical slots, 9% of these positions in production, 38% in sales, and 14% of the rest. More than one-quarter of all higher white collar positions were held by employees with academic training, mostly at technical colleges or universities. 'Technical and supervisory men' in the electrical industry were most apt to have some higher education, while those in metal fabrication were least likely to be college men.[122]

Considering that in 1920 only 1.1% of American men over twenty had a college degree,[123] one might infer that the lack of a college education would hardly have hindered skilled workers, foremen, and factory technicians from being promoted, especially in the field of production.[124] But academic background had already become an important criterion in selecting candidates for higher positions in technical and commercial fields; it was certainly more significant in the 1920s than it had been two or three decades earlier.

It is unfortunately very difficult to get a clear picture of what role secondary and special technical/commercial education played in upward mobility. Commercial education, which was already well developed by 1914, continued to expand. In 1929 2,000 private commercial schools taught vocational skills to pupils with extremely diverse educational backgrounds, who, however, were increasingly apt to have attended high school and even college. 16,000 of the approximately 20,000 public high schools in the country offered commercial courses; in 1931 they attracted about one million pupils. In addition about twenty High Schools of Commerce enrolled approximately 35,000 students in 1925, and some 300 correspondence schools (1926) had about 100,000 students. A wide variety of company training programs and public or private extension schools also offered special commercial and business education.[125]

By the 1920s, high school and some special commercial education were prerequisites for intermediate level office positions like bookkeeper or secretary.[126] In 1926 many office managers were already looking for applicants with some college education for their top secretarial positions.[127] In that year the majority of even the least skilled office employees had spent some time at a commercial school.[128] The Office Managers' Association thought that the number of business and secretarial schools was completely adequate in 1926, though they did complain that the synchronization of course content with rapidly changing office methods left something to be desired.[129]

In addition to commercial and business courses, the expanding vocational education movement concentrated on teaching mechanical and agricultural skills. Technical education below the college level developed more haltingly. Some high schools offered technical courses and the number of technical high schools was increasing, but as employers complained in 1929, many of these schools tended to become liberal arts institutions after a time.[130] Industrialists and teachers of technical subjects also criticized the lack of a system of intermediate technical education in the US comparable to Germany's that would train men for lower and middle level technical positions.

A very thorough NICB survey of US technical education in 1929 found only 39 schools to educate intermediate level technicians. After analyzing demand and surveying employers, the study concluded that at least 250 such schools were needed. It estimated that about 15,000 alumni of these special schools were at work in American industry, while 590,000 technically educated men would be necessary to end the still common practice of recruiting foremen, supervisors, and engineers from the workshop.[131] The authors strongly urged the US to emulate the German system.[132] It would seem then that in contrast to Germany a broad middle range of positions in the factory and technical fields was still open to upwardly mobile manual workers and low level technical employees in the US around 1930, although with time educational background was becoming a more important criterion for selection and advancement in these fields too.

Thus what was new in the 1920s compared to 1900 or 1910 was the greater significance of higher education; this factor most justified the common view that opportunities for career mobility were decreasing for white collar workers. Higher education separated a fairly broad top stratum of managers and well qualified white collar workers from the mass of lower and middle level employees. Even though most of the latter group had attended high school and many had some additional special education, only with great difficulty could they reach the top without college education — which was difficult to make up in later life. The other side of the coin was that many office managers wanted, among other things, employees whose background and aspirations suited them to remain happily in the same position.[133] In 1926 only 56% of a group of (mostly general) office employees surveyed expected promotion; 44% expected to stay in their current jobs. Aspirations for upward mobility were notably absent in groups where most of the employees were women such as filing clerks, addressograph and Hollerich machine operators, but ambition was also low among the predominantly male timekeepers.[134] The results of this early effort to quantify mobility expectations suggest that a large proportion of low level white collar workers did not share the American dream of climbing from the stockroom to the president's office.

The more rapid increase in higher compared to lower and middle level white collar positions and the concurrent blocking of some paths upward had opposite effects: one improved, the other narrowed lower/intermediate white collar employees' chances for upward mobility. To some extent these contrasting trends may have cancelled each other out. Table 3.7 presents the results of a study of social mobility in Norristown, Pennsylvania, a medium sized industrial city near Philadelphia. The table reveals the occupational mobility of 'clerical and sales workers' (our category of lower and middle level white collar workers except for technical employees) who lived in Norristown at the beginning and at the end of each decade; the figures denote the percentage of this group in the same occupational category or in higher or lower categories at the end of a decade.

Table 3.7
Occupational Mobility of Clerical and Sales Workers in Norristown, 1910-50[135]

	1910-20	1920-30	1930-40	1940-50
Professionals	2.5	3.6	3.0	8.0
Proprietors and Managers	15.0	12.5	12.1	18.5
Clerical and Sales Workers	67.5	75.0	60.6	49.4
Skilled Workers	3.3	0.9	5.3	6.2
Semi-skilled Workers	5.9	3.6	11.4	15.4
Unskilled Workers	5.8	4.4	7.6	2.5
Total (%)	100	100	100	100
Total (Number)	120	112	132	162

Between 1920 and 1930 only slightly fewer non-technical white collar workers in Norristown advanced into professional or managerial/proprietor positions than between 1910 and 1920. Transfers to skilled worker status and into unskilled labor declined; the tendency to remain in the lower/intermediate white collar group increased. The table does not reveal whether opportunities for lower and middle level technical employees to reach higher technical and engineering positions diminished (as one would expect in view of the increased importance of academic training), since it combined lower level technicians and higher level engineers in the same category (professionals). White collar workers' stable probability to remain at the same level distinguished them from other occupational groups in Norristown, however, since the rate of upward mobility for most groups was much higher in the 1920s than in the preceding decade. (Thus between 1910 and 1940 an increasing percentage of recruits into white collar positions were manual workers.)[136]

The following conclusions, which must of course be tested with other evidence, may be ventured: The synchronization of the educational system and the world of work continued to increase in the first third of this century. Since educational prerequisites became more significant in occupational mobility, an important decision about an individual's career was now made in school; that is, it was pushed back into the phase of life before entry into the labor force. This shift, however, did not cause a clearly discernible decline in the upward occupational mobility of lower and middle level white collar workers: either because the paths that were particularly affected — e.g., from technician to engineer — could not be isolated and analyzed due to inadequate data, or because educational barriers were still weak and their impact was counteracted by the relatively rapid increase in the number of higher white collar positions. Opportunities to transfer from manual labor to white collar status did not decrease, but tended to increase, probably because an increasing percentage of manual workers now attended high school. Thus the increased significance of educational qualifications for higher occupations did not produce a significant decline in intra or intergenerational rates of upward mobility for lower and middle level white collar workers. Access to the expanding school system in the US was always relatively open, and particularly so in these years.[137] This openness had definite limits, of course: children of businessmen and professionals continued to have easier access to the better (and more expensive) schools and universities than the children of manual workers.[138]

3. Personnel Management and Professional Ideology

Just as the trend toward synchronizing education and occupation continued during the 1920s, so did the tendency toward greater awareness of distinctions between blue and white collar workers that was already visible before 1914. Popular opinion was increasingly sensitive to the non-material status advantages of white collar occupations. More than before the desirability of a white collar job was the social esteem and practical advantages that went with white collar status, rather than its usefulness as a springboard to future independence. One example among many: after the NICB had determined that the average manual worker earned more than lower level office employees in 1926, the report went on to comment:

> But any comparison of the salaries of office employees with the wages of manual workers must take into account certain features of office employment which render it more attractive in many respects than factory work. Office work is not hazardous, although it tends to deprive the worker of the physical exercise necessary to complete physical well being. The hours of employment are uniformly shorter than in factories, averaging perhaps between seven and eight per day. The work is not seasonal and the office employee is ordinarily more secure in periods of business depression. But these considerations are probably less important than the social status attached to office employment. Because, possibly, of the closer contact of the clerical force with management, of the apparently greater opportunities for advancement, office work is generally held in greater social esteem than is manual labor.[139]

There were also signs that the collar line was growing in significance for both workers and management in industry, though company welfare and personnel policies for the most part took no formal notice of it during the 1920s.

The rediscovery of 'human relations' at the workplace, the expansion of welfare capitalism, and the increasingly systematic and professionalized personnel management movement which reached its highpoint in the 1920s were big business' answer to the wartime expansion of trade unions, high labor turnover, the postwar strike wave and threat of workers' radicalism as well as a reflection of the preoccupation with efficiency in these years. Company insurance plans, company housing, stock options and savings banks, improved working conditions and leisure time facilities — all the small integrative efforts designed to create a stable, contented workforce — continued to ignore differences between blue collar and white collar employees.[140] The recognition of the collar line that had existed before the war, e.g. separate eating facilities and vacation rights for office employees, also continued in effect.[141]

The emergence of some white collar discontent and protest in the early 1920s did lead, however, to recommendations for a personnel policy consciously directed at office employees. Some observers warned that since the 'instinctive' loyalty of white collar workers could no longer be taken for granted, and since low morale also lowered their enthusiasm and efficiency at work, companies should try 'to restore the salaried men to their logical place as the lower rank of management'. They suggested that orderly promotion channels, regular salary reviews, seniority bonuses, representation of white collar workers on general employee or separate committees, and separate white collar personnel offices should be instituted to remedy the previous neglect of these employees.[142] Even when employers' fears about their unrest disappeared, stress on the 'human factor' in personnel administration and on non-material motives for hard work and efficiency kept the special characteristics of white collar workers at least partly in view. One author advised that office costs could be reduced by giving white collar workers a sense of secure tenure and keeping the possibility of promotion before their eyes; if possible they should also be motivated with status symbols like private offices, titles, letterheads, and exclusive clubs.[143] Very little came of such suggestions, though in some companies white collar workers were granted a few more privileges. These included special insurance plans, continued salary payment in (brief) illnesses, education and training programs, and such trifles as access to company banquet rooms.[144] A mixture of egalitarian and status considerations propelled at least two large firms to transfer their entire workforce to salary payment after they had been employed for a certain length of time. Factory and office workers were then paid by the month, not docked for short absences, granted paid vacations and greater job security in slack times.[145]

Except for a few worried voices during the war and just afterwards, managers and management experts in the US viewed office workers mainly from the perspective of maximizing efficiency and reducing costs, not as a group with social problems that required attention.[146] A logical corollary of this focus was that individual white collar occupations were treated separately. The literature seldom distinguished between blue collar and white collar workers: white collar workers were not viewed as a quasi-bureaucratic middle stratum above the masses of subordinate manual workers or as a middle class between capital and labor. Criteria for receiving company benefits and the choice of different management techniques for particular groups continued to differ widely between firms, but the collar line was hardly ever decisive (and for that reason tended to remain indistinct).[147]

Company newspapers from these years[148] suggest that management's efforts to increase productivity and loyalty aimed primarily at arousing a sense of occupational identity and quasi-professional pride in their qualifications and functions in each target group. After 1923 General Electric (GE), for instance, began to publish *The G. E. Monogram. A Magazine for the Sales Organization* in addition to the factory division's *Schenectady Works News*. Twice yearly conferences of the sales staff at the firm's own island resort on a nearby lake heard lectures on the scientific character of selling, distributed professional literature, announced the results of sales contests between districts, and encouraged socializing with one's fellows — golf, tennis, picnics, sailing, etc. The magazine reported regularly on which colleges new employees had attended and lauded academic preparation for the profession of 'salesman'. It sought to foster a sense of community based on loyalty to the company and professional identity. Speeches by members of the board of directors to the sales staff usually took up themes such as 'Professionalizing Business Life' and 'Management — A Profession'. The often reiterated public service ideology of these white collar salesmen fitted well into this framework. Profit was seldom mentioned; instead, the avowed aim of salesmanship was service to the company, the customers, and the public.[149]

After January 1926 the firm issued another magazine: *P.T.M. Published by General Electric Test Alumni Association.* These alumni were graduates of two-year company courses held at various GE plants since the early 1890s. The class photos reveal that many mechanics and other skilled workers participated in the program around 1900. By the 1920s, however, it was almost exclusively college graduates who were admitted to this practical/theoretical training program for GE engineers. The graduates belonged to a company-financed club which imitated both the upper class country club and the college fraternity. They cultivated a scientific/engineering/professional image; articles in the magazine praised such values as expert, specialized knowledge; hard work; long years of theoretical preparation; duty and responsibility toward the general public.[150]

GE also sponsored other professional or semi-professional clubs. The GE Cost Accountants' Association was created in 1912; in 1904 the 'Edison Club', which had been founded by engineers with higher degrees, was coopted by the company and expanded.[151] Association Island also hosted conferences of purchasing agents, street lighting specialists, factory superintendents, the General Office and Works Engineers, the Foremen's Club, etc. Company magazines continually restated the characteristics of functional groups and occupations in terms that highlighted their professional or semi-professional qualities. Even the order clerks were extolled for their knowledge of a multitude of rules and regulations and for the precision, concentration and nerve which their job required.[152]

The progress of the personnel management movement during the war, the necessity of systematizing hiring and firing of workers to reduce fluctuation in the labor force, and the introduction of workers' committees had all directed attention to the foreman as a central figure in factory efficiency, discipline, and conflict resolution. Before the war in the US foremen had exercised vast authority; at that time almost all had risen from the ranks without any special training. Large corporations now began to impose certain controls on foremen and to define their functions. A flood of literature appeared on 'foremanship as a profession'. In just one year (1926/27) the national Chamber of Commerce held 324 training courses for foremen; most large firms and some newly founded private organizations did the same. Foremen were to be taught scientific factory and personnel management. These course materials and handbooks painted the ideal foreman as a man with a good (and not only practical) education, as a leader who commanded respect and authority because of his expertise, and as a new 'professional' with broad responsibilites.[153]

During the first world war some of the foremen's clubs founded at the company level in the wake of the turn of the century personnel management movement affiliated at the city level. The Dayton Foremen's Club, founded in 1918, became the nucleus of the Ohio Federation of Foremen's Clubs, which published its own magazine. In 1925 the National Association of Foremen was founded with strong support from corporate management. It held conferences and courses, distributed literature, and supported the creation of foremen's clubs in companies and cities. The Federation's goals included raising the standards and reputation of the 'profession', teaching personnel management, promoting cooperation and unity within management, and distributing information on occupational, technical, economic and management problems in order to foster better social relationships at work, stabilize the workforce and increase profits. These clubs did not represent the social-economic interests of their members. In later years their constitutions expressly forbade trade union activities; immediate expulsion from the Federation was threatened.[154] The efforts of these employer controlled associations in the 1930s and 1940s to counter the threat that foremen would unionize by focusing on their professional status and obligations seems fairly transparent.[155] Like the AMA and the ABA, the National Association of Foremen had a code of honor, which lauded the foreman as a responsible leader of men and an expert in industrial administration as well as a worthy citizen with a strong sense of general social responsibility.[156]

Thus the ideological tinge in this American model of the foreman did not as in Germany highlight a petty industrial official vested with the authority of his office to exercise power over subordinate workers. Instead, it revealed a professional — an expert administrator, teacher, and leader — who performed socially integrative tasks in the interest of higher productivity for his company, but who was equally committed to service to his community and society.

Again, when American industry sought to supplement older financial, compulsory, and paternalistic instruments of motivation and integration with ideological appeals, it did not turn to a general white collar let alone private bureaucratic consciousness, but rather to professional models and identification. Businessmen and managers emphasized their own claims to professional character and status,[157] and so also did large groups of lower and middle level white collar workers, unless they saw themselves simply as workers or employees. In what way and with what consequences did the economic and other pressures of the depression affect white collar workers' professionally-oriented sense of identity?

4. American White Collar Workers in the Economic Crisis and the New Deal

I. IMPACT OF THE DEPRESSION

If one measures the intensity of the economic crisis which began in 1929 by unemployment and loss of purchasing power, that is by those quantifiable indices most important for the life situation of most people, the depression hit the US and Germany equally hard. While the number of hours worked declined somewhat more precipitously between 1929 and 1932 in the US than in Germany, the total number employed dropped more sharply — a reflection of the widespread practice of job sharing in America where unemployment insurance did not exist (see Table 4.1). In 1932 30.1% of the German labor force was unemployed; in the US that year the figure was only 23.6%. That discrepancy did not arise because the US was less affected by the economic crisis, however, but was related to pre-depression unemployment figures: 9.3% in Germany in 1929 compared to 3.2% in the US. All economic indices chart the more rapid recovery of Germany after 1933 and the downward turn of the American economy in 1938, which had no parallel in an already re-arming Germany.

According to Bry's calculations (Table 4.2), the 1929-32 decline in real wages in both Germany and the US was 14-15%. This drop hit each society at a quite different point of departure, however, for the course of real wages between 1913 and 1929 had not run parallel in the US and Germany. The US went into the depression after a period of clearly expanded buying power; Germany lagged far behind the US due to the impact of war, inflation, and other factors. Furthermore, New Deal economic and financial policies brought real wages back to their pre-depression level by 1935; in the investment- and armaments-oriented Nazi economy pre-depression wage levels were not reached until 1938, and then primarily by increasing the number of hours worked.[3]

American white collar workers were hit hard by the economic crisis, though somewhat later and on the whole a little less hard than manual workers. Ohio statistics permit a representative comparison of blue collar and white collar workers (though Ohio fared somewhat better than most states during the depression). Between 1929 and 1932 the number of employed manual workers dropped

Table 4.1
Level of Employment and Unemployment, US and Germany, 1929-38[1]

	(a)	(b)	(c)	(d)	(e)	(f)	(g)	(h)
	Gainfully Occupied Employees (1929 = 100)		Hours Worked (1929 = 100)		Unemployment			
	US	Ger.	US	Ger.	US		Ger.	
					in 000s	in %	in 000s	in %
1929	100.0	100.0	100.0	100.0	1,550	3.2	1,899	9.3
1930	94.3	93.3	—	83.5	4,340	8.7	3,076	15.3
1931	86.7	81.5	—	66.4	8,020	15.9	4,520	23.3
1932	78.7	71.4	53.7	53.8	12,060	23.6	5,576	30.1
1933	79.5	74.0	56.9	61.5	12,830	24.9	4,804	26.3
1934	85.4	85.5	61.1	80.6	11,340	21.7	2,718	14.9
1935	88.1	90.6	67.9	88.4	10,610	20.1	2,151	11.6
1936	93.0	97.2	77.5	99.4	9,030	16.9	1,593	8.3
1937	96.7	104.3	82.2	110.8	7,700	14.3	912	4.6
1938	90.4	110.9	62.2	118.8	10,390	19.0	430	2.1

Table 4.2
Real Wages of Manual Workers (Weekly), US and Germany, 1913-38 (1913 = 100)[2]

	1913	1926	1927	1928	1929	1930	1931	1932	1933	1934	1935	1936	1937	1938
US	100	125	129	131	132	125	123	112	116	124	132	141	151	142
Germany	100	90	97	108	110	105	100	94	98	102	103	106	109	114

by 39.6%; in those years the number of employed bookkeepers, stenographers, and general office employees fell by 20.1%, the number of sales workers with jobs, by 25.6%. The nominal yearly incomes of blue collar workers still employed sank by 32.7% compared to 17.1% and 26.2% respectively for the two categories of white collar workers.[4] The distribution of decline by economic sector was:

Table 4.3
Decline in Employment and Per Capita Income in Ohio, 1929-32 (as a % of 1929 Levels)[4]

	No. of Gainfully Employed	Wages and Salaries
Agriculture	11.5	31.9
Construction	65.0	38.8
Manufacturing	42.8	30.0
Transportation and Energy	26.8	13.2
Commerce	17.7	18.0
Services	9.6	22.4

On the other hand, blue collar workers gained more than white collar employees from the recovery of 1933/34 which was supported by the minimum wage and maximum worktime provisions of New Deal legislation (see Table 4.4).

Table 4.4
Level of Employment and Per Capita Income of Selected Occupational Categories in Ohio, 1933/34[5]

	Level of Employment			Income		
	% Increase 1933-34	Index 1933	1926 = 100 1934	% Increase 1933-34	Index 1933	1926 = 100 1934
1. Wage workers	16.7	68.3	79.7	11.6	66.1	73.8
2. Office employees	8.5	89.7	97.3	2.8	84.7	87.1
3. Sales employees	7.6	97.1	104.5	5.9	65.7	69.6
1.-3.	14.7	72.7	83.4	9.2	69.4	75.8

In 1937, when recovery was further along and 'only' about 15% of the labor force were still unemployed, 1.17 million white collar workers (622,000 men and 548,000 women) remained out of work. They constituted 9.5% of all white collar workers (8.8% of the men and 10.5% of the women).[6]

One reason why fewer white collar than blue collar workers lost their jobs was that they were concentrated in branches of the economy that were less affected by the depression, as Table 4.3 shows. Another reason was that office work was less directly dependent on market fluctuations. Salaried employees in Germany were in roughly the same situation. The larger proportion of white collar workers in the total industrial labor force during the depression reflected their relatively greater job security in both countries (see above, Table 1.3). The wage-salary differential also followed a parallel course in both countries. It is true that American companies cut nominal salaries earlier and more drastically than wages.[7] But the actual earnings of wage workers fell further behind than those of salaried employees during the depression because wages were more directly and quantifiably linked with actual hours worked, production and the market. Short time cut more drastically into the earnings of piece rate and hourly workers than into the weekly wage or monthly salary of the white collar employee. The wage-salary diferential increased in both American and German industry between 1929 and 1932; after that, however, the distance between blue and white collar earnings in American narrowed steadily except in the crisis year 1938 (which had no parallel in Germany).

Table 4.5
Relationship Between Blue Collar and White Collar Earnings in American and German Industry, 1929, 1932, 1937[8]

	US	Germany
1929	1:2.1	1:1.5
1932	1:2.5	1:2.1
1937	1:1.9	1:1.9

In Germany the gap between wages and salaries had never been as great as in the US, and had already declined markedly before 1929.[9] The hierarchical wage policies of the Nazi government accommodated white collar workers' wishes to the extent that they kept the distance between salaries and wages from contracting as much as it did in the US during the depression. Here the hesitant economic recovery and influence of trade unions on government legislation pushed wages closer to salaries[10] even before 1939, and the armaments boom really narrowed the distance.[11] The disparity in wage-salary differentials in the US and Germany corresponded to another contrast: between 1928/29 and 1936 inequality in the distribution of income increased in Germany, while in the US it decreased slightly.[12]

These were important differences between the US and Germany: a more favorable course of earnings here before 1929, and their slower recovery after 1932; and a greater leveling of wages and salaries on the American side during the 1930s. On the other hand, the depression had a very similar impact on the economic situation of white collar workers in both societies, especially compared to blue collar workers. On both sides of the Atlantic white collar workers experienced high unemployment rates and reduced earnings, though equally they were less severely affected than blue collar workers. The social, political, and ideological conditions under which these economic changes occurred were not so similar, however.

Compared with Germany the popular reactions to the depression were remarkably calm in the US. Of course, there were protests. The farmers were particularly quick to demonstrate, for many suffered the abrupt drop in prices that came with the depression after a decade of agricultural overproduction and economic troubles. Urban hunger marches and councils of the unemployed gave radicals and communists an opportunity to agitate for a more radical response from the masses. Hunger thefts, farmers' road blocks, isolated incidents of violence against sheriffs and auctioneers, the army rout of the 20,000 bonus marchers camped in Washington, DC in the summer of 1932 — these developments sparked public debate over whether the country faced a revolution or needed a dictator.[13] On the whole, however, hope and patience, pessimism and resignation were more typical responses for the overwhelming majority of Americans than loss of faith in the governing system itself or readiness to rebel.

One basic difference underlying the divergent responses of the US and Germany to the depression was point of departure: the massive distress of the economic crisis did not find America in the same condition as Germany. War, defeat, and inflation had refueled the insecurity and skepticism about the German political system which was endemic in broad sections of the population. In the US, particularly during the early years of depression, most people expected that recovery would be as quick as it had been after the 1920/21 recession. Furthermore, the creed of individual responsibility for economic and social success kept many Americans from even perceiving their own misery as a collective group experience, let alone joining together to protest. Lengthy unemployment, impoverishment, and declining social status were therefore frequently suffered in silence because people blamed themselves for their own failure rather than looking for socio-economic or political causes.[14] When protests did occur and aggression was turned from the inside toward the outside, the state was not the target in the US as it was in Germany. Americans did not yet hold their government responsible for assuring them a secure collective existence; thus it could not be discredited for its failure.[15] Organized groups or movements (e.g., a radical labor movement) within which potential protest could have become articulate, were weak. And there was a stable political system which after twelve years of Republican rule — in stark contrast to the shaky Weimar Republic — seemed to offer still untried alternatives within itself. These characteristics of US society and politics contributed to what strikes German observers as an amazingly calm response to severe economic crisis.[16]

And in reality the Democratics did find novel ways to use government intervention to stabilize the crisis, although without the coming of the second world war. New Deal policies would not have been sufficient to overcome high unemployment and revive economic growth. Nonetheless, in the early years they did bring some relief to those who were suffering; above all, they offered hope. New Deal innovations (social security, labor legislation, public housing, state control of central bank and monetary policy, etc.) were not yet very developed in the US except for the brief interventionist interlude during the first world war. Since they had not yet been tried, these measures could not yet be dismissed as inadequate. In contrast the German state had been resorting to this kind of government intervention for decades to stabilize economy and society, with only limited success. There such remedies seemed exhausted; they inspired neither the decision-makers nor the masses. Thus the US 'lag' in the shift from competitive capitalism/economic liberalism to organized capitalism and the concomitant long period of reliance on voluntary organization by business and social groups allowed the government to tap unused reserves to reform the system in the 1930s which the interventionist German state had used up long ago. Roosevelt's administration picked up the thread of progressive reform which had been neglected in the 1920s and took the country a great step forward toward organized capitalism. Within a liberal-democratic framework the New Dealers pioneered new instruments of state economic and social intervention; their reforms were a break with American tradition, though they remained far below the level of state intervention taken for granted in Germany. At the same time New Deal programs promoted continued voluntary organization by social groups — particularly businessmen and trade unions — under the limited (and often inadequate) control of the government. Roosevelt's reforms thus stabilized the system by changing it.[17]

After 1934, however, as the New Deal's first successes were becoming as apparent as its limits, radical protest increased and the resistance of conservative elites became more rigid.[18] Demagogic politicians like Father Coughlin, Townsend and Gerald Smith, Floyd Olson and Huey Long joined socialists like Upton Sinclair in challenging the New Deal from positions which to contemporaries and historians alike have eluded clear right-left delineation. With unprecedented government assistance the labor movement began to organize previously unorganized groups and industries; within limits their demands and tactics became more radical. Strikes were more frequent and more violent. Employer reactions to labor's militancy varied; periodically, however, they organized private militia to do battle with their striking workers. Their criticism of Roosevelt for his pro-labor policies and modest reforms increased dramatically, and the New Deal faced more heated opposition from business and the well-to-do.

Thus after 1934, the US underwent a process of class polarization that marked the end of FDR's 'all class alliance'. In the Second New Deal, which began with a second wave of reform legislation, Roosevelt allied himself more decisively with the progressive forces. His strongest supporters in the 1936 victory had been the urban masses, those on modest incomes, the new ethnic groups, Negroes and organized labor; though at this highpoint of power he had also received many votes in wealthier circles.[19] The militant sit down strikes (which public opinion polls showed that a majority thought should have been suppressed), the court packing scheme, and finally the new economic crisis beginning in the summer of 1937 cost the president much of his authority over Congress and brought reform legislation almost to a standstill. Conservative demands for a return to the 'normalcy' of the 1920s increased; radical groups on the right and the left became more active. In response to this radicalism conservative legislators and organizations mounted the intolerant investigations and witchhunts which were often really aimed at Roosevelt and other New Dealers.[20] Although international tension and the consequent increase in the importance of foreign policy and defense, then the outbreak of war in Europe, helped FDR to his third victory in 1940, his margin was much narrower than in 1936. This time support from big cities and the less well off were even more clearly responsible.[21]

Under these circumstances class and socio-economic lines divided political opinions and behavior in the US more distinctly than they had before. Social and economic concerns tended to overshadow ethnic, cultural, and religious factors, even though the voting behavior of particularly first and second generation immigrants continued to be more strongly affected by the latter than by class or occupation.[22] The first systematic studies of the influence of income, employment, class situation and other socio-economic factors on political thought and behavior appeared; Gallup and Roper began to conduct public opinion polls.[23] It was in this climate of opinion that contemporary observers also began to pay more attention to white collar workers as a socio-economic group.

II. WHITE COLLAR WORKERS AS A PROBLEM IN PUBLIC DISCUSSION

There were also more specific reasons why white collar workers attracted greater public attention in the mid and late 1930s. Mass unemployment among salaried employees was a new phenomenon, and as commentators frequently repeated, it meant not only material distress but, even more for this group than for manual workers, a loss of social status.[24] Particularly in the early years of the depression white collar workers did not appear on public welfare lists to the extent that their level of unemployment would have led one to expect. They tended to keep going on their own savings for as long as possible; out of shame or fear of embarrassment they were reluctant to apply for relief.[25] In 1935, however, the number of white collar workers receiving government assistance increased rapidly (up 12%) at a time when the total number of recipients was already declining (by 2%). Relief administrators explained this atypical group behavior as primarily due to the fact that many white collar workers had completely exhausted their savings and other private reserves in their long unemployment and finally had no other alternative.[26] The 560,000 white collar workers on relief in March 1935 (including non-manual self-employed persons) were distributed as follows:[27]

	Share of All Unemployed White Collar Workers 1935 (%)	Share of All White Collar Workers in 1930 Census of Occupations (%)
Sales Employees	32.4	22.9
Office Employees	38.6	32.1
Technical and Professional Employees	14.7	20.9
Proprietors and Managers (Excluding Agriculture)	14.3	24.1

Technical and professional employees, who had shunned public assistance the longest but then increased most rapidly in 1935/36, included: over 20,000 teachers, 15,000 musicians and music teachers, 6,800 nurses, 6,200 engineers, 4,500 draftsmen and technicians, 3,800 actors, 3,000 clerics, 2,900 artists, 800 chemists, 1,400 journalists and 675 doctors.

Technically qualified white collar workers had found jobs in the public construction and conservation projects of the New Deal at an early date. At first the only refuge for unemployed white collar workers without technical skills, however, was manual labor.[28] It took a while for federal agencies like the Federal Emergency Relief Administration, the Civil Works Administration and its successor, the Works Progress Administration (WPA) under the direction of former social worker Harry L. Hopkins, to create special 'service programs' for white collar workers. Federally financed schools in isolated rural areas put teachers to work — and meant opportunities for children, which they would not have had without the depression and the New Deal. White collar workers sorted, organized, and catalogued documents at city halls and other local and state offices and worked on the collections of archives, museums and libraries at federal expense. These programs also supported survey research on a wide variety of topics: e.g., for tax purposes and transportation problems. Translation of the German classics on the white collar problem into English was subsidized as well. Public funds created jobs for doctors and nurses that improved the nation's health care. Finally, and most controversially, the government financed theater, music, music education and writers' projects and supported publicly financed recreation and educational opportunities. At the beginning of 1935 about 10% of all those employed on public works projects were involved in white collar projects. They provided jobs for about one-twelfth of the men and almost one-third of the women working on all emergency relief projects. In March 1936 there were 16,000 separate (mostly local) white collar projects under WPA auspices. In February 1936 23% of those on emergency relief were employed by 'service programs'.[29]

The wages paid by the public works projects of the WPA were not permitted to compete with private industry. Blue collar and white collar employees received a monthly check (though everyone was docked for absences). The salary scale was based on the local price level, the size of the city, and membership in one of four categories: unskilled, semi-skilled, skilled, or technical and professional work. The last category was reserved for white collar workers with the appropriate qualifications: most lower and middle level white collar workers were intermingled with manual workers in the first three categories. For relief administration purposes there was as yet no clear division between blue collar and white collar worker.[30]

These programs, however, no more solved the unemployment problems of white collar workers than those of blue collar workers. Even apart from the extremely low pay and limited hours, they provided jobs for only a small minority of those who were unemployed. In 1937, 26% of female and 28% of male white collar workers who were out of work were engaged on emergency relief projects; in that year 17% of all women and 29% of all men who were unemployed had found public works jobs.[31]

Emergency relief for non-manual workers aroused vigorous public debate. The defenders of these programs did not include in their arguments the concern that volatile lower middle class types of resentment and protest might develop from mass unemployment among white collar workers. In addition to the standard argument that public works projects increased buying power and would thus help overcome the depression, Harry Hopkins and his associates stressed the social and economic 'waste' that this level of unemployment of qualified teachers, technicians, etc. represented. They also put appropriation requests for this kind of emergency relief work in a broad, to a certain extent social democratic framework when they argued that the depression had provided the opportunity for the government to take long overdue action in some areas. These thoughts, often only intimated to a reluctant Congress, came up particularly often in arguments to support some of the service programs (for teachers, artists, technicians, doctors, researchers, librarians, etc.), since such programs were more directly connected to social reform than draining a swamp or constructing a highway.[32]

Severe critics of emergency relief for non-manual workers were not disarmed by these defenses. One relief administrator noted that many people from better off groups seemed to think it desirable to discipline unemployed and impoverished persons with physical labor. They were pleased at the idea of an unemployed musician digging canals or an impoverished child psychologist working in a garment factory. He went on to comment that this strain of 'atavistic political reaction' did not direct their work.[33] To many Americans, however, these non-manual relief projects were difficult to justify and provoked frequent charges of boondoggling.

Economic distress, unemployment, and public relief during the depression, which for the first time touched significant numbers in the middle class, stimulated public discussion of white collar workers at the very time that their middle class status was seriously threatened by that same crisis.[34] Doubts about capitalism and speculation about a possible revolution in the US flared up in public discussion in those years; they directed new attention to the political behavior of white collar workers, particularly from writers on the left. So also did the expansion and relative radicalization of the American labor movement. The concept of the 'new middle classes' seems to have been borrowed from European literature or at any rate become more widely known at this time.[35] Stratification schemas dividing white collar from blue collar or the new middle class from the working class now became more popular with statisticans and sociologists.[36] German emigrants like Emil Lederer and Hans Speier may have contributed to sharpening American perspectives on social class, especially since their writings on white collar workers from the preceding two decades were partially translated into English in these years.[37]

Other factors which helped develop previously untrained perceptions of distinctions between white collar and blue collar were the growing awareness of the impact of social-economic factors on political behavior, better understanding of the impersonal, collective elements involved in success and failure, and last but not least, the role the lower middle class played in the triumph of fascism in Europe. The 'new middle class' came to refer to a comprehensive social group. For the first time American authors (though at first rarely) began to ask the question that had animated the German debate since the turn of the century: What were the politics of this growing and potentially significant social strata; which side would they choose if political polarization increased? Answers to this question in the US echoed the answers debated in Germany from the late 19th century onward. Although most observers agreed that the political behavior of the dependent middle classes seemed fuzzy, indecisive, and internally divided, they drew widely differing conclusions from these observations. Four main approaches may be distinguished:

1. Authors who started from a European background or

perspective were particularly apt to see a danger or even probability that the sections of the lower middle class that were hard hit by the depression — small businessmen, white collar workers, and small farmers — might serve as a social base for fascism in America. They thought that lower middle class frustration, conservatism, socio-economic decline relative to the working class, and a consequent turn to the right seemed inevitable in western industrial societies where two powerful blocks — organized capital and organized labor — squeezed and threatened the lower middle classes. If the economic crisis continued, they expected the new middle class in the US to politicize in a right-radical direction just as it had in Germany. The main lines of this interpretation coincided with the European views on the relationship between capitalism, lower middle class, and fascism summarized at the beginning of this study.[38]

2. Authors who paid more attention to the actual situation in America stressed that although the dependent middle classes had been politically inactive and insignificant in the past, if the crisis continued one of two things would occur. Either there would be reactionary or even fascist white collar protests as in Europe, or white collar workers would join with the increasingly organized working class to support left-wing protests and reforms (or even revolution). In either event this school of thought predicted that the lower middle class would play a decisive political role in the future. Unlike earlier decades, political groups on the left began to view white collar workers as potential sympathizers who might become allies. For instance *Common Sense*, edited by Alfred M. Bingham and Selden Rodman after 1932, hoped for an alliance between blue collar and white collar workers. The magazine advocated an American style of radicalism that was non-communist and non-marxist but also anti-capitalist, social democratic and technocratic. Its editors warned the left not to be misled by the fiction of an inherently revolutionary working class, but instead to take seriously the attitudes and interests that white collar workers shared with large parts of the working class in America. *Common Sense* favored social reform, economic planning for a strong democratic state, and the eventual creation of a 'cooperative commonwealth'. Civil liberties and other liberal principles would be guaranteed, including private property (though not of all means of production); the editors decried talk of force or class conflict and called for respect for the patriotism and puritanism of the American middle classes. 'A sound radical movement will be one-hundred percent American, defending the home, the family, the church, and the nation'.[39] Norman Thomas' socialist party also emphasized the urgency (and the real possibility) of winning over the

masses of white collar workers and regretted its previous neglect of this group.[40] This approach to the problem distinguished white collar workers as a social group from the upper classes and the working class; its adherents were apt to view the task of winning them over to the progressive side as neither easy nor impossible.

3. A small group of authors followed an orthodox marxist interpretation. They believed that lower and middle level white collar workers would necessarily be forced to the left by the depression; they would thus swell the ranks of the revolutionary forces. The *New Masses*, a magazine sympathetic to revolution and communism, had previously ignored white collar workers as irrelevant or mocked them as mediocre pen pushers, dupes of reactionary big business.[41] But the first demonstrations by unemployed white collar workers moved the magazine to demand and predict that this previously petty bourgeois social group would fight 'shoulder to shoulder' with their working class brothers for the revolution. Relatively orthodox marxists like Lewis Corey saw the great mass of white collar workers not as a new middle class but as a new proletariat; under the impact of the depression white collar workers were in the process of becoming conscious of their true class interests. This approach excluded an elite stratum of executives and managers from this prognosis and consigned them to the forces of reaction because of their privileged relationship to big business.[42] In contrast to the first two approaches, this interpretation did not consider white collar workers an independent social group between labor and capital and did not expect them to play an independent political role. Instead, most white collar workers were placed in the working class and a small top group was aligned with the ruling class.

4. Each of these views more or less paralleled opinions which were also more or less prominent in European analyses. The most common approach to the problem in the US, however, had no parallel on the continent. Although most politicians, commentators, and observers did not anticipate a united revolutionary tide of 'head and handworkers', in one respect they shared the same premises as the orthodox marxists: they saw no reason to differentiate between the politics of the working class and those of a separate white collar class. They assumed that the political attitudes and behavior of most white collar workers would reflect the same reform sentiments, moderate liberalism, and economic distress that shaped the political views and behavior of wage workers. Thus there was no reason to single out white collar workers and direct specific arguments or promises to them; there was no need to take them into account as an independent factor in political calculations. All national party platforms (except for the Socialist Party in

1932)[43] ignored the division of the labor force into blue collar and white collar groups.[44] Roosevelt did not distinguish between blue collar workers and white collar workers or separate wage earners from salaried employees: he liked to address himself to labor, the forgotten man, the common man; to farmers, businessmen and consumers. He spoke about the problems of home owners, employed persons, and minorities, but he did not isolate white collar workers from the working and the business classes.[45] This approach rendered the lower middle classes invisible: there was as little expectation that these social groups would become centers of protest as there was room for special privileges for white collar over blue collar workers in New Deal legislation. With minor exceptions white collar workers as a social problem or a distinct group appear not to have entered into the economic, social, and practical political thought of New Dealers.[46]

Which of these four lines of interpretation came closest to describing the actual thought and behavior of American white collar workers is of fundamental significance for the received thesis presented at the outset and the questions which have framed this investigation. Did the political outlooks of white collar and blue collar workers in the US finally diverge more than they had before in these years of economic crisis? Or did lower and middle level white collar workers respond to the depression in the same basic ways as the masses of manual workers? Did white collar workers develop specifically lower middle class types of protest behavior which distinguished them — as their counterparts in Germany — from the organized working class? Or unlike German salaried employees, did the economic crisis force white collar workers who were now ready to combine to pursue collective interests to join the organized labor movement? Did the majority line up left of center, as some observers expected, or did they turn to the right? In the remainder of this chapter answers to these questions will be sought by examining three types of evidence: the history of white collar organizations during the depression, the social basis of American right-radical organizations in these years, and the raw data of early (1936 on) public opinion polls.

III. WHITE COLLAR WORKERS AND THEIR ORGANIZATIONS[47]

In 1932 about 31% of all German salaried employees (private and government) were organized, compared to 34% of all manual workers. If one isolates salaried employees in the private sector, the figure is even higher — 42%. In contrast only 12% of blue collar workers and 5% of white collar workers belonged to unions in the

Table 4.6
American White Collar Unions, 1935[50]
(Year Founded and Whether AFL or Independent [I] Union)

Organization	Membership
1. United Licensed Officers of the United States of America (1933 I)[51]	2,000
2. Air Line Pilots Association (1931 I)	600
3. Brotherhood of Railway and Steamship Clerks, Freight Handlers, Express and Station Employees (1898 AFL)	135,000
4. American Radio Telegraphists' Association (1931 AFL)[52]	2,609
5. Order of Railroad Telegraphers (1886 AFL)	50,000
6. Commercial Telegraphers' Union of North America (1903 AFL)[53]	7,500
7. International Brotherhood of Telephone Workers (1920 I)	5,400
8. Retail Clerks' International Protective Association (1890 AFL)	7,200
9. Associated Actors and Artists (1919 AFL)[54]	14,000
10. Federation of Architects, Engineers, Chemists and Technicians (1933 I)	6,000
11. International Federation of Technical Engineers', Architects' and Draftsmen's Unions (1918 AFL)	3,800
12. American Federation of Musicians (1896 AFL)	110,000
13. American Newspaper Guild (1933 I)	6,000
14. American Federation of Teachers (1916 AFL)	20,000
15. National Federation of Federal Employees (1917 I)	64,000
16. American Federation of Government Employees (1932 AFL)	18,024
17. National Association of Master Mechanics and Foremen of Navy Yards and Naval Stations (1905 AFL)	250
18. Railway Mail Association (1898 AFL)	14,494
19. National Council of Officials of the Railway Mail Service (1922 I)	330
20. National Alliance of Postal Employees (1913 I)	4,800
21. National Association of Postal Supervisors (1908 I)	6,415
22. National Association of Postmasters of the United States (? I)	5,000
23. National League of District Postmasters of the United States (1894 I)	17,000
24. National Federation of Post Office Clerks (1906 AFL)	40,000
25. United National Association of Post Office Clerks of the United States (1899 I)	45,000
26. National Association of Substitute Post Office Employees (1933 I)	3,000
Total	588,322

US in 1935.[48] Of the almost seven million organized employees in Germany in 1932, 25% were white collar workers. Out of the 4.655 million workers organized in 156 unions in the US in 1935, only 588,000 (12.6%) belonged to the 26 unions which were primarily made up of white collar workers.[49] Not only was the US labor force as a whole much less organized than the German, but white collar workers lagged far behind blue collar workers, in contrast to Germany where both categories reached similar degrees of organization in the Great Depression.

Table 4.6 presents information on the white collar unions existing in the US in 1935. Before discussing some of the German-American differences in white collar unionization, this chapter will trace the history of a few selected American white collar unions, particularly in the retail sector and in industry.

1. Sales Employees and their Unions

The depression hit retail employees hard. From 1929 to 1933 the value of all goods sold by American retail stores sank from $48.459 million to $24.517 million; taking the deflationary price index into account, this was about a 25% real drop. The number of retail establishments shrunk from 1.476 million (1929) to 1.440 million (1933); then, however, it expanded rapidly to 1.588 million stores in 1935.[55] To determine the level of employment and unemployment in retail trade compared to other economic sectors, only the number of employees who would have had full-time positions if there were no part-time or reduced hours will be counted as employed. The census defined full-time, however, as the usual number of hours per week in that industry that year — and that meant that the same factory could have considered 50 hours a normal work week in 1929, but only 30 normal in 1933. Defined in this way, the number of fully employed wholesale and retail workers dropped 22% and 24% respectively between 1929 and 1932 (the low point). Although this decline was more pronounced than that in banking (19%), it was considerably less than in most industries, where the number of fully employed workers fell by 36% (this figure excludes mining and construction, which were even harder hit). Nominal earnings for these fully employed workers sank by 29% in wholesale and 24% in retail trade between 1929 and the low point in 1933; in these years nominal earnings in industry fell by 30% (excluding mining and construction) and by 12% in construction. Since the consumer price index fell almost 25% in the same period, this contraction in retail earnings did not mean lower real wages for those who actually continued to work full-time. In fact, however, widespread part-time work during the depression meant that the nominal income of retail employees who still had jobs fell by just under 40%, about 15% more than the increase in the value of the dollar.[56]

Sales clerks not only suffered unemployment and lower earnings in the depression; company benefits for clerks as well as other workers were curtailed. Training programs, libraries, staff magazines, bonuses and raises were reduced or eliminated in many department stores. Dividends on the company stock that clerks had held approached zero and paper values also declined steeply; stock option plans were often abolished.[57] Furthermore, opportunities for promotion also contracted as the fortunes of retail stores stagnated or declined. Suffice to say that after a decade of prosperity and corresponding optimism among store employees, this onslaught of troubles shook their confidence in their employers, and thus their loyalty.[58]

The worsening economic situation of sales clerks brought new signs of life to the RCIPA. *The Advocate* began to criticize employers' pay cuts and printed sharp articles about the unemployment problem. After many years with no victories to report, the newspaper followed signs of emerging discontent closely and gave extensive coverage to the sporadic demonstrations by sales clerks. Editorials condemned employers for their greedy exploitation of the glutted labor market. The union renewed its protests which had first appeared at the end of the first world war against the practice of firing middle-aged clerks. At the end of 1931 the RCIPA vigorously protested the A & P's (with 80,000 employees) successful efforts to block union organization of its clerks by quickly signing separate contracts with blue collar unions covering the minority of manual workers employed; the company had thus undercut the clerks' support and 'destroyed the solidarity of labor'. *The Advocate* printed frequent attacks on the excessive, irresponsible power and repressive policies of the employers. Articles claimed that deep discontent over unbearable working conditions was brewing in retail stores; massive trade union organization of sales clerks appeared imminent. 'Will I have my job next week? Will they cut my wages? These are two questions uppermost in the minds of the retail employees today which are responsible for much of the spirit of dread and uneasiness that prevails'. At the end of 1932, *The Advocate* once again took on the great chain stores, predicting a 'wave of organization' in the near future. In militant tones the union declared itself well prepared to take up the struggle.[59]

The RCIPA's membership did not begin to grow before 1933, however. As in previous depressions, the strained financial situation of potential members and the resistance of anti-union employers who had the upper hand because of the oversupply of labor impeded the translation of dissatisfaction into trade union organization. The entire American labor movement reached its numerical low point in 1933.[60] Moreover, the RCIPA had gone into the depression in shakier condition than most unions. At least one-third of the locals still in existence in 1932 had no contracts with employers; only one-third reported contracts in force that covered both hours and wages.[61] Thus the appearance of widespread unrest among unorganized clerks was not sufficient to boost the union's fortunes; instead, a push 'from above' paved the way for the revival of trade union organization in retail stores.

The National Recovery Administration Act (NRA) of June 1933 was the cornerstone of Roosevelt's attempt to stimulate the economy through a moderate dose of state intervention. Modeled in part on the government's role in the economy during the first world war, the NRA foresaw a looser enforcement of anti-trust laws to allow government supervised compacts to regulate maximum work time, minimum wages, working conditions and prices in each industry or economic area. AFL lobbying efforts succeeded in including the right of employees to join (or not join) a trade union and to bargain collectively through representatives of their own choosing to establish wages and working conditions. NRA codes were to be negotiated between the employers' associations and the labor unions in each industry; once approved by the president the codes would have the force of law. If either side refused to participate, the president had authority to establish a code for that industry by decree. Laissez faire liberals, small businessmen who feared monopoly power, Jeffersonian radicals, some socialists and communists criticized the NRA as a step in the direction of a corporatist or even fascist state; they predicted that it would consolidate the power of united big business at the expense of small businesses and the public. Economists and historians have tended to be skeptical about the NRA's impact on economic recovery. For trade unions, however, the NRA provided a degree of public recognition and legitimation that was unprecedented except for the war years. Of course labor's new influence also meant a further step toward its acceptance of and integration in the private enterprise system. The president of the AFL and the RCIPA's officers celebrated Section 7(a) of the NRA as labor's magna carta.

After the conservative majority on the Supreme Court held the NRA unconstitutional in May 1935 Congress passed the National Labor Relations Act (Wagner Act) in July to continue and even strengthen the provisions of Section 7(a). The Act also created the National Labor Relations Board and gave it extensive authority over capital-labor relations. It outlawed unfair labor practices, particularly the practice of creating company unions which had mushroomed since 1933 as employers tried to circumvent Section 7(a). The right to join a union and bargain collectively could now be more stringently enforced.[62]

The RCIPA had hoped to expand with the help of the NRA. It was especially important when addressing sales clerks to be able to point out that the president and the Congress were behind union organization. As trade unions became more respectable, it was easier for the clerks who were so directly dependent on public opinion to join. Furthermore, the RCIPA could point to the obvious advantages organized groups had in shaping these new government policies and laws. And in fact, just after the NRA was passed a few new RCIPA locals were founded. However, President Coulter of the clerks' union played only a minor role in the conference which met in Washington in the summer of 1933 to establish the Retail Code. The clerks' union was still too small and weak. The Code Roosevelt signed in October of that year reduced the maximum hours that could be worked in retail stores to 48 a week. Overtime was prohibited; the minimum wage was set at $10 to $14 a week depending on the size of the locality (with some special exceptions for young trainees). Salaries could not be reduced below the level of July 1933. The Retail Code covered all employees; it did not differentiate between blue and white collar workers or between women and men. The only exception was a top group of white collar workers who were responsible for running a store or a department, and who earned at least $25-$35 a week (depending on location): they were exempted from the maximum hours provisions of the Code. Not more than one in five employees in any given store could be counted as 'executives' in this broad sense.[63]

The NRA Code reduced the hours of many clerks, and meant higher earnings for those at the bottom of the pay scale; most stores had to raise their lowest wages to conform to the Code.[64] Their improving circumstances appear to have reduced rather than increased sales clerks' interest in joining the RCIPA, however. The union grew very slowly until 1935: the long-standing indifference of clerks to union organization, anti-union campaigns by large employers (who founded company unions when necessary to thwart Section 7[a]), and inadequate RCIPA leadership in spite of a few big strikes in 1934/35 were responsible. The RCIPA also lost out in jurisdictional conflicts with other AFL unions.[65]

In 1935, however, three trends combined to change the RCIPA's fortunes: discontent among intermediate and top level sales employees; anger at wage cuts and long hours imposed after the NRA was held unconstitutional; and new directions in the

American labor movement as a whole, particularly the formation of the CIO.

The 'head clerks' or branch managers of large chain stores derived a large part of their earnings from a percentage of their store's profits. Sharp competition between branches kept these managers under constant pressure. They worked extremely long hours; they could be (and often were) transferred without notice by corporate management. This was one technique to increase profits, since it was expected that a new manager would eliminate customs and routines which relaxed sales efforts and bring aggressive new methods to his new store. He was also apt to fire a large proportion of the old manager's staff in order to start over with his own men, who were usually low paid beginners. The declining volume of sales and reduced profits in the depression hardly reduced the pressures and demands on this group of white collar workers, but they did reduce their earnings and put them under constant threat of losing their jobs. Twelve to -sixteen hour work days, competition from high school graduates seeking work, but especially the loss of earnings mobilized these 'managers', who had previously considered themselves above the labor movement.[66] As 'executives' they were not covered by the NRA's limitation on hours, and they still could be and were required to work long days. The law's minimum wage provisions did not help but hurt them; as better off white collar workers (and the AFL!) had always predicted, the minimum wage not only reduced the distance between intermediate salaries and the lowest wages paid, it often actually reduced their salary check. Employers tried to get by without raising their total wage bill by cutting middle level salaries which were not fixed by law or contract to make up for the cost of the minimum wage provisions. Or in another aggravating twist, a company might raise an employee's salary to just above the 'executive' line so that he could be required to work more than 48 hours a week.[67]

These difficulties, which stemmed at least as much from a sense of *relative* deprivation (decrease in the distance fom their inferiors) as from absolute distress, led those affected to protest and organize. Ultimately these 'managers' found a home in the labor movement. They did not organize as managers to separate themselves from ordinary sales clerks or as white collar employees to distinguish themselves from blue collar workers, but joined 'Managers and Clerks Unions' — as some locals of the RCIPA were now named — within or in close association with the AFL.[68] Many of these new elite recruits became leaders in the expanding RCIPA and worked actively to increase the union's scope and power.[69] They remained active in the RCIPA until 1948, when the

Taft-Hartley Act excluded 'supervisory employees' and thus also this group of store managers from trade union membership.

The impact of legislative and court actions on ordinary clerks also contributed to reviving the RCIPA. In 1935 the Supreme Court decided that the NRA was unconstitutional. Minimum wages were only reestablished when the Fair Labor Standards Act went into effect in 1939 (25-40 cents per hour; these levels were quickly exceeded under wartime inflation). In 1935 the number of hours worked in most industries increased and wage cuts were common. This reversal moved many poorly paid and overworked sales clerks, who had profited much more from the NRA minimum wage/maximum hours than skilled industrial workers and who had thus been less likely to organize with the NRA, in effect, to finally join the RCIPA.[70] The spectacular growth and successes of the labor movement in other industries also sparked their decision to organize.

Anger among unskilled and semi-skilled workers after the NRA was struck down may also have contributed to the schism in the American labor movement which began with the formation of the CIO in 1935/36 and lasted until the AFL-CIO reunited in 1955. The CIO's secession was due primarily to the AFL leadership's inability to modify the craft principle to allow the effective organization of unskilled and semi-skilled workers because of the opposition of powerful conservative unions like the Machinists, Boilermakers, Engravers, and the construction trades. The Congress of Industrial Organizations, whose main strength came from industrial unions in coal, textiles, garment making, steel, auto plants, oil, and rubber, stood politically to the left of the AFL. To many contemporaries it signaled the beginning of a social democratic labor movement in America. The new organization's commitment to political action, concern with broad economic, social and political problems, advocacy for the masses of unskilled workers, as well as the internal democracy in CIO unions, their militant tactics, and the relatively large number of communists (some in important positions) convinced many observers that they were witnessing the emergence of a new radical-reformist labor movement. One would not want to deny the partial truth of this contemporary view, even though in retrospect it is probably more correct to conclude that except for recruiting the unskilled (which was not completely unprecedented and, moreover, after May 1937 the AFL because challenged became more energetic in this area also), the CIO remained well within the traditional boundaries of labor organizations in the US. CIO unions also had a fairly narrow workplace orientation; they pursued primarily economic interests by unrevolutionary, non-radical means; they too accepted capitalism and management prerogative in principle and practice.[71]

The shock waves from the secession of the CIO also shook the RCIPA. Two New York locals, one under social democratic and the other under communist leadership, had rebelled against the union's executive committee in mid-1935. The dissidents' criticism of individual leaders and the executive's refusal to call the convention postponed since 1924, demands for better propaganda and membership recruitment, turned into a refusal to turn over funds to the National and an unsuccessful petition to the AFL to be recognized as an independent organization. In February 1937 the New York opposition founded a 'New Era Committee' within the RCIPA; they sponsored a turbulent mass meeting of 3,000 to 4,000 persons, including delegates from locals outside New York. In May they joined the CIO as the United Retail Employees of America, later the United Retail & Wholesale Employees of America (URWEA). The URWEA held annual conventions after 1937; in 1938 it already claimed 40,000 members (the RCIPA had just 24,000 in 1937).[72]

In addition to the personal rivalries and political differences between the New York locals and the RCIPA leadership, two structural problems also lay behind this split. In the first place, the executive committee elected in 1924 was still in office in 1936; its composition did not reflect the shift in the balance of power within the RCIPA to the large eastern cities, particularly New York. Secondly, the leadership's reluctance to call the long delayed convention alienated many members and fueled charges of incompetence from the rebellious locals.[73] Their argument that the craft union principle of the RCIPA prevented the effective organization of department store employees with their diverse occupations and levels of skill,[74] was at best only half true, however. Jurisdictional conflicts did develop between the RCIPA and the Teamsters, Butchers, and Tailors unions, but they did not block organization per se. A more important evil was the way department stores manipulated the craft unions: often they were eager to sign contracts with their relatively few blue collar workers to block the RCIPA's organizing efforts. Thus it was not the craft union principle in itself, but the way that employers could use it, that destroyed the solidarity of labor. In the US as opposed to Germany, employers did not cultivate white collar workers' separatist leanings; here the cherished craft union principle of skilled workers gave store owners the chance to court their blue collar workers and 'privilege' them with special contracts.[75] It is also true that after 1933 the RCIPA directed its main organizing efforts at department and chain stores. And according to reports in *The Advocate*, the clerks' union and local craft unions worked closely together during strikes. Moreover, in practice RCIPA locals did not strictly observe the craft principle but usually tried to organize all department store employees down to the stockroom.[76]

Only the URWEA, however, positively committed itself to industrial unionism and to organizing 'all persons employed in and about retail, wholesale, and warehouse establishments'. The RCIPA definition 'all employees of stores, mercantile and mail order establishments who are actively engaged in handling or selling merchandise' maintained the link to the sales process, though in practice this wording could include a wide variety of occupations. In fact the main difference between the two unions' membership was that the RCIPA concentrated on employees in retail establishments (respecting the domain of the International Ladies Garment Workers Union, the Teamsters, and other AFL unions) while the URWEA (without such considerations) tried to organize all employees of both wholesale and retail firms. The collar line played no role in either organization's membership criteria.[77]

Thus the growth and limited radicalization of these sales employees' trade unions were produced by the grievances of 'managing' employees, the fall of the NRA's protective provisions, and competition between the AFL and CIO — in the context of the depression and the New Deal. Leo Troy has prepared what are probably the best figures on the size of American labor unions from 1930 on, based on dues actually paid. By his calculations the RCIPA and the URWEA both grew rapidly and continuously after 1935-37 (see Table 4.7).

Table 4.7
Membership in AFL, CIO, RCIPA, URWEA, 1935-55 (in 000s)[78]

	RCIPA (AFL)	URWEA (CIO)	AFL (Total)	CIO (Total)
1935	12.0		3218.4	
1936	17.6		3516.4	
1937	23.8	40.0	3179.7	1991.2
1938	30.0	40.0	3547.4	1957.7
1939	51.0	44.0	3878.0	1837.7
1940	73.5	47.9	4343.2	2154.1
1941	83.0	47.9	5178.8	2653.9
1945	96.0	60.0	6890.4	3927.9
1950	179.1	52.7	8494.0	3712.8
1955	273.4	122.7	10593.1	4808.3

Both unions also became more radical in the late 1930s. Strikes reached a highpoint in the US in 1937; in that one year there were almost as many strikes and lockouts as in 1936 and 1938 combined: 4,740 conflicts involving 1.8 million workers. Between September 1936 and June 1937 almost 500,000 blue collar and white collar workers participated in sitdown strikes, and not only in the auto industry. In February and March of 1937 employees occupied Woolworth's and other large department stores in Detroit. Sales clerks cooperated with restaurant and kitchen workers, though they were members of different AFL unions; since police refused to intervene as long as there were no public disturbances, success was swift. Sitdown strikes by sales clerks spread to New York, Philadelphia, Providence and other cities, and many department stores prepared for trouble by hiring more detectives, spies, and supervisors. The RCIPA leadership seems to have been surprised by their members' militancy; they were followers rather than leaders in these struggles. But since there was usually no formal rebellion within the locals, the union's functionaries conducted the negotiations which wrung concessions on working conditions and union recognition from the employers. Even though the tide of sitdown strikes ebbed after April 1937, the strike wave continued throughout the summer and beyond.[79]

After mid-1937, however, boycotts, petitions to the NLRB, and other efforts to gain union recognition became more important than strikes. The goals of the RCIPA and the URWEA were essentially the same: higher salaries, a minimum wage, limited hours, the union shop, a 50% bonus for overtime, layoffs according to seniority, abolition of company unions, no reprisals against union members, better vacations — in sum, the greatest possible union control over working conditions codified in collective bargaining agreements. Labor conflicts in retail stores were not as intense and violent as the great battles in mass production industries. For one thing, department store owners capitulated more easily than Ford, US Steel, or Firestone because their business was more directly dependent on unbroken contact with the public. Furthermore, despite all their new militancy sales employees were asking for less, and were more willing to compromise, than industrial workers. Only 3% of retail employees belonged to unions in 1939, and their organizations were still somewhat shaky. The great chain stores like the A & P (with 90,000 employees at the end of the 1930s, as large as the RCIPA and URWEA combined!) gave up very little ground to the clerks' unions. Nonetheless, the demands and tactics of sales clerks' organizations were very similar to those of other trade unions; they spoke for a much larger number of clerks at the end of the decade than they had at the beginning.[80]

Speeches at the conventions of the RCIPA and the URWEA in 1939 reflected a new accent in the trade union consciousness of these white collar workers. Professional ideologies were not even indirectly mentioned; many guest speakers from friendly blue collar unions spoke to both gatherings. The programmatic parts of the RCIPA constitution had not been changed by a 1935 referendum on organizational questions, but in 1939 constitutional revision substantially altered the AFL union's stance. The new constitution stressed the identical interests of all workers, drew up rules for strikes and lockouts, and provided for a union strike fund. It referred primarily to 'fellow workers', less often to 'retail clerks', and hardly at all to 'sales people'. The new preamble, revised for the first time since the 1890s, was written in language that was at the same time more militant and more concrete.[81]

Compared to the URWEA the RCIPA remained conservative, rigid, and apolitical, however. The representatives of 200 URWEA locals who met in Detroit in December 1939 saw themselves as part of a militant, democratic, and aggressive labor movement. Although their concrete demands and conception of the trade union hardly differed from the RCIPA, and though they denied charges of communist influence and committed themselves to loyal, responsible, American trade union action within the system, they were also willing to take a decisive progressive stand on general social and political questions — in marked contrast to the reserve of AFL unions, including the RCIPA, on political questions. The URWEA passed many resolutions condemning violations of civil liberties and every form of racial, religious, and other discrimination. Its leaders opposed the European dictators and warned that the US was in danger of being drawn into the European conflict. They invoked the democratic ideals of the founding fathers to refute white supremacy claims, demand anti-lynch laws, and a halt to wartime nativism and sedition laws. Their educational programs were intended to bring about the broadest emancipation of the working class. They supported New Deal economic and social policies, agitated for greater involvement of the labor movement in politics, and supported the re-election of Roosevelt. The voice of the URWEA was infused with the spirit of progress and sometimes an almost pathetic enthusiasm for social reforms; it expressly disavowed the theory that trade unions should serve *only* as instruments to attain bread and butter goals.[82]

The composition of the URWEA's membership also differed from the RCIPA's. Middle level clerks and managers, who found the AFL's conservatism and decentralized structure hospitable, probably did not belong to the URWEA. The speakers at the 1939 convention came from the lower ranks of department and chain store clerks, and to a lesser extent from warehouse and transportation workers; some had eastern and south-eastern European surnames. The average age of the members was 25-30 years old. After 1943 40% of URWEA members were women; this proportion was higher than women's share of the total sales force (about 30% in 1940 as in the preceding two decades), though more women were probably employed in chain and department stores and during the war.[83]

Thus if sales clerks and other wholesale and retail employees organized at all in response to the depression, it was as an integral part of the American labor movement. The activities, ideologies, and aims of the RCIPA and the URWEA did not differ in principle from those of other AFL or CIO organizations — no more at any rate than the range of variation between blue collar trade unions within each federation.

The response of organized sales clerks was also typical of the great majority of white collar workers who joined collective interest organizations during the 1930s. The large unions of postal, railroad, and public employees did not claim any separate white collar identity, but were equally well integrated into the general labor movement.[84] They supported moderately progressive political platforms and focused primarily on economic and workplace related issues; though these were apt to be intertwined with larger social and political questions during the depression. Their unions expressly favored New Deal reforms, and stood to the left rather than right of center in the political spectrum of the 1930s.

2. Industrial White Collar Workers and 'Professional' Unions

During the depression unemployment was a common occurrence for white collar workers in industry as well as in commerce, though they were not as hard hit as industrial blue collar workers. Even if they kept their jobs, however, the hours of office of technical employees were often reduced when business was slow; their wages were docked accordingly.[85] Many firms also attempted to cut down their office costs by more closely supervising white collar workers, which further reduced the small privileges and freedoms that separated the office from the factory floor.[86] Furthermore, after 1932 the distance between the average white collar salary and the average blue collar wage in industry declined steadily and significantly. The economic setback in 1938 interrupted this leveling process, but it then proceeded even more rapidly after 1939 as the economy revived.[87] White collar employees were also adversely affected by cutbacks in company welfare policies: stock and profit sharing plans, subsidized housing, savings banks, cafeterias and paid vacations were often eliminated, and there were fewer recreational and educational offerings.[88]

Above all, the opportunities for advancement declined for the industrial white collar worker, just as they did for their counterparts in other economic fields during the 1930s. As Table 3.5[89] shows, the number of positions in all occupational categories increased at a much lower rate between 1930 and 1940 than in previous decades. Opportunities to move from lower/middle rank to top level white collar positions or independence (categories 1 and 2) declined — because growth of positions in these two upper categories slowed down more noticeably than positions in the third and fourth categories (in the 1930s compared to the 1920s). At the same time the number of candidates who had academic or other special training for higher positions not only did not decline, but actually increased more rapidly.[90] Both trends — the slower growth rate of positions that lower and middle level white collar workers could move up to and the rapid increase in the number of well educated candidates for such positions — must have dimmed the career hopes of those already in as well as those just entering lower and middle rank positions. Blocked career hopes was not only a problem for the new graduates who could not find work. The results of other studies suggest that the intra-generational rate of upward mobility for American society as a whole declined in the 1930s (though only temporarily, since the faster tempo of economic growth during and after the war improved mobility and career opportunities).[91] Anger at their inability to advance could only have exacerbated white collar workers' many other grievances during the depression. New Deal labor and social legislation and the general labor movement were also the framework within which these industrial white collar workers translated discontent into interest group action and collective protest.

Although New Deal legislation did not differentiate the rights and duties of social groups by the collar line, but instead along vertical or functional lines (e.g., some economic sectors, for instance agriculture, domestic service, transportation and government, were excluded from the Social Security Act in 1935), one horizontal dividing line did exist: a top stratum of professional employees and executives were set apart from the great mass of blue and white collar workers and exempted from the protective provisions of the NRA and the Fair Labor Standards Act.[92] That exemption did not hurt self-employed professionals or top executives. If they belonged to any organization based on occupation it was apt to be a professional association that disdained trade union or interest group action as incompatible with a professional sense of identity. These elite groups were the most socially and politically conservative white collar workers; with most businessmen they stood to the right of the New Deal.[93] Some professionally qualified white collar workers, below the top level, however, responded to their exclusion from the NRA by joining trade unions; in industry technicians and engineers holding moderately well paid non-managerial positions were most apt to organize.

It was also easier for technical employees of industrial firms to think about joining a labor union in the pro-union atmosphere in the US after 1933. One of their motives was to obtain political influence in order to have a say in drafting New Deal legislation; but these intermediate level employees also hoped to equal through collective bargaining the gains that non-professional workers were now guaranteed by law. And like their intermediate level counterparts in retail stores, they also sought to combat attempts by some employers to make up the cost of raising the lowest wages by lowering middle level salaries. The AFL affiliated International Federation of Technical Engineers, Architects, and Draftsmen's Unions, which had continued to limp along after the first world war, was unable to attract these new recruits to collective organization. That union limited itself almost exclusively to representing government employees who did not come under the NRA anyway; it had shown very little concern for the many technicians who lost their jobs in the economic crisis. Furthermore, the AFL's traditional distrust of middle rank employees who might promote the interests of employers was also a factor in its affiliate's failure to take on the challenge of organizing technicians and engineers in private industry. Even in the depression this older AFL technicians' union remained so insignificant that it was often ignored in contemporary discussion; its membership only began to increase after 1938.[94]

Under the impact of economic distress and the new labor legislation, spontaneous organizations of technicians and engineers were founded within companies or cities. In 1933 they came together to found the Federation of Architects, Engineers, Chemists and Technicians. The new union's purpose was 'to unite all employed and student technicians for the purpose of obtaining and preserving employment with adequate wages and proper hours and working conditions'. Membership was open to all 'who are qualified by training or experience in any professional capacity, in architecture, engineering, or any other scientific or technical work', excluding owners and supervisory employees. The new organization welcomed technicians and engineers employed by the government, private industry, or on public works projects. Its members were predominantly technicians in industrial, medical, and dental laboratories, construction draftsmen, and chemists; they undoubtedly belonged to the worst paid and least powerful ranks of these occupations. In 1936 the union reported 6,000 members in sixteen branches.[95]

The liberal press greeted this new Federation as a novel phenomenon.

> Is a technician a workingman, who can be benefited, like any other workingman, by trade-union organization? Or does he practice a profession, and is it therefore '*beneath his dignity*' to participate in joint action with his fellow technicians? *Heretofore, the technicians have always gone on the latter theory.* But today, with enormous unemployment and *with their position imperiled by developments under the NRA*, many technicians are changing their minds.[96]

The great majority of technical employees did not change their minds, of course; along with large sections of the public they continued to consider professional status incompatible with trade union organization. They stayed away from the Federation, and their purely professional associations attacked those who did join. In reply, the Federation stressed that it was possible to represent professional and economic interests at the same time; it refused to accept 'professionalism' as a barrier to collective pursuit of common economic interests. The new union proclaimed itself the 'progressive vanguard of the technical professions' and vowed to cooperate with 'fellow workers' in the factories.[97] Its goals, strategies and tactics as well as its general political line fit in well with those of the general labor movement. Attempts to join the AFL (the craft union principle was more compatible with the technicians' professional consciousness than industrial unionism) failed, however, because of strong resistance from other trade unions.[98] The Federation voted in January 1937 to join the CIO, which granted it a special status: its members were not distributed among the industrial unions by where they worked, and they were also not amalgamated into the CIO's general white collar union.[99]

At its 1938 convention the Federation behaved like a fairly typical CIO union. It raised the usual bread and butter demands without expressing any claim to special privileges over its 'fellow workers'; it regarded collective bargaining and strikes as normal trade union tactics. The leadership acknowledged aid from other CIO unions (financial contributions and assistance with organizing drives) and requested further support for a campaign against the steel and electrical industries. Speakers stated their readiness to work closely with factory hands in order to overcome the suspicions of manual workers of 'superior' white collar workers. Furthermore, the new union followed the CIO rather than the AFL in advocating a major political role for the labor movement; it also supported the New Deal, demanded more social and public works programs, polemicized against big business, passed resolutions to safeguard civil liberties, fight fascism and discrimination against Negroes and women, and demand publicly subsidized housing. In 1944 the Federation had 4,900 members, while the membership of the AFL technicians' union had climbed to 7,100. After the war the CIO expelled this union because of alleged communist inflitration. A much smaller technicians' organization merged with the CIO white collar union (UOPWA) in 1946, until in 1949 that organization was also expelled for communist leanings and disbanded. The AFL union continued to organize technical employees; in 1950 it changed its name to the 'American Federation of Technical Engineers' and in 1955 claimed 10,000 members.[100]

The short history of the Federation of Architects, Engineers, Chemists and Technicians reveals how professional groups could find a home in the American labor movement without completely renouncing their professional sense of identity or, as in Europe, forming a separate white collar trade union movement.[101] Other professional or semi-professional groups in and out of industry followed the same course. Under the impact of the economic crisis the NRA journalists founded the Newspaper Guild. Its members showed a special professional consciousness in that they avoided the name 'union' and temporarily refrained from joining the AFL. But their concrete objectives and tactics (collective bargaining, contracts, strikes) were identical with those of other American labor unions. With 5,800 members in 1936, the Newspaper Guild affiliated with the AFL; with 11,100 members in 1937 it went over to the CIO where it belonged to the left wing. The AFL-affiliated American Editorial Association (AEA) was founded only in 1940. While its anti-communist politics distinguished the AEA from the Newspaper Guild, both organizations found professionalism compatible with trade unionism.[102]

Salary cuts and layoffs also convinced the airline pilots to transform their professional organization into a trade union. 'The days of individualism and individual effort are over; now only large organizations seem able to survive. We must follow this sign of the times. From now on it is essential that we in our profession place a certain part of our time at the disposal of our organization . . .' The Air Line Pilot Association was secretly organized in 1930, and went public in 1931. It affiliated with the AFL, mainly in order to have better access to government officials. Becoming a trade union did not mean that the pilots had abandoned their sense of professional identity, however; shortly thereafter they even adopted a professional code of honor.[103]

Thus for a minority of technical employees, journalists, and pilots — teachers, musicians, and actors might also be mentioned[104] — professional identity was not an obstacle to trade union organization or to joining the general labor movement. By individual occupations, not as part of a broad white collar class, they organized within or affiliated with the AFL and the CIO. The great majority in these occupational groups who did not follow this course either remained unorganized or belonged only to professional associations which stayed away from social, political, and economic issues. Furthermore, since professional associations mingled salaried employees with independent practitioners, they cannot be equated with the German type of white collar trade union. Several factors smoothed the way for some professionals to affiliate with the American labor movement. One was the absence of a specifically middle class, white collar consciousness that rested on demarcating the middle classes or the lower middle classes from the working class in the US. Another was the character of the American labor movement; even its left wing did not demand deep ideological commitments to the proletarian cause or any broad political and social commitments. Thus it was relatively accessible to groups with primarily economic, workplace-oriented objectives that were not looking for a general reform movement. During the first world war, small groups of white collar workers had joined the labor movement for parallel reasons; despite the upheavals of depression, New Deal, and industrial unionism, the same pattern reappeared when white collar workers organized in the 1930s.

3. White Collar and Blue Collar Trade Unions in the System of Industrial Relations

The restructuring of labor relations by the Wagner Act in 1935, which was passed against a background of rapid strides for industrial unions and lost ground for white collar workers (in earnings, company benefits and legal status relative to blue collar workers), initiated a new phase in the organizational behavior of American white collar workers and in their relationship to the labor movement.

The Wagner Act guaranteed all employees (including white collar workers) the right to organize and bargain collectively with their employers through representatives of their choice, who could be union officials not employed at that company. The Act stipulated that representation elections and collective bargaining over hours, wages, and working conditions should take place in an 'appropriate bargaining unit'. In disputed cases the NLRB would decide what was an appropriate unit. The Board was also empowered to conduct elections and to oversee the implementation of the entire Act. In order to secure workers' full use of their right to organize and bargain collectively and to fulfill the purposes of the law, the Board was to decide in each case whether the appropriate unit 'shall be the employer unit, craft unit, plant unit, or subdivision thereof'.[105] The Wagner Act and the way the NLRB interpreted it in a multitude of individual decisions wrote into American law the decentralized structure of capital-labor relations which had gradually evolved in the US.[106] Furthermore, although in principle the law recognized the craft as well as the industrial basis for trade unions, in practice the Board's decisions promoted the latter. These far reaching consequences are not as important for this study, however, as is the role that NLRB decisions played in demarcating blue collar from white collar workers and in shaping the white collar organizations that emerged in the following years.

The question of whether blue collar and white collar workers should be organized together or separately did not come up as long as the craft union principle dominated the American labor movement. If organized machine tool workers in a large company were not concerned with the molders or laborers who worked alongside them, they were not apt to be interested in organizing the assistant foreman, let alone the bookkeeper or office secretaries. The only time the AFL had encountered any controversy over including white collar workers in blue collar unions was when the organization of foremen was at issue.[107] That situation changed when the craft union principle was superseded in mass production industries, however. If the Cigarmakers, who had followed the industrial principle for years, or the new and rapidly expanding UAW organized a company, should office and technical employees be included in the same bargaining unit and thus be represented by a trade union composed primarily of various categories of manual workers?

The NLRB relied on several criteria to determine the appropriate bargaining unit, but these were developed and applied quite differently in various cases. The Board's major consideration was the community of interest that existed among the employees involved. Community of interest depended of course on the choices of all workers affected, but their wishes were often contradictory. It also rested on such objective criteria as employment, function, qualifications, experience, working conditions, responsibility, relationship to management, and the possibility of mobility between groups. The past history of labor relations in a company or an industry was also taken into account. As a general rule the Board decided to exclude white collar workers from production workers' bargaining units. It based its decision mainly on the divergent interests of blue and white collar workers, which it traced to the distinction between wages and salaries and to variations in working conditions (differences in hours, vacation rights, accident risk, job security, desired improvements at the workplace, etc.).[108] In view of the emphasis on concrete workplace issues in American unions this reasoning made more sense than it would have if the labor movement — as in Germany — had pursued social reform or political objectives that might have overshadowed these distinctions between blue and white collar work.

The Board further demarcated some occupational groups — engineers, technicians, and chemists, for instance — from the mass of white collar employees because of their special qualifications and 'professional and intellectual homogeneity'.[109] Foremen and supervisory employees, who often had no special qualifications or homogeneity, were usually barred from production workers' bargaining units on the grounds that they were really part of management — an argument which was not applied to the great majority of white collar workers who did not exercise authority over others.[110] Finally, the Board supplemented these arguments by referring to the social and ideological differences between blue and white collar workers:

> ...the difference in the type of work performed, the traditional divergence in their social outlook and in their attitude toward labor organizations...are compelling reasons for the separation of the two classes of employees into separate units...There is thus no persuasive evidence tending to blur the well-defined line of demarcation existing between the clerical workers and the outside or physical workers in the operations of the company. We shall therefore not include the clerical employees in the same unit with the outside or physical employees.[111]

The policy of separating blue and white collar workers was in no way absolute; it did not prevent the Board from occasionally including some categories of white collar workers in the same bargaining unit with factory workers. But in general it was an easy rule to implement because most trade unions showed almost no interest in organizing office and technical employees or salesmen. In fact in many instances they resisted management efforts to have office workers included in the same bargaining unit. Their narrow economic goals and concentration on workplace demands apparently led them to prefer a membership with roughly the same working conditions, but blue collar resentment against the men with white collars and clean hands was also a factor. Furthermore, in the sharp confrontations between capital and labor that framed labor relations in the 1930s the unions also feared infiltration by pro-management white collar workers or spies/provocateurs. And in some cases management pressure to include white collar workers did suggest such motives, or at least the attempt to exercise a moderating influence on the new organizations through 'reliable' people.[112]

This situation began to change only toward the end of the 1930s, and then first in the CIO unions that were less exclusively concerned with narrow workplace issues but also interested in organizing entire industries and in broad social reform. The UAW and the Electrical Workers were early advocates of mixed blue collar-white collar unions within the CIO. The NLRB was increasingly receptive to their demands, except where the white collar workers involved voted decisively against the idea. (The outcome depended in any event on the election unit chosen by the Board, so that it was still possible to include large minorities of unwilling white collar workers in blue collar unions by manipulating the appropriate unit.)[113] The Steelworkers, initially extremely wary of white collar workers, reported 20,000 of them among its 858,000 members in 1947. Of the 600,000 United Electrical Workers in 1944, 50,000 were white collar employees.[114] As a rule, however, the office employees of industrial firms were not usually organized by CIO industrial unions.[115]

Thus the resurgence of the American labor movement in the 1930s and the policies of the NLRB had a great impact on white collar workers in industry. Out of the multitude of decisions by the Board on individual cases came a clearer picture of which employees were blue collar and which were white collar. For the first time in the US, the collar line acquired legal significance. (By contrast, in Germany, the distinction between wage workers and salaried employees had been significant in social insurance and labor laws since the 1880s!)

White collar workers had also watched the trade unions obtain advances for blue collar workers which were not always extended to unorganized salaried employees. Even before the Wagner Act went into effect this trend had been noticeable. Many firms, for instance, had created company unions to evade the NRA; since they were intended as a defense against trade union organization, most ignored white collar workers.[116] Thus these employees were left out of the (to be sure modest!) achievements of company unions; furthermore, separate treatment deepened the psychological distinction between factory and office. Later, when CIO unions won contracts with large corporations that benefited all factory workers, and not just select categories of skilled workers as had been the case before 1935, white collar workers were again ignored.[117] Sometimes the salaries of these unorganized and therefore relatively defenseless office employees were even cut after organized factory workers had won a wage increase.[118] Blue collar piece rate or hourly wages pulled away from the salaries of the lowest ranks of white collar workers; the wage-salary differential as a whole narrowed. Meanwhile, privileges like paid vacations that had previously been reserved for white collar workers were also becoming part of union contracts.[119] Thus in unionized industries, white collar workers shared a status that transcended the boundaries between their individual occupations: in contrast to almost all other occupational groups, they remained unorganized. Their unorganized state had been much less significant when trade unions concentrated on organizing individual crafts of skilled workers rather than the entire factory. Only with the emergence of industrial unionism in the 1930s did white collar workers' abstinence from trade union organization come to be considered a typical group characteristic — for many a conscious group choice — that distinguished them from blue collar workers as a group.

One might imagine that the experiences of white collar workers in the depression would have made them vulnerable to the sort of reactionary middle class protest movements that proved so attractive to their counterparts in Germany. Not only did they as a group suffer mass unemployment, loss of earnings, shrinking privileges and reduced chances for upward mobility, they faced these deprivations at a time when manual workers were experiencing relative social and economic advances. Moreover, the labor movement was expanding in numbers and influence and to a certain extent becoming more radical; the emerging pattern of cooperation between labor, business and government to draw up social legislation left white collar workers out in the cold. The interventionist policies of the New Deal had a slightly leveling impact and offended traditional American values — both consequences that might have been expected to upset white collar workers. And all the while radical rhetoric on the right and the left became increasingly strident; the political landscape in the US was increasingly seen as polarized. Nonetheless, there were very few traces of reactionary, anti-labor sentiment among white collar workers, though what beginnings there were will be briefly noted.

During the second world war when the NLRB became more amenable and industrial unions more eager to organize white collar workers, some technicians and engineers responded by organizing separately — often with the support of professional associations, and perhaps also with the friendly toleration of management — to avoid being absorbed into the expanding industrial unions. These organizations served not only as a bulwark against blue collar trade unions, they also represented the social and economic interests of their members. However, they did not segregate themselves from manual workers on the basis of a common white collar identity, but rather on the grounds of a well defined professional character. Most of these professional unions (of engineers, technicians, chemists, and scientists) were created between 1943 and 1947, that is, before the Taft-Hartley Act made the inclusion of professionals in industrial unions expressly dependent on their majority vote and thus more difficult. In the mid-1950s nearly 10% of the approximately 500,000 engineers in the US belonged to these unions; about half were members of the loose Federation of Engineers and Scientists of America which was formed in 1952 and declined sharply after 1956.[120]

4. Supra-occupational White Collar Unions

(a) A CIO White Collar Union

These professional unions formed during the second world war remained in the pattern of previous attempts to organize white collar workers by only joining members of the same profession or occupation. In the late 1930s the first major efforts were made to organize white collar workers as such, disregarding occupational or professional boundaries. Changes in the organization of office work had created a great number of lower and middle level positions which differed from traditional clerical occupations (bookkeeper, stenographer, secretary) either because they involved a narrowly specialized activity (using an adding machine, timekeeper) or because they entailed too broad a variety of tasks to be precisely defined (general clerks).[121] Organization along craft lines was just as impossible at the lower levels of the modern office as it was for unskilled or semi-skilled workers in modern mass production industries. Organization based on professional identity was here completely out of the question.

The antecedents of these general organizations went back to the turn of the century, when scattered Bookkeepers, Stenographers, and Accountants unions were founded. As their names reveal these unions were based on distinct clerical occupations, but they organized them together. Their greatest strength was in the offices of other trade unions. Under the leadership of a group of New York locals, they were admitted to the AFL as individual unions. The Federation refused to grant them the status of a national union, however, partly because AFL leaders thought that office workers were not worth a serious organizing effort, and partly because they were suspicious of the political radicalism of these unions (many were later expelled because of alleged communist influence).[122] During the depression the membership of the 40 Bookkeepers, Stenographers, and Accountants unions in existence grew rapidly, but they were still denied recognition as a national union by the AFL. In May 1937, thirteen locals finally followed the New York group out of the AFL. They joined with nine independent organizations to found the United Office and Professional Workers of America International (UOPWA) of the CIO with (according to their count) 8,600 members. The next year the AFL established an Office Employees International Council, which became the Office Employees International Union in 1944.[123]

Thus at the end of the 1930s the first attempts to found national trade unions of white collar workers which concentrated neither on particular industries nor on particular occupations appeared. White collar workers were now seen as a social group with sufficiently similar characteristics and problems to transcend these divisions. Labor and management both believed that long term structural changes in the office, the impact of economic crisis, and the partial leveling of social-economic differences between blue collar and white collar workers had made the latter receptive to trade union organization. The CIO leadership nonetheless decided that white collar workers required a separate organization that would take into account the group's particular characteristics, including their traditional reluctance to organize, and employ special recruiting techniques.[124] They thus approved the combined organization of insurance, banking, publishing, industrial, and other categories of white collar employees. This jurisdictional field violated the industrial union principle; it also led in reality to conflicts over boundary lines between the UOPWA and large industrial unions like the Autoworkers.[125]

Jurisdictional conflicts may have been one reason why the rapidly growing UOPWA drew almost all its members from economic sectors that were predominantly white collar; its greatest strength was in insurance and publishing, but many social workers, artists, advertising employees, and salesmen — very few banking employees — also joined.[126] Before 1943 the UOPWA had almost no success with white collar employees in major industries. This first successful white collar trade union, which won certification elections by large majorities over competing independent and company unions (particularly in insurance), was as militant in its choice of tactics as other CIO unions. Politically it stood at the extreme left of the CIO. Its legislative program did not aim at achieving special privileges for white collar workers, instead it vigorously supported the social and political program of the CIO. UOPWA leaders condemned the attacks on civil liberties during the war and discrimination against Negroes, women, and the left. In 1940 a majority of its delegates to the CIO convention voted not to support Roosevelt's re-election. In their view he had departed from his previous progressive stance and gone too far to accommodate the conservative forces in the country. UOPWA leaders, at least President Lewis Merrill, worked closely with communist groups; in consequence the union was expelled from the CIO in 1949.[127] Thus the first general white collar interest group in the US was decidedly not anti-labor, defensive about its white collar status, or filled with reactionary lower middle class sentiment.[128]

(b) The Westinghouse White Collar Association

At about the same time that the UOPWA was organized, however, white collar organizations were established within several large corporations which were not entirely free of these qualities. When Westinghouse Electric's Pittsburgh branch[129] cut salaries (but not the wages of organized factory workers) in June 1938, white collar workers organized the Association of Westinghouse Salaried Employees to protest. Engineers, draftsmen, salesmen, bookkeepers — office and factory salaried employees of all kinds — could join, but all blue collar workers were excluded. The Association soon combined with similar organizations at Westinghouse's other branches to found the Federation of Westinghouse Independent Salaried Unions (FWISU). The FWISU excluded employees in supervisory positions in order to be recognized as a valid trade union by the NLRB. In 1940 it defeated organizing drives by two CIO unions — the Technicians and the Electrical Workers — to win Board certified elections. The FWISU fought vigorously to win salary increases, orderly salary classifications, and improvements in white collar working conditions. It did not affiliate with either the AFL or the CIO, but did maintain an office outside the company in order not to arouse the NLRB's suspicion. As the elected representative of 9,000 Westinghouse salaried employees and the self-appointed spokesman for the masses of unorganized white collar workers in the US, the FWISU frequently appeared in Washington to negotiate with federal officials and testify before congressional committees on wartime labor legislation. Toward the end of the war it made contact with other independent (i.e., neither AFL nor CIO) white collar unions and proposed the formation of a national white collar association. The National Federation of Salaried Unions reported 15,000 members in 1944 and 25,000 in

1945; after the war, however, it lost strength rapidly and had declined to only 11,600 members in 1962.[130]

The FWISU was founded for the express purpose of preventing the rapidly expanding industrial unions from organizing white collar workers at Westinghouse. As far as the sources reveal, however, it avoided attacking these CIO unions and made no anti-labor statements. Its leaders frequently claimed that they had 'no antipathy' toward the AFL or the CIO; they merely asserted that salaried employees should not be swallowed up by organizations that were led by and primarily concerned with wage workers, since the two classes of employees had such different problems. A favorite FWISU theme was the advantages of independent organization for white collar workers.[131]

Even before the war, the Westinghouse union complained that organized wage workers had fared better during the depression than unorganized salaried employees: blue collar workers had caught up financially, and they had been granted privileges previously reserved for white collar workers. One of the FWISU's chief victories was to win the right to overtime pay, long a prerogative of manual workers, for salaried employees. The union also sought with some success to prevent too great a leveling of wages and salaries by establishing a regular review of the entire pay scale at Westinghouse (with their representatives participating). It attempted to write into contracts the small privileges that distinguished salaried employees (or individual occupations) from factory workers. The union protested the increased supervision of white collar workers and the employment of married women (which was standard policy in the factory but not the office at Westinghouse before the second world war).[132]

The FWISU did not rule out strikes; in 1941 its leaders called a short work stoppage to win a salary increase they had sought unsuccessfully.[133] It is doubtful, however, if this union with relatively low dues and little support from other trade unions could have conducted a major strike. Its goal was 'to provide a legal and accredited means for collective bargaining and for the promotion of the industrial, economic, and social welfare of its members'; it sought 'cooperation, understanding, and fair dealing' with management.[134] Its frame of reference clearly did not include the notion of a fundamental class conflict between labor and capital at the workplace or in society at large. While this outlook did not distinguish the FWISU from many other labor unions (particularly in the AFL), its rejection of the closed shop and the dues checkoff did. There were also other small differences between this salaried union and typical blue collar organizations: FWISU functionaries were not called shop stewards but group representatives, for instance.[135]

From the beginning the FWISU had emphasized that white collar workers would have to exert more influence on government policy and labor legislation if they did not want to fall further behind wage workers. Its representatives were active lobbyists when the Fair Labor Standards Act was passed in 1938, and they became even more active during the war. Their efforts to preserve salaried employees' advantages were not very successful, however. Wartime inflation, the shortage of labor and the power of blue collar unions, and government intervention that aided wage earners rather than salaried employees combined to further depress the real earnings of white collar workers compared to blue collar. In 1943, for the first time, the average weekly earnings of blue collar workers (in manufacturing , transportation, and some services) exceeded those of salaried employees (in manufacturing, transportation, services, government and education) (see Table 4.8).

Table 4.8
Average Weekly Earnings of Blue Collar and White Collar Workers, 1929-52 (in Dollars)[136]

Year	Blue Collar	White Collar
1929	27.14	34.78
1933	18.59	29.42
1937	25.25	32.57
1939	25.44	33.04
1944	45.27	43.63
1946	45.83	49.14
1949	56.75	57.57
1952	69.24	66.63

Thus many white collar workers were correct in perceiving that they were among the absolute and relative economic losers in the war. The UOPWA and the FWISU both demanded a special national agency for white collar workers to serve as their advocate with the National War Labor Board and the Office of Economic Stabilization to at least partially reverse this downward trend.

These wartime efforts to obtain special protection for white collar workers were buttressed with ideological arguments. The UOPWA asserted that white collar workers' constantly declining standard of living would leave them in distress and confusion; their health, ability to function, and thus — since they performed crucial tasks for society — the welfare of the nation were endangered.[137] FWISU arguments revealed traces of specifically middle class resentment. They demanded protection for the 'vast multitudes of educated, conscientious individuals receiving salaries', who had to keep up a respectable appearance they were no longer able to afford. The Westinghouse union referred to white collar workers as an intermediate group that performed most of the intellectual work necessary to keep all social institutions in existence.

As F. L. Bollens wrote in *White Collar or Noose? The Occupation of Millions*: 'Pity the poor white-collar workers!...the salaried employees are truly the forgotten Americans'. Although they were the 'real backbone of the American social structure', though as a rule they spent more on philanthropy than better paid wage workers, they were no longer able to maintain the standard of living their position demanded. Bollens predicted that their bitterness over government indifference to their plight and the economic chaos that threatened them would lead to 'moral disintegration and the decline of the principles of Christian brotherhood'.[138]

These scattered traces of lower middle class-specific types of white collar organization and protest that appeared three or four decades later in the US than comparable tendencies in Germany were still fundamentally different from the organizations and protests of the German new middle class, however. Even the FWISU, for instance, rejected anti-labor alliances and political and ideological positions.[139] It supported Roosevelt and New Deal reforms, though it also became more and more critical of what it considered excessively high taxes.[140] And even though it was founded partly in reaction to the CIO and at a time when labor was demanding sweeping social and political change, its focus was on concrete economic improvements for its members, not general social or political questions. Thus the FWISU's separation of economic from social and political issues also placed this separatist white collar union in the mainstream of the American labor movement. It is true that the Westinghouse union dwelt on the threatened or dwindling privileges of white collar workers to a greater extent than earlier white collar organizations. But with wages overtaking salaries and blue collar workers the primary beneficiaries of government intervention, their demands for special treatment for salaried employees could even be clothed in traditional egalitarian rhetoric.[141] Above all, however much FWISU protests may have expressed widespread white collar resentment, they never sparked a broad social and political protest movement in the US. With the postwar economic recovery FWISU membership stagnated and then declined.

5. White Collar Unions and the Labor Movement

To recapitulate: the economic crisis, the social and economic policies of the New Deal, and the successes of the labor movement (particularly the new industrial unions) also sparked intensive organizing drives among salaried employees in the 1930s. White collar trade unions did not really take off until the war and immediate postwar years, however. In 1935 5% of all white collar workers belonged to trade unions; the proportion was only 7% in 1939, but had climbed to 16% in 1948.[142]

There were four types of white collar organizations during the 1930s: trade unions based on individual occupations that were comparable to the skilled craft unions (e.g. the RCIPA), industrial unions that combined blue and white collar occupations (the URWEA), professional trade unions (the Federation of Architects, Engineers, Chemists, and Technicians/CIO), and white collar unions that transcended occupational boundaries (UOPWA, FWISU). All types of white collar organization, old and new, were well within the traditional framework of the American labor move-

Table 4.9
Distribution of Organized White Collar Workers by Trade Union Group, 1939 and 1945[143]

Trade Union Group	Total Membership	Number of White Collar Members	White Collar Percentage of Total Membership
1939 AFL	3,878,000	442,100	11
CIO	1,837,700	87,400	5
Independent	839,800	213,300	26
1945 AFL	6,890,400	713,100	10
CIO	3,927,900	169,000	4
Independent	1,743,800	441,000	25

ment. Efforts to set themselves apart from the working class by emphasizing the particularly middle class characteristics of white collar workers played a very small role in these organizations. There was no bifurcation of the American labor movement into blue collar and white collar divisions as there had been in Germany since the late 19th century. The organizations researched for this study, which were concentrated in industry and commerce, were not more conservative, less radical, or more susceptible to reactionary or right-wing politics than blue collar unions.

Particularly toward the end of the period under study, however, some traces of specifically white collar demands, modes of behavior, and protest did appear which were tinged with lower middle class resentment. The disproportionate distribution of white collar workers among the three groups of American labor unions also suggests a certain difference in the organizational behavior of blue and white collar workers.

More than half of all organized white collar workers belonged to AFL unions. But independent unions had a significantly higher proportion of white collar members than either the AFL or the CIO.

Table 4.10
Proportion of All Organized White Collar Workers in Each Trade Union Group, 1939 and 1945[144]

	1939	1945
AFL	59%	54%
CIO	12%	13%
Independent	29%	33%

The disproportionate tendency of white collar workers to affiliate with independent unions might indicate a certain reluctance among many organized white collar workers to merge completely with the general labor movement. Also, the fact that as a rule white collar unions could integrate themselves into the labor movement was as much a reflection of the structure and character of American labor as a clue to the true consciousness and attitudes of their members. The great tolerance of the AFL and the CIO for occupational autonomy, the fact that neither national federation demanded extensive political or ideological commitment but instead concentrated on economic and workplace issues, and that both were non-revolutionary, mostly non-radical organizations were also important factors.

And unlike their counterparts in Germany, American white collar workers did not have the option of organizing within the general labor movement or choosing a separate lower middle class, anti-labor white collar movement — either they joined the labor movement or they did not organize to pursue collective interests at all. In 1939 over 90% still chose to remain unorganized — in dramatic contrast to the highly organized salaried employees in Germany. This cross-cultural variation points up the fact that certain catalysts and motives behind white collar organization that had been present at an early date in Germany were for a long time almost completely absent in the US; they only began to appear in the 1930s, and then much less completely. As the history of white collar organizations in the depression and the war reveals, effective organization of blue collar workers and government social and economic intervention provided major stimuli for collective organization in other social groups. And it was only in the 1930s that the American labor movement made much of an effort to organize the masses of white collar workers.

The reluctance of American white collar workers to organize to pursue collective social-economic interests also rested on an individualistic concept of success, achievement, and career that was much less characteristic of German salaried employees. To put it in an oversimplified way: while most German salaried employees' belief that they belonged to superior corporate class (*Stand*) kept them from joining a labor movement defined as proletarian and politically disloyal (though not from interest group organization per se), the majority of American white collar workers refrained from joining *any* collective interest organization because of their belief in individual action and responsibility.[145] The economic crisis brought such misery, pressure, and disappointment to some white collar workers that this characteristic individualism no longer served as a barrier to joining a moderate, non-socialist labor movement. The great majority who did not take this path were left isolated rather than propelled toward separate white collar collective action, for American salaried employees lacked the corporatist/bureaucratic sense of identity and models of behavior that facilitated the organization of German salaried employees. A lower middle class 'third way' between joining the general labor movement and not organizing at all was not available in the US.

Of course, the fact that most American white collar workers did not join collective interest groups limits the conclusions about the social group that can be drawn from the absence of potential or actual reactionary attitudes and behavior in these small white collar trade unions. Thus the question of where this social group stood will now be pursued by a brief examination of the relationship between white collar workers and right-wing currents and organizations in the US during the depression.

IV. WHITE COLLAR WORKERS IN THE POLITICAL SPECTRUM OF THE 1930s

1. White Collar Workers and Right-Wing Radicalism

In this study we use the term 'right-wing radicalism' (or 'right-wing extremism') as a label for protests, ideologies, attitudes and movements characterized by an anti-democratic, anti-egalitarian, and/or anti-socialist — in short, a defensive — reaction to democratizing, egalitarian and/or socialistic tendencies in the transformation of state and society. At the same time, however, radicals on the right mount a critical, pseudo-democratic, attack on convention, traditional elites, and the status quo. This critique is not the least reason why these reactionary movements achieve power to mobilize masses.[145a]

'Fascist' we call those right-wing radical or right-wing extremist mass movements that emerged in bourgeois capitalist systems in the crisis they underwent after the first world war. They are characterized by massive terrorism, by the will to destroy the opponent who is defined as an enemy, and in the event that they attain power, by mass violence. They also preach their nation's power and expansion at the expense of other nations and eventually external aggression and war. They adhere to an extreme form of nationalism; they are ideologically and organizationally committed to the leader/follower principle; their structure is authoritarian/hierarchical; they are permeated with militaristic elements. Their mass base consists primarily of middle strata of all kinds whose composition varies according to the level of economic development. Fascist movements fight a two-front war; primarily ideological, but also in part in practical politics. They combine anti-socialism, anti-communism and anti-liberalism with resentment against those in power — capitalist and/or traditional elites. Their tone is populist, and they employ a pseudo-democratic agitation to mobilize the masses. A necessary condition for their rise and triumph is the support of established elites and ruling groups who themselves feel threatened: large landowners, business elites, the military, bureaucracy, or church may use (or hope to use) a fascist movement as a counter-revolutionary, anti-reform, reactionary, anti-democratic, anti-socialist and/or anti-communist tool. And despite their anti-elitist, populist components, the later it gets the more these elites turn to such movements. Once in power fascist movements destroy the liberal-democratic constitutional system, exterminate or markedly weaken communist, socialist, and democratic forces, and stabilize the basic foundation of capitalism — private property and private control of capital — at least in the short run.[145b]

These are ideal types derived largely from European historical experiences. One does not need an extensive study in order to discover that both right-wing extremist movements in general and fascist phenomena in particular did not play a major role in 20th century US history. But there should have been at least some tendencies, dispositions and undercurrents in the US comparable to the European right-wing extremist and fascist movements, though much weaker and different in detail. It is the purpose of these paragraphs to survey them and find out how white collar workers related to them.

If one looks for groups and movements on the American scene that were analogous to the European right-wing radical movements of the 1930s, one finds — disregarding for the moment Father Coughlin's mass following — a multitude of small, much discussed, but rather ineffective right-wing radical groups. To what extent were white collar workers represented among their members and supporters? The predominantly urban *German-American Bund* (founded 1932/33), which in 1937/38 claimed 25,000 members but probably had closer to 10,000 (half in New York City and environs), followed an explicitly National Socialist line in ideology, organization, and tactics. Newspaper reports indicated that most of its members were skilled workers, small businessmen, and white collar workers. However, no conclusions can be drawn from its composition for this study, since about one-third of the members were German citizens and most of the rest were naturalized German immigrants; only 10% had been born in the US. The Bund's money and ideas were also largely imported. The *Black Shirts* had about the same relationship to Italians and Italian fascism.[146] William D. Pelley's *Silver Shirts*, on the other hand, was a home grown fascist group. Pelley advocated a dictatorship that would forcibly suppress trade unions; he attacked Jews and communists. The Silver Shirts reached its peak strength in 1934 when it claimed 15,000 members, most of whom were native born Protestants of British and German origin living in the midwest and on the west coast. Small businessmen and economically distressed white collar workers from small towns and without much education or prestige seem to have been more strongly represented than manual workers.[147]

The members of the paramilitary *Black Legion* swore an oath to keep the secrets of the order, to follow God and the American constitution as well as the Black Legion in a holy war against Catholics, Jews, communists, Negroes and foreigners. Their rites and demonstrations copied those of the fascist Bund. The Legion had as many as 40,000 members in 1936; they were mainly unskilled and semi-skilled workers from the industrial cities of the midwest. Gerald B. Winrod's *Defenders of the Christian Faith* had no formal membership rolls. The militant anti-Catholic preacher Winrod, who attacked Roosevelt as an agent of communists and Jews, published a magazine which reached a circulation of almost 100,000. Winrod found support among the poorer classes in rural areas and small towns and cities, but not among white collar workers in large metropolitan areas.[148]

The Defenders' rural/small town fundamentalism and their hatred of Catholics and large cities placed them in the same ideological tradition as the revived (in 1915) *Ku Klux Klan*. The American tradition of nativist right-wing extremism was well past its high point by the beginning of the depression, however. In the early 1920s the Klan's rigid moralism, xenophobia, anti-Catholicism, anti-semitism, anti-modernism and racist violence had attracted at least one and a half million members; it appealed to groups who felt threatened by rapid social-economic change and whose reactions were more extreme in the intolerant atmosphere of the world war and the immediate postwar years.[149] Although a representative study of the Klan's extremely heterogeneous membership is not yet available, it is clear that in addition to its rural/small town supporters in southern, midwestern and western states the Klan also found significant support in large industrial cities.[150] Only native born adult Protestant males could join this secret order. It seems that anti-union factory workers made up the bulk of the Klan's urban support, but significant numbers of small businessmen and lower/middle level white collar workers also belonged, at least in proportion to their share of the population.[151] After 1924 the Klan's membership dropped precipitously; though it continued to exist until 1944, it played no greater role during the depression than the many other right-wing fringe groups. Its decline was due partly to the documented corruption of its leaders, but restrictions on immigration also took some of the nativist wind out of its sails. Most importantly, the Klan was unable to replace postwar hysteria with a concrete program, and the primacy of economic issues after 1930 rendered it increasingly irrelevant. Neither the independent nor the employed middle classes were significant groups among its remaining members.[152]

Many other small, often bizarre groups might be listed; they often consisted of nothing more than a leader and a list of addresses. They were highly unstable, and many of their organizers appear to have been motivated by the hope of financial gain from this sort of entrepreneurial demagogy. They played on the ignorance and grievances of people who were usually poor and often in some way socially marginal. Insofar as appeals to concrete economic and social interests played any role at all, they were seldom addressed to specific classes or groups. Of 121 anti-semitic and right-wing radical organizations counted by a critical observer in the 1930s, only four had names in which the word worker or laborer appeared. None referred to the middle class, white collar workers, salaried employees, or similar terms.[153]

The only[154] mass movement in the US in the 1930s which was clearly identified as right-wing radical and increasingly fascistic was that of the radio priest Father Coughlin. At times his organization seems to have had five million members. Public response to his radio talks was enormous. In 1938, 30% of a representative sample of Americans said that they had listened to his broadcasts regularly before the 1936 election. Of these 83% declared that in general they had been in agreement with his opinions. In April 1938, 27% of the respondents to a public opinion poll stated that they agreed with Father Coughlin's views, while 32% disagreed. In April 1940, after his rhetoric and program had become even more radical, 17% of those surveyed still proclaimed their general support for his ideas. Particularly after the election of 1936, when his candidate for president was trounced by Roosevelt, overtly fascist elements became more and more distinct in Coughlin's talks. Unlike traditional right-wing movements in the US (including the Klan), he did not warn against the danger of a strong state but demanded extensive government economic and social intervention. His attacks on elites, which were frequently couched in populist rhetoric, also became more specifically anti-capitalist. At the same time he bitterly attacked communists and socialists, and turned increasingly against even the independent trade unions and against strikes. Political parties and the American party system as such were also among his frequent targets. After 1938 Coughlin began to advocate the creation of vaguely corporatist economic and social structures in the US. He divided the world into friends and enemies, demanded belief not reasoning from his followers, and was preoccupied with conspiracy theories. Abstract anti-semitism

— attacks directed not at specific Jewish groups or individuals but at Jews as such — became an increasingly central component of his talks. His organization also introduced paramilitary elements.[155]

The decisive point for this study is that public opinion surveys taken from 1938 on reveal that white collar workers were not over-represented among the followers of this increasingly radical fascistic movement. Manual workers, the unemployed, and farmers were all more strongly attracted to Father Coughlin than salaried employees or small businessmen; 'professionals and those in business' showed the greatest skepticism about and disagreement with his movement.[156]

Right-wing radicalism has traditionally had a different ideological content in the US than in Germany. Even when its thrust has been undemocratic and reactionary, because of the prevailing egalitarian values of American society its rhetoric has been less anti-egalitarian than that of corresponding political groups in Germany. Right-wing leaders have seldom defined their targets in class, corporatist, or other social-economic categories. For that reason alone anti-labor sentiment, lower middle class resentment and anti-socialism has played a smaller role in American right-wing radicalism than ethnic, racial, and religious enemies and scapegoats. Fundamentalism, nativism, anti-semitism and racism have been the main outlets for reactionary responses to urbanization and industrialization. In further contrast to Germany, most right-wing radicals in the US (and US conservatives) had no use for a strong central government. Instead, they defended the American free enterprise system, attacked social welfare programs, and upheld state rights and the American constitutional tradition (as they saw it). It was only in the 1930s that a mass movement (albeit a comparatively small and weak one, Coughlin's movement) appeared on the extreme right of the political landscape that paralleled European right-radical movements in calling for a strong state to direct the economy and society and to maintain law and order.[157]

It would take us beyond the scope of this study to follow up and attempt to explain these differences between Germany and the US and to detail the shifts in the programs and ideologies of right-wing radical forces in America. The important point for our purposes is that at least during the 1930s, not only the ideological baggage and intensity but also the social base of right-radical currents differed in the US and Germany. With the possible exception of the Silver Shirts, old and new right-wing groups did not find above average, probably in fact below average, support among the employed lower middle classes.

There were many reasons for the extreme weakness of right-wing radical currents in the US during the depression. From the outset the US was simply not as vulnerable to right-wing attacks as Germany without the long years of economic distress which Germans had experienced before the depression even began, without the handicap of a delayed, then half imported parliamentary democracy, without the blow of a lost war. There were still unused remedies to overcome the economic crisis available within the political system; moreover, the constitutional structure insulated the political process from radical mass movements, and to a certain extent the democratic political culture and traditions immunized the country against undemocratic movements. Furthermore, the American right's traditional distrust of strong government and lack of interest in economic issues were a severe handicap in a decade in which economic and social factors became objectively and subjectively central and state intervention to ameliorate the crisis inevitable. Traditional right-wing radicalism in the US was not well adapted to the realities of organized capitalist society. In Germany, on the other hand, right-radicalism was neither anti-statist nor opposed to the centralization of power; it was thus much more compatible with the needs of the 1930s and the basic principles of organized capitalism.

However, the fact that right-wing radical groups were so small and weak and lacked public prestige in the US during the 1930s also limits their utility for this study. Would white collar workers have been more interested if such groups had been larger, more important, and not so clearly defined as a lunatic fringe? Were these splinter and fringe groups rejected by rightward leaning white collar workers only because of their lack of respectability?

Although this question cannot be answered directly, a third source provides a more representative sample to use in looking for right-wing tendencies among American white collar workers: the raw data from the first public opinion polls.

2. Voting Behavior and Public Opinion Polls

Analyzing the results of the first (about 1935) public opinion polls to use social-economic criteria to classify respondents presents methodological problems which cannot be completely solved. The abstractness and make-believe character of the question situation may elicit answers quite different from the behavior or attitudes that would emerge in a real situation with real consequences; it is difficult to test the truthfulness of replies. The wording and presentation of questions, but even the events of the day, may have affected answers given in the late 1930s in a way that is not apparent to an historian writing more than 30 years later. Technical difficulties in the art of polling, such as how to select a representative sample, were not yet fully recognized. Indirect formulation of questions and internal controls for truthfulness had not been developed. Furthermore, the data banks do not have a complete collection of these early materials. The most important drawback for this study, however, is that the categories and definitions used in these surveys to determine the socio-economic status of respondents were not sufficiently precise.[158]

When Gallup and Roper began to differentiate poll results by socio-economic and occupational groups in the 1930s, they had no generally accepted stratification scheme to rely on. The early polls used a variety of categorization systems, and it was by and large left up to the interviewer to place respondents in a particular category. The Roper polls discussed below distinguished the following groups: (1) professionals, (2) proprietors (farm), (3) proprietors (other), (4) housewives, (5) salaried (minor), (6) salaried (executive), (7) wages (factory), (8) wages (farm), (9) wages, (other), (10) retired, (11) unemployed, (12) students. Professionals (1) included both self-employed and salaried persons, the latter almost always with high status and income. The salaried (executive) (6) category covered the top rank of white collar workers who had relatively high income and authority over other employees; low level supervisors (e.g., most foremen) were not included. About two-thirds of all white collar workers surveyed were placed in the salaried (minor) (5) category; it included almost all clerical and sales employees as well as technical employees in low and intermediate positions.[159]

Table 4.11
Percentage of Votes for Roosevelt in the 1936 and 1940 Presidential Elections, by Socio-economic Groups[160]

	1936	1940
Unskilled Workers	81	69
Semi-skilled Workers	74	67
Skilled Workers	67	59
All Manual Workers	74	66
White Collar Workers	61	48
Businessmen	47	34
National Average	62.5	55

Table 4.11 presents the data, as usually published. It confirms the well known intermediate political position of white collar workers and suggests that their voting behavior more closely paralleled that of skilled workers than that of businessmen. The table also portrays a distinct white collar shift away from Roosevelt between his landslide victory in 1936 and narrower re-election in 1940. However, if one uses unpublished materials and divides white collar workers into salaried (executive) and salaried (minor) categories, the picture changes: in 1936, 67% of lower/middle level white collar workers voted for FDR, while only 50% of salaried executives supported him. Thus the voting behavior of minor salaried employees exactly matched that of skilled workers; executives deviated from businessmen by only three percentage points.[161]

A Gallup poll taken in November 1940 (using slightly different categories) confirms this alignment:

Table 4.12
Percentage of Votes for Roosevelt in 1940, by Socio-economic Groups[162]
(Votes for third party candidates not eliminated)

	%	N
Unskilled Workers (Non-farm)	68.7	(227)
Semi-skilled Workers	47.4	(318)
Skilled Workers	49.2	(270)
White Collar Workers ('Clerks') (Excluding Executives)	47.0	(617)
Professionals	27.5	(247)
Proprietors (Non-Farm)	26.1	(344)
National Average	44.5	(3127)

These results reveal a remarkable congruence between the votes of skilled (and to a lesser extent semi-skilled) and lower/middle level white collar workers. These groups formed a broad middle political position that was distinct from the voting behavior of unskilled workers, on one side, and that of professionals and businessmen, on the other.[163]

Analysis of other survey data collected in these years reveals that the greatest difference in the attitudes of lower/middle level white collar workers and those of blue collar workers was over the degree of government intervention in economy and society each group favored. White collar workers preferred the free enterprise system over a social welfare state to a slightly greater degree than blue collar workers, and were in this respect slightly more conservative. If groups with the same income level are compared the difference remains visible but becomes less pronounced.[164] The white collar category had significantly more objections to the idea of confiscatory taxes to reduce the highest incomes, the suggestion that the government should undertake to guarantee full employment,[165] and to New Deal social welfare programs.[166] There were also less pronounced differences of opinion between blue and white collar workers in the same income bracket on Roosevelt's policies toward business and his pro-union labor policy.[167] While these variations indicate that differences in the economic, social, and political orientation of blue and white collar workers were not just a function of differences in income, the data also suggest that income was usually a more important determinant of attitudes than the collar line as such.[168]

Variations between the opinions of blue and white collar workers were least evident in the lowest income group.[169] And a 1938/39 study of Akron, Ohio, found that low paid white collar workers employed on public works projects (who had thus experienced prolonged unemployment) had about the same attitudes toward trade unions, strikes, big business, and government social programs as organized blue collar workers.[170]

On questions about human and civil rights, the responses of blue and white collar workers were even more similar; if anything, white collar workers seemed to be a little more 'liberal' or 'progressive'. The Gallup poll, for instance, which distinguished between skilled and unskilled workers and also between (a minority of) highly qualified white collar workers and (the majority of) white collar workers without special qualifications,[171] asked the following questions:

1. Should America have the biggest navy in the world?
2. Do you believe that the President of the United States should have the power of a dictator over the country in time of war?
3. If you had to choose between fascism and communism, which would you choose?
4. Would you support a widespread campaign against the Jews in this country?
5. The Daughters of the American Revolution would not let a well-known Negro singer give a concert in one of their halls. As a protest against this Mrs Franklin D. Roosevelt resigned from the organization. Do you approve of her action?
6. Do you think that state and local authorities should use force in removing sit down strikers?

7. Are you in favor of the death penalty for murder?

Table 4.12[172] presents the answers of various socio-economic groups to these questions. Except on the question of the death penalty (7), white collar workers' answers were not less 'liberal' or 'progressive' than those of blue collar workers. They showed no greater interest in American naval supremacy (1), which suggests that expansionist impulses were not more rampant among white collar workers than among blue collar or other groups. They were less prepared than manual workers or the average of all respondents to see the chief executive assume emergency wartime powers (2). Presented with a fictive choice between fascism and communism (3), white collar workers without special qualifications were more decisively anti-fascist than unskilled or skilled workers. They were also more definitely opposed to an anti-semitic campaign than blue collar workers (4), even though it seems likely that their work would have brought them into direct competition with Jews more often than factory workers. Moreover, their agreement — naturally unbinding — with Eleanor Roosevelt's demonstrative protest against discrimination was higher than that of blue collar workers (who, however, were more apt to face economic competition from blacks); the highly qualified white collar group was less approving than lower/middle level employees. Other poll results suggest that while discrimination became less direct with rising socio-economic status, real tolerance did not increase.[173] On the question of the use of force against sit down strikers (6), an issue which raised both civil rights and social policy questions, the responses of skilled workers and lower/middle level white collar workers were again closer to each other than to either unskilled workers or higher white collar employees. There were also no significant differences of opinion between blue collar and white collar workers on such questions as sexual morality and prohibition.[174]

V. AMERICAN WHITE COLLAR WORKERS: SOMEWHAT LEFT OF CENTER

Thus the investigation of white collar trade unions, analysis of the social base of right-wing extremist organizations, and evaluation of early public opinion poll questionnaires all lead to the same conclusion: the collar line was not a major boundary in the American socio-political landscape during the depression. The objectives, organizational behavior, and general social/political stance of organized white collar workers hardly differed from those of organized blue collar workers. The few traces of class-specific white collar demands, protests, and organizations that did appear in the US toward the end of the era were not significant enough to alter this conclusion. Blue and white collar workers also diverged very little in their participation in right-wing extremist organizations. Skilled blue collar workers and lower/intermediate level white collar workers were similar in support for Roosevelt, and opinions on key political and social questions. The findings of this study thus support those contemporaries who grouped blue collar workers and most white collar workers together in their political analyses and programs.[175]

Two other lines of division — one cutting horizontally through the blue collar, the other through the white collar group — were more significant than the collar line itself. Organizational and voting behavior as well as social/political outlook demarcated a broad middle group of lower/intermediate level white collar and semi-skilled/skilled blue collar workers on one side from the stratum of top white collar workers (about one-third of the total) who aligned themselves with self-employed professionals and businessmen.[176] Income appeared to be the most important single factor in determining where this line should be drawn. An in-depth study of Chicago in 1937 found that about $3,000 a year was the level at which attitudes and behavior diverged.[177] This broad middle group was separated *on the other side* from the great mass of unskilled (and some semi-skilled) workers, that is from a group below them which included the majority of the most recently arrived ethnic minorities and almost all blacks.

In the American political spectrum, and especially compared to manual workers, the average American white collar worker of lower/intermediate rank stood slightly to the right of center on economic and some social questions. On civil liberties and nationalist issues, on the other hand, he was more apt to be found in the moderate center or a little to the left. If their distrust of government economic and social intervention aligned white collar workers with the traditional political right in this country, their progressive positions on civil liberties definitely did not. And both attitudes immunized them against seeking a fascist or quasi-fascist solution to their problems and distinguished them from corresponding social groups in Germany.

Thus even under the impact of a severe economic crisis which brought them massive unemployment and declining economic and social status, the lower and intermediate ranks of white collar workers still did not radicalize to the right, but instead moved closer to the attitudes and behavior of organized blue collar workers. In contrast to Germany, there was among white collar workers no specifically lower middle class protest movement

Table 4.13
Answers to Selected Questions (Gallup Poll 1937-39), by Socio-economic Groups

Question Number . . .	1		2		3		4		5		6		7	
	Yes %	No %	Yes %	No %	Yes %	No %	Yes %	No %	Yes %	No %	Yes %	No %	Yes %	No %
Unskilled Workers	45	12	15	44	23	20	14	79	62	37	46	37	57	36
Skilled Workers	39	12	17	37	25	27	12	79	61	24	63	24	55	38
Lower/Middle White Collar	44	15	15	45	19	39	8	88	65	30	63	30	69	27
Higher White Collar	38	14	14	47	30	30	9	84	59	30	70	20	62	32
Average of All Occupational Groups	38	23	16	42	25	24	17	82	59	27	61	24	60	33

directed simultaneously against economic elites and organized labor in the US. Except for the better paid upper strata (which largely shared the conservatism of businessmen and professionals), white collar workers supported Roosevelt and the New Deal to about the same degree as skilled workers (both groups less enthusiastically than the unskilled). There was no 'white collar backlash' in America comparable to the resentful protests of German salaried employees against their relative deprivation. The reforms and rhetoric of the New Deal — a little left of center, but neither radical nor socialistic — did not scare them, but either met their wishes or at least remained tolerable for them.

Thus, faced with a very similar economic situation during the depression — mass unemployment, loss of earnings, and partly blocked avenues of upward mobility — American white collar workers reacted quite differently from German salaried employees. The picture of a frustrated, resentful 'clerk', suffering from the collision between his expectations and reality and bitterly resentful of the relative gains of wage workers that was so typical for Germany in the economic crisis, bore little resemblance to the American white collar worker. In fact, when asked in 1939 if they believed that they had better opportunities to succeed than their parents had had at the same age, most white collar workers answered 'yes' — the lower/intermediate group more definitely than the highly qualified. Barely half of the industrial workers surveyed replied affirmatively.[178] Approximately two-thirds of the lower/intermediate group of white collar employees also thought that they had a good chance to advance; less than one-third assumed that they would not move into a higher position in the future.[179] This surprising optimism may have been connected to the fact that many lower/middle level white collar workers — about every fourth man and every third woman — had (one or two) immigrant parents. These children of Irish, Russian, Italian, Canadian, English, and German immigrants — to mention only the most common countries of origin for this group — were overrepresented in various sorts of low and intermediate rank white collar positions around 1940. They may have been more apt to perceive their white collar status in itself as a relative advance than the sons and daughters of families in a relatively homogeneous society like Germany, even if in most cases the positions they held no longer quite represented what they had to their parents who were stuck in unskilled or semi-skilled manual labor.[180]

Furthermore, after the prosperity of the 1920s the depression may have been experienced as a temporary interruption, not as another step in a long slide as it appeared to German salaried employees. And finally, the more modest expectations of American white collar workers compared to German, the fact that they were not similarly obsessed with maintaining an appropriate corporatist way of life that visibly demonstrated their superiority to the working class, also made them less vulnerable to a sense of threat and bitterness. The evidence suggests that American white collar workers were scarcely more likely to identify themselves, organize, or behave as a distinct social class during the depression than in previous decades. And they showed even less tendency to see themselves as part of a defensive lower middle class that was demarcated from and/or hostile to those 'above' and 'below' it on the social ladder — even though labor unions were expanding rapidly and had unprecedented power, social-economic differences between blue and white collar workers were partially leveled, and more than before American politics were polarizing along class lines. Compared to other social groups in the US, and particularly compared to manual workers, white collar workers revealed no class specific or above average inclination toward right-wing protest like that which was so characteristic of the equivalent social group in Germany.

5. The American Experience in Comparative Perspective

I. RESULTS OF THE GERMAN-AMERICAN COMPARISON

The fact that fascistic currents and groups were so insignificant in the US cannot be explained solely by analyzing the behavior of American white collar workers, of course. Many more factors were responsible than this study can take up: The first world war had a less disruptive impact on America than it did on European societies; European fascism would hardly have been possible without its inflammatory, mobilizing consequences. And America was spared the economic and political burdens of defeat which so handicapped the first German Republic during the 1920s; here rapid economic growth and relative prosperity continued until the crash in 1929. Furthermore, there was no powerful, radical labor movement in the US — an important prerequisite for the sense of collective threat that made middle class groups elsewhere receptive to anti-labor, fascistic arguments. Without a strong socialist or communist challenge to the existing political system, there was no fascist reaction. America's political culture, party structure and constitutional system was a much less vulnerable ideological and institutional framework than Weimar Germany's parliamentary system, which had not existed before 1918 and which was full of instabilities. Without the traditions of reform and social integration 'from above' which went back to absolutism in Germany, without a long tradition of state intervention to guarantee economic well being and (relative) social stability comparable to Germany's, the

US still had fresh (if in the final analysis inadequate) instruments for crisis management available within the system in the 1930s. Greater government restraint went hand in hand with the lower expectations Americans had of their government; political parties and government officials were less apt to be held responsible for individual grievances than in Germany. Finally, the American right's traditional distrust of a strong state limited its viability in an economic crisis which required government intervention.

All these — and other — factors would probably have been sufficient to prevent a fascist takeover in the US, even if a reactionary protest *potential* at all comparable to the German phenomenon had existed among American white collar workers. One of the findings of this study, however, is that this potential did not exist in the US.

Since there was no significant fascist alternative available in the US during the 1930s, it is hardly surprising that American white collar workers did not flock to fascistic parties or movements. Not so self-explanatory however, and in light of the received thesis presented in Chapter 1 unexpected, is the fact that American white collar workers did not respond to the economic crisis in specifically middle class or lower middle class ways that clearly distinguished their attitudes and behavior from the working class; they revealed no greater susceptibility to right-wing extremism than blue collar workers or other social groups in this country. The collar line as such was simply not as significant a basis for differentiating the political, legal, psychological, social-structural, and economic dimensions of life for social classes and groups in the US as it was in Germany.

This conclusion contradicts the received thesis.[1] If the findings of this study are correct, one will have to be more cautious in future about explaining visible differences between wage workers and salaried employees as a necessary function of the social and economic structure of industrial capitalist society. Nor will it be sufficient to explain petty bourgeois/lower middle class reactionary attitudes among white collar workers as a quasi-automatic byproduct of the tensions and conflicts which appear at advanced stages of industrialization: the striking divergence of white collar behavior in two societies with such similar economic structures and histories as the US and Germany discredits that assumption. Finally, one will have to be very careful about how one transfers hypotheses linking the lower middle class with susceptibility to right-wing extremism developed in the continental European context to American white collar workers — unless these theories are used as a comparative foil to identify and illuminate contrasts between societies.[2]

As has been mentioned, the contrasting social and economic experiences of German and American white collar workers after the first world war cannot be overlooked in accounting for the divergent behavior of these social groups after 1929. German white collar workers were plunged into a severe economic crisis after they had already endured years of absolute and relative economic decline. During the war and the inflationary spiral that peaked in 1923 the real income of all employed persons dropped sharply and the wage-salary differential narrowed. Though this trend was interrupted in the stabilization phase beginning in 1923/24, the distance between wages and salaries in 1929 was still less than before the war and, moreover, middle class savings which inflation had consumed remained lost. Unemployment stood at 8-9% in Germany even before it climbed to previously unknown heights during the depression. Thus like many other Germans, salaried employees experienced the great depression of the 1930s as the culmination of an already lengthy phase of misery and insecurity. The economic crash reactivated a chronic sense of crisis which the relatively good years of the Weimar Republic between 1924 and 1929 had hardly dissipated.

In contrast, the depression hit the US after a long phase of relative prosperity in which white collar workers had thoroughly participated. After a much briefer postwar depression, the distance between wages and salaries in the US did not narrow during the 1920s. The course of real earnings was more favorable for all employed persons than in Germany; economic growth continued at a more rapid pace with fewer disturbances. In 1929 the unemployment rate in the US was less than half that of Germany, just under 4%. In these circumstances the economic crash was perceived as a surprising interruption of economic progress, not as a logical continuation of long term uncertainty.[3] Thus it seems plausible to conclude that such divergent collective experiences would have made German white collar workers more receptive to reactionary extremism than American. And on top of economic distress the political and psychological burdens of the lost war, the war guilt question, and the new constitution sharpened political tensions and politicized popular discontent in Germany in ways that had no parallel in the US.

However, the contrasting experiences of German and American white collar workers in the first world war and the 1920s can only be part of the explanation. In the first place it is by no means certain that a rapidly worsening situation after a long period of uncertainty, stagnation, or partial decline makes those affected more susceptible to radicalization than a similar change in circumstances after a long period of advance and improvement. Indeed, some theories and cases make just the opposite result appear more probable.[4] Secondly, it would not be logical to expect that such a fundamental difference between societies as the varying significance of the collar line in the US and Germany could be traced entirely to the events of a few years or a decade. And in fact the investigation of German and American white collar history before 1914 found that many fundamental cross-cultural differences were already evident before the impact and aftermath of the first world war set the two societies on such divergent paths.

Even before 1914-1918, the collar line did not have the economic, social, psychological and political significance at work or in society in the US that made it a subject for reflection and investigation in Germany at an early date. Already in the prewar era the lines between unskilled laborers and skilled workers on one side and between the lower and intermediate ranks of white collar workers and executives/managerial employees on the other were objectively (e.g., in organizational behavior or in working conditions) and subjectively more important than the line between blue collar and white collar workers per se. Furthermore, all patterns of horizontal stratification in the US were cross-cut and blurred by vertical lines of differentiation (e.g., based on function, religion, ethnicity or race) to a much greater extent than in Germany. One result of the insignificance of the collar line was that the transformation of salaried employees or white collar workers from an abstract category meaningful to statisticians and later historians into a social group which had a distinct existence and characteristics for its members and other contemporaries took place later, more hesitantly, and much less completely in the US than in Germany.

In fact, just because the collar line was less significant than in Germany and because American white collar workers were not perceived as a separate social group, there is a shortage of source materials and of social scientific/historical work on this stratum. While this relative lack of information has caused this investigation special difficulties, it is also responsible for its special opportunity: to use the comparative method to define white collar workers as a subject for historical research.

The relative insignificance of the distinction between wage workers and salaried employees had vast consequences for American politics, social structure, and industrial relations in the decades of rapid industrialization before the first world war. In contrast to Germany, the collar line did not serve as a basis for interest group formation; nor was it available for efforts to divide and coopt social groups in industry and society at large. Since it was not manipulated by employers, bureaucrats, and conservative political groups here as it was in Germany, it was also not refined, strengthened, and ingrained in American society. There was no equivalent in the Progressive Era for the class-specific interest group politics of the German new middle class in the Wilhelminian Era. It would be an exaggeration to characterize the simultaneously anti-labor and anti-capitalist, status and threat conscious reactionary demands of German salaried employees before the first world war as pre- or proto-fascist. But they did formulate the basic principles of lower middle class separatism; under the difficult economic, social, and political circumstances of the Weimar Republic, separatism and resentment could be transformed into pro-fascist attitudes and behavior. Furthermore, since legislation, court decisions, the structure of organizations, and styles of social and community life embedded the special status of the lower middle class in the behavior patterns and institutions of German society, the legacy of this pre-first world war agitation was not limited to the realm of expectations, attitudes, and ideologies. Insofar as the political stance of the American new middle class before the first world war can be determined, it appears to have been part of the mass base for a heterogeneous but on the whole liberal-democratic social reform movement.

In other words: Just as the turn to the right of large sections of the German lower middle class at the end of the Weimar Replublic cannot be attributed to their postwar fate *alone*, differences between German and American white collar workers cannot be explained solely on the basis of their divergent experiences during and after the first world war. Rather, the search for causal explanations must focus again on the long term social historical differences between these two societies.

First: Differences in the structure and role of the labor movement and the working class in America and Germany during the half century 1890-1940 must be taken into account. American labor unions concentrated more exclusively on wages and working conditions than German unions; they were much less involved in broad social and political reform efforts. With a few brief and relatively unimportant exceptions, there was no working class political party in the US comparable to the Social Democratic Party in Germany. Trade union membership had comparatively little impact on other social roles; as an American of Polish descent, a Catholic, father of school children, or member of a club, a trade unionist could participate in several distinct social milieus. In contrast the German labor union (and the working class political party) tended to organize the whole person; it attempted to satisfy the economic, social, political, and cultural needs of a man and his family. The concept of a working class subculture, which so aptly describes the German situation, was with some local and temporary exceptions quite foreign to the aims or reality of the American labor movement. Behind this contrast between the two labor movements lay the differences in the two working classes: to be a worker was a more comprehensive, specific identity in Germany than in the US; one's role at work defined one's role in the most diverse social realms, including politics. Membership in the working class did not circumscribe one's political, cultural, psychological and social existence in the US to the extent that it did in Germany.

The ideological differences between the two labor movements were also significant. The radical and partly revolutionary class consciousness (and even more radical rhetoric) of German trade unions and the Social Democratic Party contrasted vividly with the instrumental 'business unionism' of most American unions, which had more forthrightly accepted capitalism and the existing economic, social, and political system. In spite of all the sporadic violence of capital-labor conflicts in the US, this labor movement did not pose the same sort of radical threat to other social groups and the status quo as the German labor movement and working class appeared to. And as a corollary, organized labor was not defined as an internal enemy and subjected to discrimination and exclusion to the same extent as in Germany.[5]

Thus American white collar workers had less reason than German salaried employees to define themselves (let alone organize) as a new middle class or as part of the lower middle class to distinguish themselves from the working class. Where the status of manual worker was less comprehensive and less apt to overshadow other social roles, whether or not one belonged to the working class was a much less urgent question; white collar workers had less reason to see themselves as members of a class that transcended occupational divisions and to behave accordingly. Because the American machinist was in the first place a machinist and only secondarily a member of the working class, the American bookkeeper could think of himself primarily as a bookkeeper — he had little objective reason or subjective motive to emphasize his membership in a white collar class. The same logic determined the way others saw and treated him. When some white collar workers did decide to organize to pursue socio-economic interests collectively, they were able to do so *within* the framework of the AFL. In this case, sales clerks or technicians did not have to identify closely as members of the working class; they did not have to commit themselves to a political, ideological, social and cultural program. Furthermore, the fact that labor presented a less serious challenge to American society also in part explains why American white collar workers as a rule felt less threatened than German salaried employees and were thus less apt to subscribe to the sort of reactionary, anti-labor or anti-socialist views so typical of German salaried employees' associations after the late 19th century. Moreover, the absence of a socialist challenge meant that American elites had less reason and opportunity to call for a united front of bourgeois social groups to defend bourgeois society. Such efforts by the ruling elites in Germany incited a good part of lower middle class political agitation and sharpened the conceptual and actual differences between wage workers and salaried employees.

Thus part of the explanation for the differences between German and American white collar workers is that since the American working class was less isolated and the American labor movement less radical than the German, the collar line and white collar workers as a distinct social group emerged later and less distinctly in the US than in Germany.

Second: The ethnic heterogeneity of the US was a serious obstacle to the formation not only of a united working class, but also of a white collar class that defined itself and behaved as such. Class formation and social stratification in Germany were based on socio-economic criteria without too many cross-cutting ethnic or racial lines of division. In the US, on the other hand, all socio-economic differentiation and stratification faced sharp and sometimes overpowering competition: sense of identity, social contacts, neighborhood, religion, and political attitudes and behavior were more often a function of race or ethnicity than class. Ethnic group organizations that encompassed a variety of classes and income levels often played about the same role in the US that the local labor organization played in Germany. Thus ethnicity rather than class was apt to dictate who would be one's friends and neighbors and how one would spend leisure time. In conjunction with the church, the ethnic community provided essential services like hospitals, kindergartens, playgrounds, old age homes, and cemeteries for its members. It also provided a framework for self-esteem and prestige and offered its members protection and community. While the ties and dependence of the immigrant generation were of course particularly strong, many of their children — the second generation who were overrepresented in lower/middle level white collar occupations — were still closely connected to their ethnic community.

Ethnicity was particularly powerful in fragmenting the working class because the overrepresentation of new immigrants (and, after the first world war, Negroes, Puerto Ricans and Mexicans) among the unskilled and their underrepresentation among skilled workers reinforced the barrier between these two halves of the working class. Yet ethnic diversity was a hindrance to white collar unity, too. Since the members of the second generation who were recruited in large numbers into lower/middle level white collar occupations kept close ties to their ethnic group, their reference group was less apt to be the working class as a whole than another ethnic group or their own group in their parents' generation. And as the case of the technical draftsmen revealed, native stock Americans often refused to combine on an occupational basis if that meant cutting across ethnic lines. There are even some examples of management using ethnic or racial lines of division for their own purpose to counteract unity based on occupation or class.[6]

Finally, native stock white collar workers may have viewed the new immigrants — first clustered in urban ghettos, but later expanding into jobs and neighborhoods previously closed to them — as a greater threat of relative deprivation[7] than the growing power of the working class and the labor movement. All in all, ethnic-racial tensions and conflicts in the US played part of the role that social-economically defined fronts played in Germany; at the very least ethnicity cross-cut classes and occupations and thus hindered their potential unity.[8]

Third: Differences in the emergence of the interventionist state in Germany and America had a significant impact on differences between white collar workers in each society. Government intervention to direct and stabilize economy and society appeared much earlier in Germany than in the US. Such state action recognized and reinforced the collar line in two ways: It gave groups a motive for collective organization in order to have some influence on the political processes that directly affected their economic and social life. Furthermore, this social legislation and its implementation by the bureaucracy and the courts differentiated the rights and benefits of groups along the collar line and thus reinforced its significance.

Bismarck's social insurance laws and the white collar movement in Imperial Germany illustrate this interaction between social divisions, interest groups, and the political decision-making process. In response to the social insurance legislation of the 1870s and 1880s, German technical employees formed collective interest groups. To interpret these statutes judges had to define who on the basis of what criteria was a worker or a non-worker (and that soon meant salaried employee). To lobby for a special insurance law for this (now legally defined) social group, German salaried employees organized on a supra-occupational basis in the first decade of this century. The Salaried Employee Insurance Law of 1911 was only the first in a long series of statutes that distinguished the insurance and labor law status of manual workers and salaried employees; these laws thus cemented lines of differentiation which might have remained more fluid, blurred, or at any rate less relevant without such legal codification. This interlocking pattern of social divisions, interest groups, and government intervention did not appear in the US because the catalyst — the interventionist state — developed much more hesitantly and much later. When widespread government intervention in economy and society began during the New Deal, it did stimulate a parallel (if weaker) process of interaction among social groups, organized interest groups, and the government, as the history of the NLRB reveals.

Fourth: Variations in the determinants and rate of social mobility in the US and Germany also contributed to the divergent significance of the collar line. This study has emphasized the significance of the links between a stratified educational system and career choice in Germany; in consequence career patterns tended to be fixed at an early age and barriers between occupations were more rigid. An individual's life chances were thus largely determined before he began work by the social and educational opportunities his family could provide; this synchronization of education and occupation emerged only after the turn of the century in the US and was never as systematic or thorough. Whether or not this qualitative difference, as one might expect, was also quantitatively expressed in different intra-generational mobility rates in the two societies — i.e., whether American workers had comparatively greater chances to work their way up to a higher position than German — cannot be determined because of insufficiently exact and comparable data. One can assume, however, that the connection between a stratified school system (to which different social strata had quite different access) and occupation was one of the reasons why intergenerational mobility from blue collar into white collar positions was apparently lower in Germany than in the US at the turn of the century. Thus the social origins of German white collar workers around 1900 more clearly demarcated them from groups below them on the social ladder than was true for their American counterparts. In the first third of the 20th century, however, the number of workers' children entering white collar positions increased markedly in Germany; at this important rung of the social ladder opportunities to advance drew about even with the rate of intergenerational upward mobility in the US, which did not increase but stayed about the same in these years.

A quantitative comparison of the opportunities for upward occupational mobility for lower/middle level white collar workers in both societies is unfortunately not possible. In addition to educational barriers, the slower growth rate of the German economy (especially in the 1920s) may have meant that chances to advance and/or become self-employed were smaller in Germany than the US. While German opportunities may have constricted in the 1920s compared to earlier decades, chances to move up may have improved for US white collar workers.[9] Rates of migration and employee turnover for the two societies cannot be systematically compared either because of insufficient data. While the first attempts to assemble comparable data appear to indicate that German and American cities showed very similar rates of migration in the late 19th century,[10] the more numerous qualitative sources used in this study point to a much greater fluidity among white collar workers in the US. In the late 19th and early 20th centuries, for instance, American sales clerks seem to have moved about as often as skilled workers, certainly more frequently than businessmen or professionals.[11]

Even more clearly than actual mobility rates, however, the preconceptions of American and German white collar workers about their chances for upwards mobility and migration differed. The belief that individual advancement by hard work and performance was really possible was widespread among American white collar workers even at the end of the 1930s; it seems to have been much more prevalent than in contemporary Germany. The vague sense that if things got too bad they could always move and begin anew — could emigrate within their own society, as Carleton advised his threatened colleagues in Boston to do — seems to have been widespread.[12] American sources do not convey the same sense of being hopelessly trapped, with no vertical or horizontal escape, that German materials do. These comparatively optimistic convictions were apparently more prevalent among white collar than blue collar workers.[13] They were cause and consequence of deeply rooted values and myths, constantly reinforced in schools, mass media and popular literature, which informed and in part still do inform tradition and political culture in North America: belief in individual success, reliance on individual problem solving, respect for work and achievement, readiness to compete and take risks, and confidence that progress is not only possible but probable.

Such a socio-psychological explanation is not enough. It was important that these preconceptions were not too decisively or lengthily contradicted by American reality; rather, much direct experience with and observation of individual mobility seemed to corroborate them. Consider the history of many immigrant families: a first generation consigned to unskilled labor was succeeded by a second generation able to enter modest sales or office positions or one of the skilled crafts. It was reasonable to expect that their children would be able to take yet another small step upward. The limits and incompleteness of this social mobility should not be overlooked: Individuals who advance, even though there are many of them, do so because there is real economic and social inequality; their individual good fortune does nothing to diminish it.

Furthermore, such small, hard steps up the social ladder usually took several generations; they bore little resemblance to the rags to riches myth of popular literature. And the top positions in business, government, and the professions remained all but closed to the children of Italians, Poles and Greeks, and difficult even for better integrated immigrant groups like the Irish to attain. Moreover, the progress of these immigrant groups was counterbalanced by the fact that more recent arrivals — rural blacks, Puerto Ricans, Mexicans — took their recently vacated places at the bottom of the social ladder. Recent scholarship has rightly stressed all these correctives to traditional claims that America was an open society, the land of opportunity. Yet, especially in comparative perspective, it is clear that upward mobility was common enough in the US to provide sufficient foundation in fact to nurture these (however exaggerated and ideologically colored) preconceptions and beliefs.[14]

Many *other factors* contributed to blurring the collar line in the US and to the related lack of definition of a white collar class and the absence of a marked susceptibility to right-wing extremism among American white collar workers. The egalitarian political culture and rhetoric of this society made it very difficult for any one group to demand special privileges. The federal structure of government and the two party system inhibited the formulation of social protest in ideological terms and its translation into protest organizations and politics: either they had a decentralizing and fragmenting effect, or they cast protest and opposition into the broad collection baskets of the major parties. But in conclusion, one cluster of differentiating conditions and causes will be singled out. Perhaps it is the most significant, because it includes the factors just enumerated and is at the same time more specifically linked to the cross-cultural contrasts this study seeks to explain.

The collar line was more pronounced and specific lower middle class protest more typical of German salaried employees than American white collar workers because of the continuing impact of certain pre-industrial, pre-capitalist, and pre-bourgeois traditions on German society even at advanced stages of industrialization which were almost completely absent in the US. Feudal/corporatist and bureaucratic traditions not only stamped the values and mentalities of social groups and the symbols, style, and political culture of German life in the 19th and early 20th centuries; they were also embedded in the legal system, organizations, social behavior, and the class structure. Both traditions dated from an era that preceded industrial capitalism, the industrial revolution and the emergence of a civil or a bourgeois society;[15] they continued, however, to operate in and to shape industrial capitalist economy and society.

Unbroken by a successful revolution from below, bureaucratic and corporatist traditions flourished in Germany to a greater extent than in other parts of western Europe, let alone the US. The German pattern of modernization 'from above', the continuing influence of pre-industrial, pre-capitalist, and pre-bourgeois elites — aristocrats, agrarians, bureaucrats and military officers — on politics, culture, and style strengthened and renewed aspects of these traditions even as Germany became a modern industrial nation. Since Marx, Engels, and Max Weber at the latest, the determinants and consequences of this unique German path to a modern society have been recognized and analyzed. Only one part of the problem was taken up in this study: the impact of these traditions on the shape and significance of the collar line.

Comparison of American sales clerks with German mercantile employees revealed that the objective and subjective boundaries dividing these equivalent social groups from their respective working classes as well as their inclination toward reactionary right-wing protest were less marked in the US primarily because of the absence of mercantile-corporatist traditions and expectations. Thus the expectations of this social group in the US were not so much on a collision course with the realities of modern economic life; socio-economic modernization and social leveling did not produce the resentment and protest that was so characteristic in Germany. Comparison of industrial white collar workers in both societies revealed that the bureaucratic traditions that shaped the actual situation, sense of identity, organizational behavior and collective expectations of the 'private bureaucrats' in Germany were also lacking in the US. Their absence partly accounts for the fact that a white collar class clearly demarcated from production workers (who were perceived as a subordinate group subject to its rule) with a vested interest in its superior status did not emerge in American industry. Government bureaucrats with high prestige and power did not serve as a normative reference group for industrial white collar workers in the US either at work or in society at large. Moreover, the state bureaucracy was also not available as a model to facilitate white collar workers' supra-occupational combination as 'private bureaucrats', simultaneously demarcated from wage workers and management.

White collar employees in American industry thus lacked both the traditional privileges and security and the lofty claims and status expectations which in Germany increasingly clashed with a changing economy and society. Without such corporatist and bureaucratic models American white collar workers were less apt to define the working class as an opposing group and a comparative reference group. A distinct lower middle class sense of identity, and reactionary attitudes, organizations and protests were almost completely absent in the US not because American white collar workers had been less dramatically affected by socio-economic change, but rather because in the absence of such traditional claims and an exalted starting point, modernization and standardization were less apt to be experienced as a challenge, threat, decline, or danger of proletarianization.

Compared with Germany and all continental societies, the US all but lacked an indigenous feudal-corporatist past. The few traces that had been brought into colonial America did not survive the Revolutionary Era and Jacksonian reforms. In the US as in England, industrialization preceded the development of large scale public bureaucracies (the reverse was true in France and Germany). Thus without corporatist or bureaucratic traditions and models, American white collar workers were apt to see themselves simply as employees, as future businessmen, or — increasingly and often with ideological overtones — as members of a professional, semi-professional, or aspiring professional group.

Up to a certain point the professional sense of identity of American white collar workers (particularly in the better qualified intermediate and upper ranks) served as a weak functional equivalent for the bureaucratic and corporatist lower middle class ideology of German salaried employees. Professionalism divided the occupational group from the mass of employees; it posited a sequence of a career steps within one's occupation and more or less negated the hope of future independence; it connoted an often ideological/illusory parallelism with highly esteemed social groups — older professions such as medicine or law — which began to assume the role of normative reference group for American white collar workers that businessmen had played in earlier decades. A professional sense of identity justified a group's claim to social recognition and prestige because they provided public 'services' (and by inference were not solely motivated by economic self-interest); it also provided a basis for group unity and organization. Flattering appeals to the professional character of a white collar group, e.g. pharmacy clerks, could be used as an argument against their trade union organization. Finally, it was also suggested that this growing sense of professionalism would contribute to defusing and solving social conflicts at work and in society.[16]

But the parallels between the functions of the lower middle class ideology of German salaried employees and the professional ideology of American white collar workers also had distinct limits. A professional self-image was much less dependent on demarcating the group from those 'above' and 'below' — from executives and owners on one side and the working class on the other — than the bureaucratic model that reinforced the lower middle class consciousness of German salaried employees. Thus decreasing social and economic differences between those paid in salaries and wages were less threatening to American white collar workers than to German salaried employees. Professional claims to social esteem and prestige were based less on (common) status than on (diverse) function; they therefore inhibited rather than promoted the supra-occupational organization of white collar workers.

Furthermore, a professional sense of identity was less centrally challenged by the risks and crises inherent in capitalism and the market economy than the bureaucratic/corporatist inspired ideology of German salaried employees. It did not imply the same right to a secure economic existence — a claim which was on a direct collision course with reality during economic crises like the depression of the 1930s. Consider: in December 1939, four-fifths of the lower/middle level white collar workers in the US surveyed (but only a little more than half of the factory workers) preferred a position with good earnings and prospects for advancement, but which also carried a 50% chance of dismissal, over a position which was secure but offered only moderate earnings and little chance to advance. The responses of men and women were about the same.[17] This marked preference for opportunity with risk over security contradicted neither the older quasi-entrepreuneurial or newer quasi-professional identification of American white collar workers. One suspects that German salaried employees would have given quite different replies to that question.

Finally, this emerging professional sense of identity provided a much less favorable basis for the type of collective, organized, simultaneously anti-capitalist and anti-labor protests that characterized the German new middle class' response to the economic crisis. For since American white collar workers' professional consciousness had developed in response to their changing economic situation in modern industrial society, it was only logical that it was less buffeted by modern economic and social reality than the cherished but increasingly obsolete corporatist/bureaucratic claims of the new middle class in Germany.

To sum up: the last few pages have sought to answer two closely related questions: why was the collar line so much less distinct in the US, and why did American white collar workers show so few signs of susceptibility to the type of right-wing extremism that so strongly attracted German salaried employees? After rejecting the divergence in the experiences of the two social groups and the two societies between the first world war and the economic crash as a *sufficient* explanation, five fundamental differences between the two societies were reviewed. *First*, variations in the structure and role of the working class and the labor movement; *second*, the ethnic-racial heterogeneity that distinguished America from Germany's more homogeneous society; *third*, differences in the timing and character of state intervention in economy and society; *fourth*, divergent patterns of and preconceptions about social mobility; and *fifth*, the continuing presence or absence of pre-industrial corporatist/bureaucratic traditions at advanced stages of industrialization. Why should this last factor be more significant than any of the others? Because with the exception of the unusual ethnic-racial heterogeneity of the US population — which is a crucial independent variable — the other clusters of causes are *partly* encompassed by and thus a function of this last cross-cultural difference. This point will be briefly illustrated.

In Germany but not in the US, pre-industrial corporatist/feudal and military/authoritarian traditions merged with and sharpened the modern tensions and contradictions inherent in industrial capitalism. The particular forms and intensity of the class conflict that accompanied German industrialization, the relatively thorough exclusion of the proletariat from civil or bourgeois society, and the logical corollary of that exclusion — an organized labor movement which seemed necessarily to threaten the status quo — were among the consequences of the continuing impact of these traditions. The militaristic and bureaucratic, sometimes even the master-servant, structure and tone of labor relations in many companies kept these traditions alive in their own way just as much as anachronistic, illiberal, and undemocratic elements in the political system did. In the ordinary encounters of daily life the middle classes and the working class continued to observe the deference due to various estates and ranks; absolutism survived in the boorish harshness of the petty government clerk or policeman, who in their own minds and to the workers represented the power of the state. The continuing impact of corporatist traditions was reflected by the fact that an individual's occupational status was apt to determine his social position and prestige, where he lived and how, his family's life style and the education he could provide for his children, his opportunities to participate in politics, and many other dimensions of his life as well. Corporatist remnants in German society help explain why working class status in itself was more important than differences between crafts or occupations; they also illuminate the relative insignificance of the line between skilled and unskilled workers in German trade unions and social structure compared to the US.[18] Bitter class conflict, a relatively homogeneous working class and a relatively closed, radical labor movement etched the collar line much more deeply into mentalities and reality in Germany than in the US. The sharpness of this line and all it stood for was a prerequisite for the emergence of a reactionary lower middle class protest potential among German salaried employees.

Bureaucratic traditions smoothed the transition to organized capitalism in Germany and perpetuated the greater significance of intervention from above over the voluntary organization of social groups. Continued reliance on old patterns of state intervention in economy and society, the presence of an extensive and efficient career bureaucracy, and the widespread acceptance of both meant that the interventionist state did not have first to overcome entrenched individualism and economic liberalism. Although bureaucratic traditions eased the early emergence of active government intervention in industrial society, they were of course not a sufficient cause.[19] The government's role was part of its reaction to the particular sharpness of class conflict and its destabilizing effects; moreover, it was not undertaken in a neutral, balancing spirit, but instead in order to determine the victor. All in all, as was illustrated above, the early emergence of an interventionist state in industrializing Germany played a major role in sharpening the collar line.

Furthermore, the bureaucracy's need for trained personnel with qualifications graded by orderly steps was a major impulse behind the creation of a highly structured and stratified educational system. Continuing corporatist preconceptions also contributed to the rigidly divided, discriminatory character of German schooling; corporatist remnants in the educational system not only mirrored but perpetuated and strengthened divisions between social classes and strata. The impact of education on social mobility and on white collar workers has been emphasized at several points in this study.

Finally, certain features of German political culture — the relative insignificance of individualism, lack of prestige accorded business success and risk taking (and related skepticism about capitalism), and the undiminished strength of pre-liberal and illiberal attitudes — suggest a German deficit in some essential ingredients of a modern bourgeois or civil society that was closely but inversely related to the strength of Germany's pre-industrial, precapitalist, and pre-bourgeois traditions. German salaried employees had not been inculcated with the social-psychological attitudes and assumptions that reinforced the individualistic aspirations for advancement, relative readiness to take risks, and belief in individual success and responsibility characteristic of their American counterparts. Instead, their anti-capitalist resentments, claims to and expectations of security at work and secure social status, and above all their capacity for collective action when threatened were well adapted to the only partially bourgeois political culture of Germany.[20]

The diverging paths of US and German societies in the 20th century illuminate the enormous consequence of the continuing impact of those pre-industrial traditions in a modern industrial nation. This comparative focus also explains America's relative good fortune by analyzing historical developments, not by conjuring up a unique American national character or similar comparative fiction.

No doubt, our analysis has often had to proceed on rather limited evidence. Inferences have frequently had to be indirect. Conclusions have been based on very aggregated data and further testing and differentiation would be desirable. Three possible avenues for further research should be briefly noted: (1) different groups of white collar workers could be compared within each society; (2) the comparison might be extended to additional countries; (3) the argument could be pursued up to the present.

II. FURTHER COMPARISONS: WHITE COLLAR WORKERS IN ENGLAND AND FRANCE

If this study has correctly stressed the significance of pre-industrial traditions for the behavior of German salaried employees before and after the first world war, it should also be possible to detect differences in the impact of these traditions on categories of employees that were more or less affected by such traditions. And indeed, there is evidence that the tendency to identify with an exalted view of one's occupation or corporate group and the corresponding tendency to view change as decline and loss were more prevalent among salaried employees who were also the sons and daughters of salaried employees or other petty to middling bourgeois families than among their colleagues who were the children of manual workers. Like the children of immigrants in the US, the latter seemed to view their position as an improvement even if it no longer offered all the status and prestige of earlier decades. This was because they compared their own situation with that of their parents rather than with an ancient, idealized era in the history of their new occupation.[21] One would also expect that men would be more attracted to such traditional orientations and thus more apt to protest than women. If a girl worked in a store or an office only before she married, she would not have the same stake in her occupation as if it were a lifetime commitment; and even if she continued to work after marriage, she would be likely to share in her husband's status rather than stand on her own. One might also assume that the force of tradition would be more powerful in small or medium sized cities than in large cities and in small and medium sized companies than in large corporations. And since corporatist traditions were not as deeply rooted among technical employees as among mercantile employees, the ideologies and attitudes discussed here should be more visible in the latter than the former group. In fact, the early results of studies comparing various groups of white collar workers in the Weimar Republic do tend to confirm these suppositions, and thus the preceding hypotheses about the significance of pre-industrial traditions.[22]

A second way to verify and perhaps modify the theses drawn from comparing the US and Germany would be to extend the comparison to other societies. The most appropriate societies would be those countries in western and central Europe, such as England, which were at about the same level of industrial development as the US and Germany. The explanation of German-American differences developed here would lead one to expect that the history of white collar workers in England would fall somewhere in between the German and American patterns. (That is roughly speaking, of course; English history also exhibits many peculiarities which escape the categories chosen for and adapted to the comparison of the US and Germany.)

Parallel to the US and distinct from the continent, industrialization in England preceded the creation of an effective public bureaucracy, and as in the US bureaucratic traditions played a much smaller role in all areas of English life than in Germany. In contrast to the US, however, a long tradition of pre-industrial, corporatist patterns of social stratification and culture continued to shape English society well into the 20th century. Yet England did not experience the same sharp clash between anachronistic but still vital traditions in socio-political life and rapid, disruptive socio-economic modernization that marred Germany's development. The structure and responses of English elites, England's liberal, democratic, and parliamentary constitutional history, the relative weakness of anti-modernist traditions and elites, and the earlier but then more gradual process of industrialization all set English history in the 19th and 20th centuries on a different path from Germany. It is also true that class lines in England were more sharply drawn than in the US; the distinction between working class and non-working class social groups stamped English social and political relationships almost as strongly as in Germany. The working class challenge was less total in England, however; marxist ideology was less influential, the Labour Party was founded later, and the gap between the skilled trades and the masses of unskilled laborers acted as a counterweight to the solidarity of the English working class.

The ethnic composition of the English population was more like Germany than the US. Later than in Germany but earlier than in the US, Great Britain forged the balancing and integrative mechanisms of an interventionist state. The quasi-bureaucratic synchronization of a stratified school system and the world of work also emerged later and more gradually than in Germany, but earlier than in the US. As far as preconceptions about the possibilities for upward mobility and belief in individual success were concerned, England was probably more like Germany than the new world.[23]

And in fact, the empirical materials that are available do seem to place the history of English white collar workers somewhere between their American and German counterparts. In the 19th and early 20th centuries the difference in status and esteem between the 'respectable black coated worker' and manual workers was quite visible. Even the lowest shop assistant ranked his own prestige — if not his income — well above that of the mechanic; his life style and social contacts were consciously kept distinct from the working class.

The actual situation of sales and bank clerks seems to have been more like the German than the American model: quasi-patriarchal traditions and dependence survived in the 'living-in system', for instance, which was still very common for shop assistants around 1900. The relationship between the boss and his assistants was more personal; at least by the second half of the 19th century, bank clerks were guaranteed regular raises and lifetime tenure. Sources repeatedly mention the 'snobbishness' of the 'clerks', their identification with the middling and better off sections of the middle class, their efforts to maintain a 'gentlemanlike' manner and their correspondingly strong reservations about trade union organization. English white collar workers began to organize hesitantly in the 1890s, and then more actively in the public sector than the private. At first the black coated workers called themselves guilds rather than trade unions and organized separately by occupation; in the beginning they also kept their distance from the trade union movement. In contrast to the US, there were some English white collar associations that ignored occupational boundaries between salaried employees while distinguishing them from all wage workers: in 1897 the National Union of Clerks, later the Clerical and Administrative Workers' Union, was founded.[24] Furthermore, the collar line was a much more meaningful indicator of political orientation and voting behavior in England than in the US. One well researched example: while the imperialistic propaganda for the Boer War had little impact on the English working class, many clerks were early and enthusiastic volunteers to fight in South Africa. As a rule white collar workers only participated in the 1926 general strike to act as strikebreakers. White collar votes did not contribute much to the Labour Party's growth after the first world war; in fact, they were almost as reluctant to vote Labour in the 1920s and just after the second world war as businessmen and managers.[25]

Yet in crucial respects the English case was more similar to the US than to Germany. Even the relative artificiality of the collective terms 'black coated workers' or 'white collar workers' common in England — compared to the paired opposites *Arbeiter-Angestellte* — indicates that the collar line and hence the sense of community of groups on both sides of it was not as strong in England as in Germany.[26] In distinct contrast to Germany the collar line had almost no significance in English law; among other things this indicates that the ruling groups in England did not think it necessary to placate salaried employees with special concessions as they did in Germany, where legal privileges were intended to keep lower middle class groups from turning to the left. The legal insignificance of the collar line also meant that it was of less *practical* importance in England whether one was counted as a member of the working class or the white collar class. Black coated workers formed narrower organizations with more specific economic goals than German salaried employees. Except for very early Friendly Societies, sales clerks organized Early Closing Associations after the late 1830s and as the National Union of Shop Assistants in 1891; however, they made no effort to join together the entire 'mercantile assistants' corporation' (including sales employees in wholesale trade and industrial firms). The normal white collar pattern of organization in England was more like the American in resting on occupation, profession, or branch of industry rather than on white collar status as such. There seem to have been no lower middle class organizations of the continental type which united small businessmen, white collar workers, and petty bureaucrats.[27]

White collar discontent increased markedly in England in response to 20th century crises: the first world war, the depression, the second world war, and the immediate postwar problems. Wartime inflation had hit clerks harder than manual workers, and the wage-salary differential declined between 1914 and 1920 (though it was almost completely restored in the 1920s). The depression brought unemployment, salary cuts, and other sacrifices, though it did not affect black coated workers as severely as manual workers (and the English were also less affected than German and American white collar workers). During the second world war and the immediate postwar years the wage-salary differential narrowed again, while taxation policies and social legislation favored manual workers over salaried employees.[28]

Many authors have reported the anxiety of lower and middle rank black coated workers about social leveling and their relative deprivation, their resentment of working class gains, and their inclination toward anti-labor, right-wing protest in these years.[29] Their own organizations, however, showed no traces of reactionary lower middle class sentiment, no tendency to turn against labor and capital at the same time. Instead, white collar associations drew closer to or affiliated with the Trades Union Congress (TUC). Their tactics — which had included the use of the strike much earlier (before 1914) than German white collar organizations — became even more similar to those of working class trade unions. White collar workers who remained unorganized — and until today, that has meant the great majority employed in the private sector — thereby chose to remain outside *any* collective interest group. As in the US, the third way of joining specifically lower middle class interest groups hostile to those above and below them was unavailable in England.[30]

It is not known to what extent white collar workers joined the reactionary middle class anti-labor militias of the 1920s and 1930s or how significantly they supported the small fascist groups of the 1930s; their number appears to have been very small, however.[31] During the 1920s white collar workers apparently voted disproportionately for the Liberal Party, but they supported the Conservative landslide in 1930. Although the majority continued to vote Conservative during the 1930s, an important and growing minority, particularly among low level clerks, chose the Labour Party. In 1945 the bottom ranks of office employees were evenly divided between Conservative and Labour voters. Office clerks, sales clerks, telegraph and postal employees and similar groups voted the way skilled workers did; their choices contrasted decidedly with businessmen's, executives', and managers' voting behavior.[32] Thus in the absence of those specifically anti-capitalist and anti-bourgeois traditions which were so pronounced in Germany, under different socio-political and cultural conditions, and perhaps also because of a less severe economic crisis, and even though in many respects English white collar workers were more similar to their German than their American counterparts, they did not develop that explosive mixture of anti-capitalist and anti-labor lower middle class protest that made such a strong contribution to the triumph of National Socialism in Germany.

The industrially advanced societies on the continent revealed even more distinct similarities to the German case than England did. The French pairing of *ouvriers* and *employés* appears quite parallel to the German *Arbeiter-Angestellte* in distinction to the vaguer English and American blue collar worker-white collar worker (though in contrast to *Angestellte*, *employé* used alone can also refer to employees in general). In further contrast to the Anglo-American pattern, the collar line became increasingly fixed in labor and social legislation everywhere on the continent after the late 19th century. In France, Belgium, and the Netherlands wage workers' and salaried employees' social status were clearly connected to their position at the workplace. The two groups were treated differently by management, and the collar line also played a large part in the distribution of social prestige and every sort of life chance. In these societies the consciousness that as a white collar worker (not just a member of a particular occupational group) one was demarcated from both the working class and the independent, rich, and powerful social groups was much more common than in England, let alone the US. At an early date white collar associations transcending occupational boundaries like the German were founded in these continental societies. And in continental western Europe as in Germany and Austria white collar workers, minor bureaucrats, small businessmen and the less well off professionals tended to be grouped in sociological writings and political propaganda (and with limited success in organizations) as a lower middle class, *Mittelstand*, or *classes moyennes*. This tendency to lump lower middle class groups together and segregate them from higher and lower social strata was much weaker or completely absent in England and the US. This contrast highlights the continuing impact of corporatist and bureaucratic patterns of thought, language, and organization on the continent that provided a framework to unite these internally diverse middle strata and simultaneously divide them from more or less united strata 'above' and 'below' them. This tendency to segregate a distinct lower middle class also presupposed the prevalence and sharpness of dichotomous class antagonisms in the political language, programs, and organizational behavior of those continental societies.[33]

However, there were also important differences among continental European societies. The collar line played a much more significant role in Italian, Belgian, and German labor and social law, for instance, than in France where other dividing lines — specialization, qualifications, and exercise of authority — provided (and still do provide) strong competition. Furthermore, securing corporatist privileges for particular groups through special legislation fit poorly in the liberal-democratic, republican-egalitarian tradition and politics of France.[34] Sociological/political literature on white collar workers appeared later in France than in Germany; the countless works on the *classes moyennes* still referred to the old middle class and the professions; lower/middle level white collar workers were usually excluded from the concept, though usage was not uniform.[35]

There were also definite differences between German and French white collar organizations and politics. To a greater degree in France than in Germany, the conflict between church and state overshadowed the collar line in structuring organizations. Most organized white collar workers in the private sector (except for small, radical, anarcho-syndicalist organizations among department store employees after the 1860s) chose the precursors of the Syndicat des Employés de Commerce et d'Industrie, in existence since 1885, formally founded in 1892. This conservative Catholic organization combined white collar workers from diverse occupations and was at least partially anti-socialist, anti-labor and probably also anti-republican. Around 1900, however, the Syndicat crossed the collar line to open its doors to Catholic workers; at the same time it distanced itself from the Catholic hierarchy and drew closer to the social democratic/socialist trade union federation (Confédération Général du Travail — CGT). After the late 1930s, when the CGT (which had split into social democratic and communist wings in 1921 but then reunited in 1935/36) came increasingly under communist influence, the Christian labor movement (CFTC) again provided a home for organized *employés* who did not want to be swallowed up in the CGT which favored manual workers.[36]

In addition, the public sector also played a different role in the organization of white collar workers in France than in Germany. Lower and middle level government officials have traditionally stood to the left of center in France; they inherit the egalitarian-administrative tradition which has so decisively distinguished the bureaucracy of the French Republic from that of the Prussian-German state, at least in the lower and intermediate ranks. Beginning in the late 19th century teachers, postal officials and other public employees organized liberal and social democratic trade unions (with the assistance of left leaning governments). Long before the first world war they campaigned vigorously for the right to strike. After the first world war highly organized lower and middle level public employees were in the vanguard of the French social democratic labor movement: the CGT in the 1920s and 1930s, the CGT-FO (Confédération Général du Travail-Force Ouvrière) after the second world war. In Germany bureaucratic tradition, law, and consistently conservative governments before the first world war had made it impossible for lower and middle level officials to ally with a labor movement that was defined as a public enemy; reactionary lower middle class sentiment not egalitarian/social democratic views were popular with large sections of the lower and intermediate ranks of the bureaucracy. Yet just across the Rhine these same groups created the leftist image of the French *employés*.[37]

Even French private sector white collar workers, who were much less organized and radical than government employees, showed earlier and more distinct tendencies to radicalize to the left and less attraction to right-wing lower middle class protest than their German counterparts. From the large and militant department store strike in 1869, the formation of the Chambre Syndicale Fédérale des Employés in 1882 (which co-founded the CGT in 1895), through the participation of some groups of private sector white collar workers in the great strikes of 1919/20 and 1936, to the cooperation of groups of white collar workers in the uprisings of May 1968, at least some white collar employees in France have showed a stronger tendency toward left-wing trade unionism and political engagement than in Germany. As far as is known — though studies which distinguished more clearly between public and private sector employees might alter this picture — white collar workers in the interwar period did not disproportionately support small right-wing groups like the Croix de Feu, Parti social français, or Parti populaire français, even though these groups made some attempts to recruit them. White collar organizations supported the anti-fascist People's Front of 1936. In fact their left-wing reached its greatest strength in that year: the great strikes and occupations also hit Parisian department stores and insurance firms. It is very probable that in the first third of this century many lower/middle level white collar workers voted for the somewhat left of center, if hardly radical, Radical Socialist Party and for the Socialists; they kept their distance from the parties of the extreme left and right. Whether or not in reaction to the People's Front and the increasing communist influence in the labor movement after 1936, as many suspect, large parts of the white collar class turned to the right and supported or at least tolerated the Vichy govenment. But this cannot be taken up here. At any rate, an organized, reactionary lower middle class white collar movement with right-wing leanings did not emerge after the second world war in France; white collar workers were hardly involved in the populist-anti-modernist protest movement of the old middle classes which peaked in the Poujadism of the early 1950s.[38]

Thus the German pattern — with right and left divided along the collar line — appears to have also characterized the French scene, though in that society the collar line was less distinctly etched and lay somewhat to the left. There were also fewer reactionary lower middle class protests in France than in Germany. This cross-cultural difference can be explained partly by the heuristic model developed from the German-American comparison: the relative insignificance of the collar line in France compared to Germany probably rested on the lower level of organization of the French working class and the much less unified (if sporadically more radical) character of the French labor movement. The conflict between secular Republican France and Catholic France overlay and blurred socio-economic lines of differentiation and conflict in ways that paralleled the function of ethnic tensions in the US. In contrast to the US, however, both France and Germany belonged to the continental old world and had deeply ingrained bureaucratic and corporatist traditions. The strong impact of these traditions on French society and politics — e.g. in economic regulations, the behavior of entrepreneurs, family life, and the social status system — is often stressed. Comparison with Germany, however, highlights the significance of successful bourgeois revolution in France. Although the French revolutions did not uproot all traditions, in some areas they weakened their impact, in others they broke their hold, and above all they reversed their political charge. The organization of sales employees in France, for instance, did not as in Germany build on the corporatist traditions of the social group. Moreover, it is not accidental that one speaks not of the middle *estate* or *Mittelstand* in France as one does in Germany, but of the middle *class*, the *classes moyennes*. These are but two examples of the way that unbroken corporatist traditions have shaped modern German social life; at least in these areas such traditions did not continue to have the same hold on France.

No one could overlook the strong bureaucratic/centralist traditions which have been an unbroken feature of French history from the Ancien Regime to the present. After 1789, however, the tradition of a strong central bureaucracy in France became amalgamated with democratic/egalitarian/republican currents that have qualitatively distinguished bureaucratic tradition in France from the Prussian-German variety. Furthermore, the French citizen's deep distrust of an authoritarian state and its bureaucracy has no parallel in Germany; the lack of respect and prestige of lower/middle rank officials in France compared to Germany has contributed to their leaning toward socialism and radicalism. Had white collar workers in the private sector in France modeled their behavior on government bureaucrats, the consequences would have been quite unlike the German 'private bureaucrat's' role modeling. All these aspects of the democratic/egalitarian repolarization of bureaucratic traditions in France would deserve attention in a comparative analysis of French white collar workers. With its early liberalization and democratization, on the one hand, and its slower, less disruptive industrialization, on the other, French society never experienced the fissures and confusion that were so characteristic of Germany's late democratization and rapid industrialization. The fact that moderate leftist governments were frequently approved by large circles of the population in France when there was still no hope of that in Germany also underlined these divergent patterns of modernization at the same time that it reflected the liberal democratic, individualistic, and anti-authoritarian nature of French political culture.

All these factors were significant determinants of the mentalities and political orientation of French white collar workers and their relationship to the working class, though the mediating channels which translated these general social structural conditions into specific white collar behavior cannot be further pursued. French white collar workers' divergent responses to the economic crisis of the 1930s may also have reflected the fact that the objective challenge they faced was weaker than that facing German salaried employees; French *employés* were not subjected to the same rapid social leveling and relative economic deprivation. But because of the constellation of factors just sketched, the French might also have perceived and responded to even similar experiences quite differently from German salaried employees.[39]

These sketches of developments in a third and a fourth society are not intended to write the histories of English and French white collar workers. All they suggest is that these cases do not contradict but instead tend to confirm the explanatory theses developed above to explain the differences which this study found between German and American white collar workers. This outline also demonstrates that the framework and categories used to compare Germany and the US can be useful in investigating other similarly industrialized societies also — though a detailed study of a third society would undoubtedly have a different focus and require modifying or extending a conceptual framework which was, after all, developed to compare the US and Germany. As interesting as this undertaking would be, it too must be left undone. Nor can the present comparison be extended to other societies like Belgium, the Netherlands, Sweden, Austria, Italy, or Japan — though that would undoubtedly further illuminate the international variations in the collar line and its economic, social, political, and cultural significance.[40]

III. OUTLOOK AND IMPLICATIONS

This study will instead conclude with a brief glance at a third approach that might be pursued to test the explanatory model drawn from the comparison of German and American white collar workers: present developments and future possibilities in these two societies. If this study has correctly explained the reasons why German salaried employees were so susceptible to right-wing lower middle class protest while their American counterparts were not, then under the conditions that have existed in both societies since the second world war white collar workers should have become less susceptible in Germany and no more so in the US. That hypothesis follows from the significance attached to the role of pre-industrial corporatist and bureaucratic traditions in differentiating the German and American cases: such traditions could naturally not have sprung up suddenly in the US, and it seems logical that they would be weaker in Germany not only because of the passage of time but also — and primarily — because of the transformation of German society by dictatorship, war, and collapse.

In fact, two important sources do substantiate this hypothesis about salaried employees in the Federal Republic of Germany. First, since 1945 organized blue collar and organized white collar workers have worked much more closely together than before the war. Today most organized white collar workers belong to industrial unions which also organize production workers in the same industry and are part of the German Federation of Trade Unions (DGB). The fact that a purely white collar trade union federation (DAG) continues to exist perhaps indicates that differences in the interests and behavior of blue and white collar workers have not completely disappeared. Still, the DAG platform reveals no basic disagreements over principles or practice with the DGB; despite occasional differences of opinion on economic and social questions, local organizations of both federations have cooperated closely, at least until 1976. Merger proposals have failed up to now, however, and tensions between the two federations have recently been on the increase. There are no lower middle class associations in the Federal Republic that are in any way comparable to the pre-second world war variety; the DHV, for instance, attempted a new start after 1945 but found little response.[41] Second, some studies of the political behavior of white collar workers in the Federal Republic suggest that the collar line has lost political significance and that white collar susceptibility to right-wing protest has diminished; thus in this respect, German salaried employees have become more like their American counterparts. White collar workers have not been over-represented among the supporters and members of the most important right-wing extremist party in the history of the Federal Republic, the NPD. The voting behavior of blue collar and white collar workers also seems to have become more similar.[42]

Thus the behavior of the new middle class since the second world war appears to support the ironic conclusion that the victory and even more the defeat of National Socialism contributed to weakening or destroying the conditions in German life which had made possible its rise and triumph.[43] The collar line has not lost all significance, of course, and there are still traces of reactionary sentiment among lower middle class groups. Furthermore, the new political attitudes and behavior of these groups have not yet been tested by a real crisis; it is impossible to predict whether new resentments and protest potential specific to white collar workers will emerge in the future. But up to now the history of the Federal Republic suggests that not much more need be feared from *this* crucial social base for right-wing extremism and fascism in Germany. Thus one important precondition for the success of fascism in the past no longer exists in the present.[44]

White collar workers in America have continued along the path marked out before the second world war. The labor movement has become less militant and radical since the 1930s, thus if anything it would have been even less likely to pose such a threat to white collar workers as to inspire reactionary attitudes and separatist organizations. Ethnicity has if anything become more significant in American life in recent decades: the civil rights struggle, greater international involvement, particularly with third world countries, and other factors have tended to increase the significance of ethnic identity in the US in recent years and also to heighten public awareness and social science interest in this problem. Moroever, since the second world war white collar workers have become more heterogeneous as blacks and other formerly excluded groups have found increased access to white collar jobs. As far as can be determined the rate of upward mobility for lower/middle level white collar workers has not declined in the last three decades; rather, it has risen from its low point in the 1930s.[45] And naturally, the preindustrial, pre-capitalist traditions which played such a major role in the emergence of a specifically white collar consciousness and class-specific types of white collar protest behavior in Germany have not suddenly appeared in this society. On the other hand, however, the interventionist state has continued to expand — though its role in economy and society is not as dramatic as during the second world war. There is some evidence that government activity has contributed to a sharper definition of the collar line, as have the industrial unions and the renewed emphasis on vocational education to prepare high school students for specific careers. There are also indications that belief in the possibility of individual success may have declined rather than increased.

In fact, the collar line does seem to have become more rather than less significant in the US during the last three decades. Recent surveys indicate that corporate management today tends to grant white collar workers special privileges in order to distinguish them from factory workers. Many industrial firms have separate personnel offices for white collar workers; management appears more involved than in the 1920s in efforts to counteract trade union organization among white collar workers. These management policies may be partly responsible for the fact that the long term tendency in the US for the wage-salary differential to narrow which began in the mid-1930s seems to have been arrested and even perhaps reversed since about 1955.[46] The special characteristics of white collar workers are taken for granted by union organizers, who employ special methods and arguments in trying to recruit them.[47] And although independent trade unions (which often function only within one large corporation) organize only a small minority of American trade union members, they have continued to have much greater success with white collar than with blue collar workers. Other indications that white collar workers have been more apt to identify with a white collar class as such have also appeared in the labor movement, where supra-occupational organizations have been founded for general office employees and for scientific/professional employees. The Office and Professional Employees International Union of the AFL-CIO attempted to expand into a general white collar union in the 1960s. One of their main arguments was that it would be easier to persuade white collar workers to join a union if it was not led and dominated by blue collar workers. Their attempts to expand ran into strong opposition from other AFL-CIO unions, however, who did not want to give up jurisdiction over white collar workers in their industry. In 1967 the AFL-CIO also formed a Council for Scientific, Professional, and Cultural Employees to coordinate the various unions of intermediate and high ranking white collar workers that were based on particular occupations.[48] And in recent years social scientific interest in the problem of white collar workers in America has also increased markedly.[49] These indications that the collar line has become more significant in the US since the second world war reflect the continuity of trends that were visible in the decades before 1940; thus from the American side as well as the German, the history of white collar workers suggests that these societies are becoming more alike. Even with these signs of the emergence of a more distinct white collar class in the US, however, very few traces of a specifically white collar type of reactionary, simultaneously anti-capitalist and anti-labor, lower middle class protest potential have appeared.

The level of organization of American white collar workers (private sector and government) declined slightly in the 1950s and 1960s: from 13% in 1956 to 11% in 1968. Yet in the same period the percentage of the labor force as a whole that was organized declined even more distinctly: from 33% to 28%. That the percentage of organized white collar workers remained this high was primarily due to the relatively well organized public sector: in 1967, 44% of government employees, but only 14% of white collar workers in the private sector, belonged to unions.[50] Even though lower/middle level office and sales work has become more like factory work in the last three decades, economic gains after the depression, legal restriction on industrial union efforts to organize office employees, and other factors have made white collar workers less willing to join trade unions since the 1930s.[51] But still if white collar workers organize at all in the US, as in the 1930s they continue to do so within the organizational and ideological framework of the general labor movement.[52] There is still no third way of separate white collar organization available in the US.[53]

These signs that the collar line has become more distinctly etched in the world of work have apparently not carried over into other dimensions of life; distinctions between blue collar and white collar workers do not seem to have acquired increased political significance, for instance. The collar line has not been a major boundary line in voting behavior or in delineating the social base for right-wing protest movements like the Wallace campaign.[54] To the extent that differences in the politics of skilled workers and lower/intermediate level white collar workers have been discernible, white collar workers continue to be found on the liberal/progressive side, not on the right.[55] The collar line has not been a front along which tensions and conflicts between a demanding, threatening working class and a threatened, resentful white collar class have crystallized. Other lines of differentiation continue to be politically more important: perhaps most important, the line between the poor, unskilled, under or unemployed marginal groups who live in the inner cities, on one side, and the diverse groups who belong to the American middle — including large sections of the working class and most lower and middle level white collar workers — on the other. Overlapping and intensifying this division is the explosive front line between ethnic and racial groups; above all, the gap between the large non-white minorities in American society and the ethnic groups which just a few decades ago occupied the lowest rungs on the social ladder. If the US should see widespread fascist protests, movements, and agitation in the forseeable future (which seems unlikely), these ethnic/racial divisions and conflicts would probably be the major battle front. It does not seem likely that in the future the collar line will play a major role in structuring political behavior and conflict.

Explicitly and by implication this study has tried to relate itself to some more general questions of historical sociology. These final pages will sum up what follows from the comparison of American and German white collar workers.

1. To what degree do similar economic transformations bring about similar social-structural and socio-cultural changes? To what extent are class, strata, and group formation shaped by changes in the economic system? To what extent is the collar line a universal, parallel phenomenon in all advanced industrial capitalist societies? In conclusion, this study emphasizes the *relative autonomy* of social-structural and socio-cultural developments. Although the tempo and structure of industrialization were quite similar in Germany and the US (particularly before 1914), the social constellations and social-psychological configurations of each society varied enormously. It is true, of course, that this study confirmed the universal character of the collar line; its existence in some form was one of the underlying assumptions on which this cross-cultural comparison rested. Yet the extreme diversity in the form and significance of the collar line in the societies studied was remarkable and perhaps not fully expected. A white collar social grouping — demarcated from manual workers and self-employed persons — existed in all advanced industrial societies. But to be a white collar worker could mean something quite different depending on where one lived; from one society to another, white collar status carried vastly different social and political weight. Thus in conclusion this study emphasizes the variations in the collar line. Sociologies of 'the' white collar workers should take this into account; and one should not be too quick to generalize about 'the' lower middle class. Furthermore, comparative studies of social mobility should also be cautious about assuming that they are using identical measures to determine vertical mobility in different societies and decades when they rely on the collar line.

2. There were, of course, a great variety of causes and conditions that were responsible for the cross-cultural differences that this study found. The German-American comparison suggests that *one* cluster of causal factors is particularly helpful in explaining the social-structural and cultural differences observed in advanced industrial societies: the impact of the continuity or lack of continuity of pre-industrial traditions. Pre-industrial corporatist and bureaucratic traditions, in combination with and intensified by the social and economic changes that accompanied industrialization, played a major role in the formation of a distinct white collar social

group or new middle class in Geramny. In the US, where such traditions scarcely existed during industrialization, white collar workers followed a quite different path. The comparative historian does not work under laboratory conditions where all other things can be held equal in order to isolate and assess the significance of one variable, of course. But by comparing 'partially modern' Germany with the 'new nation' USA, it is to some extent possible to assess the significance and determine the long term impact of corporatist and bureaucratic traditions which so strongly shaped one society but were hardly present in the other. The uneasy coexistence of social structures that originated in different eras, the tense overlayering of industrial capitalist social conflicts with pre-industrial, pre-capitalist social constellations — this 'contemporaneity of the uncontemporary' — defined Germany's path to an industrial society, but not America's. Over time, however, the significance of these older traditions has declined in Germany also. The differences between Germany and the US which were of such significance for their divergent experiences in the 20th century have diminished, and since the second world war the two societies have tended to converge rather than diverge (at least in the areas under investigation here).

3. Since the rise of fascist movements in Europe in the interwar years, there has been a lively and politically significant debate about their origins and the conditions that facilitated their rise, especially in Europe. Not only marxists have thought that the inherent tensions, frustrations, and contradictions of the bourgeois capitalist system were the primary cause of fascism. Max Horkheimer's dictum of 1939: 'Whoever does not want to talk about capitalism should keep quiet about fascism'[56] was a cautious (and influential) statement of this thesis; 'capitalism leads to fascism' translated it to the level of slogans and street demonstrations in countries like Italy, France and West Germany in the late 1960s.

To take a position on the entire problem of the relationship between capitalism and fascism would go far beyond the scope of this study, which has not discussed the functions, ideologies, and structures of fascist rule. Although the social base for fascist movements was not investigated as a whole, one important segment — the white collar component of the lower middle class — was studied in detail. Thus we have looked at the relationship between capitalism and fascism at *one* critical point.

This study's conclusion does not reject the thesis that capitalism and fascism were inextricably connected. Its findings directly support the view that the susceptibility of the new middle class to right-wing extremism which facilitated the triumph of Nazism in Germany would not have existed without the changes, tensions, and crises that accompanied the creation of an industrial capitalist society. But comparison of the German case with the US also suggests that this thesis linking capitalism and fascism must be supplemented and thus modified. The lower middle class has not always been clearly demarcated from both the working class and the ruling elites in advanced industrial capitalist societies; it has not always been a conservative or reactionary mass with a definite potential for right-wing extremist protest. Instead, that type of lower middle class protest potential and behavior emerged in response to the changes and crises of developing industrial capitalist societies only when still vital pre-industrial/pre-capitalist traditions collided with modern social needs, structures, and processes. Thus, this study also suggests that what has been confirmed about traditional social groups such as agrarians and artisans in Germany[57] also appears true of large parts of the 'modern' white collar social group: pre-industrial, pre-capitalist, and pre-bourgeois traditions continued to affect the chances for the survival and evolution of democratic social structures and behaviour even at advanced stages of industrialization. Fascism had many roots, but the interaction of two clusters of causes was particularly significant: the tensions and crises inherent in industrial capitalist systems, on one side, *and* the repercussions of the collision of older traditions with industrialization and modernization, on the other.[58]

Thus this investigation of American white collar workers has proved to be a rewarding approach to a better understanding of German history. And it may be hoped that this view of America through German eyes — that is, the application of investigative questions and analytical categories which were developed from the study of German history and society to American social history — has more clearly illuminated the problem of white collar workers in American history, suggested new interpretations, or at least contributed to defining a topic for historical research.

Perhaps specialists in American history who are accustomed to a more critical view of their past will not fully agree with all this study's conclusions, e.g. with its view of the 'Progressive reforms' and of the New Deal as a partly social democratic policy of modest reform. Labor historians who have recently stressed the more radical currents in the history of the American working class experience may be critical of the picture of a rather specific, fragmented, and basically non-radical labor movement presented here. Those who are concerned about right-wing extremist potentials in the American lower middle classes may question the relatively optimistic assessment of white collar dispositions, inclinations and attitudes presented here. On the whole, some readers may have the impression that this study has given too much credit to traditional American self-conceptions and ideologies, by stressing the international differences and, in a way, the uniqueness of the American experience.

If one confronts the realities of corporate policies around 1900 with the ideals of the 'Age of Reform', or if one compares the achievements of the New Deal with its aims and ideologies, a critical assessment will follow. The conventional image of a well integrated working class hardly matches the reality of violence, hardship, and alienation which can be found in the sources. But if one compares American businessmen of the 'Progressive Era' with German entrepreneurs in the Wilhelmine Empire, or the New Deal with fascist reactions to the Great Depression, or the American working class movements with the German, the perspectives change, and the results as well. One hopes that comparison has not distorted but instead increased the sense of proportion.

Notes

Chapter 1: The Framework and the Aims of the Study

1. For overviews on the definition of the lower middle class see L. Moulin and L. Aerts, 'Les classes moyennes. Essai de bibliographie critique d'une définition', in *Revue d'Histoire Economique et Sociale*, Vol. 32, 1954, pp. 168-86, 293-309; K. J. Gantzel, *Wesen und Begriff der mittelständischen Unternehmung*, Cologne 1962, pp. 12ff., 123ff.; recently, with a very broad definition, A. J. Mayer, 'The Lower Middle Class as Historical Problem', in *JMH*, Vol. 47, 1975, pp. 409-36, esp. pp. 424, 426-31; J. M. Wiener, 'Marxism and the Lower Middle Class', in ibid., Vol. 48, 1976, pp. 666-71.

2. This argument is found at the latest in Marx' *Communist Manifesto* (1848). For its further development cf. H. A. Winkler, *Mittelstand, Demokratie und Nationalsozialismus*, Cologne 1972, esp. pp. 21-64 and 190ff.; A. Leppert-Fögen, *Die deklassierte Klasse. Studien zur Geschichte und Ideologie des Kleinbürgertums*, Frankfurt 1974 (both works refer to the important literature).

3. Cf. G. Schmoller, 'Was verstehen wir unter dem Mittelstande? Hat er im 19. Jahrhundert zu- oder abgenommen?', in *Verhandlungen des 8. Evang.-soz. Kongresses (10. und 11. Juni 1897)*, Göttingen 1897, pp. 132-85; K. Kautsky, *Bernstein und das sozial-demokratische Programm. Eine Antikritik*, Stuttgart 1899, pp. 128ff.; P. Leroy-Beaulieu, *Essai sur la répartition des richesses et sur la tendance à une moindre inégalité des conditions*, Paris (1888) 1896[4], pp. 339-60; C.F.G. Masterman, *The Condition of England*, London 1909, pp. 69-73; S. Deming, *A Message to the Middle Class*, Boston 1915.

4. From the extensive literature cf. E. Lederer and J. Marschak, 'Der neue Mittelstand', in *GdS*, Abt. IX, Teil 1, pp. 120-41; H. Speier, 'The Salaried Employee in Modern Society', in *Social Research*, Vol. 1, 1934, pp. 111-33, reprinted in Speier, *Social Order and the Risks of War. Papers in Political Sociology*, New York 1952, pp. 68-85; S. Braun, *Zur Soziologie der Angestellten*, Frankfurt 1964; recently, U. Kadritzke, *Angestellte — Die geduldigen Arbeiter. Zur Soziologie und sozialen Bewegung der Angestellten*, Frankfurt 1975, e.g., pp. 176-98; for England: F. D. Klingender, *The Condition of Clerical Labour in Britain*, London 1935; for the US: J. Corbin, *The Return of the Middle Class*, New York 1923, pp. 6, 9, 22, passim; C. Wright Mills, *White Collar. The American Middle Classes*, Oxford 1951, 1969 edition, pp. 161-286; H. Braverman, *Labor and Monopoly Capital. The Degradation of Work in the 20th Century*, New York 1974, pp. 293-358.

5. As to the old middle class: Cf. Winkler, *Mittelstand*; R. Gellately, *The Politics of Economic Despair. Shopkeepers and German Politics 1890-1914*, London 1974; S. Volkov, *The Rise of Popular Antimodernism in Germany. The Urban Master Artisans, 1873-1896*, Princeton 1978. For the thesis of a gradual leveling between one white collar group (sales employees) and blue collar workers as well as the sense of threat already see G. Hiller, *Die Lage der Handlungsgehilfen*, Leipzig 1890, p. 11; K. Oldenburg, 'Die heutige Lage der Commis nach neuerer Literatur', in *Schmollers Jb.*, Bd. 16, 1892, pp. 749-812, e.g., p. 781; F. Goldschmidt, *Die sociale Lage und Bildung der Handlungsgehilfen*, Berlin 1894, pp. 5f.; an early American example (1915): Deming, pp. 25, 35ff., 57f.

6. Cf. E. Lederer, *Die Privatangestellten in der modernen Wirtschaftsentwicklung*, Tübingen 1912 (Ch. 4, note 37, p. 345 below for partial English translation); ibid., 'Die Umschichtung des Proletariats', in Afa (ed.), *Angestellte und Arbeiter*, Berlin 1928, pp. 39-60; S. Kracauer, *Die Angestellten* (1930) (reprinted in ibid., *Schriften*, Bd. 1, Frankfurt 1971, pp. 205-304, esp. 213f.,

273ff.); E. Grünberg, *Der Mittelstand in der kapitalistischen Gesellschaft*, Leipzig 1932.

7. Cf. above all R. Hilferding, *Das Finanzkapital* (1910), Wien 1923, pp. 443-48; A. Siegfried, *Tableau politique de la France de l'Ouest sous la Troisième République* (1913), Paris 1964, p. 477.

8. Cf. the early insights of G. Zibordi (1922), L. Salvatorelli (1923), F. Turati (1928) and in part also C. Zetkin (1923), documented and partly reprinted in E. Nolte (ed.), *Theorien über den Faschismus*, Köln 1967, pp. 79-87, 88-111, 118-37, 143-55; M. Victor, 'Verbürgerlichung des Proletariats und Proletarisierung des Mittelstandes', in *Die Arbeit*, Bd. 8, 1931, pp. 17-32 (also the articles by T. Geiger and R. Küstermeier in the same volume); T. Geiger, *Die soziale Schichtung des deutschen Volkes* (1932), Stuttgart 1967; H. de Man, *Sozialismus und Nationalfascismus*, Potsdam 1931, esp. p. 10; L. Trotsky, 'Der einzige Weg' (1932), in ibid., *Schriften über Deutschland*, Frankfurt 1971, pp. 347-410, esp. pp. 357-61; H. Lasswell, 'The Psychology of Hitlerism', in *The Political Quarterly*, Vol. 4, 1933, pp. 374ff.; W. Reich, *Massenpsychologie des Faschismus*, Kopenhagen 1933 (English: *Mass Psychology of Fascism*, New York 1970); F. Borkenau, 'Zur Soziologie des Faschismus', in *ASS*, Bd. 68, 1932/33, pp. 513-47, esp. p. 525; D. S. Saposs, 'The Role of the Middle Class in Social Development: Fascism, Populism, Communism, Socialism', in *Economic Essays in Honor of W. C. Mitchell*, New York 1935, pp. 395, 397, 400; Klingender, pp. vi-xii; E. Bloch, *Erbschaft dieser Zeit*, Zürich 1935 (reprinted in Nolte, *Theorien*, pp. 182-204); F. Sternberg, *Der Faschismus an der Macht*, Amsterdam 1935, pp. 28-35; D. Guerin, *Fascism and Big Business*, New York 1973 (first French edition 1936), pp. 41-62; O. Bauer, 'Der Faschismus', in ibid., *Zwischen zwei Weltkriegen*, Bratislawa 1936, pp. 113-42 (reprinted in ibid., et al., *Faschismus und Kapitalismus. Theorien über die sozialen Ursprünge und die Funktion des Faschismus*, Frankfurt 1967, pp. 75-141, esp. pp. 75, 117f., 131, 134f., 139f.); F. Neumann, *Behemoth, The Structure and Practice of National Socialism, 1933-1944*, New York, 1963^3, p. 411; K. Renner, *Wandlungen der modernen Gesellschaft*, Wien 1953, pp. 72-75. For a recent overview of early and later representatives of this thesis see F. L. Carsten, 'Interpretations of Fascism', in W. Laqueur (ed.), *Fascism. A Reader's Guide*, Berkeley/Los Angeles 1976, pp. 413-34, esp. p. 416.

9. Cf. above all S. M. Lipset, *Political Man. The Social Basis of Politics*, Garden City 1963, quoted here from the Anchor edition, Garden City 1963, pp. 127-97; ibid., et al., 'The Psychology of Voting', in G. Lindzey (ed.), *Handbook of Social Psychology of Voting*, Vol. 2, Reading, Mass. 1954, pp. 1124-75, p. 1136; L. Kofler, 'Das Wesen des Kleinbürgertums', in ibid., *Marxistische Staatstheorie*, Frankfurt 1970, pp. 256ff.; W. Sauer, 'National Socialism: Totalitarianism or Fascism?' in *AHR*, Vol. 73, 1967/68, pp. 404-24, pp. 410, 417; R. Dahrendorf, *Society and Democracy in Germany*, Garden City 1969; ibid., 'Recent Changes in the Class Structure of European Societies', in S. R. Graubard (ed.), *A New Europe*, Boston 1964, pp. 291-336, pp. 310-18; for N. Kogan's and G. Germani's remarks see S. J. Woolf (ed.), *The Nature of Fascism*, New York 1968, pp. 13, 73; K. D. Bracher, *Die Deutsche Diktatur*, Köln (1969) 1970^3, pp. 166-74, esp. p. 173 (English: *The German Dictatorship: The Origins, Structure, and Effects of National Socialism*, New York 1970); A. Schweitzer, *Big Business in the Third Reich*, Bloomington 1963, pp. 60-109; D. Schoenbaum, *Hitler's Social Revoltuion. Class and Status in Nazi Germany 1933-1939*, Garden City 1966 (quoted from the Anchor edition, 1967, pp. 4-5, 67-68); H. A. Winkler, 'Extremismus der Mitte?' in *VfZ*, Jg. 20, 1972, pp. 175-91 (with further references); R. de Felice, *Le interpretationi del fascismo*, Bari (1971) 1972, p. 157; with reference to the 'old middle class': Leppert-Fögen; cf. also W. Schieder, 'Fascism', in C. D. Kernig (ed.), *Marxism, Communism and Western Society. A Comparative Encyclopedia*, New York 1972, Vol. 2. Without referring so directly to the analysis of fascism and with significant varia-

tions, parts of the argumentation summarized above are found in Mills, p. 239f. and recently in Mayer, 'Lower Middle Class'. In part these arguments are also found in some analyses of right-wing radicalism in the US. Cf. S. M. Lipset and E. Raab, *The Politics of Unreason: Right Wing Extremism in America 1790-1970*, New York 1970; R. Hofstadter, 'The Pseudo-Conservative Revolt' (1955) and 'Pseudo-Conservatism Revisited' (1962), in D. Bell (ed.), *The Radical Right*, Garden City 1963[2], cited here from the Anchor edition 1964, pp. 75-103; ibid., Lipset, 'The Sources of the "Radical Right" ' and Lipset, 'Three Decades of the Radical Right', pp. 307-446.

French authors have agreed least with the argumentation sketched above, frequently emphasizing that the socio-economic changes affecting white collar workers today (particularly technical employees who are often poorly paid but well educated) will (or may) push them to the left. Cf. S. Mallet, *La nouvelle classe ouvrière*, Paris 1963; the articles in K. H. Hörning (ed.), *Der 'neue' Arbeiter*, Frankfurt 1971; J. Chatain and R. Gaudon, *Petites et moyennes entreprises: l'heure du choix*, Paris 1975 (with a forward by G. G. Valbon, member of the central committee of the French Communist Party), which tries to recruit small independent businessmen as partners in communist-led struggle against monopoly and (e.g. p. 33f) goes far toward recognizing the existence of relatively independent middle classes to which communist propaganda must be directed. Kadritzke has also recently emphasized leftist tendencies in the white collar group; he has analyzed the development of German white collar workers from about 1900 to 1933 using marxist categories, but concentrating almost exclusively on the left wing of the German white collar movement, the Afa-Bund and its precursors.

Other authors have made the leveling thesis relative, in that they strictly distinguish either between individual groups of white collar workers, between men and women, or between various epochs; cf. M. Crozier, *The World of the Office Worker* (orig.: *Le monde des employés de bureau*, 1965), New York 1973, pp. 15, 18f.; A. Giddens, *The Class Structure of the Advanced Societies*, New York 1973, pp. 179f., 181f., 190. Also critical of the received thesis: R. F. Hamilton, 'Marginal Middle Class: A Reconsideration', in *ASR*, Vol. 31, 1966, pp. 192-99; ibid., *Class and Politics in the United States*, New York 1972, esp. pp. 27ff., 194-97; ibid., *Restraining Myths. Critical Studies of US Social Structure and Politics*, New York 1975, pp. 99-146.

10. On the concept 'social-historical', cf. J. Kocka, *Sozialgeschichte. Begriff — Entwicklung — Probleme*, Göttingen 1977, pp. 97-111.

11. It must be emphasized that this is an inference that can be drawn from the argumentation sketched here, not, however, a conclusion that all authors cited in note 9 subscribe to.

12. Some methodological implications of this approach are discussed in the German version of this book (pp. 22-28).

13. Cf. above, note 1.

14. In the sense of independent vs. dependent labor (i.e. self-employed or employed by others). This is the sense in which 'class' is used in this study. Cf. more extensively J. Kocka, *Klassengesellschaft im Krieg. Deutsche Sozialgeschichte 1914-18*, Göttingen 1978[2], pp. 3-6.

15. Cf. M. Fischer, *Mittelklasse als politischer Begriff in Frankreich seit der Revolution*, Göttingen 1974, pp. 25-93; C. Baudelot u.a., *La petite bourgeoisie en France*, Paris 1974, p. 29, note 1; Winkler, *Mittelstand*, pp. 21ff.

16. Cf. M. Riedel, 'Bürger, Staatsbürger, Bürgertum', in O. Brunner et al. (eds.), *Geschichtliche Grundbegriffe*, Bd. 1, Stuttgart 1972, pp. 672-725, p. 714, esp. note 186 and pp. 718f., 721f. on the appearance of the word *Kleinbürger* (notes 210/211: its use by Marx and Engels).

17. See J. Ogilvie (ed.), *The Imperial Dictionary of the English Language*, London, new edition, 1885, Vol. 3, p. 166: 'middle class' is 'the class holding a social

position between the mechanics and the aristocracy'. *The Oxford English Dictionary*, Oxford 1933, Vol. 6, p. 421; J. Raynor, *The Middle Class*, London 1969, pp. 3-12; W. J. Reader, *The Middle Classes*, London 1972, e.g. pp. 45-57: both big businessmen, on one side, and lowly white collar workers, on the other, are counted as middle class. An example showing that tendencies to limit 'middle class' to the groups elsewhere characterized as 'bourgeois' (that is, excluding small shopkeepers, artisans and white collar workers) were not completely absent in England is R. H. Gretton, *The English Middle Class*, London 1917, pp. 8-13. On the other hand English authors close to the marxist approach tend to use 'middle class' in the sense of *classes moyennes* or *Kleinbürgertum*: see, e.g., E. J. Hobsbawm, *Industry and Empire. The Making of Modern English Society, Vol. 2: 1750 to the Present Day*, New York 1968, pp. 234, 236ff.

18. See *The Century Dictionary and Cyclopedia*, New York (1889) 1906, Vol. 5, p. 3755, where 'middle class' is described as the 'class of the people which is socially and conventionally intermediate between the aristocratic class, or nobility, and the laboring class', at the same time, however, as an 'untitled community of well-born or wealthy people, made up of landed proprietors, professional men, and merchants'; in Great Britain but not in the US the 'upper' and 'lower middle class' were distinguished. Cf. earlier, J. Stormonth, *A Dictionary of the English Language*, New York 1885, p. 612, where the definition of 'middle class' was taken almost verbatim from *Ogilvie's London Lexicon* of the same year (see note 17). See also W. G. Sumner, 'The Forgotten Man' (1883), in ibid., *The Forgotten Man and Other Essays*, New Haven 1918, pp. 465-95: 'forgotten man' as a reference to groups between the rich and the poor, between lower and upper classes; H. Croly, *The Promise of American Life* (1909), Archon Books 1963: like other progressives Croly was very concerned with groups and strata between (organized) labor and big business, but did not use the term 'middle class' to describe them; 'middle class' was used to characterize a poorly defined large middle stratum between rich and poor or big business and the working class by Deming; Corbin, esp. pp. 2ff., 8, 10; there it becomes clear how 'middle class' crystalized to describe the groups seen as squeezed between the capitalists and organized labor, and was used for the traditionally vaguer concepts like 'the forgotten man', 'the public', and 'the great range of folk in between'; A. M. Bingham, *Insurgent America. Revolt of the Middle Class*, New York 1935, pp. 47ff. thematizes and defines the concept in the context of a marxist two class schema (which he rejects). 'Lower middle class' at the latest by R. Niebuhr, 'Pawns for Fascism — Our Lower Middle Class', in *The American Scholar*, Vol. 6, 1937, pp. 144-52. In the same context, 'petite bourgeoisie' in I. Barnes, 'The Social Basis of Fascism' in *Pacific Affairs*, Vol. 9, March 1936, pp. 24-32.

19. Cf. *MEW*, Vol. 4, p. 469f.; Kautsky, *Bernstein*, p. 128f.; in part also E. Bernstein, *Evolution, Socialism, a Criticism and Aftermath*, London 1909; V. I. Lenin, *'Leftwing' Communism and Infantile Disorder*, New York 1940.

20. Cf. the titles in note 8 above by Victor, de Man, Trotsky, Reich, Bloch, Guerin, Renner and recently, without much that is new, N. A. Poulantzas, *Les classes sociales dans le capitalisme aujourd'hui*, Paris 1974, pp. 205-309.

21. Cf. Schmoller, *Was verstehen wir...*; H. Böttger, *Vom alten und neuen Mittelstand*, Berlin 1901; F. Marbach, *Theorie des Mittelstands*, Bern 1942. On the origins, development, and practical political context of the slogan *neuer Mittelstand* cf. J. Kocka, 'Angestellter', in Brunner et al., Bd. 1, pp. 110-28, p. 125f. White collar workers are more hesitantly included in *classes moyennes*. Cf. G. Deherme, *Les classes moyennes. Etudes sur le parasitisme social*, Paris 1912; L. de Chilly, *La classe moyenne en France après la guerre: 1918-1924*, Paris 1924, esp. pp. 18, 21; see also the references to the international middle class congresses after 1899, which were under strong French, Belgian, and Dutch influence and meant by *classes moyennes* small urban and rural self-employed persons; after 1905, however, on the

initiative of a German delegate, the areas of interest and groups represented were extended to private and public sector white collar workers (in Moulin/Aerts, p. 181, esp. note 73).

22. See the last note, especially the reference to the middle class congresses which after 1905 also represented dependent white collar workers; as well as the literature in Moulin/Aerts; Kocka, *Klassengesellschaft*, pp. 65-71, 93-95.

23. The problems of definition which this poses can, however, only partially be solved. Cf. for Germany: G. Hartfiel, *Angestellte und Angestelltengewerkschaften in Deutschland*, Berlin 1961, pp. 74ff.; and below, pp. 19-20 and notes 45 and 47.

24. If this investigation was only concerned with American history, it would make sense to treat white collar employees in public and private sectors together, since the distinction between public and private employees in the US is not as sharp as it is in Germany (except for a group of higher civil servants). The comparison with Germany, however, which guides this study of American white collar workers, made this procedure appear inadvisable.

25. Cf. J. Fourastié, *Le grand espoir du XXe siècle*, Paris 1950 (1972), pp. 86ff.; also C. Clark, *The Conditions of Economic Progress*, London 1940.

26. Cf. with references H. H. Hyman, 'Reference Groups,' in *IESS*, Vol. 13, New York 1968, pp. 253-361; W. G. Runciman, *Relative Deprivation and Social Justice*, Berkeley 1966, pp. 3-55; T. R. Gurr, *Why Men Rebel*, Princeton 1970, pp. 105-109; L. Festinger, 'A Theory of Social Comparison Processes', in *Human Relations*, Vol. 7, 1954, pp. 117-40; R. F. Merton, *Social Theory and Social Structure*, Glencoe, Ill. 1957[2], pp. 281-386, on the distinction between comparative reference group and normative reference group, p. 355f.; Runciman, *Relative Deprivation*, p. 11f. and p. 9f. on the concept of relative deprivation as used here; its meaning varies in Gurr, pp. 37ff.

27. Such dimensions of inequality are: income, workplace security, independence and autonomy at work, education, social origins, possibilities for upward mobility, status (in the sense of social prestige), patterns of consumption, housing, organizational behavior, access to political power, legal position, etc. These dimensions are not independent of each other, but on the other hand they are not congruent; their relative weight with reference to our problem and their interaction will be traced as far as possible. Also on this problem: J. Kocka, 'Theorien in der Sozial- und Gesellschaftsgeschichte. Vorschläge zur historischen Schichtungsanalyse', in *Geschichte und Gesellschaft*, Vol. 1, Göttingen 1975, pp. 9-42, esp. pp. 32-42. Runciman, *Relative Deprivation* (pp. 36ff.) summarizes these dimensions of inequality (as do many others in the Anglo-American tradition) using Weber's categories of 'class', 'status', and 'power'. See also Runciman, 'Class, Status, and Power?', in J. A. Jackson (ed.), *Social Stratification*, Cambridge 1968, pp. 25-61. There is no reason for such a three part schema here, since the concept of class has already been differently defined — cf. above, note 14.

28. The following discussion is limited to western societies. However, most dimensions of this difference are also found in socialist and communist societies; cf., for instance, R. Girod, *Etudes sociologiques sur les couches salariées*, Paris 1961, p. 87. Some dimensions of the distinction between blue and white collar workers are also found in pre-industrial societies, but these systems are also outside our scope.

29. One must recognize, however, that these comparisons of averages *presuppose* rather than *prove* the existence of the collar line, since in reality most distinctions are gradual, not polarized.

30. Cf. from the extensive literature: Lederer, *Die Privatangestellten*; F. Croner, *Die Angestellten in der modernen Gesellschaft*, Wien 1954; D. Lockwood, *The Blackcoated Worker*, London 1958; Mills; Girod; Crozier, *World*, E. F. Vogel, *Japan's New Middle Class*, Berkeley 1963; Giddens, pp. 177ff.

31. Cf. the literature in the last note and esp. the overview of Crozier, *World*,

pp. 9-20; very good on the example of Geneva: Girod, pp. 151ff.; for the US: Braverman, pp. 293-358; for Great Britain: Runciman, *Relative Deprivation*, pp. 55-119, esp. pp. 78-85, 115-18. Also see Giddens, pp. 179ff., who, however, rightly points out that in recent decades the average wage-salary differential has increased in some societies and that other distinctions between blue collar and white collar workers continue to be very important.

32. Cf. J. Kocka, 'Industrielle Angestelltenschaft in frühindustrieller Zeit', in O. Büsch (ed.), *Untersuchungen zur Geschichte der frühen Industrialisierung vornehmlich im Wirtschaftsraum Berlin/Brandenburg*, Berlin 1970, pp. 315-67; Braun, *Zur Soziologie*, pp. 5-22; recently, Kadritzke. All three titles contain references to other attempts of this sort. See also F. Croner, *Soziologie der Angestellten*, Köln 1962; cf. also, as an overview of white collar theories, G. S. Bain and R. J. Price, 'Who is a White Collar Employee?' in *British Journal of Industrial Relations*, Vol. 10, 1972, pp. 325-29.

33. For instance: there are office workers who like most factory workers are paid in weekly wages; their duties may include as many manual activities as those of the worker on the assembly line. On the emergence of the difference between blue and white collar workers in Germany see J. Kocka, *Unternehmensverwaltung und Angestelltenschaft am Beispiel Siemens 1847-1914*, Stuttgart 1969; Hartfiel, pp. 18ff., 52-74.

34. Cf. Crozier, *World*, pp. 12ff.

35. Cf. ibid., pp. 37ff., 184, 208f., 212f.; A. Sturmthal (ed.), *White Collar Trade Unions. Contemporary Developments in Industrial Societies*, Urbana, Ill. 1966; L. François, *La distinction entre employés et ouvriers en droit allemand, belge, français et italien*, La Haye 1963; Girod, pp. 142ff.

36. Cf. as an overview of historical-sociological white collar analyses which investigate white collar workers in the sense mentioned: Braun, *Zur Soziologie*, pp. 5-22 (who makes a contribution of this kind himself, see pp. 61-120); Kocka, 'Industrielle Angestelltenschaft', pp. 315-67; Bain/Price.

37. Thus S. M. Lipset and R. Bendix, *Social Mobility in Industrial Society*, Berkeley (1959) 1967, esp. pp. 14-17. The temporal variability of the collar line is probably also underestimated in S. Thernstrom, *The Other Bostonians. Poverty and Progress in the American Metropolis 1880-1970*, Cambridge, Mass. 1973, pp. 289-302.

38. From W. G. Hoffman et al., *Das Wachstum der deutschen Wirtschaft seit der Mitte des 19. Jahrhunderts*, Berlin 1965, pp. 196-99, 202, 204-206 (Tables 15, 18, and 20); *Historical Statistics*, p. 74. For details of calculations and limits of comparability, cf. Kocka I, p. 349, n. 55.

39. Cf. on the highly developed mercantile tradition of the US in the 18th and early 19th centuries: L. E. Davis et al., *American Economic Growth. An Economist's History of the United States*, New York 1972, pp. 17-32; T. Cochran, 'The Business Revolution', in *AHR*, Vol. 79, 1974, pp. 1449-66.

40. Cf. Girod, pp. 82ff. for comparative figures which include other societies.

41. Cf. the contributions by Kocka, Wehler and Puhle in H. A. Winkler (ed.), *Organisierter Kapitalismus. Voraussetzungen und Anfänge*, Göttingen 1974, pp. 19-57, 172-94, and the literature quoted there.

42. Cf. e. g. A. Marshall, *Industry and Trade*, London 1919, e.g., pp. 129ff.; A. L. Levine, *Industrial Retardation in Britain, 1880-1914*, New York 1967, pp. 57-78; J. Kocka, 'The Rise of the Modern Industrial Enterprise in Germany', in A. D. Chandler, Jr., and H. Daems (eds.), *Managerial Hierarchies*, Cambridge, Mass. 1980.

43. S. Kuznets, 'Quantitative Aspects of the Economic Growth of Nations, I', in *Economic Development and Cultural Change*, Vol. 5, October 1956, pp. 5-94, pp. 10, 13; cf. also ibid., *Economic Growth of Nations. Total Output and Production Structure*, Cambridge, Mass. 1971, pp. 10-99; A. Maddison, *Economic Growth*

in the West. Comparative Experience in Europe and North America, New York 1964, p. 30 estimates the yearly rate of growth of total output per capita as follows:

	1870-1913	1913-1950
Great Britain	1.3	1.3
France	1.4	0.7
Germany	1.8	0.4
US	2.2	1.7

44. Cf. below, pp. 193ff.

45. American figures from *Historical Statistics*, pp. 74-78: for purposes of comparability the figures for 'manager, officials, and proprietors', given as well as estimates of the number of independent 'professionals' (1900: 200,000; 1910: 240,000; 1920: 260,000; 1930: 290,000; 1948: 300,000), have been subtracted from the figures given for 'white collar workers', and figures for foremen have been added (1900: 140,000; 1910: 300,000; 1920: 460,000; 1930: 500,000 and 1940: 530,000). German figures include *Angestellte* and *Beamte*. For 1933 from *Statistik des Deutschen Reichs*, Bd. 458, 1937, p. 18 (territory and definitions of 1933, calculated by the Reich Office of Statistics); for 1939: *Statistisches Bundesamt Wiesbaden, Bevölkerung und Wirtschaft, 1872-1972*, Stuttgart 1972, p. 142. On the development of the statistical concept *Angestellte* in Germany: Hartfiel, pp. 16-27. Figures are given as % of the *hauptberuflich Erwerbstätige* (Germany) and of the 'economically active population' (US). On the definition: *Statistik des Deutschen Reiches*, Bd. 408, p. 7f.; *Historical Statistics*, p. 69.

46. The (estimated) proportion of women among private and public white collar workers in the sense of Table 1.2 was (in %):

	USA	Germany		USA	Germany
1895		7	1925		27
1900	25		1930	40	
1907		12	1933		31
1910	33		1939		26
1920	40		1940	44	

47. These figures refer in each case to manufacturing industries, construction and mining (in distinction to Tables 2.8 to 2.10 below). Calculated from: S. Kuznets, *National Income and its Composition 1919-1938*, New York 1941, pp. 557, 600, 643; *Statistik des Deutschen Reichs*, Bd. 408, Berlin 1931, p. 110; *Wirtschaft und Statistik*, Bd. 19, 1939, pp. 294ff. These comparative figures can also only be regarded as raw data, since the basic definition of 'salaried employee' in contrast to 'wage earner' and of *Angestellte* vs *Arbeiter* was neither clear and constant over time in the individual societies nor completely comparable between societies. Certain categories of foremen, watchmen, and production clerks, for instance, were counted as *Angestellte* in Germany but not as 'salaried employees' in the US. The distinction between wages and salaries was usually used as the dividing criterion in both societies, but not always. While in Germany a 1911 legal definition of *Angestellte* (i.e. salaried white collar employees in the private sector) (extended in 1924) was responsible for a certain uniformity, the American figures came from surveys under-

taken by the Census of Manufacturers, taken every two years between 1919 and 1939. The census questionnaire explained in general terms (and with slight variations) the distinction between the two categories and left it up to the responding firm whom to count as 'salaried' and as 'wage-earner'. Cf. US Bureau of the Census, *Biennial Census of Manufactures 1925*, Washington 1928, pp. 1193-94; ibid., *15th Census of the United States: Manufactures 1929 (Vol. 1: General Report)*, Washington 1933, pp. 4-5; ibid., *Biennial Census of Manufactures 1937*, Washington 1938, Part I, p. 7; Kuznets, *National Income*, pp. 86-88; S. Fabricant, *Employment in Manufacturing 1899-1939*, New York 1942, pp. 171ff.; G. E. Delehanty, *Nonproduction Workers in US Manufacturing*, Amsterdam 1968, pp. 2-5, 24-29.

48. Cf. A. Gerschenkron, *Economic Backwardness in Historical Perspective*, New York, 1965², pp. 5-30.

49. Cf. B. Moore, Jr., *Social Origins of Dictatorship and Democracy*, Boston 1966.

50. Cf. as an introduction to Imperial Germany: Ritter/Kocka, *Deutsche Sozialgeschichte*, pp. 62-70; further: M. Weber's inaugural address at Freiburg in 1895 in ibid., *Gesammelte politische Schriften*, Tübingen 1958² (1971³), pp. 1-25; Dahrendorf, *Society*. H.-U. Wehler, *Das deutsche Kaiserreich 1871-1918*, Göttingen 1973; F. Stern, *The Failure of Illiberalism. Essays on the Political Culture of Modern Germany*, New York 1972, pp. xi-xliv, 3-73; Winkler, *Mittelstand*, pp. 26-30, 57-64; H.-J. Puhle, *Agrarische Interessenpolitik und preussischer Konservatismus in Wilhelminischen Reich (1893-1914)*, Bonn-Bad Godesberg 1975², pp. 274-89; J. Kocka, 'Vorindustrielle Faktoren in der deutschen Industrialisierung. Industriebürokratie und "neuer Mittelstand",' in M. Stürmer (ed.), *Das Kaiserliche Deutschland*, Düsseldorf 1977², pp. 265-86.

51. Cf. e.g. H. Gutman, *Work, Culture and Society in Industrializing America*, New York, 1976.

52. Cf. A. de Tocqueville, *Democracy in America* (1835), Anchor edition, Garden City 1969; L. Hartz, *The Liberal Tradition in America*, New York 1955; S. M. Lipset, *The First New Nation*, Garden City 1967.

53. Cf. J. Kocka, 'Stand — Klasse — Organisation. Strukturen sozialer Ungleichheit in Deutschland vom späten 18. bis zum frühen 20. Jahrhundert im Aufriß', in H.-U. Wehler (ed.), *Klassen in der europäischen Sozialgeschichte*, Göttingen 1979, pp. 137-65.

54. *White Collar*. Mills treats independent artisans, shopkeepers, and small businessmen together in this work.

55. Cf. with bibliography: A. A. Blum et al., *White Collar Workers*, New York 1971; D. J. Leab, *A Union of Individuals. The Formation of the American Newspaper Guild, 1933-1936*, New York 1970.

56. Cf. above all M. D. McColloch, *White Collar Electrical Machinery, Banking and Public Welfare Workers, 1940-1970*, PhD Thesis, University of Pittsburgh 1975 (Microfilm): Braverman, Ch. 15; M. Oppenheimer, 'Women Office Workers: Petty-Bourgeoisie or New Proletarians?', in *Social Scientist*, No. 40/41, Trivandrum, Kerala (India) November/December 1975, pp. 55-75. M. W. Greenwald, *Women, War and Work: The Impact of World War I on Women Workers in the United States*, PhD Thesis, University of Pittsburgh 1977, esp. Ch. VI; M. Davies, 'Woman's Place is at the Typewriter: The Feminization of the Clerical Labor Force', in *Radical America*, Vol. 8, No. 4, July/August 1974, pp. 1-28; S. P. Benson, "The Clerking Sisterhood". Rationalization and the Work Culture of Saleswomen', in *Radical America*, Vol. 12, No. 2, March/April 1978, pp. 41-55.

57. Cf. the bibliographical essay by J. Modell, 'Die "Neue Sozialgeschichte" in Amerika', in *GG*, Bd. 1, 1975, pp. 155-77, esp. the literature in notes 20-33 (above all Thernstrom's study of Boston) as well as M. B. Katz, *The People of Hamilton, Canada. Family and Class in a Mid-Nineteenth Century City*, Cambridge, Mass.

1975; P. R. Decker, *Fortunes and Failures. White-Collar Mobility in Nineteenth-Century San Francisco*, Cambridge, Mass. 1978. This book deals with the period 1850-80, particularly with independent merchants rather than with employees.

58. For the American side see the bibliographical essay in Mills; the bibliography in McColloch; for references to the German literature see Kocka, 'Industrielle Angestelltenschaft', pp. 317ff.

59. Cf. *Historical Statistics*, p. 75f. 1.5 million (1910) to 2.9 million (1930) were 'salesmen and sales clerks' (male and female) in wholesale, retail, industry, and other sectors; the rest were insurance agents, realtors, advertising people, etc. The proportions (also those that follow) are calculated on the basis of figures given in Table 1.2 above.

60. Figures from Kuznets, *National Income*, p. 600.

61. Figures from *Historical Statistics*, p. 75.

62. In the totals in Table 1.2 managers as well as proprietors and self-employed persons are excluded. The census categories of 'sales worker' or 'clerical and kindred workers' also include hardly any higher and managing white collar workers — more likely some self-employed. In contrast the figures given above for white collar workers in manufacturing firms as well as the category 'professional, technical and kindred workers' do include these higher ranks, above all engineers, chemists, physicists, economists, and other academically trained employees of industrial firms.

63. Cf. for the period to 1914: Kocka, *Unternehmensverwaltung*, pp. 463-540; Lederer, *Die Privatangestellten*; Lederer/Marschak, 'Der neue Mittelstand'. On the Weimar Republic, the best study is now H. Speier, *Die Angestellten vor dem Nationalsozialismus*, Göttingen 1977; also F. W. Fischer, *Die Angestellten, ihre Bewegung und ihre Ideologien*. Phil. Diss., Heidelberg 1932; E. Sträter, *Die soziale Stellung der Angestellten. Rechts-und Staatswiss.* Diss., Bonn 1933; C. Dreyfuss, *Beruf und Ideologie der Angestellten*, München 1933; H. Hamm, *Die wirtschaftlichen und sozialen Berufsmerkmale der kaufmännischen Angestellten (im Vergleich mit denjenigen der Arbeiter)*. Diss. Jena, Borna-Leipzig 1931; recently, S. J. Coyner, *Class Patterns of Family-Income and Expenditure during the Weimar Republic: German White-Collar Employees as Harbingers of Modern Society*. PhD Thesis, Rutgers University, New Brunswick 1975 (based mainly on blue collar-white collar differences in consumption patterns). On the development of organizations: GDA (ed.), *Epochen der Angestellten-Bewegung 1774-1930*, Berlin 1930; Hartfiel.

64. On trends before 1914: Kocka, *Unternehmensverwaltung*; on the world war ibid., *Klassengesellschaft*, pp. 65-95; ibid., 'The First World War and the Mittelstand', in *JCH*, Vol. 8, 1973, pp. 101-24; on Weimar the works cited in note 63 by Speier, Fischer, Hamm, Sträter, Dreyfuss and Coyner; figures on shifts in social origin above all in Speier, pp. 44ff.; also in H. Kaelble, *Soziale Mobilität in Deutschland, 1900-1960* (unpublished Ms. 1976, Ch. 4.2). The various commissions of white collar associations contain very good material on the entire problem, cited in Kadritzke, p. 383; finally, Kadritzke, pp. 156-381, esp. pp. 353ff.; on the social-political situation of white collar workers: L. Preller, *Sozialpolitik in der Weimarer Republik*, Stuttgart 1949, p. 122ff., 133ff., 159-169. On the evolution of wages and salaries: G. Bry, *Wages in Germany 1871-1945*, Princeton 1960, pp. 28, 34, 467; *Statistik des Deutschen Reichs*, Bd. 408, Berlin 1931, p. 110; *Wirtschaft und Statistik*, Bd. 19, 1939, pp. 296, 299; F. Croner, 'Die Angestelltenbewegung nach der Währungsstabilisierung', in *ASS*, Bd. 60, 1928 (Ch. 4, note 37, p. 345 below for English translation), pp. 103-46, pp. 141ff., also (pp. 137-39) on the development of white collar salary rates. Further: GDA (ed.), *Die wirtschaftliche und soziale Lage der Angestellten. Ergebnisse und Erkenntnisse aus der grossen sozialen Erhebung des Gewerkschaftsbundes der Angestellten*, Berlin 1931[2], p. 101; H. Müller, *Nivellierung und Differenzierung der Arbeitseinkommen in Deutschland seit 1925*, Berlin 1954, p. 43; Fischer, *Die Angestellten*, pp. 36-41.

65. Cf. Kocka, 'The First World War'; S. Aufhäuser, *Weltkrieg und*

Angestelltenbewegung, Berlin 1918; D. Stegmann, 'Zwischen Repression und Manipulation: Konservative Machteliten und Arbeiter- und Angestelltenbewegung 1910-1918', in *AfS*, Bd. 12, 1972, pp. 351-432; Kadritzke, pp. 233-305.

66. All figures (except for 1927) from Fischer, *Die Angestellten*, pp. 44, 46; 1927 figures from Croner, 'Angestelltenbewegung', p. 115f. The 'yellow' white collar associations (1925: 59,000) and the non-trade union 'Vereinigung der leitenden Angestellten (Vela)' (1925: 23,000) are not included.

67. Cf. Fischer, *Die Angestellten*, p. 47; Kadritzke, pp. 359ff. In 1928 the Afa-Bund finally gave up the demand for a unified social insurance.

68. S. A. Pratt, *The Social Basis of Nazism and Communism in Urban Germany. A Correlation Study of the July 31, 1932, Reichstag Election in Germany.* MA Thesis, Michigan State College of Agriculture and Applied Science, Department of Sociology and Anthropology 1948; the following from pp. 118, 147, 149, 172ff. Pratt argues that the correlations for medium sized cities are the clearest since in this category the greatest differences in social composition between cities appear (p. 78f). For what follows in greater detail: J. Kocka, 'Zur Problematik der deutschen Angestellten 1914-1933', in H. Mommsen et al. (eds.), *Industrielles System und politische Entwicklung in der Weimarer Republik*, Düsseldorf 1974, pp. 792-811, esp. pp. 795ff.

69. Cf. J. Noakes and G. Pridham (eds.), *Documents on Nazism, 1919-1945*, London 1974, p. 112f.; W. Schäfer, *NSDAP. Entwicklung und Struktur der Staatspartei des Dritten Reiches*, Hannover 1956, pp. 17, 19. The slight decline in the white collar proportion of the NSDAP 1930-32 was due to the even more rapid entry of other, previously more reticent social groups.

70. Cf. e.g. B. E. Doblin and C. Pohly, 'The Social Composition of the Nazi Leadership', in *AJS*, Vol. 51, 1945/46, pp. 42-49, esp. p. 47; and H. Gerth, 'The Nazi Party. Its Leadership and Composition', in ibid., Vol. 45, 1940, pp. 517-41.

71. Cf. H.-G. Schumann, *Nationalsozialismus und Gewerkschaftsbewegung*, Hannover 1958, pp. 34, 39; and J. Noakes, *The Nazi Party in Lower Saxony 1921-1933*, Oxford 1971, pp. 174, 178. Cf. also W. S. Allen, *The Nazi Seizure of Power*, Chicago 1965, pp. 110f., 210f.

72. Cf. I. Hamel, *Völkischer Verband und nationale Gewerkschaft. Der Deutschnationale Handlungsgehilfen-Verband 1893-1933*, Frankfurt 1967, pp. 225, 228f., 232, 237, 238-61, esp. pp. 243f. 251f.; Speier, *Angestellte*, pp. 115ff.; also A. Krebs, *Tendenzen und Gestalten der NSDAP*, Stuttgart 1959, p. 16, on the formulation of the basis of consensus between the NSDAP and the DHV by a Nazi DHV official in retrospect. On the policies of the DHV leaders 1928-33 see also L. E. Jones, 'The Crisis of White Collar Interest Politics: Deutschnationaler Handlungsgehilfen-Verband and Deutsche Volkspartei in the World Economic Crisis', in *Industrielles System*, pp. 811-23; also Kocka, 'Zur Problematik', p. 800f. on the relationship between the DHV and various parties. Cf. also L. E. Jones, ' "The Dying Middle": Weimar Germany and the Fragmentation of Bourgeois Politics', in *CEH*, Vol. 5, 1972, pp. 23-54, esp. pp. 38ff.

73. Geiger, *Soziale Schichtung*, pp. 109-22, esp. pp. 120ff.; see also ibid., 'Panik im Mittelstand', in *Die Arbeit*, Bd. 7, 1930, pp. 637-54; H. Neisser, 'Sozialstatistische Analyse der Wahlergebnisse', in ibid., Bd. 7, 1930, pp. 654-59; Victor, 'Verbürgerlichung', esp. p. 30f.; also C. Mierendorff, 'Gesicht und Charakter der nationalsozialistischen Bewegung', in *Die Gesellschaft*, Bd. 7, 1930, pp. 489-504; and G. Friters, 'Who are the German Fascists?', in *Current History*, Vol. 35, 1932, p. 532-36, esp. p. 534.

74. 'Die Umschichtung des Proletariats', in *Die Neue Rundschau*, Bd. 2, 1929, p. 160f.

75. For the most recent work, see also Speier, *Angestellte*; Kadritzke, pp. 365-81.

76. Ibid., pp. 233-381, esp. pp. 306-42 (on the question of why no fusion took place between leftist white collar organizations and blue collar trade unions).

77. The sociologist Richard Hamilton (McGill University in Montreal) is working on a book on the electoral basis on the NSDAP in which he investigates various elections of the late Weimar Republic in individual cities. On the basis of new quantitative results he takes issue with the thesis of a predominantly lower middle class mass basis for the NSDAP. Hamilton has been good enough to send me some finished chapters; he has successfully demonstrated that middling and better off middle class groups were *at least* as strongly represented among NSDAP voters as lower middle class; after his book it will be more difficult to misuse the lower middle class thesis as an excuse or alibi for intermediate and upper middle class groups. He also makes it seem more probable that poorer lower middle class persons of working class origin tended less toward the right than those who were better off. He shows that there was frequently no clear correlation between the social-economic differences among election districts and the proportion of NSDAP votes in them. Yet the results I have seen so far do not weaken the thesis presented above of the over-representation of white collar workers among NSDAP voters and sympathizers as well as the thesis of the great socio-political significance of the collar line in the Weimar Republic, though the author seems to intend this (see also Hamilton, *Restraining Myths*, p. 135f.). The socio-economic composition of election districts is for the most part too mixed to permit clear conclusions from comparing election results in various districts alone.

78. Cf. from the extensive literature Lipset, *Political Man*, pp. 138-52, esp. p. 148; Sauer, 'National Socialism'; Winkler, 'Extremismus'; M. H. Kater, *Studentenschaft und Rechtsradikalismus in Deutschland 1918-1933*, Hamburg 1975; T. A. Tilton, *Nazism, Neo-Nazism, and the Peasantry*, Bloomington, Ind. 1975; P. Loewenberg, 'The Psycho-historical Origins of the Nazi Youth Cohort', in *AHR*, Vol. 76, 1971, pp. 1457-502; R. I. McKibbin, 'The Myth of the Unemployed: Who did Vote for the Nazis?', in *Australian Journal of Politics and History*, Vol. 15, 1969, pp. 25-40; Noakes/Pridham, pp. 89-116; P. H. Merkl, *Political Violence under the Swastika. 581 Early Nazis*, Princeton 1975; W. Schieder (ed.), *Faschismus als soziale Bewegung. Deutschland und Italien im Vergleich*, Hamburg 1976, pp. 25-68 (Kater), 97-118 (Winkler).

79. Cf. below, p. 267f.

Chapter 2: American White Collar Workers Before the First World War

1. Most figures from *Historical Statistics*, pp. 427, 429, 409, 139, 140, 542, 544, 556-59 and Kuznets, 'Quantitative Aspects', I, p. 13.

2. Cf. the comparisons in Bry, pp. 461-67.

3. Cf. T. V. Powderly, *Thirty Years of Labor 1859-1889*, New York 1967; N. Ware, *The Labor Movement in the United States, 1860-1895*, New York 1929 (a history of the Knights of Labor); G. N. Grob, *Workers and Utopia*, Evanston, Ill. 1961; H. G. Gutman, *Work, Culture, and Society in Industrial America*, New York 1976, pp. 1-78; ibid., 'The Workers' Search for Power. Labor in the Gilded Age', in H. W. Morgan (ed.), *The Gilded Age*, Syracuse 1963, pp. 38-68; D. Montgomery,

Labor and the Radical Republicans, New York 1972; J. Brecher, *Strike!*, San Francisco 1972; J. G. Rayback, *A History of American Labor*, New York 1959.

4. On immigration cf. O. Handlin, *The Uprooted. The Epic Story of the Great Migrations that Made the American People* (1951), Boston 1972²; P. Taylor, *The Distant Magnet. European Emigration to the US*, New York 1971 (with extensive bibliography); good statistical treatment in E. P. Hutchinson, *Immigrants and Their Children, 1850-1950*, New York 1956. J. Higham, *Strangers in the Land. Patterns of American Nativism 1960-1925* (1955), New York 1975²; ibid., *Send These to Me. Jews and Other Immigrants in Urban America*, New York 1975; S. P. Hays, *The Response to Industrialism, 1885-1914*, Chicago 1957, pp. 42ff.; W. Preston, Jr., *Aliens and Dissenters. Federal Suppression of Radicals, 1903-1933*, Cambridge, Mass. 1963.

5. An overview of the various epochs in W. T. K. Nugent, 'Politics from Reconstruction to 1900', in W. H. Cartwright and R. L. Watson, Jr., *The Reinterpretation of American History and Culture*, Washington 1973, pp. 377-400, esp. p. 390f., bibliography p. 398f., notes 36-40; K. Barkin, 'A Case Study in Comparative History: Populism in Germany and America, in H. J. Bass (ed.), *The State of American History*, Chicago 1970, pp. 373-404; also on Germany and the US: H.-J. Puhle, *Politische Agrabewegungen in kapitalistischen Industriegesellschaften. Deutschland, USA und Frankreich im 20. Jahrhundert*, Gottingen 1975, pp. 113-201.

6. On the whole problem, R. H. Wiebe, *The Search for Order 1877-1920*, New York 1967, Ch. I-IV; R. Berthoff, *An Unsettled People. Social Order and Disorder in American History*, New York 1971, pp. 301ff.; W. A. Williams, *The Contours of American History*, Chicago (1961) 1966, pp. 345-451; a very good corrective to the overly extreme criticism of the Turner thesis: C. N. Degler, *Out of Our Past. The Forces that Shaped Modern America*, New York (1959) 1970², pp. 121-34, esp. pp. 129-31; also as an overview of the frontier debate: R. Hofstadter and S. M. Lipset (eds.), *Turner and the Sociology of the Frontier*, New York 1968, esp. pp. 187-224. On Social Darwinism cf. R. Hofstadter, *Social Darwinism in American Thought, 1860-1915*, Philadelphia 1955².

7. 'Corporation Capitalism': Williams, *Contours*, pp. 343ff.; before him cf. M. H. Dobb, *Studies in the Development of Capitalism*, London 1947², p. 268; 'Political Capitalism': G. Kolko, *The Triumph of Conservatism*, Chicago (1963) 1967, pp. 57ff., 255ff. Cf. also C. H. Hession and H. Sardy, *Ascent to Affluence. History of American Economic Development*, Boston 1969, pp. 507ff.: 'The Organizational Revolution in American Economic and Political Life, 1897-1918'.

8. Cf. the outline by Kocka in Winkler, *Organisierter Kapitalismus*, pp. 19-35; H.-J. Puhle, 'Der Übergang zum Organisierten Kapitalismus in den USA — Thesen zum Problem einer aufhaltsamen Entwicklung', in ibid., pp. 172-94 (also on the following points); ibid., *Agrarbewegungen*, Ch. III, esp. pp. 113-26; P. Lösche, *Industriegewerkschaften im organisierten Kapitalismus. Der CIO in der Roosevelt-Ära*, Opladen 1974, esp. pp. 10, 36ff.

9. Cf. the statistics on combinations in *Historical Statistics*, p. 572; A. D. Chandler, Jr., *The Visible Hand: The Rise of Modern Business Enterprise in the United States*, Cambridge, Mass. 1977; G. P. Porter and H. C. Livesay, 'Oligopolists in American Manufacturing and their Products, 1909-1963', in *BHR*, Vol. 43, 1969, pp. 282-98; A. D. Chandler, Jr., and L. Galambos, 'The Development of Large-Scale Organizations in Modern America', in *JEH*, Vol. 30, 1970; R. W. and M. E. Hidy, *Pioneering in Big Business, 1882-1911: Standard Oil Company*, New York 1955; R. L. Nelson, *Merger Movements in American Industry*, Princeton 1959; L. Neal, 'Trust Companies and Financial Innovation 1897-1914', in *BHR*, Vol. 45, 1971, pp. 35-51; T. R. Navin, 'Investment Banking since 1900', in *Bulletin of the Business History Society*, Vol. 27, 1953, pp. 60-65.

10. Cf. S. Haber, *Efficiency and Uplift. Scientific Management in the Progressive Era 1890-1920*, Chicago 1964; A. D. Chandler, Jr., *The Visible Hand;* ibid.,

Strategy and Structure. Chapters in the History of Industrial Enterprise, Cambridge, Mass. 1962; ibid., and H. Daems, 'The Rise of Managerial Capitalism and its Impact on Investment Strategy in the Western World and Japan', in H. Daems and H. van der Wee (eds.), *The Rise of Managerial Capitalism*, Den Haag 1974, pp. 1-34; M. Newcomer, 'Professionalization of Leadership in the Big Business Corporation', in *BHR*, Vol. 29, 1955, pp. 54-63; D. Nelson, *Managers and Workers: Origins of the New Factory System in the United States, 1880-1920*, Madison 1975; L. Baritz, *The Servants of Power. A History of the Use of Social Science in American Industry*, Middletown, Conn. 1960. Cf. Croly, *Promise*; F. C. Howe, *Socialized Germany*, New York 1915.

11. From A. M. Edwards, *Comparative Occupation Statistics for the United States, 1870-1940* (US Bureau of the Census, 16th Census of the US, 1940), Washington 1943, pp. 100-101. In these figures sales workers in stores and professionals (technicians, engineers, economists, managers) are not included.

12. Cf. A. M. Carr-Saunders and P. A. Wilson, *The Professions* (1933), London 1964; T. Parsons, 'The Professions and Social Structure', in *Social Forces*, Vol. 17, 1939, pp. 457-67 (reprinted in ibid., *Essays in Sociological Theory*, Glencoe, Ill. 1954[2], pp. 185-99); ibid. 'Professions', in *IESS*, 1968, Vol. 12, pp. 536-47; E. Moore, *The Professions, Roles and Rules*, New York 1970.

13. Sources as for Table 2.1.

14. On the rise of the professions see especially Wiebe, *Search*, Ch. 5 (with further references).

15. Cf. *Historical Statistics*, p. 98: Membership figures for the AFL; on its development, S. Gompers, *Seventy Years of Life and Labor*, New York 1925; B. Mandel, *Samuel Gompers. A Biography*, Yellow Springs 1963; Grob, *Workers*; P. Taft, *The A.F. of L. in the Time of Gompers*, New York 1970. A. K. Steigerwald, *The National Association of Manufacturers, 1895-1914*, Grand Rapids 1964; M. Green, *The National Civic Federation and the American Labor Movement 1900-1925*, Washington 1956; J. Weinstein, *The Corporate Ideal in the Liberal State: 1900-1918*, Boston 1968; Puhle, *Agrarbewegungen*, Ch. III; Hays, *Response*, pp. 58ff.

16. A good introduction to the state of research is 'P. G. Filene, An Obituary for "The Progressive Movement",' in *American Quarterly*, Vol. 22, 1970, pp. 20-34, which refers to the most important literature, empahsizes the diversity of the reforms and denies that progressivism was a unified movement. Cf. D. P. Thelen, 'Social Tensions and the Origins of Progressivism', in *JAH*, Vol. 56, 1969/70, pp. 323-41, esp. pp. 324-30 for a critical review of the literature; R. H. Wiebe, 'The Progressive years, 1900-1917', in W. H. Cartwright and R. L. Watson, *The Reinterpretation of American History and Culture*, Washington 1973, pp. 425-42. For a short definition of 'Progressivism': R. M. Abrams, *Conservatism in a Progressive Era. Massachusetts Politics 1900-1912*, Cambridge, Mass. 1964, p. ix; another useful general history is Wiebe, *Search*. Cf. also A. A. Ekirch, Jr., *Progressivism in America*, New York 1974; very good for the points of view of interest here: Haber.

17. Cf. H. W. Faulkner, *The Decline of Laissez-Faire, 1897-1917*, New York 1951; Ekirch, pp. 67ff.; R. H. Wiebe, *Businessmen and Reform*, Cambridge 1962; ibid., *Railroads and Regulation, 1877-1916*, Princeton 1965; ibid., *Search*, Chs. 7 and 8; R. Asher, 'Business and Worker's Welfare in the Progressive Era', in *BHR*, Vol. 43, 1969, pp. 452-75; H.-U. Wehler, *Der Aufstieg das amerikanischen Imperialismus. Studien zur Entwicklung des Imperium Americanum 1865-1900*, Göttingen 1974; W. E. Leuchtenburg, 'Progressivism and Imperialism', in *Mississippi Valley Historical Review*, Vol. 39, December 1952, pp. 483-504; P. P. van Riper, *History of the United States Civil Service*, Evanston 1958, pp. 96-250, passim, esp. pp. 157-68, 223-27; Abrams, *Conservatism*; G. E. Mowry, *The Era of Theodore Roosevelt, 1900-1912*, New York 1958; R. Lubove, 'The Twentieth Century City:

'The Progressive as Municipal Reformer', in *Mid-America*, Vol. 41, 1959, pp. 195-209; S P. Hays, 'The Politics of Reform in Municipal Government in the Progressive Era', in *Pacific Northwest Quarterly*, Vol. 55, 1964, pp. 157-69.

18. Cf. on this aspect Kolko, *Triumph*; Weinstein, *Corporate Ideal.*

19. Cf. J. M. Laslett, *Labor and the Left: A Study of Socialist and Radical Influences in the American Labor Movement, 1881-1924*, New York 1970; ibid., 'Socialism and American Trade Unionism', in ibid. and S. M. Lipset (eds.), *Failure of a Dream? Essays in the History of American Socialism*, Garden City 1974, pp. 200-32; D. A. Shannon, *The Socialist Party of America. A History* (1955), Chicago 1967; H. H. Quint, *The Forging of American Socialism*, Columbia 1953; I. Yellowitz, *Labor and the Progressive Movement in New York State, 1897-1916*, Ithaca, NY 1965; M. Dubofsky, *When Workers Organize. New York City in the Progressive Era*, Amherst 1968; ibid., *We Shall be All. A History of the Industrial Workers of the World*, Chicago 1969.

20. Cf., also on the following: Puhle, 'Übergang'; on the comparison with Germany H.-U. Wehler, 'Der Aufstieg des organisierten Kapitalismus und Interventionsstaates in Deutschland', also C. S. Maier, 'Strukturen kapitalistischer Stabilität in den 20er Jahren', pp. 36-57 and 192-213 respectively in Winkler, *Organisierter Kapitalismus*; with very interesting insights already C. Lütkens, *Staat und Gesellschaf in Amerika. Zur Soziologie des amerikanischen Kapitalimus*, Tübingen 1929, pp. 5, 109ff., passim.

21. Cf. below, p. 141f. on the similarities and differences between the ideal types 'bureaucracy' and 'professionalization'. The major role of American engineers in business reform (e.g., Taylorism) and in public debate on reforms since the 1890s had only modest parallels among their German colleagues. It seems to me that this discrepancy as well as German-American differences in business organization may be interpreted in the same conteext. Cf. D. T. Farnham, *America vs. Europe in Industry. A Comparison of Industrial Policy and Methods of Management*, New York 1921; J. Kocka, 'Family and Bureaucracy in German Industrial Management, 1850-1914', in *Business History Review*, Vol. 45, 1971, pp. 133-56, here p. 155f. On the German system of chambers: H.-A. Winkler, *Pluralismus oder Protektionismus? Verfassungspolitische Probleme des Verbandswesens im Deutschen Kaiserreich*, Wiesbaden 1972.

22. Cf. Green, *National Civic Federation*; also the experiences of Lincoln Steffens with department store owner Filene in Boston around 1910 (*The Autobiography. One-Volume-Edition*, New York 1931, pp. 598-603); finally, the particular form of American radicalism in the Socialist Party ('Yankeefield' Socialism), in which Marx's *Capital* was a full step behind Edward Bellamy's *Looking Backward* (Shannon, p. 3).

23. Cf. above, pp. 160-65 for a survey of other American white collar organizations.

24. Cf. above, p. 30 and Hamel.

25. Cf. *Annual Reports of the Board of Direction of the Mercantile Library Association of the City of New York from 1821 to 1838*, New York 1868, esp. pp. 35, 54, 112; *Hunt's Merchant's Magazine*, Vol. 12, 1845, p. 393; A. S. Horlick, *Counting Houses and Clerks. The Social Control of Young Men in New York, 1840-1860*. PhD Thesis, University of Wisconsin 1969, pp. 353ff. Ibid., p. 354 on the foundation of a much more thriving Mechanics Library and Scientific Institution at the same time in New York.

26. Cf. The Society of Commercial Travellers, *The System of Commercial Travelling in Europe and the United States. Its History, Customs and Laws*, New York 1869, esp. pp. 4-8.

27. This assertion is based partly on the evidence of several contemporary handbooks for mercantile employees, in which organizations specifically for mercantile employees are not mentioned, but which do contain some references to general clubs. Cf. e.g. the advice of an old merchant in H. N. Higinbotham, *The Making of*

a Merchant (1902), Chicago 1906², p. 16f. The RCIPA newspaper frequently mentioned the membership of store clerks in the Benevolent and Protective Order of Elks (after 1868); next to actors, mercantile employees were strongly represented. Cf. *The Advocate*, September 1902, p. 8; RCIPA, *12th Convention (1905), Proceedings*, p. 67; C. W. Ferguson, *Fifty Million Brothers*, New York 1937, pp. 281-88, esp. p. 282. In contrast to the Rotary and Kiwanis Clubs, the Elks attracted few members from the upper middle class. But its membership was too occupationally heterogeneous for it to be used as a source for investigating sales employees. Cf. J. R. Nicolson and L. A. Donaldson, *History of the Order of Elks 1868-1967*, Chicago 1969². A preliminary analysis of all voluntary associations that could be found in Massachusetts between 1750 and 1830 revealed no organizations of mercantile employees (Report of Richard D. Brown, 9 November 1970 at the Charles Warren Center, Harvard University). Cf., on the contrary, on the need for sociability as a root of German mercantile organizations: *Festbuch zur Hundertjahrfeier der 'Union' Verein junger Kaufleute*, Rostock 1909, pp. 8ff.; *Denkschrift zur Feier des einhundertjährigen Bestehens des Instituts für hilfsbedürftige Handlungsdiener zu Breslau*, Breslau 1874.

28. Cf. M. Estey, 'Early Closing: Employer-Organized Origin of the Retail Labor Movement', in *LH*, Vol. 13, 1972, pp. 560-70, esp. p. 570 (on Philadelphia in the 1830s); 'The Early Closing of Stores', in *Hunt's Merchants' Magazine*, New York, Vol. 37, 1857, p. 131f. I. B. Cross, *History of Labor in California*, Berkeley 1935, p. 26 (on combinations and boycotts by clerks in San Francisco 1863). One of the founders of the RCIPA, Ed E. Mallory, mentioned similar organizations in Cleveland, Ohio after 1865, in Providence, R. I. after 1879, in New Orleans, La. and Indianapolis, Ind. after 1882 ('The Retail Clerks' National Protective Association in the U.S.', in *AFL Year Books 1892*, n.p. [Mimeograph copy in AFL-CIO Library, Washington, File: 'Labor History — International Unions, Retail Clerks']). An old member (Louis Nash) described the proceedings of one such Early Closing Society in St Paul, Minn. in 1888 in *The Advocate*, November/December 1930, p. 4f.

29. Cf. *The Advocate*, September 1907, p. 88; RCIPA, *1st Convention (1891), Proceedings*, pp. 6, 21; in the Library and Exhibition room of the Retail Clerks International Association in Washington the minutes of the 'Clerks Assembly 5929' of the Knights of Labor from 17 November 1896 to 20 January 1897 are on display (handwritten, place not identified). *15th Convention (1905), Proceedings*, p. 45: store clerks in Pittsburgh belonged to the Knights.

30. Figures from J. L. McEwen, *An Analysis of the Early Problems of the RCIPA (AFL)*, PhD Thesis, New York University, Graduate School of Business 1950, pp. 28, 46ff. These were the figures which the RCIPA turned in to the AFL; they probably exaggerated the true membership (in order to increase the organization's weight in the AFL and its prestige for new members) and furthermore do not reflect yearly fluctuations.

31. These broad goals from the Declaration of Principles in the organization's constitutions of 1891 and 1901 (which then remained basically unchanged until 1935). In 1903 nine, 1907 eight hour days were demanded. Job placement appears to have played a subordinate role in the association's activities; on the 20th anniversary, however, the leadership promised to pursue this aim. Cf. *The Advocate*, December 1910, p. 20.

32. These times were mentioned in the *1st Convention (1891), Proceedings*, p. 21; *The Advocate*, May 1896, p. 7.

33. The Early Closing Associations which were active in the 1860s at the latest in England may have served as a model for American organizations. Cf. Oldenberg, 'Die heutige Lage', esp. p. 756f.

34. Cf. *The Advocate*, September 1901, p. 19; *12th Convention (1905) Proceedings*, p. 51; similar developments already in Philadephia in 1835; Estey (see note 28).

35. Cf. P. Taft, *Organized Labor in American History*, New York 1964, pp. 123ff.

36. *11th Convention (1903), Proceedings*, p. 4; *12th Convention (1905), Proceedings*, p. 39: Employers often allowed *some* clerks to join the RCIPA in order to obtain the store card. *1st Convention (1891), Proceedings*, pp. 6, 10, 11, 12, 20: on the emphasis on the cooperation with organized blue collar workers. *The Advocate*, February 1902, pp. 11ff. and April 1902, pp. 10ff., as examples of propaganda for the union label which was specifically addressed to housewives. Cf. also *The Advocate*, January 1901, pp. 9-11.

37. *The Advocate*, May 1896, p. 7.

38. Cf. on the Consumers' League of the City of New York (founded 1889/90), *Annual Report*, 1894-1912, New York 1894ff. In 1900 there were 25 Consumers' Leagues in nine states: they joined to found the National Consumers' League (ibid., 1900, p. 11). In 1910 there were 55 leagues in sixteen states (ibid., 1910/11, p. 15). On the history of this organization, which gradually extended its field of activities: M. Nathan, *The Story of an Epoch Making Movement*, Garden City 1926; A. R. Wolfe, 'Women, Consumerism, and the National Consumers' League in the Progressive Era, 1900-23', in *LH*, Vol. 16, 1975, pp. 378-92.

39. Cf. *Official Souvenir*, Buffalo 1903 (RCIPA, 11th Convention): History of Local 212 in Buffalo with a report of activities similar to strike in 1895. Further: *The Advocate*, April 1904, p. 12 on a strike in Chicago. On other strikes: G. D. Kirstein, *Stores and Unions. A Study of the Growth of Unionism in Dry Goods and Department Stores*, New York 1950, pp. 41ff. Figures in McEwen, p. 359 (based on AFL sources): after that the RCIPA conducted the following number of strikes per year: 1899 0, 1900 2, 1901 0, 1904 3, 1905 0, 1906 0, 1901 1, 1910 0, 1911 0, 1913 1, 1914 1, 1915 0, 1916 4, 1917 9, 1918 5, 1919 8. At an early date there were isolated conflicts. In 1899 eight to ten clerks threw rotten eggs at a store which kept late hours; after that the proprietor let his assistants go earlier and manned the store himself after a certain hour (*The Advocate*, July 1899, p. 13). In 1915 the constitution (Declaration of Principles, Point 11) declared that payment of sickness and death benefits could be suspended for strike, lockout, or legal costs — but already in 1918 this point was eliminated.

40. *12th Convention (1905), Proceedings*, p. 40.

41. Cf. for the exclusively state legislation E. Brandeis, 'Labor Legislation', in J. R. Commons et al., *History of Labor in the United States, 1896-1932*, Vol. 3 (1935), New York 1966, pp. 456-500. On the more extensive coverage for female factory workers (but not female sales employees) in state legislation, esp. pp. 459, 461, 464, 466, 467; on the gradual inclusion of female employees in commerce: pp. 467, 468, 469ff., 475, 479; on the highpoint of this legislation 1911-1913: pp. 474ff.

42. Cf. *The Advocate*, December 1910, pp. 10, 20.

43. Many sales employees already were entitled to vacations in the 1890s, often without deducations from their pay. Estey (see note 28) reports that clerks in Philadelphia agitated as early as 1835 for summer vacations (p. 561). Cf. *The Advocate*, September 1902, p. 8: A union organizer excused his relatively slight success in July and August by the fact that many clerks were on vacation. But vacations depended entirely on the whim of the merchant and were not a matter of course. Cf. *The Advocate*, August 1908, p. 24; July 1916, p. 16.

44. Cf. already *The Advocate*, March 1903, p. 3; *11th Convention (1903), Proceedings*, p. 6f. The demand for a minimum wage which was raised for the first time here by the union's leadership was repeated in 1905 (*12th Convention, Proceedings*, p. 40f.) and seems only then to have found some support.

45. The demand for $9 in *The Advocate*, October 1907, p. 25f.; January 1914, pp. 7ff. The demand for a 'living wage' was made explicitly (if not

exclusively) with reference to female clerks. Cf. *The Advocate*, October 1908, p. 26f.; *12th Convention (1905), Proceedings*, p. 52f.

46. Cf. the copy of a model contract which the RCIPA recommended to its locals in 1906 in Kirstein, p. 167. McEwen, p. 84 prints a contract from 1898 which does not mention the union shop.

47. *The Advocate*, February 1908, p. 13; October 1901, p. 29; April 1917, p. 27; *11th Convention (1903), Proceedings*, p. 9.

48. Cf. *Prospectus* (1892), pp. 76ff., 101, 105; *The Advocate*, January 1903, p. 4.

49. Cf. e.g. *The Advocate*, January 1908, p. 16.

50. *The Advocate*, January 1910, pp. 21-23 on chain stores; February 1914, pp. 7-9 on the labor conflicts of the preceding years; pp. 19ff. on the up to then biggest strike (seventeen months) in Lafayette, Indiana; *The Advocate*, October 1914, pp. 7ff: 'Strife at Home — Deadly Warfare Abroad'; February 1917, p. 19: 'To Which Class Do You Belong?'

51. Compare the membership figures above, p. 55 with Table 2.3 below, p. 67.

52. That many union shop agreements were reached is demonstrated by the fact that after the war the open shop campaign by employers was also carried on in retail. Cf. *The Advocate*, July 1920, pp. 8ff.

53. *The Advocate*, January 1917, p. 19f.

54. Cf. 'The Hard Hit Class. The White Collar Slaves of Modern Industry Feel the Pinch of Poverty', in *The Advocate*, December 1916, pp. 5-7.

55. The German term is *Handlungsgehilfe*. Evidence for the following sketch of German developments: Kocka, I, p. 365f.

56. Cf. Constitution (of 1901) Article II, Section 2; Constitution (of 1907), Section 8.

57. Cf. G. Carson, *The Old Country Store*, New York 1954, p. 12f.; P. Scull, *From Peddlers to Merchant Princes. A History of Selling in America*, Chicago 1967, pp. 72-79; L. E. Atherton, *The Southern Country Store, 1800-1860*, Baton-Rouge 1949, p. 207 f.; cf. above, p. 55 on the New York Mercantile Library Association after 1821, which organized counting house as well as store clerks. Biographies and memoirs of merchants and clerks reveal frequent shifts between retail and wholesale.

58. R. M. Hower, *History of Macy's of New York 1858-1919*, Cambridge, Mass. 1943, p. 199 points out the low prestige of retail trade in the 1890s. On the transformation of merchandising practices see Scull, *Peddlers*; L. A. Johnson, *Over the Counter and on the Shelf*, Rutland, Vt. 1961.

59. *12th Convention (1905), Proceedings*, p. 75. The absence of a corporatist sense of identity and the dominance of a functional, occupational, workplace orientation made it possible for organized clerks to establish several discrete locals in the same city based on different branches of trade. In this way it was possible to organize a group which had remained apart from other clerks (among other reasons because of their greater training) in the RCIPA: drug store clerks. Cf. *The Advocate*, June 1902, p. 7f.; *13th Convention (1907), Proceedings*, p. 42. In 1903 locals composed exclusively of grocery store clerks existed in fourteen cities (*The Advocate*, March 1903, p. 15).

60. *Die wirtschaftliche Lage der deutschen Handlungsgehilfen im Jahre 1908. Bearb. nach statistischen Erhebungen des DHV, vorgenommen im Jahre 1908*, Hamburg 1910, p. 127: 'Such great disparities exist between the managing clerk in a large department store and the assistant in a small shop that the mercantile employees' association must make every effort to foster the sentiments that keep the feeling of unity among all German mercantile employees alive'.

61. Cf. *The Advocate*, April 1908, pp. 16ff.: 'The London Shop Assistant', as a report on the situation of English colleagues. W. B. Whitaker, *Victorian and Edwar-*

dian Shopworkers. The Struggle to Obtain Better Conditions and a Half-Holiday, Totowa, NJ 1973.

62. Cf. *16th Convention (1915), Proceedings*, pp. 34, 44f. The aim was the 'affiliation of all employees, whether actually engaged in selling, handling, weighing or putting up merchandise'. An opponent of the proposal declared himself in favor of 'trade autonomy' and against 'industrial unionism'. A change in statutes was voted; 'all persons regardless of sex in and around wholesale, retail and mail order establishments, other than the liquor trade in any manner engaged in the selling, soliciting or delivering of merchandise' could be organized (Constitution 1915, Section 3). This formulation was missing again in 1918. On the rejection by the AFL executive, which apparently feared interference with the rights of other unions or a further erosion of the craft principle — or perhaps was under pressure from RCIPA leaders to restrict the membership to retail trade — cf. *17th Convention (1918), Proceedings*, p. 23. On the general problem: J. O. Morris, *Conflict within the AFL. A Study of Craft Versus Industrial Unionism, 1901-1938*, Ithaca, NY 1958.

63. Constitution 1901, Article II, Section 1: 'provided they are actively employed in a retail store'; Constitution 1905, Section 3: 'Any person, regardless of sex, engaged in any branch of the retail trades, mail order house or window dressing trade...'; Constitution 1918, Section 4: 'All persons, regardless of sex, employed in mercantile and mail order establishments, who are actively engaged in handling and selling merchandise.' On the 1915 definition and its rejection, see note 62.

64. Cf. *12th Convention (1905), Proceedings*, p. 41; *16th Convention (1915), Proceedings*, p. 45; *The Advocate*, January 1916, pp. 3ff.; August 1916, p. 17f. In this last dispute with the Teamsters it was decided that the RCIPA should organize employees who spent more than 50% of their time in the store; the Teamsters those who spent more than 50% of their time working outside the store.

65. Cf. K. Bücher, *Die Arbeiterfrage im Kaufmannstande*, Berlin 1883, p. 22f.; Goldschmidt, *Die sociale Lage*, p. 19f; Hiller, p. 12; *Werden und Wirken des Verbandes Deutscher Hnadlungsgehilfen zu Leipzig, 1881-1906*, Leipzig 1906.

66. Cf. J. R. Commons et al., *History of Labor in the United States, 1896-1932*, 4 vols. (1918-35), New York 1966, Vol. 1, esp. pp. 8, 46ff.

67. Cf. T. S. Adams and H. L. Sumner, *Labor Problems. A Text Book*, New York 1905, pp. 435-59; *BLSt., Bulletin*, No. 439, Washington 1927, pp. 619-36; R. Bergewin, *Industrial Apprenticeship*, New York 1947, pp. 13-20. Mass. Bureau of Statistics of Labor, *The Apprenticeship System* (=Pt. 1 of the Annual Report, 1906) by C. F. Pidgin, Boston 1906, esp. p. 3f.; on the state of commercial education in Cleveland see R. R. Lutz, *Wage Earning and Education* (=Cleveland Education Survey [Summary]), Cleveland 1916; the development in outline from an intellectual history perspective in B. M. Fischer, *Industrial Education. American Ideals and Institutions*, Madison 1967, esp. pp. 72-137.

68. An indication that there was no functional apprenticeship system in the commercial sector was the emergence of numerous private trade schools already in the first half of the 19th century. Cf. B. R. Haynes and H. P. Jackson, *A History of Business Education in the United States*, Cincinnati 1935, pp. 15-25.

69. Cf. the early examples in Atherton, p. 207f., esp. note 66; Walter Barret (pseudonym for J. A. Scoville), *The Old Merchants of New York*, 5 vols., New York 1885, Vol. 1, p. 110.

70. Cf. e.g. D. S. Dodge, *Memoirs of William E. Dodge*, New York 1887, p. 24; K. W. Porter, *The Jacksons and the Lees*, 2 vols., Cambridge, Mass., 1937, Vol. 2, p. 1321f.; Scoville, Vol. 1, pp. 57, 195; Vol. 2, p. 101f.; (R. F. Reed), *Experience of a New York Clerk, by R. F. R.*, New York 1877; R. E. Gould, *Yankee Storekeeper*, New York 1946, pp. 25ff.

71. Cf. Horlick, pp. 135ff.

72. F. W. Roman, *The Industrial and Commercial Schools of the United States and Germany*, New York 1915, p. 246.

73. Cf. H. A. Gibbons, *John Wanamaker*, 2 vols., New York 1926, pp. 282ff.

74. Declaration of Principles (1891), Point 5; cf. *11th Convention (1903), Proceedings*, p. 7: '. . . a law should be enacted limiting the employment of an apprentice for every five (5) journeymen salesmen. . .' (President O'Brien); Constitution 1901, Article II, Section 1.

75. *13th Convention (1907), Proceedings*, p. 50 (after this time that sentence was dropped from the constitution).

76. From Edwards, *Comparative Occupation Statistics*, pp. 110, 127, 129 (after 1910). Totals for 'salesmen and saleswomen (stores)', and 'clerks in stores'. The figures all include some employees in retail stores who were not sales clerks but cashiers, for instance.

77. From G. Hohorst et al., *Sozialgeschichtliches Arbeitsbuch. Materialien zur Statistik des Kaiserreichs 1870-1914*, München 1978[2], p. 68, note 8 (there the references to the official statistics).

78. The female proportion of the total US labor force rose from 18% in 1900 to 19% in 1920 and 24% in 1940 (*Historical Statistics*, pp. 70-71). According to German government figures the female proportion of all gainfully employed persons rose from 30% in 1895 and 33% in 1907 to 36% in 1933 (*Statistisches Jahrbuch für das Deutsche Reich*, Jg. 58, 1939/40, p. 79 and Bry, p. 25). German percentage figures calculated on the basis of W. G. Hoffmann (*Das Wachstum der deutschen Wirtschaft seit der Mitte des 19. Jahrhunderts*, Berlin 1965) are even higher. The percentage of women in the labor force remains much smaller in the US than in Germany even if one excludes agriculture with its great number of female family members (in Germany) who helped out and when one remembers that the proportion of women in the US population as a whole was somewhat smaller than in Germany.

79. Cf. Hiller, p. 16; Lederer, *Die Privatangestellten*, pp. 162ff.; S. Mantel, *Die Angestelltenbewegung in Deutschland*, Leipzig 1921, pp. 38, 46, 51, 56ff, 62ff.

80. Cf. *Official Souvenir* (RCIPA), Buffalo, NY 1903 (n.p.) The Buffalo local, founded in 1895, accepted its first women members between 1901 and 1903; *The Advocate*, October 1908, p. 26: with RCIPA leaders' complaints that many locals have denied women admission.

81. Cf. ibid.; *The Advocate*, January 1914, p. 18 reported the foundation of a 'Girl's Local' in Boston (by female clerks in a department store).

82. *The Advocate*, June 1899, p. 4; July 1904, p. 7.

83. Cf. *1st Convention (1891), Proceedings*, p. 6; Declaration of Principles, Point 6; one of the first acting chairmen was a women (1891); L. Nash reported on one of the first sales clerk assemblies in St. Paul, Minn. (before 1890), where half of those present were women and girls. *The Advocate*, November/December 1930, p. 4.

84. Cf. *The Advocate*, February 1902, pp. 11ff.: the beginning of a column for women; March 1910, pp. 9ff.: 'The Saleswomen Behind the Counter and Our International Association'; June 1910, pp. 9ff.: 'Back of the Retail Sales-women Stands the RCIPA'; similar story November/December 1910, p. 20.

85. Cf. *The Advocate*, September 1901, p. 18: 'Woman as Competitor'; *The Advocate*, February 1914, p. 16: 'The Menace of the Unorganized Woman'.

86. Thus in *The Advocate*, June 1902, p. 11; similarly already in February 1902, p. 12; cf. September 1901, p. 18: 'There is no reason why sex should be arrayed against sex in the great battle for bread and butter'.

87. *The Advocate*, January 1900, p. 6. On the general topic of women and trade unionism in the 19th and early 20th centuries see E. Flexner, *Century of Struggle. The Woman's Rights Movement in the United States*, New York 1974[2], pp. 131ff., 193ff., 240ff.

88. Cf. e.g. *The Advocate*, May 1896, p. 9.

89. Thus in St Paul, Minn. in 1888 according to L. Nash in *The Advocate*, November/December 1930, p. 4.

90. Ibid.; *12th Convention (1905), Proceedings*, pp. 40, 42; *13th Convention (1907), Proceedings*, p. 53; Kirstein, p. 26.

91. E.g., in the strike in Lafayette in 1912: *16th Convention (1915), Proceedings*, pp. 21f., 26, 32; and in the Memphis strike: *17th Convention (1918), Proceedings*, p. 27; Kirstein, p. 43.

92. They characterized themselves as 'laborers', as part of the 'great industrial army of the world' (*Prospectus* 1892, pp. 83, 99), as part of the 'working classes', the 'toiling masses', as 'among the more intelligent class of wage earners' (*12th Convention* [*1905*], *Proceedings*, pp. 38, 43). They appealed to the most varied groups of blue collar workers as 'co-workers' and 'fellow-toilers' (*17th Convention* [*1918*], *Proceedings*, p. 24).

93. Cf. *Commission on the Relations and Conditions of Capital and Labor Employed in Manufactures and General Business*, Vol. 7, Washington 1901, pp. 587-91: I. B. Myers was President of the Trade and Labor Council in Memphis and at the same time representative of the local sales clerks' union, on whose situation he testified before the Senate Committee. Max Morris, Treasurer of the RCIPA from 1896-1909, was an AFL vice president and a close friend of Gompers (McEwen, p. 49f.); RCIPA President O'Brien attended the Trades and Labor Congress of Canada as a representative of the AFL (*11th Convention* [*1903*], *Proceedings*, p. 4).

94. Cf. brief and to the point: Grob, *Workers*, pp. 138-62, esp. pp. 152ff.; Taft, *The AF of L*.

95. Cf. *The Advocate*, August 1919, p. 24.

96. *The Advocate*, January 1910, p. 23.

97. *The Advocate*, September 1901, p. 18; *17th Convention (1918), Proceedings*, p. 24; August 1905, p. 108 ('Ethics of the Labor Movement'); also the president's address at the 11th Convention (*1903, Proceedings*, p. 1f.; note 92 above).

98. *The Advocate*, September 1919, p. 11f.; cf. also March 1918, p. 14 for the AFL demand for free access to education and training for everyone.

99. *The Advocate*, October 1914, p. 7; August 1916, p. 8f. On White's opposition to Gompers see R. Radosh, *American Labor and United States Foreign Policy*, New York 1969, p. 9.

100. In a satirical gloss 'Bol-she-veek!' (*The Advocate*, May 1919, p. 27).

101. E.g. *The Advocate*, February 1920, p. 17: 'Labor stands Firm Against Red Agitators'; on the whole subject: R. K. Murray, *Red Scare. A Study of National Hysteria 1919-1920*, New York 1964.

102. On the basis of Table 2.4, the table in note 103 and Hutchinson, pp. 79, 99, 122, 160, 202.

103. From Hutchinson, pp. 124-31, 161-63, 204-206; p. 77 on the use of the white labor force as a reference point after 1890. Because of slight changes in occupational categories 1890-1920 these figures are not exactly comparable. The figures in brackets may be compared with each other, but only within limits with the series before them. In 1910 and 1920 the category 'salesmen/women' was restricted to those in retail trade, for the preceding years it also included some from other fields. 'Cotton mill operatives' includes only unskilled and semi-skilled operatives; in 1910 and 1920 the category includes all unskilled and semi-skilled textile workers. Based on ibid. and pp. 101-105: Underrepresentation of immigrants among salesmen and saleswomen in the US 1870-1920:

	1870	1880	1890	1900	1910	1920
Salesmen	94	98	64	66	65	67
Saleswomen	94	71	45	55	47	52

104. Cf. *Historical Statistics*, p. 60f: Of the 448,600 immigrants in 1900, 2,400 were registered as 'professional, technical and kindred workers', 54,800 as skilled and 164,200 as unskilled workers (excluding agriculture). Expressed as a percentage of the number in these occupational categories in the US in the same year: 'professional, technical and kindred workers' 0.19%, 'clerical, sales and kindred workers' only 0.13%, skilled workers 1.78% and unskilled 4.5% (ibid., pp. 60f., 75ff.).

105. E. B. Butler, *Saleswomen in Mercantile Stores*, Baltimore 1909, p. 143f. Cf. also Hower, p. 199 on Macy's (New York) in the 1870s: '...the racial stock was almost exclusively Nordic'; ibid., p. 383: reference to greater ethnic heterogeneity of the store's personnel around 1910, when despite (reportedly) many complaints from customers, black elevator operators were hired. Hiring policies in wholesale offices were probably even more ethnically conscious than in stores. Cf. (Reed), p. 79 on discrimination against a Canadian (French Canadian?) in an office which otherwise employed only white Protestant Americans. On the general problem see above all Higham, *Strangers*, esp. pp. 68ff.

106. From Hutchinson, pp. 172-75.

107. Cf. also McEwen, p. 42: He formulates this general impression with reference to the organization's leaders in the 1890s and suggests that these were mostly of rural origins, had frequently been independent or traveling, and took an active part in local clubs.

108. *12th Convention (1905), Proceedings*, pp. 68, 72f.; cf. McEwen, pp. 54f., 165; *The Advocate*, February 1915, p. 13 (praising new immigration's law literacy test); March 1915, p. 18 (criticism of Wilson's veto of this law); February 1899, p. 8: Opposition to the imperialistic schemes of the government to acquire foreign territory and to the entry of 'coolie labor'. On the general AFL stance toward the question of immigration, see Taft, *The AF of L*, pp. 302-308.

109. Cf. on the discriminatory membership policies of some trade unions (e.g. International Association of Machinists; Brotherhood of Railway and Steamship Clerks; Brotherhood of Railway Car Men) and the AFL leadership's inability to enforce this policy: Grob, *Workers*, pp. 152ff.; Taft, *The AF of L*, pp. 308-19; H. R. Northrup, *Organized Labor and the Negro*, New York 1944, esp. p. 10f.

110. *The Advocate*, July/August 1901, p. 24; McEwen, p. 250.

111. Cf. *The Advocate*, May/June 1931, p. 20 (Arecibo local).

112. Cf. *12th Convention (1905), Proceedings*, p. 43f.; *1st Convention (1891), Proceedings*, p. 23: for factory inspection legislation and the extension of state investigations to the situation of clerks; Kirstein, p. 21 on the RCIPA demand in 1899 for a federal law prohibiting Sunday work; *11th Convention (1903), Proceedings*, p. 9: against compulsory arbitration; *13th Convention (1907), Proceedings*, p. 42 for support of the AFL 'Bill of Grievances' of 1906. *The Advocate*, November 1914, pp. 7ff. for a minimum wage for women; on the other hand ibid., January 1914, pp. 7ff. for one of the numerous arguments in favor of improved earnings through trade union organization and collective bargaining instead of through unreliable legislation.

In German mercantile assistant organizations' efforts to win better working conditions the main push was for legal regulation. There were only faint beginnings of an early closing movement like that of England or the US (e.g. 1868/69 in Berlin), but in contrast earlier, stronger, and more successful agitation for legislation to achieve that purpose. Cf. Oldenberg, 'Die heutige Lage', pp. 760-67.

113. Cf. Kocka, I, p. 374f., note 128a.

114. *2nd Convention (1892), Proceedings*, p. 12; *The Advocate* February 1908, p. 15; *13th Convention (1907), Proceedings*, p. 40.

115. *The Advocate*, October 1918, p. 16; *11th Convention (1903), Proceedings*, p. 7.

116. Around the turn of the century every male member paid 25 cents a month, every female 12½ cents; at the latest after 1903 the Convention set 50 cents for men, 25 cents for women as a monthly minimum, but for fear of discouraging members various locals continued to require less. Cf. *12th Convention (1905), Proceedings*, p. 39; per year and member every local sent at first 60 cents, after 1898 $1, and after 1905 $3 to the national union. Cf. *The Advocate* September 1907, p. 88. After 1900 death benefits, after 1905 sickness benefits were paid, primarily to make the union more attractive to potential members. Cf. McEwen, pp. 262ff.

117. The Commerce Code of 1891 strengthened the relevant sections of the 1861 Code (Allgemeines Deutschen Handelsgesetzbuch). Monthly salary payment, six weeks paid sick leave, termination notice of at least one month (as a rule six weeks) were legal rights which most blue collar workers did not enjoy. The Salaried Employees Insurance Law of 1911 expanded and solidified the legal distinction between blue collar and white collar.

118. Cf. above, p. 50 for the gradual extension of protective legislation for women and children which at first applied only to factories; cf. *The Advocate*, March 1907, p. 16: The RCIPA wished to be included in the Workman's Compensation Act.

119. Cf. *The Advocate*, May 1907, p. 5 on unpaid overtime; ibid., March 1906, p. 13: a day's absence was frequently deducted from the weekly wage in small town or country stores.

120. The *Thirty-Third Annual Report of the Massachusetts Bureau of Statistics of Labor*, Boston 1903, pp. 83-129 reported the weekly earnings of 'salesmen' in mercantile firms in selected businesses in the city of Boston, 1902 (in $):

	Maximum	Mean	Minimum
Boots and Shoes	57.50	30	14
Cigars, Cigarettes	20	13	5
Men's Clothing	60	33	5
Women's Clothing	35	20	10
Household Goods	34.62	18	3.00
Department Stores	35.00	20.00	4.50
Wallpaper	28.85	20.00	10.00
Dry Goods	26.00	16.00	6.00
Florists	25.00	18.00	10.00
Foodstuffs	60.00	36.00	6.00
Millinery	45.00	25.00	4.50
Jewelers	57.69	32.69	7.02
Liquors	30.00	18.00	8.00
Apothecary	60.00	10.00	6.00
Toys	38.00	22.50	5.00

121. From ibid. (Survey of 455 businesses with a total of 1,988 employees, of which 959 were men); *Thirty-Fifth Annual Report...*, Boston, 1905, pp. 3-17 for actual weekly earnings of skilled workers; cf. in a similar vein E. B. Gowin and W. A. Wheatley, *Occupations. A Textbook in Vocational Guidance*, Boston 1916,

pp. 66-97, 141-61, 221-44. The categories of 'clerks' and 'salesmen' are not clearly separated from each other. Most businesses reported their sales employees as 'salesmen'. Both categories can refer to wholesale employees also.

122. *Third Annual Report of the (Massachusetts) Bureau of Labor*, Boston 1872, pp. 66-91, 100-101.

123. *Thirty-Third Annual Report...*, pp. 83-129.

124. Cf. Butler, *Saleswomen*, pp. 104-20, which otherwise hardly paints a dismal picture, with excellent figures on the gradation of incomes. Cf. *The Advocate*, April 1903, p. 3: In Chicago a male clerk received $12, a female $5 weekly for the same number of hours.

125. From *The Advocate*, April 1916, pp. 5ff. 85% of those questioned said that they lived on their own earnings!

126. Cf. Butler, *Saleswomen*, p. 120. In 1890 13.5% of all working women in America were married; from *Historical Statistics*, p. 72.

127. Cf. Butler, *Saleswomen*, pp. 121, 132; on the general question see W. H. Chafe, *The American Woman. Her Changing Social, Economic and Political Roles, 1929-1970*, New York 1972, pp. 62-64.

128. Cf. also C. D. Wright, *The Working Girls of Boston*, Boston 1889, pp. 87, 92ff.; E. B. Butler, *Women and the Trades: Pittsburgh 1907-1908*, New York 1909, pp. 304ff. Cf. also the Wage Investigation of the New Orleans Chapter of the National Consumers' League (*Report to the Louisiana State Commission to Study the Conditions of Working Women and Children*, by S. M. Hartzmann) October 1914, pp. 15-23; Commonwealth of Massachusetts, *Report of the Commission on Minimum Wage Boards*, Boston 1912, pp. 113-14; further: L. Odencrantz and Z. L. Potter, *Industrial Conditions in Springfield, Illinois. A Survey by the Committee on Women's Work...*, New York 1916, pp. 8-68. Actual cases of misery are also described in F. Kelley, *Minimum Wage Boards*, New York 1911, p. 5 (on prevailing employer disregard for the modest legislation protecting women in existence). In contrast E. Ginzberg and H. Berman, *The American Worker in the Twentieth Century*, New York 1963, pp. 100-103 reprint a very satisfactory picture in the 'Salesgirl's Story' from *The Independent*, Vol. 54, No. 3, 1902, pp. 1818ff.; similarly R. W. Smuts, *Women and Work in America*, New York 1959, p. 94f. Cf. J. A. Riis, *How the Other Half Lives. Studies among the Tenements of New York* (1890), reprinted Cambridge, Mass. 1970, pp. 154-55; further, the publications of the Consumers' Leagues mentioned in note 38 above.

129. Cf. Smuts, pp. 21f., 94f.

130. Cf. *The Advocate*, April 1903, p. 3: In Chicago a male sales clerk earned $12 a week, for which in more than 34% of the businesses 74 hours were worked. A skilled worker received $24 for a 48 hour week, an unskilled worker 25c per hour (54 hour week). Cf. *12th Convention (1905), Proceedings*, p. 52.

131. Cf. McEwen, p. 42. The leaders of the RCIPA in 1914 had only grade school education (as far as sources reveal).

132. Cf. below, p. 167.

133. *Eighteenth Annual Report of the (Massachusetts) Bureau of Statistics of Labor*, Boston 1887, pp. 216ff.; see also Estey, 'Early Closing', p. 564 on Philadelphia in the 1830s. In Berlin around 1880 about 6% of the mercantile assistants were unemployed, which led to loud complaints, assemblies, and the establishment of a job referral program (Bücher, *Arbeiterfrage*, pp. 4-7).

134. This point should be emphasized, since this study does not aim at an explanation based solely on values and attitudes.

135. Cf. Gould, *Yankee Storekeeper*, pp. 25ff. for an example of a very unpatriarchal merchant-clerk relationship; similarly Horlick, pp. 73ff., 78, 82ff.; a series of articles in *The Advocate*, April 1908, pp. 16ff. and May 1908, p. 16f. on British shop assistants is also extremely revealing. The 'living-in system' of France

and England had to be explained to American readers, since it was unknown there!

136. Cf. *Hunt's Merchants' Magazine*, Vol. 19, 1948, p. 120: An English merchant recommended quasi-patriarchal methods of control to his American colleagues, among other points stricter regulation of the clerks' private lives. Horlick, pp. 260ff., who reports this, comments: this could not be instituted, for the American office was only there to transact business, not for education.

137. Cf. Higinbotham, esp. pp. 16, 28; F. Farrington, *Store Management — Complete*, Chicago 1911, pp. 113-35, 172-87; W. H. Baldwin, *Travelling Salesman*, Boston 1874.

138. Cf. J. R. Sprague, *The Middleman*, New York 1929, p. 28; a wholesale clerk after seven hours work took a 'night job in a retail hardware store' (at the end of the 19th century).

139. That did not mean that to a slight degree German mercantile assistants did not have part-time jobs. In 1908 3.5% of the DHV members surveyed stated that with the consent of their boss they had part-time work also (*Die wirtschaftliche Lage*, p. 84).

140. Cf. HGB, 59, 60, 62, 72, 76-83 (on responsibilities to the apprentice); cf. already the Commerce Code of 1861, Articles 57-65; 57 on the right of the apprentice to *Gehalt und Unterhalt* (compensation and maintenance).

141. From the surveys of the Kommission für Arbeiterstatistik: K. Oldenberg, 'Statistik der socialen Lage der deutschen Handlungsgehilfen', *Schmollers Jb.*, Jg. 17, 1893, pp. 1231-50, here p. 1246.

142. Hiller, p. 10; cf. also ibid., pp. 8, 74, 80.

143. Cf. ibid., p. 9; F. Ritter, *Zur Geschichte des Vereins der Handlungsgehilfen in Köln 1843-1893*, Köln 1893, p. 19.

144. On geographic mobility in general: Thernstrom, *The Other Bostonians*, pp. 29ff., 259f.; H. P. Chudacoff, *Mobile Americans. Residential and Social Mobility in Omaha, 1880-1920*, New York 1972; however, D. Crew, 'Definitions of Modernity. Social Mobility in a German Town 1880-1901', in *JSH*, Vol. 6, 1973, pp. 51-74, esp. p. 54f., found no significant differences between the migration rates in and out of Boston and Bochum around 1890. Cf. also D. Langewiesche, 'Wanderungsbewegungen in der Hochindustrialisierungsperiode. Regionale, interstädtische und innerstädtische Mobilität in Deutschland 1880-1914', in *VSWG*, Bd. 64, 1977, pp. 1-40, esp. p. 4.

145. Cf. Farrington, *Store Management*, p. 124; and Gibbons, Vol. 1, p. 207, on the rarity of a long career in the same store.

146. Cf. Consumers' League of the City of New York, *Annual Report 1912*, p. 10; Consumers' League of Oregon, *Report of the Social Survey Committee*, Portland 1913, p. 29.

147. *Handbuch zum Gebrauch beim Stellenwechsel* (Handbook for Use when Changing Jobs) (*Schriften des DHV*, No. 9), Hamburg n.d. (1908), pp. 50-55, esp. pp. 51, 52f.

148. *Thirty-Third Annual Report of the (Massachusetts) Bureau of Statistics of Labor*, Boston 1903, p. 83. On the significance of the monthly salary in distinguishing German white collar from German blue collar workers see Kocka, *Unternehmensverwaltung*, pp. 106ff., 110, 130f., 465, 502.

149. Cf. Butler, *Saleswomen*, p. 99: only a minority of the 60 stores surveyed in Baltimore in 1909 granted vacations.

150. Cf. *The Advocate*, January 1903, p. 3f.: many clerks were unwilling to join a union because it was 'beneath the dignity of many gentlemen clerks who draw salaries'. *The Advocate*, May 1902, p. 31: 'I hope women clerks will forgive me for calling them "wage-earners". We are all wage-earners outside the millionaire class, and there are very few of us who ever get enough per week to advance us into the "salarid" [sic!] class'.

151. Cf. Lange, *Die soziale Bewegung der Kaufmannischen Angestellten*, Berlin 1920, pp. 2-23; Kocka I, p. 379, note 171.

152. Cf. e.g. J. Hawes, *Lecture to Young Men on the Formation of Character*, Boston 1856,[2] p. 128.

153. Cf. *The Duties of Employers and Employed. Considered with Reference to Principals and their Clerks or Apprentices*, New York 1849.

154. Cf. Kocka I, p. 379f., note 175.

155. The YMCA was less interested in appropriate corporatist sociability and education than in propagating traditional puritan customs and values to new immigrants in the face of the appearance of social and cultural disintegration in the big cities. Cf. Horlick, pp. 197ff., 365; his conclusion that the YMCA was one of the new efforts by store owners to control and socialize their employees goes beyond the evidence he presents. C. H. Hopkins, *History of the YMCA in North America*, New York 1951. The New York YMCA was founded in 1852.

156. Hiller, p. 74, 80.

157. From the *Handbuch* (note 147 above), p. 51.

158. For Portland 1913: Consumers' League of Oregon, *Report*, p. 27; similarly for Pittsburgh 1909: Butler, *Women and Trades*, p. 307. Quoted from Butler, *Saleswomen*, p. 121 with reference to Baltimore in 1909.

159. Cf. also 'A Salesgirl's Story' (1902) in Ginzberg/Berman, pp. 100-103; she portrays her earlier occupation as one which permitted 'refinement and self-respect'; very similarly the interview in Smuts, p. 94f.

160. In 1890 twice as many girls as boys received a high school diploma, since they were more apt to be allowed to finish school while boys were usually sent to work (or to learn a trade) as early as possible. This behavior was not characteristic of better off Americans, however, who frequently sent their sons to private secondary schools and then to college; the number of male college graduates was four times greater than females in the same year. Cf. Smuts, pp. 49, 50.

161. *The Advocate*, January 1903, p. 3f.; January 1906, p. 11ff.; March 1906, p. 12f.

162. Retrospective by L. Nash in *The Advocate*, November/December 1930, p. 4; cf. along the same lines a memoir by Treasurer Morris in *The Advocate*, September 1904, p. 13f.; March 1902, p. 19; Kirstein, pp. 27, 106; *The Advocate*, February 1917, p. 19: 'To Which Class Do You Belong?'

163. Another source of tension was that as customers blue collar workers actually had no interest in early closing: cf. *12th Convention (1905), Proceedings*, pp. 39f., 45.

164. Although, as suggested, that was not completely absent. Cf. also Carson, p. 65; F. Hunt, *Lives of American Merchants*, Vol. 1, New York 1858, p. xli f.

165. Carson, p. 64; similarly on the early 19th century in the south: Atherton, p. 202; T. D. Clark, *Pills, Petticoats and Plows*, New York 1944, p. 27; on the tendency of the 'country boy' to go into sales positions: *Hunt's Merchants' Magazine*, Vol. 34, 1853, p. 647.

166. Cf. R. Hofstadter, *The Age of Reform. From Bryan to FDR*, New York, 1955, pp. 23-59; L. G. Wyllie, *The Self-Made Man in America. The Myth of Rags to Riches*, New York 1954; M. Rischin (ed.), *The American Gospel of Success*, Chicago 1968; C. Cochran, 'The History of a Business Society', in *JAH*, Vol. 54, 1967, pp. 5-18; L. Galambos, *The Public Image of Big Business in America, 1880-1940*, Baltimore 1975.

167. A New York office employee wrote in 1877: 'The position of an employee must, in the nature of things, be somewhat irksome to one who has passed the age of boyhood, if he has any sensitiveness or pride'. The disgrace of the position of a 'hireling' was only slightly diminished by close relationships with the boss. (Reed), p. 87f.

168. The entrepreneurial character of the salesman's position was very clear in the case of the commercial traveller or drummer of the 19th century. He was admired by the village children (cf. Sprague, p. 45; and Ginzberg/Berman, p. 182), but the office employee as such was not.

169. *The Advocate*, November 1905, p. 12; *12th Convention (1905), Proceedings*, p. 39; *The Advocate*, December 1901, p. 11; September 1902, p. 7f; November 1906, p. 18f.; *13th Convention (1907), Proceedings*, p. 40; *The Advocate*, April 1903, p. 2f.: 'No, the clerk of today is not a merchant of tomorrow, but the merchants' sons or the stockholders' sons of today are the merchants of tomorrow'; similarly, November 1917, pp. 7ff.

170. From St. Lebergott, *Manpower in Economic Growth*, New York 1964, pp. 514, 516; and *Statistik des Deutschen Reichs*, Bd. 111, p. 146f.; Bd. 202, p. 17f.; Bd. 402, I, p. 240; Bd. 458, pp. 28 and 30; Bd. 556, I, p. 8. The German figures should even be lower, by about 1-2%; in contrast to the American figures they also include managing officials and employees.

171. Cf. Hotchkin, p. 211: *The Advocate*, August 1914, p. 12: 'Competition is like the weather, it's different on different days, but it's always with us. The man who fears the weather is sure to catch cold.' *The Advocate*, January 1908, p. 17: '...the employer is a good deal like all the rest of us: He looks out for "number one". He consults his own interests first, and does what he considers is best for his business, rather than what might be considered best for his unprofitable clerks.' This was approved. A former salesman reported on the practice of his first boss (at a retail store in Boston): 'Every day the name of the leading clerk was posted, an honor based on the total of the sales he had made yesterday.' (M. P. Gould, *Where Have My Profits Gone?*, Elmira, NY 1912, p. 29).

172. Cf. *The Advocate*, February 1906, pp. 11ff.: 'Your job should be a stepping-stone to a higher one.' 'Aspire!' August 1914, p. 12: 'In every walk of life, strength comes from effort. It is the habit of self-denial which gives the advantage to the man we call self-made.' 'Business is warfare. It's a hard, constant fight to the finish.' 'Put up with hard times in a manly way and they will soon be over.' 'If there are any obstacles in your way which prevent you from advancing yourself, never get discouraged and nervous, but meet them boldly and they will pass away and your way will be clear.' Cf. further Higinbotham, p. 17; *The Advocate*, February 1914, p. 25: 'The Good Clerk' for emphasis on individualism.

173. Cf. C. Holman, *Ginger Talks; The Talks of a Sales Manager to his Men*, Chicago 1908, p. 13: 'You are in this business to make money. So is the company.' Ibid., pp. 44-46. 'Selling goods is a battle, and only fighters can win out in it. We may not like these conditions, but we didn't have the making of them and we can't alter them. They are Nature's laws...Kites always rise against the wind, not with it...Courageous men...glory in manly strife...The world in general loves a fighter and hates a quitter. It takes off its head to the man who dares...All other men it tramples on...No man ever made a three-base hit who was afraid of the pitcher — remember that...Believe that under the guise of a polite interview you are going to have A FIGHT.' Ibid., p. 113: 'But business is business. It takes live men to get orders — we can't carry dead weight and get ahead.' Employers wanted 'a salesman who has a record as a business getter — an aspiring young chap, nervous as a thoroughbred horse, and overflowing with spirit and energy.' Ibid., p. 76: the sales process is like a walk through a dynamite factory; '...the slightest misstep is likely to blow you out through the roof.'

174. Ibid., p. 22f.

175. *The Advocate*, May 1914, p. 12; *Prospectus* 1892; *The Advocate*, January 1903, p. 4; January 1906, p. 16.

176. *The Advocate*, January 1914, p. 13.

177. Cf. T. W. Arnold, *The Folklore of Capitalism*, New Haven 1937; M. H. Bloomfield, *Alarms and Divisions. The American Mind through an American*

Magazine 1900-1914, The Hague 1967; J. G. Cawelti, *Apostles of the Self-Made Man*, Chicago 1965;. S. Chase, *American Credos*, New York 1962; Hofstadter, *Social Darwinism*; N. J. Karolides, *The Pioneer in the American Novel 1900-1950*, Norman 1967; R. B. Nye, *This Almost Chosen People*, East Lansing 1966; Rischin, *The American Gospel*; F. X. Sutton et al., *The American Business Creed*, Cambridge, Mass. 1956; Weiss, *The American Myth of Success: From Horatio Alger to Norman Vincent Peale*, New York 1969; Wyllie.

178. From the maxim: 'Don't talk about bad luck. Nine to one it is one of your weaknesses that holds you back. Bad luck is nearly always only a lack of enterprise'. (*The Advocate*, March 1904, p. 19).

179. On the hopes for independence among German shop assistants cf. e.g. R. Engelsing, 'Die wirtschaftliche und soziale Differenzierung der deutschen kaufmännischen Angestellten im In- und Ausland, 1690-1900 (1967)', in ibid., *Zur Sozialgeschichte deutscher Mittel- und Unterschichten*, Göttingen 1973, pp. 51-111 for before 1850; Hiller, p. 10 (1890). In 1910 the DHV: 'Shop assistants for the most part have given up the hope of independence'; in the same breath the 'corporation of shop assistants' who must avoid proletarianization (*Die wirtschaftliche Lage*, p. 136). Each year (1903-1908) about 1% of DHV members became independent (ibid., p. 129).

180. *The Advocate*, January 1909, p. 30; September 1914, p. 11; February 1916, p. 8.

181. Cf. also on the following J. W. Fisk, *Salesmanship. A Textbook on Retail Selling*, New York 1914, pp. 5-13: 'Salesmanship a Profession'; ibid., *Retail Selling. A Guide to the Best Modern Practice*, New York, 1916; A. W. Douglas, *Travelling Salesmanship,* New York 1919, pp. 4-9; M. Sumner, *Chats on Garment Salesmanship*, Cleveland, Ohio 1917, pp. 5-11; H. E. Selecman, *The General Agent or Methods of Sales Organization and Management*, Chicago 1910; W. T. Goffe, *Problems in Retail Selling Analyzed*, n.p. 1913; H. Whitehead, *Principles of Salesmanship*, New York 1917.

182. Cf. on this above, pp. 42-54 and Haber.

183. Cf. *The Advocate*, September 1914, p. 11.

184. Cf. *The Advocate*, February 1916, p. 8f.

185. Cf. B. R. Haynes and H. P. Jackson, *A History of Business Education in the United States*, Cincinnati, 1935, pp. 26-73 (figures ibid., pp. 26, 37, 65f.); Roman, *The Industrial and Commercial Schools*, pp. 244-63; E. J. James, *Education for Business Men, III: A Plea for the Establishment of Commercial High Schools*, New York 1893.

186. Cf. Haynes/Jackson, pp. 83-96; J. H. Bossard and J. F. Dewhurst, *University Education for Business*, Philadelphia 1931; W. B. Donham, 'The Unfolding of Collegiate Business Training', in *Harvard Graduates' Magazine*, March 1921, pp. 333-47; interesting comparative references in F. Redlich, 'Academic Education for Business', in *BHR*, Vol. 31, 1957, pp. 35-91, reprinted in ibid., *Steeped in Two Cultures*, New York 1971; courses in 'salesmanship' appear to have gradually appeared only after 1910. Cf. W. A. Scott, 'Training for Business at the University of Wisconsin', in *The Journal of Political Economy*, Vol. 21, 1913, pp. 127-35, here p. 131; *The Advocate*, February 1916, p. 8.

187. Cf. e.g. Farrington, *Store Management*, p. 132; Gould, *Where Have My Profits Gone*?, p. 204f.

188. Wanamaker's Department store in Philadelphia had the beginnings of continuing education for its sales personnel after 1878, and an institutionalized 'store school' after 1890. Cf. Gibbons, Vol. 1, pp. 284ff.; The Filene Co-operative Association, *Business Course*, n.p. (Boston) 1916, esp. pp. 4-110: A. L . Filene on the history of the store; T. Mahoney and L. Sloane, *The Great Merchants*, New York 1966, p. 241; Sears and Roebuck began its educational program in 1904.

189. *The Advocate*, September 1914, p. 11; February 1916, p. 8; Sumner, *Chats*, pp. 5-11.

190. Cf. above, note 12.

191. Cf. above, pp. 42-54.

192. The professional qualities mentioned for the ideal sales person did not appear in the older sources, which were much more clearly oriented to the entrepreneurial model.

193. As in the arguments of drug store owners against the trade union organization of 'drug clerks'; cf. *The Advocate*, July 1902, p. 2; July 1915, p. 13.

194. Cf. above, pp. 11ff.

195. Cf. *Seventh Annual Report of the (Massachusetts) Bureau of Statistics of Labor*, Boston 1876, p. 3.

196.

> Although most of the salaried officers and employees are paid by the week or the month, and most wage earners on a per diem or a piece-price basis, the distinction between the two classes depends primarily on the character of work done rather than on the unit of time used in calculating rates of pay. In general, office employees are classified as 'salaried officers and employees', and factory workers as 'wage earners', while factory superintendents and foremen are treated as salaried employees if not engaged in manual labor and as wage earners if they perform manual labor in addition to their supervisory duties. (US Bureau of the Census, *Biennial Census of Manufactures 1925*, Washington 1928, p. 1193).

This definition was followed in principle after 1899. Similarly, ibid., 1929, Vol. 1 (Washington 1933), p. 4f. Cf. Delehanty, pp. 24-57; Fabricant, *Employment*, pp. 171-230; J. Kendrick, *Productivity Trends in the United States*, Princeton 1961, pp. 433-50.

197. Cf. Hartfiel, pp. 16-27, 52-74. Cf. the last note and the *Seventh Annual Report of the (Massachusetts) Bureau of Statistics of Labor*, Boston 1876, p. 205: a list of the occupations which counted as 'salaried persons'.

198. A rough overview in R. Bendix, *Work and Authority in Industry*, New York 1956; Delehanty, Appendix, Table A-2.

199. The figures are estimates based on census data, made by Fabricant (*Employment*) and Kuznets (*National Income*), used by Delehanty, Appendix, Table A-1 (there also *BLSt* estimates which differ slightly). For the years before 1919 no other series is available. P. H. Douglas (*Real Wages in the United States, 1890-1926*, Boston 1930, pp. 219, 359) comes to similar conclusions using the same material. His information for 1889 is unreliable (cf. ibid., p. 358).

200. It is, however, possible that this difference is a result of statistical methods: the American census ignored the smallest manufacturers, while the German did not. Before 1919 all firms producing goods valued at less than $500, after that less than $5,000, were excluded. Cf. Fabricant, *Employment*, pp. 217ff., 230.

201. 1895 from *Statistik des Dt. Reiches, N.F.*, Bd. 102/03, pp. 7-14, 102-10; Bd. 111, p. 61. 1907 ibid., Bd. 202, pp. 8, 14f.; Bd. 203, p. 2f. 1925 from ibid., Bd. 402, p. 221f.; Bd. 408, p. 110; Bd. 453, p. 30; Bd. 556, p. 2. The figures are the difference between the total number minus the number in mining, etc. and construction. *Beamte* are included. Through territorial changes and changes in the definition of categories the figures are not exactly comparable.

202. Cf. above the excellent discussion in Bendix, *Work and Authority*, Ch. 4. The problematic nature of many of the current assumptions about the causes of the growth in the proportion of white collar workers in industry and the difficulties involved in weighting the various causes (which probably also vary over time) are demonstrated in the special investigation by Delehanty, who treats the subject from

purely economic perspectives and discusses older literature on the problem.

203. Cf. the detailed description and analysis of this matter in Kocka, *Unternehmensverwaltung*, pp. 254-311, 463-513; G. Schulz, *Die Arbeiter und Angestellten bei Felten & Guilleaume*, Wiesbaden 1979.

204. Description from A. C. Show, 'T.-H.': or 'Among the Dynamo Builders of Lynn', in *The Electrical Engineer*, 29 June 1892, pp. 647-60, esp. pp. 655-57.

205. From the *Schenectady Electrical Handbook*, Schenectady, NY 1904, in General Electric Company, Main Library, Schenectady (henceforth cited as GEC) File L 2037, 13f., 3f.

206. Cf. W. H. Wakeman, 'The Management of Men in Mill and Factories', in *The Engineering Magazine*, Vol.8, New York 1894/95, pp. 48-53, esp. p. 51: 'Some of the officers who are lower down in the scale' apparently view it as beneath their dignity to greet the workers on the street. In *The NCR*, National Cash Register Company's magazine (Dayton, Ohio), 15 March 1904:

> At our recent large meeting, a young man from the recording forces was heard to make some unpleasant remarks about the men in the factory who were sitting near him. When this was brought to our attention, we had the man from the factory go through the offices and identify this young man and bring him up to our office. He admitted having made these remarks and was instantly told to go down, get his pay and get right out. I was glad that this was done, because such actions are outrageous. These workingmen about whom he was making remarks were perhaps making twice or three times the money that this young fellow was earning, but the class of work they were doing did not permit them to wear as good clothes.

As interesting as the antagonism itself is the effort of management to punish and end it.

207. 'Welfare Work for Employees in Industrial Establishments in the United States' (*BLSt., Bulletin*, No. 250), Washington 1919, pp. 53-55, 57-58, 73, 76; cf., however, C. M. Ripley, *Life in a Large Manufacturing Plant*, Schenectady, NY 1919, pp. 98-101, on the much better equipped white collar restaurant compared to the factory workers' canteen.

208. Cf. above, pp. 68ff., esp. Table 2.4, and below, p. 83.

209. 'Welfare Work for Employees', p. 55.

210. Thus W. A. Wykoff, *The Workers. An Experiment in Reality: The West*, New York 1899, pp. 147ff. on a factory in Chicago.

211. From W. Williams, *What's on the Worker's Mind?*, New York 1920, pp. 33, 51, 57, 59, 67, 142, 179, 181, 203 (report of a personnel manager who was a helper at many factories in the midwest in early 1919). Cf. also GEC, File E, 184 (Recollections of H.F.T. Erben): the foreman did the hiring at the factory door of the Edison Machine Works around 1890. Similarly, T. Hareven, 'The Laborers of Manchester, New Hampshire, 1912-1922', in *LH*, Vol. 16, 1975, pp. 249-65, here p. 256f.

212. On this see Kocka, *Unternehmensverwaltung*, p. 339f.

213. Cf. examples in Wyckoff, p. 156f.; Williams, *Worker's Mind*, pp. 53, 62, 225. Among the laborers that Williams worked with, he was usually the only native born American (pp. 188, 256). On the proportion of immigrants among foremen see Table 2.4 above; cf. also Hareven, p. 262 on the possible functions of ethnic uniformity between foremen and workers.

214. Williams, *Worker's Mind*, pp. 165f., 184.

215. From 1889-92 the factory at the Edison works in Schenectady worked from 7-12 and 12.30-5.30; the offices from 7.30-12 and 1-5.30. Both closed Saturday at 4.30. GEC, File E, 174 (Recollections of H. L. Baltozer and E. J. Berggren). In 1913 in a Boston evening school for women, 349 worked in offices, 230 in factories, and

103 in sales establishments. 33½% of the office employees, 4.8% of the factory workers, and 5.8% of the saleswomen worked less than eight hours a day. Less than nine hours: 89.4% of the office, 94.1 of sales, but only 59.6% of the factory workers. From M. Allison, *The Public Schools and Women in Office Service*, Boston 1914, p. 51.

216. Cf. above, pp. 92-93 on the definition of 'salary receivers' in 1876. Vacation was a very frequent perquisite. In 1914, according to a Boston survey, about 90% of those questioned — all young female office employees (not only in industry, also banking, etc) — had a paid vacation of at least one week. From Allison, pp. 102, 108. At GE, in this respect a progressive company, factory workers had paid vacations only after 1917. Cf. H. R. Northrup, *Boulwarism. The Labor Relations Politics of the General Electric Company*, Ann Arbor 1964, p. 10; cf. I. M. Tarbell, *New Ideals in Business*, New York 1916, p. 97f.: around 1900 paid vacations for 'men outside the office' were the absolute exception.

217. Cf. Allinson, p. 110f.: The average lost (around 1912) through deductions for female office employees was 8.25%, for saleswomen 13.05% and for factory workers 18.43% (female).

218. Cf. Williams, *Worker's Mind*, p. 294f. On the limits of this security see below, p. 130f.

219. The course of weekly or daily real wages (without salaries), 1913 100 (from Bry, p. 466f.):

	1890	1895	1900	1905	1910	1913
Germany	87	89	98	98	99	100
US	78	80	86	91	96	100

220 Cf. Kocka, *Unternehmensverwaltung*, p. 492 and Table 2-10.

221. Unfortunately, figures for industry as a whole are not available for Germany. On the declining distance between salaries and wages in one firm: Kocka, *Unternehmensverwaltung*, pp. 490-94.

222. Nominal earnings from Douglas, *Real Wages*, pp. 246, 361, 364, primarily based on the Census of Manufactures. Douglas calculated the average yearly earnings by dividing the total yearly wages and salaries paid by companies by the number of blue collar and white collar workers employed (data supplied by companies). The Census of Manufactures was taken in 1889, then every five years from 1899 to 1919 and every two years between 1919 and 1939. Other series, partly over the earnings of some occupational groups, partly over earnings in individual economic branches (railroads) and over salaries in the statistics of some states, were used by Douglas to extrapolate the figures for years between censuses. Cf. Douglas, *Real Wages*, pp. 73-94, 217-31, 358-62. The figures for the 1890s are less reliable than later figures. Cost of Living Index from A. Rees, *Real Wages in Manufacturing, 1890-1914*, Princeton 1961, p. 4; Lebergott, *Manpower*, p. 523.

223. Periods of stagnation/recession in the US: 1893-96, 1903/04, 1907/08, 1910/11. Cf. Hession/Sardy, p. 536f.

224. This process may be followed from contemporary special literature. Cf. F. N. Doubleday et al., *Accounting and Office Methods*, Chicago 1910, esp. pp. 1-14; J. W. Schulze, *The American Office. Its Organization, Management, and Records*, New York 1913; H. J. Barrett, *Modern Methods in the Office*, New York 1918; W. H. Leffingwell (ed.), *Making the Office Pay*, Chicago 1918, and many others. Cf. Allinson (1914), pp. 92ff. on the impact of mechanization on working relationships in the office.

225. From A. W. Edwards, *Comparative Occupation Statistics*, pp. 112, 129 (Edwards' calculations and estimates on the basis of the yearly census figures). On the office for men: B. Bliven, Jr., *The Wonderful Writing Machine*, New York 1954, pp. 6-8, 70 (photograph of a GE office in 1882). Generally on the feminization of the office: 'Women's Jobs. Advance and Growth' (*Bulletin of the Women's Bureau*, No. 232), Washington 1949, pp. 12ff.; J. Hill, *Women in Gainful Occupations, 1870-1920* (Census Monograph No. 9), Washington, DC 1929.

226. With reference to the category 'designers, draftsmen and inventors', from Edwards, pp. 111, 128.

227. These figures from a thorough investigation of Boston conditions in Allinson, pp. 122, 165f. (age, family status), 1-9, 36, 126, 128, 136 (education), 47 (ethnic composition), on this also above, Table 2.4.

228. For a comparison of female sales clerks and other occupational groups, see Table 2.6 above; Allinson, p. 118 (survey of 509 clerks), 83s (comparing their position in factory offices), pp. 113-39 (more information on levels of and factors determining earnings).

229. Cf. Bliven, pp. 8, 74; (D. Richardson), *The Long Day. The Story of a New York Working Girl. As Told by Herself*, New York 1905, pp. 268-73: the story of a woman who managed by attending evening school courses to climb into office work. M. Davies, 'Woman's Place', esp. pp. 12ff. on the changing ideologies which accompanied the entry of women into office work. On the differences between working conditions in offices compared to selling and factory work cf. Allinson, pp. 101ff. (less turnover), 102 (vacations), 105ff. (hours), 108, 110f. (fewer deductions), 107f. (good sanitary conditions), 111f. (high prestige).

230. Figures on earnings and minimum existence: ibid., pp. 113f., 118; comparative figures for men: Bliven, p. 78 (unfortunately without source); on segregation at the workplace, lower pay for women for the same work, and the ideologies to justify it: Chafe, pp. 60ff.; as well as above, p. 102f.

231. From *Historical Statistics*, pp. 202, 214. On the development of the public high school: R. Hofstadter and C. de Witt Hardy, *The Development and Scope of Higher Education in the United States*, New York 1952, pp. 31ff.

232. J. J. Sheppard, 'The Place of the High School in Commercial Education' and 'The Boston High School of Commerce' in *Journal of Political Economy*, Vol. 31, 1913, pp. 209-42; Allinson, p. 12; p. 9; a curriculum from such a school (often two-year).

233. From US Bureau of Education, *Report of the Commissioner of Education, 1899-1900*, p. 2447, cited from Allinson, p. 9. The difference between 100% were in high schools, teachers' colleges and academies. Very informative on the development of business schools: Roman, pp. 244-63.

234. US Commissioner of Labor, *17th Annual Report: Trade and Technical Education*, Washington 1912, pp. 13ff. compares European and American technical education with this result; similarly Roman, p. 158. German technical and commercial schooling came up frequently as a model in the lively American discussion of this question after the 1890s. Cf. e.g. Massachusetts Commission on Industrial Education, *Bulletin*, No. 10 (*Report on the Relations of European Industrial Schools to Labor*, by C. H. Winslow), Boston 1908, pp. 15-17.

235. Massachusetts Board of Education, *34th Annual Report (1869-70)*, Boston 1870, pp. 134-59, 163-217; cf. also above, Table 2.4: Draftsmen and technicians were the only white collar groups with an overrepresentation of immigrants (1890).

236. On this and on the reform ideas, industrial interests, and in part also social conservative ideologies behind it: Fisher, *Industrial Education*, pp. 72-84; US Commissioner of Labor, *8th Annual Report: Industrial Education*, Washington 1893, pp. 24-79 for a good but not complete survey of this government supported move-

ment and of the mechanical and industrial schools which often taught the fundamentals of technical drawing and bookkeeping in addition to manual skills.

237. A survey in ibid., pp. 79-112 under the title 'Trade and Technical Schools'. Examples: Drexel-Institute in Philadelphia (1892); New York Trade Schools (1881); Ohio Mechanics Institute (1828, one of the oldest), Technical Drawing School of Providence (1887), Art and Drawing School/St Louis (1876).

238. The next report of the US Commissioner of Labor (*17th Annual Report*, Washington 1902) to deal with this problem distinguished in contrast to the 1893 Report between 'trade schools' (preparation for factory work) and 'technical schools' (which taught the application of theory and science to specific trades) (pp. 9-12).

239. Cf. US Commissioner of Labor, *8th Annual Report*, Washington 1893, p. 132: In 1890 it had 174 students.

240. Description from ibid., pp. 132-39; C. R. Mann, *A Study of Engineering Education. Prepared for the Joint Committee on Engineering Education of the National Engineering Societies*, New York 1918, pp. 3-26. The figures are from ibid., p. 6f. They seem to be based on rather broad definitions and to be rather high. D. Wolfe (*America's Resources of Specialized Talent*, New York 1954, p. 294) estimates only 12,400 engineering graduates for 1901-10. But he has no figures for earlier decades.

241. German figures from: *Berichte aus dem Gebiete des technischen Hochschulwesens (Abhandlungen und Berichte über technisches Schulwesen*, Bd. 4), Hg. v. Dt. Ausschuss f. Technisches Schulwesen, Leipzig 1912, Anlage 2; G. Hohorst et al., *Sozialgeschichtliches Arbeitschbuch. Materialien zur Statistik des Kaiserreichs 1870-1914*, München 1975, p. 161. For a sketch of the institutional development: P. Lundgreen, 'Industrialization and the Educational Formation of Manpower in Germany', in *JSH*, Vol. 9, 1975/76, pp. 64-80 (with further literature). American figures according to Mann, *Study*, p. 6.

242. Cf. Roman, pp. 28-29; on unemployment and the related proclamations of German technicians: R. Woldt, *Das großindustrielle Beamtentum*, Stuttgart 1911, pp. 105ff. The oversupply of engineers in Germany seemed shocking to observers in the US who were not yet threatened by such a danger. Cf. M. A. Calvert, *The Mechanical Engineer in America 1830-1910*, Baltimore 1967, pp. 58-60.

243. Wolfle, *America's Resources*, p. 294. The German technical universities in the decade 1901-10 had an average enrollment of 9,500 students per year (students defined in the narrowest possible sense, excluding *Hörer* and architecture students). It is safe and probably over-conservative to assume that 50% of them passed their final examinations, sooner or later. The average duration of studies was three to four years. This would make for an annual average of 1,250 to 15,000 graduations (*Diplom*), but these are minimum figures.

244. Cf. J. Kocka, 'Bildung, soziale Schichtung und soziale Mobilität im Deutschen Kaiserreich. Am Beispiel der gewerblich-technischen Ausbildung', in B. J. Wendt and P.-C. Witt (eds), *Industrielle Gesellschaft und politisches System*, Bonn 1978, pp. 297-313.

245. Cf. Max Weber's analysis of bureaucracy, in ibid., *Economy and Society. An Outline of Interpretive Sociology*, New York 1968, pp. 956-1005. O. Hintze's analysis of the history of civil servants, in O. Hintze, 'Der Beamtenstand', in ibid., *Soziologie und Geschichte. Gesammelte Abhandlungen zur Soziologie und Geschichte*, Göttingen 1964², pp. 66-125; English translation in F. Gilbert (ed.), *The Historical Essays of Otto Hintze*, New York 1975. H. Rosenberg, *Bureaucracy, Aristocracy, and Autocracy. The Prussian Experience 1660-1815*, Cambridge, Mass. 1958.

245a. Cf. P. Ziertmann, *Das Berechtigungswesen, Handbuch für das Berufs- und Fachschulwesen* (ed.), A. Kühne, Leipzig 1929², pp. 571-605; Lundgreen, *In-*

dustrialization; F. K. Ringer, *Education and Society in Modern Europe*, Bloomington and London 1979.

246. Cf. e.g. US Commissioner of Labor, *17th Annual Report (Trade and Technical Education)*, Washington 1902, p. 871; Fisher, *Industrial Education*, p. 67; Roman, pp. 261-365ff.; *Labor Bulletin of the Commonwealth of Massachusetts*, prepared by the Bureau of Labor, No. 33 (September 1904), pp. 237-62. On the temporal precedence of private over government bureaucracies in the US: A. D. Chandler, Jr. and L. Galambos, 'The Development of Large-Scale Economic Organization in Modern America', in *JEH*, Vol. 30, 1970, pp. 205-17.

246a. Cf. Roman, pp. 1-23; M. Bloomfield, *The Vocational Guidance of Youth*, Boston 1911, p. 20 on the 'unemployables'; ibid. (ed.), *Readings in Vocational Guidance*, Boston 1915, pp. 234ff., 172ff.

247. Cf. above all the opinions of the VDI expert C. Matschoss, *Die geistigen Mittel des technischen Fortschritts in den Vereinigten Staaten von Amerika. Bericht*...Berlin 1913, pp. 4f., 7f., 37f.; A. P. M. Fleming and J. G. Pearce, *The Principles of Apprentice Training with Special Reference to the Engineering Industry*, London 1916, pp. 4-13, 45, 101.

248. Thus H. Kaelble, 'Soziale Mobilität in den USA und Deutschland 1900-1960. Ein vergleichender Forschungsbericht', in ibid (ed.), *Geschichte der sozialen Mobilität seit der industriellen Revolution*, Königstein/Ts. 1978, pp. 109-25, here pp. 113-15, 117-20 (on the basis of available mobility studies).

249. Cf. e.g. B. P. Monroe, 'Possibilities of the Present Industrial System', in *AJS*, Vol. 3, 1898, pp. 729-53 (admiring description of 'industrial relations', at the NCR). The rather uncritical biography of the founder was apparently based on archival materials from the firm: S. Crowther, *John H. Patterson, Pioneer in Industrial Welfare*, Garden City 1926.

250. Apart from the predominantly female typing division (157 women), female employees made up between 2.5% and 10% of the office employees; (all of them belonged to the category of 'clerical help'). Compiled from: *National Cash Register Factory, Dayton, Ohio, USA. As Seen by English Experts*...by Alfred A. Thomas (General Counsel and Secretary of the Corporation), n.p. (Dayton) 1904, pp. 35-41.

251. The grounds for selection were not specified; apparently the Employment Department chose these. But since the survey was made public, in view of the 'responsive' personnel administrative style of this firm the decision may also have reflected popular opinion at NCR about the 'top 50'.

252. Sources as in note 250 above, pp. 44-62. It does not say whether each man's schooling was with or without degree.

253. These were mostly private, two-year commercial colleges or business colleges; also, however, an agricultural college and a normal school (where mostly commercial subjects were taught). None had additional technical education of this level.

254. These included additional education in a 'manual training school' (in the president's case), several years attending commercial-trade evening school courses in three cases (among others in the case of the director of the European division of the company), commercial colleges and business colleges.

255. The source spoke of district schools, grade schools, and grammar schools; as a rule the number of school years was not apparent.

256. The source presents 50 persons. I exclude one — the oldest (72) — who as self-taught inventor does not appear to have had white collar status. Ibid., p. 61f.

257. The first jobs of a few cases, as helpers on their fathers' farms, have not been counted.

258. Seven of them are foremen.

259. I include the only case of attendance at an 'academy'.

260. Only three of the six high school graduates had taken a course of study that specially prepared them for their occupation. University educated were: the Assistant General Manager of the company with a degree in electrical engineering and ap-

prenticeship as a machinist, who then began as a draftsman (30 years old); the Director of the Recording Pyramid (i.e. the administrative department), who had studied at German universities and then worked as a 'clerk' and a 'salesman' at NCR (30); a District Manager, who had studied medicine for one year, but then after marrying begun as a grocery salesman (36); the Factory Engineer, also a member of the factory committee, with a college degree in civil engineering and postgraduate training in electrical engineering at Princeton (31); the second patent attorney with a Harvard College degree and some postgraduate training in 'scientific research' (29); the archivist with philological study in Europe (28).

261. Ibid., p. 34.

262. From company information in 1904, 350 or 82% of 428 male white collar employees had attended high school or its equivalent for at least some time. Ibid., p. 38.

263. Bloomfield, *Readings*, pp. 516-19.

264. Allinson, pp. 36, 113-48, esp. pp. 126, 139.

265. From Bloomfield, *Readings*, pp. 174-75, similarly pp. 118, 193f.

266. Cf. Allinson, pp. 37-39.

267. Among the 212 salaried employees of a Berlin Siemens factory (one part of the large electrical manufacturing firm) there were in 1890: 49 with an academic technical education; eighteen with a technical school education on the level below the university; two had attended a commercial school; 31 had been to a general secondary school; 33 had no more than elementary school education; in 79 cases educational background was unclear. In 1910 20% of all Siemens' salaried employees had an academic technical education, 35% had attended a technical school below the university level; 25% had had some commercial schooling. Cf. Kocka, *Unternehmensverwaltung*, pp. 280, 470. Of course the usefulness of this comparison is limited due to different educational requirements in an electrical manufacturing firm and in a firm producing registration machines.

268. For the following cf. M. Lazerson, *Origins of the Urban School. Public Education in Massachusetts 1870-1915*, Cambridge, Mass. 1971; M. L. Barlow, *History of Industrial Education in the United States,* Peoria, Ill. 1967, pp. 57-66.

269. Massachusetts Commission on Industrial Education, *Bulletin*, No. 11: *Report on the Advisability of Establishing One or More Technical Schools or Industrial Colleges* (Boston) 1908, pp. 4-5. Massachusetts established this commission in 1905/06 under pressure from employers (particularly in the shoe industry) to reform the educational system.

270. Cf. e.g. National Association of Manufacture's (NAM), *Proceedings*, 1912, p. 157f.; Massachusetts Commission on Industrial Education, *1st Report* (Boston) 1907, p. 15f.

271. A good overview of this discussion in Fisher, *Industrial Education*, pp. 83-137.

272. A frequently cited defense of the new life career principle against older American ideals of mobility: W. Eliot, 'The Value During Education of the Life-Career Motive' (Address to the National Education Association), Boston 1910.

273. This distinction was made in investigations at the latest by 1902, but not yet in 1893. Cf. above, notes 237 and 238; also: US Commissioner of Labor, *25th Annual Report: Industrial Education*, Washington 1911, p. 14: 'Industrial education' was defined as 'training for the mechanical trades and other manual occupations' and was distinguished from 'technical education. . .that is designed to fit students for supervisory, professional, or semi-professional vocations'.

274. Cf. NAM, *Proceedings*, pp. 158-64; Massachusetts Commission on Industrial Education, *1st Report* (Boston) 1907, p. 17; ibid., *Bulletin* No. 11, 1908, p. 4-15, 17-21: demands for industrial schools and industrial colleges, the latter for factory supervisors, foremen, technicians of all sorts on the model of German and Swiss schools.

275. Terms 1912 in NAM, *Proceedings*, p. 158.

276. The earliest use of the term known to me is in the magazine *The Draftsman*, Cleveland, Ohio, Vol. 2 (September 1903), p. 275. Some technical draftsmen got a 'swelled head' when they passed the $18 a week line. 'Men of this type are usually the ones the men in the shops call "white collars" or "silk glove men". They are often very much afraid of soiling their hands.' For further examples of the early use of 'white collar' cf. last note (1912); G. H. Mead, 'The Larger Educational Bearing of Vocational Guidance (1913)', in Bloomfield, *Readings*, p. 48f. C. E. Funk, *Heavens to Betsy! And Other Curious Sayings*, New York 1955, p. 29 dates the term too late when he asserts that it arose in the first world war.

277. Cf. e.g. B. F. M. Leavitt, *Examples of Industrial Education*, Boston 1912.

278. Thus in traces before the war, but particularly 1919 and 1922 in schools in the greater Boston area. Cf. Lazerson (see note 268 above), Ch. VII, n. 20.

279. Cf. Leavitt, pp.95-128 and Lazerson.

280. Cf. the survey of the debate up to the Smith-Hughes Act of 1917, which provided federal funds for vocational education, in Fisher, *Industrial Education*, pp. 128-37; on the multi-faceted extension of trade and industrial schools with state subsidies and strong business influence: US Commissioner of Labor, *25th Report*, Washington 1911.

281. Donham; Bossard/Dewhurst, esp. pp. 247-63; Haynes/Jackson.

282. For further details cf. Kocka I, p. 394, n. 314.

283. Cf. Lutz, pp. 47ff.

284. Cf. F. Parsons, *Choosing a Vocation*, Boston 1909; Bloomfield, *Vocational Guidance*; E. B. Woods, 'The Social Waste of Unguided Personal Ability', in *AJS*, Vol. 19, 1913, pp. 358-69; Bloomfield, *Readings*.

285. In a mining region in northeastern Pennsylvania in 1904 the sons of miners went to high school only in exceptional cases; they were sent to work as soon as possible, and at night they were too tired for school. Cf. P. Roberts, *Anthracite Coal Communities*, New York 1904, p. 171. The daughter was more apt to be sent to high school, so that she could then — before she married — support herself as a school teacher.

286. In 1914, 142 of 310 girls in a Boston day high school came from workers' families, as did 209 of 349 girls attending evening high school. Most of their fathers were skilled. Only 20% of the pupils from workers' households had fathers who were unskilled. Most of these working class children attended commercial rather than academic high schools. Cf. Allinson, p. 163.

287. Cf. US Commissioner of Labor, *25th Annual Report*, Washington 1911, p. 23f.

288. Very positive: Allinson, pp. 43ff.; very skeptical: Lutz, pp. 76ff. According to Allinson's survey of 1914, 27% of 861 Boston female evening high school students worked in a factory during the day, 41% worked in offices, and 12% were sales clerks (p. 54).

289. Pioneering corporation schools or apprenticeship schools were founded at Hoe and Co., a printing press factory in Philadelphia, in 1872 and at Westinghouse in East Pittsburgh, Pa. in 1888; in 1901 General Electric and Baldwin Locomotive Works followed, 1903 International Harvester, many railroad corporations in 1905 (in 1915 there were 108 such schools under the direction of railroads); in 1913 the National Association of Corporation Schools was founded, to which in 1902 146 companies belonged. In 1914 a survey of 51 businesses found that they had a total of 8,089 persons in company schools. Cf. US Commissioner of Labor, *25th Annual Report*, Washington 1911, pp. 145ff. Further evidence in Kocka I, p. 395, note 325.

290. On preference given to high school graduates in white collar careers at General Electric, cf. Ripley, *Life*, p. 131. New York examples mentioned in Bloomfield, *Readings*, pp. 295f., 509.

291. This impression emerges from the correspondence over the consolidation of McCormick and Deering, from which the International Harvester Company was formed, for instance, as well as from the correspondence over the necessary reorganization of departments. Cf. Cyrus H. McCormick Jr. Papers, Series 2C, Box 33, File: Traffic Department. Reorganization 1903; File: Consolidation Sales Department 1903; File: Consolidation Purchasing Department 1903 (State Historical Society of Wisconsin. Madison, Wisc.). Cf. further A. Kolb, *Als Arbeiter in Amerika. Unter deutsch-amerikanischen Grosstadt-Proletariern*, Berlin 1904, p. 67; W. Williams, *Worker's Mind*, pp. 250-51; also C. B. Spahr, *America's Working People*, London 1900, pp. 146-47 on the completely unbureaucratic promotion at Carnegie in Homestead; further: Farnham, *America vs. Europe*, p. 324.

292. From Fisher, *Industrial Education*, p. 8.

293. My data are not sufficient to support this quantitatively by measuring actual upward mobility. The studies of social mobility that are available do not show such a decline in occupational mobility. Cf. H. Kaelble, *Historische Mobilitätsforschung. Westeuropa und die USA im 19. und 20. Jahrhundert*, Darmstadt 1978, p. 72: comparing the findings of Thernstrom (Boston), Griffen (Ploughkeepsie), Gitelman (Waltham), Hopkins (Atlanta), Chudacoff (Omaha) and Worthman (Birmingham) with studies on European cities (without finding a clear pattern). Cf. particularly St. Thernstrom, *The Other Bostonians*, Ch. 4; ibid., *Poverty and Progress. Social Mobility in a Nineteenth Century City*, Atheneum edition, New York 1969, pp. 96-104. These studies do not usually permit a distinction to be made between moves of blue collar workers into employed (clerks, etc.) and self-employed (small business, etc.) white collar positions; rather, they measure moves into 'non-manual' or 'white collar' positions in general. The same is true of most materials collected in S. M. Lipset and R. Bendix, *Social Mobility in Industrial Society*, Berkeley and Los Angeles 1959. An exception is: M. B. Katz, *The People of Hamilton, Canada West. Family and Class in a Mid-Nineteenth-Century City*, Cambridge, Mass. 1975, p. 146. Most studies do not permit the differentiation between economic sectors which would be necessary to test the above hypothesis. Finally, the growing rigidity of the collar line (as hypothesized above) may not have resulted in a net decline of career mobility from blue collar into white collar employee positions because of counteracting tendencies, especially the relative increase of the latter. It would be necessary to control for this factor.

294. Cf. Wiebe, *Search*, cf. above, pp. 66-79.

295. Cf. the evidence in Kocka, *Unternehmensverwaltung*, pp. 136ff., 166ff. 272f., 478f.; and with some modifications, Schulz, *Arbeiter*, p. 363f.

296. The *Seventh Annual Report of the Massachusetts Bureau of Labor*, Boston 1876, which placed draftsmen in both categories; the *27th Annual Report*..., Boston 1897, p. 118f. placed draftsmen as well as foremen in the 'wage earners' category.

297. *The Draftsman*, Chicago, Vol. 1, March 1902, p. 117; Vol. 2, April 1903, pp. 90ff.; Vol. 1, May 1902, p. 275; Vol. 1, December 1902, p. 368.

298. Ibid., Vol. 1. December 1902, p. 370; Vol. 2, November 1903, p. 273 on the 'traveling draftsman'; p. 270 on the draftsman as 'floater'.

299. Ibid., Vol. 1, March and May 1903, pp. 117, 185; cf. also Matschoss, *Die geistigen Mittel*, p. 33. *The Draftsman* became *Browning's Industrial Magazine* in 1906 and ceased to address itself specifically to technical draftsmen.

300. Cf. the citation from 'Railway Mechanical Engineering' in *Minnesota Engineering Year Book*, Vol. 4, 1896, p. 20, quoted by Calvert, p. 114-45.

301. In 1896 28% of a sample of 47 engineering school graduates worked in a drawing room (ibid., p. 149).

302. Unpublished autobiography of Anton Bem, written as a letter to his family, dated Bartlesville, Oklahoma, 4 May 1924. For access to the typewritten ms. I thank

Prof. Oscar Handlin of Harvard University.

303. This expression appeared in the name of a technicians' association founded in Germany in 1904: Bund technisch-industrieller Beamter.

304. Cf. on the interdependence of the academization of technical education and the emergence of the engineering profession: Kocka, *Unternehmensverwaltung*, pp. 166-71, 173-80, 271-77.

305. Cf. the evidence in Calvert, pp. 51, 53f., 67f., 71-74, 76f., 153-67.

306. Cf. Calvert, pp. 23ff., 109ff. 197ff.; D. Calhoun, *The American Civil Engineer*, Cambridge 1910; E. T. Layton, *The Revolt of the Engineers*, Cleveland 1971, pp. 25-52, esp. pp. 30, 33, 36, 39 on the membership requirements of various organizations.

307. *The New Webster Encyclopedic Dictionary of the English Language*, Chicago 1969, p. 289: 'one who manages an engine or has to do with the construction of engines and machinery; or a person skilled in the principles and practice of engineering, either civil or military'. In contrast H. Schimank, 'Das Wort "Ingenieur",' in *Zeitschrift des VDI*, Bd. 83, 1939, pp. 325-31.

308. Cf. *The Draftsman*, Vol. 2, September 1903, p. 202:

> But any Tom, Dick and Harry in this whole free country can be an engineer if he chooses... What mechanical engineer has not had the humiliating experience of being mistaken for them (common machine-webbers and coal-heavers)... [We are] a butt for the just ridicule of every educated European that lands on our shores, to wit, that every bootblack is a professor in America, every stoker an engineer, every journeyman carpenter an architect, and every successful politician an LL.D.

309. Cf. Kocka, *Unternehmensverwaltung*, pp. 106-11, 129ff., 303ff., 500ff.

310. The archives of the Baker Library, Harvard School for Business Administration, holds materials from this firm. Cf. above all: *Wage Rages 1874-78* (v.KB-1), p. 27: daily rates for white collar employees in the factory office; *Wage Rates 1878-81* (v. KB-2), pp. 4, 59, 139, 228 (includes office-like factory personnel in daily wages); *1906-07* (v.KB-23), pp. 1-13. Cf. H. M. Gitelman, 'The Labor Force at Waltham Watch During the Civil War Era', in *JEH*, Vol. 25, 1965, pp. 214-43; ibid., *Working Men of Waltham: Mobility in American Urban Industrial Development 1850-1890*, Baltimore 1974.

311. From Deering Harvester Factory, Time and Payroll Book 1883ff. In McCormick-Collection, State Historical Society of Wisconsin, Madison, Wisc.; Entry 2: 3M/6H4-13.

312. Cf. above, p. 82f.

313. After 1887, at least in Massachusetts, legislation — apparently to protect the worker — required that every employee be paid his wages by the week, unless written contracts between employer-employee established another method of payment. The law differentiated neither categories of employees nor economic sectors. Cf. *Twenty-First Annual Report of the (Massachusetts) Bureau of Statistics of Labor*, Boston 1891, pp. 47-49; US Commissioner of Labor, *22nd Annual Report: Labor Laws of the US*, Washington 1908, p. 602f.

314. A. F. Hadley, 'Ethics of Corporate Management', in *The North American Review*, Vol. 194, 1907, pp. 120-34; and S. Morris, 'The Wisconsin Idea and Business Progressivism', in *JAS*, Vol. 4, 1970, pp. 39-60.

315. On the situation before the beginning of the war see: 'Welfare Work for Employees in Industrial Establishments in the United States' (*BLSt., Bulletin*, No. 250), Washington 1919 (p. 119f.: almost all of the schemes presented were established in the last ten-twelve years); D. D. Lescohier in J. Commons et al., *History of Labor*, Vol. 3 (1935), New York 1966, pp. 293-345; D. Brody, 'The Rise and Decline of Welfare Capitalism', in J. Braeman, et al. (eds.), *Change and Con-*

tinuity in Twentieth-Century America, Ohio State University Press 1968, pp. 147-78; further, W. J. Ghent, *Our Benevolent Feudalism*, New York 1902; E. D. L. Otey, *Employers' Welfare Work*, Washington 1913; Tarbell; National Civil Federation, Conference on Welfare Work. Held at the Waldorf-Astoria, New York City, 16 March 1904, under the Auspices of the Welfare Department of the National Civic Federation, New York 1904. For an interpretation of the NCF's concentration on welfare work after 1903/04, see Weinstein, *The Corporate Ideal*.

316. Cf. the overviews in C. C. Ling, *The Management of Personnel Relations*, Homewood, Ill. 1965, pp. 49-82; C. R. Milton, *Ethics and Expediency in Personnel Management*, Columbia, SC 1970, pp. 1-99; Baritz, *Servants*. The connections between the personnel management movement and the much narrower and earlier scientific management movement are made clear in The American Society of Mechanical Engineers, *50 Years of Progress in Management, 1910-1960*, New York 1960, pp. 277-323 (reprint of two reports from 1912 and 1922); 'Proceedings of Employment Managers' Conference, January 19 and 20, 1916' (*BLSt., Bulletin*, No. 196), Washington 1916, esp. pp. 21-24 (on the key problem of labor turnover), p. 48 (on the training of technicians); D. Bloomfield (ed.), *Selected Articles on Employment Management*, New York 1919 (the first Reader on the new subject). Recently, D. Nelson, *Managers and Workers: Origins of the New Factory System in the United States, 1880-1920*, Madison, Wisc. 1975.

317. On the whole subject see above, pp. 42-54.

318. On the creation of company welfare provisions, cf. A. Günther and R. Prevot, *Die Wohlfahrseinrichtungen der Arbeitgeber in Deutschland und Frankreich*, Leipzig 1905; on the collar line's significance in efforts to integrate some employees into the company: Kocka, *Unternehmensverwaltung*, pp. 500-13; on its significance at the societal level ('new middle class' politics and white collar insurance law), pp. 536-44.

319. Cf. above, p. 123f.

320. Probably the most comprehensive investigation of 370 pension programs before the first world war: A. Epstein, *The Problem of Old Age Pensions in Industry. An Up-to-date Summary*. . ., Harrisburg, Pa. 1926, esp. pp. 71-72, 77-79. Only in five cases were the pension benefits limited to 'clerks and salaried employees only', in one other case to 'administrative, selling and supervisory forces.' 88% of the pension plans in existence in 1925 (in this investigation) had been founded after 1910, 99% after 1900. Around 100,000 or 5-6% of all those over 65 in the US received a pension from a private employer (ibid., p. 407).

321. Cf. US Commissioner of Labor, *23rd Annual Report 1908: Workmen's Insurance and Benefit Funds in the US*, Washington 1909, pp. 387-603 for a representative survey and investigation of 461 'Benefit Funds' (85% were voluntary); only nine of these excluded white collar employees, and fourteen excluded certain departments from participation (p. 396); pp. 400-41, 440-47 on the gradation of rights and duties.

322. Cf. e.g., Cyrus H. McCormick, Jr. Papers (McCormick Collection), Series 2C, Box 30, File: Consolidation: Pension Plans for Employees, Stock Distribution; Boxes 39-42. This material provides detailed information on the development of company welfare programs at International Harvester 1901-10. Although the factory workers were undoubtedly the main focus of these policies, white collar workers (not executives, however) were usually also covered, and in any case there was no consciously separate policy for white collar workers. Factory workers and office employees sat together, for example, on recreational committees (Box 39., File 'Welfare 1903', S. M. Darling to Cyrus McCormick 3/22/1904), played on the same football teams (Box 39, File 'Company Outings 1901-1903', Miss Beeks to Cyrus McCormick 7/24/1903), worked together on the 'sociological committee' (Box 39, File 'Welfare 1903', S. M. Darling on 6/2/1904). Cf. further the extensive descriptions in W. H. Tolman, *Industrial Betterment*, New York City 1900; 'Wage-

Earning Pittsburgh' (*Pittsburgh Survey*, Vol. 6), New York 1914, pp. 266ff.; O. W. Nestor, *A History of Personnel Administration 1890 to 1910*, PhD Thesis, University of Pennsylvania 1954.

323. *Welfare Work for Employees*, pp. 90, 82-83.

324. Cf. details and evidence from Rockefeller's Colorado Fuel and Iron Company, McCormick, and other firms: Kocka I, p. 399f., n. 366.

325. Cf. on McCormick/International Harvester: Cyrus H. McCormick Jr. Papers, Series 2C, Box 37, File 'IHC. Profit Sharing' for changing and unsystematically organized lists of participants (State Historical Society of Wisconsin, Madison, Wisc.). Cf. also R. Ozanne, *A Century of Labor — Management Relations at McCormick and International Harvester*, Madison 1967, p. 36f. (profit sharing only for top executives and salesmen), pp. 57 and 82f. on other privileges separating executives from the mass of employees; pp. 33 and 91 for inclusion of shifting groups in profit sharing and bonus plans.

326. 'Notice' of 16 September 1921, in Ford Archives, Dearborn, Michigan, Acc. 121). Cf. also A. Nevins, *Ford*, 3 vols., New York 1954ff. For an account of a middle level white collar worker's dismissal without notice after twenty years see W. Carleton, *One Way Out. A Middle-Class New Englander Emigrates to America*, Boston 1911, pp. 38-39.

327. Cf. (NCR), *The Model Factory of the World*, n.p., n.d. (1900), without pagination; on the NCR 'Advance Club': Monroe, 'Possibilities', p. 739. Members were executives and managers, foremen, department heads and — for a fixed term —50 representatives chosen from the 'rank and file'. Cf. various company magazines of General Electric in the firm's library in Schenectady, NY, e.g. *Schenectady Works News*, Vol. 1ff., 1917ff; *The G. E. Monogram. A Magazine for the Sales Organization*, Vol. 1ff., 1923ff.; *P.T.M. Published by General Electric Test Alumini Association*, Vol. 1ff., 1926ff.

328. J. D. Rockefeller, Jr. *Address to the Joint Meeting of the Officers and the Representatives of the Employees of the Colorado Fuel and Iron Company*, Pueblo, 2 October 1915, p. 3f.; cf. on the significance of this speech, which accompanied the establishment of an unprecedented model company union: C. J. Hicks, *My Life in Industrial Relations*, New York 1941, pp. 44-48; I. Bernstein, *The Lean Years*, Baltimore 1960, pp. 157-64.

329. Carleton, *One Way Out*.

330. Ibid., p. 3, cf. also 1916: Tarbell, p. 257: There were often reservations against the word pension, since it carried 'the idea of something given, not earned'. An electrical company thus chose the term 'service annuity' to describe the same thing. Such considerations would have probably been superfluous in Germany.

331. Carleton, *One Way Out* pp. 4-16, 97, 128-30.

332. Based on S. B. Warner, *Street Car Suburbs. The Process of Growth in Boston, 1870-1900*, Cambridge 1962, esp. pp. 154-65; R. A. Woods, *The City Wilderness. A Settlement Study by Residents and Associates of the South End House*, Boston/New York 1898; cf. also Farnham, *America vs. Europe*, p. 71f. on the connection between individual striving for success and the lack of social reform efforts in the US (in contrast to Europe).

333. Carleton does not specify his suburb. Those named were heavily settled by professionals. Cf. Warner, *Street Car Suburbs*. p.65.

334. Carleton, *One Way Out*, pp. 17-54, esp. pp. 19, 25, 33, 28f.

335. Ibid., pp. 55-301.

336. Carleton paints a rosy view of life in this poor part of Boston. He describes the switch to hard physical labor (after twenty years in an office!) as liberation and the change in life for himself and his family as a return to the best American traditions! He presents his experience as a way open to all, without acknowledging the special conditions in his situation — such as the fact that he alone in his housing project spoke and wrote perfect English.

337. The source is used carefully here. Extreme criticisms of white collar life in order to romanticize his new manual labor-pioneer existence have been disregarded, for instance. Cf. e.g. ibid., pp. 97, 128-29, 150. No conclusions can be drawn about what is not covered: references to religion or church, efforts to educate himself or political opinions.

338. Roberts, pp. 97, 200.

339. Cf. A. M. Low, 'What is Socialism?' (IV), in *The North American Review*, Vol. 197, II, April 1913, p. 564.

340. Figures compiled from G. L. Coyle, *Present Trends in the Clerical Occupations*, New York 1928, p. 14 and *Historical Statistics*, p. 9; on the general question M. A. Jones, *American Immigration*, Chicago 1960, p. 218.

341. Cf. e.g. the contradictory explanations in M. and S. Chase, *A Honeymoon Experiment*, Boston 1916, p. 20 (on Rochester, NY) and Williams, *Worker's Mind*, p. 252 (on a city on Lake Michigan) on the question whether landladies gave preference to white collar over blue collar workers or not.

342. Cf. Low, 'What is Socialism?' (1913), p. 560, who stresses that members of this class are addressed as 'Mister' in contrast to workers. He treats this statement as novel. My survey of contemporary literature is naturally very limited, and it cannot be ruled out that other and earlier references of this sort could be found.

343. Cf. Bloomfield (ed.), *Readings*, pp. 48-49, 74-75, 118; pp. 48-49 on the significance of hopes of upward mobility as cause for preferring white collar positions.

344. Cf. Allinson, pp. 64f., 111f. based on a survey of female office employees in Boston.

345. Kolb, *Arbeiter*, p. 90.

346. Cf. J. D. Burn, *Three Years Among the Working-Classes in the United States during the War*, London 1865, p. 19: '[L]abor as a profession is more dignified in America than in [this] whole country'; which he explained among other reasons by the greater demand for labor in the US. Even more definite, though less convincing, since the observation of an American (not a foreigner): 'American Manufactures' in *Hunt's Merchants' Magazine*, Vol. 5, August 1841, p. 140f. and 'Labor, Its Relations, in Europe and in the United States Compared', ibid., Vol. 11, September 1845, pp. 217-23.

346a. It would be difficult to make this point with respect to the status of unskilled labor which carried little esteem in the US as well. Cf. examples in Thernstrom, *Poverty*, p. 28.

347. On this, W. Sombart, *Warum gibt es in den Vereinigten Staaten keinen Sozialismus?* (1906, Darmstadt 1969, pp. 127-29; T. Cassau, *Die Gewerkschaftsbewegung*, Halberstadt 1930, pp. 126, 157-62; Bergewin, *Apprenticeship*, p. 12; François, pp. 352-57.

348. There are numerous sources for such estimates. Cf., for instance, *Report of the Committee of the Senate upon the Relations between Labor and Capital...*, 5 vols., Washington 1885, Vol. 2, pp. 964, 1113; Chase, *Honeymoon*, p. 5; P. H. Douglas, *American Apprenticeship and Industrial Education*, New York 1968, p. 210.

349. An overview of the whole problem: B. Fisher, *Industrial Education*, esp. pp. 14-18, 38ff., 47f., 72-84, 114-119. On the entire question also, R. Hofstadter, *Anti-Intellectualism in American Life*, New York 1962, pp. 233ff., 393ff.

350. Cf. Kolb, *Arbeiter*, pp. 47, 60; Chase, *Honeymoon*, pp. 11.

351. Sombart, *Warum*, pp. 188-221; Kolb, *Arbeiter*, p. 45; *Mosley Industrial Commission to the United States of America, October-December 1902. Reports of the Delegates*, Manchester 1903, p. 9; Farnham, *America vs. Europe*, p. 72.

352. It is revealing that contemporary investigations of patterns of consumption did not as a rule use the collar line to organize their data. Cf. e.g. B. L. B. More,

Wage-Earners' Budgets. A Study of Standards and Cost of Living in New York City, New York 1907: lower white collar workers such as draftsmen were included among 'working men'; a large group of 'professionals', which included the better off white collar workers, was set off from workers. While this mingling makes it difficult to compare blue and white collar consumption, it implicitly supports our thesis about the relatively unimportant role of the collar line in distinguishing standards of living. On the for German eyes middle class eating habits of American workers see Sombart, *Warum*, pp. 106, 117ff., 121ff.

353. Cf. *Seventh Annual Report of the (Massachusetts) Bureau of Statistics of Labor*, Boston 1876, pp. 32, 322. Further comparative averages (ibid., pp. 24f., 214f., 40f., 230f., 440f., 234f., 40, 46f., 230f).

354. Cf. Sombart, *Warum*, pp. 96f., 116.

355. Cf. Woods, *City Wilderness*, pp. 48f., 86, 88, 96f., 100; 100f. on the overall character of the South End. In better tenements lower level white collar workers and better off workers lived together. Cf. US Commissioner of Labor, *8th Special Report: The Housing of the Worker*, Washington 1895, pp. 186-89 (New York), 200-206 (Boston); Warner, *Street Car Suburbs*, p. 56; and pp. 46, 64, 75f., 80 on neighborhood segregation by income rather than nationality or occupation.

356. Cf. Jones, *American Immigration*, pp. 218, 225, 254.

357. Cf. the description of the Chicago 'Hill District'' in *Wage Earning Pittsburgh* (*The Pittsburgh Survey*, ed. by P. U. Kellogg, Vol. 6), New York 1914, p. 351; similarly also Kolb, *Arbeiter*, p. 136f.

358. Without much evidence, a contrary position is taken by Thernstrom, *Poverty*, pp. 91-92.

359. Penetrating reflections on the connection between egalitarian traditions and weakly developed corporatism on one side and individual striving for profit and success as well as the primary significance of income and consumption (instead of occupation as such) on the other: Lipset, *First New Nation*, pp. 66, 119, 125ff., 206-208, 332, passim.

360. Cf. *The Draftsman*, Vol. 4, March 1905, p. 91; November 1905, p. 177f.; Vol. 6 (titled *Browning's Industrial Magazine*), June 1906, p. 233f.

361. Cf. W. Sauer, 'Das Problem des deutschen Nationalstaates', in *Politische Vierteljahrsschrift*, Bd. 3, 1962, pp. 159-86; R. Dahrendorf, *Gesellschaft und Demokratie in Deutschland*, München 1965; Stern, *The Failure of Illiberalism*; H.-U. Wehler, *Das Deutsche Kaiserreich 1871-1918*, Göttingen,[3] 1977. G. Roth, *The Social Democrats in Imperial Germany. A Study in Working-Class Isolation and National Integration*, Totowa, 1963; G. A. Ritter, *Arbeiterbewegung im wilhelminischen Reich. Die Sozialdemokratie und die Freien Gewerkschaften 1890-1900*, Berlin[2] 1963. Cf. E. M. Kassalow, *Trade Unions and Industrial Relations. An International Comparison*, New York 1969, esp. pp. 6-28 for a good introduction to the comparative treatment of the American labor movement; and the conclusions in Lösche, *Industriegewerkschaften*, pp. 190ff.; on the absence of feudal traditions in the US and its significance: Tocqueville, pp. 561ff., passim; Hartz, pp. 234ff., passim; Lipset, *First New Nation*, pp. 101, 148, passim. K. Lewin, 'Social-Psychological Differences between the United States and Germany', in ibid., *Resolving Social Conflicts. Selected Papers on Group Dynamics*, New York 1948, pp. 3-33.

362. Shown in Kocka, *Unternehmensverwaltung*, pp. 463-544.

363. Cf. ibid., pp. 513-17.

364. Review of the halting development of American labor and social law: Brandeis, in Commons et al., Vol. 3, pp. 399-698; M. Derber and E. Young, *Labor and the New Deal*, Madison 1957, pp. 121-55, 193-274. For Germany: Friedrich Syrup, *100 Jahre staatliche Sozialpolitik 1839-1939. Aus dem Nachlass bearb. v. O. Neuloh*, Stuttgart 1957; A. Gladen, *Geschichte der Sozialpolitik in*

Deutschland. Eine Analyse ihrer Bedingungen, Formen, Zielsetzungen und Auswirkungen, Wiesbaden 1974.

365. Cf. below, pp. 211f, 219, 224f.

366. Cf. Kocka, *Unternehmensverwaltung*, pp. 148-96, 523-44; a summary in ibid., 'Vorindustrielle Faktoren'.

367. H. Rosenberg, *Bureaucracy*.

368. Classically formulated by Weber, *Economy and Society*, pp. 956-1005.

369. See note 366. On the concept of 'normative reference group': Runciman, *Relative Deprivation*, p. 12.

370. Cf. US Civil Service Commission, *A History of the Federal Civil Service 1789-1939*, Washington 1939; cf. F. C. Howe, *Wisconsin. An Experiment in Democracy*, New York 1912, p. 46: 'Wisconsin has created a new profession, the profession of public service. It has adopted the German idea to American soil'. Ibid., *Socialized Germany*, p. 21f.; Morris, 'The Wisconsin Idea', p. 46, passim.

371. Cf. Chandler/Galambos, on the later development of public than private bureaucracies in the US; on the influence of business management methods on public administration: D. Waldo, *The Administrative State*, New York 1948, pp. 9, 24, 42-45.

372. Cf. on this mainly K. Wiedenfeld, *Kapitalismus und Beamtentum*, Berlin 1932; T. Wilhelm, *Die Idee des Berufsbeamtentums*, Tübingen 1933.

373. E. Fraenkel, *Das Amerikanische Regierungssystem*, Köln 1960 ^{2}, p. 214; pp. 211-19: an extremely illuminating and relevant introduction to the issue only touched on here.

374. Cf. E. B. K. Foltz, *The Federal Civil Service as a Career. A Manual*, New York 1909, pp. 255ff., 59, 65-69, 283-84, 304-305.

375. Cf. O. Hintze, 'Der Beamtenstand', pp. 66-125, esp. p. 77 on the status of German bureaucrats before 1914.

376. Cf. above, pp. 89ff.

377. What follows from *The Draftsman*, Vol. 1 (1902), pp. 77, 79, 97, 117f., 191, 368; Vol. 2 (1903), pp. 16f., 66, 128, 130; Vol. 3 (1904), p. 86f.; Vol. 4 (1905), pp. 91, 185, 220f., 278f., 314; Vol. 5 (1906), pp. 37, 234.

378. Cf. above, pp. 149ff. and Layton, *Revolt*, pp. 25-52 for a useful overview of professionalization among engineers.

379. After 1896 some states legally protected the title 'certified public accountant'. Overview in J. D. Edwards, *History of Public Accounting in the United States*, East Lansing, Mich. 1960, pp. 1-100 (history to 1914); pp. 34-41 on the definition of the profession; further: C. W. Haskins, *Business Education and Accountancy*, New York 1904, esp. pp. 138ff.

380. On the *Vereinigung der leitenden Angestellten in Handel und Industrie e.V. (Vela)*, founded 1918, see G. Kleine, *Die leitenden Angestellten in der gegenwärtigen Wirtschaftsgesellschaft*, Köln 1955.

381. Cf. W. H. Lange (Industrial Relations Counselors, Inc.) 'The American Management Association and Its Predecessors' (American Management Association, Special Paper, No. 17), New York 1928; W. E. Wickenden, 'Is Management a Profession?' (AMA, Special Paper, No. 3), New York 1924; cf. National Association of Office Managers, *Proceedings, 2nd Annual Conference, Buffalo*, NY 1921; in general: Weibe, *Search*, p. 123.

382. Cf. A. von Haller Carpenter, *Glimpses of the Life and Time of...*, Chicago 1890, p. 120f. This autobiography is interesting anyway as the story of a man who in the US was a professional with a definite specialization, but who would have been a senior railroad bureaucrat in Germany.

383. Cf. American Institute of Bank Clerks, *Bulletin*, New York, Vol. 1ff., 1902ff., Vol. 2, 1903, No. 9, p. 17f.: 'The avocation of a bank clerk — more a profession than a business — is no mean life work for any man, and there ought not to

be mean or inferior men in it!' The Institute was founded and partly financed by the American Bankers Association in 1900, allegedly at the urging of the clerks. It grew rapidly, and in 1905 the contributing banks feared that their clerks were transforming the Institute into a sort of trade union (from ibid., Vol. 7, 1906, p. 950f.). Yet the cover of the *Bulletin* continued to proclaim: 'The Institute is conducted under the auspices of the American Bankers Association to promote the educational and social welfare of bank men, through the organization of chapters, and otherwise, and to fix and maintain a recognized standard of banking education by means of official examinations and the issuance of certificates.' (e.g. in Vol. 8, 1907, February). After 1907: 'Institute of Banking'.

384. Cf. L. A. Cremin, *The Transformation of the School: Progressivism in American Education, 1876-1957*, New York 1961; T. D. Martin, *Building a Teaching Profession. A Century of Progress 1857-1957*, Middletown, NY 1957; E. B. Wesley, *NEA (National Education Association). The First Hundred Years, The Building of the Teaching Profession*, New York 1957. J. Barzun, *Teacher in America*, Boston 1945; American Federation of Teachers, *Organizing the Teaching Profession. The Story of the American Federation of Teachers*, Glencoe, Ill. 1955; R. J. Braun, *Teachers and Power. The Story of the American Federation of Teachers*, New York 1972.

385. Cf. e.g. Allinson, p. 140. Also frequently 'office service'.

386. Cf. above, pp. 89ff.

387. On the rising professions: above, pp. 44ff. The declining chances for independence were emphasized in contemporary vocational guidance literature. Cf. Gowin/Wheatley, p. 144; L. Brandeis, *Business. A Profession*, Boston 1914, p. 65.

388. Cf. on this and the following, above all C. L. Gilb, *Hidden Hierarchies. The Professions and Government*, New York 1966, pp. 34ff.: Professionalization from 1890 to 1920 seen as a striving for status in an increasingly urban society.

389. Cf. on this, above all Parsons, 'Professions and Social Structure', p. 189f.; Layton, *Revolt*, p. 6f.

390. This dual basis for the authority of the bureaucracy was already presented from many sides as an unsolved problem in Max Weber's concept of bureaucracy. Cf. e.g. B. H. Hartmann, *Funktionale Autorität*, Stuttgart 1964, pp. 36ff. I am following here, as in the next sentences, Max Weber's ideal type (cf. note 245 above), which fully met the *claims* (if not the real situation) of German industrial private bureaucrats before 1914. The following statements on the German side from Kocka, *Unternehmensverwaltung*, passim.

391. Cf. above, pp. 144ff. for the draftsmen: the wish for higher professional status could be formulated as a wish to be a 'first-class workman'. Cf. also above, pp. 89ff. on the closeness of the 'trade' consciousness and semi-professional consciousness of sales clerks. Cf. finally below, pp. 218ff. on the compatibility of professional consciousness and trade union action in the labor movement.

392. On the conflict between the bureaucratic and the capitalist principles Wiedenfeld; Kocka, *Unternehmensverwaltung*, p. 534f. on the anti-capitalist potential of German private bureaucrats in industry before 1914.

393. Business and profession were not opposites in American popular literature before 1914. Cf. Brandeis, 'Business a Profession; The Business Professions', in *Annals*, Vol. 28, July 1906; also Hofstadter, *Age*, p. 144f. That professional modes of thought also contained uncapitalistic and even anti-capitalistic elements was rightly emphasized in Th. Veblen, *The Engineers and the Price System*, New York 1933; Layton, *Revolt*, pp. 1-52 on correspondence and tensions between professionalism and capitalism.

394. Evidence in Kocka, *Unternehmensverwaltung*, pp. 463-90, 523ff.

395. On typical professional protest against bureaucratic controls and limitations on professional autonomy: cf. Gilb, pp. 34f., 93f., 98ff.

396. In addition to the explanations above, pp. 101ff. see P. F. Brissenden and E. Frankel, *Labor Turnover in Industry. A Statistical Analysis*, New York 1922, esp. pp. 52-55, 76f.

397. Cf. above, p. 130.

398. Low, 'What is Socialism?', passim, esp. pp. 560-66; cf. also C. T. Herrick, 'Concerning Race Suicide', in *The North American Review*, Vol. 184, February 1907, p. 407; R. S. Baker, 'Capital and Labor Hunt Together', in *McClure*'s, Vol. 21, September 1903, p. 463; Hofstadter, *Age*, pp. 171 (n. 4), 216.

399. Cf. above, p. 42f.

400. Low, 'What is Socialism?' pp. 564, 565. Cf. on this literature of social criticism: H. S. Wilson, *McClure's Magazine and the Muckrakers*, Princeton 1970. Involved were magazines like *McClure*'s, *Collier*, *Cosmopolitan* and *American Magazine*, and authors like Lincoln Steffens, Ida M. Tarbell, William A. White, Upton Sinclair and Gustavus Myers. References to the participation of some white collar workers in these political currents are unclear. Apart from the article by Low cited here, see Hofstadter, *Age*, pp. 216-17; further, the comments in *The Draftsman*, Vol. 1, 1902, pp. 326ff.; Vol. 2, 1903, p. 205, which followed a moderate progressive line. Similarly, American Institute of Bank Clerks, *Bulletin*, Vol. 7, 1906, pp. 956-59. RCIPA politics also fit into the progressive reform movement — on this see Ch. 2, Part 2, above.

401. Thus (limited to Wisconsin 1900-12): R. E. Wyman, 'Middle Class Voters and Progressive Reform: The Conflict of Class and Culture', in ***APSR***, Vol. 68, 1974, pp. 488-504; the precincts on which the analysis rests, however, were occupational and social-economically very mixed; furthermore, the proportion of progressive voters in middle class and upper class precincts was so high — in part higher than in working class precincts (see p. 496) — that no direct information over the white collar groups under investigation here is possible. Cf. also M. P. Rogin and J. L. Shover, *Political Change in California: Critical Elections and Social Movements, 1890-1966*, Westport, Conn. 1970, pp. 35-89 (gradual shift of the progressive electoral basis from the middle class to the working class).

Chapter 3 American White Collar Workers in the World War and the 1920s

1. Cf. B. Baruch, *American Industry in War*, New York 1941; G. S. Watkins, *Labor Problems and Labor Administration During the World War*, 2 vols., Urbana/Ill. 1919; Taft, *Organized Labor*, pp. 309-21; S. Shapiro, 'The Great War and Reform: Liberals and Labor 1917-19', in *LH*, Vol. 12, 1971, pp. 323-44; A. S. Link, *The Impact of World War I*, New York 1969; R. D. Cuff, 'Woodrow Wilson and Business-Government Relations During World War I', in *Review of Politics*, Vol. 31, 1969, pp. 385-407; ibid., *The War Industries Board. Business-Government Relations during World War I*, Baltimore 1973; W. E. Leuchtenburg, 'The New Deal and the Analogue of War', in Braeman et al., *Change*, pp. 81-143.

2. Cf. Corbin, *The Return of the Middle Class* (1923), a book that complains of the neglect of the middle classes, white collar workers in particular, in the last years:

> Capital is organized, class-conscious — and so manages to care for its own. Labor is organized, class-conscious; it takes its own abundantly. But the great range of folk in between have no organization, no sense of their collective in-

terests, of their relation to the state as a whole. And so they are forgotten. (p. 8)

3. The course of earnings and the cost of living from Table 2.10 (above). Cf. in general also: Douglas, *Real Wages*, pp. 238-43; on the declining wage-salary differential outside industry see R. K. Burns, 'The Comparative Economic Position of Manual and White-Collar Employees', in *The Journal of Business*, Vol. 27, Chicago 1954, pp. 257-67, esp. p. 258. On the declining distance between wages and salaries internationally: Bureau International du Travail, *Fluctuations des salaires dans différents pays de 1914 à 1922*, Geneva 1923; on Germany cf. for instance: *Deutsche Handels-Wacht*. Zs. d. DHV, Bd. 25, 1918, p. 40; *Zahlen zur Geldentwertung 1914-23* (Sonderheft 1 zu 'Wirtschaft und Statistik'), Berlin 1925, p. 43.

4. From A. G. Maher, *Bookkeepers, Stenographers and Office Clerks in Ohio, 1914-1924* (US Department of Labor. Women's Bureau, *Bulletin*, No. 95), Washington 1932, pp. 11, 12, see also above, Tables 2.3 and 2.11.

5. The proportion of white collar workers was not much higher in the recession years 1921 and 1922 than in the years of upswing. For every ten white collar workers there were 61 blue collar workers in 1919, 63 in 1920, 60 in 1921, 62 in 1922, 65 in 1923, and 60 in 1924 and 1925; cf. Table 3.2 and also above, p. 124, the 'Notice' from Ford. Further: E. S. Cowdrick, *Manpower in Industry*, New York 1924, pp. 154-56 on the 'surplus of clerical help'.

6. Cf. The Hard Hit Class. 'The White Collar Slaves of Modern Industry Feel the Pinch of Poverty', in *The Advocate*, December 1916, pp. 5-7. 'White collar slaves' came up repeatedly in the 1920s and 1930s in a social criticial context. Cf. E. Rice, *The Adding Machine. Seven Scenes*, Garden City 1923, p. ix (social critical play over a failed bookkeeper); used ironically: F. Ray, 'White Collary', in *The New Republic*, Vol. 42, April 1925, p. 155; once again in earnest during the depression: 'White-Collar Slavery (by an Ex-Slave)', in *The Forum*, Vol. 87, New York 1932, pp. 242-47 (report on the experiences of a commercial employee).

7. Cf. *The Advocate*, October 1919, p. 25: 'Low-Salaried Men and Clerks Seek Charity', an article that treats the economic distress of 'office men, bank clerks, public employees' and 'clerks in big business' together. The 'small salaried pen-and-ink-toiler', the 'small salaried citizen', now are said to appear for the first time at public welfare institutions.

8. From Kuznets, *National Income*, pp. 576-604, as follows: Col. 1 from p. 597 (col. 9); Col. 2 from p. 600 (col. 11); Cols. 3 and 4 calculated by dividing the yearly total wages and salaries of all industrial firms (p. 579, col. 9 and p. 582, col. 11) by the number of wage earners and salary receivers respectively. The figures from Douglas (*Real Wages*) used in Table 2.11 above extend only to 1926. Kuznets also (like Douglas) relied on data from the Census of Manufactures. Cf. on this the remarks in the note to Table 2.11. Comparing the Douglas and Kuznets figures for 1919-26 (in Tables 2.11 and 3.2), one finds small differences (due to varying methods of calculation) which are not important for our purposes.

9. Cf. Deming, pp. 25, 35ff., 57f.; Corbin, pp. 4, 6, 9, 23.

10. Cf. Corbin, p. 10f.:

> Labor and capital live in separate spheres; no question arises of social discrimination. Their struggle is purely economic. The brain worker rubs elbows everywhere. The clerk knows that in most ways that count he is inferior to the skilled and prosperous mechanic out in the factory, yet he cherishes his white collar though it ruins him for it means that his standing is that of an educated man.

Cf. also A. C. White, 'An America Fascismo', in *The Forum*, Vol. 72, 1924, pp. 636-42, esp. p. 638f.

11. R. Hofstadter and S. M. Lipset have attempted to distinguish 'status politics' and 'class politics' by the fact that the former is based on social resentment

and desires to maintain or improve one's status, while the latter rests only on economic conflicts of interests. Cf. Lipset, 'Sources', esp. pp. 308-15. This division, as the case in point reveals, is entirely too artificial; furthermore, it directs attention away from the economic preconditions for status protests. See the in this respect justified criticism in G. A. Brandmeyer and R. S. Denisoff, 'Status Politics', in *Pacific Sociological Review*, Vol. 12, 1969, pp. 5-11.

12. Cf. Corbin, pp. 11, 23, 28, 32-35, 46-48; Deming, p. 75; White, 'American Fascismo'.

13. Cf. Rice, *Adding Machine*, esp. pp. ix, 4f.: Mrs Zero, worn out, speaking in relatively uneducated slang, at bedtime in their very modest bedroom: 'If you was any kind of man you'd have a decent job by now, an' I'd be getting some comfort out of life...'. P. 21f.: Zero talks to himself and phantasizes about his confrontation with the boss and the latter's response — promoting him to the front office. P. 25-29:the reality. The boss does not even know his name, Mr Zero twitches expectantly, proudly says that in 25 years he has not missed a day, and on the advice of the 'efficiency expert' is replaced by an adding machine. P. 35: his wife's opinion: 'All they gotta do is put an ad in the paper. There's ten thousand like you layin' around the street'. P. 40f: the visit to his house.

14. Cf. K. T. Jackson, *The Ku-Klux-Klan in the City, 1915-1930*, New York 1967, pp. 62-65, 108, 119, 120: in Knoxville, Tenn., Chicago, Aurora, Ill. and Winchester, Ill. one third, 60-70% (twice), then ca. one-quarter of the members respectively were reported as white collar workers (though the categories were not absolutely clear).

15. Cf. Cowdrick, p. 197; G. L. Coyle, ' "White Collars" and Trade Unions', in *American Federationist*, Vol. 35, 1928, p. 1211 on 'law and order leagues' organized by employers during industrial conflicts which included white collar workers among other groups.

16. Cf. J. C. Burnham, 'New Perspectives on the Prohibition "Experiment" of the 1920s' in *JHS*, Vol. 2, 1968, pp. 50-58; J. Gusfield, *Symbolic Crusade and the American Temperance Movement*, Urbana, Ill. 1963; reprinted in Braeman et al., *Change*, pp. 257-308; N. Clark, *The Dry Years: Prohibition and Social Change in Washington*, Seattle 1965, pp. 113-22.

17. Thus e.g. in New York the 'American Society of Engineering Draftsmen', mentioned in International Federation of Draftsmen's Unions (AFL), *2nd Convention, Proceedings*, New York 1919 (cited as IFDU henceforth), p. 53f.

18. *International Federation of Technical Engineers, Architects and Draftsmen (AFL), 1918-43. Silver Anniversary*, Washington 1943 (cited *IFTEAD* in following), pp. 9f., 14, 19, 9f.; IFDU, *2nd Convention*, p. 29; L. Wolman, *Ebb and Flow in Trade Unionism*, New York 1936, p. 175.

19. IFDU, *2nd Convention*, pp. 56, 62-64, 43f.; *IFTEAD*, pp. 10, 18, 9: 'The disparity existing between the shop crafts and those in the drafting office grew more and more pronounced. To add to the burden, when all of the crafts were being paid for overtime work, the draftsmen were required to work extended hours without compensation.'

20. Cf. *25 Jahre Techniker Gewerkschaft. 10 Jahre Bund technischer Angestellter und Beamter, hg. v. Bund technischer Angestellter und Beamter im Afa-Bund*, Berlin 1929, pp. 13ff.: Bismarckian social legislation as the impetus for the beginning of the organization of the 'Technikerstand' (technicians' corporation) in the early 1880s.

21. Formulated in the constitution: 'Composed of all men and women performing work of a drafting nature'. From IFDU, *2nd Convention*, p. 55.

22. But strikes were rare, among other reasons because the organization considered itself too weak. Cf. IFDU, *2nd Convention*, p. 17, 19; cf. however *IFTEAD*, p. 19 on strikes and lockouts in San Francisco in 1919 in which the local

received strong support from the local labor council.

23. The debate ibid., pp. 52ff., 65-69, 77, 105; also on the decision *IFTEAD*, pp. 10, 12: Of the seventeen local organizations founded from mid-1916 to mid-1918 which then joined the national federation, four were 'marine Draftsmen's Unions', seven were 'Draftsmen's Unions', one was a 'Civil Engineering Union', one was an 'Engineering Inspectors' Union'. Membership definition from International Federation..., Constitution 1937, Article III, Section 1.

24. The references to these obstacles are frequent. Cf. *IFTEAD*, pp. 14, 19.

25. *Report of President to the Officers and Delegates of the 7th Annual Convention, Washington 1924* (typewritten carbon copy, AFL-CIO Library, Washington), pp. 3, 5 (quote), 6.

26. The membership figures were (from Wolman, p. 175) 1919: 1800; 1920: 3500; 1921: 2200; 1922: 1000; 1923: 600; 1924: 600; 1925: 600; 1926: 700; 1927: 1600; 1928: 1900; 1929: 1500.

27. Cf. *President's Report and Resumé of Action 10th Annual Convention...*, Washington 1927, p. 7: Notably a decided critique of Italian fascism and the Carnegie Foundation, which had brought out Alfredo Rocco's 'The Political Doctrine of Fascismo' without a distancing comment. P. 6f. a brief critique of communist efforts, which did not actually surface in this organization; p. 7f. on the successful 24 hour strike of 'technical men' who worked for the city in Chicago.

28. The up to then largest strike took place in St Louis in the spring of 1918 (5,000 participants). It was directed primarily against the large department stores and aimed at winning higher salaries and union recognition; the strikers were defeated. *The Advocate*, April 1918, p. 7; May 1918, p. 15f. Ibid., April 1919, p. 15f. on a successful strike in Belleville, Ill.; August 1919, p. 14f. and September 1919, p. 17f. on two defensive strikes in Chicago. An overview of retail clerks' strikes to the beginning of 1918: *17th Convention (1918), Proceedings*, p. 27. *The Advocate*, April 1919, p. 15f.: The RCIPA leadership recommended as a model the contract just reached in Belleville by strike with the merchants of the city. It contained the union shop principle, the establishment of a store committee, exact regulations over work and lunch times, one week paid vacation, 50% overtime bonus payment, minimum wage of $7/week in the first half year, $8 in the second, pay raises of $2-$3 for all currently employed clerks (with a leveling tendency for higher salaries), limitation on the number of apprentices (i.e., helpers under sixteen) to one per five clerks, rehiring drafted employees, no reduction in previous commissions and bonuses. On the course of membership: Wolman, p. 188f.

29. From H. J. Clermont, *Organizing the Insurance Worker. A History of Labor Unions of Insurance Employees*, Washington 1966, pp. 4-9.

30. Cf. ibid., pp. 1-3.

31. Cf. K. Baarslag, *History of the National Federation of Post Office Clerks*, Washington 1945, pp. 5-122; Wolman, p. 198. Cf. also S. D. Spero, *The Labor Movement in a Government Industry*, New York 1924, esp. pp. 229ff.; ibid., *Government as Employer*, reprint Carbondale 1972; M. R. Godine, *The Labor Problem in the Public Service*, Cambridge, Mass. 1951; L. Troy, 'White-Collar Organization in the Federal Service, in A. A. Blum et al., *White Collar Workers*, New York 1971, pp. 166-210.

32. Cf. H. Henig, *The Brotherhood of Railway Clerks*, New York 1937, pp. 3-78, esp. pp. 38-40, 50-57 on the war years, 285 on membership figures. After 1919 the union's name was the 'Brotherhood of Railway and Steamship Clerks, Freight Handlers, Express and Station Employees'. Cf. also A. M. McIsaac, *The Order of Railroad Telegraphers. A Study in Trade Unionism and Collective Bargaining*, Princeton 1933, esp. pp. 28-47 on the war. The union (AFL) organized blue and white collar workers.

33. Cf. J. Barbash, *Unions and Telephones. The Story of the Communications Workers of America*, New York 1952, pp. 4-15.

34. Cf. V. Ulriksson, *The Telegraphers. Their Craft and Their Unions*, Washington 1953, pp. 101-17.

35. Cf. above, note 31 and Wolman, p. 189. Membership: 1917: 8,100, 1920: 38,500.

36. Cf. 'AFT, A 50-year Assessment', in *Changing Education. A Journal of the American Federation of Teachers*, Summer 1966, pp. 10ff., passim; C. L. Zitron, *The New York City Teachers Union 1916-1964*, New York 1968, pp. 15-21; R. J. Braun. Membership figures from Wolman, p. 188f.

37. Cf. also R. D. Leiter, *The Musicians and Petrillo*, New York 1953; A. Harding, *The Revolt of the Actors*, New York 1929.

38. Cost of living index in Lebergott, p. 525.

39. Cf. S. Fabricant, *The Trend of Government Activity in the United States since 1900*, New York 1952, pp. 3-148.

40. Cf. *Historical Statistics*, p. 97 and below note 53 on the declining membership of the AFL; for analysis of the causes: Wolman, pp. 33ff.

41. On this particularly P. H. Douglas, *Wages and the Family*, Chicago 1925, p. 5f.; M. Leven et al., *America's Capacity to Consume*, Washington 1934, pp. 54-56, 93, 103-104; summarized in Bernstein, *Lean Years*, pp. 64-70.

42. Cf. ibid., pp. 1-43; L. Pope, *Millhands and Preachers*, New Haven 1942; C. Heer, *Income and Wages in the South*, Chapel Hill 1930; J. J. Rhyne, *Some Southern Mill Workers and their Villages*, Chapel Hill 1930.

43. Lebergott, p. 525.

44. From *BLSt., Bulletin*, No. 409, Washington 1926, pp. 25-28.

45. Cf. *MLR*, Vol. 30, 1930, p. 227; Bernstein, *Lean Years*, pp. 58-60.

46. Cf. for the American development from 1919 to 1929: Kuznets, *National Income*, p. 216f.; the comparative estimates from Bry, p. 23.

47. From figures in Lebergott, pp. 524, 523.

48. See the illuminating reports of foreign visitors to America, e.g.: A. Siegfried, *America Comes of Age*, New York 1927, esp. p. 159; *Amerikareise deutscher Gewerkschaftsführer*, Berlin 1926. The exploitation and harassment of workers in spite of higher wages and high consumption, their dependence and organizational weakness compared to Australian workers is emphasized in H. G. Adam, *An Australian Looks At America*, Sydney 1927, pp. 50f., 54-55, 85ff. In general: G. Soule, *Prosperity Decade: 1917-1929* (1947), New York 1968, pp. 208-28; W. E. Leuchtenburg, *The Perils of Prosperity, 1914-1932*, Chicago 1958, pp. 178-203; Bernstein, *Lean Years*, pp. 47-82.

49. Cf. Wolman, p. 188f.

50. Cf. Table 2.7 above; Lebergott, p. 513f.: in 1919 17% of American employees (blue and white collar) were engaged in commerce; in 1929 20%, and in 1939 21%; *Historical Statistics*, p. 518: in 1919 there were 3,977,000 persons employed in retail trade; in 1929, 6,077,000.

51. *18th Convention (1924), Proceedings*, pp. 55ff., Kirstein, p. 215f.

52. Cf. e.g. *The Advocate*, February 1925, pp. 15ff.: 'Militant Organization Essential. This Quality Lacking Among Retail Salespeople'.

53. From the calculations in Wolman, p. 188f. and *Historical Statistics*, p. 97, the membership (in thousands) was:

	1899	1903	1909	1919	1929	1933
RCIPA	10	50	15	21	10	5
AFL	611	1,914	2,006	4,125	3,461	3,048

54. Figures in Lebergott, pp. 525-28.

55. F. C. and F. E. Croxton, 'Average Wage and Salary Payments in Ohio, 1918-1932', in *MLR*, Vol. 38, 1934, pp. 143-59 and the continuation in ibid., Vol. 42, 1936, pp. 706-17. The figures are based on the yearly surveys of the Statistical Office of Ohio, which sent questionnaires to a large number of firms (1929: 42,000 with ca. 1.3 million employees, among them: 168,000 bookkeepers, stenographers and office employees as well as 87,000 sales employees). Higher white collar workers such as 'officials', 'super-intendants' and 'managers' were not included in the income figures or in the employment data. The average number of persons employed per year was reported directly by the firms; yearly income averages were obtained by dividing the total yearly sums for wages and salaries (as given by the companies) by the average yearly employment figures (in other words, temporary workers are included).

56. From La Dame, *The Filene Store. A Study of Employees' Relation to Management in a Retail Store*, New York 1930, p. 146f.

57. From an investigation by the 'Women's Bureau of Labor', reprinted in *The Advocate*, March/April 1932, p. 12f.

58. E.g. *The Advocate*, March 1925, p. 10: Kresge paid on the average only $7.25 to women clerks. In Massachusetts in 1916 the minimum wage for female sales clerks had already been set at $8.50. Cf. *The Advocate*, October 1922 (Editorial).

59. From *Historical Statistics*, p. 523. In 1928 315 of them sold groceries, 220 shoes, 294 apparel. The statistics covered 26 branches. A chain store had at least two subsidiaries.

60. Calculated from *Historical Statistics*, pp. 519, 520.

61. Cf. Scull, *Peddlers*, p. 250 on probably the first shopping center outside Baltimore (1907) and p. 228.

62. Cf. the story of a 'grocery clerk' in Ginzberg/Berman, p. 181.

63. Cf. *The Advocate*, February 1920, p. 17f.; January 1921, p. 15; July 1920, pp. 9ff.; May 1921, pp. 11ff: 'The Open Shop Drive'.

64. Cf. *The Advocate*, September/October 1930, p. 31: 'Sensitive Clerks Drive Customers from Scores of Stores Everywhere'. The article lectured clerks against taking offense at customers and criticized the tendency of some clerks to assert their own opinions contrary to those expressed by customers. 'Their [the customers'] notions may be crazy but there are many persons in a better position to criticize than the family grocer... [E]educated people are those able to adapt themselves to the conditions of life.'

65. Cf. on sources and literature, pp. 121ff.

66. 'Welfare' was defined: 'Anything for the comfort and improvement, intellectual or social, or the employees, over and above wages paid, which is not a necessity of the industry nor required by law'. From *BLSt., Bulletin*, No. 250, Washington 1919, p. 8.

67. The following from ibid., pp. 14f., 34f., 43, 54, 70, 73, 82, 89, 101, 108.

68. Cf. *BLSt., Bulletin*, No. 458, Washington 1928 ('Health and Recreation Activities in Industrial Establishments, 1926'). Medical care at work, extension of vacation rights and group insurance (by private insurance companies, arranged by the companies) were the areas where progress was most clear.

69. A. Epstein (*Problem of Old Age Pension*) is perhaps the most extensive survey of company pension plans in existence in 1925. 88% of the 370 plans had been created after 1910. Only eight were in 'mercantile industry'. Ibid., p. 21; L. Hahn and P. White, *The Merchants' Manual*, New York 1924, p. 554f.: no sickness insurance was mentioned, and there were no rules about continued salary payments during sicknesses. Length of service usually played a role, but in any case support was at the discretion of management.

70. Hahn/White, p. 55: in 1924 of 875 businesses questioned by the National Dry Goods Association, 12% gave no vacation time (these were primarily small

businesses), 50% one week and 38% two weeks. *BLSt., Bulletin*, No. 491 ('Handbook of Labor Statistics', 1929 edition), pp. 749-53; *The Advocate* July/August 1930, p. 13; J. R. Boubman, *Principles of Retail Merchandising*, New York 1936, p. 75.

71. Cf. the summary in Bernstein, *Lean Years*, pp. 171-74.

72. Cf. H. Baker, *Personnel Programs in Department Stores*, Princeton 1935, p. 9; in 1924 the personnel department in department stores was still a rare innvoation. Cf. Hahan/White, pp. 487ff.

73. Dartnell Corporation Chicago, *Survey of Retailing Practices...*, New York 1931, Vol. 1, pp. 80, 84.

74. Cf. ibid., pp. 86, 88; very clearly the typical handbook of the Retail Dry Goods Association: Hahn/White, pp. 534ff.

75. Dartnell Corporation, *Survey*, p. 89f. with the suggestion that this should be introduced in every business. Cf. also Baker, *Personnel Programs*, p. 30: Reprint of a typical teaching plan for 1934/35, which also included an 'Inspirational Talk'.

76. Cf. National Retail Dry Goods Association, *Preliminary Report on Commission and Bonus Methods. The Committee for the Study of Wage Problems*, New York 1920; M. H. Tolman, *Positions of Responsibility in Department Stores and Other Retail Selling Organizations. A Study of Opportunities for Women*, New York 1921; 'Methods of Compensation for Department Store Employees. A Survey by Industrial Relations', in *Bloomfield's Labor Digest*, Boston 1921 (p. 11: even for bookkeepers piece rates were recommended); Hahn/White, pp. 487-555; an excellent case study: La Dame, *Filene*, which was exceptional in providing liberal opportunities for employee co-determination (mostly not used); Dartnell Corporation, *Survey*, pp. 80-111.

77. Cf. Baker, *Personnel Programs*, p. 19.

78. La Dame, *Filene*, pp. 94-97, 382-83.

79. A forerunner, the Prince School of Education for Store Service, had already existed in Boston in 1905. In 1918 the Carnegie Institute of Technology in Pittsburgh established a Research Bureau for Retail Training; in 1919 the School of Retailing at New York University was founded. Cf. Hahn/White, p. 505. National Retail Dry Goods Association, *Addresses and Reports, 2nd Annual Convention — Store Manager's Division, May 13-15, 1925 (Atlantic City)*; ibid., *Proceedings, Sixth Annual Convention. Store Managers' Group, May 20-23, 1929 (Chicago)*.

80. Cf. *The Advocate*, March/April 1932, p. 2 (on 1929 practices).

81. From *BLSt., Bulletin*, No. 439, Washington 1927, p. 586f. (These figures appeared normal to the author of this piece.)

82. *Historical Statistics*, p. 520f. Of just under 3,000 employees at Filene's in 1926, only 21% had been there less than one year, 38% had worked 1-5 years, 39% 5-20 years, and 2% even longer. Furthermore, only 9% were less than 20. 22% were 20-25 years old, 17% 25-30, 15% 30-35, 13% 35-40, 16% 40-50, and 8% were over 50 (LaDame, *Filene*, pp. 95, 99); cf. also the empirical investigation of 50 department stores in 1934 by Baker, *Personnel Programs*, pp. 49ff.

83. Cf. Conway's article 'The Hard Hit Class. The White Collar Slaves of Modern Industry Feel the Pinch of Poverty' (*The Advocate*, December 1916). See also *The Advocate*, October 1919, p. 25: 'Low-Salaried Men and Clerks seek Charity', an article which treats the economic distress of 'office men, bank clerks, public employees' and 'clerks' together; *The Advocate*, January 1924, p. 17: '...there are indications of unrest and dissatisfaction among the so-called "white-collar" workers'. *The Advocate*, January 1925, p. 16f.: 'White Collar Workers Organize' (an article which presents the organizational efforts of Washington teachers as a model for other 'white collar workers').

84. Cf. e.g. M. A. Bills, 'Social Status of the Clerical Worker', in *Journal of Applied Psychology*, Vol. 9, 1925, pp. 424-27; H. B. Bergen, 'Social Status of the Clerical Worker', in ibid., Vol. 11, 1927, pp. 42-46. The following rank order of

social status groups was used as a measure by the authors: (1) unskilled laborer; (2) semi-skilled mechanical worker; (3) skilled mechanical worker; (4) clerical worker; (5) salesman or manager of a department in a company; (6) proprietor of a small business; (7) professionals, managers, owners of large business concerns.

> The classes are given above in the order which, we believe, the average clerk would consider that of their social status. The order of grouping is not that of financial returns. The salary of the skilled mechanical worker and even of the semi-skilled would in many cases exceed that of the clerical worker; however, anyone who has known a large number of clerical workers, especially those employed in an office that is connected with a factory, will, we believe, agree that women, particularly, consider a clerical job to carry higher social standing than a mechanical job. (Bills, 'Social Status', p. 424).

This categorical division hardly appears (or not at all) in earlier stratification investigations. Cf. e.g. W. F. Ogburn and D. Peterson, 'Political Thought of Social Classes', in *PSQ*, Vol. 31, 1916, pp. 300-17: Differentiation between 'upper class', 'middle class', some 'clerks' counted in the 'laboring class' (by income and prestige); S. A. Rice, *Farmers and Workers in American Politics*, New York 1924 (no mention of 'white collar' or 'clerical workers'). Also revealing is C. C. North, *Social Differentiation*, Chapel Hill 1926, p. 13: the self-evident use of a two class schema, which placed 'clerks' and 'salesmen' in the 'laboring class'.

85. Cf. F. R. Donovan, *The Saleslady*, Chicago 1929, p. 1f.: The girls questioned by the author clearly chose a secretarial position over a sales clerk's. 'But you don't get any money in a department store, and you won't have a chance to meet any men. I don't want to marry a ribbon-counter clerk'.

86. Thus, e.g. R. Leigh, *The Human Side of Retail Selling. A Textbook for Salespeople in Retail Stores...*, New York 1921, p. 7: 'Salesmanship a Skilled Profession'; N. A. Hawkins, *Certain Success*, Detroit 1920,[3] pp. 29ff.: 'The Universal Need for Sales Knowledge'; F. Farrington, *The Successful Salesman*, Chicago 1918, p. 15; N. A. Brisco and J. W Wingate, *Retail Buying*, New York 1925, p. v; N. A. Brisco et al., *Store Salesmanship (Retail Series Secondary Schools)*, New York 1934, p. 2. National Retail Dry Goods Association, *Proceedings, Fourth Annual Convention, Store Managers' Division, May 10-13, 1927* (Chicago), pp. 5-11 (L. Hahn: 'Retailing — a Profession'); Leigh, p. 9f. On the now frequent offerings of 'retail selling courses' in public secondary schools and special schools: F. G. Nichols et al., *A New Conception of Office Practice*, Cambridge, Mass. 1927, p. 53.

87. Cf. the interviews with several sales clerks in Ginzberg/Berman, pp. 183, 184, 185, 328f.; Baker, *Personnel Programs*, p. 76 on the frequent identification of young female clerks with the business where they were employed.

88. Very distinctly in D. K. Beckley and W. B. Logan, *The Retail Salesperson at Work*, New York 1948, p. 2.

89. Cf. *The Advocate*, March/April 1931, p. 6f.: 'The Retail Salesman — He Can Make Business — Or Break It'.

90. *18th Convention (1924), Proceedings*, p. 24f. Even in this tame period in the RCIPA's history it was astonishing and unusual for the union's convention to listen to such openly employer ideologies. It is possible that financial dependence was behind it.

91. Cf. *The Advocate*, July/August 1930, p. 14f.: May/June 1932, p. 1f.

92. Cf. Tables 2.10 and 3.2.

93. Cf. Kuznets, *National Income*, pp. 551-57, 576-604, 659-77.

94. Yearly earnings (per capita) for employees (blue and white collar) in selected economic areas:

	Nominal Earnings in 1914 $				Real Earnings in Current $			
	Banks	Insur-ance	Private Schools	Federal Govt.	Banks	Insur-ance	Private Schools	Federal Govt.
1920	1,364	2,071	885	1,451	683	1,004	444	726
1923	1,575	1,974	1,120	1,412	928	1,116	660	832
1928	1,698	2,232	1,275	1,600	995	1,307	746	935

Nominal earnings from Kuznets, *National Income*, pp. 731-37, 761-66, 811-14. Cost of living index from Lebergott, p. 523.

95. Cf. W. W. Rostow, 'The Past Quarter-Century as Economic History and the Tasks of International Economic Organization', in *JEH*, Vol. 30, 1970, pp. 150-87, esp. pp. 157-60.

96. Cf. F. C. and F. E. Croxton (see note 55 this ch.), esp. Vol. 38, pp. 148-54 and Vol. 42, pp. 713-15; also H. F. Clark, *Live Earnings in Selective Occupations*, New York 1937, p. 364. The term 'white collar' in Table 3.8 includes: 'bookkeepers, stenographers, and office clerks' as well as 'sales people [not travelling]'. Of the 1.2 million employees included in 1928, 9,500 were engaged in agriculture, 79,500 in construction, 750,000 in industry, 139,000 in private services and 82,000 in transportation and public service.

97. Cf. Bry, p. 467; Victor, 'Vernbürgerlichung', p. 23; Fisher, *Die Angestellten*, p. 39; cf. S. Kuznets, *Modern Economic Growth. Rate, Structure and Spread*, New Haven, Conn. 1966, p. 168f.: Wages and salaries amounted to 47% of national income in Germany in 1913, 1925-29 64%; in the US, however, 54% from 1899-1908, 58% 1919-28, and also 58% in 1929.

98. Cf. below, Ch. 4.

99. Cf. the most extensive: Coyle, *Present Trends*.

100. Four examples: The otherwise extremely well informed book of the American, D. T. Farnham (*Europe vs. America*, 1921) completely ignored the collar line in comparing company organization and social structure (pp. 352-55). W. MacDonald, *The Intellectual Worker and His Work*, New York 1923, had an international scope but almost completely excluded American history (except for p. 326f.). The famous study by R. S. and H. M. Lynd, *Middletown. A Study in American Culture* (1929), New York 1956, used a two-class schema ('working class' and 'business class') as if it was self-evident and gave only very peripheral attention to white collar workers (p. 22). The commission appointed by President Hoover to investigate American society at the beginning of the crisis ignored white collar workers and problems to the greatest extent. Cf. *Report of the President's Research Committee on Social Trends. Recent Social Trends in the United States*, New York 1934; cf. also above, note 84.

101. The railroads were a special case: in spite of reprivatization after 1920 they remained under government control; competition between companies was increasingly restricted. Like large public agencies such as the post office, they were highly bureaucratized. Government agencies and the railroads were less hostile to trade unions than private enterprise. White collar trade unions mentioned continued to exist in government, railroads and in artistic areas during the anti-union 1920s. Their membership (which declined 18%) was in fact more stable than the labor movement as a whole (down 33%). Calculated from Wolman, pp. 172-92. From the same source the following presentation of membership in the more important American white collar unions.

	1910	1920	1930
Draftsmen		2,200	1,200
Commercial Telegraphers	1,000	2,200	4,000
Railroad Station Agents	600	8,800	
Railroad Telegraphers	20,000	78,000	41,000
Railroad Clerks	5,000	186,000	97,000
Federal Employees		38,500	33,500
Postal Supervisors			5,800
Post Office Clerks (Independent)	21,000	29,000	41,000
Post Office Clerks (AFL)	1,400	25,000	44,800
Teachers		9,300	5,200
Actors and Artists		9,000	9,700
Musicians	42,000	70,000	100,000
Retail Clerks	15,000	20,800	10,000
White Collar Unions	107,000	478,000	393,000

102. Cf. International Federation of Commercial, Clerical and Technical Employees, *Ten Years*, Amsterdam (International Salaried Employees, Secretariat) 1930, pp. 21-23 (membership list).

103. 'Living on the Ragged Edge. Family Income vs. Family Expenses', in *Harper's Monthly Magazine*, New York, December 1925, pp. 55-58. Quotes from p. 58.

104. Ray 'White Collary': Satirical sketch of a conversation between the bookkeeper Quiggley and his boss, a small merchant, about the unsatisfactory situation of the 'white collar gang'.

105. Cf. NICB, *Clerical Salaries in the United States*, New York 1926, pp. 29ff.: comparison of the earnings of lower level white collar workers (clerks, ledger clerks, payroll clerks, cost clerks, order clerks, shipping clerks) with the average earnings of blue collar workers in 25 industries in the same year: the former came to about $25, the latter to $27.27.

106. Cf. Cowdrick (1924), pp. 154-56; Coyle, *Present Trends* (1928), p. 32; B. R. Morley, *Occupational Experience of Applicants for Work in Philadelphia* (Diss., University of Pennsylvania) Philadelphia 1930, p. 15: 25.7% of the employed population of Philadelphia and 26% of the unemployed group investigated (1,132 persons altogether) belonged to the category 'trade and clerical'; the figures for factory workers were 47.5 and 59.2%; for professionals: 5.2 and 1.7%.

107. The best contemporary summary of this industrial revolution in the office is Coyle, *Present Trends*, pp. 17ff.; p. 25f. Thoughts on the shifts in status it implied: ibid., ' "White Collars" and Trade Unions (1928)'; and 'What can the Office Workers Learn from the Factory Worker?', in *The American Federationist*, Vol. 36, 1929, pp. 917-18. From the massive literature on efficient, rational office organization: C. C. Parsons, *Office Organization and Management*, Chicago 1918; W. H. Leffingwell, *Office Management. Principles and Practice*, Chicago 1925; also the Proceedings of the National Association of Office Managers from 1920.

108. Cf. above, pp. 113ff. The chance for office workers to advance was emphasized for instance in the 'Opportunity Monographs' published for disabled veterans: Federal Board for Vocational Education, Vocational Rehabilitation Series, No. 23: 'Commercial Occupations', Washington 1919, e.g., pp. 6, 12. On the apparent reduction of these chances already: S. Nearing, *Poverty and Riches*,

Philadelphia 1916, pp. 132-37, 144-45, which presents the industrial white collar workers' problem primarily as a mobility problem of 'men half-way-up'. W. B. Catlin, *The Labor Problem in the United States and Great Britain*, New York 1926, p. 41.

109. Cf. on this comparison with the most important literature: Kaelble, 'Soziale Mobilität', pp. 113-115, 117-120; more exact figures for German commercial employees in Hamm, p. 52: in 1908 19% of the members of the DHV (male) came from working class families; in 1929 24% of the male and 29% of the female members of the GDA did, and in the same year 65% of the female members of the relatively leftist Zentralverband der Angestellten had working class origins: above all: Speier, *Angestellte*. An excellent comparison of one county in 1910 and 1940: N. Rogoff, *Recent Trends in Occupational Mobility*, Glencoe, Ill. 1953; Lipset/Bendix, *Social Mobility*, esp. pp. 33ff., 101ff., 122ff.; Thernstrom, 'Class and Mobility in a Nineteenth-Century City', in R. Bendix and S. Lipset (eds.), *Class, Status and Power*, New York 1966,[2] pp. 602-15, p. 613f.; Thernstrom, *The Other Bostonians*, esp. Chs. 5 and 9 (with further references). Cf. on England Klingender, p. 64f., who estimates that 30-35% of English 'clerks' (industry, insurance, banks, etc.) came from working class families (1930).

110. Especially Rogoff, pp. 47, 48, 50f., 54, 56f., 61: comparison of intergenerational rates of mobility in Indianapolis and surroundings 1910 and 1940.

111. Cf. Thernstrom, 'Class', p. 612 (with the literature cited); Lipset/Bendix, *Social Mobility*, pp. 288ff., 27, 90, 184ff. Very good, however: S. Goldstein, 'Migration and Occupational Mobility in Norristown, Pennsylvania', in *ASR*, Vol. 20, 1955, pp. 402-408; more extensively, ibid., *Patterns of Mobility, 1910-1950. The Norristown Study. A Method for Measuring Migration and Occupational Mobility in the Community*, Philadelphia 1958. Without long time comparisons: G. L. Palmer, *Labor Mobility in Six Cities*, New York 1954, esp. p. 115; for the 1960s: J. L. Stern and D. B. Johnson, *Blue- to White-Collar Job Mobility*, Madison 1968.

112. Based on *Historical Statistics*, p. 74. Categories 1, 2 and 4 include some self-employed persons, especially in 1. With reference to the above statements this is not a great distortion, however, if one views independent and dependent positions in the first two categories as an advance for persons in the third category.

113. Cf. Nichols, *Conception*, pp. 80ff., 86.

114. The overqualification of many office employees (at the bookkeeper and secretarial level) and the preference of office managers for high school graduates is shown for 1926 on the basis of broad survey results in ibid., pp. 50-65.

115. Federal Board of Vocational Education, Vocational Rehabilitation Series No. 25 ('Occupation in the Electrical Manufacturing Industries'), Washington 1919, p. 5f. and No. 29 ('Drafting'), Washington 1919, pp. 5-7. In 1950 86% of the professional and technical employees had spent at least four years in high school, as had 59% of the sales employees, 56% of clerks, 29% of skilled workers and 20% of unskilled workers (from Lipset/Bendix, *Social Mobility*, p. 92).

116. Cf. above, pp. 107ff.

117. Thus also the Society for Promotion of Engineering Education, *Report of the Investigation of Engineering Education 1923-29*, Vol. 2, Pittsburgh 1934, Part 2, p. 6.

118. Cf. Bossard/Dewhurst, esp. pp. 247-63.

119. From Wolfle, pp. 294.

120. Ibid., p. 31.

121. D. M. Blank and G. J. Stigler, *The Demand and Supply of Scientific Personnel*, New York 1957, p. 4f.

122. Figures organized by branches from the not precisely dated, probably unpublished investigation of the NICB are partly reprinted in Society for the Promotion of Engineering Education, *Report*, Vol. 2, Part 2, pp. 64, 66 (around 1925/27).

The formulation 'college trained' included former college students with or without degree. Cf. also Kocka I, p. 426, note 145.

123. This number from F. W. Taussig and C. S. Josyln, *American Business Leaders. A Study in Social Origins and Social Stratification*, New York 1932, p. 166.

124. Cf. above, pp. 101-17.

125. Overview in B. R. Haynes and H. P. Jackson, *A History of Business Education in the United States*, Cincinnati 1935, esp. pp. 37f., 50f., 65f., 99, passim.

126. Thus already in 1918: Federal Board for Vocational Education, Vocational Rehabilitation Series, No. 23 ('Commercial Occupations'), Washington 1919, pp. 9, 12.

127. Cf. Nichols, *Conception*, p. 51f.

128. Cf. above, pp. 167ff.

129. Nichols circles this problem, esp. pp. 23ff., 50-65.

130. Cf. E. P. Cubberley, *Public Education in the United States. A Study and Interpretation of American History*, Boston 1934, pp. 554-8, 631ff., 644ff.; Barlow, p. 292ff.; Society for the Promotion of Engineering Education, *Report*, Vol. 2, Part 2, p. 2.

131. Cf. ibid., pp. 11, 40ff., 56, 71, 81ff.

132. Cf. ibid., pp. 247-69, esp. p. 267.

133. Cf. Nichols, *Conception*, p. 63. These attitudes were also expressed in *The G. E. Monogram. A Magazine for the Sales Organization*. Cf. e.g. the poem 'Be the Best' (inside back cover) in Vol. 1, December 1923 which concluded:

> If you can't be a highway, then just be a rail
> If you can't be the sun, be a star;
> It isn't by size that you win and fail —
> Be the best of whatever you are.

134. Nichols, *Conception*, pp. 90ff., 79. Correspondents, who were over 90% male, showed the highest expectations of upward mobility.

135. From Goldstein, 'Migration', pp. 405-407.

136. From ibid., pp. 405 and 405-407: mobility into white collar positions (clerical and sales) in %:

	1910-20	1920-30	1930-40	1940-50
By Skilled Workers	1.7	4.0	5.3	3.1
By Semiskilled Workers	4.9	8.1	9.1	4.5
By Unskilled Workers	4.2	2.7	4.7	5.2

137. Cf. Lipset/Bendix, *Social Mobility*, pp. 93 ff.

138. The number of Junior Colleges, founded primarily in the west and the south in order to give more youths a chance at college education and considered both a major lever and proof of democracy, increased between 1902 and 1929 from 1 to 400. Cf. Cubberley, p. 557; Society for the Promotion of Engineering Education, *Report*, Vol. 2, Part 23, p. 47. Yet even in the relatively unstratified west and at this education level in 1929/30 the children of executives, proprietors, and professionals were clearly overrepresented, while children of blue collar and lower/intermediate level white collar workers were clearly underrepresented. Cf. the survey in H. D. Anderson, 'Whose Children Attend Junior College?', in *Junior College Journal*, Vol. 4, 1934, pp. 165-72, esp. p. 169. The disproportionate representation of

various classes and occupational groups at colleges would, of course, be even more distinct, if one compared the occupations of fathers of students at private schools or universities such as Harvard (ibid., p. 171).

139. NICB, *Clerical Salaries*, p. 35; cf. similarly, Douglas, *Real Wages* (1930), p. 367f.; and Cowdrick (1924), p. 153; Coyle, *Present Trends*, p. 38; and above, note 84.

140. A good, brief analysis of this movement with rich source materials and many illustrations: S. H. Slichter, 'The Current Labor Policies of American Industries', in *The Quarterly Journal of Economics*, Vol. 43, 1929, pp. 345-64. I have gone through a great number of sources for variations in the treatment of blue and white collar workers, mostly with negative results. Cf. e.g. 'Health and Recreation Activities in Industrial Establishments 1926' (*BLSt., Bulletin*, No. 458), Washington 1928; 'Handbook of Labor Statistics', 1921 Edition (*BLSt., Bulletin*, No. 541), Washington 1931, esp. pp. 379ff., 415ff., 469ff., 673ff., 891ff.; J. T. Broderick, *Pulling Together*, Schenectady, NY 1922 (on General Electric); The Goodyear Tire and Rubber Company, Akron, Ohio, *The Work of the Labor Division*, Akron 1920; D. Bloomfield (ed.), *The Modern Executive*, New York 1924; H. Feldman, 'A Survey of Research in the Field of Industrial Relations. A Preliminary Report to the Advisory Committee on Industrial Relations of the Social Science Research Council, New York June 8, 1928' (this typewritten carbon copy lists a number of current problems under debate, but contains no references to white collar workers); S. A. Lewinsohn, *The New Leadership in Industry*, New York 1926; NICB, *Industrial Relations Programs in Small Plants*, New York 1929; ibid., *Industrial Pensions in the United States*, New York 1925; ibid., *Industrial Relations*, New York 1931; also material from the AMA. Recently: G. E. Kahler and A. C. Johnson, *The Development of Personnel Administration, 1923-1945*, Madison 1971.

141. Cf. AMA, Survey Report No. 5 (*The Negro in Industry*), New York 1923, p. 25: 'The office worker and the grimy mechanic of the same race do not care to mingle at lunch; the latter is at a disadvantage which is not felt when they are separate'. 'Handbook of Labor Statistics 1924-1926' (*BLSt., Bulletin*, No. 439), Washington 1927, pp. 611-16: differing vacation rights; also Bloomfield and Bloomfield, *Employee Vacation Plans*, Boston 1923; Metropolitan Life Insurance Company, Home Office, New York, *Vacation for Industrial Workers*, New York revised edition (1930), p. 5.

142. Cowdrick (1924), pp. 156-60.

143. E. J. Benge, *Cutting Clerical Costs*, New York 1931, pp. 260ff., 265, 269, 272f.

144. Cf. 'Unemployment-Benefit Plans...' (*BLSt., Bulletin*, No. 544), Washington 1931, p. 13; K. J. Adams, *Humanizing a Great Industry (Armour & Co.)*, n.p., n.d. (1919), pp. 18, 20, 22, 30: gyms, massage, medical check ups for correspondents; female office employees had their own courses, dances, gymnastic programs; 'salaried employees' had certain pension privileges; office employees had their own orchestra, separate garages and separate hairdressers (on company property). Eastman Kodak Company, *Industrial Relations*, Rochester, NY 1924, pp. 5, 7ff., 15f., 17: psychological tests only for white collar workers and for blue collar workers who 'rose' into the office; special educational opportunities for white collar workers; greater pension rights for 'office and salaried employees' in contrast to 'hour and piece workers'; white collar vacation privileges. 'Handbook of Labor Statistics 1924-26', pp. 330-33: continued pay checks in cases of sickness much more frequent for white collar workers. Further: AMA, Survey Report No. 18 (*Payment to Employees When Absent on Account of Jury and Military Duty*), New York 1925; ibid., Survey Report No. 6 (*Wage Payment in Cash or Check*), New York 1923: blue collar paid in cash, white collar in check.

145. Cf. Slichter, p. 415f. on the Commonwealth Edison Company in Chicago and Standard Oil in California.

146. Cf. Nichols, *Conceptions*; Benge; the bibliography in Coyle, *Present Trends*, pp. 42-44; the literature on office organization in note 107 above; and A. M. Ruggles, *A Diagnostic Test of Aptitude for Clerical Office Work*, New York 1924; D. M. Andrew, *Measured Characteristics of Clerical Workers*, Minneapolis 1934.

147. Cf. A typical example from the 1920s: The National Cash Register Company's profit sharing plan had four steps: (a) 35 executives; (b) 100 department heads and foremen; (c) 400 assistant foremen and assistant department heads; (d) 5,000 employees in the office and the factory (with no differentiations within each category); from Crowther, *John H. Patterson*, pp. 260-61. If companies provided clubs and recreational facilities, it was either for all employees together (whether or not all made the same use of them is a second question) or for departments or occupational groups (foremen or technicians, e.g.) separately: from *Health and Recreation Activities*, p. 37.

148. Cf. NICB, *Employee Magazines in the United States*, New York 1925.

149. Cf. the lead article in *The G. E. Monogram*, Vol. 2, July 1925, p. 18: 'Somewhere in the inner consciousness of every salesman is graven the proudly humble motto of the Prince of Wales: "I Serve"... No salesmen can get away from it. By the very nature of things, service is his life motif'. The above presentation is based on reviewing Vols. 1-8, 1923-30.

150. Based on: *PTM*, Vol. 1, 1926 to Vol. 7, 1932.

151. Cf. *Schenectady Works News*, Vol. 1, March 1917, p. 2; *PTM*, Vol. 2, October 1927, pp. 5ff.

152. *PTM*, Vol. 1, April 1924, p. 33.

153. Cf. G. F. Buxton, *A Report of Foremanship Conferences; 7 Years Services to the Industries of Indiana 1923-1930* (1931); Bloomfield, *Selected Articles*, pp. 301-29; ibid., *Executive*, pp. 197-222; H. Diemer et al., *The Foreman and His Job. The First Work Manual of the Modern Foremanship Course*, Chicago 1921; 'Bibliography on Foreman Training. A Selected and Annotated List of References on Recent Books, Pamphlets and Magazine Articles' (Federal Board for Vocational Education, *Bulletin*, No. 128), Washington 1928; cf. also Slichter, p. 412f.

154. Cf. The National Association of Foremen, *A Present Day Necessity. The Foremen's Club. Its Purpose and Organization*, Dayton, Ohio (1938) 1946^2, pp. 12f., 5.

155. In 1946 the National Association of Foremen had 30,000 members: 79% were foremen, supervisors, and department heads; 13% top white collar workers like members of the board of directors and factory directors; 8% were engineers, purchasing agents, or highly qualified skilled workers. Two hundred clubs existed (especially in the midwest), 165 at the company level. It seems likely that the employer paid the membership dues. After 1935 a second federation, the National Council of Foremen's Clubs, existed with ca. 100 clubs (1946), each with 150-300 members. Altogether it had 27,000 members in 23 states. At both organizations' yearly meetings most speakers were top industrial managers. From: W. W. Mussmann, 'Foremens' Clubs', in *Management Record*, November 1946, p. 375.

156. NAF (National Association of Foremen), *Code of Ethics*, Dayton, Ohio (1944) 1945 (in Acc. 354, Ford Archives, Dearborn, Mich.).

157. Cf. C. E. Noyes, 'The Profession of Management', in *The Antioch Review*, Vol. 5, March 1945, pp. 16-23; Milton, pp. 100-34.

Chapter 4: American White Collar Workers in the Economic Crisis and the New Deal

1. Columns (a) and (b): International Labour Office, *Year-Book of Labour Statistics*, Geneva 1939, p. 24f.; columns (c) and (d): ibid., p. 28 (wage earners only); columns (e) and (h): United Nations, *Statistical Yearbook 1948*, Vol. 1, New York 1949, p. 84. In view of the high number of estimates, varying definition of terms and methods of collection, these are only approximate figures; cf. on the problems in determining unemployment figures the literature in Lösche, *Industriegewerkschaften*, p. 203, n. 7, as well as: 'Labor Force, Employment, and Unemployment, 1929-1939. Estimating Methods', in *MLR*, Vol. 67, 1948, pp. 50-53. Cf. on the entire chapter also J. Kocka, 'Amerikanische Angestellte in Wirtschafskrise und New Deal 1930-1940', in *VfZ*, Jg. 21, 1972, pp. 333-75.

2. Bry, p. 467. The figures exclude agricultural workers. Detailed figures on unemployment and real earnings in Germany in T. W. Mason, *Arbeiterklasse und Volksgemeinschaft. Dokumente und Materialien zur deutschen Arbeiterpolitik 1936-1939*, Opladen 1975, esp. pp. 60-77, 1249-86. From this data unemployment declined a little more slowly after 1933/34 and real earnings recovered still more slowly after 1933 than the above figures indicate. Ibid., pp. 1241-43 on increase in number of hours worked and p. 1266 on hour earnings, which rose only slightly after 1933 and remained distinctly lower than the level of 1929. Mason's figures allow differentiation of the highly aggregated figures presented above. They do not, however, permit a comparison of blue and white collar workers.

3. Cf. D. Petzina, 'Germany and the Great Depression', in *JCH*, Vol. 4, October 1969, pp. 59-74. W. Bowden, 'Labor in Depression and Recovery, 1929-1937', in *MLR*, Vol. 45, November 1934, pp. 1045-81.

4. From F. C. and F. E. Croxton, esp. p. 159.

5. *MLR*, Vol. 42, 1936, p. 713. Cf. above, note 4.

6. Unemployment figures (1937) from US Bureau of the Census, *Census of Partial Employment. Final Report on Total and Partial Unemployment. U.S. Summary*. Washington 1938, p. 5. These figures also include those engaged on public relief projects, but not temporary or part-time workers. Figures for total employed in 1940 from D. L. Kaplan and M. C. Casey, *Occupational Trends in the United States 1900 to 1950* (US Bureau of the Census, Working Paper No. 5), Washington 1958, p. 6.

7. In the spring of 1932, of 1,718 private businesses surveyed 1,383 had reduced the salaries of managers and executives, 1,391 those of other white collar employees, and 1,195 had cut the wages of blue collar workers. If one compares the weighted averages, the salaries of executives/managers declined 14.9% from 1929 to March/May 1932, those of other white collar workers droped 13.1% and wages declined 11.1%. Salary reductions increased going up the salary scale. From NICB, *Salary and Wage Policy in the Depression*, New York 1932, pp. 48, 56.

8. Because of source problems, these are very rough comparisons (yearly averages per capita). The figures for the US refer to 'manufacturing industries', that is, excluding mining and construction. Based on Kuznets, *National Income*, from Table 3.12 above. The figures for Germany are calculated from *Wirtschaft und Statistik*, Jg. 19, 1939, pp. 296, 299; they refer to all industry, that is including mining and construction.

9. Cf. A. Sturmthal (ed.), *Contemporary Collective Bargaining in Seven Countries*, Ithaca, NY 1957, p. 355: Variations in earnings between skilled and unskilled workers were also more pronounced after the second world war in the US than in Germany.

10. The National Industrial Recovery Act of 1933 provided for establishing minimum wages by industrial branches. The codes, which also regulated hours,

seem to have had a leveling effect on wages and salaries. Cf. M. H. Schoenfeld, 'Analysis of the Labor Provisions of N.R.A. Codes', in *MLR*, Vol. 40, 1935, pp. 574-603, esp. pp. 579ff.

11. Burns, 'Comparative Economic Position'.

12. Evidence in Kocka I, p. 432 (note 14) and Lorenz-Curve, p. 433.

13. Cf. e.g. G. R. Leighton, 'And If the Revolution Comes?', in *Harper's Monthly Magazine*, Vol. 164, March 1932, pp. 466-76; D. Wecter, *The Age of the Great Depression 1929-1941*, New York (1948) 1969, pp. 36ff. Further: E. Leuchtenburg, *Franklin D. Roosevelt and the New Deal 1923-1940*, New York 1963, pp. 18ff., 23f., 25, 30f., 51ff., 74, 78.

14. Cf. E. W. Bakke, *The Unemployed Worker*, New Haven 1940, pp. 25-26; M. Komarovsky, *The Unemployed Man and His Family*, New York 1940, pp. 23-27; J. C. Furnas et al., *How America Lives*, Oxford 1941, p. 3. Cf. in contrast the completely different reactions in M. Jahoda et al., *Die Arbeitslosen von Marienthal* (1933), Neuaufl. Allensbach 1960, esp. pp. 80-100.

15. Cf. M. Wallace, 'The Uses of Violence in American History', in *American Scholar*, Vol. 40, 1970/71, pp. 82, 97f.

16. Cf. the interview with the psychiatrist D. F. Rossmann in S. Terkel, *Hard Times. An Oral History of the Great Depression*, New York 1970, p. 80f.; similarly pp. 77, 86, 92, 196f. A graphic description of the mood of the 'American middle class' (from a practicing physician to bank clerks and skilled workers) at the end of 1931, in G. W. Johnson, 'The Average American and the Depression', in *Current History*, Vol. 35, New York 1932, pp. 671-75; Leuchtenburg, *Roosevelt*, p. 26 with further references.

17. An overview of social and economic legislation in the New Deal in B. Mitchell, *Depression Decade. From New Era through New Deal, 1929-1941* (1947), New York 1969. An interesting comparison from quite other perspectives: J. A. Garraty, 'New Deal, National Socialism, and the Great Depression', in *AHR*, Vol. 78, 1973, pp. 907-44; the stabilizing effects are emphasized in B. J. Bernstein, 'The New Deal: The Conservative Achievements of Liberal Reform', in ibid. (ed.), *Towards a New Past. Dissenting Essays in American History*, New York 1968, pp. 263-88. Cf. also E. W. Hawley, *The New Deal and the Problem of Monopoly: A Study in Economic Ambivalence*, Princeton 1969; J. Braeman et al. (eds.), *The New Deal*, 2 vols., Columbus, Ohio 1975; F. Freidel, *Launching the New Deal*, Boston 1973.

18. The extent to which disappointment over New Deal reforms had replaced initial confidence among intellectuals, who as a group were increasingly turning to the left, by the middle of 1934 is shown in the collection of articles from *Common Sense*: A. M. Bingham and S. Rodman (eds.), *Challenge to the New Deal*, New York 1934.

19. On protest politicians and the agitation, which like Townsend and Long pushed the president toward more decisive social welfare policies: A. M. Schlesinger, Jr., *The Politics of Upheaval* (1960), Boston 1966, pp. 15-207; and pp. 282ff. as well as the next note. On trade union history: I. Bernstein, *Turbulent Years. A History of the American Worker 1933-1941*, Boston 1970; Lösche, *Industriegewerkschaften*; D. Brody, 'Labor and the Great Depression', in *LH*, Vol. 13, 1972, pp. 231-44. On the level of organization and strikes: *Historical Statistics*, p. 98. On the Second New Deal: Schlesinger, *Politics*, pp. 211-657; F. Freidel in A. L. Hamby (ed.), *The New Deal*, New York 1969, pp. 11-32, esp. pp. 25ff.; Leuchtenburg, *Roosevelt*, pp. 147-96; S. Lubell, *The Future of American Politics*, New York 1951, pp. 232-34; R. S. Kirkendall, 'The Great Depression', in Braeman et al., *Change*, pp. 167-74 (with bibliography); W. F. Ogburn and E. Hill, 'Income Classes and the Roosevelt Vote', in *PSQ*, Vol. 50, 1935, pp. 186-93; W. F. Ogburn and L. C. Coombs, 'The Economic Factor in the Roosevelt Elections, in *APSR*, Vol. 34, 1940, pp. 719-27, here p. 719; Terkel, p. 135.

20. Cf. S. Fine, *Sit-Down. The General Motors Strike of 1936-1937*, Ann Arbor 1969; Bernstein, *Turbulent Years*, pp. 519ff. on trade union history; J. MacGregor Burns, *Roosevelt*; Vol. 1: *The Lion and the Fox*; Vol. 2: *The Soldier of Freedom*, New York 1956 and 1970, here Vol. 1, pp. 291-478 on New Deal history after 1937; W. E. Leuchtenburg, 'Franklin D. Roosevelt's Supreme Court "Packing" Plan', in W. H. Droz et al., *Essays on the New Deal*, Austin 1969, pp. 69-115; on the revival of conservative forces: Leuchtenburg, *Roosevelt*, pp. 254, 273. An extensive survey of the for the most part numerically insignificant but extremely vocal fascist or fascistic fringe groups in D. S. Strong, *Organized Anti-Semitism in America*, Washington 1941; recently Lipset/Raab, *Politics*, pp. 150-208. On the growing influence of the communists in the CIO: I. Howe and L. Coser, *The American Communist Party*, Boston 1957, esp. pp. 368-86; Rayback, p. 366f.; D. R. McCoy, *Angry Voices, Left-of-Center Politics in the New Deal Era*, Lawrence, Kansas 1958. On the House Committee on Un-American Activities, primarily directed at the left, cf. A. R. Ogden, *The Dies Committee*, Washington 1945.

21. Cf. Kirkendall, 'Great Depression', p. 170; Lubell, pp. 51ff., who for 1940 found that a monthly rent of $45-60 (in the cities) was the dividing line between Roosevelt and Landon voters and discovered 'class consciousness' and 'economic voting' among workers and rich Republicans; Burns, *Roosevelt*, Vol. 1, pp. 442-55.

22. Cf. J. L. Shover, 'Ethnicity and Religion in Philadelphia Politics, 1924-40', in *American Quarterly*, Vol. 25, 1973, pp. 499-515, who can demonstrate that in Philadelphia the vote for or against Roosevelt varied more strongly between ethnic groups than between social-economic categories.

23. Cf. Kocka I, p. 435, n. 27.

24. Cf. V. Shlakman, 'Status and Ideology of Office Workers', in *Science and Society*, Vol. 16, 1952, pp. 1-26, here p. 16; further: L. Corey, *The Crisis of the Middle Class*, New York 1935, p. 256f.; as well as the evidence in Leuchtenburg, *Roosevelt*, p. 119f.

25. On the problem of unemployed white collar workers cf. already (Hoover's) *The President's Organization of Unemployment Relief. Second brief report on made work for white-collar unemployed*, Washington, 10 March 1932, 'Effect of Depression on Office Workers', in *MLR*, Vol. 33, 1931, pp. 1057-59; 'Middle Class Misery', in *Survey*, Vol. 68, 1932, pp. 402-404; A. M. Edwards, 'The "White-Collar Workers",' in *MLR*, Vol. 38, March 1934, pp. 501-505; *Monthly Report of the FERA*, Washington, October 1935, pp. 25-30: in thirteen cities ca. 40% of the labor force were in white collar occupations (according to the 1930 census), but only 18% were on relief.

26. Cf. WPA, *Government Aid During the Depression to Professional, Technical and Other Service Workers*, New York 1936, p. 11f.

27. *Monthly Report of the FERA*, Washington, December 1935, pp. 59-63; WPA, *Government Aid*, p. 3f.

28. Cf., for instance, WPA, *Weekly Progress Report*, Washington, 20-25 January, 1936, p. 3f.: in 108 counties in twelve states (mostly rural) 3.9% of the WPA employees had white collar occupations, but only 1.7% were placed in them.

29. Cf. *Monthly Report of the FERA*, Washington, December 1933, p. 7; June 1935, pp. 16-19; December 1935, p. 62. An overview of ongoing white collar programs in *The Project*, issued by the Work Division of the FERA, Washington, January 1935, pp. 39-42; ibid., May 1936, pp. 20-33. On events after mid-1935: 'White Collar Work under the WPA', in *MLR*, Vol. 45, 1937, pp.1364-70; D. S. Howard, *The WPA and Federal Relief Policy*, New York 1943, pp. 138ff. (on the controversy about the allegedly too 'left' publicly financed theater project 1939), pp. 187, 232, 449, 607; see also R. D. McKinzie, *The New Deal for Artists*, Princeton 1973.

30. Cf. WPA, *Government Aid*, pp. 10-12, 71: The maximum monthly income

(which was only paid in cities with a population of over 10,000 and in expensive states like New York and Massachusetts) in 1936 was: $55 for unskilled, $65 for semi-skilled, $85 for skilled and $94 for technical and professional work. The lowest income paid was $19, $27, $35, and $39 respectively (in places with fewer than 500 inhabitants in most southern states).

31. Calculated from US Bureau of Census, *Census of Partial Employment . . . Summary*, p. 5. On this also A. E. Burns, 'Work Relief Wage Policies, 1930-36', in *Monthly Report of the FERA*, Washington, June 1936, pp. 22-55.

32. Cf. in particular WPA, *Government Aid*, pp. 5, 7, 13f., 15, 17; on emergency relief projects generally, the head of the WPA: H. L. Hopkins, *The Realities of Unemployment*, Washington n.d. (1936); cf. further: H. Swados, *The American Writer and the Greater Depression*, Indianapolis 1966.

33. WPA, *Government Aid*, pp. 9, 12f., 15, 17, 41, 52ff.

34. Cf. the titles above in notes 24 and 25; 'The Plight of the White Collar Army', in *The Literary Digest*, Vol. 105, 7 June 1930, pp. 69-70; 'The Middle Class Unemployed', in *Spectator*, 9 March 1934, p. 361; 'Significance of White-Collars', in *The World Tomorrow*, Vol. 16, 1933, p. 198; cf. also the evidence in Shlakman, p. 17.

35. Still used with quotation marks by L. Corey, *Crisis*, pp. 112, 147ff., passim; Bingham, *Insurgent America*, p. 50, passim, who refers to G. D. H. Cole, *What Marx Really Meant*, London 1934, p. 99.

36. Cf. the still commonly used reclassification of the results of the American occupational census, which in contrast to Germany and Prussia was originally organized only on functional criteria (economic area or occupation), by A. M. Edwards, 'A Social-Economic Grouping of the Gainful Workers of the United States', in *JAStA*, Vol. 28, 1933, pp. 377-91, esp. pp. 377ff. Edwards, an official in the Census Bureau, attempted to regroup the census results by stratification criteria; the difference between head and hand work served as the main dividing line. There had been forerunners, but the division between hand and head worker was much less clearly defined in them. Cf. I. A. Hourwich, 'The Social-Economic Classes of the Population of the United States', in *Journal of Political Economy*, Vol. 19, 1911, pp. 188-215, 309-37, esp. pp. 190-94, 310ff.; A. H. Hansen, 'Industrial Class Alignments in the United States', in *QPAStA*, Vol. 17, 1920, pp. 417-25; ibid., 'Industrial Classes in the United States in 1920', in *JAStA*, Vol. 18, 1922, pp. 503-506; and A. M. Edwards, 'Social Economic Groups of the United States', in *QPAStA*, Vol. 15, 1917, pp. 643-61, esp. pp. 644ff.

37. Cf. E. Lederer, 'The Problem of the Modern Salaried Employee: Its Theoretical and Statistical Basis' (Chs. 2 and 3 of *Die Privatangestellten*, 1912) (published by the State Department of Social Welfare and the Department of Social Science, Columbia University, as a Report on Project No. 165-6999-6027 Conducted Under the Auspices of the WPA), New York 1937; Speier, 'The Salaried Employee in Modern Society'; ibid., *The Salaried Employee in German Society* (translated as a Report on Project No. 465-97-3-81 under the Auspcies of the WPA), New York 1939 (part of Speier's unpubl. diss. *Soziologie der Angestellten*, 1932, which appeared in revised form in 1977 under the title, *Die Angestellten vor dem Nationalsozialismus*); in mimeographed form also under the auspices of the same project a translation was available of F. Croner, *The White Collar Movement in Germany since the Monetary Stabilization*, New York 1937 (German original in *ASS*, Vol. 60, 1928, pp. 103-46 entitled 'Die Angestelltenbewegung nach der Währungsstabilisierung'); C. Dreyfuss, *Occupation and Ideology of the Salaried Employees*, New York 1938 (German original entitled: *Beruf und Ideologie der Angestellten*, München 1933).

38. Cf. Such a line of thought in Niebuhr, 'Pawns'; similarly: H. N. Brailsford, 'The Middle Class and Revolution', in *The World Tomorrow*, Vol. 16, 1933,

pp. 465-66; 'Hitler and the Middle Classes', in ibid., p. 147; Barnes, 'Social Basis', who like many others analyzed the 'petite bourgeoisie' as the social basis of fascism. Implied also in the critical novel recommended by the *New Masses*: E. Seaver, *The Company*, New York 1930, pp. 110ff. and 145ff. (on the anti-socialist hysteria and anti-semitism of office employees).

39. Cf. *Common Sense*, ed. by A. M. Bingham and S. Rodman, Vol. 1ff. (New York 1932/33ff.), reprinted New York 1968; evidence and quotes from *CS* in Kocka I, p. 438f., n. 48; Bingham, *Insurgent America*, pp. 36f., 104ff., 179-93. See also F. A. Warren III, 'Alfred Bingham and the Paradox of Liberalism', in *The Historian*, Vol. 28, February 1966, pp. 252-67. On technocratic ideas in the group: Bingham, *Insurgent America*, pp. 189-92, 223-35. On this in general: S. Chase, *Technocracy. An Interpretation*, New York 1933; H. Elsner, Jr., *The Technocrats: Prophets of Automation*, Syracuse, NY 1967.

40. Cf. N. Thomas, *The Choice Before Us*, New York 1934, pp. 54, 77, 78, 186, 220. 'The Significance of White-Collars', in *The World Tomorrow*, Vol. 16, 1933, pp. 198-99; H. W. Laidler, 'The White-Collar Worker', in *The American Socialist Review*, Vol. 3, Fall 1934, pp. 53-58. A moderately progressive politics from the 'middle income skill group' ('the small farmers, the small business men, the low salaried intellectuals, and the skilled workers') was also hoped for by H. D. Lasswell, 'The Moral Vocation of the Middle Income Skill Group', in *The International Journal of Ethics*, Vol. 45, 1935, pp. 127-37, esp. pp. 127, 133, 136f.; cf. also Saposs, pp. 414ff.

41. Cf. the *New Masses*, Vol. 5, May 1930, p. 17: 'White-Collar Slaves' (including the description of a police attack on a demonstration by radical workers in Manhattan:

> Up on the Treasury Building steps, out of the windows of office buildings, skyscrapers, twenty dollars-a-week clerks in striped collegiate cravats howled with delight as the police swung their clubs at the hopeless heads of the manifestants.

Cf. M. Gold, 'Hemingway — White Collar Poet', ibid., Vol. 3, March 1928, p. 21; ibid., Vol. 4, August 1928, p. 8: S. Burnshaw, 'White Collar Slaves', a poem glorifying manual labor and pitying or castigating the 'movers of pencils'. On the magazine itself: J. North, (ed.), *New Masses. An Anthology of the Rebel Thirties*, New York 1969, p. 5, 13, 19-33.

42. S. E. Seaver and M. W. Mather, 'White Collar Workers and Students Swing into Action', in *New Masses*, Vol. 22, 5 July 1934, p. 17; Vol. 11, 19 June 1934, p. 9: 'On the White Collar Front'; Vol. 12, 4 September 1934, pp. 16ff.: S. Hill, 'Technicians in Revolt'; ibid., Vol. 14, 22 January 1935: 'A Year of the Guild' (positive treatment of the Newspaper Guild's first year); Corey, *Crisis* (1935), pp. 163ff., 247-77, 344.

43. The Socialist Party at least took specific notice of white collar workers, though it also did not make special demands for their benefit. Cf. the platforms 1932, 1928, and 1912 in K. H. Porter and D. B. Johnson (eds.), *National Party Platforms 1840-1968*, Urbana (1956) 1970, pp. 351, 352, 292, 189.

44. From surveying the platforms, ibid., pp. 325-401. Naturally that did not mean that many points were not *also* addressed to white collar workers. But the benefits were promised to the people, the needy, the unemployed, and white collar workers were not mentioned. In contrast agriculture was always addressed as a separate group, as was labor, business, industry, the Negroes, Indians, youth, veterans and slumdwellers. In fact, references to specific social groups such as these became more common from 1932 to 1940.

45. From a cursory survey of his speeches in S. J. Roseman, *F. D. Roosevelt, The Public Papers and Addresses*..., Vols. 1-13, New York 1950-69; cf. *Roosevelt,*

Complete Presidential Press Conferences, Vol. 1-25 (1933-45), reprinted New York 1972.

46. From statements by Raymond Moley, who in the first years of the New Deal was one of the most important members of Roosevelt's 'Brains trust', in a conversation in Cambridge, Mass. on 11 December 1970. A similar impression emerges from reviewing the special literature on economic and social policies of the New Deal.

47. On the following section: J. Kocka, 'Die Organisationen amerikanischer Angestellter in Wirtschaftskrise und New Deal', in H.-A. Winkler (ed.), *Die grosse Krise in Amerika. Vergleichende Studien zur politisichen Sozialgeschichte 1929-1939*, Göttingen 1973, pp. 40-80.

48. Figures for the German side calculated from Bry, pp. 28 and 43; *Geschäftsbericht des Bundesvorstandes des Deutschen Gewerkschaftsbundes 1950/51*, Köln 1952, p. 733. For the American side I am following the estimates by Mills, pp. 302, 363f.

49. From 'Handbook of American Trade-Unions. 1936 Edition' (*BLSt., Bulletin*, No. 618), p. 7ff.; p. 21f. on the method of collection (figures reported by the unions).

50. From 'Handbook of American Trade-Unions (1936)', pp. 56-234. Organizations ≠3, 15 and 16 included a large number of self-employed, and it cannot be entirely ruled out that at times employed white collar workers were a minority of their members. Not included are purely local organizations that were unaffiliated with the AFL (including all company unions); a few Canadians are included in the figures. Messengers and letter carriers were not considered white collar workers. The sources used here do not contain a definition of 'trade union', only a description which probably conformed to ordinary usage ('Handbook of American Trade Unions' [1936], pp. 17-52). The decisive characteristic of a trade union was the representation of workers' interest against the employer, primarily by seeking to control or influence wages, hours, and working conditions through various tactics: mainly collective bargaining and wage contracts, but without ruling out the strike (p. 17). The definition became sharper only in the course of 1936 (Wagner Act). Cf. Bernstein, *Turbulent Years*, p. 326.

51. Founded in 1933 from the Neptune Association (1912) and Ocean Association of Marine Engineers (1918).

52. Forerunners since 1913.

53. Forerunners since 1897.

54. Forerunners since 1896.

55. Cf. *Historical Statistics*, p. 519f.

56. Calculated from E. F. Denison, 'Revised Estimates of Wages and Salaries in the National Income, 1929-1943', in *Survey of Current Business*, ed. by US Department of Commerce, Bureau of Foreign and Domestic Commerce, June 1945, pp. 17-24, esp. pp. 20 and 21; p. 17 on the definition of terms. Cf. Table 4.4.

57. An exact survey of the decline of these company welfare programs in all economic areas from 1927 to 1936 in NICB, 'What Employers are Doing for Employees' (*NICB Studies*, No. 221), New York 1936, pp. 12, 14, 16, 20, 22. For department stores in particular see the representative survey by Baker, *Personnel Programs*, pp. 21, 29, 32, 40.

58. On the general problem see D. Brody, 'The Emergence of Mass-Production Unionism', in Braeman et al., *Change*, pp. 221-62, esp. p. 248.

59. Cf. *The Advocate*, January/February 1931, pp. 1-4, 7; March/April 1931, pp. 1ff.: the beginning of a boycott against a chain store in Casper, Wyoming with the aid of local blue collar unions; May/June 1931, pp. 12f., 7; November/December 1931, pp. 1-14; March/April 1932, pp. 1-3, 12 (quote); May/June 1932, pp. 14, 20; September/October 1932, p. 3.

60. The membership of the AFL declined from 4.1 million (1920) to 2.3 million (1933). *Historical Statistics*, p. 97. Cf. in general on trade union and labor history

1929-32: Bernstein, *Lean Years*, pp. 245-513, esp. pp. 334ff., 416ff.

61. From a survey by the RCIPA leadership. The absolute number of locals is not reported. Cf. *The Advocate*, May/June 1932, p. 13.

62. Cf. Bernstein, *Turbulent Years*, pp. 19-36 on the creation of the NRA and the interests behind it; pp. 318-51 on the origins of the Wagner Act; R. W. Fleming, 'The Significance of the Wagner Act', in Derber/Young, pp. 121-55; best on the NRA and its critics: Hawley, *New Deal*; recently Lösche, *Industriegewerkschaften*, pp. 46-96: a good analysis of the emerging system of labor law and industrial relations. On the RCIPA's position on the NRA: *The Advocate*, July/August 1933, pp. 1-4; November/December, p. 2 on Section 7(a): 'We predict that this act of emancipation will go down in history as marking the doom of industrial tyranny in the United States'.

63. *The Advocate*, September/October 1933, pp. 1-5; November/December 1933; January/February 1934, pp. 14, 18.

64. Baker, *Personnel Programs*, p. 44 comes to this conclusion in 1935; similarly *The Advocate*, November/December 1933, p. 4.

65. Cf. *The Advocate*, July/August 1933, pp. 3, 15; November/December 1933, pp. 1, 2, 4; January/February 1934, p. 1f.; May/June 1934, p. 1; on an unsuccessful strike in December/January 1934/35 against the Boston Store in Milwaukee cf. 'White-Collar Strike', in *The Nation*, New York, 9 January 1935, p. 49f; *The Advocate*, January/February 1935, pp. 1-10.

66. Cf. the study of the Boston University School of Theology cited in *The Advocate*, November/December 1931, p. 1f.; September/October 1932, p. 1f.: 'Chain Store Managers Rebel'; November/December 1932, p. 3.

67. Baker, *Personnel Programs*, p. 44; St Louis AFL Retail Stores Employees Union, *20 Years of Progress, 1934-54 (Local Union 655)*, n.p., n.d., p. 6.

68. On the fight of the 'Managers and Clerks Union', allied with the Teamsters, Meat Cutters, Warehousemen, Auto Mechanics, and Typographical Union, against the A&P in Cleveland, Ohio in 1934, cf. *The Advocate*, November/December 1934, pp. 1-3; St Louis AFL Retail Stores Employees Union, *20 Years*, p. 7, on the decisive role of the store managers in the foundation of this RCIPA local.

69. Cf. ibid., p. 8 on the career of Vernon A. Housewright, a store manager, who co-founded the first local in St Louis and later (1947) became president of the RCIPA. His successor as leader of the St Louis local, Renschen, was chairman of the St Louis Central Trade and Labor Union Council in 1946; he too had originally been a store manager.

70. For disappointment over extended working hours and wage reductions after the fall of the NRA cf. the examples in *The Advocate*, July/August 1935, pp. 1-5; September/October 1935, pp. 1-3.

71. Thus Brody, 'Labor'. Brody confirms S. Perlman, 'Labor and the New Deal in Historical Perspective', in Derber/Young, pp. 363-70; pp. 45-76 in the same volume a summary of the most important data: E. Young, 'The Split in the Labor Movement'. Cf. also the analysis in Lösche, *Industriegewerkschaften*, esp. pp. 20-39. Extensive and non-analytical: W. Galenson, *The CIO Challenge to the AFL*, Cambridge, Mass. 1960; Bernstein, *Turbulent Years*, pp. 363ff.; M. M. Kampelman, *The Communist Party vs. the CIO*, New York 1957; R. Radosh, 'The Corporate Ideology of American Labor Leaders from Gompers to Hillman', in J. Weinstein and D. W. Eakins (eds.), *For a New America*, New York 1970, pp. 125-52.

72. After 1940 the United Retail, Wholesale and Department Store Employees of America. Figures from L. Troy, *Trade Union Membership, 1897-1962* (National Bureau of Economic Research, Occasional Paper No. 92), New York 1965, pp. A-5, A-22; Troy's figures computed from dues payments (on the method: ibid., pp. 10-17). On the history of the schism: Kirstein, pp. 55-62.

73. Cf. URWEA, *2nd Biennial Convention (Detroit 1939)*, pp. 8-10; Kirstein, pp. 56-60.

74. Thus the URWEA, *2nd Convention (1939), Proceedings*, p. 9f.; Kirstein, p. 56 accepts this argument uncritically in my opinion; cf. also 'White Collar Unions on their Way', in *Business Week*, 19 August 1939, pp. 30-36 on AFL and CIO efforts to organize department store employees.

75. Examples of such employer tactics: *The Advocate*, November/December 1931, p. 3; September/October 1936, p. 3.

76. Cf. e.g. the foundation of the St Louis local in May 1934. It organized 'salespeople and allied workers in their industry'; in 1935 stockroom workers were accepted (St Louis AFL Retail Store Employees Union, *20 Years*, pp. 7, 8). Cf. RCIPA, *19th Convention (1939), Proceedings*, p. 42 on conflicts with stronger craft unions.

77. URWEA, *Constitution 1939*, Article III, Section 1; RCIPA *Constitution 1939*, Section 6(a); very similar already in 1918. URWEA and RCIPA organizers often began a new local with a nucleus of stockroom workers, packers, restaurant workers and truckdrivers who were ready to organize; they then made the first breakthrough against employer resistance, after which the sales personnel found it easier to join. From *Business Week*, 19 August 1933, p. 33.

78. Cf. Troy, *Trade Union Membership*, A-8, A-18, A-22, A-26, and pp. 10-20. Based on his own calculations Troy gives the membership of the RCIPA in 1935 as larger than the figures based on the organization's own reports. This might be explained by the efforts of the organization to save money by submitting lower figures to the AFL (and thus having a lower assessment). In 1939 this relationship was reversed: According to Troy the RCIPA had 51,000 members, the URWEA 44,000; the two unions reported their membership as 85,000 and 75,000 respectively. Cf. RCIPA, *18th Convention (1939), Proceedings*, p. 43; URWEA, *2nd Convention (1939), Proceedings*, p. 56.

79. Cf. *The Advocate*, March/April 1937, pp. 1ff.: description of five department store strikes which were in progress at press time. RCIPA, *19th Convention (1939), Proceedings*, p. 36f. on the distribution of the newly created strike fund; p. 43 on struggles against chain stores; H. A. Millis, *How Collective Bargaining Works*, New York 1942, p. 941 on the AFL-run, successful 55-day strike in the Fall of 1938 in San Francisco against a 'Retailer's Council' of 43 department stores and other businesses; Kirstein, pp. 63-74; *Historical Statistics*, p. 99.

80. Cf. the report on his activities of the URWEA president Wolchok, in URWEA, *2nd Convention (1939), Proceedings*, pp. 56ff.; Millis, p. 941f.; *The Advocate*, March/April 1937, p. 2f.: reprint of strike demands; URWEA, *2nd Convention (1939), Proceedings*, pp. 56ff. (Report by President Wolchok); NICB, *Unions of White Collar Employees*, New York 1943, p. 5. 95,000 trade union members (including some few wholesale employees) compared to 4.47 million employees in retail trade. Cf. *Historical Statistics*, p. 420; Lebergott, p. 518; on the A&P: URWEA, *2nd Convention (1939), Proceedings*, p. 63; *The Advocate*, July/August 1938, p. 1ff.; March/April 1939, p. 12.

81. Cf. RCIPA, *19th Convention (1939), Proceedings*, pp. 9, 10, 80, pp. 14ff.; on the RCIPA after 1945 see also M. Harrington, *The Retail Clerks*, New York 1962; M. Estey, 'The Retail Clerks', in Blum et al., *White-Collar*, pp. 46-82.

82. Cf. URWEA, *2nd Convention (1939), Proceedings*, pp. 7-12, 30f., 33, 41, 52f., 58, 66, 92, 80f. The only black delegate — it was stated that in many locals black members were common — spoke for solidarity between races.

83. The sources permit no systematic analysis of the memberships. The statements above are based on the lists of delegates, ibid., pp. 15ff. and occasional references to occupation in the debates; also NICB, *Unions of White Collar Employees*, p. 5. Cf. generally on the URWEA: B. Stolberg, *The Story of the CIO*, New York 1938, pp. 261-64. On the proportion of women cf. above, Table 2.3 as

well as 'Women's Jobs. Advance and Growth' (*Bulletin of the Women's Bureau*, No. 233), Washington 1949, p. 21: according to the figures there (slightly different from Table 2.3) the proportion of women salespersons was 30% in 1920, 27% in 1930, and 29% in 1940.

84. Cf. below, p. 207: list of white collar organizations. I have not investigated organizations outside commerce and industry on a primary source base. The statements above are based on the secondary literature; as well as N. Denton, *History of the Brotherhood of Railway and Steamship Clerks, Freight Handlers, Express and Station Employees*, Cincinnati, Ohio 1965; H. Hollander, *Quest for Excellence*, Washington 1968 (on the National Federation of Federal Employees); A. A. Hyman, *Significant Factors Relative to the Growth and Potential of the American Federation of State, County and Municipal Employees, AFL-CIO*. Diss. University of Pennsylvania 1963; L. Kramer, *Labor's Paradox. The American Federation of State, County, and Municipal Employees, AFL-CIO*, New York 1962; The American Federation of Government Employees (AFL-CIO Library Washington, Labor History-International Unions, File: Government Employees); Spencer Miller, Jr., *Brief Outline of the National Federation of Post Office Clerks*, New York 1940; F. Monroe, 'The Story of the National Federation of Post Office Clerks', in *The Union Postal Clerk*, August 1936, pp. 2-4; National Association of Letter Carriers (AFL-CIO), *Seminar Booklet* (ca. 1960) (AFL-CIO Library Washington, Labor History-International Unions); F. B. Powers, 'Fifty Years of Union History. An Article About the Commercial Telegraphers Union', in *The American Federationist*, July 1952, pp. 22-24; Troy, 'White-Collar'. An overview of the subject, but without attention to the question of interest here: E. M. Kassalow, 'White-Collar Unionism in the United States', in Sturmthal, *White-Collar*, pp. 305-64; a general confirmation of this thesis in Mills, p. 316f.

85. Cf. L. F. Bollens, *White Collar or Noose? The Occupation of Millions*, New York 1947, p. 184f.

86. Cf. the magazine (after 1891), *Factory and Industrial Management*, Vol. 83, New York 1932, p. 17f.: 'Gone are the Good Old Days': recommends reducing overhead by transferring office employee salaries into cost-related methods of payment based on achievement; pp. 190-99: 'If Fixed Salaries Were Not Fixed' (propaganda for tying white collar salaries to supply and demand considerations); p. 459f.: 'Down with Overhead'.

87. Cf. Table 3.2; for the years after 1939: Burns, 'Comparative Economic Position', p. 260f.

88. Cf. NICB, *Effect of the Depression on Industrial Relations Programs*, New York 1934, pp. 3, 4, 6. In a group of 233 firms studied because of their progressive stance in this area:

	In Existence 1933	Discontinued 1929-1933
Stock Sharing Plans	24	25
Profit Sharing	13	7
Pension Plans	128	7
Suggestion Boxes	102	22
Company Housing	25	8
Cafeterias/Restaurants	124	25
Paid Vacations		
for White Collar Workers	194	18
for Blue Collar Workers	37	28
Athletic Clubs	115	23

Musical Activities	34	20
Outings and Picnics	83	39
Apprenticeship Courses	106	17
Foremen's Courses and Conferences	147	38
Courses of College Graduates	34	15

For further reductions in the course of the depression cf. ibid., *What Employers are Doing for Employees* (1936).

89. Cf. above, p. 180.

90. Cf. above, Table 3.11.

91. Cf. above, Table 3.12; Thernstrom, *The Other Bostonians*, pp. 51f., 56, 59, 233.

92. This presents the problem of boundaries in individual cases, which was only gradually clarified by employer practice and court decisions. The Taft-Hartley Law (1947) drew the conclusion from this clarification process and in Title I, Section 2(12) defined the 'professional employee':

> (a) any employee engaged in work (1) predominantly intellectual and varied in character as opposed to routine mental, manual, mechanical, or physical work; (2) involving the consistent exercise of discretion and judgement in its performance; (3) of such a character that the output produced or the result accomplished cannot be standardized in relation to a given period of time; (4) requiring knowledge of an advanced type in a field of science or learning customarily acquired by a prolonged course of specialized intellectual instruction and study in an institution of higher learning or a hospital, as distinguished from a general academic education or from an apprenticeship or from training in the performance of routine mental, manual, or physical process; or (b) any employee, who (1) has completed the courses of specialized intellectual instruction and study described in clause (4) of paragraph (a), and (2) is performing related work under the supervision of a professional person to qualify himself to become a professional employee as defined in paragraph (a).

From N. S. Falcone, *Labor Law*, New York 1962, p. 424..

93. On the engineering societies, which had largely abandoned their earlier social reform traces and expressed increasingly anti-union, anti-social legislation and New Deal opinions: E. L. Brown, *The Professional Engineer*, New York 1936, pp. 40-59; Layton, *Revolt*, pp. 225-42. J. S. Auerbach, *Lawyers and Social Change in Modern America*, Oxford 1975.

94. Cf. *International Federation of Technical Engineers, Architects and Draftsmen, 1918-1943*, n.d. (1943), p. 24: A local organization of technicians in New York met distrust and rejection when it applied to affiliate with the AFL in 1936; ibid., *Resume of Action Taken at the 15th Annual Convention*, Washington, June 1932; ibid., *Synoptic Report of Proceedings of the 20th Annual Convention*, Washington, September 1937; ibid., *Report of Proceedings, 21st Annual Convention, Philadelphia 1938* (typewritten carbon copy reports in the AFL-CIO Library, Washington).

95. Ibid., *1918-1943*, p. 24 on the foundation of a New York technicians' organization, the Architectural and Engineering Guild, which came into existence in 1933 to influence NRA legislation and only joined the AFL technicians' union in 1937; 'Handbook of American Trade Unions (1936)', p. 291f.; Labor Research Association, *Labor Fact Book III*, New York 1936, p. 116; S. Hill, 'Technicians in Revolt', in *New Masses*, Vol. 12, 4 September 1934, pp. 16-18; Stolberg, p. 264f.

96. 'Unions for Technicians', in *The New Republic*, 24 January 1934, pp. 195-96; also Hill, 'Technicians', p. 17.

97. Cf. NICB, *Unions of White Collar Employees*, New York 1943, p. 6; *Minutes of the Third Annual Convention of the Federation of Architects, Engineers, Chemists, and Technicians (CIO)*, Detroit 1937, pp. 11f., 20f. (on attacks by the National Association of Professional Engineers and the American Society of Civil Engineers); the Federation's responses pp. 2, 8, 9, 22.

98. Cf. International Federation of Technical Engineers, Architects and Draftsmen (AFL), *Synoptic Report of Proceedings (1937)*, p. 32; the reasons remain unclear. Possibly the fact that the 'Federation' already had the reputation of being a communist-led union played a role. Cf. Stolberg, p. 264.

99. Cf. the discussion in United Office and Professional Workers of America (UOPWA), *Proceedings, 2nd Convention*, Washington 1938, p. 40f.

100. Cf. *Minutes of the Third Annual Convention of the Federation of Architects, Engineers, Chemists and Technicians (CIO)*, Detroit 1937 (the only protocoll from these years, typewritten carbon copy in the AFL-CIO Bibliography, Washington); Troy, *Trade Union Membership*, A-20; Stolberg, p. 264; Kampelman; 'Directory of Labor Unions in the United States' (*BLSt., Bulletin*, No. 1127), Washington 1953, p. 5; and typewritten notice of 9 May 1957 in File 'History of Organizations' (AFL-CIO Library Washington); on the UOPWA, 'Directory of National and International Labor Unions in the United States, 1955' (*BLSt., Bulletin*, No. 1185), Washington 1955, p. 30. In 1953 the organization was briefly called the International Federation of Technical Engineers, Architects and Draftsmen.

101. In the spring of 1938 e.g. 2,000 members of the midwest auto industry-based Society of Designing Engineers joined the Federation. Cf. Stolberg, p. 265.

102. Cf. NLRB. Division of Economic Research, *Collective Bargaining in the Newspaper Industry*, Washington 1939, esp. pp. 104-40; very informative on the early history: D. J. Leab, *A Union of Individuals. The Formation of the American Newspaper Guild, 1933-1936*, New York 1970; ibid., 'Toward Unionization', in *LH*, Vol. 11, 1970, pp. 3-22; B. Kritzberg, 'An Unfinished Chapter in White-Collar-Unionism. The Formative Years of the Chicago Newspaper Guild...,' in *LH*, Vol. 14, 1973, pp. 397-413; B. Minton and J. Stuart (eds.), *Men Who Lead Labor*, New York 1937, pp. 115-42 on Heywood Brown, the founder and leader of the Newspaper Guild; Stolberg, pp. 245-56; Bernstein, *Turbulent Years*, pp. 127-37; Kampelman, pp. 18f., 32, 42, 43, 46, 47, 112, 118, 211; on the founding of the American Editorial Association (AFL): 'The Story of a Newspaper Union', in *The American Federationist*, November 1940, p. 11; membership figures from Troy, *Trade Union Membership*, A-6, A-22.

103. Quoted from Air Line Pilots Association International, *News and Progress Bulletin*, Vol. 1, No. 3, January 1932, p. 3f. (lead article by Chairman Behncke); cf. *The Alpa Story. A Study of History, Purposes, Functions and Organization of the Air Line Pilots Association International (AFL-CIO)*, by the APA Public Relations Department, n.p. (1957)^2, 1966, esp. pp. 1f., 16; and *Stenographic Report of Excerpts of the Proceedings of an Organization Meeting. July 27, 1931* (typewritten), in Wayne State University, Labor Archives (Detroit): ALPA, Ser. I, Box 3, Folder 'First ALPA Election' among others; there also a complete collection of *The Air Line Pilot* (the organization's magazine). The union counted 700 members in 1935, 1,000 in 1939. From Troy, *Trade Union Membership*, A-1, Cf. also G. E. Hopkins, *The Airline Pilots: A Study in Elite Unionization*, Cambridge, Mass. 1971.

104. The American Federation of Teachers (AFL) had 4,200 members in 1929; 7,000 in 1932; 13,700 in 1935; and 32,100 in 1939. The Musicians' Union (AFL) had 100,000 members 1929-34; 127,000 in 1939. The actors' and artists' union of the AFL had 4,300 in 1935; 20,100 in 1939. From Wolman, p. 189; Troy, *Trade Union Membership*, A-6, A-9. On the musicians, R. D. Leter, *The Musicians and Petrillo*, New York 1953; cf. also M. Ross, *Stars and Strikes: Unionization of*

Hollywood, New York 1941.

105. Overview of the law, the Board, and its work: Bernstein, *The New Deal Collective Bargaining Policy*, Berkeley 1950, pp. 112-60; pp. 153-60: Reprint of the law (above quote from Section 9[b]); a reliable commentary by a member of the Board: J. Rosenfarb, *The National Labor Policy and How It Works*, New York 1940; an exact survey of the actual impact in Millis.

106. On this now Lösche, *Industriegewerkschaften*, pp. 52-69; L. emphasizes that this decentralization contributed to the fragmentation of the activities of American unions, the isolation of labor conflicts, to maintaining the significance of individual large corporations and to stabilizing the entire system.

107. Traditionally, foremen had been admitted to the printers', construction crafts', and partly also the metal workers' unions (a consequence of the emphasis on the craft); in part this was also true for railroad workers. In commercial shipping, railroads and the post office some foremen's organizations had been created in the 19th century. At the end of the 1930s the situation was thus: Of 186 trade union constitutions studied 120 did not mention foremen; 29 (mostly craft unions in the AFL) admitted them; 37 (mostly CIO) expressly excluded them. It was assumed that as a rule the 120 that did not mention them did not organize foremen. From C. Cabe, *Foremen's Unions, A New Development in Industrial Relations*, Urbana, Ill. 1947, p. 30f.

108. NLRB, *Annual Reports*, Washington, *I* (1936), pp. 112-20, *II* (1937), pp. 122-39; *III* (1938), pp. 156-97; *IV* (1939), pp. 83-97; *V* (1940), pp. 63-71; *VI* (1941), pp. 63-71; ibid.; *II* (1937), pp. 134, 136.

109. Cf. ibid., *I* (1936), p. 119; *II* (1937), p. 133; *III* (1938), p. 188f.

110. On the exclusion of foremen and other supervisory employees: ibid., *II* (1937), p. 136f.; *III* (1938), pp. 180ff.; *IV* (1939), pp. 93ff.; cf. also Rosenfarb, p. 342; C. O. Gregory, *Labor and the Law*, New York 1949[2], p. 323f. After 1941 foremen began to draw the lesson from this and organize separately in the Foremen's Association of America. Cf. Cabe, p. 32f. In 1947 Taft-Hartley stated:

> The term 'supervisor' means any individual having authority, in the interest of the employer to hire, transfer, suspend, lay off, recall, promote, discharge, assign, reward, or discipline other employees, or responsibility to direct them, or to adjust their grievances, or effectively to recommend such action if in connection with the foregoing the exercise of such authority is not of a merely routine or clerical nature, but requires the use of independent judgement.

'Supervisors' were not permitted to be represented by the same bargaining unit as white collar and blue collar workers without 'supervisory status'. (Sources in note 92, above.)

111. NLRB, *III* (1938), p. 184.

112. Cf. ibid., *I* (1936), p. 115; *II* (1937), p. 132f.; *IV* (1939), p. 95. *Minutes of the Third Annual Convention of the Federation of Architects, Engineers, Chemists and Technicians (CIO)*, Detroit 1937, p. 17; Rosenfarb, p. 343; Shlakman, p. 25.

113. Cf. NLRB, *III* (1938), p. 185 and *IV* (1939), p. 85; corroborating: UOPWA, *Proceedings, 2nd Convention*, Washington 1938, pp. 38, 41f.

114. Shlakman, p. 26 (notice of the United Steelworkers); on the situation in the electrical industry: McColloch, p. 177; further: C. D. Snyder, *White-Collar Workers and the UAW*, Urbana, Ill. 1973, pp. 57ff.

115. Cf. a parallel division between the Oil Workers International Union (CIO) and the UOPWA (CIO) in Los Angeles, which the 'general officers' of the UOPWA approved: UOPWA, *Proceedings, 2nd Convention (1938)*, p. 42.

116. 'Characteristics of Company Unions 1935' (*BLSt., Bulletin*, No. 634), Washington 1937, p. 112: of 126 company unions studied, 50 excluded white collar

workers, 37 included them, and 39 did not mention them.

117. Cf. examples in NLRB, Division of Economic Research, *Written Trade Agreements in Collective Bargaining* (Bulletin, No. 4), Washington 1940, pp. 305, 309ff., 285, 194ff., 269ff. The contract between the Ford Motor Company and the United Automobile Workers (CIO) of 20 July, 1941, excluded most white collar categories by enumeration (Ford Archive, Dearborn, Michigan, Settlement File).

118. Thus for 3,000 office employees at General Electric in 1937, from UOPWA, *Proceedings, 2nd Convention*, p. 42.

119. Cf. for the complaint of a white collar worker: Bollens, p. 3f.

120. Cf. H. Northrup, *Unionization of Professional Engineers and Chemists*, New York 1946; R. E. Walton, *The Impact of the Professional Engineering Union*, Boston 1961, pp. 18-22 with comprehensive bibliography; G. Strauss, 'Professional or Employee-Oriented: Dilemma for Engineering Unions', in *Industrial and Labor Relations Review*, Vol. 17, Ithaca, NY 1964, pp. 519-33; A. Kleingartner, 'Professionalism and Engineering Unionism', in *Industrial Relations*, Vol. 8, May 1969, pp. 224-35; J. W. Kuhn, 'Engineers and their Unions', in Blum et al., *White Collar*, pp. 85-125, here pp. 90ff.

121. Cf. Nichols, *Conception*, esp. pp. 42-47; Coyle, *Present Trends*, esp. pp. 17ff.

122. UOPWA, *Proceedings, 2nd Convention (1939)*, p. 7; Clermont, pp. 4-8; Stolberg, p. 257f.

123. In 1937 the New York local of the Bookkeepers, Stenographers, and Accountants Union alone reported 2,500 members; on it and the exit from the AFL, which was accused of hindering organization in white collar areas: Clermont, pp. 8-12.

124. Cf. UOPWA, *Proceedings, 2nd Convention (1939)*, pp. 6f., 18, 51; ibid., *3rd Convention (1940)*, pp. 3, 5, 7; NICB, *Unions of White Collar Employees*, p. 3.

125. The UOPWA territory was restricted in favor of the separate CIO technicians' union, the CIO government employees' union, and in part the industrial unions. Cf. Art. 1 (Sec. 2) of the UOPWA Constitution of 1942:

> The UOPWA shall have jurisdiction over all employees in office and with offices as headquarters in those industries in which such employees predominate and also in those industries where they form a minority of the employees but are not organized by the industrial unions existing in the industries in which they are employed. The primary jurisdiction of the UOPWA shall be all employees in the graphic arts and related fields; all financial institutions (including insurance companies), and all non-profit institutions such as the social service agencies.

126. From Troy, *Trade Union Membership* (A-22 and A-7) the UOPWA membership was 8,700 in 1937; 13,800 in 1939; 13,000 in 1941; 22,200 in 1943; 31,500 in 1945 and 50,800 in 1948. The first separate parallel organization in the AFL (1944) had 13,600 in 1945 and 26,200 in 1948. The various categories of office employees were usually organized in the same local. In 1939 there were 36 'mixed' locals, 28 locals for insurance employees, two for publishing employees, one for advertising employees, one for artists, one for sales representatives. From UOPWA, *2nd Convention (1939)*, p. 16.

127. From the *Proceedings of the 2nd and 3rd Conventions*; details in Kocka I, p. 455, note 184. Cf. Clermont, pp. 9-138 on the UOPWA in insurance up to expulsion from the CIO; McColloch, pp. 47-53; on the communist orientation of Merrill: Kampelman, pp. 96-100.

128. I did not find material on the AFL office employees' organization for the years of interest here. Cf. P. R. Hutchings (President, Office Employees International Union), 'Office Workers Look at their Trade', in *American Federationist*, March 1947, pp. 11, 13, 31f.

129. What follows is based primarily on the in part printed, in part typewritten data, that I received from the Central Library, Westinghouse Electric Corporation in a parcel mailed 4 December 1970; and on Bollens, *White Collar or Noose?*; Bollens was the first president of the still existing Association of Westinghouse Salaried Employees and the FWISU and the National Federation of Salaried Unions that grew from it.

130. Which other company white collar associations joined must remain open. After 1937, however, a New Jersey Esso Employees Association (clerical) existed, with 500 members. Cf. Troy, *Trade Union Membership*, A-32, A-33, A-41, also on the National Federation. On its foundation: Bollens, pp. 212ff.; 'NFSU Expands', in *Business Week*, 19 May 1945, pp. 106-107.

131. Ibid., p. 106; Bollens, pp. 212-18.

132. Cf. ibid., pp. 5f., 126-31, 200f.; McColloch, p. 167f.

133. Cf. ibid., p. 162.

134. Bollins, p. 78 (Constitution of the FWISU).

135. Ibid., p. 212; 'N.F.S.U. Expands', p. 106.

136. From Burns, 'Comparative Economic Positions', pp. 257-67, esp. p. 260f. (also for a more exact definition of categories, sources, and computation methods).

137. Cf. Bollens, pp. 2-11, 184, 212; but also UOPWA, *Push Salaries UP!*, New York 1944[2]; L. Merrill, *A Salary Policy to Win the War*, n.p. (UOPWA) September 1943, p. 3f. ibid., *The White Collar Workers and the Future of the Nation (Testimony before the Senate Sub-Committee on Wartime Health and Education, January 25-29, 1944)*, pp. 6, 17, 20.

138. Bollens, pp. 13, 201, 181, 193, 204, 210.

139. Ibid., p. 36f.; but see also p. 44f.: rejection of any form of radicalism.

140. Ibid., pp. 28ff., 195.

141. They demanded 'equity', 'justice', 'equality', referred to the discrimination against white collar workers, and their undemocratic neglect as 'orphans of labor' (ibid., pp. 14, 202, 213).

142. For 1935 and 1948: Mills, p. 302. For 1939: 'White Collar Unions on their Way', in *Business Week*, 19 August 1939, p. 31 as well as my own estimates.

143. Calculated from the following table:

Union	1939	1945
AFL:		
Actors and Artists	20,100	24,300
Air Line Pilots	1,000	6,000
Architects and Draftsmen	1,900	7,800
Musicians	127,300	133,100
Office Employees		13,600
Post Office Clerks	43,700	44,800
Railroad Telegraphers	44,000	48,800
Railway and Steamship Clerks	91,000	225,000
Retail Clerks	51,000	96,800
State County and Municipal Employees	27,000	61,000
Teachers	32,100	31,100
Telegraphers	3,500	20,800
CIO:		
Architects, Engineers, Chemists and Technicians	3,400	

American Communications Association	6,000	12,000
Newspaper Guild	14,400	15,100
Office and Professional Workers	13,800	31,500
Retail, Wholesale and Department Store Union	44,000	60,000
State, County and Municipal Workers	5,800	10,400
Independent:		
Empire State Telephone Union		2,600
Federal Employees	64,600	82,000
Maryland Telephone Traffic Union	1,700	2,700
Maryland Telephone Workers	1,100	1,800
Motion Picture Art Directors	100	200
New England Telephone Operators	7,600	12,100
New Jersey Esso Employees Association	500	500
Post Office Clerks	34,500	35,000
Postal Employees	2,500	12,000
Postal Supervisors	8,800	11,000
Railway Conductors	33,000	37,800
National Federation of Salaried Unions		25,000
Screen Directors' Guild	500	500
Screen Writers	700	1,300
United Telephone Organizations	10,000	10,000
National Federation of Telephone Workers	45,000	176,000
Telephone Workers of New Jersey	2,700	2,500

Calculated from Troy, *Trade Union Membership*. Cf. notes 50 and 72 above, and next note.

144. Source as in note 143. In these as in the above figures white collar workers in organizations with predominantly blue collar membership are not included. Particularly in the CIO this led to error, but not more than 2 or 3%.

145. This is difficult to prove. But see the relevant passages in Mills, pp. 7-9, 259-65, 308ff. on the individualistic ideologies of this middle class, which would not have applied to the corporate group-conscious mercantile assistants, private bureaucrats, and salaried employees in Germany before or after the first world war.

Finally, in the US white collar workers in bureaucratic public or semi-public areas such as the railroads, post office, and government agencies organized much earlier and more strongly than those in private firms, banks and commercial enterprises.That was due not only to the greater anti-union resistance of private employers, but may also be explained by the fact that railroad, post office, and government employees were not as affected by the most important factor limiting organization: individual success, career, and achievement orientation. (155b)

145a. Helpful in approaching this concept is: A. J. Mayer, *Dynamics of Counterrevolution in Europe, 1870-1956*, New York 1971 (with extensive bibliography). But as used here the concept also includes right-radical phenomena which were in reaction to changes and challenges brought by reform (not only revolution). See further Lipset/Raab, Ch. 1.

145b. Cf. the overview on fascist movements, systems and theories of fascism in: W. Schieder, 'Fascism', in: C. D. Kernig (ed.), *Marxism, Communism, and Western Society. A Comparative Encyclopedia*, New York 1972, Vol. 2. On the question of Japanese fascism not discussed there, cf. M. Maruyama, *Thought and Behavior in Modern Japanese Politics*, Oxford 1969, pp. 25-83 (also pp. 52ff. on the weak mass basis of Japanese fascism, which has led many to consider Japanese developments in the 1930s and 1940s as not fascistic); an overview of recent literature: W. Wipermann, *Faschismustheorien*, Darmstadt 1975[2]. Different interpretations of and introductions to local fascisms: W. Laqueur (ed.), *Fascism. A Reader's Guide. Analyses, Interpretations, Bibliography*, Berkeley 1976. Materials on fascist movements in different countries are found in: E. Weber, *Varieties of Fascism. Doctrines of Revolution in the Twentieth Century*, New York 1964. A good critical discussion of neo-marxist theories of fascism: H. A. Winkler, *Revolution, Staat, Faschismus*, Göttingen 1978, pp. 65, 117; also: A. G. Rabinbach, 'Toward a Marxist Theory of Fascism and National Socialism', in *New German Critique*, Vol. 1, No. 3, 1974, pp. 127-153; W. Schieder (ed.), *Faschismus als soziale Bewegung. Deutschland und Italien im Vergleich*, Hamburg 1976.

146. On the Bund: Strong, *Organized Anti-Semitism*, pp. 21ff.; G. Myers, *History of Bigotry in the United States* (1943), reprint New York 1960, pp. 326ff.; L. V. Bell, 'The Failure of Nazism in America, in *PSQ*, Vol. 85, 1970, pp. 85-99; ibid., *In Hitler's Shadow. The Anatomy of American Nazism*, Port Washington, NY 1973, p. 21f.; S. A. Diamond, *The Nazi Movement in the United States, 1924-41*, Ithaca, NY 1974. On the Black Shirts: *76th Congress, 3rd Session House of Representatives Report No. 1476*. Investigation of the Un-American Propaganda Activities in the United States, 3 January 1940. Ogden, *Dies Committee*, pp. 110ff.

147. From Strong, *Organized Anti-Semitism*, pp. 52-54. The best description is in T. Hoke, *Shirts*!, New York (American Civil Liberties Union) 1934, pp. 5-20; (pp. 21ff. on other, even smaller, similar organizations).

148. Cf. Lipset/Raab, *Politics*, pp. 157ff.; M. Janowitz, 'Black Legions on the March', in D. Aaron (ed.), *America in Crisis*, New York 1952, pp. 305-25, esp. p. 323; Myers, pp. 363ff.; Strong, *Organized Anti-Semitism*, p. 71ff.

149. This interpretation follows Jackson (p. 251f. on membership of 1.5 million); in contrast, Lipset/Raab (*Politics*, p. 21) give the Klan three-six million members. O. Handlin (*Al Smith and this America*, Boston 1958, p. 118) estimates four million.

150. Whether it was really primarily new residents from rural areas — thus C. C. Alexander, *The Ku Klux Klan in the South West*, University of Kentucky Press 1965, p. 29 and Lipset/Raab, *Politics*, pp. 121ff. — or instead the old residents, who wished to set themselves apart from the newcomers, is unclear. The latter thesis in Jackson (partly), p. 241, who presents the numerical strength and the power of the Klan in the cities; cf. also R. A. Goldberg, 'The Ku Klux Klan in Madison, 1922-1927', in *Wisconsin Magazine of History*, Vol. 58, Fall 1974, pp. 31-44.

151. Cf. above, p. 160.

152. Cf. e.g. R. S. and H. M. Lynd, pp. 481-83 as well as further evidence in Lipset/Raab, *Politics*, p. 123ff. (on the exit of the more 'respectable' members after the mid-1920s). Further on the decline: Jackson, pp. 251ff.; D. M. Chalmers, *Hooded Americanism*, Chicago 1968, pp. 291ff. and 304-18 on the remnants of the Klan in the 1920s. A useful summary of the Ku Klux Klan in the 1920s (without an analysis of the social basis): R. M. Miller, 'The Ku Klux Klan', in Braeman et al., *Change*, pp. 215-55 (with bibliography).

153. On the other hand the conspicuous frequent references to Christendom and the American constitution. Cf. the list in Strong, *Organized Anti-Semitism*, pp. 138-43.

154. Huey Long's dramatic actions and large following cannot be considered right-radical or fascistic despite the contrary opinions of many contemporaries (who confused his authoritarian-demagogic methods, anti-elitist and anti-capitalist radicalism as well as his associations with shady figures with fascism). Furthermore, his followers came primarily from rural areas and small towns in the south, and thus not from the urban middle classes of interest here. Cf. T. H. Williams, *Huey P. Long*, New York 1969; R. E. Snyder, 'Huey Long and the Presidential Election of

1936', in *Louisiana History*, Vol. 16, Spring 1975, pp. 117-43. The 'Liberty League', a conservative anti-New Deal organization, remained an organization of rich businessmen without a mass base and cannot be considered either right-radical or fascistic. Cf. G. Wolfskill, *The Revolt of the Conservatives*, Boston 1962.

155. Cf. on the early years: D. H. Bennett, *Demagogues in the Depression*, New Brunswick 1969, pp. 29ff., 190ff. (especially on his cooperation with William Lemke and Francis Townsend); C. J. Tull, *Father Coughlin and the New Deal*, Syracuse 1965, esp. pp. 173-238 on the more radical phase after 1936 (on the foundation of the Christian Front in 1938, p. 189f.); recently: S. Marcus, *Father Coughlin. The Tumultuous Life of the Priest of the Little Flowers*, Boston 1973; on the survey results: H. Cantril, *Public Opinion, 1935-1946*, Princeton 1951, p. 147f.

156. From Lipset, 'Three Decades'; Lipset/Raab, *Politics*, pp. 171-78. Agreement with the Catholic priest Coughlin correlated most strongly with religious factors, particularly with membership in the Catholic Church. Catholic white collar workers supported Coughlin to a much greater extent than Protestant.

157. Cf. Lipset/Raab, *Politics*, esp. pp. 3-33; 110-49 on the 1920s; pp. 150-208 on the Depression; pp. 338-427 on George Wallace. Higham, *Strangers*; ibid., *Send These*; J. H. Bunzel, *Anti-Politics in America*, New York 1967; D. Bell (ed.), *The Radical Right*, Garden City 1964; Hofstadter, *Anti-Intellectualism*; ibid., *The Paranoid Style in American Politics*, New York 1966, pp. 3-141.

158. The for the most part unpublished results of the early Gallup Polls (American Institute of Public Opinion — AIPO) and Roper-Fortune Polls referred to in the following were made available to me with the financial help of Harvard University by the Roper Public Opinion Research Center in Williamstown, Mass.

159. According to a letter of 10 August 1971, from Mrs Carolyn W. Crusius to the author. Mrs Crusius worked on the first Roper Polls. She confirmed that written specifications were not kept.

160. E. G. Benson and E. Wicoff, 'Voters Pick their Party', in *POQ*, Vol. 8, 1944, pp. 168-69. The figures for professionals: 49 and 38, for the farmers, 59 and 54. The business group appears to have included only independents, while academically trained employed persons were counted as professionals. It remains unclear exactly where the line between white collar and professionals ran for the interviewers.

161. Based on Roper, Study 3, Question III, 7 of January 1939. The absolute numbers were 464 'salaried minor', 218 'salaried executive' and 490 'wage workers'. (Results recalculated so that Roosevelt plus Landon = 100, i.e. votes for third party candidates and invalid ballots eliminated.)

162. AIPO, No. 224 of 19 November 1940, Question 8B. In rural areas and small cities (under 10,000 inhabitants) the percentage for Roosevelt among white collar workers (excluding higher level) was even higher than among skilled and semi-skilled workers.

163. Even when one considers 'white collar employees' as one group, their membership in the Democratic Party (40%) was only 4% different from skilled workers (44%), but 11% from businessmen (29%). From Cantril, p. 576.

164. Placing the respondents in one of four income categories or 'economic groups' was left up to the interviewer: 'it is a classification of respondents based on how well off and how poorly off they seemed to be financially as shown by the way they live, the things they have and do'. (From an undated specification 'Economic Level', which was apparently used by interviewers, sent to me with correspondence of 19 April 1971 by the Roper Public Opinion Research Center.) A was the best off, D the poorest, and B and C the middle groups. This categorization was only used by the Roper-Fortune polls.

165. Roper Study 5, Question II, 1 (March 1939). In economic groups C and D 72.8% and 79.4% respectively of factory workers, but only 56.3% and 65.5% of salaried-minor employees favored such government responsibility.

166. Roper Study 9, Question I, 4 (September 1939). In favor of Roosevelt's welfare program: in income group A: 30%; in B: 38%; in C: 51%; in D: 64%. Within group C: salaried minor 55% and factory workers 70%; within group D: salaried minor 61% and factory workers 80%. Similar differences existed in attitudes toward government spending and the Townsend Plan, which would have guaranteed state old age pensions, and was more strongly approved of by blue collar workers than white collar.

167. Roper Study 9, Question I, 4h and i (September 1939): As a whole in agreement with Roosevelt's 'attitude toward business and businessmen': income group A: 17%; B: 28%; C: 36%; D: 43%.

Within C:	proprietors (non-farm) 32%	Within D:	proprietors (non-farm)	43%
	salaried (min.) 39%		salaried (min.)	47%
	factory workers 43%		factory workers	53%

As a whole in agreement with Roosevelt's 'attitude toward labor and labor unions': income group A: 20%; B: 29%; C: 41%; D: 50%.

Within C:	proprietors (non-farm) 41%	Within D:	proprietors (non-farm)	42%
	salaried (min.) 48%		salaried (min.)	64%
	factory workers 55%		factory workers	68%

168. That was also true for the electoral results in themselves. Compare the following figures (for 1940) with the distribution by occupational groups.

Income Received	% voting for Roosevelt 1936	1940
$50 Per Week and up	42	28
$20 to $50 Per Week	60	53
Less than $20/Week (Including Welfare)	76	69
Welfare Recipients, Emergency Relief Employees (Blue and White Collar)	84	80

From D. Katz, 'The Public Opinion Polls and the 1940 Election', in *POQ*, Vol. 5, 1941, p. 71 (Roosevelt votes plus Wilkie votes = 100).

169. Roper, Study 4, Question I, 7 (January 1939). According to this in 1936 in income group C 68% of salaried (minor) and 77% of factory workers voted for Roosevelt; in group D salaried minor 77% and factory workers 80% (Roosevelt votes plus Landon votes = 100).

170. Cf. A. W. Jones, *Life, Liberty and Property*, Toronto 1941, pp. 289-99, 326.

171. More exact division is also not possible here. In addition to these two white collar categories, which corresponded approximately to Roper's distinction between 'salaried-executives' and 'salaried-minor', Gallup also had a group for 'professionals', which included academically trained employed persons and self-employed and which remains unnoted in the following.

172. The sum of 'yes' and 'no' answers is less than 100, because undecided and no response answers are not given. Other occupational groups not considered here: professionals, businessmen, relief workers, housewives, students, and retired. Question 1: AIPO No. 113, Q. 1 of 26 February 1938; Question 2: AIPO No. 113, Q 4 of 26

February 1938; Question 3: AIPO No. 145, Q 11 of December 1938; Question 4: AIPO No. 121 Q 6c of May 1938; Question 5: AIPO No. 150, Q 1 of 2 March 1939; Question 6: AIPO No. 105, Q 3 of 30 November 1937; Question 7: AIPO No. 105, Q 1 of 30 November 1937.

173. Cf. evidence in Kocka I, p. 463f., note 241.

174. From Roper, Study 2, Question II, 3 (Question on disapproval of sexual activity of women before marriage) and AIPO No. 135 (October 1938).

175. Cf. above, p. 203f.

176. A. W. Kornhauser, 'Analysis of "Class" Structure of Contemporary American Society. Psychological Bases of Class Divisions', in *Industrial Conflict: A Psychological Interpretation*, New York 1939, pp. 199-244, confirms that, pp. 254ff., on the basis of an investigation of several thousand inhabitants of Chicago (1937): 'The largest gap is rather between the business group together with the associated professions of engineering and law, on the one hand, and the worker groups composed of manual laborers and the lower levels of white-collar employees, on the other'.

177. Cf. ibid., pp. 254-55.

178. Their present chances of success were considered better than those of their fathers or mothers (in the case of unmarried women) (in%):

	Income Group		
	B	C	D
Proprietors (non-farm)	60.1	56.5	53.7
Professionals	66.3	60.6	—
White Collar (Exec.)	67.8	(66.6)	—
White Collar (Minor)	70.8	72.7	63.6
Factory Workers	—	46.1	52.0
Average of All Categories	64.4	62.4	50.4

Roper, Study 13, Question 7A (December 1933).

179. Ibid., Question 13.

180. See primarily Table 2.4.

Chapter 5: The American Experience in Comparative Perspective

1. Cf. above, pp. 1ff.

2. Cf. above, p. 345f., notes 37 and 38 for examples of 'exports' of German white collar interpretations into the US in the 1930s. The most important study of American white collar workers — Mills — also appears to me too strongly influenced by interpretative models which are more applicable to German and other European white collar groups than to America.

3. On this generally, see R. Vierhaus, 'Auswirkungen der Krise um 1930 in Deutschland. Beiträge zu einer historischpsychologischen Analyse', in W. Conze and H. Raupach (eds.), *Die Staats und Wirtschaftskrise des Deutschen Reichs 1929/33*, Stuttgart 1967, pp. 155-75, esp. p. 158.

4. Cf. Gurr, Ch. 2-4; J. C. Davies, 'Toward a Theory of Revolution', in *ASR*, Vol. 27, 1962, pp. 5-19.

5. A good introduction with further references is Kassalow, *Trade Unions*, esp. pp. 6-28; Lösche, *Industriegewerkschaften*, esp. pp. 190-201.

6. H. M. Gitelman, 'No Irish Need Apply: Patterns and Responses to Ethnic Discrimination in the Labor Market', in *LH*, Vol. 14, 1973, pp. 56-82; Hareven, 'Laborers'.

7. Cf. above, pp. 11ff.

8. The great role of nativism in US history is confirmed here. Cf. Higham, *Strangers*. Generally: J. A. Kahl, *The American Class Structure*, New York (1953) 1957, pp. 221-50; a good contemporary study of South Chicago: W. Kornblum, *Blue Collar Community*, Chicago 1974; Hamilton, *Class*, pp. 198f., 216f.

9. Thus Speier, *Angestellte*, pp. 52ff.; see also for emphasis on the international similarity of mobility rates: Lipset/Bendix, *Social Mobility*, esp. Ch. II; cf. also S. M. Miller, 'Comparative Social Mobility: A Trend Report and Bibliography', in *Current Sociology*, Vol. 9, 1960, pp. 1-89 (with slightly different conclusions); Thernstrom, *The Other Bostonians*, p. 259 predicts a slightly greater rate of mobility in the US compared to Europe; Crew, 'Definitions', esp. p. 54f. seems to confirm this.

10. Cf. D. Crew, 'Regionale Mobilität und Arbeiterklasse. Das Beispiel Bochum 1880-1901', in *GG*, Vol. 1, 1975, pp. 99-120, here p. 102f.

11. Cf. above all, C. Griffen, 'Workers Divided: The Effect of Craft and Ethnic Differences in Ploughkeepsie, NY 1850-1880', in S. Thernstrom and R. Sennett (eds.), *Nineteenth Century City*, New Haven 1969, p. 62; Chudacoff, *Mobile Americans*, pp. 86f., 92f.; Goldstein, 'Migration', p. 404 for 1901-50.

12. Cf. the very stimulating study by A. Hirschman, *Exit, Voice, and Loyalty. Response to Decline in Firms, Organizations, and States*, Cambridge, Mass. 1970, pp. 106ff.

13. Cf. above, pp. 246ff.

14. Cf. Lipset/Bendix, *Social Mobility*, pp. 76-113; Thernstrom, *The Other Bostonians*, pp. 256-61; very good comparison by a German emigré social scientist: K. Lewin, 'Social-Psychological Differences', pp. 3-33.

15. Cf. G. A. Ritter and J. Kocka, *Deutsche Sozialgeschichte. Dokumente und Skizzen. Bd. II: 1870-1914*, München 1974, pp. 62ff.

16. On the similarities and differences between trade unions and professional organizations see also R. M. Blackburn, *Union Character and Social Class. A Study of White-collar Unionism*, London 1967, pp. 24-27; G. S. Bain et al., *Social Stratification and Trade Unionism. A Critique*, London 1973, pp. 70-78.

17. Based on a survey by Roper, Study 13, Question VI (cf. on source Ch. 4, note 153ff.) The question read: 'If you had a choice, which would you prefer: (a) A steady job earning just enough to get by on, but with no prospect for advancement? (b) A job which pays a high wage, but with a fifty-fifty chance of getting promoted or fired? (c) Depends; (d) Don't know'. The answers in percentages:

	Men			Women		
	Yes(a)	Yes(b)	N	Yes(a)	Yes(b)	N
Professionals	13	83	(167)	16	75	(57)
Proprietors (Excl. Agr.)	20	75	(450)	25	69	(64)
Lower/Middle White Collar	18	78	(413)	24	73	(196)
Higher White Collar	9	87	(152)	7	93	(27)
Factory Workers	45	53	(110)	41	59	(17)
Other Blue Collar Wkrs. (Excl. Agr.)	33	63	(405)	43	52	(159)

18. Hartz, pp. 3ff., 234ff. contains part of this argument (from an intellectual history perspective). Parts of this argument also in Lösche, *Industriegewerkschaft*, pp. 190-92, 195, 242, esp. note 786 with interesting references to Marx and Engels, who in part support the line of thought developed above; also Kassalow, *Trade Unions*, pp. 6-28. Traces of this argumentation are frequently found, but as yet there is no systematic analysis of the German labor movement from this perspective.

19. Cf. Wehler, *Der Aufstieg des Organisierten Kapitalismus*, passim; esp. p. 49.

20. On the concept of bourgeois or civil society (*bürgerliche Gesellschaft*), as used here, and on the *Defizit an Bürgerlichkeit* in Germany, cf. more precisely: Ritter/Kocka, *Deutsche Sozialgeschichte*, Bd. II, pp. 62-70; Stern, *Failure*, esp. the introduction and part I; Dahrendorf, *Society*.

21. Cf. Hamilton, *Class*, pp. 336ff.; ibid., 'Marginal Middle Class'.

22. Cf. also on further differentiations Kocka I, pp. 316-19, 469-70.

23 Cf. Hobsbawm, *Industry*; H. Perkin, *The Origins of Modern English Society, 1780-1880*, London 1969; S. G. Checkland, *The Rise of Industrial Society in England 1815-1885*, London 1964; R. Lewis and A. Maude, *The English Middle Class* (1949), New York 1950, pp. 15, 18f. (on the significance of the 'gentry' and 'gentleman' tradition for the English middle classes). A very interesting comparison is M. R. Gordon, 'Domestic Conflict and the Origins of the First World War: The British and the German Cases', in *JMH*, Vol. 46, 1974, pp. 192-226. See also on the more general context: Gerschenkron, pp. 5-30.

24. Still the best: Lockwood, *Blackcoated Worker* (though without consideration of technical white collar workers) and G. Anderson *Victorian Clerks*, Manchester 1976; G. Crossick (ed.), *The Lower Middle Class in Britain 1870-1914*, New York 1977. Further: Klingender (with the emphasis on bank clerks and the situation of the 1930s); further: J. R. Dale, *The Clerk in Industry. A Survey of the Occupation Experience, Status, Education, and Vocational Training of a Group of Male Clerks Employed by Industrial Companies*, Liverpool (1962) (history and intensive study of 208 clerks based on interviews 1956/57). On white collar trade unions in addition to Lockwood, Ch. V, esp.: G. Routh, 'White-Collar Union in the United Kingdom', in Sturmthal, *White-Collar*, pp. 165-204; also G. S. Bain, *The Growth of White-Collar Unionism*, New York 1970; R. Lumley, *White-Collar Unionism in Britain. A Survey of the Present Position*, London 1973; Material on the history of sales clerks in Whitaker; Blackburn (above all pp. 130-93: history of bank clerks and the Bank Officers' Guild); further also: B. Humphreys, *Clerical Unions in the Civil Service*, London 1958; A. Spoor, *White-Collar Union. Sixty Years of NALGO (National Association of Local Government Officers)*, London 1967. See also K. Prandy, *Professional Employees. A Study of Scientists and Engineers*, London 1965; A. Tropp, *The School Teachers*, London 1957; W. J. Reader, *Professional Men: The Rise of the Professional Classes in 19th Century England*, London 1966.

25. Cf. R. Price, *An Imperial War and the British Working Class: Working Class Attitudes and Reactions to the Boer War 1899-1902*, London 1972, pp. 8-10, 153, 199, 217, 219, 228f., 241; Klingender, p. 82; J. Bonham, *The Middle Class Vote*, London n.d. (1954?), pp. 71, 74, 94, 129 and 153f.

26. Cf. Crozier, *World*, pp. 7 (note), 39f.

27. Cf. M. Crozier, 'White-Collar Unions — the Case of France', in Sturmthal, *White-Collar*, pp. 90-126, p. 97f. on the comparative insignificance of the collar line in England; Whitaker, pp. 21f., 30; Dale, p. 46 (on the Lancashire Commercial Clerks Association of 1802); Klingender, p. 110 (list of trade unions which organized white collar workers in 1934); Routh, 'White-Collar', p. 171f. (list of white collar organizations, 1961).

28. Cf. Klingender, pp. 73, 76, 77, 85ff.; D. H. Aldcroft, *The Inter-War Economy: Britain, 1919-1939*, New York 1971, p. 41 (on the relative mildness of the depression in England); Lockwood, *Blackcoated Worker*, pp. 41-57; Lewis/Maude, pp. 247ff.

29. Cf. already Masterman, *Condition*, pp. 69-73; ibid., *England after the War*, New York 1923, pp. 71-121, esp. pp. 106ff.; Hobsbawm, *Industry*, p. 236f.; Dale, pp. 29ff.; Runciman, *Relative Deprivation*, pp. 78ff., 109-11, 115, who emphasizes, however, that these attitudes appeared more often among white collar workers after 1945 than in the interwar years, when leveling tendencies were not yet as strong; cf. also Raynor, p. 53, as well as Lewis/Maude, p. 87f. on parallel presentation of white collar workers in novels and plays.

30. Cf. Lockwood, *Blackcoated Worker*, Ch. V and p. 194f.; Blackburn, pp. 154, 134f. and 148ff.; J. Henry Lloyd, *Guilds and the Salary Earner*, London 1921; L. Benjamin, *The Position of the Middle-Class Worker in the Transition to Socialism*. Published by the Labour Party, London 1935, p. 22: List of white collar organizations which had already joined the TUC in 1935; for the period around 1960: Routh, 'White-Collar', p. 169f. (white collar workers in labor unions), pp. 170, 192 (much higher level of organization in public sector than private), p. 173 (most affiliated with TUC), pp. 179, 180f. (strikes by sales clerks and teachers before 1914), p. 181f. (on the first world war). The similarities between blue and white collar unions today and in the last decades is emphasized (or overemphasized) in Bain et al., *Social Stratification*.

31. Thus Lockwood, *Blackcoated Worker*, p. 194f.; see also note 1 on p. 195; Klingender, p. 81f.; cf. also C. Cross, *The Fascists in Britain*, London 1961; R. Benewick, *The Fascist Movement in Britain* (1969), London 1972^2, pp. 108-32, esp. pp. 121ff.

32. Statements on the 1920s based on a comparison of London districts in Bonham, pp. 150, 153, 154, 156, 158; p. 154 on the growth of Labour votes in 1935 and 1945 in 'Blackcoatia'. Ibid., p. 129 on the distribution of votes by socio-economic groups 1945, 1950 and 1951 from survey data. If one looks at the 'intermediate group' (sales clerks, letter carriers, telegraphers, police, waiters) alone, the labor percentage predominated in 1945 and 1950 — but no longer entirely in 1951 (pp. 129, 125). Cf. also M. Kahan et al., 'On the Analytical Division of Social Class', in *British Journal of Sociology*, Vol. 17, 1966, pp. 122-32: Differences in the distribution of votes between lower and middle level white collar workers are more pronounced than between blue collar and white collar workers as such; this is implicitly supported in Lewis/Maude, pp. 88, 106.

33. On this Moulin/Aerts; Marbach; on middle class organizations of this type in France in reaction to the Popular Front cf. H. Mougin, 'Un projet d'enquête sur les classes moyennes en France', in R. Aron et al., *Inventaires III. Classes moyennes*, Parison 1939, pp. 287-341, here pp. 327-41; comparative law: François, also: Crozier, *World*; ibid., 'White-Collar Unions'; M. Collinet, *Essai sur la condition ouvrière (1900-1950)*, Paris, 1951; ibid., 'Structure des classes salariées en France depuis cinquante ans', in *Revue internationale du travail*, Vol. 67, 1953, pp. 229-53; C. Gide, *Travail intellectuel et travail manuel*, Paris 1901; Girod, *Etudes*; C. Marenco, *Employés des banque*, Paris 1959.

34. The legal comparison from François, esp. pp. 11, 155-78; p. 359 on legal (1922 and 1924) and company privileges of white collar over blue collar workers in Italy and Belgium in order to (and with the effect of) preventing the creation of a united labor organization; on Austrian white collar insurance, which was established even before the German (1906) cf. E. Lederer, 'Die österreichische Sozialversicherungsvorlage', in *Schmollers Jb.*, Bd. 39, 1909, pp. 1643-72.

35. Cf. e.g. de Chilly, p. 18, 21; A. Desqueyrat, *Classes moyennes*, Paris 1939, p. 25; in contrast G. Izard, *Les classes moyennes*, Paris 1938, p. 11; Moulin/Aerts, p. 172.

36. Cf. Crozier, 'White-Collar Unions', pp. 103-109; P. Verdin, *La fondation du syndicat des employés de commerce et de l'industrie*, Paris 1929; R. P. S. Piat, *Jules Zirnheld, Président de la C.F.T.C.*, Paris 1948; T. B. Caldwell, 'The Syndicat des

Employés du Commerce et de l'Industrie (1887-1919). A Pioneer French Catholic Trade Union of White Collar Workers', in *IRSH*, Vol. 11, 1966, pp. 228-66; P. Delon, *Les employés. De la plume d'oie à l'ordinateur. Un siècle de lutte. Origines et activité de la Fédération C.G.T.*, Paris 1969, pp. 52ff.

37. Cf. Crozier, *World*, pp. 43-54; ibid., 'White-Collar Unions', pp. 109-14; ibid., 'Les attitudes politiques des employés et des petits fonctionnaires', in M. Duverger (ed.), *Paris politiques et classes sociales en France*, Paris 1955, pp. 85-99; ibid., 'L'ambiguité de la conscience de classe chez les employés et les petits fonctionnaires, in *Cahiers internationaux de sociologie*, Vol. 28, 1955, pp. 78-97; ibid., 'Le rôle des employés et des petits fonctionnaires dans la structure française contemporaine', in *Transactions of the Third World Congress of Sociology*, Amsterdam 1956, Vol. 3, pp. 311-19; B. Laurent, *Postes et Postiers*, Paris 1922. On German development: Hintze, 'Beamtenstand'; K. Ritter v. Scherf, *Die Entwicklung der Beamtenbewegung und ihre Interessenvertretung*, Diss. Greifswald (1919); A. Lotz, *Geschichte des deutschen Beamtentums*, Berlin 1909.

38. Cf. Crozier, *World*, p. 48f.; divergent S. Hoffmann, 'Aspects du Régime de Vichy', in *Revue française de sciences politique*, Vol. 6, 1956, pp. 44-49, here p. 48: on the participation of the 'fractions plus réduites des fonctionnaires des administrations publiques ou syndicales, des employés et travailleurs indépendants', which felt threatened by the leftist policies and strength of the labor movement after 1936 and turned away from the radical socialist party. Not very helpful on the social basis of French right-wing groups: R. Remond, *The Right Wing in France. From 1815 to de Gaulle*, Philadelphia (1966) 1969^2; pp. 273-307 on right-wing groups of the 1920s and 1930s and on the question why no strong fascist movement emerged in France; further: P. J. Larmour, *The French Radical Party in the 1930s*, Stanford 1964; E. J. Weber, *Action française. Royalism and Reaction in Twentieth Century France*, Stanford 1962. S. Hoffman,, *Le mouvement poujade*, Paris 1956 (p. 9 on the historical context). The certainly not exactly leftist, but indecisive and shifting, unideological and fairly apolitical atmosphere of these groups, which left the individual wide discretion over political decisions, are described in Crozier, *World*, Part 3; C. Baudelot et al., *La petite bourgeoisie en France*, Paris 1974, pp. 293-301.,

39. On the whole cf. H. Lüthy, *Frankreichs Uhren gehen anders*, Stuttgart 1954; S. Berger, *The French Political System*, New York 1974, pp. 3ff.; the anti-authoritarian state distrust of the French is mentioned e.g. in R. Lowenthal, 'Secessio Plebis', in *The Twentieth Century*, May 1951, pp. 350-62, here p. 361f.; on the labor movement in comparative perspective: Kassalow, *Trade Unions*, pp. 100-29.

40. Cf. the essays on Australia, Austria, Japan, Sweden, and the comparative summary of the editor in Sturmthal, *White-Collar*; Bain et al., *Social Stratification*; Kassalow, *Trade Unions*, pp. 195-232 (with bibliography on various countries: pp. 225-32); D. Lockwood, 'Der Angestellte: Eine international vergleichende Darstellung', in H. Bayer (ed.), *Der Angestellte zwischen Arbeiterschaft und Management*, Berlin 1961, pp. 145-69; International Labour Office, *Bibliography on Non-Manual Workers*, Geneva 1959; International Labour Office *(Reports for the) Advisory Committee on Salaried Employees and Professional Workers. General Report. First Item on the Agenda*, Geneva 1951 and 1954; François; E. G. Erdman, *Das Recht der Arbeitnehmer auf Beteiligung an der Verwaltung der Betriebe der gewerblichen Wirtschaft. Ein internationaler Rechtsvergleich*, Köln 1952; E. Lakenbacher, *Die österreichischen Angestelltengewerkschaften. Geschichte und Gegenwart*, Wien 1967; H. Oesch, *Wesen und Ziele der schweizerischen Mittelstandsbewegung*, Diss. Zurich 1928; Marbach; Croner, *Die Angestellten*; E. Dahlström, *Management, Unions and Society. A Study of Salaried Employees' Attitudes*, Stockholm 1954; F. Höök, *Salaried Employees and the Industrial Transformation*, Stockholm 1955; E. M. Kassalow, 'Professional Unions in Sweden', in *Industrial Relations*, Vol. 8, 1969, pp. 119-34; R. Torstendahl, *Dispersion of*

Engineers in a Transitional Society. Swedish Technicians 1860-1940, Uppsala 1975; Vogel; M. Maruyama, 'The Ideology and Dynamics of Japanese Fascism', in ibid., *Thought and Behavior in Modern Japanese Politics*, Oxford 1969, pp. 25-83, here pp. 57-65; S. Punekar and M. G. Savur, *Management/White-Collar Relations*, Bombay 1969.

41. A useful overview of the development of German white collar organizations in the Federal Republic is G. Hartfiel, 'Germany', in Sturmthal, *White-Collar*, pp. 127-64, esp. pp. 133-60.

42. Cf. H. Maier and H. Bott, *Die NPD. Struktur und Ideologie einer 'nationalen Rechtspartei*', München 1968^2, p. 14; H. D. Klingemann and F. U. Pappi, 'Die Wählerbewegungen bei der Bundestagswahl am 28. September 1969', in *PVS*, Bd. 11, 1970, pp. 111-38, esp. p. 124; ibid., 'Parteiensystem und Sozialstruktur in der Bundesrepublik', in *PVS*, Bd. 14, 1973, pp. 191-225, here p. 199; ibid., 'Sozialstruktur, gesellschaftliche Wertorientierungen und Wahlabsicht', in *PVS*, Bd. 18, 1977, pp. 195-229, here pp. 215, 217. On the whole problem J. Kocka and M. Prinz, 'Angestellte zwischen Faschismus und Demokratie. Traditionen und Neuansätze vom Reich zur Bundesrepublik', in R. M. Lepsius (ed.), *Sozialgeschichtliche Grundlagen der Bundesrepublik Deutschland* (forthcoming).

43. Cf. Dahrendorf, *Society*. The same might be said with reference to other traditional burdens of democracy in Germany: the power of the Junkers, the strength of militarism, the extreme nationalism and pronounced authoritarian tendencies. J. Kocka, '1945: Neubeginn oder Restauration?', in C. Stern and H. A. Winkler (eds.), *Wendepunkte deutscher Geschichte, 1848-1945*, Frankfurt 1979, pp. 141-68.

44. The thesis of the continuity of the conditions which produced fascism in the present is very influentially stated in T. W. Adorno, 'Was bedeutet: Aufarbeitung der Vergangenheit?' in ibid., *Eingriffe*, Frankfurt 1963, pp. 125-47, esp. p. 125; explicitly and implicitly this thesis is part of many marxist analyses in the recent past and present in West Germany. Our findings do not support it.

45. Cf. M. Kilson, 'Blacks and Neo-Ethnicity in American Political Life', in N. Glazer and D. Moynihan (eds.), *Ethnicity, Theory and Experience*, Cambridge, Mass. 1975, pp. 236-66; ibid., pp. 141-74: D. Bell, 'Ethnicity and Social Change'. Cf. McColloch, p. 169: After the second world war there were blacks in white collar positions at General Electric, not before; see also Mills, p. 248. In 1966 5.2% of white collar employees in New York were black; of 4,249 New York companies in 1967, 43% had no black white collar workers. From J. S. Morgan and R. L. Van Dyke, *White-Collar Blacks: A Breakthrough?* New York 1970. Thernstrom, *The Other Bostonians*.

46. Cf. A. A. Blum, *Management and the White-Collar Union* (AMA Research Study, No. 63), New York 1964, esp. p. 11f. (on differential treatment of white collar and blue collar workers); also, NICB, *Personnel Practices in Factory and Office: Manufacturing* (Personnel Policy Study, No. 194), New York, 1964; ibid., *Office Personnel Practices: Nonmanufacturing* (Personnel Policy Study, No. 197), New York 1965; A. A. Blum, 'The Office Employees', in ibid., et al., *White-Collar*, pp. 3-45, here pp. 26f., 29; ibid., p. 12f. on the course of wages and salaries.

47. Cf. ibid., p. 30f.; Bain et al., *Social Stratification*: report on the literature and critique of a variety of publications which treat white collar unions and discuss their differences from blue collar labor unions.

48. Cf. Blum, 'Office Employees', pp. 35f., 39f.

49. Cf. McColloch (extensive bibliography); Hamilton, 'Marginal Middle Class'; M. Oppenheimer, 'What is the New Working Class?' in *New Politics*, Vol. 10, 1972, pp. 29-43; M. K. Benet, *The Secretarial Ghetto*, New York 1973; Blum et al., *White Collar* (with bibliography); Hamilton, *Restraining Myths*, pp. 99-146. Also the discussion on post-industrial society has revived interest in white collar workers. Cf. D. Bell, 'The Post-Industrial Society: The Evolution of an Idea', in *Survey*, Vol. 17,

1971, pp. 102-68; S. P. Huntington, 'Postindustrial Politics: How Benign Will It Be?', in *Comparative Politics*, Vol. 7, 1974, pp. 163-91.

50. Cf. Blum, 'Office Employees', pp. 3, 6f.; Troy, 'White-Collar', here pp. 186ff. (also on the particular organizing conditions in the public sector and the occupational categories legally prohibited from trade union organization).

51. On the continuation of the tendencies to routinization, other-directed work parallel to the factory, changes in the method of payment, lowering of qualifications and mechanization in lower and middle office areas, which are thereby ever more distinctly distinguished from the area of higher and executive employees, cf. McColloch; also in general: Braverman, Chs. 15 and 16. The much higher level of organization in the public sector in the US (as in France and England) seems to indicate that employer resistance to white collar unions, which is still very strong in American industry, but missing in most government agencies, remains an important cause for the modest degree of organization among American white collar workers.

52. Cf. McColloch, pp. 255-71 on the increasing discontent and interest in trade unionism in the electrical industry during the 1960s, as well as his summary, pp. 386-418; on the relatively radical teachers: W. A. Wildman, 'Teachers and Collective Bargaining', in Blum et al., *White-Collar*, pp. 126-65, esp. pp. 133ff.; on the sales clerks: Estey, 'Retail Clerks'; on 'professional' white collar workers: E. C. Ladd and S. M. Lipset, *Professors, Unions, and American Higher Education*, Berkeley 1973; A. Etzioni (ed.), *The Semi-Professions. Teachers, Nurses, Social Workers*, New York 1969; Huntington, p. 181.

53. McColloch, pp. 197, 209, 249f., 264ff. on the stagnation of the FWISU. The degree to which certain organizational tendencies in higher white collar areas, as in the case of engineers and their professional associations, in the 1940s and 1950s were defensive reactions against the threat of inclusion in expanding industrial unions is shown by Kuhn, *Engineers*, here pp. 90ff.; the Taft-Hartley Act of 1947 reduced this danger decisively.

54. This is shown in detail in Hamilton, *Class*, pp. 198f., 214ff., 218, 378, 402-407, 452ff. and 460-67 (on the electoral base of George Wallace in 1968); the distinction between 'manuals' and 'non-manuals' is somewhat more pronounced in small cities and in the south (pp. 244-46, 356f.); see also ibid., *Restraining Myths*, pp. 99-146.'

55. Cf. Lipset, *Political Man*, pp. 87-114; together with Hamilton, *Class*, pp. 434-67 (criticism of Lipset's influential thesis of working class authoritarianism, but also, however, with data which — esp. pp. 434ff. — show the greater liberalism of 'non-manuals' on questions of human and civil rights); also J. D. Wright, 'Working Class Authoritarianism and the War in Vietnam', in *Social Problems*, Vol. 20, Fall 1972, pp. 133-49 (with the most important literature).

56. 'Die Juden in Europa', in *Zs. f. Sozialforschung*, Jg. 8, 1939, pp. 115-37, here p. 116. Many authors in varying ways have connected capitalist crises and fascism. Cf. the titles in notes 8 and 9 on p. 286f. by Trotsky, de Man, Reich, Bloch, Sternberg, Guerin, Bauer, Kofler; cf. also P. Togliatti, *Lektionen über den Faschismus* (1935), Frankfurt 1973. Further: R. Kühnl, 'Probleme einer Theorie über den internationalen Faschismus, in *PVS*, Bd. 16, 1975, pp. 89ff.; ibid., *Formen bürgerlicher Herrschaft. Liberalismus-Faschismus*, Reinbek 1971; E. Hennig, *Bürgerliche Gesellschaft und Faschismus in Deutschland. Ein Forschungsbericht*, Frankfurt 1977; H. Grebing, *Aktuelle Theorien über den Faschismus und Konservatismus. Eine Kritik*, Stuttgart 1974, pp. 82ff.; H. C. F. Mansilla, *Faschismus und eindimensionale Gesellschaft*, Neuwied 1971; N. Kadritzke, *Faschismus und Krise. Zum Verhältnis von Politik und Ökonomie im Nationalsozialismus*, Frankfurt 1976; N. Poulantzas, *Faschismus und Diktatur. Die Kommunistische Internationale und der Faschismus*, München 1973. A report on the literature and the German debate in English: Rabinbach.

57. Cf. Moore, *Social Origins*; Winkler, *Mittelstand*; F. Stern, *The Politics of Cultural Despair*, New York 1961; ibid., *Failure*; Dahrendorf, *Society*; H. A. Turner, Jr., *Faschismus und Kapitalismus in Deutschland*, Göttingen 1972; Winkler, 'Extremismus'; very early and to the point: Ernst Bloch, *Erbschaft dieser Zeit* (1935), new revised edition Frankfurt 1962, esp. pp. 104-32; A. F. K. Organski, 'Fascism and Modernization', in Woolf, pp. 19-41.

58. Italian fascism is partly discussed from parallel perspectives. Cf. e.g. L. Salvatorelli, *Nationalfascismo*, Torino 1923 and F. Borkenau, 'Zur Soziologie des Faschismus', in *Archiv f. Sozialwissenschaft und Sozialpolitik*, Bd. 68, 1933, pp. 513-47; as quoted in Nolte, *Theorien*, pp. 118-27, esp. pp. 126f., 156-81, esp. pp. 165, 170f., 179f. Since Italy was at a distinctly less developed stage of industrialization than the societies investigated in this study, however, white collar workers there necessarily played a weaker, non-parallel role and found themselves in a different, non-comparable situation. The frequently mentioned lower middle class support for Italian fascism may thus have been correspondingly more strongly composed of small independents, members of the professions, and government officials. Cf. J. Peterson, 'Wählerverhalten und soziale Basis des Faschismus in Italien zwischen 1919 und 1928', in W. Schieder (ed.), *Faschismus als soziale Bewegung*, Hamburg 1976, pp. 119-56.

Bibliography

1. Unpublished Sources

AFL-CIO Library, Washington (File 'Labor History — International Unions').
Baker Library, Harvard School of Business Administration, Cambridge, Mass.: Materials on the history of the (American) Waltham Company in the 19th century.
Ford Archives, Dearborn, Michigan: Materials on the history of the firm.
General Electric Company, Central Library, Schenectady, NY: Materials on the history of the firm.
Interview with Mr. Samuel J. Meyers, Vice President of the Retail Clerks Union (previously RCIPA), 12 August 1970 in Washington, DC.
The Roper Public Opinion Research Center, Williams College, Williamstown, Mass. (Databank): Questionnaires (raw data) from Gallup and Roper polls 1936-40.
State Historical Society of Wisconsin, Madison, McCormick Collection: History of the McCormick/International Harvester firm, late 19th and early 20th centuries.
Wayne State University, Detroit, Labor History Archives: Materials on the early history of ALPA and the Newspaper Guild.
Westinghouse Electric Corporation, Central Library, East Pittsburgh: Materials on the history of the FWISU/NFSU sent 12 April 1970.

2. Periodical Publications

American Institute of Bank Clerks, *Bulletin*, Vol. 1ff., New York 1902ff.; after Vol. 9 (1907) under the title American Institute of Banking, *Bulletin*.
American Labor Legislation Review, Vol. 1ff., New York 1911ff.
American Management Association (AMA), Special Papers, No. 1ff., New York 1924ff.
—— , Survey Reports, No. 1ff., New York 1923ff. (in part mimeographed).
——, Convention Address Series, No. 1ff., New York 1922ff.
The American Socialist Quarterly, Vol. 1-4, New York 1932-35, *American Socialist Monthly*, Vol. 5-6, 1936-37, *Socialist Review*, Vol. 6ff., 1937ff.
Common Sense (CS), Vol. 1ff., New York, 1932-33ff.
The Draftsman, Vol. 1-4, Cleveland, Ohio, 1902-05; earlier under the title: *Draftsman's Bulletin* (August-December 1901); after 1906: (*Browning's*) *Industrial Magazine*.
The Draftsman, Vol. 1, Philadelphia 1927/28.
Factory and Industrial Management, Vol. 1ff., New York 1891ff.
Federal Emergency Relief Administration (FERA), Monthly Reports, Washington 1933-36.
Federation of Architects, Engineers, Chemists and Technicians, *The Bulletin*, Vol. 1-5, 1934-38.

General Electric (ed.), *Schenectady Work News*, Vol. 1ff., Schenectady, NY 1917ff.
General Electric News. General Office, Vol. 1ff., Schenectady, NY 1944ff.
General Electric Test Alumni Association, *P.T.M.*, Vol. 1ff., Schenectady, NY, 1926ff.
Guild Reporter. Ed. by American Newspaper Guild, Vol. 1ff., New York 1933ff.
The Ledger. Office and Professional News (UOPWA). Vol. 1ff., New York 1935ff.; 1939-40 under the title: *UOPWA News*.
The Literary Digest, New York 1929-39.
(Massachusetts) Bureau (of Statistics) of Labor, Annual Reports, Vol. 1-44, Boston 1870-1913.
Monthly Labor Review (MLR). Ed. by US Department of Labor, Bureau of Labor Statistics (BLSt.), Vol. 1ff., Washington 1915ff.
National Association of Office Managers, *Proceedings of Annual Conference*, Philadelphia 1920ff.
National Labor Relations Board (NLRB), Annual Reports, Vol. 1ff., Washington 1936ff.
——, *Decisions and Orders*, Vol. 1 (1935/36)ff., Washington 1936ff.
New Masses. A Magazine of Workers and Literature, Vol. 3ff., New York 1928ff.
The Public Opinion Quarterly. School of Public Affairs, Vol. 1ff., Princeton, NJ 1937ff.
Retail Clerks' National (after 1899: *International*) *Advocate*. Official Organ of the Retail Clerks' National (after 1899: International) Protective Association (RCIPA), Vol. 1-44, Cleveland, Ohio 1896-1940.
Retail Clerks' National (after 1899: International) Protective Association (RCIPA), Proceedings of the First (Second. . . Nineteenth) Annual Convention, 1891-1939.
The Retail, Wholesale and Department Store Employee (URWEA), Vol. 1ff., Philadelphia 1937ff.
Saturday Evening Post, Philadelphia 1927/28-1939/40.
Survey, Vol. 65-75, New York 1929-39.
US Bureau of the Census, Census of Manufacturers, 1879, 1889, 1899, 1904, 1909, 1914, 1919, 1921-39 (every two years), Washington, DC.
US Commissioner of Labor, Annual Reports, Vol. 1-31, Washington 1886-1917.
US Department of Labor, *Bureau of Labor Statistics (BLSt), Bulletin*, No. 249-694, Washington 1919-42.
The World Tomorrow, Vol. 11-22, New York 1928-39.

3. Published Sources*

Abrams, R. M., *Conservatism in a Progressive Era. Massachusetts Politics 1900-1912*, Cambridge, Mass. 1964.
Adam, H., *An Australian Looks at America*, Sydney 1927.
Adams, K. J., *Humanizing a Great Industry* (= Armour & Co.), ca. 1919.
Adams, T. S. and H. L. Summer, *Labor Problems. A Text Book*, New York 1905 (1914[8]).
Afa (ed.), *Angestellte und Arbeiter*, Berlin 1928.
Aldcroft, D. H., *The Inter-War Economy: Britain 1919-1939*, New York 1971.
Alexander, C. C., *The Ku Klux Klan in the Southwest*, Lexington 1965.
Allen, W. S., *The Nazi Seizure of Power*, Chicago 1965.
Allinson, M., *The Public Schools and Women in Office Service*, Boston 1914.
Amerikareise deutscher Gewerkschaftsfuhrer, Berlin 1926.
Anderson, G., *Victorian Clerks*, Manchester 1976.
Andrew, D. M., *Measured Characteristics of Clerical Workers*, Minneapolis 1934.

* Only sources cited in the text are listed. For complete bibliography see Kocka I, pp. 478-550.

Arnold, T. W., *The Folklore of Capitalism*, New Haven 1937.

Aron, R. et al., *Inventaires III. Classes Moyennes*, Paris 1939.

Asher, R., 'Business and Worker's Welfare in the Progressive Era: Workmen's Compensation Reform in Massachusetts, 1880-1911', in *BHR*, Vol. 43, 1969, pp. 452-75.

Atherton, L., *The Southern Country Store 1800-1860*, Baton Rouge 1949.

Auerbach, J. S., *Lawyers and Social Change in Modern America*, New York 1975.

Aufhauser, S., *Weltkrieg und Angestelltenbewegung*, Berlin 1918.

Baarslag, K., *History of the National Federation of Post Office Clerks*, Washington DC 1945.

Bain, G. S. and R. J. Price, 'Who Is a White Collar Employee?' in *British Journal of Industrial Relations*, Vol. 10, 1972, pp. 329-39.

Bain, G. S. et al., *Social Stratification and Trade Unionism. A Critique*, London 1973.

Baker, H., *Personnel Programs in Department Stores*, Princeton, NJ 1935.

Bakke, E. W., *The Unemployed Worker*, New Haven 1940.

Baldwin, W. H., *Travelling Salesmen. Their Opportunities and their Dangers. An Address...*, Boston 1974.

Barbash, J., *Unions and Telephones. The Story of the Communications Workers of America*, New York 1952.

Baret, Walter (J. A. Scoville), *The Old Merchants of N.Y.* (5 vols), New York 1885.

Baritz, L., *The Servants of Power. A History of the Use of Social Science in American Industry*, Middletown, Conn. 1960.

Barkin, K., 'A Case Study in Comparative History: Populism in Germany and America', in H. J. Bass (ed.), *The State of American History*, Chicago 1970.

Barlow, M. L., *History of Industrial Education in the United States*, Peoria, Ill. 1967.

Barnes, I., 'The Social Basis of Fascism', in *Pacific Affairs*, Vol. 9 (March 1936), pp. 24-32.

Barrett, H. J., *Modern Methods in the Office. How to Cut Corners and Save Money*, New York 1918.

Baruch, B., *American Industry in War*, New York 1941.

Baruch, B., *The Radical Right. The New American Right*, Garden City 1963².

Barzun, J., *Teacher in America*, Boston 1946.

Baudelot, C. et al., *La petite bourgeoisie en France*, Paris 1974.

Bauer, O., 'Der Faschismus', in ibid., *Zwischen zwei Weltkriegen*, Bratislawa 1936.

Bayer, H. (ed.), *Der Angestellte zwischen Arbeiterschaft und Management*, Berlin 1961.

Beckley, D. K. and W. B. Logan, *The Retail Salesperson at Work*, New York 1948.

Bell, L. V., 'The Failure of Nazism in America. The German American Bund, 1936 to 1941', in *PSQ*, Vol. 85, 1970, pp. 85-99.

Bell, L. V., *In Hitler's Shadow. The Anatomy of American Nazism*, Port Washington, NY 1973.

Bendix, R., *Work and Authority in Industry. Ideologies of Management in the Course of Industrialization*, New York 1956.

Benet, M. K., *The Secretarial Ghetto*, New York 1973.

Benewick, R., *The Fascist Movement in Britain* (1969), London 1972².

Benge, E. J., *Cutting Clerical Costs*, New York 1931.

Benjamin, L., *The Position of the Middle-Class Worker in the Transition to Socialism*. Published by the Labour Party, London 1935.

Bennett, D. H., *Demagogues in the Depression. American Radicals and the Union Party 1932-1936*, New Brunswick, NJ 1969.

Benson, E. G. and E. Wicoff, 'Voters Pick Their Party', in *POQ*, Vol. 8, 1944.

Benson, S. P., ' "The Clerking Sisterhood". Rationalization and the Work Culture of Saleswomen', in *Radical America*, Vol. 21, No. 2, March/April 1978, pp. 41-55.
Bergen, H. B., 'Social Status of the Clerical Worker', in *Journal of Applied Psychology*, Vol. 11, February 1927, pp. 42-46.
Bergewin, R., *Industrial Apprenticeship*, New York 1947.
Bernstein, B. J. (ed.), *Towards a New Past: Dissenting Essays in American History*, New York 1968.
Bernstein, E., *Evolutionary Socialism, A Criticism and Aftermath*, London 1909.
Bernstein, I., *The New Deal Collective Bargaining Policy*, Berkeley 1950.
Bernstein, I., *The Lean Years. A History of the American Worker 1920-1933*, Boston 1960.
Bernstein, I., *Turbulent Years. A History of the American Worker 1933-1941*, Boston 1970.
Berthoff, R., *An Unsettled People. Social Order and Disorder in American History*, New York 1971.
Bills., 'Social Status of the Clerical Worker', in *Journal of Applied Psychology*, Vol. 9, December 1925, pp. 424-27.
Bingham, A. M. and S. Rodman (eds), *Challenge to the New Deal*, New York 1934.
Bingham, A. M., *Insurgent America. Revolt in the Middle Classes*, New York 1935.
Blackburn, R. M., *Union Character and Social Class. A Study of White-Collar Unionism*, London 1967.
Blank, D. A. and G. J. Stigler, *The Demand and Supply of Scientific Personnel*, New York 1957.
Bliven, B., Jr., *The Wonderful Writing Machine*, New York 1954.
Bloch, E., *Erbschaft dieser Zeit*, Zurich 1935, new edition Frankfurt/M. 1962.
Bloomfield, D., *The Modern Executive*, New York 1924.
Bloomfield, D. (ed.), *Selected Articles on Employment Management*, New York 1919.
Bloomfield, Meyer (ed.), *The Vocational Guidance of Youth*, Boston 1911.
Bloomfield, Meyer (ed.), *Readings in Vocational Guidance*, Boston 1915.
Bloomfield, M. H., *Alarms and Diversions: The American Mind Through American Magazines 1900-1914*, The Hague 1967.
Blum, A. A., *Management and the White-Collar Union*, New York 1964.
Blum, A. A., 'The Office Employee', in ibid et al., *White-Collar Workers*, New York 1971, pp. 3-45.
Blum, A. A., *White Collar Workers*, New York 1971.
Bollens, L. F., *White Collar or Noose? The Occupation of Millions*, New York 1947.
Bonham, J., *The Middle Class Vote*, London 1954.
Borkenau, F., 'Zur Soziologie des Faschismus', in *ASS*, Vol. 68, 1932/33, pp. 513-47.
Bossard, J. H. S. and J. F. Dewhurst, *University Education for Business. A Study of Existing Needs for Business*, Philadelphia 1931.
Böttger, H., *Vom alten und neuen Mittelstand*, Berlin 1901.
Boubman, J. R., *Principles of Retail Merchandising*, New York 1936.
Bracher, K., *The German Dictatorship. The Origins and Effects of National Socialism*, New York 1970.
Braeman, J. et al. (eds), *The New Deal*, 2 Vols., Columbus, Ohio 1975.
Brailsford, H. N., 'The Middle Class and Revolution', in *The World Tomorrow*, Vol. 16, 1933, pp. 465-66.
Brandeis, A., *Business a Profession*, Boston 1914.

Brandeis, E., 'Labor Legislation', in H. J. Commons et al., *History of Labor in the United States, 1896-1932*, Vol. 3, 1935, New York 1966, pp. 456-500.

Brandmeyer, G. A. and R. S. Denisoff, 'Status Politics: An Appraisal of The Application of a Concept', in *The Pacific Sociological Review*, Vol. 12, 1969, pp. 5-11.

Braun, R. J., *Teachers and Power. The Story of the American Federation of Teachers*, New York 1972.

Braun, S., *Zur Soziologie der Angestellten*, Frankfurt/M. 1964.

Braverman, H., *Labor and Monopoly Capital. The Degradation of Work in the Twentieth Century*, New York 1974.

Brecher, J., *Strike!*, San Francisco 1972.

Brisco, N. A. and J. W. Wingate, *Retail Buying*, New York 1925.

Brisco, N. A. et al., *Store Salesmanship*, New York 1934.

Brissenden, P. F. and E. Frankel, *Labor Turnover in Industry. A Statistical Analysis*, New York 1922.

Broderick, J. T., *Pulling Together*, Schenectady, NY 1922.

Brody, D., 'The Rise and Decline of Welfare Capitalism', in J. Braeman et al. (eds), *Change and Continuity in Twentieth-Century America*, Columbus, Ohio 1968, pp. 147-78.

Brody, D., 'Labor and the Great Depression: The Interpretative Prospects', in *LH*, Vol. 13, 1973, pp. 231-44.

Brown, E. L., *The Professional Engineer*, New York 1936.

Bry, G., *Wages in Germany 1871-1945*, Princeton 1960.

Bucher, K., *Die Arbeiterfrage im Kaufmannsstande*, Berlin 1883.

Bunzel, J. H., *Anti-Politics in America. Reflections on the Anti-Political Temper and its Distortions of the Democratic Process*, New York 1967.

Burn, J. D., *Three Years Among the Working-Classes in the United States During the War*, London 1865.

Burnham, J. C., 'New Prospectives in the Prohibition "Experiment" of the 1920's', in *JSH*, Vol. 2, 1968, pp. 50-68.

Burns, A. E., 'Work Relief Wage Policies, 1930-36', in *Monthly Report of the FERA*, Washington, June 1936, pp. 22-55.

Burns, J. M., *Roosevelt: The Lion and the Fox*, New York 1956.

Burns, J. M., *Roosevelt: The Soldier of Freedom*, New York 1970.

Burns, R. K., 'The Comparative Economic Position of Manual and White-Collar Employees', in *The Journal of Business*, Vol. 27, Chicago 1954, pp. 257-67.

Butler, E. B., *Saleswomen in Mercantile Stores*, Baltimore 1909.

Butler, E. B., *Women and the Trades. Pittsburgh 1907-1908* (= *The Pittsburgh Survey*, Vol. 1), New York 1909.

Buxton, G. F., *A Report of Foremanship Conferences; 7 Years' Services to the Industries of Indiana 1923-1930*, 1931.

Cabe, J. C., *Foreman's Unions. A New Development in Industrial Relations*, Urbana, Ill. 1947.

Caldwell, T. B., 'The Syndicat des Employés du Commerce et de l'Industrie (1887 to 1919). A Pioneer French Catholic Trade Union of White Collar Workers', in *IRSH*, Vol. 11, 1966, pp. 228-66.

Calhoun, D. H., *The American Civil Engineer. Origins and Conflict*, Cambridge, Mass. 1960.

Calvert, M. A., *The Mechanical Engineer in America 1830-1910. Professional Cultures in Conflict*, Baltimore 1967.

Cantril, H., *The Psychology of Social Movement*, New York 1941.

Cantril, H., *Public Opinion, 1935-1946*, Princeton 1951.

Carlton, W., pseud., *One Way Out. A Middle-Class New Englander Emigrates to America*, Boston 1911.

Carpenter, A. v. Haller, *Glimpses of the Life and Times of A. v. H. Carpenter (General Passenger and Ticket Agent, Chicago, Milwaukee and St. Paul R. R.)*, Chicago 1890.
Carr-Saunders, A. M. and P. A. Wilson, *The Professions* (1933), London 1964.
Carson, G., *The Old Country Store*, New York 1954.
Cassau, T., *Die Gewerkschaftsbewegung*, Halberstadt 1930.
Cawelti, J. G., *Apostles of the Self-Made Man*, Chicago 1965.
The Century Dictionary and Cyclopedia, New York (1889), 1906.
Chafe, W. H., *The American Woman. Her Changing Social, Economic, and Political Roles, 1920-1970*, New York 1972.
Chalmers, D. M., *Hooded Americanism: The History of the Ku Klux Klan*, Chicago 1968.
Chandler, A. D., Jr., and L. Galombos, 'The Development of Large-Scale Economic Organizations in Modern America', in *JEH*, Vol. 30, 1970, pp. 205-17.
Chandler, A. D., *The Visible Hand: The Rise of Modern Business Enterprise in the U.S.*, Cambridge, Mass. 1977.
Chandler, A. D. (ed.), *The Rise of Big Business*, Cambridge, Mass. 1980.
Chase, M. and S., *A Honeymoon Experiment*, Boston 1916.
Chase, S., *Technocracy. An Interpretation*, New York 1933.
Chase, S., *American Credos*, New York 1962.
Chatain, J. and R. Gaudon, *Petites et moyennes entreprises: l'heure du choix*, Paris 1975.
Chechland, S. G., *The Rise of Industrial Society in England 1815-85*, London 1964.
Chilly, L. de, *La classe moyenne en France apres la guerre: 1918-1924. Sa Crise: Causes, conséquences et remedes*. These de doctorat en sciences politiques et economiques, Paris 1924.
Chudacoff, H. P., *Mobile Americans. Residential and Social Mobility in Omaha, 1880-1920*, New York 1972.
Clark, G., *The Conditions of Economic Progress* (1940), New York 1960^2.
Clark, H. F., *Life Earnings in Selected Occupations in the United States*, New York 1937.
Clark, N., *The Dry Years: Prohibition and Social Change in Washington*, Seattle 1965.
Clark, Th.D., *Pills, Petticoats and Plows*, New York 1944.
Clermont, H. J., *Organizing the Insurance Workers. A History of Labor Unions of Insurance Employees*, Washington 1966.
Cochran, Th. C., 'The History of a Business Society', in *JAH*, Vol. 54, 1967, pp. 5-18.
Cochran, Th. C., 'The Business Revolution', in *AHR*, Vol. 79, 1974, pp. 1449-66.
Collinet, M., *Essai sur la condition ouvrier (1900-1960)*, Paris 1951.
Collinet, M., 'Structure des classes salariées en France depuis cinquante ans', in *Revue internationale du travail*, Vol. 67, 1953, pp. 299-53.
Corbin, J., *The Return of the Middle Class*, New York 1923.
Corey, L., *The Crisis of the Middle Class*, New York 1935.
Cowdrick, E. S., *Manpower in Industry*, New York 1924.
Coyle, G. L., *Present Trends in the Clerical Occupations*, New York 1928.
Coyle, G. L., 'White Collars and Trade Unions', in *The American Federationist*, Vol. 35, 1928, pp. 1211-15.
Coyner, S. J., *Class Patterns of Family-Income and Expenditure during the Weimar Republic: German White Collar Employees as Harbingers of Modern Society*. PhD Thesis, Rutgers University, New Brunswick, NJ 1975.
Cremin, L. A., *The Transformation of the School: Progressivism in American Education 1897-1957*, New York 1961.

Crew, D., 'Definitions of Modernity. Social Mobility in a German Town 1880-1901', in *JSH*, Vol. 6, 1972, pp. 51-74.

Crew, D., 'Regionale Mobilitat und Arbeiterklasse. Das Beispiel Bochum 1880-1901', in *GG*, Vol. 1, 1975, pp. 99-120.

Croly, H., *The Promise of American Life* (1909), Archon Books 1963.

Croner, F., *The White Collar Movement in Germany since the Monetary Stabilization*, New York 1937.

Croner, F., *Die Angestellten in der moderne Gesellschaft*, Wien 1954.

Croner, F., *Soziologie der Angestellten*, Köln 1962.

Cross, C., *The Fascists in Britain*, London 1961.

Cross, I. B., *History of Labor in California*, Berkeley 1935.

Crossick, G., *The Lower Middle Class in Britain. 1870-1914*, New York 1977.

Crowther, S., *John H. Patterson. Pioneer in Industrial Welfare*, Garden City, NY 1926.

Croxton, F. C. et al., 'Average Wage and Salary Payments in Ohio, 1918-1932', in *MLF*, Vol. 38, 1934, pp. 143-59; and Vol. 42, 1936, pp. 706-17.

Crozier, M., 'Les attitudes politiques des employés et des petits fonctionnaires', in M. Duverger (ed.), *Partis politiques et classes sociales en France*, Paris 1944, pp. 85-99.

Crozier, M., 'L'ambiguité de la conscience de classe chez les employés et les petites fonctionnaires', in *Cahiers internationaux de sociologie*, Vol. 28, 1955, pp. 78-97.

Crozier, M., 'Le role des employés et des petits fonctionnaires dans la structure française contemporaine', in *Transactions of the Third World Congress of Sociology*, Amsterdam 1956, Vol. 3, pp. 311-19.

Crozier, M., *The World of the Office Worker*, New York 1973.

Cubberley, E. P., *Public Education in the United States. A Study and Interpretation of American Educational History*, Cambridge, Mass. 1934^2.

Cuff, R. D., *The War Industries Board. Business-Government Relations During World War I*, Baltimore 1973.

Dahlström, E., *Management, Unions and Society. A Study of Salaried Employees' Attitudes*, Stockholm 1955.

Dahrendorf, R., 'Recent Changes in the Class Structure of European Societies', in S. R. Graubard (ed.), *A New Europe*, Boston 1964.

Dahrendorf, R., *Society and Democracy in Germany*, Garden City, 1969.

Dale, J. R., *The Clerk in Industry. A Survey of the Occupation, Experience, Status, Education and Vocal Training of a Group of Male Clerks Employed by Industrial Companies*, Liverpool 1962.

Davies, J. C., 'Toward a Theory of Revolution', in *ASR*, Vol. 27, 1962, pp. 5-19.

Davies, M., 'Woman's Place is at the Typewriter: The Feminization of the Clerical Labor Force', in *Radical America*, Vol. 8, No. 4, July/August 1974, pp. 1-28.

Davis, L. E. et al., *American Economic Growth. An Economist's History of the United States*, New York 1972.

Decker, P. R., *Fortunes and Failures. White Collar Mobility in Nineteenth Century San Francisco*, Cambridge, Mass. 1978.

Degler, C. N., *Out of Our Past. The Forces that Shaped Modern America*, New York (1959), 1970^2.

Deherme, G., *Les classes moyennes. Etudes sur le parasitisme social*, Paris 1912.

Deimer, H. et al., *The Foreman and His Job. The First Work Manual of the Modern Foremanship Course. Being the Expression of Practical Foreman*, Chicago 1921.

Delehanty, G. E., *Nonproduction Workers in U.S. Manufacturing*, Amsterdam 1968.

Delon, P., *Les employés de la plume d'oie a l'ordinateur, un siècle de lutte, origines et activité de la Federation C.G.T.*, Paris 1969.
Deming, S., *A Message to the Middle Class*, Boston 1915.
Denison, E. F., 'Revised Estimates of Wages and Salaries in the National Income, 1929-1943', in *Survey of Current Business*, ed. by US Department of Commerce, Bureau of Foreign and Domestic Commerce, June 1945.
Denton, N., *History of the Brotherhood of Railway and Steamship Clerks, Freight Handlers, Express and Station Employees*, Cincinnati, Ohio 1965.
Derber, M. and E. Young (eds.), *Labor and the New Deal*, Madison, Wisc. 1957.
Desqueyrat, A., *Classes moyennes*, Paris 1939.
Dobb, M. H., *Studies in the Development of Capitalism*, London 1947^2 (1903).
Doblin, B. E. and C. Pohly, 'The Social Composition of the Nazi Leadership', in *AJS*, Vol. 51, 1945/46, pp. 42-49.
Dodge, D. S., *Memoirs of William E. Dodge*, New York 1887.
Donham, W. B., 'The Unfolding of Collegiate Business Training', in *Harvard Graduates' Magazine*, March 1921, pp. 333-47.
Donovan, F. R., *The Saleslady*, Chicago 1929.
Doubleday, F. N. et al., *Accounting and Office Methods*, Chicago 1910.
Douglas, A. W., *Travelling Salesmanship*, New York 1919.
Douglas, P. H., *Wages and the Family*, Chicago 1925.
Douglas, P. H., *Real Wages in the United States 1890-1926*, Boston 1930.
Douglas, P. H., *American Apprenticeship and Industrial Education*, New York 1968.
Dreyfuss, C., *Beruf und Ideologie der Angestellten*, München 1933.
Dreyfuss, C., *Occupation and Ideology of Salaried Employees*, New York 1938.
Droz, W. H. et al., *Essays on the New Deal*, Austin, Texas 1969.
Dubofsky, M., *When Workers Organize: New York City in the Progressive Era*, Amherst, Mass. 1968.
Dubofsky, M., *We Shall Be All: A History of the Industrial Workers of the World*, Chicago 1969.

Edwards, A. M., 'Social-Economic Groups of the United States. Gainful Workers of United States Classified by Social-Economic Groups or Strata', in *QPAStA*, Vol. 15, 1917, pp. 643-61.
Edwards, A. M., 'A Social-Economic Grouping of the Gainful Workers of the United States', in *JAStA*, Vol. 28, 1933, pp. 377-91.
Edwards, A. M., 'The "White-Collar Workers",' in *MLF*, Vol. 36, 1934, p. 501.
Edwards, A. M., *Comparative Occupation Statistics for the United States, 1870-1940*, Washington 1943.
Edwards, J. D., *History of Public Accounting in the United States*, East Lansing, Mich. 1960.
Ekirch, A. A., Jr., *Progressivism in America. A Study of the Era from Theodore Roosevelt to Woodrow Wilson*, New York 1974.
Elsner, H., Jr., *The Technocrats. Prophets of Automation*. Syracuse, NY 1967.
Engelsing, R., 'Die wirtschaftliche und soziale Differenzierung der detuschen kaufmannischen Angestellten im In — und Ausland, 1690-1900', in *Zs. f.d. gesamte Staatswissenschaft*, Vol. 123, 1967, pp. 347-80, 482-514; also ibid., *Zur Sozialgeschichte duetscher Mittel — und Unterschichten*, Gottingen 1973, pp. 51-111, 271-83.
Epstein, A., *The Problem of Old Pensions in Industry. An Up-to-Date Summary of the Facts and Figures Developed in the Further Study of Old Age Pensions*, Harrisburg, Pa. 1926.
Erdmann, E. G., *Das Recht der Arbeitnehmer auf Beteiligung an der Verwaltung der Betriebe der gewerblichen Wirtschaft. Ein internationaler Rechtsvergleich*, Koln 1952.

Estey, M., 'Early Closing: Employer-organized Origin of the Retail Labor Movement', in *LH*, Vol. 13, 1972, pp. 560-70.
Etzioni, A. (ed.), *The Semi-Professions. Teachers, Nurses, Social Workers*, New York 1969.

Fabricant, S., *Employment in Manufacturing 1899-1939. An Analysis of Its Relations to the Volume of Production*, New York 1942.
Fabricant, S., *The Trend of Government Activity in the United States since 1900*, New York 1952.
Falcone, N. S., *Labor Law*, New York 1962.
Farnham, D. T., *America versus Europe in Industry. A Comparison of Industrial Policy and Methods of Management*, New York 1921.
Farrington, F., *Store Management — Complete*, Chicago 1911.
Farrington, F., *The Successful Salesman*, Chicago 1918.
Faulkner, H. W., *The Decline of Laissez-Faire, 1897-1917*, New York 1951.
Felice, R. de, *Le interpretazioni del fascismo*, Bari (1971) 1972.
Ferguson, Ch. W., *Fifty Million Brothers. A Panorama of American Lodges and Clubs*, New York 1937.
Festinger, L., 'A Theory of Social Comparison Processes', in *Human Relations*, Vol. 7, 1954, pp. 117-40.
Filene, P. G., 'An Obituary for "The Progressive Movement",' in *American Quarterly*, Vol. 22, 1970, pp. 20-34.
Fine, S., *Sit-down: The General Motors Strike of 1936-1937*, Ann Arbor, Mich. 1969.
Fischer, F. W., *Die Angestellten, ihre Bewegung und ihre Ideologien*. Phil. Diss., Heidelberg 1932.
Fischer, M., *Mittelklasse als politischer Begriff in Frankreich seit der Revolution*, Gottingen 1974.
Fischer, B. M., *Industrial Education; American Ideals and Institutions*, Madison, Wisc. 1967.
Fisk, J. W., *Salesmanship. A Text Book for Retail Selling*, New York 1914.
Fleming, A. P. M. and J. G. Pearce, *The Principles of Apprentice Training with Special Reference to the Engineering Industry*, London 1916.
Flexner, E., *Century of Struggle: The Women's Rights Movement in the United States*, Cambridge, Mass. 1959.
Foltz, E. B., *The Federal Civil Service as a Career. A Manual for Applicants for Positions and Those in the Civil Service of the Nation*, New York 1909.
Fourastie, J., *Le grand espoir du XXè siècle*, Paris 1950 (1972).
Fraenkel, E., *Das Amerikanische Regierungssystem*, Koln 1960^2.
Français, L., *La distinction entre employés et ouvriers en droit allemand, belge, francais et italien*, Le Hage 1963.
Freidel, F., *Franklin D. Roosevelt. Launching the New Deal*, Boston 1973.
Friters, G., 'Who are the German Fascists?', in *Current History*, Vol. 35, 1932, pp. 532-36.
Funk, C. E., *Heavens to Betsy! And Other Curious Sayings*, New York 1955.
Furnas, J. C. et al., *How America Lives*, Oxford 1941.

Galambos, L., *The Public Image of Big Business in America, 1880-1940. A Quantitative Study in Social Change*, Baltimore 1975.
Galenson, W., *The CIO Challenge to the AFL. A History of the American Labor Movement 1935-1941*, Cambridge, Mass. 1960.
Gantzel, K. J., *Wesen und Begriff der mittelstandischen Unternehmung*, Koln 1962.
Garraty, J. A., 'The New Deal, National Socialism, and the Great Depression', in *AHR*, Vol. 78, October 1973, pp. 907-44.

GDA, *Die wirtschaftliche und soziale Lage der Angestellten. Ergebnisse und Erkenntnisse aus der frühen sozialen Erhebung des Gewerkschaftsbundes der Angestellten*, Berlin 1931[2].

GDA (ed.), *Epochen der Angestellten — Bewegung 1774-1980*, Berlin 1930.

Geiger, Th., 'Panik im Mittelstand', in *Die Arbeit*, Vol. 7, 1930, pp. 637-54.

Geiger, Th., *Die soziale Schichtung des deutschen Volkes* (1932), repr. Stuttgart 1967.

Gellately, R., *The Politics of Economic Despair. Shopkeepers and German Politics 1890-1914*, London 1974.

Gerschenkron, A., *Economic Backwardness in Historical Perspective*, New York 1965[2].

Gerth, H., 'The Nazi Party. Its Leadership and Composition', in *AJS*, Vol. 45, 1940, pp. 517-41.

Ghent, W. J., *Our Benevolent Feudalism*, New York 1902.

Gibbons, H., *John Wanamaker*, 2 Vols, New York 1920.

Giden, C., *Travail intellectuel et travail manuel*, Paris 1901.

Gidens, A., *The Class Structure of Advanced Societies*, New York 1973.

Gibb, C. L., *Hidden Hierarchies. The Professions and Government*, New York 1966.

Gilbert, F. (ed.), *The Historical Essays of Otto Hintze*, New York 1975.

Ginzberg, E. and H. Berman, *The American Worker in the Twentieth Century. A History Through Autobiographies*, Glencoe 1963.

Girod, R., *Etudes sociologiques sur les couches salariées. Ouvriers et employés*, Paris 1961.

Gitelman, H. M., 'The Labor Force at Waltham Watch during the Civil War Era', in *JEH*, Vol. 25, 1965, pp. 214-43.

Gitelman, H. M., 'No Irish Need Apply: Patterns and Responses to Ethnic Discrimination in the Labor Market', in *LH*, Vol. 14, 1973, pp. 56-82.

Gitelman, H. M., *Working Men at Waltham: Mobility in American Urban Industrial Development 1850-1880*, Baltimore 1974.

Gladen, A., *Geschichte der Sozialpolitik in Deutschland. Eine Analyse inhrer Bedingungen, Formen, Zielsetzungen und Auswirkungen*, Wiesbaden 1974.

Godine, M. R., *The Labor Problem in the Public Service*, Cambridge, Mass. 1971.

Goffee, W. R., *Problems in Retail Selling Analyzed. What Some of the Problems Are and How to Overcome Them Day to Day*, 1913.

Goldberg, R. A., 'The Ku Klux Klan in Madison, 1922-1927', in *Wisconsin Magazine of History*, Vol. 58, Fall 1974, pp. 31-44.

Goldschmidt, F., *Die soziale Lage und Bildung der Handlungsgehilfen*, Berlin 1894.

Goldstein, S., 'Migration and Occupational Mobility in Norristown, Pennsylvania', in *ASR*, Vol. 20, 1955, pp. 402-408.

Goldstein, S., *Patterns of Mobility, 1910-1950. The Norristown Study. A Method for Measuring Migration and Occupational Mobility in the Community*, Philadelphia 1958.

Gompers, S., *Seventy Years of Life and Labor*, New York 1925.

Gordon, M. R., 'Domestic Conflict and the Origins of the First World War: The British and the German Cases', in: *JMH*, Vol. 46, 1974, pp. 192-26.

Gould, M. P., *Where Have My Profits Gone?*, Elmira, NY 1912.

Gould, R. E., *Yankee Storekeepers*, New York 1946.

Gowin, E. B. and W. A. Wheatley, *Occupations. A Textbook in Vocational Guidance*, Boston 1916.

Grebing, H., *Aktuelle Theorien uber Faschismus und Konservatismus. Eine Kritik*, Stuttgart 1974.

Green, M., *The National Civic Federation and the American Labor Movement 1900 to 1925*, Washington 1956.

Greenwald, M. W., *Women, War and Work. The Impact of WWI on Women Workers in the US.* PhD thesis, University of Pittsburgh 1977.
Gregory, C. O., *Labor and the Law*, New York (1946), 1949².
Gretton, R. H., *The English Middle Class*, London 1917.
Griffen, C., 'Workers Divided: The Effect of Craft and Ethnic Differences in Poughkeepsie, New York, 1850-1880', in S. Thernstrom and R. Sennett (eds), *Nineteenth Century Cities*, New Haven 1969, pp. 49-97.
Grob, G. N., *Workers and Utopia*, Evanson, Ill. 1961.
Grunberg, E., *Der Mittelstand in der kapitalistischen Gesellschaft*, Leipzig 1932.
Guerin, D., *Fascism and Big Business*, New York 1973 (first published 1936).
Gunther, A. and R. Prevot, *Die Wohlfahrseinrichtungen der Arbeitgeber in Deutschland und Frankreich*, Leipzig 1905.
Gurr, T. R., *Why Men Rebel*, Princeton, NJ 1970.
Gusfield, J. R., *Symbolic Crusade and the American Temperance Movement*, Urbana, Ill. 1963.
Gutman, H. G., 'The Worker's Search for Power. Labor in the Gilded Age', in H. W. Morgan (ed.), *The Gilded Age*, Syracuse, NY 1963.
Gutman, H. G., *Work, Culture and Society in Industrializing America; Essays in American Working Class and Social History*, New York 1976.

Haber, S., *Efficiency and Uplift. Scientific Management in the Progressive Era 1890 to 1920*, Chicago 1964.
Hadley, A. T., 'Ethics of Corporate Management', in *The North American Review*, Vol. 184, 1907, pp. 120-34.
Hahn, L. and P. White, *The Merchant's Manual. Published under the Auspices of the National Retail Dry Goods Association*, New York 1924.
Hamby, A. L. (ed.), *The New Deal*, New York 1969.
Hamel, I., *Volkischer Verband und nationale Gewerkschaft. Der Deutschnationale Handlungsgehilfen-Verband 1893-1933*, Frankfurt/M. 1967.
Hamilton, R. F., 'Marginal Middle Class: A Reconsideration', in *ASR*, Vol. 30, 1966, pp. 192-99.
Hamilton, R. F., *Class and Politics in the United States*, New York 1972.
Hamilton, R. F., *Restraining Myths. Critical Studies of U.S. Social Structure and Politics*, New York 1975.
Handlin, O., *Al Smith and His America*, Boston 1958.
Handlin, O., *The Uprooted. The Epic Story of the Great Migrations that Made the American People*, Boston (1951), 1973².
Hansen, A. H., 'Industrial Class Alignments in the United States', in *QPAStA*, Vol. 17, 1920, pp. 417-25.
Hansen, A. H., 'Industrial Classes in the United States in 1920', in *JAStA*, Vol. 18, 1922, pp. 503-506.
Harding, A., *The Revolt of the Actors*, New York 1929.
Hareven, T. K. (ed.), 'The Laborers of Manchester, New Hampshire, 1917-1922: The Role of Family and Ethnicity in Adjustment to Industrial Life', in *LH*, Vol. 16, 1975, pp. 249-65.
Harrington, N., *The Retail Clerks*, New York 1962.
Hartfiel, G., *Angestellte und Angestelltengewerkschaften in Deutschland. Entwicklung und gegenwärtige Situation von beruflicher Tatigkeit, sozialer Stellung und Verbandswesen der Angestellten in der Gewerblichen Wirtschaft*, Berlin 1961.
Hartmann, H., *Funktionale Autoritat*, Stuttgart 1964.
Hartz, L., *The Liberal Tradition in America. An Interpretation of American Political Thought Since the Revolution*, New York 1955.
Haskins, C. W., *Business Education and Accountancy*, New York 1904.
Hawes, J., *Lecture to Young Men on the Formation of Character*, Boston 1865².

Hawley, E. W., *The New Deal and the Problem of Monopoly: A Study in Economic Ambivalence*, Princeton, NJ 1969.
Haynes, B. R. and H. P. Jackson, *A History of Business Education in the United States*, Cincinnati 1935.
Hays, S. P., *The Response to Industrialism, 1885-1914*, Chicago 1957.
Hays, S. P., 'The Politics of Reform in Municipal Government in the Progressive Era', in *Pacific Northwest Quarterly*, Vol. 55, 1964, pp. 157-69.
Heer, C., *Income and Wages in the South*, Chapel Hill, NC 1930.
Henig, H., *The Brotherhood of Railway Clerks*, New York 1937.
Hennig, E., *Burgerliche gesellschaft u. Faschismus in Deutschland. Ein Forschungsbericht*, Frankfurt 1977.
Hession, C. H. and H. Sardy, *Ascent to Affluence. History of American Economic Development*, Boston 1969, pp. 890ff.
Hicks, C. J., *My Life in Industrial Relations. Fifty Years in the Growth of a Profession*, New York 1941.
Hidy, R. W. and M. E. Hidy, *Pioneering in Big Business, 1882-1911: Standard Oil Company*, New York 1955.
Higham, J., *Strangers in the Land. Patterns of American Nativism 1860-1925*, New York 1975[2].
Higham, J., *Send These to Me. Jews and Other Immigrants in Urban America*, New York 1975.
Higinbotham, H. N., *The Making of a Merchant*, Chicago (1902) 1906[2].
Hilferding, R., *Das Finanzkapital* (1910), Wien 1923.
Hill, J., *Women in Gainful Occupations 1870-1920* (Census Monograph No. 9). Washington, DC 1929.
Hiller, G., *Die Lage der Handlungsgehilfen*, Leipzig 1890.
Hintze, O., 'Der Beamtenstand', in ibid., *Soziologie und Geschichte*, Gottingen 1964, pp. 66-125.
Hirschman, A., *Exit, Voice and Loyalty. Response to Decline in Firms, Organizations, and States*, Cambridge, Mass. 1970.
Hobsbawm, E. J., *Industry and Empire. The Making of Modern English Society, Vol. 2: 1750 to the Present Day*, New York 1968.
Hoffmann, S., 'Aspects ud regime de Vichy', in *Revue française de Science politique*, Vol. 6, 1956, pp. 44-69.
Hoffmann, S., *Le mouvement Poujade*, Paris 1956.
Hofstadter, R., *The Age of Reform: From Bryan to F.D.R.*, New York 1955.
Hofstadter, R., *Social Darwinism in American Thought, 1860-1915*, Philadelphia 1955[2].
Hofstadter, R., *The Paranoid Style in American Politics*, New York 1966.
Hofstadter, R. and S. M. Lipset (eds), *Turner and the Sociology of the Frontier*, New York 1968.
Hofstadter, R. and C. de Witt Hardy, *The Development and Scope of Higher Education in the United States*, New York 1952.
Hohorst, G. et al., *Sozialgeschichtliches Arbeitsbuch. Materialien zur Statistik des Kaserreichs 1870-1914*, Munchen 1975.
Hoke, T., *Shirts! A Survey of the New 'Shirt' Organizations in the United States Seeking a Fascist Dictatorship*, New York 1934.
Hollander, H., *Quest for Excellence*, Washington 1968.
Holman, W. C., *Ginger Talks. The Talks of a Sales Manager to His Men*, Chicago 1908.
Hook, E., *Salaried Employees and the Industrial Transformation (The Industrial Institute for Economic and Social Research)*, Stockholm 1955.
Hopkins, C. H., *History of the YMCA in North America*, New York 1951.

Hopkins, G. E., *The Airline Pilots: A Study in Elite Unionization*, Cambridge, Mass. 1971.
Hopkins, H. L., *The Realities of Unemployment*, Washington n.d. (1936).
Horlick, A. St., *Counting-Houses and Clerks. The Social Control of Young Men in New York, 1840-1860*. PhD thesis, University of Wisconsin 1969.
Horning, K. H. (ed.), *Der 'neu' Arbeiter*, Frankfurt/M. 1969.
Hourwich, I. A., 'The Social-Economic Classes of the Population of the United States', in *Journal of Political Economy*, Vol. 19, 1911, pp. 188-215, 309-37.
Howard, D. S., *The WPA and Federal Relief Policy*, New York 1943.
Howe, F. C., *Wisconsin. An Experiment in Democracy*, New York 1912.
Howe, I. and L. Coser, *The American Communist Party*, Boston 1957.
Howe, R. M., *History of Macy's of New York 1858-1919. Chapters in the Evolution of the Department Store*, Cambridge, Mass. 1946.
Humphreys, B., *Clerical Unions in the Civil Service*, London 1958.
Huntington, S. P., 'Postindustrial Politics, How Benign Will It Be?', in *Comparative Politics*, Vol. 7, 1974, pp. 163-91.
Hutchinson, E. P., *Immigrants and Their Children, 1850-1950*, New York 1956.
Hyman, A. A., *Significant Factors Relating to the Growth and Potential of the American Federation of State, County, and Municipal Employees, AFL-CIO*, PhD thesis, University of Pennsylvania 1963.
Hyman, H. H., 'Reference Groups', in *IESS*, Vol. 13, New York 1968, pp. 253-361.

Izard, G., *Les classes moyennes*, Paris 1938.

Jackson, J. A. (ed.), *Social Stratification*, Cambridge 1968.
Jackson, K. T., *The Ku Klux Klan in the City, 1915-30*, New York 1967.
Jahoda, M. et al., *Die Arbeitslosen von Marienthal* (1933), new edition Allensbach 1960.
James, E. J., *Education of Business Men III: A Plea for the Establishment of Commercial High Schools. An Address Before the Convention of the American Bankers' Association...*, New York 1893.
Janowitz, M., 'Black Legions on the March', in D. Aaron (ed.), *America in Crisis*, New York 1952, pp. 304-25.
Johnson, G. W., 'The Average American and the Depression', in *Current History*, Vol. 35, 1932, pp. 671-75.
Johnson, L. A., *Over the Counter and on the Shelf; Country Storekeeping in America 1620-1920*, Rutland, Vt. 1961.
Jones, A. W., *Life, Liberty and Property. A Story of Conflict and a Measurement of Conflicting Rights*, Philadelphia 1941.
Jones, L. E., ' "The Dying Middle": Weimar Germany and the Fragmentation of Bourgeois Politics', in *CEH*, Vol. 4, 1972, pp. 23-54.
Jones, L. E. 'The Crisis of White Collar Interest Politics: Deutschnationaler Handlungsgehilfen-Verbund und Deutsche Volkspartei in the World Economic Crisis', in H. Mommsen et al. (eds), *Industrielles System und politische Entwicklung in der Weimarer Republik*, Dusseldorf 1974, pp. 811-23.
Jones, M. A., *American Immigration*, Chicago 1960.
Josyln, C. S., *American Business Leaders. A Study in Social Origins and Social Stratification*, New York 1932.

Kadritzke, U., *Angestellte. Die geduldgien Arbeiter. Zur Soziologie und sozialen Bewegung der Angestellten*, Frankfurt/M. 1975.
Kadritzke, N., *Faschismus und Krise. Zur Verhältnis von Politik und Ökonomie in Nationalsozialismus*, Frankfurt 1976.
Kaelble, A., 'Soziale Mobilität in Deutschland 1900-1960', unpublished Ms. 1976.

Kaelble, H., 'Sozialer Aufstieg in den USA und Deutschland, 1900-1960. Ein vergleichender Forschungsbericht', in H.-U. Wehler (ed.), *Sozialgeschichte Heute. Fs. fur Hans Rosenberg zum 70. Geburstag*, Gottingen 1974, pp. 525-42.
Kahan, M. et al., 'On the Analytical Division of Social Class', in *British Journal of Sociology*, Vol. 17, 1955, pp. 122-32.
Kahl, J. A., *The American Class Structure*, New York (1953) 1957.
Kahler, G. E. and A. C. Johnson, *The Development of Personnel Administration, 1923 to 1945*, Madison, Wisc. 1971.
Kampelman, M. M., *The Communist Party vs. the CIO. A Study in Power Politics*, New York 1957.
Kaplan, D. I. and M. C. Casery, *Occupational Trends in the United States 1900 to 1950* (= US Bureau of Census, Working Paper, No. 5), Washington 1958.
Karolides, N. J., *The Pioneer in the American Novel 1900-1950*, Norman, Oklahoma 1967.
Kassalow, E. M., 'Professional Unions in Sweden', in *Industrial Relations*, Vol. 8, 1969, pp. 119-34.
Kassalow, E. M., *Trade Unions and Industrial Relations: An International Comparison*, New York 1969.
Kater, M. H., *Studentenschaft und Rechtsradikalismus in Deutschland 1918-1933*, Hamburg 1975.
Katz, D., 'The Public Opinion Polls and the 1940 Election', in *POQ*, Vol. 5, 1941.
Katz, M. B., *The People of Hamilton, Canada. Family and Class in a Mid-Nineteenth Century City*, Cambridge, Mass. 1975.
Kautsky, K., *Bernstein und das sozialdemokratische Programm. Eine Antikritik*, Stuttgart 1899.
Kelley, F., *Minimum Wage Boards*, New York 1911.
Kendrick, J., *Productivity Trends in the United States*, Princeton, NJ 1961.
Kernig, C. D. (ed.), *Marxism, Communism, and Western Society. A Comparative Encyclopedia*, New York 1972.
Kilson, M., 'Blacks and Neo-Ethnicity in American Political Life', in N. Glazer and D. P. Moynihan (eds.), *Ethnicity. Theory and Experience*, Cambridge, Mass. 1975, pp. 236-66.
Kleine, G., *Die leitenden Angestellten in der gengenwärtigen Wirtschaftsgesellschaft*, Koln 1955.
Klingemann, H. D. and F. U. Pappi, 'Die Wählerbewegungen bei der Bundestagswahl am 28. September 1969', in *PVS*, Vol. 11, 1970, pp. 11-38.
Klingender, F. D., *The Condition of Clerical Labor in Britain*, London 1935.
Kocka, J., 'Family and Bureaucracy in German Industrial Management, 1850-1914', in *BHR*, Vol. 45, 1971, pp. 133-56.
Kocka, J., *Klassengesellschaft im Krieg. Deutsche Sozialgeschichte 1914-1918*, Göttingen 1973.
Kocka, J., 'Theorien in der Sozial- und Gesellschaftsgeschichte, Vorschläge zur historischen Schichtungsanalyse', in *GG*, Vol. 1, Göttingen 1975, pp. 9-42.
Kocka, J., *Sozialgeschichte. Begriff — Entwicklung — Probleme*, Göttingen 1977.
Kocka, J., *Angestellte zwischen Faschismus und Demokratie, Zur politischen Sozialgeschichte der Angestellten: USA 1890-1940 im internationalen Vergleich*, Göttingen 1977.
Kocka, J., 'Stand — Klasse — Organization. Strukturen sozialer ungleichheit in Deutschland vom späten 18. bis zum frühen 20. Jahrhunder im Aufriss', in H.-U. Wehler (ed.), *Klassen in der europäischen Sozialgeschichte*, Göttingen 1979.
Kofler, L., 'Das Wesen des Kleinburgertums', in ibid., *Marxistische Staatstheorie*, Frankfurt/M. 1970, pp. 256ff.
Kolb, A., *Als Arbeiter in Amerika. Unter deutsch-amerikanischen Grosstadt-Proletariern*, Berlin 1904.

Kolko, G., *The Triumph of Conservatism*, Chicago 1963.
Komarovsky, M., *The Unemployed Man and His Family*, New York 1940.
Kornblum, W., *Blue Collar Community*, Chicago 1974.
Kornhauser, A. W., 'Analysis of "Class" Structure of Contemporary American Society. Psychological Bases of Class Divisions', in ibid., *Industrial Conflict: A Psychological Interpretation*, New York 1939, pp. 199-244.
Kracauer, S., 'Die Angestellten (1930)', in ibid., *Schriften*, Vol. 1, Frankfurt/M. 1971, pp. 205-304.
Kramer, L., *Labor's Paradox. The American Federation of State, County, and Municipal Employees, AFL-CIO*, New York 1962.
Krebs, A., *Tendenzen und Gestalten der NSDAP*, Stuttgart 1959.
Kritzbert, B., 'An Unfinished Chapter in White-collar Unionism. The Formative Years of the Chicago Newspaper Guild, Local 71, American Newspaper Guild, AFL-CIO', in *LH*, Vol. 14, 1973, pp. 397-413.
Kühnl, R., *Formen Burgerlicher Herrschaft. Liberalismus-Faschismus*, Reinbeck b. Hamburg 1971.
Kühnl, R., 'Probleme einer Theorie uber den internationalen Faschismus', in *PVS*, Vol. 16, 1975, pp. 89ff.
Kuznets, S., *National Income and its Composition 1919-1938*, New York 1941.
Kuznets, S., 'Quantitative Aspects of the Economic Growth of Nations, I', in *Economic Development and Cultural Change*, Vol. 5, October 1956, pp. 5-94.
Kuznets, S., *Modern Economic Growth. Rate, Structure and Spread*, New Haven, Conn. 1966.
Kuznets, S., *Economic Growth of Nations. Total Output and Production Structure*, Cambridge, Mass. 1971, pp. 10-99.

Ladd, E. C. and S. M. Lipset, *Professors, Unions and American Higher Education*, Berkeley 1973.
La Dame, *The Filene Store. A Study of Employees' Relation to Management in a Retail Store*, New York 1930.
Laidler, H. W., 'The White Collar Worker', in *The American Socialist Review*, Vol. 3, 1934, pp. 53-58.
Lakenbacher, E., *Die österreichischen Angestelltengewerkschaften, Geschichte und Gegenwart*, Wien 1967.
Lange, P., *Die soziale Bewegung der Kaufmannischen Angestellten*, Berlin 1920.
Lange, W. H., *The American Management Association and Its Predecessors* (=AMA, Special Paper, No. 17), New York 1928.
Laqueur, W. (ed.), *Fascism. A Reader's Guide*, Berkeley and Los Angeles 1976.
Larmour, P. J., *The French Radical Party in the 1930's*, Stanford 1964.
Laslett, J. H. M., *Labor and the Left: A Study of Socialist and Radical Influences in the American Labor Movement, 1881-1924*, New York 1970.
Laslett, J. H. M., and S. M. Lipset, *Failure of a Dream? Essays in the History of American Socialism*, Garden City, NY 1974.
Lasswell, H. D., 'The Psychology of Hitlerism', in *The Political Quarterly*, Vol. 4, 1933, pp. 374ff.
Lasswell, H. D., 'The Moral Vocation of the Middle-Income Skill Group', in *The International Journal of Ethics*, Vol. 45, January 1935, pp. 127-37.
Laurent, B., *Postes et postiers*, Paris 1922.
Layton, E. T., Jr., *The Revolt of the Engineers. Social Responsibility and the American Engineering Profession*, Cleveland 1971.
Lazerson, M., *Origins of the Urban School in Massachusetts 1890-1915*, Cambridge, Mass. 1971.
Leab, D. J., 'Toward Unionization: The American Newspaper Guild and the Newark Ledger Strike of 1934-35', in *LH*, Vol. 11, 1970, pp. 3-22.

Leab, D. J., *A Union of Individuals. The Formation of the American Newspaper Guild, 1933-1936*, New York 1970.
Leavitt, F. M., *Examples of Industrial Education*, Boston 1912.
Lebergott, S., *Manpower and Economic Growth*, New York 1964,
Lederer, E., 'Die österreichische Sozialversicherungsvorlage', in *Schmollers Jb. f. Gesetzgebung, Verwaltung und Volkswirtschaft*, Vol. 39, 1909, pp. 1643-72.
Lederer, E., *Die Privatangestellten in der modernen Wirtschaftsentwicklung*, Tübingen 1912.
Lederer, E., *The Problem of the Modern Salaried Employee* (= Report on Project No. 165-6999-6027 conducted under the auspices of WPA), New York 1937. Translation of Chs. 2 and 3 of *Die Privatangestellten*. . ., Tubingen 1912.
Lederer, E., 'Die Umschichtung des Proletariats', in *Die Neue Rundschau*, Vol. 2, 1929, pp. 145-61.
Lederer, E. and J. Marschak, 'Der neue Mittelstand', in *GdS*, Abt. 9, Teil 1, Tubingen 1926, pp. 120-41.
Leffingwell, W. H. (ed.), *Making the Office Pay. Tested Plans, Methods, and Systems*. . ., Chicago 1918.
Leffingwell, W. H. (ed.), *Office Management. Principles and Practices*, Chicago 1925.
Leigh, R., *The Human Side of Retail Selling. A Textbook for Salespeople in Retail Stores*, New York 1921.
Leighton, G. R., 'And If the Revolution Comes. . .?', in *Harper's Monthly Magazine*, Vol. 164, 1932, pp. 466-76.
Leiter, R. D., *The Musicians and Petrillo*, New York 1953.
Lenin, W. I., *'Leftwing' Communism, an Infantile Disorder*, New York 1940.
Leppert-Fögen, A., *Die deklassierte Klasse. Studien zur Geschichte und Ideologie des Kleinburgertums*, Frankfurt/M. 1974.
Lepsius, R. M. (ed.), *Sozialgeschichtliche grundlagen der Bundesrepublik Deutschland*, Stuttgart 1980.
Leroy-Beaulieu, P., *Essai sur la répartition des richesses et sur la tendance a une moindre inégalité des conditions*, Paris (1888) 1894[2].
Leuchtenburg, W. E., *The Perils of Prosperity, 1914-1932*, Chicago 1958.
Leuchtenburg, W. E., *Franklin D. Roosevelt and the New Deal, 1932-1940*, New York 1963.
Leven, M. et al., *America's Capacity to Consume*, Washington 1934.
Levine, A. L., *Industrial Retardation in Britain 1880-1914*, New York 1967.
Lewin, K., 'Social-Psychological Differences Between the United States and Germany', in ibid., *Resolving Social Conflicts. Selected Papers on Group Dynamics*, New York 1948, pp. 3-33.
Lewis, R. and A. Maude, *The English Middle Classes* (1949), New York 1967.
Lewisohn, S. A., *The New Leadership in Industry*, New York 1926.
Ling, C. C., *The Management of Personnel Relations. History and Origins*, Homewood, Ill. 1965.
Link, A., *The Impact of World War I*, New York 1969.
Lipset, S. M., *Political Man, The Social Basis of Politics*, New York 1960.
Lipset, S. M., *The First New Nation*, Garden City, NY 1967.
Lipset, S. M. and R. Bendix, *Social Mobility in Industrial Society*, Berkeley and Los Angeles 1959.
Lipset, S. M. and E. Raab, *The Politics of Unreason: Right-Wing Extremism in America 1790 to 1970*, New York 1970.
Lloyd, J. H., *Guilds and the Salary Earner*, London 1921.
Lockwood, D., *The Blackcoated Worker. A Study in Class Consciousness*, London 1969[2].
Loewenberg, P., 'The Psychohistorical Perspectives on Modern German History', in *JMH*, Vol. 47, 1975, pp. 229-79.

Losche, P., *Industriegewerkschaften im Organisierten Kapitalismus. Der CIO in der Roosevelt Ara*, Opladen 1974.

Lotz, A., *Geschichte des deutschen Beamtentums*, Berlin 1909.

Low, A. M., 'What Is Socialism? Some Reasons for the Present Discontent (IV)', in *The North American Review*, Vol. 197/I, 1913, pp. 556-65.

Löwenthal, R., 'Secessio Plebis', in *The Twentieth Century*, May 1951, pp. 350-62.

Lubell, S., *The Future of American Politics*, New York 1951.

Lubove, R., 'The Twentieth Century City: The Progressive as Municipal Reformer', in *Mid America*, Vol. 41, 1959, pp. 195-209.

Lumley, R., *White Collar Unionism in Britain. A Survey of the Present Position*, London 1973.

Lundgreen, P., 'Industrialization and Educational Formation of Manpower in Germany', in *JHS*, Vol. 9, 1975, pp. 64-80.

Luthy, H., *Frankreichs Uhren gehen anders*, Stuttgart 1954.

Lutz, R. R., *Wage Earning and Education* (= Cleveland Education Survey, Summary), Cleveland 1916.

Lynd, R. S. and H. M. Lynd, *Middletown. A Study in American Culture*, New York (1929), 1956.

MacDonald, W., *The Intellectual Worker and His Work*, New York 1923.

Maddison, A., *Economic Growth in the West. Comparative Experience in Europe and North America*, New York 1964.

Maher, A. G., *Bookkeepers, Stenographers and Office Clerks in Ohio, 1914 to 1924* (= US Department of Labor, Women's Bureau, Bulletin No. 95), Washington 1932.

Mahoney, T. and L. Sloane, *The Great Merchants; America's Foremost Retail Institutions and the People who Made Them Great*, New York 1966.

Maier, H. and H. Bott, *Die NPD. Struktur und Ideologie einer 'nationalen Rechtspartei'*, München 1968[2].

Mallet, S., *La nouvelle classe ouvrier*, Paris 1963.

Man, H. de, *Sozialismus und Nationalfascismus*, Potsdam 1931.

Mandel, B., *Samuel Gompers, A Biography*, Yellow Springs 1963.

Mann, C. R., *A Study of Engineering Education*. Prepared for the Joint Committee on Engineering Education of the National Education Societies, New York 1918.

Mansilla, H. C. F., *Faschismus und eindimensionale Gesellschaft*, Neuwied 1971.

Mantel, S., *Die Angestelltenbewegung in Deutschland*, Leipzig 1921.

Marbach, F., *Theorie des Mittelstandes*, Bern 1942.

Marcus, S., *Father Coughlin: The Tumultuous Life of the Priest of the Little Flower*, Boston 1973.

Marenco, C., *Employés de banque*, Paris 1959.

Marshall, A., *Industry and Trade*, London 1919.

Martin, T. D., *Building a Teaching Profession. A Century of Progress 1857-1957*, Middletown, Conn. 1957.

Maruyama, M., *Thought and Behaviour in Modern Japanese Politics*, Oxford 1969, pp. 25-83.

Mason, T. W., *Arbeiterklasse und Volksgemeinschaft. Dokumente und Materialien zur deutschen Arbeiterpolitik 1936-1939*, Opladen 1975.

Masterman, C. F. G., *The Condition of England*, London 1909.

Masterman, C. F. G., *England After The War. A Study*, New York 1923.

Matschoss, C., *Die geistigen Mittel des technischen Fortschritts in den Vereinigten Staaten von Amerika*, Berlin 1913.

Mayer, A., *Dynamics of Counterrevolution in Europe, 1870-1956*, New York 1971.

Mayer, A., 'The Lower Middle Class as Historical Problem', in *JMH*, Vol. 47, 1975, pp. 409-36.

McColloch, *White Collar. Electrical Machinery, Banking and Public Welfare Workers, 1940-1970*. PhD thesis, University of Pittsburgh 1975.
McCoy, D. R., *Angry Voices. Left-of-Center Politics in the New Deal Era*, Lawrence, Kansas 1958.
McEwen, J. L., *An Analysis of the Early Organizing Problems of the Retail Clerks International Association (AFL)*. PhD thesis, Graduate School of Business Administration, New York 1950.
McIsaac, A. M., *The Order of Railroad Telegraphers. A Study in Trade Unionism and Collective Bargaining*, Princeton, NJ 1933.
McKibbin, R. I., 'The Myth of the Unemployed: Who Did Vote for the Nazis?' in *Australian Journal of Politics and History*, Vol. 15, 1969, pp. 25-40.
McKinzie, R. D., *The New Deal for Artists*, Princeton, NJ 1973.
Merkl, P. H., *Political Violence under the Swastika. 581 Early Nazis*, Princeton, NJ 1975.
Merrill, L., *A Salary Policy to Win the War*, New York (UOPWA) September 1943.
Merrill, L., *Which Side Are You on? Raises or Reaction for White Collar Workers?*, New York (UOPWA ca. 1944).
Merrill, L., 'The White Collar Workers and the Future of the Nation' (Testimony before the Sub-Committee on Wartime Health Education, 25-29 January 1944), Washington 1944.
Mierendorff, C., 'Gesicht und Charakter der nationalsozialistischen Bewegung', in *Die Gesellschaft*, Vol. 7, 1930, pp. 489-504.
Miller, S., Jr., *Brief Outline of the National Federation of Post Office Clerks*, New York 1940.
Mills, C. W., *White Collar. The American Middle Classes*, Oxford 1951.
Mills, H. A., *How Collective Bargaining Works*, New York 1942.
Milton, C. R., *Ethics and Expediency in Personnel Management: A Critical History of Personnel Philosophy*, Columbia, SC 1970.
Minton, B. and J. Stuart (eds), *Men Who Lead Labor*, New York 1937.
Mitchell, B., *Depression Decade. From New Era Through New Deal 1929-1941*, New York (1947) 1964.
Modell, J. 'Die "neue Sozialgeschichte" in den Vereinigten Staaten', in *GG*, Vol. 1, 1975, pp. 155-70.
Monroe, F., 'The Story of the National Federation of Post Office Clerks', in *The Union Postal Clerk*, August 1936, pp. 2-4.
Monroe, P., 'Possibilities of the Present Industrial System', in *AJS*, Vol. 3, 1898, pp. 729-53.
Montgomery, D., *Labor and the Radical Republicans*, New York 1972.
Moore, B., *Social Origins of Dictatorship and Democracy*, Boston 1966.
Moore, W. E., *The Professions: Roles and Rules*, New York 1970.
More, L. B., *Wage-Earner's Budgets. A Study of Standards and Cost of Living in New York 1907*.
Morgan, J. S. and R. L. Van Dyke, *White-Collar Blacks: A Breakthrough?*, New York 1970.
Morley, B. R., *Occupational Experiences of Applicants for Work in Philadelphia*. PhD thesis, Philadelphia 1930.
Morris, J. O., *Conflict Within the AFL: A Study of Craft versus Industrial Unionism, 1901-1938*, Ithaca, NY 1958.
Morris, S., 'The Wisconsin Idea and Business Progressivism', in *JAS*, Vol. 4, 1970, pp. 39-60.
Moulin, L. and L. Aerts, 'Les classes moyennes. Essay de bibliographie critique d'une définition', in *Revue d'histoire économique et sociale*, Vol. 32, 1954, pp. 168-86 and pp. 293-309.
Mowry, G. E., *The Era of Theodore Roosevelt, 1900-1912*, New York 1958.

Muller, H., *Nivellierung und Differenzierung der Arbeitseinkommen in Deutschland seit 1925*, Berlin 1954.
Murray, R. K., *Red Scare. A Study of National Hysteria 1919-1920*, New York 1964.
Myers, G., *History of Bigotry in the United States*, New York 1969.

The National Association of Foremen, *A Present Day Necessity. The Foremen's Club. Its Purpose and Organization*, Dayton, Ohio (1938), 1946[2].
National Industrial Conference Board, *Employee Magazines in the United States*, New York 1925.
NICB, *Industrial Pensions in the U.S.*, New York 1925.
NICB, *Clerical Salaries in the United States*, New York 1926.
NICB, *Salary and Wage Policy in the Depression*, New York 1932.
NICB, *Effect of the Depression on Industrial Relations Programs*, New York 1934.
NICB, *What Employers Are Doing for Employees, A Survey of Voluntary Activities for Improvement of Working Conditions in American Business Concerns*, New York 1936.
NICB, *Unions of White Collar Employees*, New York 1943.
NICB, *White Collar Unionization*, New York 1949.
Nathan, M., *The Story of an Epoch Making Movement*, Garden City, NY 1926.
Navin, T. R., 'Investment Banking since 1900', in *Bulletin of the Business History Society*, Vol. 27, 1953, pp. 60-65.
Neal, L., 'Trust Companies and Financial Innovation 1897-1914', in *BHR*, Vol. 45, 1971, pp. 35-51.
Nearing, S., *Poverty and Riches. A Study of the Industrial Regime*, Philadelphia 1916.
Neisser, H., 'Sozialstatistische Analyse der Wahlergebnisse', in *Die Arbeit*, Vol. 7, 1930, pp. 654-59.
Nelson, D., *Managers and Workers: Origins of the New Factory System in the U.S. 1880-1920*, Madison 1975.
Nelson, R. L., *Merger Movement in American Industry, 1885-1956*, Princeton, NJ 1959.
Nestor, O. W., *A History of Personnel Administration 1890 to 1910*. PhD thesis, University of Pennsylvania 1954.
Neumann, F., *Behemoth. The Structure and Practice of National Socialism, 1933 to 1944* (1942[2]) New York 1963[3].
Newcomer, M., 'Professionalization of Leadership in the Big Business Corporation', in *BHR*, Vol. 29, 1955, pp. 54-63.
Nicholls, F. G. et al., *A New Conception of Office Practice, Based on an Investigation of Actual Office Requirements*, Cambridge, Mass. 1927.
Nicholson, J. R. and L. A. Donaldson, *History of the Order of the Elks 1868-1967*, Chicago 1969[2].
Niebuhr, R., 'Pawns for Fascism — Our Lower Middle Class', in *The American Scholar*, Vol. 6, 1937, pp. 144-52.
Noakes, J., *The Nazi Party in Lower Saxony 1921-1933*, Oxford 1971.
Noakes, J. and G. Pridham (eds), *Documents on Nazism, 1919-1945*, London 1974.
Nolte, E. (ed.), *Theorien uber den Faschismus*, Koln 1967.
North, C. C., *Social Differentiation*, Chapel Hill, NC 1926.
North, J. (ed.), *New Masses. An Anthology of the Rebel Thirties*, New York 1969.
Northrup, H. R., *Organized Labor and the Negro*, New York 1944.
Northrup, H. R., *Unionization of Professional Engineers and Chemists*, New York 1946.
Northrup, H. R., *Boulwarism. The Labor Relations Policies of the General Electric Company*, Ann Arbor 1964.

Noyes, C. E., 'The Profession of Management', in *The Antioch Review*, Vol. 5, March 1945, pp. 16-23.
Nugent, W. T. K., 'Politics from Reconstruction to 1900', in W. H. Cartwright and R. L. Watson, Jr. (eds), *The Reinterpretation of American History and Culture*, Washington 1973.
Nye, R. B., *This Almost Chosen People: Essays in the History of American Ideas*, East Lansing, Mich. 1966.

Odencrantz, L. and Z. L. Potter, *Industrial Conditions in Springfield, Illinois. A Survey by the Committee on Women's Work...*, New York 1916.
Oesch, H. W., *Wesen und Ziele der schweizerischen Mittelstandsbewegung*, Zurich 1928.
Ogden, A. R., *The Dies Committee*, Washington 1945.
Ogburn, W. and L. C. Coombs, 'The Economic Factor in the Roosevelt Elections', in *APSR*, Vol. 34, 1940, pp. 719-27.
Ogburn, W. and E. Hill, 'Income Classes and the Roosevelt Vote', in *PSQ*, Vol. 50, 1935, pp. 186-193.
Ogilvie, J. (ed.), *The Imperial Dictionary of the English Language*, new edition, London 1885.
Oldenberg, K., 'Die heutige Lage der Commiss nach neuerer Literatur', in *Schmollers Jb.*, Jg. 16, 1892, pp. 749-812.
Oldenberg, K., 'Statistik der socialen Lage der deutschen Handlungsgehilfen', in *Schmollers Jb.*, Jg. 17, 1893, pp. 1231-50.
Oppenheimer, M., 'What Is the New Working Class?', in *New Politics*, Vol. 10, 1972.
Oppenheimer, M., 'Women Office Workers: Petty-Bourgeoisie or New Proletarians?,' in *Social Scientist*, No. 40/41, Trivandrum, Kerala (India), November/December 1975, pp. 55-75.
Otey, E. L., 'Employers' Welfare Work' (= BLSt, *Bulletin*, No. 123), Washington 1913.
Ozanne, R., *A Century of Labor-Management Relations at McCormick and International Harvester*, Madison 1967.

Palmer, G. L., *Labor Mobility in Six Cities*, New York 1954.
Parsons, C. C., *Office Organization and Management*, Chicago 1918.
Parsons, F., *Choosing a Vocation*, New York 1909.
Parsons, T., 'The Professions and Social Structure' (1939), in ibid., *Essays in Sociological Theory, Pure and Applied* (1949), Glencoe, Ill. 1954², pp. 34-49.
Perkin, H., *The Origins of Modern English Society, 1780-1880*, London 1969.
Pertzina, D., Germany and the Great Depression, in *Journal of Contemporary History*, Vol. 4, No. 4, October 1969, pp. 59-74.
Piat, R. P. S., *Jules Zirnheld. President de la C.F.T.C.*, Paris 1948.
Pope, L., *Millhands and Preachers. A Study of Gastonia*, New Haven 1947.
Porter, G. P., 'Oligopolists in American Manufacturing and Their Products, 1909-1963', in *BHR*, Vol. 43, 1969, pp. 282-98.
Poulantzas, N. A., *Faschismus und Diktatur. Die Kommunistische Internationale und der Faschismus*, München 1973.
Poulantzas, N. A., *Les classes sociales dans le capitalisme aujourd'hui*, Paris 1974.
Powderly, T. V., *Thirty Years of Labor, 1859-1899*, New York 1967.
Powers, F. B., 'Fifty Years of Union History, An Article About the Commercial Telegraphers' Union', in *The American Federationist*, July 1952, pp. 22-24.
Prandy, K. L., *Professional Employees; a Study of Scientists and Engineers*, London 1965.
Pratt, S. A., *The Social Basis of Nazism and Communism in Urban Germany. A*

Correlation Study of the July 31, 1932, Reichstag Election in Germany. MA thesis, Michigan State College of Agriculture and Applied Science, Department of Sociology and Anthropology 1948.
Preller, L., *Sozialpolitik in der Weimarer Republik*, Stuttgart 1949.
Preston, W., Jr., *Aliens and Dissenters. Federal Suppression of Radicals, 1903-1933*, Cambridge, Mass. 1963.
Price, R., *An Imperial War and the British Working Class: Working-Class Attitudes and Reactions to the Boer War, 1899-1902*, London 1972.
Puhle, H.-J., *Agrarische Interessenpolitik und preussischer Konservatismus im wilhelminischen Reich (1893-1914)*, Bonn-Bad Godesberg 1975[2].
Puhle, H.-J., *Politische Agrarbewegungen in kapitalistischen Industriegesellschaften. Deutschland, USA und Frankreich im 20. Jahrhundert*, Gottingen 1975[2].
Punekar, S. and M. G. Savur, *Management-White Collar Relations*, Bombay 1969.

Quint, H. H., *The Forging of American Socialism*, Columbia 1953.

Rabinbach, A. G., 'Toward a Marxist Theory of Fascism and National Socialism', in *New German Critique*, Vol. 1, No. 3, Fall 1974, pp. 127-53.
Radosh, R., *American Labor and United States Foreign Policy*, New York 1969.
Radosh, R., 'The Corporate Ideology of American Labor Leaders from Gompers to Hillman', in J. Weinstein and D. W. Eakins (eds), *For a New America*, New York 1970, pp. 125-52.
Rayback, J. G., *A History of American Labor*, New York 1959.
Raynor, J., *The Middle Class*, London 1969.
Reader, W. J., *Professional Men: The Rise of the Professional Classes in 19th Century England*, London 1966.
Reader, W. J., *The Middle Classes*, London 1972.
Redlich, F., 'Academic Education for Business', in *BHR*, Vol. 31, 1957, pp. 35-91, repr. in ibid., *Steeped in Two Cultures*, New York 1971.
Rees, A., *Real Wages in Manufacturing 1890-1914*, Princeton, NJ 1961.
Reich, W., *Mass Psychology of Fascism*, New York 1970.
Remond, R., *The Right Wing in France from 1815 to de Gaulle*, Philadelphia 1969[2].
Renner, K., *Wandlungen der modernen Gessellschaft*, Wien 1953.
RFR (Reed, F. R.), *Experience of a New York Clerk*, New York 1877.
Rhyne, J. J., *Some Southern Mill Workers and Their Villages*, Chapel Hill, NC 1930.
Rice, E. L., *The Adding Machine. A Play in Seven Scenes*, Garden City, NJ 1923.
Rice, S. A., *Farmers and Workers in American Politics*, New York 1924.
Richardson, D., *The Long Day. The Story of a New York Working Girl. As Told by Herself*, New York 1905.
Riedel, M., 'Bürger, Staatsburger, Bürgertum' , in O. Brunner et al. (eds), *Geschichtliche Grundbegriffe*, Vol. 1, Stuttgart 1972, pp. 672-725.
Riis, J. A., *How the Other Half Lives. Studies Among the Tenements of New York (1890)*, Cambridge, Mass. 1970.
Ringer, F. K., *Education and Society in Modern Europe*, Bloomington and London 1979.
Riper, P. P. van, *History of the United States Civil Service*, Evanston, Ill. 1958.
Ripley, C. M., *Life in a Large Manufacturing Plant*, Schenectady, NY 1919.
Ritter, F., *Zur Geschiechte des Vereins der Handlungsgehilfen in Koln 1843-1893*, Koln 1893.
Roberts, P., *Anthracite Coal Communities. A Study of the Demography, the Social, Educational and Moral Life of the Anthracite Regions*, New York 1904.

Rockefeller, J. D., Jr., 'Address to the Joint Meeting of the Officers and the Representatives of the Employees of the Colorado Fuel & Iron Company, Pueblo, 2 October 1915', n.p. n.d.

Rogin, M. P. and J. L. Shover, *Political Change in California: Critical Elections and Social Movements, 1890-1966*, Westport, Conn. 1970.

Rogoff, N., *Recent Trends in Occupational Mobility*, Glencoe, Ill. 1953.

Roman, F. W., *The Industrial and Commercial Schools of the United States and Germany*, New York 1915.

Rosenberg, H., *Bureaucracy, Aristocracy and Autocracy. The Prussian Experience 1660-1815*, Cambridge, Mass. 1958.

Rosenfarb, J., *The National Labor Policy and How It Works*, New York 1940.

Ross, M., *Stars and Strikes. Unionization of Hollywood*, New York 1941.

Rostow, W. W., 'The Past Quarter Century as Economic History and the Tasks of International Economic Organization', in *JEH*, Vol. 30, 1970, pp. 150-87.

Ruggles, A. M., *A Diagnostic Test of Aptitude for Clerical Office Work. Based on an Analysis of Clerical Operations*, New York 1924.

Runciman, W. G., *Relative Deprivation and Social Justice*, Berkeley 1966.

Saposs, D. J., 'The Role of the Middle Class in Social Development. Fascism, Communism, Socialism', in *Economic Essays in Honor of Wesley Clair Mitchell*, New York 1935, pp. 395-424.

Sauer, W., 'National-Socialism: Totalitarianism or Fascism?', in *AHR*, Vol. 73, 1967, pp. 404-24.

Schafer, W., *NSDAP. Entwicklung und Struktur der Staatspartei des Dritten Reiches*, Hannover 1956.

Scherf, K. Ritter v., *Die Entwicklung der Beamtenbewegung und ihre Interessenvertretung*. Diss., Greifswald 1919.

Schieder, W., 'Faschismus', in *SDG*, Vol. 2, Freiburg 1968, pp. 438-77.

Schlesinger, A. M., Jr., *The Age of Roosevelt*, 3 Vols., Cambridge, Mass. 1957-60 (Vol. 1: *The Crisis of the Old Order*; Vol. 2: *The Coming of the New Deal*; Vol. 3: *The Politics of Upheaval*).

Schmoller, G., 'Was verstehen wir unter dem Mittelstande? Hat er im 19. Jahrhundert zu-oder abgenommen?', in *Verhandlugen des 8. Evan-soz. Kongresses*, Gottingen 1897, pp. 132-85.

Schoenbaum, D., *Hitler's Social Revolution. Class and Status in Nazi Germany 1933 to 1939*, Garden City, NY 1966.

Schoenfield, M. H., 'Analysis of the Labor Provisions of NRA Codes', in *MLR*, Vol. 40, 1935, pp. 574-603.

Schull, P., *From Peddlers to Merchant Princes. A History of Selling in America*, Chicago 1967.

Schulze, J. W., *The American Office. Its Organization, Management and Records*, New York 1913.

Schumann, H.-G., *Nationalsozialismus und Gewerkschaftsbewegung*, Hannover 1958.

Schweitzer, A., *Big Business in the Third Reich*, Bloomington 1964.

Scott, W. A., 'Training for Business at the University of Wisconsin', in *The Journal of Political Economy*, Vol. 21, 1913, pp. 127-35.

Seaver, E., *The Company*, New York 1930.

Selecman, E. H., *The General Agent or Methods of Sales Organization and Management*, Chicago 1910.

Shannon, D. A., *The Socialist Party of America: A History*, New York 1955.

Shapiro, S., 'The Great War and Reform: Liberals and Labor, 1917-1919', in *LH*, Vol. 12, 1971, pp. 323-44.

Sheppard, J. J., 'The Place of High School in Commercial Education', in *The Journal of Political Economy*, Vol. 31, 1913, pp. 209-42.

Shlakman, V., 'Status and Ideology of Office Workers', in *Science & Society*, Vol. 16, 1952, pp. 1-26.
Shover, J. L., 'Ethnicity and Religion in Philadelphia Politics, 1924-40', in *American Quarterly*, Vol. 25, 1973, pp. 499-515.
Siegfried, A., *America Comes of Age*, New York 1927.
Siegfried, A., *Tableau Politique de la France de l'Ouest sous le Troisième République* (1913), Paris 1964.
Slichter, S. H., 'The Current Labor Policies of American Industries,' in *The Quarterly Journal of Economics,* Vol. 43, 1929, pp. 393-435.
Smuts, R. W., *Women and Work in America*, New York 1959.
Snyder, C. D., *White-Collar Workers and the UAW*, Urbana, Ill. 1973.
Snyder, R. E., 'Huey Long and the Presidential Election of 1936', in *Louisiana History*, Vol. 16, 1975, pp. 117-43.
Sombart, W., *Warum gibt es in den Vereinigten Staaten keinen Sozialismus?* Darmstadt (1906) 1969.
Soule, G., *The Coming American Revolution*, London 1934.
Spahr, Ch. B., *America's Working People*, London 1900.
Speier, H., *The Salaried Employees in German Society* (= A Report on Project No. 465-97-3-81 under the auspices of the WPA), New York 1939.
Speier, H., 'The Salaried Employee in Modern Society', in *Social Research*, Vol. 1, 1934, pp. 111-33, repr. in ibid., *Social Order and the Risks of War*, Papers in Political Sociology, New York 1952, pp. 68-85.
Speier, H., *Angestellte vor dem Nationalsozialismus*, Gottingen 1977.
Spero, S. D., *Labor Movement in a Government Industry*, New York 1924.
Spero, S. D., *Government as Employer*, repr. Carbondale, Ill. 1972.
Spoor, A., *White-Collar Union. Sixty Years of NALGO (National Association of Local Government Officers)*, London 1967.
Sprague, J. R., *The Middleman*, New York 1929.
Stegmann, D., 'Zwischen Repression und Manipulation: Konservative Machteliten und Arbeiter- und Angestelltenbewegung 1910-1918', in *AfS*, Vol. 12, 1972, pp. 351-432.
Steigerwalt, A. K., *The National Association of Manufacturers 1895-1914. A Study in Business Leadership*, Michigan 1964.
Stern, C. and H. Winkler (eds.), *Wendepunkte deutscher Geschichte 1848-1945*, Frankfurt 1979.
Stern, F., *Kulturpessimismus als politische Gefahr*, Stuttgart 1963.
Stern, F., *The Failure of Illiberalism. Essays on the Political Culture of Modern Germany*, New York 1972.
Stern, J. L. and D. B. Johnson, *Blue to White-collar Job Mobility*, Madison 1968.
Sternberg, F., *Der Faschismus an der Macht*, Amsterdam 1935.
Stolberg, B., *The Story of the CIO*, New York 1938.
Stormonth, J., *A Dictionary of the English Language*, New York 1885.
Strater, E., *Die soziale Stellung der Angestellten*. Diss., Bonn 1933.
Strauss, G., 'Professional or Employee-Oriented?: Dilemma for Engineering Unions', in *Industrial and Labor Relations Review*, Vol. 17, Ithaca, NY 1964, pp. 519-33.
Strong, D. S., *Organized Anti-Semitism in America*, Washington 1941.
Sturmthal, A. (ed.), *Contemporary Collective Bargaining in Seven Countries*, New York 1957.
Sturmthal, A. (ed.), *White Collar Trade Unions. Contemporary Developments in Industrial Societies*, Urbana, Ill. 1966.
Sumner, M., *Chats on Garment Salesmanship*, Cleveland 1917.
Sumner, W. G., 'The Forgotten Man' (1883), in ibid., *The Forgotten Man and Other Essays*, New Haven 1918.
Sutton, F. X. et al., *The American Business Creed*, Cambridge, Mass. 1956.

Swados, H., *The American Writer and the Great Depression*, Indianapolis 1966.
Syrup, F., *100 Jahre staatliche Sozialpolitik 1839-1939. Aus dem Nachlassbearb. v. O. Neuloh*, Stuttgart 1957.

Taft, P., *Organized Labor in American History*, New York 1964.
Taft, P., *The A.F. of L. in the Time of Gompers*, New York 1970.
Taussig, F. W. and C. S. Joslyn, *American Business Leaders. A Study in Social Origins and Social Stratification*, New York 1932.
Taylor, P., *The Distant Magnet. European Emigration to the U.S.A.*, New York 1971.
Terkel, S., *Hard Times. An Oral History of the Great Depression*, New York 1970.
Thelen, D. P., 'Social Tensions and the Origins of Progressivism', in *JAH*, Vol. 56, 1969/70, pp. 323-41.
Thernstrom, S., *The Other Bostonians. Poverty and Progress in the American Metropolis 1880 to 1970*, Cambridge, Mass. 1964.
Thernstrom, S., *Poverty and Progress: Social Mobility in a Nineteenth-Century City*, Cambridge, Mass. 1964.
Thomas, N., *The Choice Before Us. Mankind at the Crossroads*, New York 1934.
Tilton, T. A., *Nazism, Neo-Nazism, and the Peasantry*, Bloomington, Ind. 1975.
Tocqueville, A. de, *Democracy in America*, Garden City, NY 1969.
Togliatti, P., *Lectures on Fascism* (1935), New York 1976.
Tolman, W. H., *Industrial Betterment*, New York 1900.
Tolman, M. H., *Positions and Responsibility in Department Stores and Other Retail Selling Organizations. A Study of Opportunities for Women* (=Studies in Occupations, No. 5), New York 1921.
Torstendall, R., *Dispersion of Engineers in a Transitional Society. Swedish Technicians 1860-1940*, Uppsala 1975.
Tropp, A., *The School Teachers*, London 1957.
Trotzky, L., 'Der einzige Weg', in ibid., *Schriften uber Deutschland*, Frankfurt/M. 1971, pp. 347-410.
Troy, L., *Trade Union Membership, 1897-1962*, New York 1965.
Tull, C. J., *Father Coughlin and the New Deal*, Syracuse, NY 1965.
Turner, H. A., Jr., *Faschismus und Kapitalismus in Deutschland*, Göttingen 1972.

Ulriksson, V., *The Telegraphers. Their Craft and Their Unions*, Washington 1953.

Veblen, T., *The Engineers and the Price System*, New York 1933.
Verdin, P., *La fondation du syndical des employés du commerce et de l'industrie 1886-1891*, Paris 1929.
Victor, M., 'Verbürgerlichung des Proletariats und Proletarisierung des Mittelstandes', in *Die Arbeit*, Vol. 8, 1931, pp. 17-32.
Vierhaus, R., 'Auswirkungen der Krise um 1930 in Deutschland. Beitrag zu einer historisch-psychologischen Analyse', in W. Conze and H. Raupach (eds), *Die Staats-und Wirtschaftskrise des Deutschen Reichs 1929/33*, Stuttgart 1967, pp. 155-75.
Vogel, E. F., *Japan's New Middle Class. The Salary Man and His Family in a Tolugo Suburb*, Berkeley, Calif. 1968.
Volkov, S., *The Rise of Popular AntiModernism in Germany. The Urban Master Artisans, 1873-1896*, Princeton, NJ 1978.

Wakeman, W. H., 'The Management of Men in Mills and Factories', in *The Engineering Magazine. Devoted to Industrial Progress*, Vol. 8, New York 1895, pp. 48-53.
Waldo, D., *The Administrative State. A Study of the Political Theory of American Public Administration*, New York 1948.

Wallace, M., 'The Uses of Violence in American History', in *American Scholar*, Vol. 40, 1970/71, pp. 81-102.
Walton, R. E., *The Impact of the Professional Engineering Union: A Study of Collective Bargaining Among Engineers and Scientists and its Significance for Management*, Cambridge, Mass. 1961.
Ware, N., *The Labor Movement in the United States, 1860-1895*, New York 1955.
Watkins, G. S., *Labor Problems and Labor Administration During the World War*, 2 Vols., Urbana, Ill. 1919.
Weber, E., *Action Francaise*, Stanford, Calif. 1962.
Weber, E., *Varieties of Fascism*, Princeton, NJ 1964.
Weber, M., *Economy and Society. An Outline of Interpretative Sociology*, New York 1968.
Weber, M., *Gesammelte politische Schriften*, Tubingen 1958^2 (1971)^3.
Wecter, D., *The Age of the Great Depression 1929-1941*, New York (1948), 1969.
Wehler, H.-U., *Der Aufstieg des amerikanischen Imperialismus. Studien zur Entwicklung des Imperium Americanum 1865-1900*, Göttingen 1974.
Wehler, H.-U., *Das Kaiserreich 1871-1918*, Göttingen 1975.
Weinstein, J., *The Corporate Ideal in the Liberal State, 1900-1918*, Boston 1968.
Weiss, R., *The American Myth of Success: From Horatio Alger to Norman Vincent Peale*, New York 1969.
Wesley, E. B., *NEA (National Education Association): The First Hundred Years. The Building of the Teaching Profession*, New York 1957.
Whitaker, W. B., *Victorian and Edwardian Shopworkers. The Struggle to Obtain Better Conditions and a Half-Holiday*, Totowa, NJ 1973.
Whitehead, H., *Principles of Salesmanship*, New York 1917.
Wiebe, R. H., *The Search for Order, 1877-1920*,New York 1967.
Wiedenfeld, K., *Kapitalismus and Beamtentum*, Berlin 1932.
Wiener, J. M., 'Marxism and the Lower Middle Class', in *JMH*, Vol. 48, 1976, pp. 666-71.
Wilhelm, T., *Die Idee des Berufsbeamtentums*, Tübingen 1933.
Williams, T. H., *Huey P. Long*, New York 1969.
Williams, W. A., *The Contours of American History*, Chicago (1961) 1966^2.
Williams, W., *What's on the Worker's Mind*, New York 1920.
Winkler, H. A., 'Extremismus der Mitte?', in *VfZ*, Vol. 20, 1972, pp. 175-91.
Winkler, H. A., *Mittelstand, Demokratie und Nationalsozialismus*, Köln 1972.
Winkler, H. A., *Pluralismus oder Protektionismus? Verfassungspolitische Sozialgeschichte 1929-39*, Göttingen 1973.
Winkler, H. A., *Organisierter Kapitalismus. Voraussetzungen und Anfänge*, Göttingen 1974.
Winkler, H. A., *Revolution, Staat, Faschismus*, Göttingen 1978.
Wilson, H. S., *McClure's Magazine and the Muckrakers*, Princeton, NJ 1970.
Woldt, R., *Das grossindustrielle Beamtentum*, Stuttgart 1911.
Wolfle, D., *America's Resources of Specialized Talent. A Current Appraisal and a Look Ahead. The Report of the Commission on Human Resources and Advanced Training*, New York 1954.
Wolfskill, G and J. A. Hudson, *The Revolt of the Conservatives: A History of the American Liberty League, 1934-1940*, Boston 1962.
Wolman, L., *Ebb and Flow in Trade Unionism*, New York 1936.
Woolf, S. J. (ed.), *The Nature of Fascism*, New York 1968.
Woods, R. A. (ed.), *The City Wilderness. A Settlement Study by Residents and Associates of the South End House (South End Boston)*, Boston 1898.
Wright, C. D., *The Working Girls of Boston*, Boston 1889.
Wykoff, W. A., *The Workers. An Experiment in Reality: The West*, New York 1899.
Wyllie, I. G., *The Self-Made Man in America*, New Brunswick, NJ 1954.

Wyman, R. E., 'Middle-Class Voters and Progressive Reform: The Conflict of Class and Culture', in *APSR*, Vol. 68, 1974, pp. 488-504.

Yellowitz, I., *Labor and the Progressive Movement in New York State, 1897-1916*, Ithaca, NY 1965.

Ziertmann, P., 'Das Berechtigungswesen', in H. Kuhne (ed.), *Hb. f.d. Berufs- u. Fachschulwesen*, Leipzig 1929[2], pp. 571-604.

Zitron, C. L., *The New York City Teachers Union 1916-1964*, New York 1969.

List of Abbreviations

Advocate	*Retail Clerks' International Advocate*
AfA-Bund	Allgemeiner freier Angestelltenbund
AFL	American Federation of Labor
AfS	*Archiv für Sozialgeschichte*
AFT	American Federation of Teachers
AH	*American History*
AHR	*American History Review*
AJS	*American Journal of Sociology*
AIPO	American Institute of Public Opinion
ALPA	Airline Pilots' Association
AMA	American Management Association
Annals	*Annals of the American Academy of Political and Social Science*
A&P	Great American and Pacific Tea Company
APSR	*American Political Science Review*
ASR	*American Sociological Review*
ASS	*Archiv für Sozialwissenschaft und Sozialpolitik*
BA	Bachelor of Arts
BHR	*Business History Review*
BLSt	US Department of Labor, Bureau of Labour Statistics
Bull.	Bulletin
CEH	*Central European History*
CFTC	Confédération Française des Travailleurs Chrétiens
CGT-FO	Confédération Géneral-Force Ouvrière
CGT	Confédération Général du Travail
CIO	Congress of Industrial Organization
CS	*Common Sense*
CSSH	*Comparative Studies in Society and History*
CWA	Civil Works Administration
DAG	Deutsche Angestellten-Gewerkschaft
DGB	Deutscher Gewerkschaftsbund
DHV	Deutschnationaler Handlungsgehilfenverband
FDR	Franklin D. Roosevelt
FERA	Federal Emergency Relief Administration
Fs.	Festschrift
FWISU	Federation of Westinghouse Independent Salaried Unions
GDA	Gewerkschaftsbund der Angestellten
GdS	*Grundriß der Sozialökonomik*
GE(C)	General Electric (Company)
Gedag	Gesamtverband deutscher Angestellten-Gewerkschaften
GG	*Geschichte und Gesellschaft*
Hb.	*Handbuch*
HGB	*Handelsgesetzbuch*
Historical Statistics	*US Bureau of the Census, Historical Statistics of the United States, Colonial Times to 1957*, Washington 1960
HZ	*Historische Zeitschrift*
IESS	*International Encyclopedia of the Social Sciences*
IFDU	International Federation of Draftman's Unions
IFTEAD	International Federation of Technical Engineers
IRSH	*International Review of Social History*
JAH	*Journal of American History*

JAS	*Journal of American Studies*
JAStA	*Journal of the American Statistical Association*
JCH	*Journal of Contemporary History*
JEH	*Journal of Economic History*
JIH	*Journal of Interdisciplinary History*
JMH	*Journal of Modern History*
JSH	*Journal of Social History*
Kocka I	J. Kocka, *Angestellte zwischen Faschismus und Demokratie. Zur politischen Sozialgeschichte der Angestellten. USA 1890-1940 im internationalen Vergleich,* Gottingen 1977.
KPD	Kommunistische Partei Deutschlands
KZSS	*Kölner Zeitschrift für Soziologie und Sozialpsychologie*
LH	*Labor History*
MEW	K. Marx and F. Engels, *Werke,* Berlin 1956ff
MGM	Militärgeschichtliche Mitteilungen
MLR	*Monthly Labor Review*
NAF	National Association of Foremen
NAM	National Association of Manufacturers
NCR	National Cash Register Company
NEA	National Education Association
NFSU	National Federation of Salaried Unions
NICB	National Industrial Conference Board
NLRB	National Labor Relations Board
NPL	*Neue Politische Literatur*
NRA	National Recovery Act
NSBO	Nationalsozialistische Betriebszellen-Organisation
NSDAP	Nationalsozialistische Deutsche Arbeiterpartei
PCF	Parti Communiste Français
POQ	*Public Opinion Quarterly*
PSQ	*Political Science Quarterly*
PVS	*Politische Vierteljahresschrift*
QPAStA	*Quarterly Publication of the American Statistical Association*
RCIA/RCIPA	Retail Clerks' International (Protective) Association
RP	*Review of Politics*
Schmollers Jb.	*Schmollers Jahrbuch für Gesetzgebung, Verwaltung und Volkswirtschaft*
SDG	Sowjetsystem und Demokratische Gesellschaft
SPD	Sozialdemokratische Partei Deutschlands
TH	Technische Hochschule
TUC	Trade Union Congress
UAW	United Automobile Workers
UOPWA	United Office and Professional Workers of America, International
URWEA	United Retail, Wholesale Employees of America
VDH	Verband deutscher Handlungsgehilfen
VDI	Verein Deutscher Ingenieure
VfZ	*Vierteljahrshefte für Zeitgeschichte*
VwA	Verband der weiblichen Handels- und Büroangestellten
WSWG	*Vierteljahrschrift für Sozial- und Wirtschaftsgeschichte*
WPA	Work Progress Administration
YMCA	Young Men's Christian Association
ZdA	Zentralverband der Angestellten
ZK	Zentralkomitee
Zs.	Zeitschrift

Index

Jürgen Kocka

is professor and director of the Institute of History at the University of Bielefeld. He has published many books and articles in the fields of social and political history, including *Klassengesellschaft im Krieg. Deutsche Sozialgeschichte 1914-1918* (Gottingen, 1973) and *Sozialgeschichte. Begriff — Entwicklung — Probleme* (Gottingen, 1977).

Maura Kealey

has a PhD in Comparative History from the University of California, Berkeley (1978). She is a former lecturer in Modern Society and Social Thought at the University of California at Santa Cruz.